Handbook of Asian Aging

Edited by
Hyunsook Yoon
Hallym University

and

Jon Hendricks
Oregon State University

CRC Press
Taylor & Francis Group
Boca Raton London New York

CRC Press is an imprint of the
Taylor & Francis Group, an **informa** business

First published 2006 by Baywood Publishing Company, Inc.

Published 2018 by CRC Press
Taylor & Francis Group
6000 Broken Sound Parkway NW, Suite 300
Boca Raton, FL 33487-2742

First issued in paperback 2018

ISBN 13: 978-0-415-78455-9 (pbk)
ISBN 13: 978-0-89503-316-1 (hbk)

Library of Congress Catalog Number:

Library of Congress Cataloging-in-Publication Data

Handbook of Asian aging / edited by Hyunsook Yoon and Jon Hendricks.
p. cm.
Includes bibliographical references and index.
ISBN 0-89503-316-X (cloth)
1. Older people--Asia. 2. Older people--Government policy--Asia. 3. Older people--Services for--Asia. 4. Aging--Asia. I. Yoon, Hyunsook. II. Hendricks, Jon, 1943-

HQ1064.A78H35 2005
305.26'095--dc22

2005048001

Dedication

To Dr. Samuel Aroni, Professor Emeritus of UCLA, who, through his initial enthusiasm and motivation for a worthwhile project on global aging, brought together some of his well-known colleagues from the United States, Israel, and Australia. His faith, encouragement, and support make him, in essence, the godfather of this book. This book affirms the philosophical belief that people joining forces can achieve great things that one person acting alone cannot do.

KON SIK
&
HAZEL O'REAR REEVES

Table of Contents

PART III: LIVING ARRANGEMENTS, FAMILY CAREGIVING, AND SOCIAL SUPPORT

PART IV: HEALTH AND LONG-TERM CARE

PART V: COMMUNITY SOCIAL SERVICES

FOREWORD

Mapping Intersections in the Atlas of Asian Aging

The 20th century was marked not just by technological and medical breakthroughs but also by striking increases in life expectancy and a shrinking of the world stage (Hendricks and Cutler, 2002). By the dawn of the 21st century, these shifts had encircled the globe and were being felt in all quarters. Many people, regardless of where they live, can now anticipate up to three or more decades beyond the point at which the formal economic sector moves them into retirement, and there can be little doubt that the quality of their lives will be influenced by events well beyond their horizon.

In many respects, population aging in developing countries in Asia represented a "gray dawn" to the new century, just as it had earlier in what are now thought of as developed countries. At the same time, worldwide commerce has brought unprecedented changes in custom and traditions long established across the continent (Peterson, 1999). Providing insight into how those transformations are playing out, along with giving Asian experts their own voice in describing the experience of aging, were abiding priorities for us as this *Handbook of Asian Aging* took shape.

Given the vast reach of the Asian landscape, making hasty generalizations from one to another country is an endeavor fraught with drawbacks and missteps. Yet, as Liang (2004) and others have long observed, cross-cultural comparisons are invaluable for double-checking inferences and causal mechanisms for whatever aspect of aging the professional community examines. Adding to the complexities of such analyses is the fact that the experience of aging is itself paradoxical: Individuals are convinced their lives are like no one else's, whereas gerontologists are intent on making generalizations reflecting identifiable patterns. Obviously there is undeniably validity to both positions. As nation states experience economic change, population aging is a simultaneous occurrence foreshadowing consequences for governments as well as for individuals. The processes are inextricably interwoven. As developing nations move toward being countries of the old (Hendricks, 1980), they have to create policies that provide some semblance of balance between what are often less than parallel priorities. Complicating the process even further, they must do so in the midst of competing claimants.

In Asia, where market economies took root somewhat later than in other quarters of the globe, populations are aging at staggering rates, and economic growth is hard-pressed to keep pace. Add in the undeniable healthcare crises posed by population aging, and we see national governments being forced to make hard choices as to where to put their scarce resources. No single scenario is likely to carry the day. As will be seen in the chapters to follow, few solutions provide a cure-all—and just as few are indemnified in the face of economic setbacks. Each prospective strategy affects differing constituency in conflicting ways; subvention and redirection are abiding facts of life. Policies firmly supported today may fall prey to new priorities tomorrow.

Arbitrating the Conflict Between Economic Security and Old-Age Security

So how do states arbitrate between conflicting social priorities in order to adequately sustain all citizens, young and old? Hudson-Rodd (2001) reiterated a familiar admonition as she noted that an equitable and just society is the best chance for creating a healthy old age, especially a healthy old age for women. But what constitutes equitable and just? Such tenets are based on underlying moral and ethical principles that have evolved in every culture. In times of plenty and relative stability, a given set of values can be espoused, despite some differences of opinion. These moral precepts provide the social adhesive that nurtures communality across members of a group despite various centrifugal tendencies. However, when surrounding conditions are altered in any significant way, values are redefined as the terms of the social contract are written, rewritten, and amended again, depending on macro-level circumstances well beyond the ken of the individuals whose lives are affected (Hendricks and Leedham, 1991; Thompson, 1971).

Of course it is essential to ensure a sense of social solidarity and belonging under any circumstances—but especially as social and economic development take place. Nowhere is this any more apparent than in Asian nations moving rapidly from overarching traditional values of filial piety, communal harmony, and self-subjugation to Westernized notions of materialism, personal happiness, and individualism. The shift is having a palpable effect across generations, leading to an increasingly fractured existence in which generations have come to hold dramatically different worldviews and in which global economic trade is also bringing distinct values, priorities, and material interests. Townsend (1981) spoke of the structured dependence of the elderly in addressing exactly these sorts of alterations wherein societal-level redefinitions play out by creating what may be described as asymmetrical dependencies accruing to the aged. In this fashion, the social meaning of aging is shaped as a social status, based on what are ostensibly earned credits and entitlements is redefined. How individuals experience their later years is in no small measure a product of circumstances encountered in earlier stages of life—on both an individual level and on a structural level—and what is regarded as their "due" is a reflection of the socioeconomic contexts in which they find themselves when they are old.

For example, in a prophetic analysis of changes accompanying the marketization of China, Liu (2002) highlighted the effect structural changes have on the everyday life and subjectivity of individuals born in an earlier era. Though Liu's emphasis is not restricted to aging *per se*, the discussion helps contextualize the impact of changes in China insofar as individuals are concerned. In a nutshell: Imagine anticipating a life script focused on one definition of productivity, filial responsibility, community, individualism, and temporality—then becoming old under the auspices of a different script. What is true of China is pretty much true in all developing nations: One series of generations has internalized one set of values and expectations, but their younger cohorts, on which they now depend, operate with slightly to very different expectations.

The Sword of Damocles

Greek legend has it that the courtier Damocles was seated beneath a sword hanging by a single hair as an object lesson for how precarious entitlements can become. With dramatic growth in the aged populations of developing countries, resources are squeezed between riding the economic tide or tending to those who have given what they could and are now defined as old.

Add in some persistent disadvantages—education, rurality, and gender come readily to mind—and the situation becomes even more tentative. China and India are two places where quality of life for the elderly, and especially the oldest old, older rural residents, and old women, is anything but heartening. As will be seen in several of the chapters to follow, the new economy in Asia is an urban economy, and to the extent that social insurance is made available to those in need, it is frequently an urban policy. Wage labor is normally an urban phenomenon in modern economies, so it should not be too surprising that benefits follow suit. The consequences of these shifts for older people, growing old as the world changes around them, can be profoundly unsettling.

Dependence on the benevolence of others, regardless of normative expectations and whether they are family members, can yield a delicate hold on any elder's sense of well-being or quality of life. Add in local gender-based disparities, ethnic favoritism, changing employment patterns of younger workers competing in a market economy, episodic scarcity, or any of a myriad of local circumstances or structural arrangements, and the prospect of adequate old-age security does not necessarily grow any brighter. As Yung-Ping Chen and John Turner point out in chapter two, actual benefits accruing to the elderly reflect the invisible hand of market forces, the invisible handshake of tradition and custom, and the invisible foot of political decisions. Questions of political economy and issues of well-being among the elderly are inextricably intertwined.

As if national variability were not enough, there is not a universal old person in Asia any more than there is one anyplace else in the world. Furthermore, as Mason (1992) and others have asserted, it is also misleading to posit a single model of family. However, regardless of unique attributes of family life in various Asian cultures, the nature of broad-reaching gender relations is somewhat comparable. That is, the gendered and generational stratification within families that leads to the relative power and prestige of women and men is played out in one Asian culture after another with substantially the same effect. This means that women are disproportionately accorded responsibility for caregiving and prone to economic vulnerability. Even in Asian cultures with more egalitarian familial relationships, old-age security is not guaranteed even when need-based assistance is provided. The reach of the family hearth or, put in more Western terms, the household of care, may be broader in the East than in the West, but it is undeniably under siege (Bengtson, Kim, Myers, and Eun, 2000).

Aging Policy in the Face of Economic Hardship

As will be seen in the demographic discussion to follow and in several other chapters, the pace of population aging is likely to be one of the more unwieldy issues in Asia even under the best of circumstances. Then, too, the relative weight of long-cherished past and emerging future orientations is being changed as capitalism and market mentalities are suffused across the region, thereby altering the perceived script for an individual's life. Even the notion of individual life scripts represents a sea change. The challenge for nation states is to maintain elders' sense of well-being in the face of a changing social and economic landscape that profoundly alters the measure of life.

What is more, Kinsella (2000) pointed out that the shift in healthcare provisions from acute care to coverage for chronic and degenerative conditions will subvert other efforts to offer a social safety net or old-age security, even as this shift opens the door to more market-driven solutions and lessened family support. At present, composite social security and old-age assistance provisions account for an estimated 40 percent of government expenditures in some Asian nations, and these expenditures are being roundly challenged by those who say that first the nation needs to ensure its prosperity before tending to benefits for the elderly.

Complicating the picture, the much-lauded Asian economic boom came in for hard times in the 1990s. As bubble trouble swept over one nation after another, the noble intentions of Asian policymakers concerned about the welfare of older adults came face to face with the realities of economic stagnation or worse. Under those circumstances, it is hard to claim anything is sacrosanct or any provision inviolate. Of course demographic transitions alone are not sufficient to portend hardship or disparagement; political decisions are at the core of what it means to be old. It should never be doubted that social policies are prisms that both focus and provide perspective on societal values and the significance of social groups.

To put a slightly sharper focus on the obduracy of the issues: China, as a case in point, must kindle economic growth at a rate of no less than 7 percent annually (actual growth has averaged about 10 percent) just to sustain current rates of employment and economic solvency. As the planned economy under the centralized Chinese government of the late 20th century waned, the country's participation in the global economy grew at a furious pace. One result of this transition was that as China developed a robust market economy, tens of millions of workers previously in the employ of state-run enterprises found themselves out of work; unfortunately, they will be followed by equal numbers in coming decades as further economic transformations take place (Chow and Xu, 2001; Yardley, 2004). The contradictory demands of national policies supporting economic growth, managing unemployment in a country where a remarkable 200 million people are unemployed, and providing reasonable benefits to older adults do not foster a situation in which simple fixes are easily implemented. The volatility of the Chinese economy will bring a setback, as inevitably happens, and a delicate balancing act will be demanded to protect the gains obtained and impose no further privation on older citizens.

Japan provides another object lesson in coping with paired economic priorities. In late 2003, Prime Minister Koizumi signed orders to cut ¥1 trillion in subsidies to needy families and elder-care services along with a range of other retrenchments designed to prop up Japan's faltering economic engine. Elsewhere across Asia comparable problems, though smaller in scale, are making themselves felt. The gray dawn may have arrived before Asian governments had moved far enough in their economic aspirations to finance promises made in the drive to promote economic development (Hermalin, 2001; Phillips, 2000).

As difficult as localized social and fiscal inequalities may prove to be, global economic challenges accompanying rapidly shifting old-age dependency ratios portent hardships in developed and underdeveloped countries alike. Some go so far as to say that these hardships may affect global prosperity itself (Hashimoto, Mondale, and Pöhl, 2002). Regardless of the ultimate outcome, the stakes are high and the debate is sure to be heated—as will become abundantly clear in the chapters to follow.

Standing at the Crossroads

Asia is indeed at a crossroads, and the situation of older adults is very much at a crucial intersection (Hermalin, 2001). Traditional provisions and values stressing family and communal responsibilities have slowed the advent of formal governmental programs. But as economic transformation occurred, revamped public policies were very much needed. Now, with aspirations exceeding realities, retrenchments—and thereby, hardships—are a specter looming large on the horizon. Positive reforms and staunch social security provisions are widely heralded and much lauded; let us hope the pillars on which they are built are able to withstand the countercurrents swirling round.

The contributors to this *Handbook of Asian Aging* are keenly aware of conflicting pressures and threats posed to the quality of life for older adults. Each brings his or her own perspective to the volume and outlines pressing issues facing the elderly in their particular context. The fact that common threads appear, then disappear, in the warp and woof of the fabric of Asian aging ought not come as a complete surprise as this fabric is more tapestry than broadcloth. Part I sets forth a matrix of key issues crisscrossing demographic, economic, political, and cultural realms. These stage-setting chapters provide essential conceptual tools applicable for interpreting the substantive country-specific reports that follow. In Parts II and III, contributors carefully examine a variety of topical facets of the aging experience ranging from work, retirement, and economic well-being to living arrangements and social interaction. Part IV takes up the abiding issue of healthcare and long-term care, key ingredients of aging policies if national governments are to claim they are doing well by their elderly. Community-based social services are the topic of Part V, germane for the same reasons.

We recognize that not all Asian countries are included and that those that do appear are not necessarily representative of their sister nations. For advocates of countries not represented here, we ask your forbearance; omissions were not intentional. We believe readers will find that what the contributors have to say will provide substantial insights into what is going on in their respective countries.

Jon Hendricks
Hyunsook Yoon

REFERENCES

Bengtson, V., Kim, K.-D., Myers, G., and Eun, K.-D. (Eds.). (2000). *Aging in East and West: Families, states, and the elderly.* New York: Springer.

Chow, N., and Xu, Y. (2001). *Socialist welfare in a market economy.* Aldershot, United Kingdom: Ashgate.

Hashimoto, R., Mondale, W. F., and Pöhl, K. O. (2002). *Meeting the challenge of global aging.* Washington, DC: CSIS Press.

Hendricks, J. (1980). Preface. In J. Hendricks (Ed.), *In the country of the old* (pp. iii–v). Amityville, NY: Baywood.

Hendricks, J., and Cutler, S. (2002). The future of gerontology and geriatrics. *Contemporary Gerontology, 9,* 7–10.

Hendricks, J., and Leedham, C. (1991). Dependency or empowerment? Toward a moral and political economy of aging. In M. Minkler and C. L. Estes (Eds.), *Critical perspectives on aging: The political and moral economy of growing old* (pp. 55–74). Amityville, NY: Baywood.

Hermalin, A. (2001). Ageing in Asia: Facing the crossroads. *Hallym International Journal of Aging, 3,* 133–167.

Hudson-Rodd, N. (2001). Women's lives: Social development implications of the demographic change in the Asia Pacific region. *Journal of Social Work Research and Evaluation, 2,* 73–81.

Kinsella, K. (2000). Demographic dimensions of ageing in East and Southeast Asia. In D. R. Phillips (Ed.), *Ageing in the Asia-Pacific region* (pp. 35–50). London: Routledge.

Liang, J. (2004). Cross-cultural comparative social gerontology: Current state and future prospects. *Contemporary Gerontology, 10,* 59–64.

Liu, X. (2002). *The otherness of self: A genealogy of the self in contemporary China.* Ann Arbor: University of Michigan Press.

Mason, K. O. (1992). Family change and support of the elderly in Asia: What do we know? *Asia-Pacific Population Journal, 7,* 13–32.

Peterson, P. (1999, January/February). Gray dawn: The global aging crisis. *Foreign Affairs,* 42–55.

Phillips, D. (2000). Ageing in the Asia-Pacific region: Issues, policies, and contexts. In D. Phillips (Ed.), *Ageing in the Asia-Pacific region* (pp. 1–33). London: Routledge.

Thompson, E. P. (1971). The moral economy of the English crowd in the eighteenth century. *Past and Present, 50,* 76–136.

Townsend, P. (1981). The structured dependency of the elderly: A creation of social policy in the twentieth century. *Ageing and Society, 10,* 5–28.

Yardley, J. (2004, May 28). It's out of college and onto jobless rolls in China. *New York Times,* p. A3.

Acknowledgments

We would like to offer acknowledgments and great appreciation for invaluable assistance to Ms. Amber Richards for the editing and research in the United States; to Ms. Stella Sarkisyan for compiling demographic information in the United States; to Ms. Claudette Butler for the multiple liaison tasks with the Australian contributors and the international editors; to Ms. Odelia Pollak for all her work and efforts with the publishers, the editors, and the Israeli contributors.

The editors also wish to acknowledge all the remarkable and diverse older people who in so many ways provided the essential data and insights that enabled the respective contributors to present their cases. In a very real way, this book is a testimony to the fact that people of any age share so much with each other, regardless of nationality, race, religion, cultural heritage, or status.

Too soon old, too late prosperous is an aphorism that captures the aftermath of the silver tsunami surging across Asia. Unlike the West where national economies and per capita income improved prior to the demographic transition to an aging population, much of Asia is traversing the other route. Add to the mix the dramatic differentiation that characterizes the nations in the region and forecasting the future is daunting.

The contributors to this *Handbook of Asian Aging* are due major appreciation. The goal was to have individual authors establish their own focus, set forth aging priorities in their own countries, and speak in a voice grounded in local circumstances. Thanks to their efforts, we have a sense of the ways in which institutions matter and aging is affected. As barriers to entry have been dismantled, breathtaking economic changes have swept over national economies. Even so, as is the case with China, it is apparent that rates of change reflect starting points and growth even as localized disparities and stagnation in some sectors is shrouded by sheer growth in others. In 2005 China was projecting a $300 billion shortfall in meeting the needs of existing retirees despite the fact that private sector productivity had increased at a remarkable rate since the mid-1990s. Certainly that shortfall is larger than any other nation on earth but it is prescient perhaps in terms of the issues that will preoccupy Asia in the decades ahead.

As the authors make clear, changing policies, institutions, and population structures affect individual well-being on the most personal of levels. They also point out that the social consequences of market restructuring, the shift away from traditional family hearths, and the importation of market-based solutions leave the most vulnerable segments of the population in even more precarious positions. As others have noted, the health and social security issues looming on the horizon will dwarf those receiving so much attention in Western nations.

Jonathan Kauffman must be singled out for special acknowledgment. Working as a free-lance editor in San Francisco, he gave unstintingly to all contributors. His thoughtful touch and keen abilities not only add luster to this effort, but ensured that it would see the light of day. There was no aspect of the task which has not benefitted from his attention. In the final phases he was joined by Audrey Wong who demonstrated a masterful touch of her own. The good people at Baywood Publishing Co. are also deserving of recognition for their willingness to publish this volume.

Without the generous support of Hallym University and the Ilsong Foundation in Seoul, Korea, bringing this book to fruition would have been considerably more arduous. We appreciate their support and their belief that an enhanced understanding of aging will help create a better tomorrow. The bridge to that prospect rests on sound scholarship.

INTRODUCTION

The Sweep of Asian Aging: Changing Mores, Changing Policies

Jon Hendricks and Hyunsook Yoon

The advent of global economic relationships has brought extensive changes to the nations of Asia—that sweep of the world from Pakistan and India, to Japan, the Philippines, and Indonesia. We have also included Australia in this volume because of its prominence in the affairs of the Asian-Oceania region. In addition to potent demographic transitions that place Asia among the most rapidly aging areas in the world, there have been essential economic and policy challenges throughout the region that affect familial, social, and cultural relationships. In a region where communal accord and familial interdependence have long been revered, far-reaching changes are afoot. Ironically, as much as filial responsibilities have been a vital precept, public provisions for the aged have lagged behind cultural and ideological shifts. To understand the issues looming large for many Asian governments and to put change in context, it is essential to recognize both the convergence and divergence of these patterns among the peoples of Asia.

Admittedly, gerontology is an emerging specialty in some nations in Asia, better established in others, and virtually nonexistent in a few. There are a variety of vibrant professional and learned assemblages serving to advance what we know about aging. One of the most significant intentions of this *Handbook of Asian Aging* is to give Asian scholars and experts voice in describing the situation the elderly encounter in their country. There is no denying that both that voice and the challenges facing the elderly are firmly rooted in the local circumstances. Another overriding objective is to expand the knowledge base and the armamentarium professionals may bring to their efforts to contribute to our understanding of Asian aging.

CONVERGENCE AND CHANGE

Asia embodies such a medley of cultures, economies, and shifting social patterns that it boggles the mind. Dissimilarities notwithstanding, there remain a number of shared threads running all through the region—the fleet pace of social change, the rapid aging of the population, and the intersection of traditional morality with global market forces. Such changes, along with attendant transformations, are redefining what it means to grow old in Asia. Many factors pose quandaries to national and local governments—add to the equation quandaries posed by episodic economic fluctuations, delays in designing and implementing appropriate policies in areas where kinship networks, the reach of the family hearth, and mutual assistance have customarily been the principal source of support, or the task of balancing priorities of emerging market forces with social assurances—and the predicaments proliferate as pressures intensify (Bengtson, Kim, Myers, and Eun, 2000; Ingersoll-Dayton and Saengtienchai, 1999).

Paradoxically, even in light of its admiration of the wisdom associated with age, Asia is a region where children have long been celebrated. In certain countries—Cambodia, Malaysia, the Union of Myanmar, and Vietnam among them—children retain primacy on the policy agenda, while the same countries have not or are only just implementing comprehensive national policies to provide for their aged. However, many Asian nations are formulating or reformulating aging policies as the countries experience dramatic demographic conversions due to the rapid increase of the populations (Kinsella, 2000; Phillips, 2000).

At present, more than half the world's population over the age of 60 (the standard demarcating old age in most non-Western countries) lives in Asia. According to United Nations (U.N., 2001) projections, the portion of Asian populations ages 65 and older will more than quadruple by 2050. Concurrently, the population under age 15 will diminish as birthrates spiral downward. Though Asia's age distribution is still more youthful than that of the West, conspicuous reductions in birthrates and significant increases in life expectancy are having extensive effects on the distribution of the population. This swift population aging presents a challenge to policymakers, political stability, social equality for the elderly (especially older women), and to the preservation of time-honored ways of life. Seemingly, abuse, neglect, and homelessness have reared their ugly heads in places where they were seldom documented in the past (Han and Kim, 2000; Kim, 1998; Sung, 2001). Under the circumstances currently characterizing many Asian countries, it is reasonable to ask whether old age in Asia will ever resemble the retirement years as they are portrayed in the West (Hermalin, 2001; Phillips, 2000).

Contributors to this *Handbook of Asian Aging* address the interaction among demographic transitions, market economies, traditional values and their implications for quality of life, healthcare, labor and retirement policies, public pension programs, social services, and economic growth across Asia. As the

U.N. Economic and Social Commission for Asia and the Pacific (ESCAP, 1999) pointed out, the interface between economic prosperity and population aging is far-reaching and shapes many facets of a culture, its customs, and its social policies. As one undercurrent changes direction, attendant alterations reverberate throughout society, affecting familial, social, and cultural practices. In a part of the world where communal consensus, filial obligation, and familial interdependence have long been venerated, comprehensive challenges are in the offing (Ingersoll-Dayton and Saengtienchai, 1999; Phillips, 2000; Sung, 2001).

AGING POPULATIONS

Although the figures vary widely from region to region within Asia, rapidly declining birthrates and improvements in infant mortality following World War II produced an increasingly younger population profile throughout the region until the mid-1970s. Moving into the 1980s, a striking shift in family planning policies resulted in reduced fertility rates in many Asian countries, and the proportion of the population under age 15 began to wane, especially in Asian-Pacific nations. During the same period, improving health and abatement of chronic conditions resulted in increases in the proportion of the elderly, but at a somewhat slower rate. As a consequence, there has been a considerable expansion of the present portion of the population that is of working age. In fact, the remarkable economic changeover in Asia may be attributed to an increased capacity of working-age adults to foster productivity and discretionary financial gains (Mason, 2001; Williamson and Higgins, 2001).

In 2000, it was estimated that 30 percent of Asia's aggregate population was under age 15, 6 percent age 65 or older, and 64 percent in the working-age interval of 15 to 64; the average age was 29. U.N. medium projections estimate that the population of working-age adults will be approximately the same in 2050, at 64 percent, but there will be a signal turnabout in the distribution of children and old people. The portion under age 15 will drop to 19 percent, while those age 65 and older will rise to 18 percent. To illustrate the overall impact of these swings: Countries such as Singapore or Malaysia will experience upsurges of their elderly populations of up to 372 percent by 2050. The Philippines and Indonesia will each evidence gains of 240 percent, while South Korea will see a 216 percent increase. In Bangladesh or Thailand, the increase will be in the neighborhood of 200 percent more elderly in 2050 than in 2000. The average age will rise to 40, and the aging index (number of those age 65 and older compared to number of those under age 15) will shift, as birthrates fall to below steady-state levels (Kinsella and Velkoff, 2001; U.N., 2001).

At present, Asia's elderly are concentrated in the younger segments of the old-age population range. In the next few decades, however, the greatest growth will happen in the older age groups. This will occur as life expectancy rises and as the large cohorts born in the decades immediately following World War II move into old age. Of all Asians age 55 or older, over more than half are now between the ages of 55 and 64, about one third are between 65 and 74, and nearly one sixth are 75 or older.

These patterns will remain fairly stable over the next 25 years, but during the subsequent 25-year period leading to 2050, the relative size of the oldest age group (those ages 75 and older) is expected to swell substantially. Estimates are that the oldest old, accounting for about 15 percent of the aged population at present, will increase to 17 percent in 2025 and then climb to roughly 27 percent by 2050 (U.N., 2001). The challenges posed by this distribution of the population will be felt across all realms of life and throughout the value structure and political agenda of each country. In fact, traditional values are evidently already under siege if press reports and readily available research findings are any indication (Ingersoll-Dayton and Saengtienchai, 1999; Sung, 2001).

Not surprisingly, the percentages of the aged population are highest in the more economically integrated nations of the Asian-Pacific region, while those in south-central and Southeast Asia will remain less than 10 percent for several decades. To illustrate: Japan, the first country in the region to undergo a transition to low fertility in the 1950s and already the third oldest country in the world, has one of the longest life expectancies in the world. The number of older Japanese has been on the ascent since the 1970s and will continue to climb until midcentury, when more than half of its older population will be over the age of 75 (Kinsella and Velkoff, 2001; Masuda, 2001). Already, 22 percent of the Japanese population is over age 60, with 17 percent over the age of 65. Nearly one quarter of those Japanese above age 60 fall into the oldest-old category of 75 or more years, making Japan the oldest of the Asian countries—followed by Hong Kong, Taiwan, South Korea, and Singapore. By 2025, one in three Japanese will be at least 60 years old, with a national median age of 50. The proportion of the oldest old is projected to surpass 35 percent of the elder population by 2050. Countries generally described as among Asia's economic tigers—Japan, South Korea, Taiwan, Hong Kong, and Singapore—will see at least one in four citizens over the age of 60 by 2025.

By contrast, the South Asian nations of Bangladesh, Nepal, India, Sri Lanka, and Pakistan are representative of countries somewhat behind in economic terms and just shifting from high to low fertility. Fertility is a far more complicated issue that is sometimes apparent. For example, in India, which already accounts for 17 percent of the world's population, the number of children a woman bears is, in part, her in-law's decision and reflects the culture's emphasis on male offspring. Yet even these countries are beginning to age even before they undergo economic transformations comparable to those experienced in other Asian nations. In India, only 14 percent of the elderly population currently falls into the 65-and-older category, projected to increase to 22 percent by 2050 (U.N., 2001). Though relatively small by comparison, Sri Lanka's population over the age of 65 is presently estimated to be approximately 6.5 percent and is likely to grow to nearly 12 percent by 2025. According to rough estimates, in the neighborhood of slightly more than 30 percent of elderly Sri Lankans either receive pensions or have access to provident funds (Martin, 1990).

At this point in time, two out of three Asians over the age of 60 live in the People's Republic of China. Its elderly population will more than double by 2025 and may reach 439 million by 2050. In contrast, in the Philippines or Malaysia, approximately 6 percent of the population is over age 60, and this figure is projected to increase to around 10 percent by 2025. Interestingly, Cambodia and Laos will actually see lower percentages of older adults in the first two decades of the 21st century than they had at the close of the 20th century (Phillips, 2000). As will be seen in a couple of the chapters to follow, each country's pattern of population aging is unique and each calls for a contextualized appraisal.

Aging of the population in the Asian-Pacific and Southeast Asian regions has occurred far more rapidly than it did in Western countries, with doubling rates that have spawned what Kinsella and Velkoff refer to as "fractious debates" about how best to resolve dilemmas that must be accommodated without delay (Kinsella and Velkoff, 2001; Lee and Mason, 2000; Westley, 1998; Westley, Lee, and Mason, 2000). As is true in the West, women have lower mortality rates throughout life; consequently, older Asian women outnumber older men, particularly in the oldest age intervals. At this time, among the population ages 55 and older, there are about 90 men for every 100 women. Among those ages 75 and older, there are roughly 70 men for every 100 women. This sex ratio is a persistent feature of Asia's population that is not expected to change appreciably over the next 50 years, despite patriarchal cultural values in some countries that favor the survival of male infants.

Traditionally, nearly everyone in Asia married and few divorced. Accordingly, nearly all older men and women have lived their lives in marital households of one or another type. In Japan, divorce among young couples has been on the increase for the past decade or more, but midlife divorces have taken a stark upward swing as the old cultural ideal of *gaman*—self-denial—has been supplanted by more Westernized ways of thinking. Even so, as life expectancies rise for both genders, the proportion of the elderly who are widowed is projected to decline as partners grow older together—but the proportion of elderly living in extended families is not. Japanese time-series data for the last four decades suggest that the proportion of elderly living with kin in extended families is declining, and the number living as couples, alone, or in institutions is climbing linearly (Kinsella and Velkoff, 2001).

THE ELDERLY IN FAMILY CONTEXTS

Across Asia, families have traditionally assumed virtually exclusive responsibility for providing old-age security. Up until recently, aging has been a family affair; the Confucian ideal of filial piety is ubiquitous and even codified into law in

China and elsewhere. As the authors of the chapters in this volume make clear, in the past most elderly lived in extended, multigenerational families and relied on adult children, spouses, or other family members for material needs and personal care. Today, even when children live separately from parents, as is commonly the case in urban economies, contact is more frequent and resources flow more substantially than in the West. In South Korea, for example, more than three quarters of the elderly report that the greater part of their expressive and instrumental support derives from family sources. Despite alternative accommodations coming to the fore, in Seoul more than 65 percent, and in Tokyo and Osaka approximately 54 percent of the elderly continue to live with their families. However, these percentages are in near freefall, notwithstanding enduring ideological prescriptions to the contrary (Masuda, 2001; Sung, 2000).

By and large, the family-based model of providing care for the elderly has been successful, especially given the potential for substantial intergenerational income disparities in the context of the rapidly developing economics of Asia. When the current generation of old people were young, their earnings were a pittance compared to what present-day workers command. Without kin care these elders would be in even more dire straits in today's escalating economies. Norms regarding family support are a two-edged sword, however. On the one hand, there is every indication that they help ensure that the elderly share in the region's economic abundance. At the same time, the custom of familial responsibility has served to delay design of public policies more suited to modern market economies and changing familial circumstances (Choi, 2000; Yoon, Eun, and Park, 2000).

Despite its historic status, the ethic of family support is under siege from demographic, social, and economic transformations sweeping across Asia, and the confluence of these forces is likely to erode quality of life among the elderly in coming decades. As traditional values are assailed by the new agenda, the ramifications play out vividly on societal arrangements at the macro level as well as on the psychological functioning of individuals. The same demographic forces propelling a decline in aggregate support ratios also portend a flagging of the support ratio within families as they downsize. These changes, in turn, are aggravating stressors levied on older adults, as evidenced by a variety of indicators of inequality and well-being (Hu, 1995; Kim, 1998; Phillips, 2000). In many Asian countries, Japan being a prime case in point, the attenuation of close ties with offspring is construed as shameful (Maeda and Ishikawa, 2000). Increases in life expectancy not only mean that adults are more likely to have surviving elderly parents, but the persistence of low fertility also implies that sons and daughters have fewer siblings with whom to share responsibilities for parental care. Long-term low fertility also means fewer workers and an erosion of the tax bulwark upon which public pensions and healthcare depend, thereby leaving the elderly in exposed and tenuous circumstances (Kinsella, 2000). In South Korea, the percentage of older women with no surviving male offspring has been on the upswing and will continue to climb; therefore, these women will likely find themselves increasingly dependent on formal support systems sustained by public policies. The fact that an increasing number of women are also entering the paid labor force—in South Korea, nearly half of all women currently work outside the home—means fewer kin caregivers are available (Kinsella and Velkoff, 2001; Sung, 2000).

Changing economic patterns are reinforcing demographic trends, especially in China, Hong Kong, Japan, Singapore, and other Asian-Pacific nations where family planning policies have yielded fewer young people moving into the labor force or available to assume caregiving responsibilities for aging relatives. In contrast, Cambodia, Malaysia, the Union of Myanmar, the Philippines, Thailand, Vietnam, and elsewhere where fertility rates have not declined as precipitously are not likely to face comparable near-term pressures. Even so, in many instances young people are leaving their ancestral homes for urban locales and new employment prospects, thereby leading to greater geographic separation from parents. At the same time, women are entering the workforce in ever greater numbers, thereby constricting time available to buttress family support.

Exposure to Westernized worldviews may also be introducing new ideas about marriage, family, and individualism. To highlight one example, marriage rates have dropped substantially in a number of countries—an unthinkable pattern a generation ago. If a sizeable number of men and women forgo marriage altogether, this, too, will have significant implications for families in the not-too-distant future. Not to be overlooked is the fact that the advent of employee-based and public pension programs, as well as paid caregiving and greater financial capability on the part of individuals, offer alternative mechanisms for securing old-age support as the availability of age-old informal family sustenance dwindles. The World Bank summarized the situation succinctly: "It is inevitable that formal systems should eventually replace informal systems as the dominant form of old age support" (World Bank, 1994, p. 67).

Indeed, in Asia's most prosperous countries, the multigenerational extended family has clearly waned. In 1950, 65 percent of Japanese young women said they expected to depend on their children in old age; by 1990, only 18 percent still expected to do so. In South Korea, just 8 percent of women surveyed in 1997 said they wanted to live with their children in old age, while 70 percent preferred substitute living situations (Lee, 1998; Mason, Lee, and Russo, 2002). Cross-sectional survey data from Taiwan imply that this attitude is reciprocal; declining numbers of children favor coresidence with aged parents, favoring alternative, more tenable arrangements (Hsu, Lew-Ting, and Wu, 2001). Even in Nepal, where roughly 83 percent of elderly Nepalese live with an adult child, the sense of filial obligation is eroding in the face of social and economic transformations (Pienta, Barber, and Axinn, 2001). Comparable trends have emerged across Asia. As the chapter on Australia by Kendig and Quinn points out, there is considerable controversy over the sustainability of informal support and family ties to meet the needs of elderly Australians.

Continuing reassessments of public policies will have significant ramifications for the role of the family in the future. Having said that, it is important to point out that in most instances, Asian age policies have been formulated with the family milieu taken as normative, no matter the extent to which economics or preferences may contravene such provisions. As might be expected, global economic forces are producing conflicting pressures, and there is considerable effort being devoted to maintaining traditional or quasi-traditional family arrangements in the face of the marketization of so much else. A number of Asian nations have explicitly recognized the desirability of preserving strong kinship networks and have adopted pro-family policies in an attempt to bolster family support. In Singapore, children are now legally responsible for support and guardianship of the welfare of elderly parents. In Malaysia and Singapore, public housing policies have been rewritten to promote multigenerational living arrangements. Throughout Asia, many governments are providing daycare and other supplemental services aimed at helping adult children care for aged parents. Almost as an exception to the pattern found in Southeast Asian nations with relatively younger populations, Malaysia provides tax incentives and a number of welfare provisions to care for its old people, and other governments are considering comparable policies (Sim, 2002; World Bank, 1994).

AGING AND PUBLIC POLICY

As the World Bank (1994) points out, and as several of the authors of this volume make clear, the design of policies for old age involves multiple pillars. In the section to follow, we will review a number of crucial elements that affect quality of life for the elderly. Our listing is not exhaustive, but it is illustrative of agenda items that cannot be denied.

Healthcare Policy

Healthcare policy is a prevailing issue as healthcare costs skyrocket across Asia, according to the World Health Organization (WHO). Between the grinding toll of diseases linked to poverty and lifestyle adversities, and exacerbated by the spotty nature of health insurance for those in greatest need, healthcare in many Asian nations is teetering on the brink of collapse—or at least inordinate cost ("WHO Cautions," 2002). The aging of the Asian population will necessitate restructuring of healthcare provisions, since long-term care is near bedrock status in the design of supportive environments for old people in general, not merely institutionalized elderly. As Phillips and Chan (2002) asserted, long-term care needs to be conceived most broadly and should contain an array of social services, healthcare and personal care provided at home, in the community, and in institutions. Adopting a fee-for-service model at the same time as Asian countries are experiencing what appears to be a breakdown in their intergenerational support culture implies that the marketplace of misfortune is on the verge of leaving vulnerable older people on the outside looking in.

It is virtually a given that in the developing countries of Asia, the elderly will require greater and different kinds of healthcare than their younger counterparts, and the plea for long-term care policy will only become more conspicuous as costs escalate and survival curves mean more elderly will be in need of medical assistance. As governments respond to population aging and changing patterns of morbidity, they will find it difficult to balance healthcare demands against other pressing public programs. Equally difficult will be prioritizing the shortfalls facing the elderly against continuing demands for therapeutic and palliative services, especially from children, women of reproductive age, the poor, and those who have contracted communicable diseases, including raging numbers of people with HIV/AIDS and tuberculosis.

In the chapters to follow, important insights on epidemiological patterns in Asia are provided, along with suitable rationales for dependable long-term care provisions (Choi, 2000; Leung, 2000; Phillips and Chan, 2002). As several of the authors aver, it would be misleading to unequivocally assert a pattern of morbidity compression comparable to that of the West will take place in Asia, or even to typify differential morbidity by gender, though women do have longer life expectancies. Chances are that over the near term, disability rates will climb as Asian countries age. And, in all likelihood, the complexity of gender-related issues pertaining to aging and to healthcare provisions will escalate among future cohorts, as educational attainment for women is on the rise throughout Asia. Most commentators believe that major healthcare policy reformations are vital if quality of life is to be protected (Hermalin, 2001; Phillips and Chan, 2002).

In more affluent Asian nations, spending on medical services has soared, reflecting both rising costs and population aging. In Japan, for example, healthcare expenditures have more than doubled as a percentage of gross domestic product (GDP) between 1960 and 1997. Of course other factors also contribute to mounting costs. For one thing, people who are better off with greater discretionary income tend to spend more on healthcare. In all likelihood, disability rates will increase as more people live long enough to reach old age, and new technologies will bring a wide range of inventive, expensive health services to the medical marketplace. Interestingly, the National Health Insurance in South Korea expressly precludes technologically expensive treatment and includes a copayment of 20 percent for those services that are covered. A factor that should not be overlooked is variable tax revenues associated with economic stagnation, which result in relatively larger percentages of GDP going to mandated provisions, including medical care. Current approaches to health may be costly, and even Japan's much-lauded Gold Plan for providing healthcare for older citizens is increasingly being subjected to criticism on the basis of its expense—not only within the Koizumi cabinet, but by a number of nongovernmental organizations (NGOs) as well. Major retrenchments are being proposed in light of economic recession and internal national discord, and the future of the defined-benefits of the Gold Plan is tarnished.

Around the world, expenditures for medical intervention expand in the last two years of life. In the United States in 1996, for example, Medicare beneficiaries in the final year of life comprised 6 percent of all beneficiaries while accounting for 21 percent of program payments. Thus, even if older people are healthier and living longer, expenditures for medical and palliative care will escalate. As will be seen in many of the chapters in this volume, a comparable pattern is found in Asian countries with burgeoning older populations, and the elderly are having to vie with other pressing priorities.

As Asian populations live longer, the call for healthcare will not lessen. Epidemiological studies suggest that cardiovascular diseases, cancer, obstructive pulmonary disease, and osteoporosis will burgeon. At the same time, informal and familial resources are increasingly strained and are insufficient in the face of structural changes in the economy, and the demand for long-term care associated with disability will spiral upward as more people live into their 70s, 80s, and beyond. Obviously, general public health issues will remain important, reflecting hardship and lifestyle privations. Rising demand for treatment of both communicable and noncommunicable diseases cannot be ignored and is likely to result in loudly competitive appeals for national resources.

Healthcare demands mount as nations undergo economic development, per capita income rises, and life expectancies increase. In combination, these factors are reflected in the increased resources allocated to and rising expectations for health and quality-of-life issues. Whatever the level of economic affluence, population aging challenges the financing and delivery of medical intervention. Asian countries will be faced with decisions about what types of healthcare to provide, to whom it should be provided, and how to effectively and efficiently treat the greatest number of people. Interestingly, Japan has recognized the importance of family care as one facet of a panoply of formal provisions amid contradictory clashes imposed by need to work and need to care. Beginning in 2001, eligible Japanese families began receiving payments for providing care to their most needy older relatives; and no matter how small the recompense, it was an ameliorative step in the provision of what are termed "silver services" (Morikawa, 2001).

In countries that have yet to ensure primary care for all, and where aging has not yet emerged as an abiding issue, paying for long-term care of the elderly is neither a priority nor the subject of much controversy. As will be seen, many developing nations in Asia, including India, Indonesia, and the Philippines, currently channel the majority of public spending to maternal and child health as the principal groups deserving of healthcare. Even in these countries, however, older adults constitute the fastest growing demographic group, and their needs are becoming increasingly perceptible and poignant. Interestingly, the Philippines had one of the earliest retirement systems, but it has not kept pace with social or economic change, and fewer than about 20 percent of the elderly currently receive any benefits.

The economic tigers of the Asian-Pacific region—Hong Kong, Singapore, Japan, South Korea, and Taiwan—have opted for employment-based health insurance with governmental subsidization for the poor, disabled, and elderly. These governments have followed comparable historical patterns of health insurance implementation to achieve universal coverage. First, national governments as employers opt to cover public-sector employees with health insurance financed by taxes and receipts from public enterprises. Second, private employees in the formal sector are covered through government-mandated employment-based health insurance. Third, agricultural workers, the self-employed, and workers in small enterprises (the stereotypical "mom and pop" firms) are brought under a public health umbrella through government-regulated insurance groups financed by means of a combination of taxes and premiums. This incremental pattern is being essentially replicated in the Philippines and Thailand and in other Asian countries beginning to formulate preliminary public programs. These schemes ultimately achieve universal coverage but at high expenditure levels. In the final step, price controls and other governmental stipulations attempt to restrain health expenditures through regulatory control. These employment-based systems are costly and lead to cost shifting at the same time as they grant license to employers to cut jobs, particularly among older workers, and also sanction overuse of healthcare services. As populations age, these costs and the need for reform will become more imperative, especially if economic expansion slows as population aging continues unabated.

Retirement and Labor-Force Policies

Economic development, the global restructuring of labor markets, and internal financial realignments are having far-reaching ramifications in Asia (Kinsella, 2000). Reflecting gains in life expectancy, the number of older workers in Asia has mushroomed over the past half century and will continue to climb as the size of the older cohort grows. Yet, because of policy changes and economic pressures, labor-force participation rates are actually projected to diminish slightly—from 25 percent of the population ages 65 and older in 2000 to 22 percent in 2050. This decline is explained in part by the shift away from agricultural subsistence farming and small-scale marginal occupations to larger-scale enterprises focused on export-oriented economic gains or to public-sector employment. As recent economic reports suggest, long-term employment prospects and security are also undergoing redefinitions so that mid- to late-life unemployment rates are likely to increase in the near term (Phillips, 2000).

Labor-force participation rates for older workers do vary widely across specific countries, however, but are generally low overall and lowest in more affluent Asian economies. Interestingly, structural adjustments appear to have a salient influence on women's work histories and ability to balance work and family demands. For example, in Taiwan, where small-scale economic enterprises and labor-intensive production predominate, women's labor-force participation, relative earnings power, and lifetime patterns are more comparable with those of men than they are in South Korea or Japan. Taiwanese women may also live in a society where gender equality more closely approximates the West and where there is a smaller gendered wage differential than elsewhere in Asia (Brinton, 2001; Yu, 2001). They also have greater flexibility in moving into and out of the labor force, are reported to have greater negotiating power with their employers as family demands ebb and flow, and appear to cope well with conflicting demands of work and family life as childcare becomes more easily accessible (Yu, 2001). It is still the case, however, that women tend to find work primarily in domestic arenas and in service and export-processing industries subject to the influence of economic decisions some distance removed from where they are employed.

In Asia's most prosperous nations, primarily Japan and South Korea, older workers, especially men, may have accumulated sufficient personal assets and pension benefits to retire earlier than in the past. Among Japanese men ages 55 and older, labor-force participation rates are expected to drop from 41 percent in 2000 to 29 percent in 2050. By contrast, among comparably aged Indian men, labor-force participation is higher and predicted to decline much less—from 46 percent in 2000 to 41 percent in 2050. As the overview of economics by Chen and Turner in this volume makes abundantly clear, economic policies are inextricably interwoven with all other public policies and decisions.

In Asia as in much of the rest of the world, workers are exiting the labor market at younger and younger ages. For a portion, deteriorating health may dictate early retirement, but generally speaking this is not the case. Fifty years ago, the majority of Asia's workers were self-employed, either in agriculture or in small-scale enterprises. The decision to work or not was predicted on personal circumstances—wealth, health, responsibilities, preferences, and local conditions. As economies industrialized, more and more workers became employees of governments and large-scale private corporations, where decisions to work or not are often beyond their control and perhaps in the hands of decision-makers remote from where the work is actually done. The pattern across Asia is that decisions to work are progressively governed by public policies and corporate bureaucracies that may discourage or, in some instances, prohibit continued employment by older workers. Labor markets themselves are no longer discrete places controlled by local decision-makers but are often global in nature or attempting to gain leverage in a global marketplace (Rai, 2002).

Obviously, retirement may not be an option where levels of economic development are low or economies are volatile, and many elderly have little choice but to work as long as they are able. Nonetheless, across Asia, the trend is for many workers to retire at younger ages. They do so, in part, because they can afford to as economic prosperity permits and the advent of modern fiscal markets, public and private pension policies, and cash economies facilitate accumulation of personal resources sufficient to support an extended retirement. Studies in several Asian countries have shown that expanding pension and social security provisions tend to encourage early retirement, just as they do in the West. Recent trends appear to suggest that an increasing number of Asian corporations are utilizing compensation programs to encourage early retirement in order to trim payrolls as they seek to retain corporate viability. Such measures have been widely utilized in Japan and South Korea over the past decade or so as economic hard times have eroded the vitality of their economic giants. In many instances, older workers have little voice in the matter, as their jobs are in precarious economic pursuits.

Most Asian governments impose a statutory retirement age below 65—for example, age 60 in the Philippines and South Korea and age 55 in Indonesia and India. As has been the case around the world, Asian nations have been slow to adjust mandatory retirement ages despite rapid improvements in health and life expectancy that potentially enable people to continue to be economically engaged. Workers today may actually prefer to postpone retirement beyond where laws permit as a way to offset erosion of their purchasing power. In the United States, the elimination of a mandatory retirement age several years ago slowed the downward trend in employment rates for older workers, without affecting employment among younger workers. As pointed out in several chapters, in an effort to adapt to market fluctuations, many Asian governments allow businesses and firms to compel older workers to retire when there are widespread economic downturns necessitating greater liquidity, when particular sectors or corporations are challenged, or when firms restructure production processes. Despite evidence to the contrary, dismissing older workers is generally assumed to enhance job prospects for younger workers, predominantly men who are viewed as primary family breadwinners.

Older women are especially vulnerable workers. To a large extent, they work in marginal economic sectors; and even when they are employed in large-scale firms, decisions about whether to retire may be beyond their personal volition. Even in the best of circumstances they are frequently perceived as secondary breadwinners and regarded as nonessential. It was certainly true that during South Korea's recent economic tumult, female employment rates declined more precipitously than did male employment rates. The same has been true in Japan as it has dealt with its own economic stagnation (Brinton, 2001). Furthermore, unemployed women were more likely to become discouraged and to withdraw from the labor market, and even when reemployed, less likely than their male counterparts to obtain comparable or even stable positions in the face of highly constrained employment options. Although unemployment rates for older workers in most of the developing economies in Asia are fairly low, the rate among workers in the 55–64 age interval is markedly higher than among their younger counterparts (Kinsella and Velkoff, 2001). As Olson points out in her chapter, the arrival of export economies and technology is leaving older workers attenuated and obsolete.

There is little reason, though, for governments to endorse early retirement. In fact, the practice reduces employment rates and individual incomes, dampens national economic well-being, and curbs tax revenues. Reducing the number of older workers does not increase employment among younger workers but sunders an important lifeline for many workers not ready or able to retire. Older and younger workers frequently have disparate skills, and labor markets rarely shrink or expand in the same sectors or occupations. In well-functioning economies, the number of jobs is not fixed; rather, it ebbs and flows in dynamic fashion with the number of persons participating in the labor market.

Obviously, retirement policies are not singularly responsible for joblessness or underemployment incurred by older workers. The wage system in some Asian countries—Japan and South Korea especially—reflects seniority rather than performance and is a deeply engrained employment principle. A recurrent charge has been that the wage profiles for senior workers are out of balance with what they are sometimes said to be contributing to the bottom line. Efforts to tie wages more closely to performance and to increase flexibility in job assignments or hours worked are intended to ease pressures that force older workers into retirement. Customarily, seniority-based wage systems have not facilitated options that allow older workers who may contribute diminished productivity to remain employed at reduced wages. Structural impediments, created by corporations, or labor unions, or imposed by governments, also have profound and intractable effects on older workers by limiting the pliability of employment practices. Governments throughout the world establish mandatory retirement ages, and many firms have inflexible rules about work hours that make it problematic for older workers to retire gradually by sliding into part-time employment.

As the authors of this volume point out at several junctures, mandatory retirement ages tend to be lower in developing nations than in their more economically advanced counterparts. Asian retirement ages range from a low of 50 to the long-established 65. In Singapore, for instance, the retirement age is 55, as it is in several nations. Younger retirement ages initially reflected shorter life expectancies and poor health status in developing countries, yet governments have been slow to adjust retirement ages as health and life expectancy have improved. China, Vietnam, Pakistan, and Sri Lanka impose younger retirement ages for women than for men, despite the fact that women characteristically live longer and may spend more years in old age without employment or a spousal support to afford financial stability.

As Olson's review of politics and policies, as well as other chapters, make clear, there is a multitude of policy options that might be considered. One obvious option is either to increase mandatory retirement ages or simply to eliminate them. A second option would be to introduce a scale of sliding pension benefits indexed to retirement age. Monthly benefits might be lower for workers who retire early and higher for others who work longer so that lifetime benefits are equalized. Such a pension scenario provides no incentives for retiring either early or late but facilitates a range of options. Of course, an absence of effective pension provisions is itself an option that cannot be disregarded.

Employers might be less reluctant to hire or retain older employees if they have opportunities to offer part-time positions, the flexibility to vary responsibilities as capabilities of older workers change, or the latitude to structure wages commensurate with productivity. Such pliable employment alternatives may become increasingly attractive to Asian employers as the growth of the labor-force slackens or economies stagnate. The implementation of flexible and part-time employment options may be especially attractive to women. Occupational retraining programs and general educational upgrading will permit older men and women to take up new occupations, to cope with technological change in the workplace, or to exercise personal choice.

Public Pension Programs

With personal and national prosperity, workers around the world retire at younger ages. In Asia, the estimated median age of retirement for men declined from 67 in 1960 to 63 in 2000. In 1950, 30 percent of Asian men and women ages 65 and older were still in the labor force. In 2010, only 22 percent of this age group will be working under current parameters. Obviously, this trend has important implications for workers, families, public coffers, and national economies.

If workers retire earlier yet live longer than in the past, greater resources will be required to support extended periods of retirement. Some workers may be hard-pressed to make ends meet, although others may amass sufficient assets to support themselves through old age. In fact, such an accumulation of wealth may be related to why Asian workers elect early retirement. Still others may be forced to retire because of ill health, economic downturns, or mandatory retirement policies. This latter group will draw additional resources—from families, social security, or pension programs—in order to maintain financial wherewithal in old age.

Though governmental agencies around the world have come to play an increasingly important role in tackling the economic and social security of elderly citizens, many Asian governments assume a more diffident approach. The pensions systems of Malaysia, Singapore, and Japan provide close to universal coverage, but few other countries have followed suit. In 1992, for example, the percentage of workers in India covered by any kind of old-age benefits was scarcely 1 percent, in Indonesia it was 7 percent, and in South Korea, 26 percent. Generally, Asian nations are spending less than 2 percent of GDP on pension benefits, compared to 6 percent in the United States or 18 percent in Sweden. As global economic forces sweep across Asia, the principles they entail may well run counter to traditional value structures and emergent economic needs; accordingly, one consequence is cautiousness in formulating public policies. As

Hermalin (2001) and others have noted unequivocally, Asia is at a crossroads, and many monumental decisions loom large.

As populations age and social security programs mature, the relative share of public resources devoted to pensions and other provisions will increase. Whether or not they will duplicate levels seen in Western countries will depend on policies currently being formulated. Certainly, policy recommendations promulgated by the World Bank might lead one to assume that Western-style social security provisions are in the offing across Asia. An obvious question is whether the local economic state of affairs can accommodate corresponding public policies.

Given the paucity of comprehensive pension programs in Asia, it is somewhat problematic to forecast future directions. In countries that provide effective old-age support funded by payroll taxes, population aging will present persistent challenges. The problems are especially imminent in Japan and they may be a portent of things to come. Japan has spent heavily from public coffers to try to sustain its economic potency in the region and in the world, even cutting the wages of public employees to prop up overextended corporations and financial institutions. Yet Japan has an inclusive social welfare agenda, built upon a heavy reliance on pay-as-you-go financing. Benefits for retirees are a pass-through from current payroll taxes, as is the case in the United States (U.S. Social Security Administration, 1999). As the number of retirees rises relative to the number of workers and the wage base during coming decades, taxes will have to be raised to very high levels, benefits reduced to very low levels, or both in some combination. In the United States, a similar situation prevails: The public pension system is generally said to be unsustainable, partly for demographic reasons but also in light of the shift to a service economy and the changing nature of the wage base on which payroll taxes are withheld. Reforms are necessary and perhaps urgently needed in Japan because of the economic struggle following the prosperity of the late 1980s and early 1990s and because the aging of the population is occurring so swiftly.

In contrast, Singapore has pre-funded its future pension pool by accumulating large fund balances built from the mandatory contributions by current workers and employers. As its population ages, rising pension payouts will be underwritten from pension fund earnings and by drawing down assets in each retiree's individual provident accounts (mandatory savings accounts managed by governmental agencies). Population aging will have no immediate impact on either taxes paid or benefits received by Singapore's workers in the decades just ahead. Despite some of the issues pointed to in the overview chapter on economic resources, Singapore stands out for anticipating future needs and establishing an Inter-Ministerial Committee on the Ageing Population charged with designing an integrative and comprehensive strategy that might well be emulated by sister nations. Typical of the long-range approach adopted in Singapore, the government has also set up a mandatory medical savings scheme for the entire population, with governmental contributions indexed according to individual incomes.

As will be evident in the chapters to follow, given the pace of aging in Asia, there is a relatively narrow window in which to adopt programs and policies to support its elderly. In many countries, the necessary preconditions for establishing sound public and private pension systems have not yet been cultivated. Many countries lack appropriate legal provisions, financial institutions, markets, or administrative capacity to provide economic security for their elderly. Indeed, to date, some countries have scarcely begun to address the consequences of rapidly changing circumstances.

IMPLICATIONS FOR ECONOMIC GROWTH

The demographic transformations of the past several decades have helped stimulate Asia's prosperity. As fertility declined, a smaller percentage of the population consisted of dependent children, while the labor force continued to grow, boosting saving and investment rates, fueled by rising per capita income levels. Demographic conditions will continue to favor economic expansion for several more decades, except in Japan, where the economy has stagnated, cash flows have waned, and the population has aged, all three factors combining to depress saving rates. Japan's population, not to mention its economy, matured earlier than elsewhere in Asia, and it is currently experiencing liquidity concerns barely on the horizon elsewhere in Asia. Though Japan's fiscal situation is lethargic, at best, the other powerhouses, including South Korea and China, continue to thrive.

The impact of demographic transformations on savings and investments has been especially important in Pacific, central, and Southeast Asian countries. For the most part, saving and investment rates were modest in the 1960s—near zero or even negative in Indonesia, Thailand, South Korea, Singapore, and Taiwan. By 1990, there was a major turnaround, and saving and investment rates in several Asian nations ranked among the highest in the world. The accumulation of wealth—prompted in part by demographic change and low dependency ratios—has been vital to ensuring economic vigor. Declining birthrates and the number of working-age adults have spurred investments and savings, and also have had a profoundly positive effect on reducing dependency on foreign capital (Williamson and Higgins, 2001). There are exceptions to be sure; in Indonesia, being a case in point where real wages and purchasing power have declined substantially in the past few years, the economic forecast is dubious. Despite fluctuations and variations across the region, most economies have been kindled by industrialization and global investments (Mason, 2001; Williamson and Higgins, 2001).

The concentration of the population at the working ages should continue to stimulate economic expansion in a number of Asian economies for the near term. Eventually, however, conditions will turn less favorable as the working-age population begins to decline relative to retired cohorts, a trend likely to characterize the foreseeable future. In many countries, the period of extraordinarily high rates of saving and investment is likely to give way to an era of lower rates of saving and investment, resulting in slower economic expansion and unstable revenue streams, both public and private.

To the extent that economic growth decelerates because of aging, rather than imperfect fiscal policy, this slowdown should not be viewed with alarm, especially among Asia's more sustainable economies. The extremely high rates of economic expansion that some countries achieved late in the 20th century have been intrinsically transitory—in part, catching up with the West, but also a consequence of the transition from high to low fertility, improvements in life expectancy and health, not to mention consumer spending. Countries that have successfully ridden the economic wave accompanying these trends have been able to attain higher standards of living that will enable them to cope with the challenges of population aging. In the future, as their populations age further still, their economic growth may yet languish to levels comparable to the world's more mature economies.

Prospects are much less promising for governments struggling with their development agenda or which have not established fiscal and political institutions essential to encourage economic productivity while meeting the social needs of an aging society. The pace of change and the rapidity of Asian aging are happening so quickly that governments have little time to squander. Furthermore, as van Willigen and Lewis and multiple other authors point out in this volume, time-honored ideologies and global fiscal priorities can be less than harmonious, with the resulting conflict echoing across future generations. As such struggles are waged, pensions, health needs, and the social well-being of the aged become unquestionably subject to strenuous debate.

THE FACE OF THE FUTURE

Asia is at a crossroads, and policy choices loom. There are remarkable divergences as well as convergences in issues facing governments across the region. The need for innovative approaches formulated in light of traditions has come to the fore across all the nations of Asia as they encounter global economic entanglements (Hermalin, 2001). Demographic projections for the region suggest that the elderly population will expand considerably over the next 50 years—both in absolute numbers and as a proportion of overall populations. This changing situation presents palpable challenges to policymakers in terms of the interaction of economic and social security, family life, living arrangements and lifestyles, health, and labor-force policy, or for reconciling changing circumstances and cultural customs. Generally speaking, old people in Asia have been supported and sustained by extended families, but there are indications that kinship systems and filial values are eroding in the face of economic and demographic transformations. The obvious question is: Who will provide Asia's growing elderly population with social, economic, and healthcare support?

Not surprisingly, in Japan, where resolutions regarding provision of public healthcare and social services may be further advanced than in South Korea, stress levels are reported to be lower among a sample of caregivers than among their opposite number in South Korea. If appropriate policies are in any way implicated, then Japan may be a model for other Asian nations (Rhee and Lee, 2001). As will be seen repeatedly in the chapters to follow, problems proliferate far faster than solutions.

The rapid increase in numbers, especially among the oldest old, will compel governments to anticipate the resultant demand for healthcare and a host of related infrastructural needs. In many countries, the future elderly will be better educated, urban, and more professional than current cohorts. This means they are likely to be more effective in making their needs known and may be resolute in their insistence on sophisticated and costly services. At the same time, education and income gains may be associated with improved health status at older ages, mitigating the anticipated operating costs of service provisions. As a number of chapters assert, decision-makers must fashion programs to look after present elderly, yet avoid getting locked into policies and approaches that may not be suitable for the changing composition of tomorrow's elderly (Mason, Lee, and Russo, 2001, 2002).

Only a few Asian governments, Japan and Singapore foremost among them, provide pension programs that cover more than a scant fraction of the population. Some provinces and cities in China are experimenting with localized approaches to financing retirement benefits, but these afford rather limited coverage to date. In several countries in the region, however, pension programs exist in theory, but cover few workers in practice. Modest resources are allocated to support pension programs in these countries—only 0.22 percent of GDP in India or 0.14 percent in South Korea, for example. Statutory retirement ages among public and other covered employees are relatively young in much of Asia, and governments may be tempted to increase those thresholds to older ages as a way to preserve productivity and control costs. In the near term at least, such a tactic may conflict with changing skills requirements for technological jobs or run counter to the drive to create more jobs for young people coming to adulthood as a result of previously elevated fertility rates. In many Asian nations, the absence of broad-ranging retirement provisions with strong vesting provisions permits policymakers a relatively free hand in fashioning new programs, but it will be a challenge to build in sufficient flexibility to reflect existing and emergent needs.

Not to be overlooked is the fact that religious and ideological precepts have historically played a prominent role in shaping utile ethical prescriptions and, thereby, public pronouncements. It is important to keep in mind that three influential moral traditions—Buddhism, Confucianism, and Islam—have commingled with Christian sentiments in the region and continue to play a tangible role in influencing idealized views of the elderly. The strong emphasis on family values has colored public practices even as the availability of family resources has waned. Not surprisingly, in a region as ethnically diverse as Asia, ethnicity is yet another factor relevant to how old people are perceived. Needless to say, there are plentiful variations. Overall, one might not be wrong in assuming that the moral economy of more agrarian and less market-driven economies not yet dealing with severe shortages has a more supportive, idealized exchange perspective toward older members, especially during times of plenty. Yet, not surprisingly, activist age-based coalitions have emerged in the past few years in Japan, Hong Kong, the Philippines, Singapore, and elsewhere in Asia in an effort to help shape aging policy and to address equality and quality-of-life issues. Such concerns are only going to become more pressing in the face of the intermingling of economic, social, and global change.

REFERENCES

Bengtson, V., Kim, K.-D., Myers, G., and Eun, K.-S. (2000). *Aging in East and West: Families, states, and the elderly.* New York: Springer.

Brinton, M. (2001). Married women's labor in East Asian economies. In M. C. Brinton (Ed.), *Women's working lives in East Asia* (pp. 1–37). Stanford, CA: Stanford University Press.

Choi, S.-J. (2000). Aging in Korea: Issues and policies. In D. Phillips (Ed.), *Aging in the Asia-Pacific region* (pp. 223–242). London: Routledge.

Economic and Social Commission for Asia and the Pacific [ESCAP]. (1999). *Promoting a society for all ages in Asia and the Pacific.* New York: United Nations.

Han, E.-J., and Kim, T.-H. (2000). An ecological study on causes of elder abuse. *Journal of the Korea Gerontological Society, 20,* 71–89.

Hermalin, A. I. (2001). Aging in Asia: Facing the crossroads. *Hallym International Journal of Aging, 3,* 133–167.

Hsu, H.-C., Lew-Ting, C.-Y., and Wu, S.-C. (2001). Age, period, and cohort effects on the attitude toward supporting parents in Taiwan. *The Gerontologist, 41,* 742–750.

Hu, Y. H. (1995). Elderly suicide risk in family contexts: A critique of the Asian family care model. *Journal of Cross-Cultural Gerontology, 10,* 199–217.

Ingersoll-Dayton, B., and Saengtienchai, C. (1999). Respect for the elderly in Asia: Stability and change. *International Journal of Aging and Human Development, 48,* 113–130.

Kim, H.-G. (1998). Public perceptions of elder mistreatment and its reality in Taegu. *Journal of Korean Gerontological Society, 18,* 184–197.

Kinsella, K. (2000). Demographic dimensions of aging in East and Southeast Asia. In D. Phillips (Ed.), *Aging in the Asia-Pacific region* (pp. 35–50). London: Routledge.

Kinsella, K., and Velkoff, V. A. (2001). *An aging world: 2001* (U.S. Census Bureau, Series P95/01-1). Washington, DC: U.S. Government Printing Office.

Lee, H.-T. (1998). *Family welfare and reproductive health: The Korean experience.* Seminar on Population and Development Policies in Low Fertility Countries. Seoul: KIHASA.

Lee, S.-H., and Mason, A. (2000). Population aging raises questions for policymakers. *East-West Center: Asia-Pacific Population and Policy, 53,* 1–4.

Leung, E. M.-F. (2000). Long-term care issues in the Asia-Pacific region. In D. Phillips (Ed.), *Aging in the Asia-Pacific region* (pp. 82–92). London: Routledge.

Maeda, D., and Ishikawa, H. (2000). Aging in Japan: Retirement, daily lives, pensions, and social security. In D. Phillips (Ed.), *Aging in the Asia-Pacific region* (pp. 113–132). London: Routledge.

Martin, L. G. (1990). The status of South Asia's growing elderly population. *Journal of Cross-Cultural Gerontology, 5,* 93–117.

Mason, A. (Ed.) (2001). *Population change and economic development in East Asia: Challenges met, opportunities seized.* Stanford, CA: Stanford University Press.

Mason, A., Lee S.-H., and Russo, G. (2001). Population momentum and population aging in Asia and Near-East countries. *East-West Center Working Papers: Populations, 107,* 1–146.

Mason, A., Lee S.-H., and Russo, G. (2002). As Asia's population ages, worries grow about the future. *East-West Center: Asia Pacific Issues, 58,* 1–8.

Masuda, M. (2001). Characteristics and the background of the Japanese long-term care insurance system. *Hallym International Journal of Aging, 3,* 169–179.

Morikawa, M. (2001). Problems and future directions of the long-term care insurance system in Japan: Rethinking substitution and compensation for family care. *Hallym International Journal of Aging, 3,* 181–189.

Phillips, D. R. (2000). Aging in the Asia-Pacific region: Issues, policies, and contexts. In D. Phillips (Ed.), *Aging in the Asia-Pacific region: Issues, policies, and future trends* (pp. 1–34). London: Routledge.

Phillips, D. R., and Chan, A. C. M. (2002). National policies on aging and long-term care in the Asia-Pacific: Issues and challenges. In D. R. Phillips and A. C. M. Chan (Eds.), *Aging and long-term care: National policies in the Asia-Pacific* (pp. 1–22). Singapore: Institute of Southeast Asian Studies.

Pienta, A. M., Barber, J. S., and Axinn, W. G. (2001). Social change and adult children's attitudes toward support of elderly parents: Evidence from Nepal. *Hallym International Journal of Aging, 3,* 211–235.

Rai, S. M. (2002). *Gender and the political economy of development: From nationalism to globalization.* Malden, MA: Polity Press.

Rhee, K.-O., and Lee, M. J. (2001). Comparison of caregiving burden among Korean and Japanese caregivers. *Hallym International Journal of Aging, 3,* 191–210.

Sim, O. F. (2002). Aging in Malaysia: A review of national policies and programmes. In D. R. Phillips and A. C. M. Chan (Eds.), *Aging and long-term care: National policies in the Asia-Pacific* (pp. 107–149). Singapore: Institute of Southeast Asian Studies.

Sung, K.-T. (2000). An Asian perspective on aging East and West: Filial piety and changing families. In V. Bengtson, K.-D. Kim, G. Myers, and K.-S. Eun (Eds.), *Aging in the East and the West: Families, states, and the elderly* (pp. 41–56). New York: Springer.

Sung, K.-T. (2001). Elderly respect: Exploration of ideals and forms in East Asia. *Journal of Aging Studies, 15,* 13–26.

United Nations [U.N.]. (2001). *World population prospects: The 2000 revision.* New York: Author.

U.S. Social Security Administration. (1999). *Social security programs throughout the world.* Washington, DC: Author.

Westley, S. B. (1998). Asia's next challenge: Caring for the elderly. *East-West Center: Asia-Pacific Population and Policy, 45,* 1–4.

Westley, S. B., Lee, S.-H., and Mason, A. (2000). Policy options to support Asia's growing elderly population. *East-West Center: Asia-Pacific Population and Policy, 54,* 1–4.

WHO cautions rising health care costs in Asia. (2002, September 9). *The Korean Herald,* p. 3.

Williamson, J., and Higgins, M. (2001). The accumulation and demography of connection in East Asia. In A. Mason (Ed.), *Population change and economic development in East Asia: Challenges met, opportunities seized* (pp. 123–154). Stanford, CA: Stanford University Press.

World Bank. (1994). *Averting the old age crisis: Policies to protect the old and promote growth.* New York: Oxford University Press.

Yoon, G., Eun, K.-S., and Park, K.-S. (2000). Korea: Demographic trends, sociocultural contexts, and public policy. In V. Bengtson, K.-D. Kim, G. Myers, and K.-S. Eun (Eds.), *Aging in the East and the West: Families, states, and the elderly* (pp. 121–137). New York: Springer.

Yu, W.-H. (2001). Family demands, gender attitudes, and married women's labor force participation: Comparing Japan and Taiwan. In M. C. Brinton (Ed.), *Women's working lives in East Asia* (pp. 70–95). Stanford, CA: Stanford University Press.

PART 1

Asian Aging in Social Context

CHAPTER ONE

Demography of Aging Across Asia

Andrew Mason, Sang-Hyop Lee, and Gerard Russo

The year 2000 was a demographic watershed in Asia. After a century of growth, the number of children in the region peaked in 1999 and, with the turn of the millennium, has begun a slow, gradual decline. At the same time, mortality has dropped dramatically across the region. Three phenomena—the enormous, sustained baby boom that characterized the 20th century, the decline in fertility that will characterize the 21st, and the continuing, steady decline in mortality—all have major implications for the size and the age structure of Asian populations.

All across Asia, the proportions of older adults ages 65 and older in national populations are expected to grow rapidly over the next 50 years. This process of population aging is already clearly visible in the economically advanced countries of East Asia. Population aging is beginning in the Southeast Asian countries that have successfully increased life expectancy and reduced fertility, and can be anticipated even in the South Asian countries where the number of children today is still high. Population aging will present many challenges—such as providing healthcare for the elderly, assuring economic security for the elderly, and sustaining economic growth—to the societies and economies of Asian nations, and this demographic trend will have a sustained and irreversible impact on the nature of the support system on which the elderly rely.

AGING AND POPULATION CHANGE

Population aging began in Asia during the 1970s. Before then, rapid growth in the number of children was producing a younger population. Between 1950 and 1975, the percentage of the Asian population ages 15 and younger rose from 37 percent to 40 percent and the median age for the region dropped from

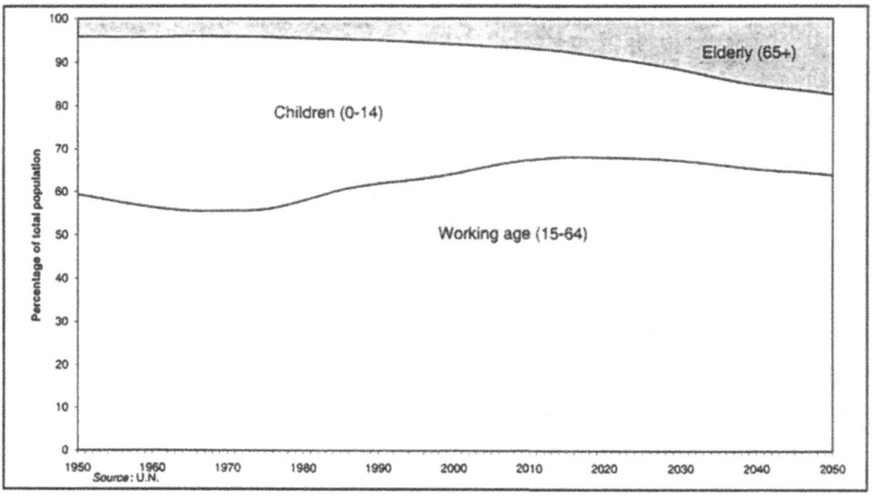

Figure 1. Asia's age transition.

21.9 to 19.7. By the mid-1970s, this trend had reversed itself. Growth in the number of children slowed relative to the numbers of working-age adults and elderly (Figure 1). By 2000, if U.N. values are accurate, children accounted for only 30 percent of Asia's population, and the percentage of Asians who were working age had risen to 64 percent. The proportion of older adults in the population had increased gradually from the 1970s to 2000 and will continue to rise for the foreseeable future. By 2050, 17 percent of those living in Asia are expected to be age 65 or older; 19 percent will be younger than 15; and 64 percent will be between the ages of 15 and 64. The median age will have reached 39 (United Nations [U.N.], 1999, medium projections).

More detailed snapshots of Asia's projected age and sex structure are provided by the age pyramids for 2000, 2025, and 2050 shown in Figure 2. The age pyramid for 2000 is similar to those found in other relatively young populations. There is a broad base consisting of large numbers of children and a narrow top consisting of smaller numbers of older adults. In the past, new cohorts of ever-increasing size entered the population, enlarging the base. In the future, however, the base of the age pyramid is expected to remain stable while population growth will be concentrated at older ages.

The relative stability of Asia's young population is already apparent among the youngest age groups. In 2000, the 0-to-4-year-old cohort and the 5-to-9-year-old cohort have essentially the same population size, and neither cohort is as large as the 10-to-14-year-old cohort. In the future, entering cohorts are projected to be of similar size or somewhat smaller than preceding ones. The major demographic phenomenon will be a "filling out" of the pyramid at older ages. As this occurs, all

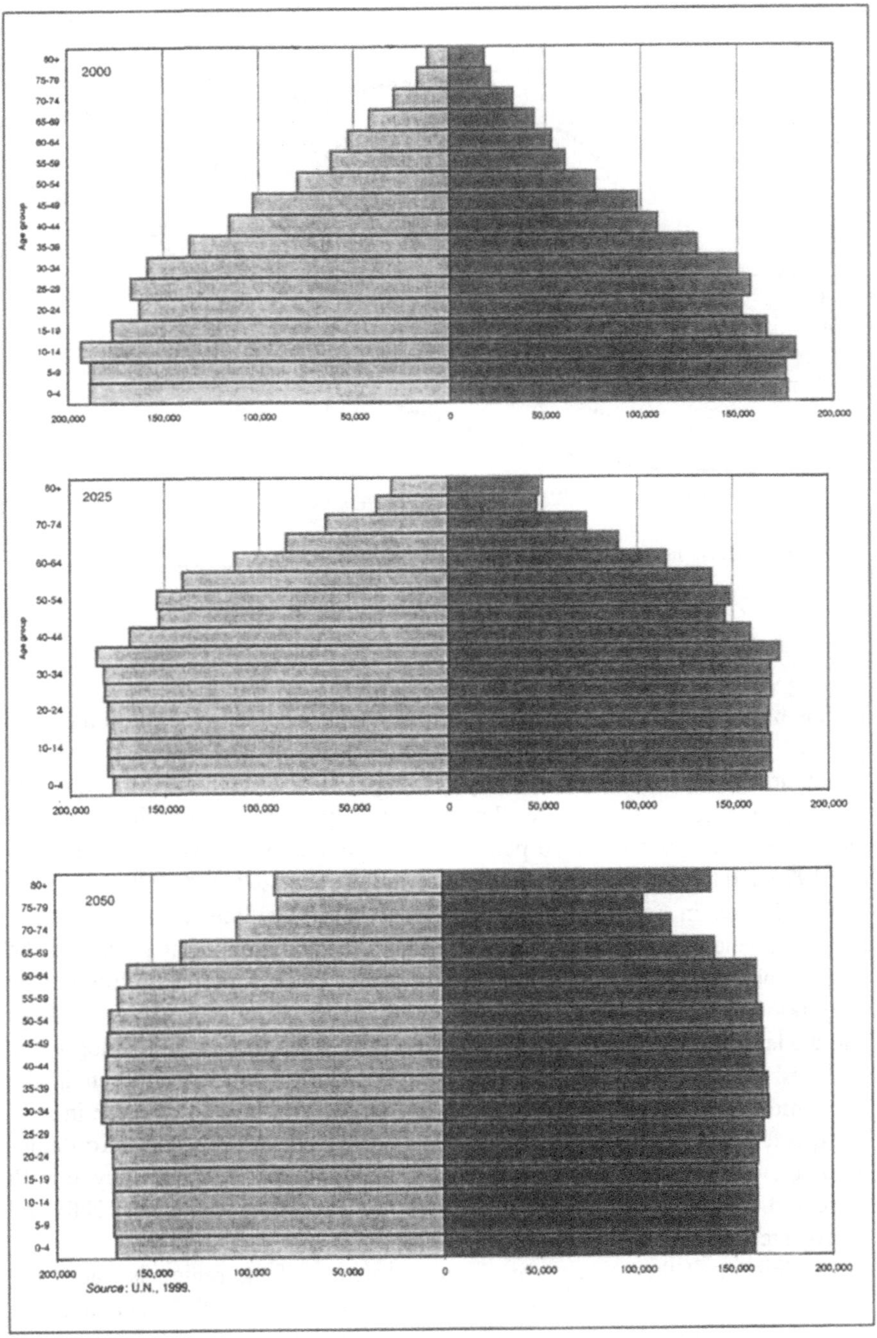

Figure 2. Age pyramid for Asia. (light gray = females, dark gray = males.)

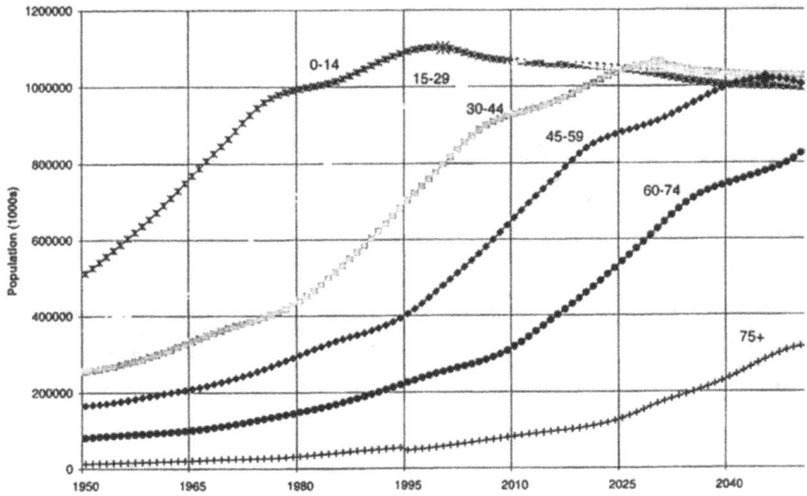

Source: U.N., 1999.

Figure 3. Population of Asia, 1950–2050.

but the oldest cohorts are projected to stabilize at around 300–350 million people per five-year age group. Between 2000 and 2025, 99 percent of Asia's projected population growth is accounted for by those ages 30 and older and only 1 percent by the population of those under the age of 30. By contrast, individuals ages 30 and younger accounted for 70 percent of the population growth between 1950 and 1975 and nearly 40 percent of the growth between 1975 and 2000.

The changes in Asia's population are being driven by three interrelated demographic phenomena. The first is a sustained "baby boom" that produced the largest cohort of youth in the past and, possibly, in the foreseeable future. The baby boom led to accelerated growth in the number of children between 1950 and the late 1970s and more modest growth until 1999. The second demographic event is the emergence of relative stability in the number of children in the population. After more than a century of growth, the number of children in Asia is expected to begin a period of very slow, sustained decline. The third demographic event is the shift in the region's mortality rates. Life expectancy at birth increased from 41 years in the early 1950s to 60 years by the early 1980s and is projected to reach 68 years in 2000–05.

The impact of these events on the age structure of the region is traced out in Figure 3, which charts Asia's population from 1950 to 2050 separately for 15-year age groups. This representation of age structure is advantageous in that it facilitates following cohorts over time. The impact of the baby boom is evident in the accelerated growth of the child population, those ages 0–14, between 1950 and 1980 and more gradual growth during the last two decades of the 20th century. The child population more than doubled in size, increasing from about 500 million in 1950 to about 1.1 billion in 2000.

Asia's baby boom was different than the post–World War II baby boom that occurred in the United States and many other Western countries. The Asian baby boom was much longer lasting and occurred for different reasons: The Western baby boom resulted from an increase in rates of childbearing, whereas Asia's baby boom primarily resulted from a decline in infant and child mortality.

The Asian baby boom had an enormous impact on the age structure of the population, and its effects will continue well into the 21st century. The first group of baby boomers reached young adulthood in 1965, and in 1995 reached 45 years of age. This means that in the next few decades, the most rapid growth in Asia's population will be among those in the prime working ages (30–59). Growth in the older adult population will accelerate beginning in 2010, when the first baby boomers turn 60.

The future age structure of Asia will be influenced by the near stability of future cohorts of children and by the rapid growth of the baby boom generation. The year 2000 produced a generation of children in Asia, the Y2K generation, that is smaller than the preceding one. As this generation ages, growth in the number of young adults and prime-age adults will stabilize and possibly begin to decline.

Concurrently, the baby boomers will continue to enlarge the absolute and relative numbers belonging to older age groups. The impact of continuing changes in mortality on age structure is less apparent in Figure 3 than changes in the size of cohorts of children. However, declining mortality at older ages will have an important impact. As life expectancy rises in the future, the gains in survival rates will be increasingly concentrated at older ages. As a consequence, older age groups grow more rapidly during their high-growth period than do younger age groups. Likewise, once growth ceases older cohorts decline somewhat more gradually than do young cohorts. Thus, declining mortality in the future will reinforce the shift to an older population.

In percentage terms, the older adult population will be the most rapidly growing segment of Asia's population during the first half of the 21st century. The average annual rate of growth for the population ages 60–74 is projected at 2.9 percent and that of the population ages 75 and older, at 3.4 percent. By contrast, the population ages 0–14 is projected to decline at an annual rate of 0.2 percent, the size of the population ages 15–29 is projected to remain essentially the same from 2000 to 2050, and the populations of the 30–44 and 45–59 age groups are projected to increase at 0.5 percent and 1.5 percent annually, respectively.

The aggregate patterns for Asia are dominated by the region's two most populous countries, China and India. However, the general trends and demographic forces that are influencing regional trends are also operating in other Asian countries. The speed and timing of population aging will vary considerably among the countries in the region. In general, the countries of East Asia are furthest along in the aging process, followed by Southeast Asia and then South Asia. Japan and Singapore have the oldest populations in Asia. Among Asia's major countries, Pakistan has the youngest population (as measured by median age in 2000). There, 42 percent are under the age of 15 and only 5 percent are ages 65 and older.

For projection purposes, in this study we will take a more detailed look at seven Asian countries in each subregion. They include the Philippines, Thailand, Indonesia, India, Japan, Korea, and Bangladesh, which are at various stages of demographic transitions. Detailed data on other countries can be found in two recent surveys by the East-West Center (2002) and by Asian Development Bank (Mason, 2002). Aging measures for these study countries examined in detail in this chapter are reported in Table 1.

PROJECTED GROWTH OF THE ELDERLY POPULATION AND THE LABOR FORCE

In this section we present population and labor-force projections recently prepared by the United Nations (U.N., 1999) and the International Labour Organization (ILO, 1996).

Population Projections, 2000–2050

This section makes detailed use of population projections from the United Nations (U.N., 1999). Any population projection is based on a set of assumptions

Table 1. Summary Measures of Aging for Asia, Major Subregions, and Seven Asian Countries

	Elderly population (1000s)			Growth rate of elderly population		Old-age dependency ratio		
	2000	2025	2050	2000-25	2025-50	2000	2025	2050
Asia	207,349	454,964	864,614	3.14	2.57	0.086	0.144	0.25
East Asia	114,390	241,217	389,089	2.98	1.91	0.113	0.21	0.383
Southeast Asia	24,503	58,253	131,138	3.46	3.25	0.074	0.124	0.262
South Asia	68,457	155,494	344,388	3.28	3.18	0.076	0.112	0.216
Japan	21,614	32,383	33,323	1.63	0.11	0.250	0.447	0.584
South Korea	3,152	8,020	12,665	3.74	1.83	0.094	0.226	0.417
Indonesia	10,001	23,078	51,500	3.34	3.21	0.073	0.123	0.26
Philippines	2,758	7,786	18,558	4.15	3.47	0.061	0.105	0.216
Thailand	3,576	8,924	17,077	3.66	2.60	0.084	0.178	0.382
Bangladesh	4,149	10,494	29,787	3.71	4.17	0.081	0.123	0.232
India	50,466	111,934	231,266	3.19	2.90	0.068	0.112	0.221

Note: All data employ the medium fertility variant.
Source: U.N. Population Division, 1998.

about long-range trends in demographic variables. The reality that emerges during the coming decades may differ considerably from projected values depending on a variety of social, political, economic, and demographic forces. Political instability, new rounds of economic crisis, the emergence of new infectious diseases, and the increasingly rapid spread of HIV/AIDS could lead to substantial, unanticipated deterioration in mortality conditions and depressed levels of fertility. More optimistically, medical breakthroughs could lead to a substantial extension of life and more rapid increases in life expectancy than anticipated. The future course of fertility is very uncertain. How low fertility will decline, how long it remains at subreplacement levels, and whether new baby booms will occur are primarily a matter of speculation.

Despite these uncertainties, population projections provide an important and useful framework for thinking about the future. At this point, the authors will rely on a single projection—the medium variant—to describe the broad demographic trends in Asia. Below, alternative projections are considered in some detail. The U.N. projections do not consider alternative mortality variants, but two such variants have been prepared.

The methodology is summarized here, but the interested reader can find a more detailed explanation in Zlotnik (1999). The methodology used by the United Nations requires estimates of the population by sex and age category in a base year (1995) and subsequent trends in age-specific rates of fertility, mortality, and international immigration from 1995 to 2050. An estimate of the base-year population in each country is obtained by revising and updating the most recent population census using available data on fertility, mortality, and, in principle, immigration. Decennial population censuses are conducted in most Asian countries in years ending with 0 or 1; hence, the most recent direct data on population were collected in 1990 or 1991. In most countries, more recent estimates of fertility and mortality are available from surveys and civil registration systems. The most comprehensive data are available for fertility and child mortality. Many countries do not have recent data on adult mortality. Few countries have reliable information on international immigration. Of the 32 countries of East, Southeast, and South Asia that have populations of 150,000 or more, 21 have estimates of fertility available after 1993; 18 have estimates of child mortality available after 1993; and 5 have estimates of adult mortality after 1993. Thirteen additional Asian countries have estimates of adult mortality for the 1990–93 period (Zlotnik, 1999, Table 1).

The U.N. Population Division prepares three sets of projections used here. They differ in their assumptions about future trends in fertility. The medium variant distinguishes three groups of countries. The first consists of countries with total fertility rates (TFRs) above replacement level (2.1 births per woman). (The TFR is the average number of children women would bear were they subject to the age-specific birthrates prevailing during the period in question.) In these countries, the TFR is projected to decline smoothly until it reaches 2.1 births per woman, at which time it remains constant throughout the remainder of the projection. The second group consists of countries with a TFR between 1.5 and 2.1 births per woman. In these countries, the fertility rate is projected to converge to 1.9 births per woman. The third group consists of countries with very low fertility, that is, a TFR below 1.5 births per woman. In these countries, the TFR is projected to rise to a target level of 1.7 births per woman.

Of the seven countries examined in this chapter, four belonged to the high-fertility group. Of these seven, Indonesia is projected to reach replacement level first, in 2000–05; India five years later; and the Philippines and Bangladesh, in 2010–15. Two countries, South Korea and Thailand, are low-fertility countries where the TFR is projected to increase to 1.9 births per woman during the first part of the 21st century (Table 2).

In the low-fertility variant, the TFR for high-fertility countries is projected to decline to 1.6 births per woman. For low-fertility countries, the TFR is projected to decline to 0.4 births per woman below the target fertility level used in the medium-fertility variant; thus, the TFRs in South Korea and Thailand are projected to decline to 1.5 births per woman. In the high-fertility variant, the TFR for high-fertility countries is projected to decline to 2.6 births per woman. The TFR for the low-fertility countries is projected to rise to 0.4 births per woman above the target level, for a TFR of 2.3 births per woman in South Korea and Thailand (Zlotnik, 1999).

U.N. population projections are based on a single set of mortality assumptions, instead of providing alternative variants. In most countries in Asia, life expectancy at birth is expected to increase steadily, based on recent or medium-term experience, but more slowly as high levels of life expectancy are reached. Countries with a life expectancy of less than 65 years, for example, are projected to gain 2–2.5 years in life expectancy per quinquennium. When life

Table 2. Fertility Assumptions, Medium U.N. Projections

Country	1990-95	1995-2000	2000-05	2005-10	2010-2015	2015-2020
Japan	1.43	1.47	1.54	1.61	1.68	1.73
South Korea	1.65	1.69	1.76	1.83	1.89	1.90
Indonesia	2.58	2.26	2.10	2.10	2.10	2.10
Philippines	3.62	3.19	2.76	2.33	2.10	2.10
Thailand	1.74	1.74	1.78	1.85	1.90	1.90
Bangladesh	3.11	2.82	2.53	2.24	2.10	2.10
India	3.13	1.72	2.31	2.10	2.10	2.10

Note: For countries included in this table, the TFR is constant after 2015-2020.
Source: U.N., 1998.

expectancy reaches 70, the gain per quinquennium is only 1.0 year of life. At higher levels, the increase per quinquennium drops to 0.3 to 0.5 years. The mortality pattern is assumed to converge to an ultimate life expectancy of 82.5 for males and 87.5 for females, although no country reaches the ultimate life expectancy by the end of the projection period (Zlotnik, 1999). Mortality assumptions for three Asian countries—Cambodia, India, and Thailand—explicitly include the impact of HIV/AIDS. Details of the procedures followed are available in Zlotnik (1999).

The projected life expectancy, at 10-year intervals, for each of the study countries is reported in Table 3. In every country, a steady increase in life expectancy is anticipated. The most rapid projected increase occurs in countries with low levels of life expectancy in 1990–95: Bangladesh, Indonesia, India, and the Philippines. Slower increases are anticipated in Thailand and South Korea. The projections anticipate substantial convergence in mortality conditions. By 2040–45, the difference between the lowest and the highest country, Bangladesh and South Korea, is only 5.4 years. In comparison, the difference in 1990–95 was estimated at 15.3 years.

The final component of the U.N. population projections is international migration. The information about international migration is limited and unreliable, but in most instances international migration is a relatively small component of population growth. In some instances, however, political instability or natural disasters have generated large-scale movements between countries. These movements are largely unpredictable in nature, and no attempt is made to capture them in the U.N. projections, although the projections do anticipate the return of refugees to the country of origin in some instances. The six study countries (except for Japan) are all classified as population "exporters," although Thailand

Table 3. Projected Life Expectancy in Seven Asian Countries

	Life expectancy (years)						Projected increase (years)
	1990-95	2000-05	2010-15	2020-25	2030-35	2040-45	
Japan	79.5	80.3	81.1	81.9	82.7	83.4	3.9
South Korea	70.9	73.5	75.4	77.1	78.4	79.4	8.5
Indonesia	62.6	67.3	70.5	72.9	74.9	76.6	14.0
Philippines	66.3	69.8	72.3	74.4	76.3	77.7	11.4
Thailand	68.8	69.4	72.8	75.4	76.0	76.6	7.8
Bangladesh	55.6	60.7	65.3	69.2	71.9	74.1	18.5
India	60.3	64.2	67.3	70.4	72.7	74.2	13.9

Note: All data employ the medium fertility variant.
Source: U.N. Population Division, 1998.

is a net exporter only for the period between 2000 and 2005. Thereafter, no net international migration is projected. Net outflows by South Koreans are projected to decline and stabilize at zero by 2020–25. The other study countries are projected to experience net outflows on a continuing basis. The Philippines has the largest projected net outflows, averaging 0.1 percent of the population per year between 2000 and 2050.

Indonesia and Bangladesh both have net outflows equal to 0.06 percent of their population per year. The absolute number of emigrants from India exceeds that from the other study countries but represents only 0.01 percent of the population per year. Obviously, net migration is a relatively small component of population growth even in the Philippines. The impact on age structure may be substantially larger than these net rates suggest to the extent that the age distribution of those who migrate is heavily concentrated in particular age groups. Data on the age distribution of projected migrants are not available from the United Nations. Hence, the extent to which immigration is influencing population aging in Asia cannot be directly assessed. This is an issue, however, to which we return below.

Labor-Force Projections to 2050

The previous section examines the impact of population momentum on population aging in Asia. Population momentum also had deep implications for the size and the age distribution of the labor force (the economically active population). The broad labor-force trends for Asia are summarized by Figures 4 and 5, which show both the historical and projected labor forces in 10-year age groups for males and females. In many respects, the labor-force trends are similar to the population trends described above. This is hardly surprising, as a key determinant of the size of the labor force in any age group is the size of the population in that age group. The values presented here, unless otherwise indicated, are based on the United Nations' medium-variant population projections.

In some countries, labor-force trends differ from population trends because of important changes in labor-force participation rates (activity rates). The activity rates of three demographic groups in particular are changing in many countries. First, many teenagers and young adults are extending their time in school and delaying their entry into the labor force. Second, activity rates among women have increased as rates of childbearing have declined. Third, activity rates among older males have dropped. Estimates and projections of participation rates primarily rely on the 1996 study published by the International Labour Organization (ILO), *Economically Active Population Estimates and Projection* (EAPEP). The EAPEP provides estimates and projections of labor-force participation rates by sex and five-year age groups for the period 1950–2010 at 10-year intervals and for 1995. These projections were extended to 2050 by making additional assumptions.

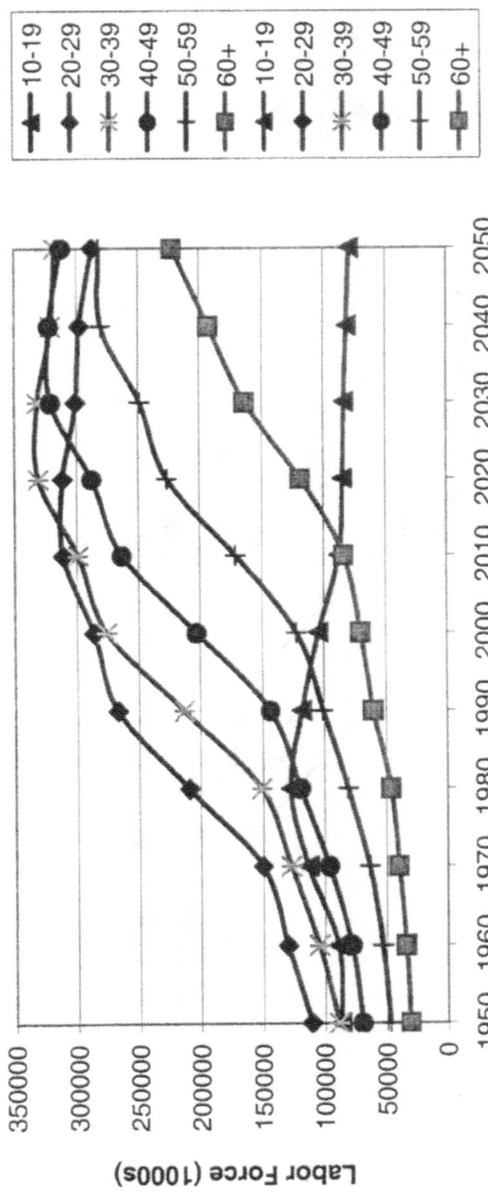

Sources: ILO, 1996; U.N., 1999. Calculations by authors.

Figure 4. Male labor force of Asia by ten-year age group, 1950-2050.

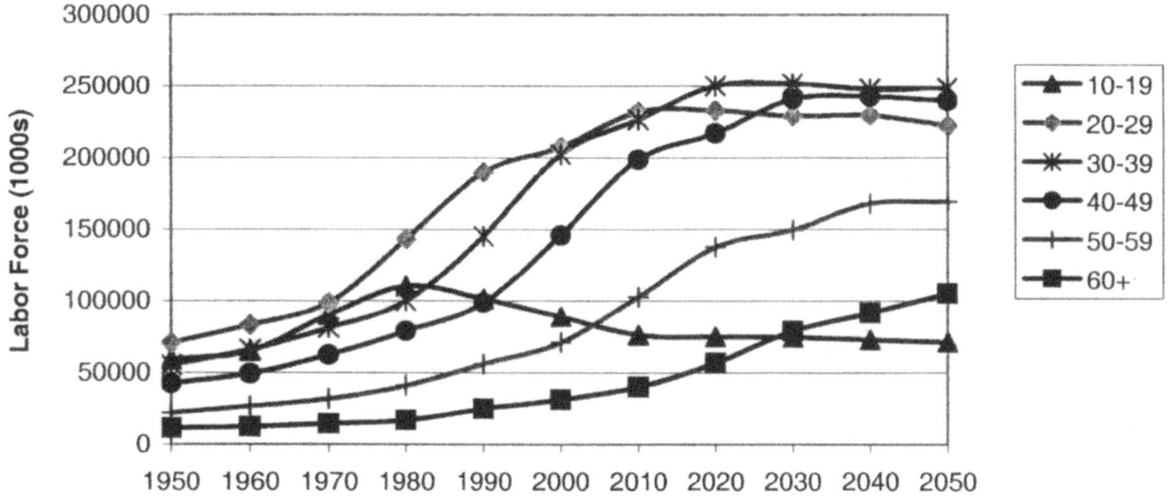

Sources: ILO, 1996; U.N., 1999. Calculations by authors.

Figure 5. Female labor force of Asia by ten-year age group, 1950-2050.

The participation rates were combined with U.N. population projections from the 1998 revision to the United Nations' *World Population Prospects* to yield estimates and projections of the labor force by age and sex.[1]

The labor-force transition for Asia is dominated by its two largest countries, China and India. However, most Asian countries have similar experiences, with slight variation in the timing and speed of the transition. Asian countries have experienced waves of substantial labor-force growth, affecting the youngest age groups first, followed by successively older age groups. This phenomenon is very similar to what we have seen in the previous section and directly reflects the impact of demographic transition. The size of the child labor force, those ages 10–19, accelerated during the 1960s and 1970s, reached a peak in 1980, and then entered a period of decline that is projected to continue.[2] Growth in the size of the labor force in this age group ceased earlier than corresponding population figures because of the rapid decrease in activity rates of 10-to-19-year-olds since 1980. The young-adult labor force, those ages 20–29, increased most rapidly during the 1970s and 1980s and is projected to peak in 2010. The prime-age male and female labor force, those ages 30–49, has been increasing rapidly for the last two decades and is projected to reach its apex in 2030. The oldest segment of the labor force, those ages 60 and older, is relatively small and has increased slowly during the last 50 years. Its era of rapid increase is not expected to begin until 2010 or later. In percentage terms, the elderly labor force is projected to increase most rapidly during the next 50 years. However, declining activity rates among older adults could slow this growth considerably.

Table 4 profiles the total labor force and the older adult labor force of Asia, including several subregions and seven countries. Note that the broad changes experienced in individual Asian countries are similar to those seen in the region as a whole. There are differences in timing and magnitude, however. South Korea and Thailand are further along in their labor force transitions and their labor forces are expected to grow little or not at all between 2000 and 2050. The older adult labor forces of these two countries are expected to grow substantially, but less so than in India, Bangladesh, or elsewhere. Japan is also much further along in the transition and, unlike most Asian countries, population decline in Japan is anticipated by the U.N. projections. Although Japan's older adult labor force is expected to grow modestly, its total labor force is projected to decline by 20 million workers between 2000 and 2050.

Changes in activity rates have an important impact on the size and key characteristics of the labor force. The changes that have occurred in the entire Asian region, shown in Figures 6 and 7, are similar to those that individual Asian countries have also experienced. Three general changes have been pervasive.

[1] The 1996 labor-force projections published by the ILO use earlier U.N. population projections.

[2] The activity rates for those in this age group are assumed to be constant after 2010, but one can well imagine continued decline in those rates with further reductions in the size of the child labor force.

Table 4. Total Labor Force and Older Adult Labor Force in Asia

	Total labor force (1000s)			Labor force ages 65 and older (1000s)		
	1950	2000	2050	1950	2000	2050
Asia	687,012	1,786,136	2,478,075	20,774	50,671	193,278
East Asia	366,935	874,564	853,782	9,115	20,562	53,051
Southeast Asia	84,805	260,621	426,501	3,456	8,469	45,054
South Asia	235,272	650,951	1,197,792	8,203	21,640	95,173
Japan	36,650	68,164	48,178	1,465	4,837	5,633
South Korea	7,449	23,881	23,789	201	700	2,239
Indonesia	32,149	102,856	163,584	1,834	3,518	14,673
Philippines	8,194	32,067	67,555	279	1,080	6,196
Thailand	10,894	37,173	40,340	269	932	3,772
Bangladesh	24,153	68,471	127,918	946	1,903	12,310
India	169,907	445,770	738,140	5,278	16,199	65,206

Source: ILO, 1996. Calculations by authors.

First, adult men ages 25–54 are reducing their participation in the labor force slightly, while adult women are increasing theirs. Second, young men and women ages 15–24 are postponing their entry into the labor market. Third, elderly men are withdrawing from the labor force at a younger age. The effects of these changes are to concentrate the labor force at prime ages and to increase the number of women in the labor force as compared to men.

The inverse U-shaped profile of activity rates by age for men (Figure 6) is typical of most countries. The activity rates of men ages 24–54 are slightly decreasing in some countries because of weak labor markets. Younger male workers ages 15–24 show declining activity rates, mostly due to the increase in the age limit for compulsory schooling and the growing trend among the young for pursuing higher education. In some instances, young people are not seeking work because they think no work is available for their skills.

For men ages 55 and older, activity rates have declined substantially over the last 50 years and are projected to continue to decrease, although more gradually, in the future. This is mostly because older men have been discouraged from working and have ceased seeking work as employment opportunities for this age group have shrunk. Rapid technological progress has made their skills and competencies obsolete, reducing their productivity. Employers appear to be reluctant to employ or even to retain older workers on the grounds that aging reduces productivity and seniority-based remuneration raises the cost of employing older workers. Many older people have lost job opportunities because employment has shifted out of agriculture. Jobs in agriculture have been the most

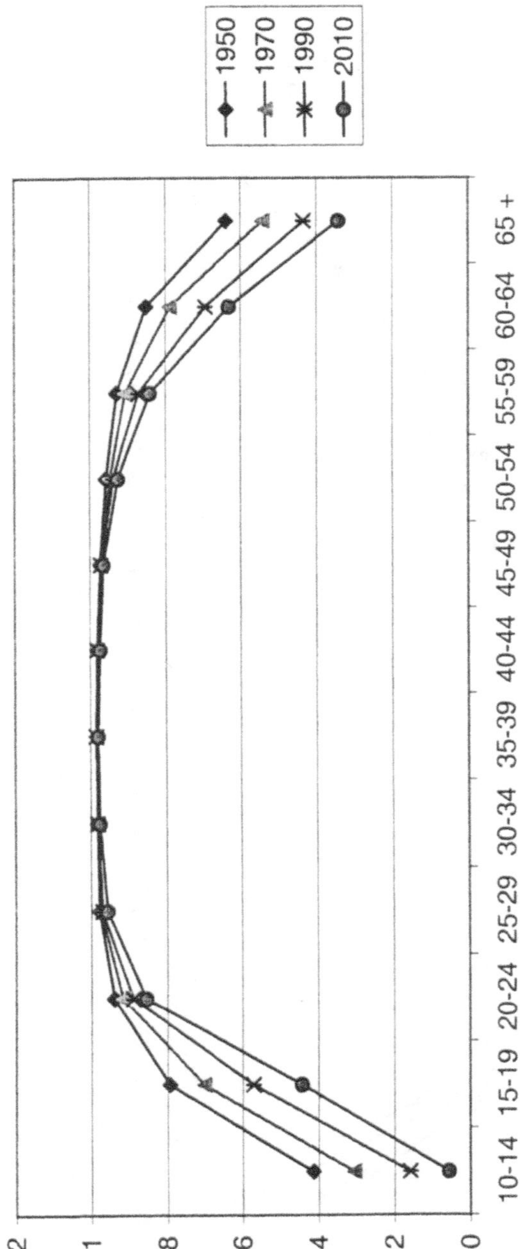

Source: ILO, 1996.

Figure 6. Male labor-force participation rates in Asia by age group.

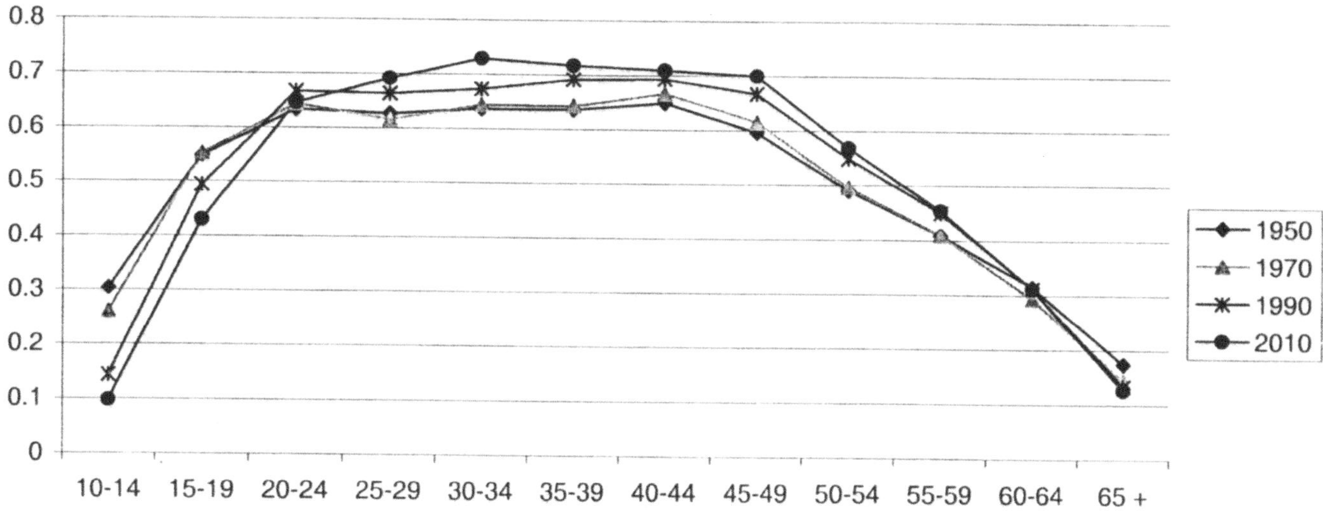

Source: ILO, 1996.

Figure 7. Female labor-force participation rates in Asia by age group.

important source of employment for the elderly, and this sector is not subject to the rigidities of the labor market that exist in an urban setting. Rapid changes in educational systems might also have given middle-aged and younger workers a competitive advantage over their older counterparts. In some countries, mandatory early-retirement provisions have affected activity rates among the elderly. Finally, for developed countries such as Japan and South Korea, higher standards of living, an increased preference for retirement, and the development of pension systems have contributed to lower activity rates among older men.

In most Asian countries, though, pension programs are sufficiently small that they have had a modest influence on retirement. However, as Asian countries begin to implement new programs for the elderly, elderly activity rates could decline more rapidly than projected.

The profile of the activity rates of women (Figure 7) is moving closer to that of men, although, even in 2010, women are considerably less likely to be in the labor force than are men. The increase in female labor-force participation, concentrated in the 25–59 age group, can be traced to a variety of important developments. Changes in family responsibilities, particularly delayed marriage and the decline in child-rearing responsibilities, have played a particularly important role. The development of such elements of social infrastructure as the following have contributed to the increased feminization of the labor force: childcare, preschool, and elder-care facilities; changes in the work organization and the development of part-time work; and the growth of new industries that require workers with dexterity and intelligence rather than brute strength. Improved survey procedures also measure women's activities more accurately by asking women what they do rather than asking them for their profession.

The trend toward higher female labor-force participation rates in Asia is not replicated in the experience of Bangladesh or Thailand. Women ages 25–59 in both of these countries have much higher activity rates than do women in other countries in the region. As their levels are already so high, a small decrease is foreseen for the next 50 years. For younger women in Asia, the trend in activity rates is similar to that for younger men. As they remain in school longer their labor-force participation rates have declined. The gender gap in labor-force participation has largely disappeared at this age, as young women are as likely to be in the labor force as are young men. For women ages 55 and older, activity rates are generally low, have changed very little, and are projected to remain relatively constant.

Activity rates vary widely among countries or subregions, reflecting varying labor market conditions, industrial structures, educational systems, gender bias, and pension systems. Two differences are particularly important. First, participation by elderly men in the labor force varies widely. Whereas most of countries in Southeast and South-Central Asia recorded participation rates for this population ranging from 50 percent to 60 percent in the mid-1990s, Japan and South Korea recorded rates of around 35 percent. Second, there are differences in the pattern of women's participation in the labor force. The M-shaped women's activity profile found in relatively developed countries in the region, such as Japan and South Korea, was characteristic of the female life cycle in the 1950s through the 1970s. The bimodal shape was the result of women leaving the workforce at around the age of 25 to marry and raise children; a proportion returned to it at around age 35 once their children had entered school or once older children could take care of younger ones. This M-shape is not characteristic of less developed countries in the region, probably because of such factors as the dominance of the agricultural sector and differing ways of child rearing. Even where the M-shape is found, the increase in female activity rates is causing its gradual disappearance.

The changing age structure of the Asian labor force reflects changes both in activity rates and in the underlying population. Declining activity rates among the young are reinforced by declining population growth rates among the young. Declining activity rates among the elderly, however, are more than offset by the rapid growth of elderly populations throughout Asia. The resulting transition of the Asian labor force is shown in detail in Figures 8 and 9.

The proportion of Asian workers, both male and female, who are ages 10–19 has experienced a sharp decline for the last two decades. Although India and Bangladesh still will have a relatively high proportion of young workers for the next few decades, their workforces too will begin to experience the same shift. Prior to 1990, Asia as a whole did not experience any change in the proportion of the labor force who were ages 50 and older, although in Japan this figure had already increased very substantially by 1990. South Korea and Thailand are also beginning to experience an increase in the proportion of the labor force who are over the age of 50, and this proportion is projected to increase markedly over the next 10 years. By 2050, one third of the male labor force is projected to be age 50 or older; a somewhat smaller fraction of the female labor force will be concentrated at these ages.

If the projections presented here prove to be accurate, declining labor-force participation rates and stable or declining populations will lead to a decline in the number of young workers across Asia. Continued increases in female labor-force participation rates, combined with larger populations in the prime working ages, will lead to a significantly larger female labor force. The number of elderly workers will also grow substantially, even though the proportion of elderly men participating in labor force is expected to decline.

DEMOGRAPHIC CHARACTERISTICS AND SUPPORT SYSTEMS FOR THE ELDERLY

Currently, Asia's older adult population is concentrated at the younger edge of this age group, but over time the numbers of older population will increase disproportionately. Of the population ages 55 and older in 2000, roughly half

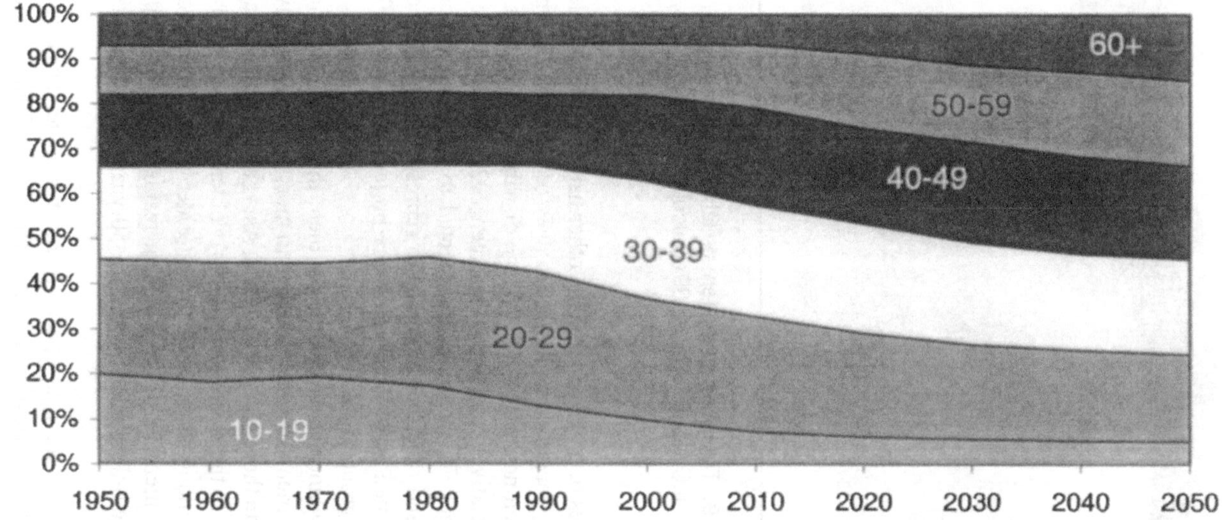

Sources: ILO, 1996; U.N., 1999. Calculations by authors.

Figure 8. Transition of the male labor force in Asia.

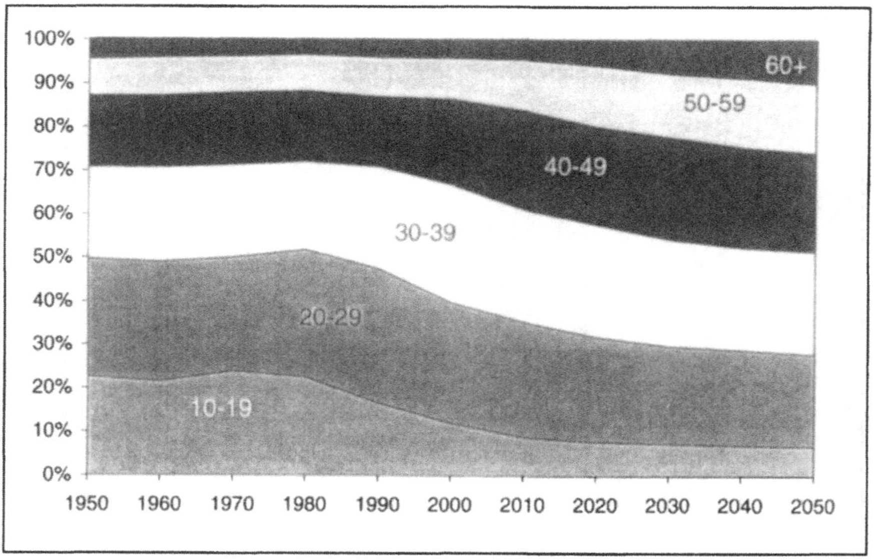

Figure 9. Transition of the female labor force in Asia.
Sources: ILO, 1996; U.N., 1999. Calculations by authors.

were between the ages of 55 and 64 and the other half were 65 or older. Of those above the age of 65, roughly two thirds are ages 65–74 and the remainder are 75 and older. Between now and 2025, the age distribution of Asia's older adult population will be relatively stable, but between 2025 and 2050 the percentage of the population ages 75 and older is expected to increase substantially. By 2050, men ages 75 and older are projected to represent 23 percent of the older male population; women ages 75 and older are projected to reach 30 percent of their age and gender group (Table 5).

In general, older women outnumber older men; they are also concentrated at older ages than older men. The reason is that, in most countries, survival rates for women are higher than those for men. In 2000, Asia had about 9 men ages 55-plus for every 10 women in the same age group. At older ages, the sex ratio is even more unbalanced. Among those ages 75 and older, there are approximately 7 men for every 10 women. This is a persistent feature of Asia's population and is expected to change only modestly over the 50-year projection period covered in this chapter.

The older adult labor force is concentrated at younger ages, reflecting the decline in labor-force participation rates at older ages. In 2000, about 70 percent of workers in the 55-and-older age group were ages 55–64, and about 30 percent were 65 or older. After 2025, a modest shift in the distribution toward older ages is anticipated.

Table 5. Demographic Characteristics of the Older Adult Population and Labor Force in Asia

	Ages 55-59	Ages 60-40	Ages 65-74	Ages 75+	Total
Age distribution of men ages 55 and older (%)					
2000	29.0	24.7	33.2	13.1	100.0
2025	29.8	24.0	31.8	14.4	100.0
2050	22.5	21.9	32.5	23.1	100.0
Age distribution of women ages 55 and older (%)					
2000	26.2	23.0	33.4	17.3	100.0
2025	27.1	22.4	31.8	18.6	100.0
2050	19.7	19.6	31.3	29.4	100.0
Sex ratio (100 × men/women)					
2000	101.9	98.8	91.6	69.3	92.1
2025	100.9	98.0	91.8	71.1	91.8
2050	103.9	101.2	94.0	71.5	90.7
		Ages 55-59	Ages 60-64	Ages 65+	Total
Age distribution of the labor force (%)					
2000		43.6	27.8	28.6	100.0
2025		44.5	27.6	27.9	100.0
2050		38.5	27.6	33.9	100.0
Sex ratio (100 × male workers/ female workers)					
2000		193.4	210.6	254.1	213.6
2025		187.8	201.4	235.5	203.6
2050		193.0	207.4	238.7	211.3

Sources: ILO, 1996; U.N., 1999. Calculations by authors.

Older men are much more likely to be in the labor force than older women. In 2000, there were about 190 older men for every 100 older women in the labor force. The dominance of men among older workers is even greater at later ages. Among those ages 65 and older, there were 250 men in the labor force for every 100 women. Again, little change in these figures is anticipated for the next 50 years.

The demographic characteristics of national older adult populations vary across subregions. The proportion of adults ages 75 and older is higher in East

Asia than in other regions. Over time the differences between subregions are expected to increase. By 2050, one third of the older adult population in East Asia is expected to be ages 75 and older. In South Asia and Southeast Asia, about one quarter will fall into the oldest age group. Japan's older population is much more heavily concentrated at the oldest age group than is true of other countries. By 2050, more than 40 percent of Japan's older adult population are projected to be 75 or older (Table 6).

The gender balance of this age group also varies among the regions and countries of Asia. Currently, Southeast Asia has a lower sex ratio, that is, relatively few older men as compared to older women, than East and South Asia. Among the individual Asian countries, the older populations of Japan, South Korea, and Thailand are most heavily weighted toward women. Bangladesh, on the other hand, has an unusually high sex ratio. Over the projection period, these differences of sex ratios become attenuated, although Japan, South Korea, and Thailand are projected to continue to have a relatively low sex ratio among their older populations.

In addition, the activity rates of the older population are projected to decline during the coming decades. In part, this reflects earlier retirement ages and changes in the age distribution of the older population. The most rapid changes tend to be in the countries experiencing the most rapid aging: Japan, South Korea, and Thailand. As activity rates decline, the older population will depend more on private and public transfers and on their financial assets and less on labor earnings.

Table 6. Demographic Characteristics of the Older Adult Population

	Percentage of population ages 55+			Sex ratio, population ages 55+			Population ages 55+ in labor force (%)		
	2000	2025	2050	2000	2025	2050	2000	2025	2050
Asia	12.1	20.1	29.8	92.1	91.8	90.7	41.6	39.6	35.3
East Asia	16.8	18.4	33.6	92.2	90.5	88.8	36.9	33.8	28.4
Southeast Asia	13.9	14.1	24.2	84.8	86.6	87.4	51.4	52.8	47.3
South Asia	15.4	16.6	26.6	92.1	91.5	90.7	45.8	44.3	41.1
Japan	22.9	37.5	43.1	81.6	82.7	83.7	40.7	33.8	29.2
South Korea	13.9	17.6	34.7	77.5	82.7	83.5	43.0	39.1	31.4
Indonesia	12.1	13.7	23.4	87.4	87.4	86.0	52.7	50.8	44.5
Philippines	13.4	13.9	21.0	90.9	91.6	89.6	55.9	53.4	49.6
Thailand	16.2	17.1	31.2	83.6	85.1	84.6	47.5	45.2	37.4
Bangladesh	12.2	12.4	17.0	106.8	96.6	96.3	65.0	64.9	57.3
India	13.7	15.6	21.6	94.1	95.6	93.9	45.7	43.7	40.8

Sources: ILO, 1996; U.N., 1999. Calculations by authors.

Demographics and the Support System for the Elderly

Many older adults rely on their marital partner for both personal and financial support. In the following paragraphs, the authors will deal only with broad demographic changes that bear on the support system for Asian elders. Several important studies provide more detailed information on the family support system in Asia (Cho and Yada, 1994; Hermalin, 2002; Mason, Tsuya, and Choe, 1998).

Marital Status

Over time the proportion of the elderly who are married can shift substantially because of changes in the proportion who are celibate (i.e., those who never marry), the proportion who divorce, mortality rates, and the proportion who remarry after divorce or the death of a spouse. In most Asian countries, relatively low percentages of people never marry and divorce rates are low. In the future, however, these two factors may become more significant. The proportions of young adults who have married have declined precipitously in many Asian countries. The decline may be entirely the result of a preference for a later age at marriage, but it may be that the proportion who never marry will rise. Likewise, rates of divorce have also increased in many Asian countries and, if rates of remarriage are low, the impact on the support system for the elderly could become considerable.

Changes in mortality rates are having and will continue to have a large impact on the proportion of older adults who are married. A substantial portion of the elderly, particularly elderly women, are widowed. For example, we estimate that for the year 2000, once women reach their late 60s (ages 65–69) that about half of all South Korean and Indonesian women and about 40 percent of all Thai and Filipino women are widows. Among women in older age groups the proportions are even greater. Depending on the nature of the support system, the loss of a spouse can have a devastating impact on the surviving marital partner. The proportions of elderly men who are widowed are much lower. Of men in their late 60s, for example, we estimate that fewer than 15 percent were widowed in 2000.

Women are much more likely to be widowed than men for several reasons. First, men are subject to higher mortality rates and typically die at a younger age than do women. Second, wives are typically younger than their husbands, adding further to the number of years by which they can expect to outlive their husbands. Third, in Asia older women are relatively unlikely to remarry should their husband die. A final issue is whether or not the mortality of husbands and wives is independent. If the loss of a spouse greatly increases mortality risks among women, for example, we would expect to see lower proportions who are widowed. Although the evidence is indirect, statistical analysis suggests that wives do not face substantially elevated mortality risks at the loss of their husband.[3]

[3] A detailed discussion of the methodology is available from the authors upon request.

However, husbands who experience the loss of a wife may be subject to greater mortality risks. As mortality rates decline in the future, in the absence of offsetting changes, the proportion of men and women at any age who are widowed will decline. Changes in any of the factors mentioned above could also influence the proportion of older adults who are married. The results presented here, however, are based on the assumption that these other factors will remain constant and that only mortality changes will influence the proportion who are widowed.

Projections of the proportion of older adults who are widowed have been prepared for four Asian countries for which the requisite data were available. The trends are similar in all four countries, suggesting that it may be safe to generalize from their experiences. As expected, the age profiles of the proportions widowed shift steadily downward during the projection period. The changes are very substantial. A rough characterization is that, for women, the proportions widowed drops in half at each age group between 2000 and 2050. For men, the percentage changes are even greater and the proportions of males who are widowed will reach low levels by 2050 (Figure 10).

Although these changes are large, they are not out of keeping with trends in Japan, where the proportion of older Japanese who were widowed dropped rapidly between 1970 and 1995. The steep decline reflected the very substantial increase in the proportion of men and women who survived to advanced ages. The changes in widowhood have potentially far-reaching, but complex, implications for the support system for the elderly. In the future, older men and women can expect to have a surviving spouse much later in life. That spouse may be an important resource providing personal care, companionship, and financial resources. However, the spouse also may be a burden and a drain on the limited human and financial resources of his or her elderly partner.

Population Dependency Ratio and the Economic Support Ratio

In all economic settings, the existence of large populations that are not currently productive requires that economic resources be transferred from the productive population to the nonproductive population. The relative sizes of those two groups determine in part the relative size of the transfers or the "burden" of the nonproductive population on the productive one.

The nonproductive population consists of two age groups, the young and the elderly. As described above, the demographic transition in Asia is accompanied by important changes in the relative sizes of the productive and nonproductive populations. In many Asian populations, rapid decline in fertility rates has led to a rapid drop in the relative size of the child population and, consequently, a substantial rise in the productive population relative to the nonproductive population. As the transition has proceeded, however, the relative size of the elderly dependent population has increased, producing a decline in the productive relative to the nonproductive population. This demographic phenomenon undermines the capacity of the productive population to support the nonproductive population.

These demographic changes are measured in two ways. The first makes use of the population dependency ratio. This is a standard measure. The child dependency ratio is conventionally constructed as the ratio of the population ages 0–14 to the population ages 15–64. The old-age dependency ratio is constructed as the ratio of the population ages 65 and older to the population ages 15–64. The total dependency ratio is the sum of these two or the ratio of the dependent population (0–14 plus 65-plus) to the productive population (15–64).

The second measure is the economic support ratio, which is the ratio of the productive population to the consuming population. Often the productive population is calculated using weights to adjust for age variation in the labor-force participation rates and for the productivity of the working-age population. The consuming population is constructed using weights to adjust for age variation in material "needs." We use a simple variant of the economic support ratio here. For the productive population, we use the labor force unadjusted for age variation in productivity; for the consuming population, we count children ages 0–14 as 0.5 and all adults as 1.0.

To summarize:

Child dependency ratio:	Pop(0–14) / Pop(15–64)
Old-age dependency ratio:	Pop(65+) / Pop(15–64)
Total dependency ratio:	(Pop(0–14) + Pop(65+)) / Pop(15–64)
Economic support ratio:	(Total labor force) / (0.5 Pop(0–14) + Pop(15+))

Dependency ratios and the economic support ratio are provided for the regions of Asia and specific countries in Table 7. The table summarizes the important trends highlighted above. The major trends anticipated in the region are a decline in the child dependency ratio and a rise in the old-age dependency ratio during the next 50 years.

In East Asia, the rising old-age dependency ratio is the most significant factor in the modest increases seen in the region's total dependency ratio between 2000 and 2025 and in the more substantial increases between 2025 and 2050. In Southeast and South Asia, the trend in the total dependency ratio is dominated by the child dependency ratio between 2000 and 2025. Thereafter, the total dependency ratio begins to rise in step with the old-age dependency ratio. The pattern for the economic support ratio is similar to the pattern for the total dependency ratio.

The support ratio moves inversely to dependency ratio because producers are in the numerator and consumers in the denominator in the support ratio. In 2000, the number of workers per effective consumer varies from 0.52 in South Asia to 0.66 in East Asia, giving East Asia an advantage. By 2050, the demographic advantage of East Asia disappears entirely with its economic support ratio dropping to 0.52. In both Southeast and South Asia, the support ratio increases between 2000

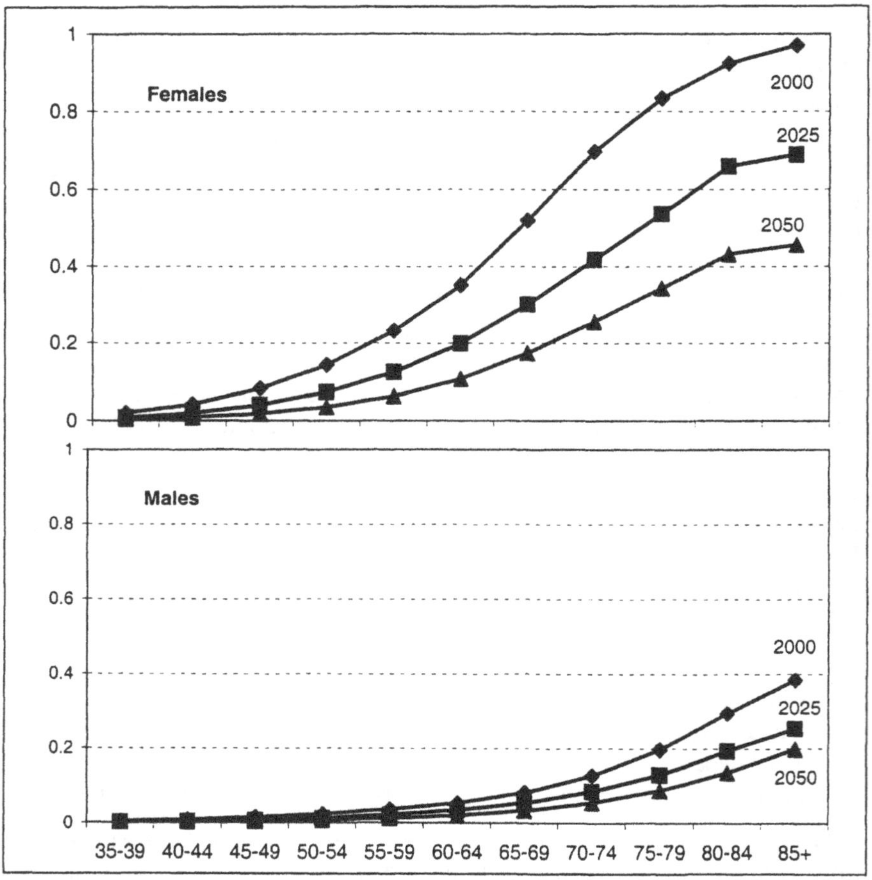

Figure 10.
(a) Projections of proportion of the adult population who are widowed, South Korea.

and 2025 but begins to drop after 2025. Note, however, that the support ratios in Southeast Asia and South Asia do not reach the level achieved in East Asia.

IMPLICATIONS OF AGING: POLICY OPTIONS[4]

As population aging proceeds in Asia, the region must deal with three broad sets of social and economic changes: changes in the size and basic character of healthcare; the need to develop a larger and comprehensive approach to old-age

[4] See Mason, Lee, and Russo (2001) for a detailed discussion of this section.

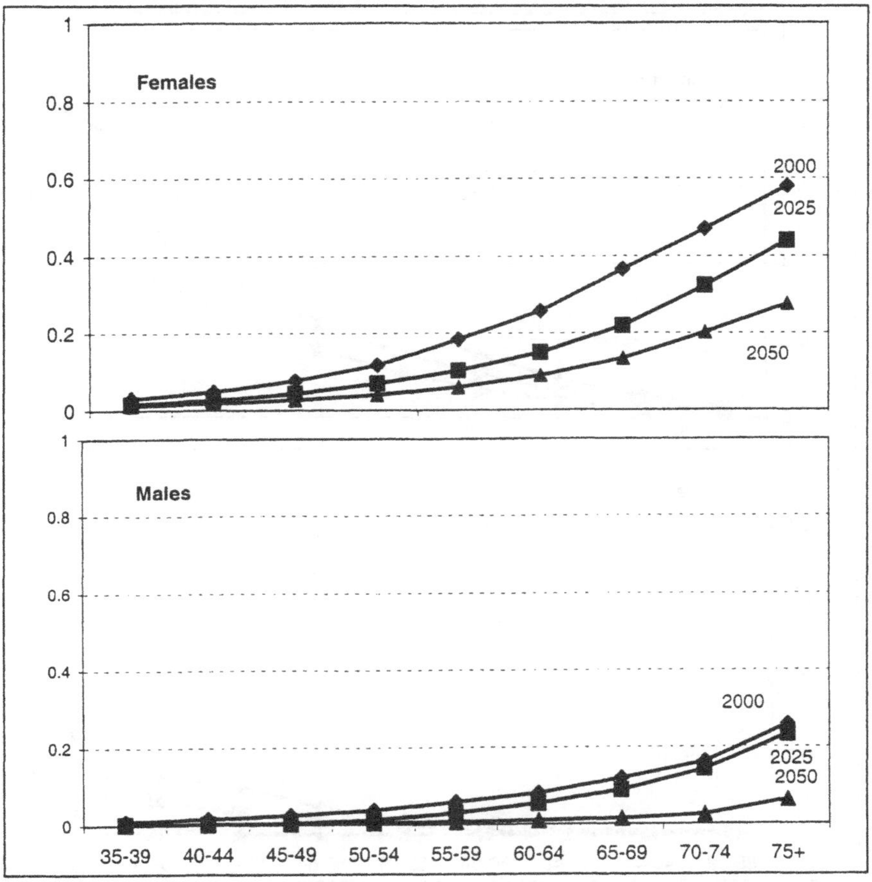

Figure 10. (Cont'd.)
(b) Projections of proportion of the adult population who are widowed, Philippines.

security; and changes in economic conditions. The authors discuss the implications of population aging for these changes.

Healthcare for the Elderly

A key challenge for Asian countries is to adapt to the population's changing healthcare needs. Population aging will place an increasing burden on national healthcare systems. Among the world's economically advanced countries, including Japan, healthcare spending per capita is about four times higher among people ages 65 and older than among those under age 65.

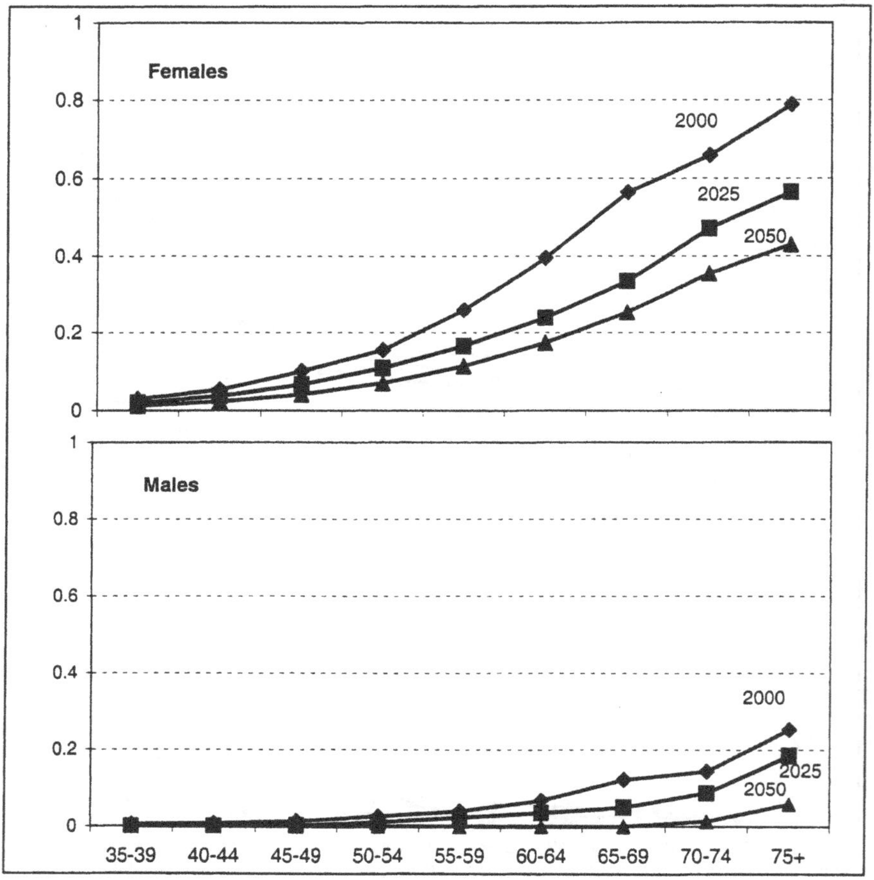

Figure 10. (Cont'd.)
(c) Projections of proportion of the adult population who are widowed, Indonesia.

As people live longer, demand grows for care related to such acute and chronic conditions as cardiovascular diseases, cancer, obstructive pulmonary disease, and osteoporosis. At the same time, general public health issues remain important. Furthermore, new and resurgent infectious diseases increasingly emerge around the world. Rising demand for treatment of both communicable and noncommunicable diseases will place increasing claims on national resources. In developed countries, spending on healthcare already has risen, in part reflecting population aging. In Japan, for example, healthcare spending more than doubled as a percentage of gross domestic product (GDP) between 1960 and 1997.

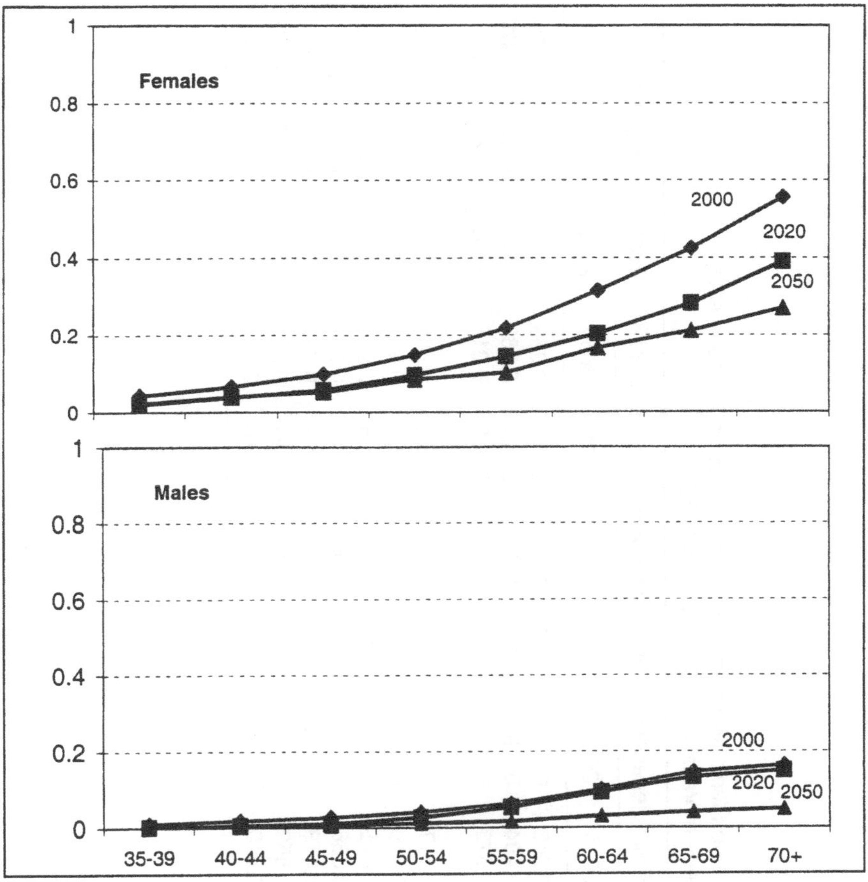

Figure 10. (Cont'd.)
(d) Projections of proportion of the adult population who are widowed, Thailand.

The main determinant of individual healthcare spending is not age itself but the number of years remaining until a person's death. Studies have shown that individual healthcare expenditures increase substantially in the last two years of a person's life. In the United States in 1996, for example, Medicare beneficiaries in their last year of life comprised just 6 percent of all beneficiaries but accounted for 21 percent of program payments (Health Care Financing Administration, 1998). Thus, even if older people are healthier than in the past and live longer, spending on healthcare will rise because the proportion of the population in its last few years of life will rise. Similarly, spending for long-term care associated with disability

Table 7. Summary of Dependency Ratios and Economic Support Ratios in Asia, Medium Variant, 2000, 2025, and 2050

	Total dependency ratio			Child dependency ratio			Old-age dependency ratio			Economic support ratio		
	2000	2025	2050	2000	2025	2050	2000	2025	2050	2000	2025	2050
East Asia	0.462	0.474	0.649	0.349	0.265	0.266	0.113	0.210	0.383	0.761	0.675	0.575
Southeast Asia	0.568	0.460	0.570	0.494	0.336	0.308	0.074	0.124	0.262	0.709	0.705	0.661
South Asia	0.649	0.472	0.522	0.573	0.360	0.306	0.076	0.112	0.216	0.658	0.660	0.623
Japan	0.468	0.673	0.838	0.217	0.226	0.254	0.250	0.447	0.583	0.583	0.582	0.545
South Korea	0.393	0.477	0.678	0.299	0.252	0.270	0.094	0.226	0.417	0.647	0.622	0.564
Philippines	0.676	0.458	0.521	0.615	0.353	0.305	0.061	0.105	0.216	0.677	0.672	0.649
Thailand	0.450	0.453	0.660	0.366	0.274	0.278	0.084	0.178	0.382	0.787	0.728	0.653
Indonesia	0.546	0.456	0.573	0.473	0.333	0.313	0.073	0.123	0.260	0.683	0.695	0.652
Bangladesh	0.622	0.428	0.523	0.569	0.344	0.309	0.052	0.084	0.213	0.753	0.761	0.728
India	0.620	0.459	0.531	0.540	0.336	0.300	0.081	0.123	0.232	0.641	0.638	0.601

Source: See text.

will rise. Even though the prevalence of severe disability among people ages 65–75 is falling in many developed countries, as the absolute older adult population grows so too will the number of elders with severe disabilities.

Demand for healthcare increases as countries develop and per capita income rises, reflecting the increased resources available to meet the demand. Whatever the level of development, however, population aging presents challenges in the finance and delivery of healthcare. Asian countries increasingly will be faced with decisions about what type of healthcare to provide, for whom, and how to do so efficiently.

Many developing countries, including India, Indonesia, and the Philippines, currently focus on maternal and child health because they view it as the most cost-effective health measure in lives saved. In countries that have yet to achieve primary care for all, and where aging has not yet emerged as an important issue, paying for long-term care for older adults is not a high priority. In Japan, South Korea, and Taiwan, the Asian countries where population aging is furthest along, however, the situation is different. Japan, like the United States, heavily subsidizes healthcare for the elderly and subsidizes long-term care insurance as well.

Providing health insurance helps expand access to healthcare. In developed countries, most public insurance schemes explicitly involve some type of financial subsidy from high-income to low-income groups. People with few resources of their own typically need assistance in paying for insurance itself as well as in making copayments for health services received. The developed countries of the region (Japan, South Korea, and Taiwan) have opted for employment-based health insurance schemes with government subsidies for the poor, disabled, and elderly. These countries have followed similar historical patterns of health insurance development to achieve universal coverage. First, the government, as employer, covered public-sector employees with health insurance financed through tax revenues and receipts from public enterprises. Second, private employees in the formal sector began to be covered through government-mandated employment-based health insurance, tantamount to a wage tax. Third, agricultural workers, the self-employed, and workers in the informal sector began to be covered through government-sponsored insurance groups financed through a combination of taxes and premiums.

This incremental pattern is being largely replicated by the Philippines and Thailand. These national systems ultimately achieve universal coverage of their populations, but at high expenditure levels. In the final step, price controls and other government regulations attempt to restrain healthcare expenditures. These employment-based systems amount to distortionary labor taxes, which are costly because they discourage work and encourage overuse of the healthcare system.

Job Opportunities for Older Workers

As populations age, the labor-force decisions made by older workers will become increasingly important to the workers and their families, to employers, and to governments. For some older workers, continued employment will be crucial to maintaining an adequate standard of living. Many will be supporting not only themselves but also their aging parents. Employers will look increasingly to older workers as working-age populations begin to decline and labor shortages emerge. Governments will depend on the taxes paid by older workers as tax revenues fall short of the resources required to fund public pension programs, costly healthcare programs, and other important public services.

Throughout Asia and much of the world, however, older workers are withdrawing from the labor force at younger and younger ages. For some, deteriorating health may dictate early retirement but, in general, older adults are healthier and have lower rates of disability than in the past. Why then are they withdrawing just when they are needed most? What, if anything, can be done to reverse this trend?

Fifty years ago, the great majority of Asia's workers were self-employed, mostly in agriculture. The decision to work or not to work was dictated by personal circumstances—such as wealth, health, responsibilities, or preferences. As economies have industrialized, more and more workers have become employees of governments and private firms. Individuals' decisions to work are increasingly governed by complex policies that reflect the influence of firms, labor unions, and public officials. The resulting rigidities in the labor market often discourage or, in some instances, virtually prohibit continued employment by older workers.

The trend toward earlier retirement is a persistent feature of economic development. In developed countries, men now retire much earlier than was the case in the 1950s. This trend is occurring in Asia, although older Asian men are much more likely to be working than are men in the West. The picture is more complex for women. In most Asian countries, labor-force participation rates among older women are generally low and have not changed in any systematic fashion over the past few decades. The situation for women is likely to change dramatically in the future because younger cohorts of women have much higher rates of labor-force participation.

The direct correlation between rising levels of economic development and earlier retirement suggests that many people are spending longer in retirement because they can afford to do so. Retirement may not even be an option where levels of development are low, because most people have no choice but to work as long as they are able. Retirement is a luxury available only to the relatively well-off. Rising incomes are only partly responsible for the decline in work among older adults. Labor market rigidities and a wide range of disincentives shoulder much of the blame.

In Asia as throughout the world, most governments impose mandatory retirement ages. For most Asian countries, the statutory retirement age is either 65 or below 65—for example, 65 in South Korea, 60 in the Philippines, and 55 in Indonesia and India. Many countries have been slow to adjust mandatory retirement ages upward despite rapid improvements in health and life expectancy that enable people to continue to be productive longer than in the past. Many people today want to work longer than laws permit them to. In the United States, the elimination of a mandatory retirement age several years ago reversed the downward trend in employment rates for older workers, and it did not reduce employment among younger workers.

Many Asian governments allow firms to force older workers into early retirement when there are general downturns in the economy, when particular sectors or firms decline, or when firms restructure their production processes. Despite evidence to the contrary, dismissing older workers is thought to help job prospects for young employed men, who are viewed as the primary breadwinners for their families.

Older women may be especially vulnerable to such policies as they are frequently viewed as secondary rather than primary breadwinners in the family. During South Korea's recent economic crisis, for example, female employment declined more rapidly than male employment, unemployed female workers were more likely to withdraw from the labor force, and when women were reemployed they were less likely to obtain full-time regular positions than their male counterparts.

There is little reason, however, for governments to encourage early retirement. In fact, the practice can reduce employment and income and can dampen economic welfare in general. Cutting the number of older workers does not increase employment among young workers. Older and younger workers frequently have different skills, and labor markets rarely shrink and grow in the same sectors or occupations. In well-functioning economies, the number of jobs is not fixed but changes with the number of individuals willing to work.

Public policies are not entirely to blame for job losses among the elderly. The wage system in some Asian countries, Japan and South Korea in particular, is based on seniority rather than on performance. Firms find themselves paying older workers far more than they are contributing to the bottom line.

Efforts, some of which are underway, to tie wages more closely to performance and to increase flexibility in job assignments and hours worked could greatly ease pressures to force older workers into retirement. In developed countries, public pension programs have had a substantial effect on retirement. In the United States, large increases in Social Security benefits have been partly responsible for the decline in the percentage of older people who remain in the labor force. Even more generous programs in Europe have led to low rates of employment among older Europeans. Pension programs have undermined work incentives by cutting the link between work effort and standards of living among the elderly.

In Asia, public pension programs have been modest to this point and, consequently, have not greatly influenced older workers. However, it is likely that the expansion of public benefit programs currently being considered in many Asian countries would lead to further declines in the average age at retirement.

Particularly in aging societies, policies that undermine labor-force participation or dictate early retirement are damaging. Under such policies older workers who are not yet prepared for retirement are forced to accept a lower standard of living during their retirement years. Given the importance of the family support system in Asia, some of the extra burden of support imposed by such policies is shouldered by the families of the elderly.

The Role of the Family Support System in Providing Old-Age Security

In most traditional Asian societies, older adults live in extended, multigenerational households and rely on their adult children, their spouses, and other family members for material needs and personal care. During the 1980s, more than three quarters of elders in Asia were living with children or family (World Bank, 1994). During the 1990s, about two thirds were living with their adult children, ranging from about one half in Kazakhstan to more than four fifths in Pakistan and Bangladesh (Bongaarts and Zimmer, 2001).

Today, demographic, social, and economic changes have put the traditional family support system under pressure. In countries where fertility has been low for decades, the elderly have few adult children to provide support, and many of these children have moved away from their family homes. Marriage rates have dropped sharply in some countries, and women are entering the workforce in increasing numbers. Middle-aged women, the traditional caregivers, may have less time than they did in the past to care for elderly family members. Increasing exposure to the West may also be introducing new ideas about marriage, family, and individualism—ideas that clash with the traditional sense of responsibility for the elderly.

It is not clear how quickly or to what extent these pressures will undermine traditional family support systems. Family support for the elderly is already on the decline in some of Asia's most economically advanced countries. The percentage of Japanese elders living with their children dropped from 80 percent in 1950 to 50 percent in 1990 (Ogawa and Retherford, 1997). In South Korea, the proportion of elderly women living with their children declined from 78 percent in 1984 to 47 percent in 1994. In Taiwan, the proportion of elderly parents living with a married son declined from 82 percent in 1973 to 70 percent in 1986 (Weinstein, Sun, Chang, and Freedman, 1994).

In 1997, only 8 percent of South Korean women of childbearing age indicated that they wished to live with their children when they grow old (Lee, 1998). Although the actual proportion of elders living with their children has not gone down in the Philippines, fewer working-age adults wish to live with their children in the future (Natividad and Cruz, 1997).

The changes in living arrangements probably indicate a broader decline in family support. In 1996, only 15 percent of elderly men and women in Japan mentioned children as a source of income, down from 30 percent in 1981 (Ogawa and Retherford, 1997). Even if the elderly continue to live with their children, the family support system will become less effective as elders live longer and have fewer children. Lee, Mason, and Miller (2000) showed that by 2050 a fully functioning family support system would be able to meet only about one-half of the retirement needs of the elderly in East Asia's low-fertility countries. To meet their retirement needs fully, older adults will have to work longer, save more, or rely on substantially enhanced public programs.

The challenge for public policy is to assess the viability of family support systems and to devise programs that will be supportive or complementary. Several governments have adopted such policies. In Singapore, children are now legally responsible for the support of their elderly parents. Many East and Southeast Asian countries are providing adult daycare and other support services aimed at helping children care for their elderly parents, and Malaysia and Singapore have revised their public housing policies to accommodate multigenerational living arrangements. Malaysia also provides families with tax incentives for elder care (World Bank, 1994).

Public Support Programs for the Elderly

During the past 60 years, national governments around the world have come to play an increasingly important role in providing old-age security for their citizens. Many Asian countries offer some type of support for the elderly. Japan and Singapore have large-scale programs with close to universal coverage, but in most countries coverage is restricted to narrow population groups (Table 8). The Employees' Provident Fund in India, for example, restricts coverage to employees in one of 177 prescribed occupations who are working in establishments with at least 20 workers.

The relatively modest scope of such programs in most Asian countries is also reflected in financial measures of their size. In 1993, the proportion of public expenditure earmarked for social security programs was only 2 percent in the Philippines and 8 percent in South Korea, compared with 22 percent in the United States and more than 40 percent in most European countries.

Public pension programs offer two important advantages. First, they represent a politically acceptable means of providing an economic safety net for those elders who might otherwise experience severe levels of poverty. Second, national programs allow risk pooling. Individuals who must provide for their own retirement needs may make poor investments. They may suffer a disability that curtails their income-earning capacity or experience unusual longevity and outlive their

Table 8. Coverage of Schemes Providing Cash Benefits to the Elderly, Disabled and/or Survivals

Countries (coverage rate in 1992)	Coverage of schemes (1999)	Special schemes
Japan (100%)	National pension program: All residents ages 20-59. Voluntary coverage for residents ages 60-64 and citizens residing abroad ages 20-64 (employees' pension insurance: employees of firm in industry and commerce)	Public employees; private school teachers; workers in the agriculture, fishery, and forest sectors
Singapore (100%)	Employed individuals earning more than $50 a month and some self-employed workers	Public workers
Philippines (52.6%)	All private employees ages 60 or younger. House helpers and self-employed individuals earning at least 1,000 pesos a month	Government employees, military personnel
Thailand (n.a.)	Employees of firms with 10 or more workers; voluntary coverage for the self-employed	Civil servants, private school teachers
Indonesia (6.9%)	Establishments with 10 or more employees or with a payroll of 1 million rupees or more a month	Public employees, military personnel
Bangladesh (0.0%)	None	Public employees
India (0.9%)	Employees of establishments with 20 or more employees in 177 categories of industries; employees earning more than 5,000 rupees a month are excluded	Public employees, employees of the railway industry, and coal miners
China (21.1%)	Employees in state-run enterprises; private-collective, and foreign-invested companies depend on local government regulations	Government and Communist party employees; employees of cultural, scientific, and educational institutions

Sources: ILO, 1995; U.S. Social Security Administration, 1999.

savings. Public programs can spread these risks and provide a monthly benefit that lasts as long as the beneficiary survives. Most also include some form of disability insurance.

Public programs entail their own set of risks, however. First, providing wide coverage may entail enormous administrative hurdles, particularly in low-income countries with large numbers of agricultural, self-employed, casual, domestic, and informal-sector workers. It is notoriously difficult to collect pension payments in sectors where labor turnover is high and documentation is weak (Bailey, 1997). Recent legislation in the Philippines, for example, requires that household help and self-employed workers be covered, but there is a substantial gap between coverage under the law and coverage in practice.

Second, public pension programs are only feasible in countries with a substantial degree of political stability. The ability of a government to collect taxes may decline, or the political regime may change, with new leaders backing out of promises made by their predecessors. As governments obtain privileged access to large pension reserves, they may also make unwise investments or pursue large-scale public infrastructure projects without adequate scrutiny of potential risk and return (World Bank, 1994).

Third, public pension programs that are not carefully designed will prove to be unsustainable as the number of elderly increases relative to the working-age (and taxpaying) population. Many countries have pay-as-you-go systems in which current retirees are supported not by their own savings but by contributions from current workers. Current workers will, in turn, be supported in old age by the next generation of workers. As the number of retirees increases relative to the number of workers, either payroll taxes must rise to high levels, or benefits must be reduced to low levels, or some combination of the two. There is little doubt, for example, that Japan's public pension program will face enormous difficulties in the coming years.

Economic Conditions

During the past few decades, demographic changes have favored economic growth in many Asian countries. Changes in age structure have contributed to rapid labor-force growth, higher saving and investment rates, and unprecedented increases in per capita income (Bloom and Williamson, 1998; Mason, 2001). Demographic conditions will continue to favor economic growth in Asia for several decades or more except in Japan, where labor-force growth has turned negative and population aging may begin to depress saving rates.

The impact of demographics on national saving and investment rates has been especially important in East Asia (Lee, Mason, and Miller, 2001; Williamson and Higgins, 2001). For the most part, East Asian countries had very low rates of saving and investment in 1960—about 10 percent or less. By 1990, saving and investment rates ranked among the highest in the world, between 20 to

35 percent in the study countries (Figure 11). The rapid accumulation of wealth caused in part by demographic change has been crucial to East Asia's rapid economic growth.

The current heavy concentration of the population at the working ages should continue to favor economic growth in most Asian countries. Eventually, however, as the working-age population declines relative to the retired population, conditions will turn less favorable to economic growth. In many Asian countries, the period of extraordinarily high rates of saving and investment may give way to an era of lower rates of saving and investment and slower economic growth.

Aggregate economic growth will almost surely slow as population aging becomes more pervasive and countries begin to experience negative labor-force growth and lower saving rates. Living standards may continue to improve because of productivity increases and greater investment in human capital. With continued increases in life expectancy, further increases in per capita wealth are possible, although at a slower pace than in the past.

Slower economic growth should not be viewed with undue alarm, especially among Asia's most successful economies. The extremely high rates of economic growth that some Asian countries have achieved in recent decades have been inherently transitory—in part, catching up with the West and, in part, coming from the demographic transition from high to low fertility and mortality. Countries that have successfully seized the economic opportunities presented by the demographic transition have been able to reach higher standards of living that will enable them to cope better with the challenges of population aging. In the future, as their populations age, their economic growth is likely to slow to the levels seen in the world's mature economies. Prospects are much less promising for countries that are struggling with their development efforts and are not developing the economic and political institutions that are essential for meeting the needs of an aging society. The process of population aging is so rapid in Asia that little time is left to respond.

CONCLUDING REMARKS

Asia has entered a new demographic era. The number of children, those ages 0–14, reached a peak in the year 2000 after decades of rapid and sustained growth. During the 21st century, the number of children in the region may stabilize at the current level of around 300–350 million. Or, if fertility rates drop to low levels, Asia could experience a period of sustained decline in the number of children.

During the next few decades, the adult population will continue to grow, older populations especially rapidly. Between 2000 and 2050, the 60–74 age group is expected to increase at an annual rate of 2.9 percent and the 75-plus age group at 3.4 percent. By 2050, 17 percent of Asia's population will be 65 and older while the percentage under 15 will shrink to 19 percent. This is a remarkable change

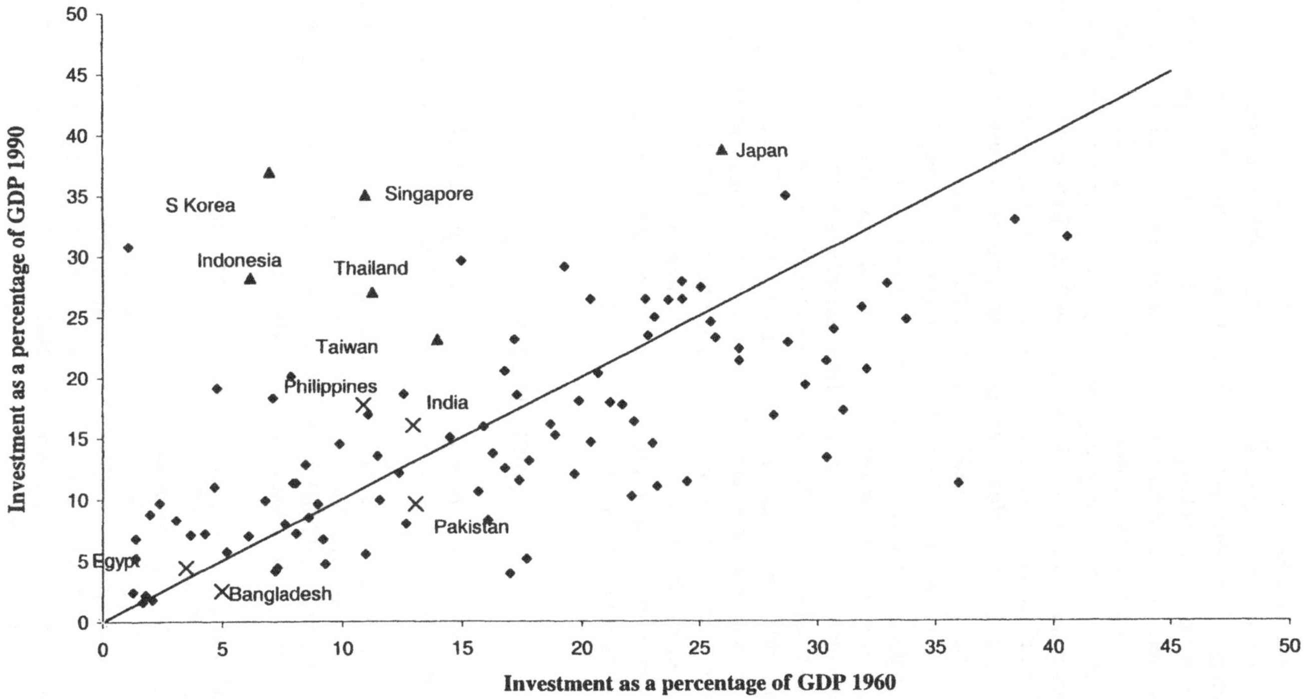

Source: Summers and Heston, 1991.

Figure 11. Comparison of investment rates of the countries of the world, 1960 versus 1990.

from the 1970s, when the percentage under age 15 reached 40 percent of the total and the percentage ages 65 and older was only 4 percent.

In the absence of demographic solutions to the problems accompanied with population aging, Asian countries must depend on economic and social policies that meet the needs of the elderly and promote strong economic performance. What aging societies lose in sheer numbers of workers they can gain back through more productive economies. A top priority is to tap the productive potential of older workers by eliminating mandatory retirement ages and rigidities in the labor market that hurt both older workers and the firms that employ them. Public pension reform must pay close attention to potentially adverse effects on incentives to work and save. Healthcare policy must insure that efforts to provide high-quality healthcare do not lead to waste and inefficiency in the health sector. Well-functioning financial markets and institutions are essential so that older workers can earn an adequate return on their retirement savings and protect themselves against the risks of old age. A favorable investment environment, integration into the global economy, and developments making it relatively easier for older adults to participate in the global economy (such as through the Internet) will help many older adults maintain their economic independence.

Countries in Asia can cope with the demographic changes ahead, but only if they begin to prepare now. Governments must take immediate steps that will both help the elderly and benefit broad development concerns. While political crises and short-term economic problems engage the attention of many Asian leaders, preparing for the needs of an aging society can no longer be postponed.

REFERENCES

Bailey, C. (1997, October). *Coverage under social security pension schemes.* Tripartite regional consultation with Asian countries, ILO Social Security Department, Bangkok, Thailand.

Bloom, D. E., and Williamson, J. G. (1998). Demographic transitions and economic miracles in emerging Asia. *World Bank Economic Review, 12*(3), 419–456.

Bongaarts, J., and Zimmer, Z. (2001). *Living arrangement of older adults in the developing world: An analysis of DHS household surveys* (Working Paper No. 148). New York: Population Council.

Cho, L.-J., and Yada, M. (Eds.). (1994). *Tradition and change in the Asian family.* Honolulu, Hawaii: East-West Center.

East-West Center. (2002). *The future of Asia's population.* Honolulu, Hawaii: Author.

Hermalin, A. I. (Ed.). (2002). *The well-being of the elderly in Asia: A four-country comparative study.* Ann Arbor: University of Michigan Press.

Health Care Financing Administration. (1998). *Health care financing review: Medicare and Medicaid statistical supplement, 1998.* Baltimore, Maryland: U.S. Department of Health and Human Services.

International Labour Organization [ILO]. (1996). *Economically active population, 1950–2010.* Geneva, Switzerland: Author.

Lee, H.-T. (1998). *Family welfare and reproductive health: The Korean experience.* Seminar on Population and Development Policies in Low Fertility Countries. Seoul: KIHASA.

Lee, R. D., Mason, A., and Miller, T. (2000, March). *From transfers to individual responsibility: Implications for savings and capital accumulation in Taiwan and the United States.* Paper presented at the annual meeting of the Population Association of America, San Diego, California.

Lee, R. D., Mason, A., and Miller, T. (2001). Saving, wealth, and the demographic transition in East Asia. In A. Mason (Ed.), *Population change and economic development in East Asia: Challenges met, opportunities seized* (pp. 155–184). Stanford, California: Stanford University Press.

Mason, A. (Ed.) (2001). *Population change and economic development in East Asia: Challenges met, opportunities seized.* Stanford, California: Stanford University Press.

Mason, A. (2002). Population and human resource trends and challenges. In V. N. Gnanathurai (Ed.), *Key indicators of developing Asian and Pacific countries 2002* (pp. 1–37). Manila: Asian Development Bank.

Mason, K. O., Tsuya, N. O., and Choe, M. K. (Eds.). (1998). *The changing family in comparative perspective: Asia and the United States.* Honolulu, Hawaii: East-West Center.

Mason, A., Lee, S.-H., and Russo, G. (2001). *Population momentum and population aging in Asia and Near-East countries* (Working Paper, Population Series, No. 107). Honolulu, Hawaii: East-West Center.

Natividad, J. N., and Cruz, G. T. (1997). Patterns in living arrangements and familiar support for the elderly in the Philippines. *Asia-Pacific Population Journal, 12*(4), 17–34.

Ogawa, N., and Retherford, R. D. (1997). Shifting costs of caring for the elderly back to families in Japan. *Population and Development Review, 23*(1), 59–74.

United Nations [U.N.]. (1999). *World population prospects: The 1998 revision.* New York: Author.

U.S. Social Security Administration. (1999). *Social security programs throughout the world.* Washington, D.C.: Author.

Weinstein, W., Sun, T. H., Chang, M. C., and Freedman, R. (1994). Co-residence and other ties linking couples and their parents. In A. Thornton and H.-L. S. Lin (Eds.), *Social change and the family in Taiwan.* Chicago: University of Chicago Press.

Williamson, J. G., and Higgins, M. (2001). The accumulation and demography connection in East Asia. In A. Mason (Ed.), *Population change and economic development in East Asia: Challenges met, opportunities seized* (pp. 123–154). Stanford, California: Stanford University Press.

World Bank. (1994). *Averting the old age crisis.* Washington, D.C.: Author.

Zlotnik, H. (1999, May). *World population prospects: The 1998 revision, joint ECE-Eurostat work session on demographic projections* (Working Paper No. 19). Paper presented at the National Institute of Statistics of Italy (ISTAT), Perugia, Italy.

Author's Note: The authors are grateful to Kokila Agarwal, Phil Estermann, James Gribble, Charles Llewellyn, Jerre Manarolla, Christopher McDermott, Robert Retherford, Zynia Rionda, John Stover, and Hania Zlotnik for comments and suggestions, and to Piya Sereevinyayut and Ann Takeyasu for their research assistance.

CHAPTER TWO

Economic Resources: Implications for Aging Policy in Asia

*Yung-Ping Chen and John Turner**

As has been made apparent in preceding chapters, population aging will occur more rapidly in Asia than in any other region of the world over the next few decades (West and Kinsella, 1998). Because of rapid demographic transition and the size of the population in the region, the challenges of population aging worldwide will largely be fielded by Asian nations. This chapter addresses the role of economic resources in social policy for the aged in Asia and the Pacific region.

SOCIETAL FORCES AND SOCIAL POLICY

Scarcity is the point of departure in the study of economics. Economists start from the fundamental notion that society's ability to satisfy human wants is limited. At any one time, an economy has only a limited command over the human and material resources required to produce goods and services. Human desires for goods and services seem limitless, whereas the resources needed for producing these things are restricted. Scarcity, as the basic fact of economic life, pervades all societies, irrespective of political orientations or levels of economic development. People simply do not have all the resources needed to produce all the things they would want to have. This fundamental constraint is as true in a rich country as it is in a poor country; this same constraint exists in countries with differing ideologies. Although the condition of scarcity always imposes the ultimate constraint, it is more acute in a poor country than in a rich one.

*The views, opinions, and judgments expressed here are solely the responsibility of the authors and do not represent the position of AARP.

Because society does not have all the material and nonmaterial resources with which to produce all the goods and services its population wants, choices are inevitable. When a society allows economic priorities to operate through the market relatively freely, the process is referred to under the rubric of market forces. Market forces deal with the scarcity of goods and services by adjusting their relative prices accordingly. Market forces are sometimes called the "invisible hand"—the rise and fall of prices guide buying and selling.

Societies cannot choose whether or not to allow economic forces to operate because they always do. Societies can only choose whether or not to allow market forces to predominate. Other forces also play major roles in deciding how market determinations are allowed to operate. Social and historical forces often circumscribe how the invisible hand works. These other forces are captured by the metaphor "the invisible handshake." Yet still other forces, metaphorically called by some the "invisible foot"—political and legal influences—may preclude economic forces from becoming market forces.

In short, the functioning of economics in society can be understood as a reaction to and interaction of the invisible hand (market forces), the invisible handshake (social and historical forces), and the invisible foot (political and legal forces). Economics is integral to the sociology, history, and politics within a society, just as sociology, history, and politics have roles to play in its economics (Colander, 2004). A basic understanding of how economics operate is essential to an appreciation of the situation of the elderly.

DEMOGRAPHIC AND ECONOMIC CONSIDERATIONS

When the direction of social policies changes, people often ascribe the shift to changes in ideology or to political maneuvering. Frequently lost in these considerations are the powerful roles demography and economics play in shaping social policy. In analyzing the one, the other must be kept front and center; the two operate in light of one another.

Demographics

As has been noted in earlier chapters, many countries in Asia and the Pacific are facing extremely rapid population aging. For example, while the percentage of the U.S. population ages 60 and older is expected to take 81 years (1933–2014) to increase from 10 to 20 percent, in Singapore such an increase is expected to occur in only 18 years (1999–2017), with Singapore reaching the doubling point only three years later than the United States. Other countries in the region are aging at rates somewhere in between. Rapid population aging means that countries have less time to make the necessary adjustments to their public policies and institutions, including social security programs. Rapid population aging and the ensuing rapid shifts in policy may make the politics of social security reform more problematic. Depending on resolutions proffered, birth cohorts that are relatively close together may deal with social security programs of considerably different levels of generosity.

As Mason, Lee, and Russo pointed out in chapter two, the major cause of rapid population aging is low fertility, but increasing life expectancy also plays a role. Though it is often thought that fertility rates below the replacement rate of 2.1 live births per female only occur in developed countries, in fact, fertility rates below that level are occurring in China, South Korea, Taiwan, and Thailand, Australia, Japan, and Singapore. In Japan, the estimated long-term fertility rate—the number of children a woman is expected to bear in her lifetime—fell to 1.39 children per woman in 2002. By contrast, Asian countries with large segments of the population who are Muslim or Catholic and have not yet attained rapid economic transformation have significantly higher fertility rates. To illustrate, in 2001 the fertility rate of the Philippines was 3.6 children per woman and that of Malaysia, 3.2.

Population aging, which virtually all countries are now experiencing, obviously raises many problems at all levels—for individuals, families, and societies. Old-age economic security is but one rubric under which many of these problems and their possible solutions may be discussed.

As pointed out throughout this book, the societal burden imposed by population aging has major policy implications. Such burden is captured to a large extent by the old-age dependency ratio—the ratio of older people to working-age adults in the general population. Currently, older people are generally defined as those ages 65 and older. Using this benchmark, information in the U.S. Census Bureau's International Data Base projections for future years shows large and frequently dramatic increases in the old-age dependency ratio in many countries (Table 1). For the 25 countries in Asia for which we have data, only by shifting the calculation to age 70 as the benchmark instead of age 65 do we find that for 12 countries the old-age dependency ratios in 2030 would be the same or lower, and in some cases much lower, than their ratios in 2003 (which are based on age 65). As was noted by the editors in their introductory chapter, age 60 may actually be a more realistic old-age benchmark at the present time and in light of relative life expectancies. The higher age may be justified by the improvements in mortality and health trends, but it is not intended to define away old-age dependency. Rather, it is meant to stimulate new directions for policymaking in both the public and private sectors.

Economics

Rapid economic development across the region has drawn many workers from self-employment or casual employment into wage employment, especially in East Asia. Between 1980 and 1996, the portion of the economically active population who were wage workers grew in Malaysia from 54 to 73 percent, in

Table 1. Measuring Old-Age Dependency Ratios in Asia—Age 65 versus Age 70

Country	Age 65+/Age 18–64 in 2003 (%)	Age 65+/Age 18–64 in 2030 (%)	Age 70+/Age 18–69 in 2030 (%)	Change from 65+ to 70+ in 2030 (%)
Afghanistan	6.3	7.8	4.2	–3.5
Bangladesh	6.8	10.7	6.2	–4.5
Bhutan	8.7	9.9	5.5	–4.3
Burma	8.6	15.4	8.6	–6.8
Cambodia	6.8	10.3	5.7	–4.6
China	12.2	27.2	16.0	–11.2
East Timor	6.1	12.1	6.9	–5.3
Hong Kong, S.A.R.	16.8	44.2	26.0	–18.2
India	9.0	15.0	8.8	–6.2
Indonesia	8.8	18.0	10.7	–7.4
Iran	9.2	14.3	8.4	–5.9
Japan	30.3	52.7	37.4	–15.3
Laos	7.5	7.6	4.4	–3.3
Malaysia	8.5	16.9	10.0	–6.9
Mongolia	6.8	13.1	6.8	–6.3
Nepal	7.9	9.3	5.4	–3.9
North Korea	12.1	23.9	13.7	–10.3
Pakistan	9.2	10.9	6.3	–4.6
Philippines	7.8	13.3	8.0	–5.3
Singapore	10.3	22.9	13.8	–9.1
South Korea	12.2	34.4	20.8	–13.6
Sri Lanka	11.7	25.2	15.6	–9.5
Taiwan	14.7	35.7	22.0	–13.8
Thailand	11.6	27.0	16.4	–10.5
Vietnam	10.5	18.2	10.4	–7.9

Source: U.S. Census Bureau, International Data Base, as analyzed in Chen and Velkoff, 2003.

Pakistan from 22 to 33 percent, and in Thailand from 22 to 37 percent (Gillion, Turner, Bailey, and Latulippe, 2000). This trend has also contributed to the growing need for revamping public policies, especially social security pensions. In large parts of Asia that are also becoming more industrialized and urbanized, Indonesia and Vietnam providing relevant examples, the majority of the workforce continues to work in agriculture or the urban informal sector, relying on family support once they reach old age.

The financial crisis that started in Thailand and rolled across the Asia-Pacific region in the late 1990s resulted in many jobs being lost and savings eroded for countless individuals. Even those who remained employed saw the value of their savings decline due to steep falls in the prices of financial assets, particularly equities, and by currency devaluation and inflation. In Indonesia, for example, the stock market fell from US$91 billion in 1996 to US$15 billion at the end of 1998, a move reflecting both the decline as measured in Indonesian currency and the sharp depreciation in the value of the currency relative to the U.S. dollar.

The family is another important mainstay of economic life in Asia and the Asian-Pacific region. The extended family is fundamental to most Asian societies and plays an important role in providing retirement income security. Most Asian elders live with one or more of their children, though the prevalence of this practice is declining across Asia, but nowhere more clearly than in Japan. In many Asian countries, it has traditionally been thought that the family should care for its elderly and that the development of social security systems might undermine the family's role. The traditional Confucian values that emphasize family responsibility for the economic support of older family members have served to slow the development of social security programs.

The impact of these traditional views can be seen in the development of formal mechanisms to meet the needs of the elderly. In part because of these views, a national social security program was not introduced in South Korea until 1988; Thailand waited until 1999. The relatively late development of national social security programs in these countries may also have been influenced by the fact that while many of the countries in this part of Asia were colonized by European countries, neither South Korea nor Thailand were, and thus they were less influenced by European thinking on the establishment of social security programs. With increasing urbanization and declining fertility rates, however, families are becoming smaller and more geographically dispersed. As a result, traditional support systems are under pressure, and social security benefits are increasingly seen as appropriately supplementing traditional family support.

SOCIAL SECURITY OLD-AGE BENEFITS IN ASIA

Worldwide, countries provide social security old-age benefits in remarkably diverse ways, reflecting differences in level of development and in historical experience. Such differences also are prompted by differing political philosophies and cultural views concerning the roles of the public and private sectors. Social security old-age benefits programs are provided by at least 172 countries around the world, which constitutes most but not all nations (United States Social Security Administration [U.S. SSA], 1999).

Because of the diverse ways social security old-age benefits are structured, it is necessary to consider what constitutes an old-age social security program. Essential elements include that such programs are employment-related, provide cash benefits in old age, and are mandatory, on the general supposition that many workers would not save adequately for retirement on their own. Thus, pensions voluntarily provided by employers are not included in this survey.

The diversity of mandatory old-age benefits programs can be seen by examining the major forms they take:

1. The large majority of countries provide old-age benefits through a *defined-benefit social security system* based on principles of social insurance, where workers contribute to the system and subsequently receive a benefit linked to their earnings. In a defined-benefit program, benefits are calculated using a formula usually based on the number of years of contributions and the worker's earnings. Pakistan, Saudi Arabia, and the Philippines are examples of countries employing this system.

2. An increasing number of countries provide benefits through a *mandatory individual-account defined-contribution program*. In a defined-contribution program, benefits are based on the worker's lifelong contributions to his or her individual account and the investment earnings on the funds in the account. A number of countries in Latin America adopted these programs during the 1990s, with the trend continuing into the first decade of this century and spreading to such Asian countries as Kazakhstan and Hong Kong.

3. A number of countries that were formerly British colonies in Africa and Asia have *provident funds*. Provident funds are mandatory savings plans that are fully funded and managed by government organizations. While other types of social security programs generally provide benefits as an annuity, provident funds usually only provide a lump-sum retirement benefit. Singapore and Malaysia are examples of countries using this system.

4. *Notional account plans* are a relatively new type of plan, recently adopted by Mongolia, as well as by Italy, Latvia, Poland, and Sweden. Each worker has an individual account, but the system is financed on a pay-as-you-go basis. A contribution is attributed to each worker's account as a bookkeeping entry. The return that is credited on the accumulated bookkeeping balance in each worker's account takes into consideration current and prospective demographic and productivity change.

5. Some countries give workers the option of contributing to a state-run plan versus contributing to a private-sector managed plan. This approach is often called *contracting out,* but is also called "opting out" or "voluntary carve-outs."

Workers or employers can choose between the state-run program and a private sector program. This approach is used by Peru with respect to its individual accounts system, by Japan and the United Kingdom with respect to their defined-benefit social security systems, and by India with respect to its Employees' Provident Fund.

6. Some countries mandate employer-provided pension plans, an approach used by Australia and Switzerland. Under a mandate, employers are required to provide their employees with pension plans meeting minimum requirements. These mandated plans can be either defined-benefit or defined-contribution plans, and in Switzerland cash-balance plans—a hybrid plan combining features of both defined-benefit and defined-contribution plans—are common. This type of plan is not found in Asia.

7. Some countries have contractual agreements that are widespread. The mandate is not a legal requirement imposed by the state but is the result of a contractual agreement between labor unions and employers that covers most workers in the country. This approach only is feasible in countries with widespread coverage of workers by unions or where union-negotiated pension arrangements can be required to be extended to nonunionized employers in the same industry. The Netherlands and Sweden are examples of this approach, but there are no examples in Asia.

Some countries provide flat benefits to individuals based on their having worked, but the benefits are not tied to earnings or to past contributions. The benefits may increase with years of contributions, or may be financed out of government general revenue. Japan provides flat benefits based on the number of years the person paid a flat-rate contribution.

Coverage

Probably the most important social security issue in Asia is the low level of workforce coverage in many countries. Social security programs in this region vary considerably in coverage and benefit levels, but generally tend to be less developed than in other parts of the world at comparable levels of economic development. Increasing the level of coverage is one of the most important policy issues facing social security programs in the region. Differences across the region in the level of per capita income partially explain differences in the extent of social security coverage. Middle- and high-income countries tend to have high coverage rates; the coverage rate in Malaysia is 60 percent, and that in Singapore, 73 percent. The high-income OECD countries of Australia, New Zealand, and Japan have near universal coverage.

Some countries in the region have very low coverage rates. For example, India has a coverage rate of about 10 percent, while the Philippines has a coverage rate of 28 percent (Fox and Palmer, 2001). In 1993, Vietnam extended compulsory social security coverage to the private sector, but coverage remains below 10 percent of the workforce because of extremely low compliance. China, Indonesia, and Thailand each have less than 30 percent coverage of private-sector workers and government workers combined (Holzmann, MacArthur, and Sin, 2000).

The low coverage rate in several Asian countries is due in part to the high percentage of workers in informal employment, as contributory programs in the region usually exclude the self-employed and those working in small firms (Gillion, Turner, Bailey, and Latulippe, 2000). Also, workers in small enterprises in the formal sector often are not covered. For example, the Provident Fund in Indonesia excludes workers in enterprises with 10 or fewer workers, while enterprises with 20 or fewer workers are excluded in India (Subrahmanya, 2002). Contribution evasion on the part of both employers and workers also contributes to low coverage rates (Bailey and Turner, 2001).

Expanding coverage, in particular to workers in the informal sector, is widely regarded as a priority across the region. One issue is whether workers in the informal sector should be included in a separate social security program specific to them rather than being included in the program for employees in the formal sector. In some countries, high contribution rates may pose an insurmountable hurdle for the social security program to appeal to low-income workers in the informal sector. Some analysts have argued that programs funded by worker contributions are not appropriate for the poorest workers because of their inability to contribute (Subrahmanya, 2002).

Malaysia has extended coverage to all employees regardless of the size of the enterprise in which they are employed. This example may provide useful information with respect to extending social security coverage to small employers. The Malaysian model may not be useful, however, for extending coverage to the informal sector because informal-sector workers by definition do not have formal, stable employer-employee relationships.

South Korea has taken another approach, extending coverage to the self-employed in 1995 by obliging farmers, fishermen, and rural self-employed individuals to contribute 3 percent of their earnings, a rate which is being increased by 3 percent every five years until it reaches 9 percent. Brunei Darussalem provides all citizens and permanent residents with a pension starting at age 60, but the pension is minimal (West and Kinsella, 1998). Vietnam also has a novel program that attempts to serve the needs of agricultural workers. In the farmers' program, farmers make an annual contribution of 80 kilos of rice, entitling them to approximately 6 kilos of rice per month when they are eligible to retire (Gillion, Turner, Bailey, and Latulippe, 2000).

Sri Lanka has established a Farmers Pension Scheme to provide pension coverage for agricultural workers and fishermen. This plan is run by the Agricultural and Agrarian Insurance Board, which is part of the national Agriculture Ministry. The plan provides disability and survivor benefits as well as pension benefits.

A few countries in Asia do not have a national social security program at all. In Cambodia, no such program exists, and older people are forced by their poverty to continue working until very late in life (Kato, 2000). Bangladesh, Nepal, and the Union of Myanmar have programs for government employees only but lack a social security system for private-sector employees (U.S. SSA, 1999). Afghanistan enacted a social insurance system in 1987 (U.S. SSA, 1999), but benefits have not yet been dispensed.

New Zealand and Japan are among only a small number of countries around the world that provide a universal pension to the aged that is not based on having worked. In Japan, the pension increases with the number of years that the person paid contributions. New Zealand is practically unique in that its social security earnings-related old-age benefit is financed out of general government revenue, with no contribution by either employee or employer (Willmore, 2001). This system became universal in 1938. It provides flat benefits that are neither earnings related nor means tested. The benefits received from the system are taxable as income, however.

Australia also provides old-age benefits through a program that is not based on workers' contributions but rather is financed out of general government revenue. Entitlement is based on age, residency, income, and assets but not on employment history (Bateman and Piggott, 2001). Currently the age of eligibility is 61.5 for women and 65 for men, but the age for women is being raised and will reach 65 by 2014. Australia's program is means tested, but participating in it is not stigmatized, an aspect of the perception of means-tested programs in other countries that causes many people who are eligible to not participate. In Australia, most older adults receive benefits through the program. The means-tested benefit is supplemented by a mandatory employer-provided pension, called the Superannuation Guarantee System (Barrett and Chapman, 2001). That pension can be either a defined-benefit or defined-contribution pension but, in nearly all cases, is provided as a defined-contribution pension. Employers must contribute 9 percent of wages to these plans. While the major source of income for retired workers is currently the means-tested program, it will be supplanted by the mandatory Superannuation Guarantee System once the latter has fully matured (Bateman and Piggott, 2001).

PATTERNS OF REFORM

Pension reform in Asia and the Pacific is taking place in three patterns. First, some national provident funds are being changed to defined-benefit plans. Second, some market-oriented countries with existing defined-benefit social security programs are reforming their programs. Third, some socialist countries are moving toward market economies, and this change is affecting their provision of old-age benefits.

Reform of Provident Funds

Income transfers as a means of income redistribution play a relatively small role in most Asian social security programs, thus placing greater responsibility on individuals and families for assuring adequate retirement income. A striking feature across the region is the large number of countries with no social insurance program, most of which are former British colonies that rely on a provident-fund model dating from the colonial period. Provident funds are mandatory savings plans that are fully funded individual accounts. The provident funds considered here in the context of social security programs are mandatory and are managed by governmental agencies. Provident funds provide personal-savings accounts but have no aspect of redistribution and thus provide no assurance that low-wage workers will receive adequate benefits. Provident funds in some countries are similar to savings accounts, where the account of each worker is credited an interest rate, which tends to vary with market rates of return but may be less than the interest rate earned on the underlying funds. Many of the provident funds have been criticized for providing low coverage and low benefits. They often allow workers to withdraw their money for various reasons before retirement age.

Provident funds originated in Asia. While they have been terminated by some countries in the Caribbean and Africa in favor of the social insurance type of social security program, none of the Asian countries have terminated their provident funds as of the publication of this chapter. Of the 19 countries around the world that have national provident funds in the early 2000s, 12 are in Asia and the Pacific (Saunders, 2001), and three of these have had a provident fund for more than 50 years—Indonesia (established in 1951), Malaysia (established in 1951), and India (established in 1952). The provident fund in Singapore began in 1955. India, Sri Lanka, Nepal, and Fiji allow workers with equivalent private-sector plans to opt out of the provident fund, while Malaysia allows a voluntary opt-out for teachers, soldiers, the self-employed, and domestic workers (Ferrara, Goodman, and Matthews, 1995).

Provident funds are sometimes used by governments to finance development projects and thus may aid in the economic development of a country. However, a common criticism of the provident funds is that they have done a poor job of managing investments (World Bank, 1994). The provident fund in Sri Lanka, started in 1958, produced real annual returns in the late 1990s of less than 2 percent (Iglesias and Palacios, 2000). In Singapore, where the Central Provident Fund is invested in government bonds, for the period 1987–1997 the real return was approximately zero (Asher, 1999b). Across the region, debate is ongoing over whether government supervision of provident funds is inherently doomed to mismanagement, or whether institutional and regulatory frameworks can be developed to assure that the provident funds are invested in a way that yields good returns. Such a change may require reforms in capital and financial markets as well as institutional developments concerning corporate governance and financial disclosure.

Lump-sum benefits typically provided by provident funds do not protect against the risk of a retired person outliving his or her income, and for this reason provident funds have been criticized by the International Labour Office for not ensuring social insurance protection (Gillion, Turner, Bailey, and Latulippe, 2000). This problem is increasingly acknowledged among the countries with national provident funds. For example, the Fiji National Provident Fund, started in 1966, offers its members a choice between a lump-sum benefit and a life annuity. However, members are encouraged by the fund to take annual pension benefits, as the annuity factors used to convert individual account balances into pensions are extremely generous—25 percent for single-life pensions and 16.7 percent for joint life pensions, compared with actuarial annuity factors of 10 and 8 percent. Despite the annuity being offered on very favorable terms, only about 10 percent of members actually choose that option. Other countries have recognized that compulsion is necessary. For example, Singapore has decided that members of its Central Provident Fund must set aside a minimum sum in their retirement account at age 55 to finance an annuity benefit (Gillion, Turner, Bailey, and Latulippe, 2000).

The Central Provident Fund, which was established by the British colonial administration in 1955, is the main component of Singapore's social security system (Asher, 1999a). This tiny country of 3 million people is unusual in that the government has greatly expanded the role of the Central Provident Fund to use it to provide financing for a wide variety of social and political objectives. To accommodate these objectives, the government gradually raised the individual contribution rate, which was initially 10 percent of wages but was ramped-up to 50 percent in 1984 (Asher and Karunarathne, 2001).

Singapore has used the rate of individual contribution to its provident fund as a policy tool for macroeconomic stabilization. To combat the recession in 1985–86, Singapore reduced the rate to 35 percent. In 1994, the national government raised the rate to 40 percent but reduced it to 30 percent in 1999 to offset effects of the East Asian financial crisis. The contribution rates apply to earned incomes less than 2.4 times the average monthly wage for Singaporeans. In part because of the high mandatory contribution rates, Singapore has the highest saving rate in the world (Asher, 1995).

Contributions to the Central Provident Fund in Singapore are allocated to three accounts. The ordinary account, which is about 75 percent of the total, may be used for housing and for investments. The Medisave account goes toward health insurance premiums and unreimbursed medical expenses. Only the Special Account is specifically for retirement. This account receives contributions of 4 percent, but with the reduction in the overall contribution rate in 1999, the Special Account did not receive any contributions in the early 2000s. In 2002, the contribution rate to the Special Account was reset at 4 percent for workers ages 35 and younger, 6 percent for workers ages 36 to 55, and 0 percent for workers ages 56 and older (Central Provident Fund, 2003).

Most of the monies in the Central Provident Fund have been invested in government bonds, but over time this restriction has been loosened. The bonds pay a low rate, equal to the average of the rates paid by four local banks, with a guaranteed minimum rate of 2.5 percent (Turner and Rajnes, 2001). The low nominal rate paid by the Central Provident Fund has roughly equaled the rate of inflation over long periods (Holzmann, MacArthur, and Sin, 2000). The low yield constitutes an implicit tax on the pension funds of workers, with the government benefitting by obtaining financing at below-market rates. Starting in 1986, participants have been allowed to invest a portion of their balances in approved domestic stocks. Since 1995, participants could invest in foreign stocks and bonds traded on the stock exchange of Singapore. In 1997, the limit on foreign currency–denominated investments increased from 20 to 40 percent. Starting in 1999, participants were allowed to invest in capital markets outside Asia, such as the United States (West and Kinsella, 1998).

In India, most people work in the informal sector and are not covered by social security programs for old-age benefits (Subrahmanya, 2002). The first programs established to provide social security benefits to different groups of workers were provident funds. The Employees' Provident Fund, by far the largest in India, was introduced in 1952 to cover workers in formal employment. The fund is invested in approved government securities, mainly fixed-interest bonds. It provides lump-sum benefits to people who are retired or who have been out of the covered sector for a specified period. Allowing withdrawals to finance house building, medical treatment, marriage expenses, and higher education, however, undermined its basic objective of assuring retirement benefits. If an employer sets up a provident fund at least as generous as that from the Employees' Provident Fund, the employer's provident fund may replace the Employees' Provident Fund—a form of contracting out (Chatterjee, 1999).

Starting in 1971, part of the Indian provident-fund contributions has also been used to provide monthly pensions to surviving dependents. In 1995, India partially converted the Employees' Provident Fund into a defined-benefit pension plan. Approximately 50 percent of contributions to the fund are now used to finance a defined-benefit annuity payable through the Employees' Pension Scheme. This program applies to firms with more than 20 employees, effectively excluding a large percentage of the workforce. In addition to the provident fund, the National Old Age Pension plan provides pensions to individuals ages 65 and older who have little or no income. The plan pays a pension of 75 rupees a month from general revenue of the central government. The level of the pension was set at 75 rupees a month in 1995 and as of 2002 remained at that level (Subrahmanya, 2002).

The Malaysian Employees Provident Fund has a high contribution rate of 23 percent. It is conservatively invested; in 2000, 34 percent of its portfolio was invested in Malaysian government securities, 24 percent in money market instruments, and 21 percent in equity (Malaysian Employees Provident Fund, 2003).

Indonesia, the third most populous country in Asia (after China and India), and the fourth most populous country in the world, has three separate provident funds: one for the military, one for the civil service, and one for the private sector. As is typical of this region and of many countries around the world, the retirement benefits provided by the funds for the military and civil service are considerably more generous than those for the private sector.

The Indonesian provident fund for private-sector employees provides lump-sum retirement benefits at age 55 based on contributions of 5.7 percent of earnings, the employer paying 3.7 percent (plus 0.3 percent for death benefits) and the employee paying 2.0 percent (Ramesh, 2000). It has provided low benefits, however, in part because of the low returns received by workers—but also because of high administrative expenses, including expensive office facilities for some staff. It is widely believed that the government uses part of the investment funds for political purposes (Dailey and Turner, 1996). In addition, the government does not credit all the returns received on investment of the funds to workers. Furthermore, the returns that are credited are subject to a tax.

This provident fund covers only 10 percent of the labor force, primarily because of the large informal sector in Indonesia, but also because of widespread contribution evasion. The military and civilian government service provident funds cover a slightly larger percentage of the total workforce (Ramesh, 2000).

Reform of Social Insurance Programs

Countries in Asia less exposed to British influence—such as Pakistan, the Philippines, South Korea, Taiwan, and Thailand—have generally established defined-benefit social insurance pension programs to cover employees. As in the West, the social insurance systems in the region are generally financed by contributions from both employers and employees.

In South Korea, for example, employers and employees both contribute 4.5 percent of wages. The program is temporarily accumulating large balances because it will not pay out retirement disbursements until 2008. South Korea has accumulated sizable reserves in its social security funds, equivalent to 10 percent of the GDP, but these funds are projected to dissipate as the system matures (Holzmann, MacArthur, and Sin, 2000). Currently, South Korea promises to pay a high replacement rate of 60 percent of wages to workers who have contributed to the program for 40 years. The program's funds are primarily invested in government securities and quasi-government projects, such as public housing. However, because of the drop in interest rates and the aging of the population, the investment fund is projected to be depleted by 2044, necessitating increases in the contribution rate to meet promised obligations.

Social security benefits in South Korea are supplemented by mandatory severance-pay allowances. Employers are required to pay severance settlements equal to 30 days of wages per working year, at the average wage, to retiring employees with at least one year of service. Employers are not required to fund such benefits in advance, and for the most part the benefits are paid out of current revenues. To pay these benefits in the case of the bankruptcy of a firm, the government has created a Wage Claim Guarantee Fund that is financed by a tax of 0.2 percent of wages.

Most countries in the region have a serious problem of contribution evasion, with workers and employers underreporting wages or simply not paying mandatory contributions (Bailey and Turner, 2001). In some countries, the weak connection between the worker's contributions and benefits encourages contribution evasion. The Social Security Old Age Pension in Thailand first received contributions in 1999. Pensions will only be available to workers who have contributed at least 15 years and are at least 55 years old. However, benefits are only based on the final five years of earnings, which gives workers an incentive to overstate earnings for those years and understate them all other years. In 1996, Thailand required all employers listed on the stock exchange, all financial institutions supervised by the country's central bank, and several other categories of employers to provide a provident fund for their workers. However, workers may opt not to participate in the fund, which differs from other countries in the region where participation is mandatory and the fund is managed by the government (Ramesh, 2000).

Although the system in the Philippines, established in 1957, has provided a high replacement rate of more than 70 percent for retired workers who have reached age 60 and have contributed to the system 120 months (Ramesh, 2000), benefits are still based on the final five years of earnings (U.S. SSA, 1999). This system provides a minimum pension benefit for workers with at least 10 years of contributions and provides a higher minimum for workers with at least 20 years of credits.

Pakistan has a unique scheme combining a traditional social insurance program with a mandatory charity based on the scriptures of the Qur'an. The social insurance system applies to employees in firms with 10 or more workers and is financed by a 5 percent payroll tax on employers, with employees paying nothing (U.S. SSA, 1999). However, because of widespread contribution evasion, relatively few people receive benefits from the system; those who do are mainly wage earners in large industries.

Partly in response to this evasion, partly in recognition of the growing influence of Islam as a political and ideological force in Pakistan, the country has implemented an Islamic social policy called *zakat*. *Zakat* is one of the five pillars of Islam and involves the giving of alms to certain deserving groups listed in the Qur'an. With the national *zakat* system, on the first day of the holy month of Ramadan, every bank account above a certain level is taxed 2.5 percent. The money is collected by the national government and then redistributed through 40,000 volunteer groups across the country. The groups identify and select the neediest poor to receive the benefit, with more than half going to the poor elderly, mainly widows. Because the system has been motivated by religious ideals, it has been less affected by corruption than have secular government–run programs. Pakistan is not alone in sampling this arrangement; Bangladesh and Malaysia have also adopted national *zakat* plans at different times. This stands as an example of Muslim countries trying to help their most vulnerable older citizens using a system based on traditional Muslim religious practices rather than on Western models of social security pensions (Clark, 2001).

The Japanese government has a long history of providing public pensions. As early as 1873, pensions for samurai and lords placed the largest burden on the central government, and the government attempted reforms in that year to reduce the burden (Michael and Taylor, 1964). Present-day Japan has a complex social security system. Its National Insurance Plan pays a flat-rate universal basic pension benefit that every resident above age 60 is eligible to receive. Its Employees' Insurance Plan pays an earnings-related benefit to employees in the private sector (Watanabe, 2002). Japan's social security system incorporates a feature that the United Kingdom's system shares: contracting out, or voluntary carve-outs. With carve-outs, workers in large enterprises can contribute to an alternative private-sector plan, called Employees' Pension Funds, reducing their mandatory contributions to the earnings-related part of social security in exchange (Watanabe, Turner, and Rajnes, 1994). The decision to participate in contracting out is not made by individual workers but is made collectively by workers at the enterprise level. Both plans are partially funded, meaning that they have accumulated assets that are less than sufficient to fully pay their accumulated liabilities.

Social Security Reform in Socialist Countries

A number of countries in Asia have socialist governments that are moving toward market-oriented economies, including Cambodia, the People's Republic of China, the Lao People's Democratic Republic, Mongolia, and Vietnam. Most pensioners in these countries are former public-sector employees, but in the future an increasingly large percentage of contributors—ultimately perhaps the majority—will be retired from the private sector. In some of the socialist countries in the region, state-owned enterprises are individually liable to provide retirement benefits for their shareholder-employees. This type of arrangement makes it virtually impossible, both socially and politically, for the state to allow outmoded enterprises to go bankrupt. The significance of the general socialist model is substantial; civil service and state-owned enterprises have accounted for a high proportion of total formal employment in China, the Lao People's Democratic Republic, and Vietnam. In all those countries, however, economic policies are being reformulated in an effort to trim the civil service, reduce the role of state-owned enterprises, and come to grips with the large number of such enterprises that are losing money and are not competitive in a global economy.

Given the vastness of the country and the population, China does not have a single national social security plan. Sizeable differences exist in the types of pensions provided in different cities and provinces. Different economic sectors also have different plans. During the 1980s and 1990s, the Chinese government's decentralization policies allowed certain provinces to experiment with different types of social security reform with little centralized oversight (Sin, 2000).

Changes in China during the 1990s and early 2000s, including economic reform and migration of large segments of the population from rural to urban areas, have reduced the coverage provided by the social security system so that by 2000 it covered considerably less than 50 percent of the urban workforce. These changes have increased significantly the number of non-state-sector employees left uncovered by China's social security programs. State-sector workers represented more than 90 percent of the urban workforce during the central planning era—from the 1950s to about 1990—but in 2000 made up only about 50 percent (Liu and MacKellar, 2001). In the meantime, most rural elderly are still supported by their families.

In 1997, China began to gradually move toward a three-pillar system congruent with the World Bank model (World Bank, 1994). A basic defined-benefit plan constitutes the first pillar and will provide benefits equal to 20 percent of average wages in the province where the recipient lives. The second tier is a provident-fund type of individual accounts system with a mandatory worker contribution rate of 8 percent: employers contribute 7 percent and employees contribute 1 percent. The government manages the investment of these accounts. The third tier is a voluntary system of individual contributions to individual account funds. Different cities are pursuing different approaches within this general three-legged framework. Some cities, including Shanghai, Ningbo, and Shenzhen, have experimented with a pension system based solely on individual accounts (West, 1999). Shanghai has since moved away from this approach, however.

The transition to a reformed social security system will doubtlessly occur over a period of a number of years. China currently lacks some of the prerequisites for reliance on individual accounts invested in capital markets: It does not yet have competitive capital markets even though it is making rapid progress in this regard. It also does not have clearly defined private property rights, which would be necessary for the ownership and full transferability of stock shares. Seemingly, social problems familiar in the West are making themselves known throughout China and involve everything from homelessness to elder abuse.

Hong Kong, though now part of China, has a separate social security system. It began a mandatory individual accounts system in 2000 whereby workers and employers both contribute 5 percent of wages into funded individual accounts. Higher amounts can be contributed voluntarily and, once in the accounts, are treated the same as the mandatory portion. The pension fund managers are chosen by the employers, leaving employees able to choose only from among the funds offered by that particular manager (Fox and Palmer, 2001). The pension funds may invest in stock listed on recognized stock exchanges and on investment-grade debt. This system is designed to provide lump-sum benefits, as is common in the provident funds in Asia. It maintains a fund to compensate participants for losses due to illegal activities by fund managers. Unlike the rest of China, the system in Hong Kong is not a multipillar system, since when it matures, the individual accounts system will be the primary source of retirement income for most participating workers. Hong Kong also maintains a means-tested program to provide poverty relief.

Pensions for workers in state-owned enterprises are a major issue in the Lao People's Democratic Republic. In the past, these workers were covered by the civil service pension scheme. A reform in 1993, however, excluded them from the scheme. While most state-owned enterprises have been privatized, a social security program has not yet been established for workers in the private sector. Also, the problem of paying for pensions based on past entitlements under the civil service pension has not been resolved. Some retired employees are being paid pensions by the ministries formerly responsible. For example, individuals who have retired from Lao Beer are receiving pensions from the Ministry of Industry. The state-owned enterprises that remain have had to assume responsibility for paying pensions (Gillion, Turner, Bailey, and Latulippe, 2000).

In Vietnam, certain groups have, with the guidance of the government, established pension plans for their members. These groups include both urban informal-sector workers who are members of cooperatives and rural workers who are members of the Farmers' Union. Vietnam's social security program has a relatively high contribution rate for the region, 15 percent, with monthly old-age pension benefits providing a replacement rate of 69 percent of the average covered wage. However, once taxes are taken into account the replacement rate for total compensation is about half that figure as wages subject to taxes are only about half of total wages (MacArthur, 2000). Due in large part to the mortality rate among young men during the war from 1954 to 1975, Vietnam is not currently facing a problem with population aging (MacArthur, 2000).

Mongolia has a contribution rate of 19 percent, of which employers pay 13.5 percent with employees responsible for the remaining 5.5 percent. The self-employed can voluntarily join the system at a rate of 9.5 percent. Probably in part due to the high contribution rates, contribution arrears (nonpayment) are a serious problem. In 1999, Mongolia approved a reform establishing unfunded notional accounts. A notional account system establishes individual accounts for each worker and credits contributions and interest earnings to these accounts. These accounts are notional or hypothetical, however, because they are unfunded, with benefits paid out of current payroll taxes. This system was established to deal with ongoing fiscal problems; however, the reform resulted in a substantial cut in benefits (Fox and Palmer, 2001).

LONG-TERM CARE

As was pointed out by the editors in the introductory chapter, across Asia, long-term care is already a significant policy concern that will grow in importance as populations continue to age. No place are the priorities of the economic development agenda and the demographic transformation of the population more apparent than in the provision of palliative long-term care services.

Demand for Long-Term Care

Population aging brought about by declining fertility and mortality rates has become a worldwide phenomenon. In fact, some projections suggest that, due to breakthroughs in genetic research and biomedicine, longevity gains may accelerate, not slow (Schieber and Hewitt, 2000). The projected growth of the older adult population of many countries, especially in the numbers of elders in their 80s, certainly invites concern because frailty is more common at advanced ages.

However, what proportion of the oldest old will need long-term care is difficult to forecast because of uncertainty about the effects of better health and improved lifestyles (Campion, 1994; Fiatarone, O'Neill, Ryan, et al., 1994; Skoog, Nilsson, Palmertz, Andreasson, and Svanborg, 1993). It would be instructive to learn about disability trends in all the other countries covered in this volume. Absent such information, however, it may be useful to refer to the comparison of life expectancy based on mortality data alone versus "disability-adjusted life expectancy" (DALE) as reported by the World Health Organization. DALE is derived by subtracting years lost to disability from the overall length of life based on mortality data only. In other words, DALE deducts the estimated years of ill health from the expected overall life expectancy, yielding the equivalent years of healthy life (Table 2). One implication of this discussion is that policy development for long-term care needs to recognize the likely effects of lifestyle practices on incidence of disability.[1]

According to calculations of DALE, Japan ranks number one in the world, with an average health-life expectancy of 74.5 years at birth in 1999 (Table 2). Several factors may account for Japan's ranking. One is the low rate of heart disease, associated with the traditional low-fat diet of the Japanese. But Japan's

[1] A recent report of a longitudinal study of 724 men over a 60-year period identified seven factors that appeared to predict successful aging: moderate alcohol use, no smoking, a stable marriage, exercise, appropriate weight, positive coping mechanisms, and no depressive illness. Mental depression was the only factor beyond individual control that affected the quality of aging (Vaillant and Mukamal, 2001).

Table 2. Comparison of Life Expectancy: Mortality-Based versus Disability-Adjusted

Country	Mortality-based life expectancy (years)	Disability-adjusted life expectancy (years)	Expectation of disability at birth (years)	Lifespan lived with disability (percent)
Japan	80.9	74.5	6.4	7.9
Australia	79.5	73.2	6.3	7.9
Canada	79.1	72.0	7.1	9.0
United States	76.8	70.0	6.8	8.9
Singapore	78.0	69.3	8.7	11.2
China	69.7	62.3	7.4	10.6

Note: Because Hong Kong and Taiwan, two of the seven countries studied in this volume, are not reported in the source, data for China are listed here as a proxy.

Source: Taken from or estimates based on data in annex table 2 and annex table 5 in World Health Organization, 2000.

national diet is reportedly incorporating higher amounts of high-fat foods such as red meat. Another factor is low cancer rates resulting from less tobacco use. However, smoking became more common after World War II, and the long-term effects of its increased popularity may cause the incidence of cancers to rise in the future.

Over the years, there has been much speculation about how long the average human lifespan may be extended. Longevity is the quantitative aspect of life. To make life more worth living is life's qualitative dimension. Living longer without reasonable physical and mental health is a blessing to no one—the individuals themselves, their families and friends, or society at large.

In policy terms, therefore, biomedical and pharmaceutical research should be complemented with research to prevent diseases, promote wellness, and enhance socioeconomic aspects of life. Preferably, both types of research should increase. When confronted by a choice, however, it may be argued that more attention should be paid to improving socioeconomic considerations as opposed to investing in biological dimensions of aging so as to improve quality of life rather than lengthen it. In other words, better quality of life is preferred over more quantity of life.

Supply of Long-Term Care

Throughout this volume the point is made that in Asia and the Pacific, the bulk of long-term care services has traditionally been provided by informal (unpaid) caregivers. However, such care has become less and less available due to geographic dispersion of family members, increased labor-force participation by women, fewer children in the family, more childless families, higher divorce rates, more single-parent families, and the rising incidence of family members being unable to care for others because of their own advanced age or their own health impairment. In light of the last factor, the traditional reliance of elders on the family may require a closer examination when improving mortality becomes a significant factor. When people live to be in their 80s and 90s, their children would be in their 60s and 70s, and their grandchildren would be in their 40s and 50s. In this multigenerational setting, it is not difficult to appreciate the logistical issues younger members of the family must grapple with in rendering assistance to their older relatives. Although informal care is still very important, as it is replaced by formal caregiving, the demand for the latter increases. The supply of a formal-care workforce is an important issue and one that some trace to the strong cultural traditions of the Asian world. Shortages are already evident everywhere.

As is apparent in some of the chapters of this volume, a useful policy initiative may be to channel some of each country's long-term care budget toward paying informal caregivers for the services provided to the elderly. Cash payment in exchange for in-kind benefits under the German social insurance program for long-term care may be a useful approach. Such a policy will enable beneficiaries to pay their informal caregivers, thus helping to alleviate worker shortage.

Another supply issue relates to the nature of the long-term care services that are needed. As is clear from existing literature, criticisms abound everywhere against the so-called institutional bias—premature or inappropriate placement of disabled people in a nursing home. Concomitantly, there have been movements in all countries toward home and community-based care. Although there are still cases of inappropriate admission to nursing facilities, the problem may be regarded as part of an evolutionary process: Those who needed long-term care in the past were most likely to have suffered from strokes or other acute diseases, often requiring constant medical supervision or custodial care. As longevity increases, a larger portion of older adults may be inflicted with such chronic conditions as arthritis, osteoporosis, lung and heart diseases, or Alzheimer's and Parkinson's diseases and may consequently need assistance with normal daily activities. As disease patterns change, so will the methods by which long-term care services are provided.

While there will always be a need for medical services and institutional living arrangements, most people requiring long-term care also need social services and personal care to assist them in their daily tasks. Adequate provision of the homecare services focusing on social and personal care would help people live at home. Homecare entails a large demand for in-home supportive workers able to render assistance beyond those that might be classified as medical or palliative.

Funding for Long-Term Care

In regard to funding for long-term care, the adoption of social insurance for long-term care in Germany and in Japan provides an encouraging model for other nations to consider. In 1995, the Long-Term Care Insurance Program was introduced in Germany, based on the pay-as-you-go principle. It is a mandatory insurance scheme that covers the entire population. Those who are eligible for the benefits of the plan can choose between cash and in-kind benefits or a combination of both.

In April 2000, Japan implemented its Long-Term Care Insurance Law, creating a system of unique financing and service delivery in Asia. Financing for long-term care consists of (a) general revenue (bearing one half of the total cost of services) from three levels of government on a 2:1:1 formula (50 percent from the national government and 25 percent each from prefectures and municipalities); and (b) premium payments (bearing the other half of the total cost) from individuals ages 40–64 (covered only for age-related disability such as Alzheimer's disease or stroke) and from individuals ages 65 and older, with the premiums for many of the latter group deducted from their social security pensions. There is no coverage for people under age 40. The insurer is the municipal government, which is responsible for determining eligibility. Service delivery is carried out by both municipalities and private nonprofit and for-profit service providers. The advantages and drawbacks of these policy experiments in Germany and Japan should be studied closely. In our view, the application of insurance principles in the public sector is a major step in the right direction.

CONCLUDING REMARKS

Population aging is occurring more rapidly in Asia than in any other region of the world. The rapidity of Asian demographic change will shorten the lead time governments have for implementing reforms and will cause cohorts of individuals to receive considerably less generous publicly provided benefits than their older counterparts. The interconnectedness of economics with a panoply of social and population changes portends major readjustments in the not-too-distant future. We point to two areas of concern: social security and long-term care.

Many workers in the region lack social security coverage. Extending social security to workers lacking such coverage is, and will continue to be, a major problem in the region. Related to this problem is a lack of compliance with social security contribution requirements, which causes workers who are legally covered to not accrue benefits because they and their employers are not contributing as mandated. The long-term consequence is to risk destitution in old age.

Finally, a word about transferability of experiences across countries may be in order. Doubtless a country may adopt or adapt certain technical information from another country. However, given that a country's social institutions express a long legacy of traditions, it appears unlikely that there will be wholesale adoption of approaches or programs from abroad. For example, for a country whose policy emphasizes individual and family responsibility with only helping hands from private volunteer organizations as a safety net, it is doubtful that it would adopt a social insurance model for income security or health security inclusive of long-term care, which may prove more successful in another country, or vice versa. However, we remain hopeful that researchers, practitioners, and policymakers in different countries will endeavor to learn from one another and adopt best practices.

REFERENCES

Asher, M. G. (1995, September). *Compulsory savings in Singapore: An alternative to the welfare state* (National Center for Policy Analysis Report No. 198). Retrieved September 12, 2003, from http://www.ncpa.org/studies/s198/s198.html

Asher, M. G. (1999a, August 23). *The pension system in Singapore.* World Bank Pension Reform Primer. Retrieved November 17, 2003, from http://wbln0018.worldbank.org/HDNet/HDdocs.nsf/65538a343139acab85256cb70055e6ed/58a20e0a641943e8852567d6007b63ae/$FILE/9919.pdf

Asher, M. G. (1999b). *Social security system and its reform: Interview with Dr. Byeong-Ho-Gong.* Retrieved November 17, 2003, from http://www.cfe.org/english/publi/view17.htm

Asher, M. G., and Karunarathne, W. (2001, March). *Social security arrangements in Singapore: An assessment.* Paper presented at the International Seminar on Pensions, Tokyo.

Bailey, C., and Turner, J. (2001). Strategies to reduce contribution evasion in social security financing. *World Development, 29,* 385–393.

Barrett, J., and Chapman, K. (2001). The Australian superannuation system. In *Private pension systems: Administrative costs and reforms* (pp. 185–199). Paris: Organization for Economic Cooperation and Development.

Bateman, H., and Piggott, J. (2001, March 22). *Australia's mandatory retirement saving policy: A view from the new millennium.* Washington, D.C.: World Bank. Retrieved November 17, 2003, from http://wbln0018.worldbank.org/HDNet/HDdocs.nsf/65538a343139acab85256cb70055e6ed/0310a48d5288b8b785256a1700504806/$FILE/0108.pdf

Campion, E. W. (1994). The oldest old. *New England Journal of Medicine, 330,* 1819–1820.

Central Provident Fund. *Central Provident Fund website.* Retrieved September 17, 2003, from http://www.cpf.gov.sg

Chatterjee, B. (1999). India. In D. Callund (Ed.), *International benefits yearbook, 1999* (pp. 162-166). London: Sweet and Maxwell.

Chen, Y.-P., and Velkoff, V. A. (2003, November). *Projecting older support ratios around the world for 2030: Alternative estimates.* Presented at the 2003 Gerontological Society of America Annual Meeting, San Diego, California.

Clark, G. (2001). Pakistan's zakat system: A policy model for developing countries as a means of redistributing income to the elderly poor. In F. L. Ahearn Jr. (Ed.), *Issues in global aging* (pp. 47–76). New York: The Haworth Press.

Colander, D. C. (2004). *Economics.* New York: McGraw-Hill/Irwin.

Dailey, L., and Turner, J. (1996). *Indonesia's social security system for employees: A baseline study.* Report for the Asian-American Free Labor Institute, Washington, DC.

Federal Interagency Forum on Aging-Related Statistics. (2000). *Older Americans 2000: Key indicators of well-being.* Washington, DC: U.S. Government Printing Office.

Ferrara, P. J., Goodman, J. C., and Matthews, M., Jr. (1995, October). *Private alternatives to social security in other countries* (National Center for Policy Analysis Report No. 200). Retrieved September 12, 2003, from http://www.ncpa.org/studies/s200/s200.html

Fiatarone, M. A., O'Neill, E. F., Ryan, N. D., Clements, K. M., Solares, G. R., Nelson, M. E., Roberts, S. B., Kehayias, J. J., Lipsitz, L. A., and Evans, W. J. (1994). Exercise training and nutritional supplementation for physical frailty in very elderly people. *New England Journal of Medicine, 330,* 1769–1775.

Fox, L., and Palmer, E. (2001). New approaches to multipillar pension systems: What in the world is going on? In R. Holzmann and J. E. Stiglitz (Eds.), *New ideas about old age security* (pp. 90–132). Washington, DC: World Bank.

Gillion, C., Turner, J., Bailey, C., and Latulippe, D. (2000). *Social security pensions: Development and reform.* Geneva, Switzerland: International Labour Office.

Holzmann, R., MacArthur, I. W., and Sin, Y. (2000, June). *Pension systems in East Asia and the Pacific: Challenges and opportunities.* Social Protection Unit, the World Bank. Retrieved November 17, 2003, from http://wbln0018.worldbank.org/HDNet/HDdocs.nsf/5b9b9684435b3a4585256c0500 0515ab/4304337865f1a7788525690c0054f031/$FILE/0014.pdf

Iglesias, A., and Palacios, R. (2000). *Managing public pension reserves: Evidence from the international experience* (Social Protection Discussion Paper No. 0003). Washington, DC: World Bank.

Kato, E. U. (2000). Ageing in Cambodia: Tradition, change, and challenges. In D. R. Phillips (Ed.), *Ageing in the Asia-Pacific region: Issues, policies, and future trends* (pp. 360–374). London: Routledge.

Liu, S., and MacKellar, L. (2001, January). *Key issues of aging and social security in China* (International Institute for Applied Systems Analysis Interim Report IR-01-004). Retrieved September 20, 2003, from http://www.iiasa.ac.at/cgi-bin/pubsrch?IR01004

MacArthur, I. (2000). Country profile for Vietnam. In R. Holzmann, I. W. MacArthur, and Y. Sin, *Pension systems in East Asia and the Pacific: Challenges and opportunities* (Appendix). Washington, DC: World Bank. Retrieved November 17, 2003, from http://wbln0018.worldbank.org/HDNet/HDdocs.nsf/5b9b9684435b3a4585256c0500 0515ab/4304337865f1a7788525690c0054f031/$FILE/vietnam.pdf

Malaysian Employees Provident Fund. (2003). *Malaysian Employees Provident Fund* website.

Michael, F. H., and Taylor, G. E. (1964). *The Far East in the modern world* (Rev. ed.). New York: Holt, Rinehart, and Winston.

Ramesh, M. (2000). *Welfare capitalism in Southeast Asia: Social security, health, and education policies.* New York: St. Martin's Press.

Saunders, P. (2001). Economic growth and social security: Aspects of recent Asian experience. In D. D. Hoskins, D. Dobbernack, and C. Kuptsch (Eds.), *Social security at the dawn of the 21st century* (pp. 69–98). New Brunswick, New Jersey: Transaction Publishers.

Schieber, S. J., and Hewitt, P. H. (2000). *Demographic risk in industrial societies.* Mimeographed September 6, 2000, draft.

Sin, Y. (2000). Country profile for China. In R. Holzmann, I. W. Mac Arthur, and Y. Sin, (Eds.), *Pension systems in East Asia and the Pacific: Challenges and opportunities* (Appendix), Washington, DC: World Bank. Retrieved November 17, 2003, from http://wbln0018.worldbank.org/HDNet/HDdocs.nsf/5b9b9684435b3a4585256c0500 0515ab/4304337865f1a7788525690c0054f031/$FILE/china.pdf

Skoog, I., Nilsson, L., Palmertz, B., Andreasson, L.-A., and Svanborg, A. (1993). A population-based study of dementia in 85-year-olds. *New England Journal of Medicine, 328,* 153–158.

Subrahmanya, R. K. A. (2002). Income security for older people: An Asian perspective. *International Social Security Review, 55,* 49–65.

Turner, J., and Rajnes, D. (2001). Rate of return guarantees for mandatory defined contribution plans. *International Social Security Review, 54,* 49–66.

U.S. Social Security Administration [U.S. SSA]. (1999). *Social security programs throughout the world* (SSA Publication No. 13-11805). Washington, DC: Author.

Vaillant, G. E., and Mukamal, K. (2001). Successful aging. *American Journal of Psychiatry, 158*(6), 839-847.

Watanabe, N. (2002). Social security reform ideas in Japan. *Journal of Aging and Social Policy, 14,* 81–94.

Watanabe, N., Turner, J., and Rajnes, D. (1994, November-December). 'Pay or play' pensions in Japan. *Contingencies,* 63–65.

West, L. A. (1999). *Pension reform in China: Preparing for the future.* Washington, DC: U.S. Census Bureau. Retrieved November 17, 2003, from http://www.census.gov/ipc/www/ebsum97b.htmlhttp://www.census.gov/ipc/www/ebsum97b.html

West, L. A., and Kinsella, K. (1998). *Pension management and reform in Asia: An overview* (Report No. 11). Seattle, Washington: The National Bureau of Asian Research.

Willmore, L. (2001, September). *Universal pensions in low income countries.* Paper presented at the Oxford IPD Workshop, Oxford, England.

World Bank. (1994). *Averting the old age crisis.* Oxford, England: Oxford University Press.

World Health Organization. (2000). *The world health report 2000: Health systems—Improving performance.* Geneva, Switzerland: Author.

CHAPTER THREE

The Politics and Policies of Aging, Asian Style

Laura Katz Olson

Approximately three fourths of the world's population live in Asia (Mehta, 1997). As noted in the chapter on demography, countries across the region are facing rapid demographic aging, fostering a stark increase in absolute numbers as well as in the percentage of older adults in their populations. By the dawn of the current century, slightly more than 50 percent of the world's population ages 60 and older and nearly 40 percent of those ages 80 and over lived in Asia; these figures are projected to rise to 57 percent and 48 percent, respectively, over the next 20 years (Phillips, 2000).

Though Asian nations share many social and cultural characteristics, especially in regard to their attitudes toward the elderly, the vast diversity of historical and contemporary circumstances, conditions, and institutional arrangements must be taken into account when considering each nation's policies related to aging. Certainly, Asian nations are at varying stages of social and economic development, which affects the extent of their resources for meeting the needs of older adults and their families. Japan and South Korea are the most globalized and economically advanced, followed by Taiwan, Hong Kong, and China; the latter has one of the fastest growing economies in the world. Much of the southeast—Singapore, Indonesia, Laos, Malaysia, and Thailand—also is developing rapidly, although progress in the Philippines has lagged somewhat compared with its neighbors. The poorest, least developed countries in Asia are in the south-central region: Afghanistan, Bangladesh, India, Nepal, Pakistan, Sri Lanka, Tajikistan, Turkmenistan, and Uzbekistan (Lee and Mason, 2000).

INDUSTRIALIZATION, MODERNIZATION, AND THE CHANGING SITUATION OF OLDER ASIANS

Social and economic change does not occur within a vacuum: Public officials and commercial interests make concrete decisions that affect the entire fabric of society. Over the last several decades, developing nations have placed programs fostering rapid economic development and modernization at the forefront of their agendas. Such policies inevitably have affected the overall experience of aging, disadvantaging a considerable percentage of older people and their families. Political leaders throughout Asia now are facing the profound ramifications of their actions. As nations become more industrialized and urbanized, larger numbers of their elderly citizens have been thrust on their own, thereby requiring increasing amounts of financial aid as well as social services. Outside of Japan, South Korea, Hong Kong, and Taiwan, which all experienced rapid economic development and urbanization earlier than other Asian nations, a large percentage of people in Asia—including three fourths of the populations of China and India—still live in small villages and on farms (Mehta, 1997). However, most nations in the region are steadily moving from peasant-agrarian economies to metropolitan, industrial societies, and all are looking to assume a place on the world economic stage. In 20 years, it is expected that more than half of the population of Asia will reside in urban areas, mostly because of the accelerating rate of migration to cities by younger generations (Economic and Social Commission for Asia and the Pacific, 1999). Despite ongoing economic support from their families, elders remaining in rural communities are increasingly left to fend for themselves. In addition, even when adult children are willing to take their parents to the city with them, affordable accommodations are frequently too tiny to house multigenerational households. For example, according to Chow (2000), in Hong Kong "housing units are generally very small . . . due to lack of space, and it is almost impossible for more than two generations to live in the same household." However, because dwellings are relatively expensive, many adult children are forced to live with their elderly parents.

Concomitantly, as the economies of most Asian nations shift from either rural or small family-based enterprises to large manufacturing and service industries, there are fewer opportunities for the aged to work. Furthermore, increasing numbers of older adults lose their jobs as new types of technology render them obsolete (ESCAP, 1989). Asia currently has the highest labor-force participation rates for individuals ages 65 and older. But this rate is projected to decline progressively as countries continue to pursue economic development and to modernize (ESCAP, 1999; Lee and Mason, 2000). Consequently, elders who have been able to support themselves throughout their lives are becoming financially dependent on others, especially their families. As other chapters in this volume make clear, rapid economic change has drawn increasing participation of women into the paid labor force, leaving them less available for elder-care duties. In Hong Kong, for example, half of all women are now employed. In its overall assessment of the repercussions of economic development on the lives of older people and their families in Asia, ESCAP (1999) recently concluded: ". . . while there is obviously room for debate about the extent and duration of the adverse impact on older persons, and certainly wide variation between countries, . . . the final outcome will depend very much on policy responses" (p. 15).

GLOBALIZATION

Developing nations in Asia, similar to developing nations in other regions of the world, have had to adopt certain programs and policies in order to secure loans from international agencies. Since the 1980s, the World Bank and the International Monetary Fund have imposed structural adjustment policies (SAPs) on industrializing countries such as Malaysia, India, Sri Lanka, and the Philippines. These austerity measures, intended to spur the growth of each nation's gross domestic product (GDP) and economy, have had devastating effects on large sectors of its population. Severe cutbacks in social welfare spending, reductions in wages, implementation of export-oriented policies, increased foreign investments, and privatization of state enterprises have fostered greater unemployment and poverty, poorer health, and reductions in the provision of public health care. For instance, between 1969 and 1985, public-sector healthcare expenditures in Asian nations subject to SAPs declined from 5.5 percent to 2.2 percent of national budgets (Chang, 2000). SAPs also have led to the demise of small family enterprises, including the breakdown of family farms.

As a result, women increasingly have been forced into the labor force in order to help sustain their families financially. In some countries, such as Thailand, the Philippines, Sri Lanka, Bangladesh, and Indonesia, they have had to migrate to other nations in search of work, mostly as domestics (Parrenas, 2001). At the 1995 Nongovernmental Organizations (NGOs) Forum on Women in Beijing, China, "Asian women organizers in particular pointed to the massive migration from countries as a result of SAP-driven poverty" (Chang, 2000, p. 124). A large number of these women are wives and mothers who form transnational households, leaving their children in the care of their spouses and parents.

Moreover, women often are encouraged to depart from their homeland in order to alleviate unemployment. In the Philippines, for instance, low economic growth, compounded by a large and growing working-age population, has spurred large-scale migration of women to other nations as contract workers. Such migration also bolsters the economy: Emigrants are viewed as export commodities, generating much-needed foreign currency for their debt-ridden countries. Nearly all of the female workers with transnational families send the bulk of their wages home, thus supporting both the nation as well as family members. In the Philippines, where the labor outflow is state sanctioned, such remittances are the second largest source of foreign currency. At the same time, it is estimated that 30 to 50 percent of the Filipino population—especially the aged—is dependent on this form of financial assistance. More than half of the 6.5 million emigrants from the Philippines are female, the majority providing elder care, childcare, and housecleaning services in private homes in more than 130 nations. Importantly, though many Filipinas travel to the United States and Western Europe, a large number serve as low-wage domestics in the more advanced industrial nations of Asia, including Japan, Hong Kong, Singapore, and Malaysia, illustrating the cleavage between the "have" and "have-not" nations in the region (Parrenas, 2001).

WHO CARES FOR THE AGED?

Filial piety has been and continues to be the mainstay of elder care across the region. Confucian moral prescriptions in countries such as Japan, Korea, and China, as well as Islamic, Buddhist, and Hindu value systems in other Asian nations, all uphold the notion that older people must be respected and esteemed. In the Philippines, a predominantly Christian country, the value of *utang na loob* (a debt of gratitude) also instills a comparable sense of obligation to one's parents. Indeed, the extended family is regarded as central to an individual's social, political, and economic life. Regardless of subtle cultural differences among the various religions and nations in Asia, adult children are viewed as responsible for the well-being of their parents or parents-in-law, beliefs that have endured despite rapid social and economic changes. In most places, the idea of filial obligation is reinforced by a culture of shame that renders people subject to the approval of others. These values often are backed by legal mandates and sanctions.

Though families in Western countries also take primary responsibility for the care of their elders, the commitments expected from Asian children are far more extensive. Among other factors, older people—including couples—expect to live with their adult children; Americans and Europeans prefer "intimacy at a distance." Not only do many more elders in Western nations live alone, but increasing numbers tend to prefer that arrangement. By contrast, in nearly all Asian countries, relatively fewer people live by themselves; for example, only 2 percent in Korea; 3 percent in China; 6 percent in Malaysia and the Philippines; and 8 percent in Indonesia live in one-person households (International Labour Office, 1997). Multigenerational households also are far more common in Asia than in the West. In some places, such as Thailand, the Philippines, Malaysia, and Singapore, more than 80 percent of the population ages 60 and older reside with their families. Multigenerational shared-housing arrangements range from 44 percent of the elderly in Hong Kong, 55 percent in South Korea, and 66 percent in Taiwan to nearly 70 percent in India (more than 90 percent in rural areas) and 76 percent in Indonesia. The vast majority of the aged in China and Malaysia also are similarly situated (Bartlett and Wu, 2000; Chow, 2000; ESCAP, 1999; International Labour Office, 1997). Even in economically advanced Japan, where multigenerational households are declining, fully 50 percent of elders coresided with an adult child at the end of the 20th century (Ogawa and Retherford, 1993). Clearly, a sense of obligation persists among the young and old alike, even though cracks are beginning to appear in the filial mandates. For one thing, the ability to form multigenerational households has become increasingly more difficult because of population aging (four- and five-generation families are emerging), distance from parents (rural-to-urban and international migration), inadequate resources (growing unemployment), smaller houses (urbanization), and other adverse social and economic factors associated with development.

In addition, in Asia the elderly tend to be more reliant on their families for at least some financial support than in the United States or Western Europe. For instance, in South Korea, two thirds of older people depend on their adult children for their economic needs. An older woman, in particular, must turn to her son if her spouse dies or if he can no longer provide for her (Kinsella, 2000). Greater unemployment rates among the aged and their forced retirement as a result of industrialization are placing even greater economic burdens on young families. Furthermore, declining fertility in many places reduces the likelihood of having a son who can support his aging parents and portends further changes in the decades immediately ahead. The reality is that there are and will be fewer children to care for parents who are living longer.

Critically, in Asian societies mutual obligations and reciprocity among generations is common, rendering such words as *dependency* misnomers (ESCAP, 1999). In fact, Mehta (1997) argues, "So far as family care is concerned, elderly women in Asian societies appear to be more on the giving rather than the receiving end" (p. 16). Though élderly women are less likely to be in the labor force than older men, the former are usually responsible for domestic chores such as cooking and cleaning as well as full-time care of grandchildren, especially when both the adult child and his or her spouse are employed. In the Philippines, grandmothers often raise the children when a mother must go overseas to work support her family from afar. Indeed, nearly 75 percent of elders in the Philippines who have grandchildren care for them on a regular basis (Natividad, 2000). Modernization can undermine traditional notions of reciprocity, leading to resentment by adult children providing financial aid and to a sense of shame on the part of the older parents who are forced to receive it.

THE ROLE OF THE STATE: ECONOMIC SUPPORT OF THE ELDERLY

As this section will show, political leaders in the region, reinforced by Asian cultural values, have eschewed the establishment of comprehensive retirement systems, leaving older people dependent on their family for financial support. For the most part, any available government assistance is confined to the impoverished aged who have no living kin to assist them.

Income Security Systems

Nearly all developed Western nations have instituted a combination of government and private pension schemes to cover the vast majority of the labor force, along with some form of national healthcare coverage (except for the United States). Though in many places there are sharp economic divisions among the aged based on gender, class, race, and ethnicity, some form of public assistance generally is available, especially in Western Europe, to meet their minimum income needs as well.

In contrast, only a few Asian countries, Japan and Singapore being the foremost examples, have retirement schemes that cover more than a fraction of workers or pay any meaningful retirement income (Lee and Mason, 2000). The Asian political culture is so steeped in family values that it has impeded the establishment and growth of social welfare programs for the elderly, including pension systems. Rather than viewing older people as a social responsibility, national governments have relied primarily on adult children to support their aged parents financially. Thus, there are few state-sponsored programs aimed at providing retirement income, and even then coverage is seriously restricted. In addition, only limited public resources have been appropriated to support the programs that do exist. In India and South Korea, for example, the government contributes only 0.22 percent and 0.14 percent, respectively, of their GDPs to such systems (Lee and Mason, 2000). In addition, a strong ethic of individual and family responsibility for economic support has influenced the structuring of retirement programs. In most of Southeast Asia, for example, there tends to be an "aversion to social insurance" (ESCAP, 1999, p. 67).

Pension policy, Asian style, tends to be restricted largely to employee-supported provident-fund arrangements with limited government financing. These publicly mandated and managed schemes—basically government-administered savings plans—have been in existence in the former British colonies of India, Malaysia, and Singapore for a long while; in the last decade, they also have been set up in Indonesia, Hong Kong, and Thailand (Asher, 1998). The latter nation, for example, which does not have an extensive income support system for its retirees in the private sector, has attempted to introduce more comprehensive provisions under its newly enacted Social Security Act of 1990 (Asher, 1998; Phillips, 2000). However, the primary emphasis of this legislation is on expanding provident funds, thus "encouraging" more workers to save for their own old age (Asher, 1998). Though such schemes have accumulated significant assets that are used as investment capital in certain Asian nations, the benefits tend to be too low to provide sufficient retirement income. Since workers generally can draw from them prior to old age, the total amounts (which generally are paid out as a lump sum at retirement) often are whittled down over the years. Inflation also deflates their value considerably (International Labour Office, 1997).

For the most part, even where some type of pension system has been enacted, the coverage is exceedingly narrow. Whereas nations such as Japan, Singapore, and South Korea have relatively high coverage rates (95 percent, 76 percent, and 76 percent, respectively), most other nations in the region have a more limited scope: approximately 24 percent in China, 11 percent in India, 12 percent in Indonesia, 4 percent in Pakistan, 19 percent in the Philippines, and 50 percent in Malaysia (Asher, 1998; ESCAP, 1999; Heller, 1999). These retirement schemes generally include only organized sectors of the labor force; few plans include agricultural or other informal workers. Yet in most developing Asian countries, a large percentage of the population—in many places, the majority—still labors outside the formal labor market (Lee and Mason, 2000; Phillips, 2000). Apart from Japan, Singapore, South Korea, Hong Kong, and Taiwan, significant numbers of people also still live in agricultural areas, working on farms or in small, family-owned enterprises (Mehta, 1997). In addition, many Asian nations, including Taiwan, Indonesia, and Thailand, have established special retirement systems exclusively for their government workers, police, and military personnel, many of whom constitute a "pension elite" within these countries as they have significantly more assets and income. However, because of the economic crisis of the late 1990s, even these schemes are beginning to be reevaluated. Thailand, for instance, recently has restructured its plan for its government employees, implementing a two-tiered system and reducing benefits for new participants (Asher, 1998).

Clearly, a combination of factors—restricted, generally wage-related, pensions; inadequate provident plans; limited national funding; and relatively recent, immature pension systems—has left most retirees in Asia without economic resources to maintain their independence. Despite declining fertility rates, urbanization, and the development of nuclear families, adult children and other family members continue to bear most, often all, of the financial burden of sustaining their aged mothers and fathers. Notwithstanding Taiwan's labor insurance scheme, which pays out lump-sum payments at age 60, more than 50 percent of older people in the nation count on their adult children for their economic sustenance (Bartlett and Wu, 2000).

Indonesia, a predominantly rural country, has relatively few workers participating in any of its pension plans. Its defined-contribution provident fund covers about 35 percent of the formal sector but only 11 percent of the total labor force. Moreover, according to Hugo (2000), it is "poorly managed and provides very low returns to its members" (p. 304). The nation's three other existing schemes—the civil-service pension program, special military and police scheme, and the employer-sponsored pension plan (mostly sponsored by state enterprises)—include but a fraction of workers (Asher, 1998; ESCAP, 1999). Consequently, pensions serve as the main source of income for only 13 percent of males and 4 percent of females, most of whom live in urban areas. Not surprisingly, then, 20 percent of older men and nearly 50 percent of older women have to rely on their children for most of their economic support and 50 percent and 70 percent, respectively, for at least some income (Hugo, 2000).

Even in nations with more substantial provident-fund coverage, such as Malaysia, which offers the Employees Provident Fund, and especially Singapore, which offers the Central Provident Fund, there are decided class divisions; average total fund amounts per worker are low in both locales, with a small percentage of high-wage earners retaining disproportionate shares of the accumulated assets. Notably, in Singapore, ". . . seven in ten older people rely on family members, particularly children, to support them in old age, while only 1 percent use the Central Provident Fund as their main source of retirement income" (Asher, 1998, p. 14). In Malaysia, since few elders obtain significant retirement income and many fall into poverty whether or not they had been covered under the provident fund, the majority of older people require full or partial support from their children.

The Philippines actually has one of the oldest retirement systems in Asia; private-sector workers are covered under a compulsory wage-based, defined-benefit Social Security System and government employees through the Government Service Insurance System, both of which have been in existence for decades. Yet, only about one fifth of the country's labor force, most of whom live in urban areas, are receiving any retirement income. The explanation, at least in part, is that the Philippines is primarily agricultural and most of its aged population live in rural areas, laboring as farmers or are otherwise self-employed in small-scale, marginal economic activities (Somera, 1995). Despite the existence of the Social Security System and the Government Service Insurance System, it is estimated that more than half of older Filipinos rely on adult children for economic support (Natividad, 2000). Moreover, the Social Security System faces serious administrative and fiscal problems (Asher, 1998).

Furthermore, as developing nations in the Asian region are transitioning into large-scale market economies, their policy initiatives are increasingly relying on the private sector, leading to serious problems of inadequate regulations, market failures, and growing income inequalities (Heller, 1999). In some places, notably China, intricate and generous community and enterprise-based welfare provisions were established in earlier decades for all sectors of society. In urban areas, the majority of workers were covered by the state sector through work unit–based social security for retirement income, medical services, and other social supports. Since the introduction of market-oriented reforms and the reduction in state-owned production over the last two decades, fewer employees are covered by the public sector or are receiving its social benefits than was previously the case. Currently, only about one fourth of retired older people, predominantly urban men, are receiving pensions. At the same time, some provinces and cities are experimenting with new ways to provide retirement income, placing a greater emphasis on individual responsibility through the establishment of individual savings accounts (Lee and Mason, 2000; Phillips, 2000). As with other Asian nations, the reality is that nearly 60 percent of all older people must depend primarily on their families for financial support (Peng and Zhi-Gang, 2000). In the near future, many older Chinese may have to fend for themselves, especially since more will have only one—or no—child upon whom they can rely.

Though the more economically advanced Asian nations, notably Japan and South Korea, have developed Western-style defined-benefit, pay-as-you-go public programs similar to those in the United States and Western Europe, these programs are of more recent origin, subject to the effects of rapid population aging. Consequently, there is a shorter period for them to mature, and hence higher levels of under funding will characterize even the relatively well-designed programs. These types of retirement schemes generally require many years to fully develop (Asher, 1998; Mehta, 1997). Accordingly, Japan and South Korea are now confronting many of the same issues that have plagued other economically advanced nations, but such problems have occurred with greater intensity in the two Asian nations and are unlikely to be easily resolved (Heller, 1999).

Established in 1961, Japan's social security system covers fully 95 percent of the labor force (ESCAP, 1999). However, it faces an imminent fiscal crisis as the number of retirees are rapidly growing relative to the percentage of workers supporting the system. These problems have been compounded by economic setbacks since the summer of 1997 and by ongoing political struggles over the nation's priorities. Moreover, the provision of decent pensions to certain sectors of the population, along with a growth in personal savings, increasingly has encouraged early retirement. The labor-force participation rate of Japanese men ages 55 and older, currently at 41 percent, is projected to decline to 29 percent in 2050 (Lee and Mason, 2000). There also is some indication that the availability of pensions has seriously eroded the expectations of workers who are currently middle aged that their children should, or will, support them in the future (Ogawa and Retherford, 1993).

South Korea also has a compulsory wage-based contributory program: The National Pension Program (NPP), established in 1988, covers about one third of the workforce and lump-sum benefits are available to individuals at age 60 (Kwon, 1998a). However, because workers must have participated in the NPP for at least 20 years to become eligible for benefits, relatively few older people (6 percent) currently are receiving anything from the system. There are additional systems for government workers, military personnel, and teachers. Though a significant number of people are retiring earlier than in the past, many workers are supporting both themselves and their aging parents. Furthermore, several factors—a widespread slowdown in economic growth, shrinking public revenues, and fewer numbers of workers relative to the number of pensioners—already are threatening the viability of the new, relatively immature pension scheme. As suggested earlier and in other chapters in this volume, Asian governments have been more concerned with economic growth than with the social problems such growth engenders for older adults and their families. With greater industrialization, work patterns have been vastly altered, and more older workers have lost their independent sources of income. "Older men in Asia have traditionally worked in agriculture, and many find it increasingly difficult to earn a living as Asian economies shift toward manufacturing and the service industries" (Lee and Mason, 2000, p. 5). Few people among the older population in the region have savings that they can fall back on. Moreover, the current emphasis on developing export-related economies as well as structural adjustment policies have led to lower wages for some sectors of society, making it even more difficult for individuals in these sectors to put money away. Thus, without pension income, a large percentage of the aged are or will become destitute. Even in places that recently have introduced some type of retirement system, today's elderly comprise a transitional generation who are not eligible for a stipend.

Alternative Governmental Responses

At the same time, the age of mandatory retirement in the existing or newly established pension programs for industrial and public-sector workers is generally much lower than that imposed by the developed nations in the West: usually between ages 55 and 60 for men and between 50 and 55 for women. In Asian countries undergoing high unemployment, these measures are viewed as protections for younger workers (ESCAP, 1999). However, such policies also have increasingly added to the economic dependency among middle-aged and older people across the region. Evidently, the enduring notions of family support are not only rendered out of filial obligation, but often out of financial necessity.

Indeed, abject poverty is prevalent among older Asians nearly everywhere, especially in the countryside (Mehta, 1997). Moreover, similar to more economically advanced regions of the world, Asia has experienced a feminization of poverty. Older women are particularly reliant on their children since they are more likely to be widowed and have no other sources of income. Not only do women generally lack a pension, but fewer older women than men participate in the formal labor force, particularly at more advanced ages. Paradoxically, in many Asian nations women face a lower mandatory retirement age than men, even though they tend to live longer.

Although more rural elders live in multigenerational households than their urban counterparts, older women are increasingly forced to live by themselves and depend on the remittances of city-dwelling adult children (Phillips, 2000). Given the low incomes among most young workers and their uncertain economic prospects and conditions, this obviously can place a hardship on adult children who may be supporting two households. In Hong Kong, since city dwellings are relatively small, adult children must either leave their elderly mothers and fathers behind or finance separate households. These pressures, however, have been partially alleviated through extensive subsidized public housing programs, which currently accommodate a significant percentage of elders (Chow, 2000).

Filial obligation and individualism in Asia foster a strong sense of self-reliance that renders any government help an option of last resort: Welfare programs are restricted to impoverished elders who have no available family to assist them. Thus, low-income and poverty-stricken families, forced to support their elders, receive no help from the government. In South Korea, as noted elsewhere in this volume, the majority of older people have incomes below the poverty level. Yet a recently enacted public assistance law guarantees a minimum subsistence-level income, along with access to medical and housing aid, only to individuals who have no kin (Choi, 2000). There is also an old-age allowance, the Elder-Respect Pension, for older people ages 65 and older who have no other sources of income. Since the pension amounts are minuscule, even elders who are eligible for this pension continue to be financially dependent on their children.

Hong Kong has made selected public assistance for older people available since 1971, and India has provided modest support since 1995, but in these countries, too, assistance is restricted to elders who are both destitute and abandoned. In both nations, older people are the poorest sector of society; regardless of their country's welfare programs, most are dependent entirely on their family for economic support. Until 2000, Hong Kong lacked any type of retirement system. Young workers now must save for their own old age while also assisting their parents; the recently enacted Mandatory Provident Fund (MPF) will not provide retirement income for at least another 20 years. Given that there are not any significant pension programs in India, well over half of older adults are totally reliant on their kin, a significant percentage of whom are indigent themselves: One third of the overall population lives in grinding poverty.

Despite demographic aging, many Asian nations worry that implementation or expansion of government-supported pension systems would be too costly, depleting resources from other priorities, especially investments necessary to compete in the world market. Moreover, as workers increasingly are being required to save for their own retirement and as traditional values of filial responsibility are flagging, a major response to the income needs of the elderly has been to strengthen legally mandated filial responsibilities. In countries such as China, South Korea, Thailand, India, and the Philippines, families already have a legal mandate to support their parents (Formanek and Linhart, 1997; Phillips, 2000). In the latter nation this duty has been reinforced in the government's recently declared political commitments to older people in need, which included the insistent statement, "The family has the duty to care for its elderly members although the state may also do so through just programs for social security" (Somera, 1995, p. 32).

In 1996, China enacted the Protection of the Rights and Interests of the Elderly, reiterating the dictate that families must care for their elders (both parents and in-laws), including paying for medical care, housing, income, and other services (Peng and Zhi-Gang, 2000). Singapore, through the 1995 Maintenance of Parents Act, now has authorized parents to claim upkeep from their children through the judicial process (Asher, 1998). Hong Kong, along with a number of other governments in the region, also is instituting educational programs aimed at preserving and transmitting the value of filial responsibility to the young. Concomitantly, some governmental programs are using tax incentives to promote ongoing family support, such as the 1996 tax rebate in Malaysia for children funding the medical care of their older parents (Tan and Ng, 2000).

THE ROLE OF THE STATE: HEALTH-RELATED SERVICES

Similar to pension policies in the region, Asian nations tend to provide only limited publicly-supported medical services. There is an even greater paucity of government programs to assist the frail elderly, whether at home or in nursing homes.

Medical Care

Healthcare is arguably one of the most formative fiscal concerns experienced by nations throughout the world in the 21st century. In Asia, population aging and industrialization are generating increased demand for health services, and reports by international agencies suggest the whole panoply of healthcare is teetering on the brink of collapse. Not only do the aged require greater amounts of medical care than younger people, demographic changes are fostering an epidemiological transition from acute diseases to more costly chronic, degenerative ailments such as cancer, cardiovascular diseases, and dementia. Hence, medical expenditures are likely to increase steadily, and in some places to spiral, as nations in the area confront both growing demographic aging and greater longevity among the aged. Many developing nations in Asia also are dealing with childhood diseases as well as infectious and parasitic illnesses, including polio, measles, malaria, tuberculosis, and HIV/AIDS, which infect large numbers of people in all age groups (Lee and Mason, 2000). Western medical standards and technologies also are increasingly penetrating the region, adding to the demand for more expensive procedures and contributing to the emergent crisis (Heller, 1999).

Unlike nearly all developed nations of the West, except for the United States, comprehensive government-funded medical services are lacking in Asia. Most of the region is heavily reliant on the private sector for the financing and delivery of healthcare. Yet even these services and insurance schemes are not well organized. In many places, they are less capable of meeting the healthcare needs of the population than in more economically advanced nations in other parts of the world (ESCAP, 1989). As with retirement income, the preferred method in many Asian countries is to encourage people to pay for their own healthcare needs; government programs generally include heavy consumer cost-sharing. The poor, especially in Southeast Asia, tend to rely on underfunded public hospitals, health centers, and clinics—and these facilities are vastly inadequate to meet the demand for services

(Mehta, 1997). Concomitantly, the area is witnessing the steady growth of private practitioners and hospitals, affordable only for well-off households.

Rapidly increasing healthcare costs have been compounded by the widespread slowdown in economic growth, rising unemployment and inflation, and shrinking public revenues. Consequently, public officials across Asia are enacting cost-containment measures, restructuring systems by placing greater burdens on individuals and their families and by reducing public medical services despite growing needs. In fact, healthcare has been particularly affected by government cuts and policy restrictions.

Nevertheless, Japan, South Korea, Hong Kong, Singapore, and Taiwan have achieved comprehensive, mandated healthcare coverage. Relying on employment-based systems, these schemes generally are dominated by the private sector in the delivery of services and tend to be primarily fee-for-service systems. They also have become extraordinarily costly, far outstripping revenues, and are verging on insolvency. Consequently, the programs rely on relatively high copayments and expensive premiums that impose the greatest burden on lower-income workers. Moreover, the health needs of the aged are placing growing pressures on both the capacity and the costs of these schemes. Where the elderly utilize the medical systems for social hospitalization (see Rhee, Chapter 12), the fiscal pressures are exacerbated: Because of shortages in long-term care services, older people are increasingly using more costly hospital care, when available, in their stead. In Hong Kong, for example, older adults occupy about half of all hospital beds (Mehta, 1997). In Singapore, although older adults make up 7 percent of the population, they represent 17 percent of all hospitalizations, and their hospital stays average more than 11 days per person as compared to 5 days per person for other age groups (Phua, 2000).

Along with its pension system, Japan instituted a comprehensive healthcare program in 1961 that steadily developed into a high-technology, high-cost medical system; its older population is the heaviest user of the system, accounting for 40 percent of total costs in 2000 (Lai, 2001). As early as the 1980s, Japan began reigning in its social welfare costs both by cutting medical services for the elderly and by instituting copayments. It also unsuccessfully attempted to shift costs back to families by revitalizing notions of filial obligation (Eto, 2001; Ogawa and Retherford, 1993).

In 2000, South Korea, which has had medical insurance programs since 1976, established new policies for a single-payer, compulsory program, National Health Insurance (NHI), which covers nearly the entire population. Unlike Japan, new, high-tech procedures and equipment generally are not included under NHI, though the system does cover traditional healthcare practices as well as dental care and prescription drugs. In addition, because of substantial cost-sharing charges, including a copayment of 20 percent or more for services and high deductibles, patients often have to pay about half of all medical expenses themselves. Taiwan's universal healthcare system is more recent; prior to the enactment of its National

Health Insurance program in 1995, only about 15 percent of the population had any type of medical coverage (Bartlett and Wu, 2000). Though individuals ages 70 and older do not have to pay any premiums, as with the rest of the beneficiaries they are responsible for the varying copayments for services.

In Singapore, the National Health Plan and its Medisave scheme, established in 1983, have attempted to encourage greater individual responsibility by imposing a mandatory medical savings plan on the population, with the government contributing a variable portion of the costs. At the same time, the plan has reinforced filial responsibility by allowing any accumulated assets in the accounts to pay for the medical costs of older parents. By 1995, more than half of all older people in the nation relied on their children's Medisave to finance medical services, and only 20 percent used their own or their spouse's funds. In effect, the current generation of workers bears a significant proportion of both their own and their parents' healthcare needs (Phua, 2000). The country also established an optional contributory MediShield insurance plan that covers catastrophic illness. Overall, cost containment has been one of the most important governmental policy priorities, achieved by such steps as lowering demand for services, reducing subsidies for those who can afford to pay, and implementing cost controls on high-technology medicine (Vasoo, Ngiam, and Cheung, 2000).

Other developing Asian nations have recently, and gradually, introduced policies supporting comprehensive, compulsory healthcare coverage. Indonesia began to do so in 1993 and Thailand in 1989 (Heller, 1999; Phillips, 2000). The national Health Insurance Act, enacted by the Philippine government in 1995, currently only covers inpatient care. It pays a relatively small portion of hospital bills, though elders are entitled to free medical and dental services in some government facilities (Natividad, 2000). Each of these newer insurance systems varies in detail, but all are patterned on the existing Asian approach to funding and delivering healthcare services.

China, on the other hand, has implemented policies that protect only the civil service and large state-owned enterprises under its health insurance system, thus covering about 20 percent of the population. Furthermore, its commune-based healthcare system in agricultural areas has largely broken down; only a small fraction of the rural population has access to any medical services (Heller, 1999). Most of the poorer nations, especially in South Asia, also have not established universal healthcare systems; in these places, medical services are the most backward, and even primary care tends to be unavailable to the vast majority of the population.

Home and Community-Based Long-Term Care

The establishment and development of social and support services are conspicuously lagging across Asia and nonexistent in many places, with the exception of Japan, because policymakers assume that families will fully meet the long-term care needs of their frail elders. As Mehta (1997) observes, in economically advanced nations, rapid industrialization and the social and economic dislocations it has fostered have been ". . . accompanied by a clear trend in population aging, but not by any comparable trend of social welfare expansion for elderly people" (p. 74). In nations with only limited medical care, such as India, supportive services are even scarcer and policymakers are the least attuned to the needs of older people and their families.

The most critical role that adult children are expected to play in their aging parents' lives is not income support or meeting their medical needs but caring for them if they become frail or chronically ill. At the same time, parents and adult children alike regard any paid hands-on assistance as inferior to the care that they could provide themselves (Mehta, 1997). In many Asian countries, it is assumed that sons (usually the eldest one) should support their parents financially while their wives will provide the actual caregiving labor. Such concepts are still dominant across the region, especially in rural areas, though middle-class daughters—particularly unmarried ones—are helping their own parents more than in the past. Though family members, mainly wives and adult daughters, are responsible for the vast majority of long-term care in the United States, the antipathy of the population toward government-supported assistance tends to be far lower than in Asia. Furthermore, in developed European nations, hands-on help from the public sector generally is eagerly sought, allowing families to focus on other aspects of elder care.

For the most part, supportive community services in Asia tend to be in scarce supply, even in nations where such services are attainable, and are offered primarily to older people with significant needs but no living relatives to provide for them (Mehta, 1997). The quality of formal services is in question across the region as well, further discouraging their use. In the more economically advanced Asian nations, the rich can take advantage of private facilities and services, often hiring domestic servants from other nations; middle- and working-class families generally cannot afford paid help. Consequently, the vast majority of adult children, especially women, are increasingly burdened as market-driven changes and economic development foster growing numbers of physically or mentally impaired aged in need of assistance, fewer family members available to provide it, and no government services to aid them.

In China, private entrepreneurship has come to dominate many sectors of the service trades (Formanek and Linhart, 1997). However, neither for-profit firms nor the national government offers supportive community services such as home help and daycare centers. Frail or childless older people, who are guaranteed food, clothing, medical services, housing, and burial expenses by the state or collective policies, tend to be institutionalized in nursing homes scattered around the country (Peng and Zhi-Gang, 2000). Though local governments are attempting to develop community-based services for the elderly, many of them are restructuring their programs to include market and commercial considerations, including the imposition of fees (Asher, 1998). Neighborhoods, too, are playing a larger role in providing social welfare, but since they target assistance to those people without any relatives, the vast majority of older people continue to rely solely on their families for care (Peng and Zhi-Gang, 2000).

Though Filipino elderly are included under the National Health Insurance as dependents of their adult children, the program doesn't cover any long-term care, not even in-home nursing or rehabilitation services. Publicly supported elder care, mostly provided in nursing homes, is available only for the "abandoned, destitute, and disadvantaged" (Natividad, 2000, p. 275). And even these facilities are severely limited; most are established and operated by religious and charitable organizations rather than by the national government (Somera, 1995). Similarly, Indonesia does not offer long-term care as part of its national healthcare system. The few services that are available in the nation also are run by private charities and other NGOs; again, they focus almost exclusively on the abandoned poor.

Asian nations with relatively well-developed healthcare schemes also fail to provide supportive elder-care services. South Korea's system excludes visiting nurses, home help, and other community assistance such as daycare (Choi, 2000). Here, too, there are very few publicly supported long-term care services at all, including institutional facilities; the small number of program recipients are destitute older people who have no kin. Likewise, with the exception of home nursing, there are not many subsidized formal services in Hong Kong, where the emphasis has remained almost entirely on retaining frail elders in the community by promoting family care (Vasoo, Ngiam, and Cheung, 2000). In fact, public officials have expressed ongoing resistance to any policies that would undermine or replace filial responsibilities: "The role that the government would play is still to complement, or at most supplement, . . . the caring functions traditionally performed by the family or the 'community'" (Chow, 2000). The government also encourages adult children to live with their older parents through such public policies as giving preference in public housing to young families who reside with or attend to their frail parents.

In nations where social service systems for the elderly are in the formative stages, the fiscal crisis of the late 1990s seriously constrained development of public policies (Phillips, 2000). For example, Taiwan's Welfare Law for the Aged, revised in 1997, made frail older adults (again, primarily those without family support) eligible for a wide range of services and benefits, including a variety of institutional, community and home-based services (Bartlett and Wu, 2000). Even with the resumption of economic growth, however, Taiwan's fiscal problems have engendered ongoing retrenchment in public spending on social provisions overall; long-term care tends to be of low priority. Thus, relatively few such services have been established to date.

One recent policy shift, as in the United States, is to induce young people to save for their own potential disability needs as they age. Singapore recently enacted an ElderShield scheme providing for long-term care insurance, similar to its method of funding medical services. Currently, there are very limited government services provided, though a government-funded Medifund policy has been established for indigent older people without any family.

As suggested earlier, Japan is an exception among Asian nations. However, its social services remained relatively underdeveloped until recently, notwithstanding the comprehensive medical and pension schemes the country established in 1961. Similar to programs in other countries across the region, Japan's publicly supported assistance for the elderly was once means tested, focusing exclusively on elders with disabilities who had no relatives to care for them. Furthermore, in the 1980s, Japan revised a number of policies and began reining in social welfare costs both by cutting medical services for older people and by instituting copayments. It also attempted to shift costs back to families by revitalizing notions of filial obligation (Eto, 2001; Ogawa and Retherford, 1993). Public officials, however, were not very successful: According to Eto (2001), attitudes toward formal services in the country were changing, especially among middle-class households where two earners were necessary to maintain their standard of living. Japan rapidly emerged as one of the oldest nations in the world. More and more working females struggled to meet their elder-care burdens, and by the early 1990s a number of women's groups began publicizing their plight and actively demanding government assistance. Political leaders also were swayed by the growing medical costs resulting from large numbers of older people using costly and lengthy hospitalization stays to meet their long-term care needs (Maeda and Ishikawa, 2000).

As a result, in 1994 the government substantially increased long-term care services through the New Gold Plan, which covers home help, visiting nurse services, daycare centers, respite services, and residential facilities. The main goal of the plan is to allow elders to continue living in the community by supplementing rather than replacing family care. Political leaders also established a compulsory insurance system under the 1997 Long-Term Care Insurance (LTCI) law that covers institutional and community-based services. It is funded both through private premiums and government outlays and includes for-profit, nonprofit, and public-sector providers (Eto, 2001). Most importantly, older adults in Japan will be entitled to services regardless of whether they have children to care for them. Though Japan is one of the only Asian nations to introduce a relatively comprehensive long-term care program, both the supply and quality of services continue to be a problem; there are substantial shortages in community-care services and institutional facilities relative to demand (Maeda and Ishikawa, 2000).

Institutional Long-Term Care

Few elders in Asia live in nursing homes: Only about 1 to 2 percent of the older population on average (ESCAP, 1999). The percentages range from

0.3 percent in South Korea and Malaysia, 0.6 percent in China, and 1.6 percent in Japan and Singapore to 3 percent in Taiwan and a high of 7 to 8 percent in Hong Kong (Bartlett and Wu, 2000; Leung, 2000; Mehta, 1997; Ogawa and Retherford, 1993). However, with the rapid aging of the population occurring across the region and the growth in the numbers of old old, demand for residential care has been increasing everywhere.

Overall, government-run nursing homes are rare and are underwritten by policies designed mainly for the destitute and abandoned. Where private-pay facilities are available, such as in Japan, Hong Kong, Singapore, Taiwan, and South Korea, they are too expensive for the vast majority of families (Phillips, 2000). In China, private-pay homes are both costly and of low quality, thus restricting demand considerably. In comparison, Hong Kong provides government-funded homes of relatively decent quality. Consequently, they are in short supply, and demand continues to grow: "Most [elders] have to wait between three and five years for a place and, indeed, a high proportion of people on the waiting list never gain entry to these institutions as they have died by the time a vacancy occurs for them" (Leung, 2000, p. 85). As a result, elders in Hong Kong who can afford to pay (or whose families can) are forced into high-priced, lower-quality places that are being established to meet the shortfall (Chow, 2000).

SOME POLITICAL CONSIDERATIONS

Politics, of course, plays a considerable role in the provision of publicly-supported benefits. In Western Europe, the existence of strong social democratic parties, along with the influence of interest groups—especially organized labor—has been instrumental in fostering the emergence and growth of universal health-care systems, relatively comprehensive retirement systems, and an array of social services, particularly for the elderly. In addition, older people and old-age advocacy groups, representing a significant percentage of the electorate, are becoming increasingly vocal throughout Western Europe (Phillips, 2000). In the United States, the aged have emerged as a strong political force, successfully defending both the Social Security System and Medicare despite ongoing retrenchment in social programs overall. On the other hand, since the 1980s, private pension systems have been eroding commensurate with the steady decline in the power of organized labor.

Until recently, the vast majority of Asian nations were characterized by authoritarian rule or semi-despotic paternalism that prevented or limited the political participation of the populace, opposition parties, and interest groups. As a result, they have conspicuously lacked powerful, unified labor movements and grassroots pressure groups. At the same time, European-style social democratic parties are altogether absent. For the most part, "the truncated nature of the political spectrum, limitations on interest groups, and outright repression meant that any nascent political demand for state-run social safety nets was attenuated" (Haggard, 2000, p. 186).

For instance, in 1967 and 1968, Singapore's Prime Minister Lee Kuan Yew and his People's Action Party (PAP) introduced the Industrial Relations Act and the Employment Act, respectively, which among other impacts severely curtailed trade union power (Kwon, 1998b). Trade unions in Malaysia, a semi-democratic nation, have been relatively weak political actors because of low levels of unionization, legal restrictions, and both formal and informal government controls over their organization and activities. The Malaysian government has a particularly strong resistance to any type of transfer social insurance program, including those for workers, the aged, and the poor (Haggard, 2000).

The level and scope of social welfare programs also is limited in Hong Kong and Taiwan. In the former nation, trade unions, along with interest groups overall, have not been actively engaged in politics, and political parties are of recent origin (Kwon, 1998b). Similarly, Taiwan has had a "dominant party political system with weak social and labour movements" (Tyabji, 1993, p. 61). A limited number of welfare services were instituted only after social unrest: ". . . some of the laws were enacted under political pressure rather than to meet perceived social welfare needs" (p. 61). In Thailand, organized labor has consisted primarily of the "relatively privileged segments of the working class, such as workers in the state-owned enterprise sector" (Haggard, 2000, p. 208).

A number of Asian governments have manipulated social policy over the years to enhance their legitimacy. Authoritarian capitalist regimes maintained control of the nation partly through their paternalistic pact with the middle class. In Singapore, for example, the government provided social benefits in exchange for acquiescence to the political status quo. Specifically, after the emergence of social unrest in 1966 and 1967, Lee introduced social welfare measures (Tyabji, 1993). He used the Central Provident Fund, established in 1950 when Singapore was still a British colony, to promote support for his regime: "The Central Provident Fund and its components, such as housing and medical schemes, have played an important role in the political success of the PAP government" (Kwon, 1998b, p. 38). Similarly, the limited welfare system in Taiwan was first introduced by the government in the 1940s and 1950s to enhance its political legitimacy (Kwon, 1998b).

The original South Korean welfare system was largely brought into effect by the military government when it seized power in 1961 "to compensate for its lack of political legitimacy (Kwon, 1998b, p. 54). The political strategy of legitimization occurred again after the 1980 military coup d'etat with the *promise* of more government benefits (Kwon, 1998b). Even Japan, which has a relatively liberal system longer than any other East Asian country, has developed a de facto one-party system vis-à-vis its paternalistic appeals to the middle class (Haggard, 2000). In addition, its early social welfare policies, initiated by Prime Minister Kakuei Tanaka in 1973, was primarily a response to citizens' movements and the emergence at the time of leftist local governments. His welfare initiatives can, in effect, be viewed as "a pre-emptive strike" (Kwon, 1998b, p. 63).

Beginning in the 1980s, nations such as South Korea, Taiwan, Thailand, and the Philippines made the transition to democratic forms of government, followed by Indonesia and others. Because of electoral competition, older parties revitalized themselves and new competing unions, federations, interest groups, and social movements emerged with varying degrees of vitality (Haggard, 2000). In Korea, the actual expansion of National Health Insurance, and the introduction of the National Pension Programme, did not emerge as salient political concerns until after President Doo Hwan Chun agreed to hold popular elections for president in 1987 and general elections the following year: Both the governing and opposition parties included these programs in their platforms (Kwon, 1998b). Additionally, since 1987, interest group activity has increased, including the rise of militant labor groups (Gomez, 2000). South Korea's labor movement is one of the strongest in the area and has had some input into policymaking since the Kim Dae Jung government. Consequently, there has been a relatively larger broadening of the social agenda than in some other countries in the region (Haggard, 2000).

Political reforms in Taiwan since the late 1980s, including the lifting of martial law in 1987, also has transformed social policy. The nation's political opposition movements, which "developed into a full-fledged political party" (the Democratic Progressive Party—DPP), fought elections on a number of issues, including the implementation of the National Health Insurance (NHI) scheme. In response to the political and social pressures, the governing party (the Kuomintang—KMT) decided to introduce the healthcare measure earlier than it previously had intended "to help it to hold on to power" (Kwon, 1998b, p. 49). Political parties also have competed for popular support at the national and local levels through other social issues such as old-age allowances.

Regardless of political form, since Asian nations have placed primary emphasis on capital accumulation and economic development, especially export-led growth, welfare measures (except those that aid in this goal) have been of lesser concern (Tyabji, 1993). Nearly all of the countries tend to have close business-government relations, viewing this as necessary for achieving high levels of overall growth (Haggard, 2000). Private economic actors, even in the newly democratic countries, are the most politically powerful entities; they generally go "unchecked by countervailing interests" (Haggard, 2000, p. 223). Indeed, Rudolph (2000) calls it a collusion between business conglomerates (including banks) and politicians. Certainly, the privileged position of big-business leaders has played and continues to play a crucial role in eschewing social insurance schemes.

As suggested earlier, the conservative nature of the democratic transitions re-enforce adherence to cultural mandates, especially the strong work ethic, self-reliance, and filial responsibility. At the same time, both governments and powerful business leaders harbor a deep-seated political resistance to Western models of the welfare state that they argue do not fit with Asian values. However, their overriding premise is that they are working in an increasingly competitive global environment and they should "not be burdened with additional costs" (Haggard, 2000, p. 184). Asian political and economic leaders assert that the "Asian Model" of economic growth, with its relatively low labor and social costs, works best. Both the "Asian values" doctrine and increasing material benefits through rapid economic growth have been used to justify centralized state authority, champion business interests, and appeal to the middle class (Johannen, Gomez, and Rudolph, 2000).

Thus, provident funds, which were initially introduced by Britain into many of its colonies, continue to be the most popular form of welfare program among elites in the region. These schemes are mostly compulsory savings plans that also provide an ongoing flow of revenue to the governments (Tyabji, 1993). Singapore as well as other Asian nations rely heavily on the accumulated assets in their pension systems for capital. In 1994, the Central Provident Fund represented 73 percent of Singapore's GDP (Kwon, 1998b). Moreover, from the beginning, one major goal of South Korea's pension measures has been to mobilize capital for public investments (Kwon, 1998a). In Malaysia, any growth in social security programs tends to be tied to its contribution to economic development rather than to what is viewed as "nonproductive" welfare protections (Tyabji, 1993).

The financial crisis of 1997, however, showed the urban and middle classes, which had grown steadily during the period of high growth, that they were quite vulnerable to the vicissitudes of the economy. As Haggard (2000, p. 230) puts it, "the achievements of the nascent working and middle classes were more fragile than thought. With the aging of the population, urbanization, more open economies, and the recurring risk of financial shocks, the holes in the safety net became more apparent, leading to new insecurities." Many households, confronted with the possibility of slow growth, inflation, unemployment, and the like, could no longer count on accumulating their own assets for healthcare, retirement, and other current and future needs.

As a result, the Asian financial crisis has fostered new, diverse demands for social and political reforms from the general population, including the establishment and expansion of social safety nets. In particular, national debate on such topics as social insurance and retirement systems is increasing where progressive political pressures, especially labor, have managed to gain a voice in policy-making. As Gomez points out (2000, p. 248): "Many civil society groups have taken on a more political role, given the space created for criticism by the economic crisis."

Notwithstanding, for the most part, trade unions are not well-represented in government, countervailing interest groups remain relatively ineffectual, and, with the partial exception of South Korea, they do not have strong parties representing their interests (Haggard, 2000). As Rudolph (2000, p. 52) puts it, "For most countries in the region, political parties and democratic institutions allowing for opposition politics are weak, unstructured, suppressed and marginalized." In particular, "labor's overall influence has been small because of the newness of democratic rule, in part because of structural factors such as the size of the small-firm and informal sectors and the emphasis on export-oriented manufacturing" (Haggard, 2000, p. 234). It is uncertain whether Asian leaders now and in the future will begin to address more fully the social needs of their people, including the aged, or just attempt to co-opt the new and growing political forces.

CONCLUSION

Most Asian nations are facing rapid population aging, along with a decline in mortality at older ages. Consequently, greater numbers of elders in the region are living longer. Concomitantly, the region is experiencing fast-paced economic development, industrialization, forced retirement at early ages, urbanization, and the steady influx of women into the labor force, all of which have had adverse effects on older people and their families. Public policies are being challenged to keep up with the pace of change and to ensure the quality of life for older citizens. Moreover, older adults across Asia increasingly are left without the means to support themselves, and greater numbers of adult children must care for their parents with fewer siblings to share the burden.

Few Asian countries have comprehensive or effective pension policies to take up the slack. Where such systems exist, they tend to be limited in scope and poorly funded, rely on the worker's own savings, and provide only meager retirement benefits relative to need. Although Japan and South Korea have established Western-style pension programs, their relatively recent systems, burdened with providing for a high and growing percentage of retirees, are encountering even greater financial problems than the economically advanced nations with more mature pension systems.

Not surprisingly, older adults tend to be the poorest sector of society across Asia, and abject poverty is common, especially in rural areas. Few countries offer even limited social welfare supports, whether financial assistance, in-home care, community services, or institutional facilities, and those programs that exist tend to be available only to the destitute and abandoned. In certain areas, the private sector offers some services, but at exorbitant charges and of questionable quality. Where medical and social services must be purchased, elderly women are at a particular disadvantage since they generally have very low— or no—income.

Throughout the region the primary support system for the elderly has been and continues to be their adult children. In deference to a tradition of filial piety, children are expected to subsidize their parents' everyday needs, shelter them (preferably in multigenerational households), pay for their medical services, and, particularly for daughters and daughters-in-law, provide full-time, hands-on care when their elderly parents become ill or chronically disabled. Despite their best efforts, it is becoming increasingly difficult for adult children to comply with these mandates, especially in the absence of any real government support.

Help for overburdened families does not seem imminent. Since the end of the 1990s, the region has experienced a slowdown in economic growth, rising unemployment and inflation, and mounting medical costs for both acute and chronic diseases, fostering a steady retrenchment in social spending, especially for healthcare. Some nations that have relied on loans from the International Monetary Fund—Malaysia, India, and the Philippines among others—are subject to structural adjustment policies that also have led to cuts in government benefits. Certainly, the prospects for the establishment and expansion of formal long-term care programs in the foreseeable future are not promising. Instead, most Asian nations are strengthening filial obligations and shifting greater pension and medical expenses to workers while disregarding the increasingly overwhelming financial, physical, psychological, and emotional costs these policies entail.

REFERENCES

Asher, M. (1998). The future of retirement protection in Southeast Asia. *International Social Security Review, 51*(1), 3–30.

Bartlett, H. P., and Wu, S.-C. (2000). Ageing and aged care in Taiwan. In D. R. Phillips (Ed.), *Ageing in the Asia-Pacific region: Issues, policies, and future trends* (pp. 210–222). New York: Routledge.

Chang, G. (2000). *Disposable domestics: Migrant women workers in the global economy.* Cambridge, Massachusetts: South End Press.

Choi, S.-J. 2000. Ageing in Korea: Issues and problems. In D. R. Phillips (Ed.), *Ageing in the Asia-Pacific region: Issues, policies and future trends* (pp. 223–242). New York: Routledge.

Chow, N. W. S. (2000). Ageing in Hong Kong. In D. R. Phillips (Ed.), *Ageing in the Asia--Pacific region: Issues, policies, and future trends* (pp. 158–173). New York: Routledge.

Economic and Social Commission for Asia and the Pacific [ESCAP]. (1989). *Emerging issues of population aging in Asia and the Pacific* (Asian Population Studies Series No. 99). New York: United Nations.

ESCAP. (1999). *Promoting a society for all aged in Asia and the Pacific: Information materials for International Year of Older Persons* (U.N. Publication ST/ESCAP/1982). New York: United Nations.

Eto, M. (2001, November). *Confusion in the introduction of Japan's long-term care insurance system: Who is responsible for care of the disabled elderly.* Paper presented at the Northeastern Political Science Association meeting, Philadelphia.

Formanek, S., and Linhart, S. (1997). *Aging Asian concepts and experiences past and present.* Vienna: Der Österreichischen Akademie Der Wissenschaften.

Gomez, J. (2000). A political evaluation of the Asian crisis: Prospects for democracy. In U. Johannen, J. Rudolph, and J. Gomez (Eds.), *The political dimensions of the Asian Crisis* (pp. 189–250). Singapore: Select Books.

Haggard, S. (2000). *The political economy of the Asian financial crisis.* Washington, D.C.: Institute for International Economics.

Heller, P. S. (1999). Aging in Asia: Challenges for fiscal policy. *Journal of Asian Economics, 10,* 37–63.

Hugo, G. (2000). Lansia: Elderly people in Indonesia at the turn of the century. In D. R. Phillips (Ed.), *Ageing in the Asia-Pacific region: Issues, policies, and future trends* (pp. 299–321). New York: Routledge.

International Labour Office. (1997). *Ageing in Asia: The growing need for social protection.* Geneva, Switzerland: Author.

Johannen, U., Gomez, J., and Rudolph, J. (2000). Introduction. In U. Johannen, J. Rudolph, and J. Gomez (Eds.), *The political dimensions of the Asian Crisis* (pp. 1–10). Singapore: Select Books.

Kinsella, K. (2000). Demographic dimensions of ageing in East and Southeast Asia. In D. R. Phillips (Ed.), *Ageing in the Asia-Pacific region: Issues, policies, and future trends* (pp. 35–50). New York: Routledge.

Kwon, H.-j. (1998a). The South Korean National Pension Programme: Fulfilling its promise? In R. Goodman, G. White, and H.-j. Kwon (Eds.), *The East Asian welfare model: Welfare orientalism and the state* (pp. 106–118). New York: Routledge.

Kwon, H.-j. (1998b). Democracy and the politics of social welfare: A comparative analysis of welfare systems in East Asia. In R. Goodman, G. White, and H.-j. Kwon (Eds.), *The East Asian welfare model: Welfare orientalism and the state* (pp. 27–74). New York: Routledge.

Lai, O.-K. (2001). Long-term care policy reform in Japan. In I. Chi, K. Mehta, and A. Howe (Eds.), *Long-term care in the 21st century: Perspective from around the Asia-Pacific rim* (pp. 5–20). New York: Haworth Press.

Lee, S.-H., and Mason, A. (2000). Population aging raises questions for policymakers. *Asia-Pacific Population and Policy, 53,* 1–3.

Leung, E. M. F. (2000). Changing needs and changing service delivery for long-term care in Hong Kong. In D. R. Phillips (Ed.), *Ageing in the Asia-Pacific region: Issues, policies, and future trends* (pp. 155–168). New York: Routledge.

Maeda, D., and Ishikawa, H. (2000). Ageing in Japan: Retirement, daily lives, pensions, and social security. In D. R. Phillips (Ed.), *Ageing in the Asia-Pacific region: Issues, policies, and future trends* (pp. 113–132). New York: Routledge.

Mehta, K. (Ed.). (1997). *Untapped resources: Women in ageing societies across Asia.* Singapore: Times Academic Press.

Natividad, J. N. (2000). Ageing in the Philippines: An overview. In D. R. Phillips (Ed.), *Ageing in the Asia-Pacific region: Issues, policies, and future trends* (pp. 267–283). New York: Routledge.

Ogawa, N., and Retherford, R. D. (1993). Care of the elderly in Japan: Changing norms and expectations. *Journal of Marriage and the Family, 55*(3), 585–597.

Parrenas, R. S. (2001). *Servants of globalization: Women, migration, and domestic work.* Stanford, California: Stanford University Press.

Peng, D., and Zhi-Gang, G. (2000). Population ageing in China. In D. R. Phillips (Ed.), *Ageing in the Asia-Pacific region: Issues, policies, and future trends* (pp. 194–209). New York: Routledge.

Phillips, D. R. (2000). *Ageing in the Asia-Pacific region: Issues, policies, and contexts.* In D. R. Phillips (Ed.), *Ageing in the Asia-Pacific region: Issues, policies, and future trends* (pp. 1–34). New York: Routledge.

Phua, K. H. (2000). Financing health and long-term care for ageing populations in the Asia-Pacific region. In D. R. Phillips (Ed.), *Ageing in the Asia-Pacific region: Issues, policies, and future trends* (pp. 93–112). New York: Routledge.

Rudolph, J. (2000). The political causes of the Asian Crisis. In U. Johannen, J. Rudolph, and J. Gomez (Eds.), *The political dimensions of the Asian Crisis* (pp. 13–93). Singapore: Select Books.

Somera, R. D. (1995). *Invisible kin: Filipino aging in a bureaucratic context.* New Delhi, India: Reliance Publishing House.

Tan, P. C., and Ng, S. T. (2000). Ageing in Malaysia: Issues and problems. In D. R. Phillips (Ed.), *Ageing in the Asia-Pacific region: Issues, policies, and future trends* (pp. 284–298). New York: Routledge.

Tyabji, A. (1993, May). Social security in the Asian-Pacific region. *Asian-Pacific Literature, 2*(1), 53–72.

Vasoo, S., Ngiam, T.-L., and Cheung, O. (2000). Singapore's ageing population: Social challenges and responses. In D. R. Phillips (Ed.), *Ageing in the Asia-Pacific region: Issues, policies, and future trends* (pp. 174–193). New York: Routledge.

CHAPTER FOUR

Culture as the Context of Aging

John van Willigen and Denise C. Lewis

The context of human aging is culture. Culture is the web of meaning, values, and other structures that serves as a basis for the decisions that guide an individual's behavior. As such, culture can be thought of as structuring the experience of aging and, indeed, the entire life course. In order for gerontological researchers, service providers, and policymakers to understand the circumstances of the older people for whom they work, they must first understand the content of the cultures of the people with whom they deal.

The influence of culture is pervasive. Culture constitutes the values and roles that define the interrelationships between people of different ages in each family and in other kinds of social organizations where physical and emotional care for older people is provided. In many Asian settings, these core values and roles are associated with the multigenerational family structure reported to be important to the welfare of older people. Noteworthy examples of this are the Confucian ideal of filial piety (Ogawa and Retherford, 1993) and traditions underlying the South Asian joint family (van Willigen and Chadha, 1999).

The cultural dimension of aging has many aspects besides the concepts and values that support the family life of older people. Aging processes are expressed through all the cultural institutions within a person's community. Concomitantly, all human behavior is expressed through cultural media. It is impossible to definitively separate cultural dimensions from social, economic, or political dimensions. Perhaps most relevant relationships between such dimensions with regard to aging are those that often exist between government policies relating to older people and the cultural context within which these policies were created. Policy can resonate with the cultural context. Conversely, in some cases national policy may lag behind or not reflect the existing cultural diversity of the nation.

In this chapter the authors will explore a number of aspects of aging that are influenced by culture, using examples from the literature on aging in Asia. The chapter has two major foci: the concept of culture itself and salient aspects of

Asian cultures as the context of aging. Such salient aspects of culture include (a) cultural models of the life course and nature of old age; (b) conceptions of old people in the family; (c) caregiving roles within the family; and (d) cultural knowledge about health, "successful aging," and the aging body.

METHODS OF CULTURAL ANALYSIS

Research that attempts to understand culture is most often done using ethnographic research methods (Bernard, 1994). This research tradition makes use of naturalistic observation and interviewing. The research process is calculated to preserve the integrity of the person's categories of meaning as used in his or her specific community, not to capture research subjects' responses to discipline-defined measures. Therefore, ethnographic researchers pay great attention to language, engaging words and the nuances of their meanings in the social context.

Ethnographic research practice is very diverse; however, all the individual strains of practice share certain tendencies. These include the emphatically participatory manner of research, relying as it does on participant observation in which the researcher lives in the community being researched and develops multi-stranded relationships with what ethnographers call "key informants." The capturing of social experience is an important aspect of the process. In addition to stressing participation, the ethnographic approach is usually based on the creation of complex narrative or graphic depictions of the situation being studied in the form of field notes, maps, photos, videos, and other representations. Although ethnographers may use surveys based on random samples as well as standardized or close-ended interview questions, neither is stressed nor required. Furthermore, when a survey is implemented its results are deeply contextualized.

Survey research, in which the same questions are asked of each research subject in order to test theoretical constructs, contrasts with ethnography, which relies on a diverse range of data sources to construct a narrative that presents the rich complexity of the cultural context. This product sometimes includes "thick description," an idea introduced to anthropology by Clifford Geertz in 1973. Thick description conveys the multiple layers of meaning in lived cultural experience. The research goals of these two strategies are quite different. Survey research, with its concern for samples and standardization of measurement, has as its goal production of propositions that can be generalized. Ethnography relies on a process of inductive interpretation rather than the logico-deductive hypothesis testing associated with survey research.

Each of these approaches has both strengths and weaknesses. The two research strategies can be combined effectively. John van Willigen and N. K. Chadha used a mixed approach in their 1999 study of the social relationships of older people in a neighborhood in Delhi, India. In that study, in-depth ethnographic interviews were used to help make survey questions more appropriate to the context and to provide a context of meaning for the analysis. Project AGE (Age, Generation, and Experience) also used a hybrid quantitative and ethnographic approach in its comparative study of aging in various sites in North America, Europe, Africa, and Asia (Keith, Fry, Glascock, Ikels, Dickerson-Putman, Harpending, and Draper, 1994).

CROSS-CULTURAL RESEARCH VERSUS CROSS-NATIONAL RESEARCH

It is important to make a clear distinction between cross-cultural and cross-national research in aging-related studies (Albert and Cattell, 1994; Rubinstein, 1992). According to Albert and Cattell (1994, p. ix), both forms of research are useful for understanding the aging process and "represent two alternate streams of information on the aging experience." Cross-national studies sometimes appear to assume that "national boundaries represent cultural boundaries." Nations contain much internal cultural variation that relates to significant differences in lived experience. Cross-national research rarely captures this variation. Such variation is often dealt with through the use of ethnic, racial, or religious categories as key research variables. There are significant problems associated with these categorizations: conceptualizations of a given category that vary from researcher to researcher and from study to study; shifting self-concept of the people being researched; and historical changes in the terminology deemed appropriate. These difficulties tend to be ignored when the research results are published and used.

Cross-national and cross-cultural studies also vary methodologically to a considerable degree. Cross-cultural studies make significant use of ethnographic methods with the goal of increasing the contextualization and the capturing of meanings associated with the lived experience of individuals. Cross-national research often relies on classic survey methods. Just because research is done in a setting where cultural difference occurs does not mean that it is cross-cultural. One needs a specific research strategy that operationalizes culture.

The amount of literature reporting ethnographically oriented research on aging in Asian cultures varies a great deal country by country. Although there is not much literature in any country, the literature from Southeast and Central Asia seems to be the most limited. More has been conducted in Japan, Hong Kong, and India. Even in these countries, though, the urban mainstream is represented in more depth than are rural or ethnic minorities. Some recent examples include ethnographic research on aging in Asia concerning adaptation (Ikels, 1983); health experiences (Cohen, 1998; Lamb, 2000; Lock, 1993); intergenerational relations (Thang, 2001); social aging (van Willigen and Chadha, 1999), and daily life (Somera, 1997).

THE CULTURE CONCEPT

Expressed in the most basic terms, culture is what humans learn and what they create from what they learn. It contrasts with what humans acquire through genetic inheritance. Culture consists of at least three different kinds of phenomena: cognition, emotion, and motor patterns. The cognitive dimensions of culture include a wide range of phenomena that can be conveyed with such terms as *knowledge, concepts, models, techniques, beliefs, values, symbols, aesthetic forms,* and *customs.* Many aspects of the emotions appear to be uniform across cultures, but some aspects of how emotions are expressed and triggered are learned and are therefore culture specific. They also vary both among different cultures and within each culture. Just as we learned emotions, we also learn motor patterns. There are significant cultural differences in this regard.

Individuals acquire culture through their experiences. Young children learn their culturally based behavioral repertoire very early. As individuals age they learn new knowledge and forms of behavior. The ongoing process of learning culture is *enculturation.* Of special interest to researchers, policymakers, and service providers in the field of aging is enculturation later in the life course, and the enculturation of the values that define family life in a particular way, as well as the cultural implications of dementia. Cultural content flows to new members of the social group through enculturation, which normally means young members learning from their elders. There is much more research on enculturation early in the life course than on enculturation later in the life course.

Culture is often regarded as synonymous with tradition or that which is passed down from generation to generation. It is important to understand that culture includes the knowledge that we have acquired through this means; however, culture also includes new, nontraditional knowledge. Furthermore, tradition is subject to many different interpretations and revisions. Traditions may not even be rooted in the past; instead, they may be created as a means of adapting to new conditions. Moreover, the cultural past is often idealized, somehow made better through time. Much discourse on aging in Asian countries identifies a kind of golden age of relentless expression of filial piety—an age that probably never existed. When we think about traditional culture, we need to recognize that, though rooted in the conditions of the past, it is transformed to fit contemporary circumstances or purposes. Tradition is a product of a dialogue between the past and present. Knowledge and practices associated with the past are blended with present circumstances and beliefs to mold a dynamic cultural milieu and provide relevant traditions.

What is learned varies from person to person; yet when social scientists normally speak of culture they speak of "learned content" that is widely shared. Among cultural anthropologists it is conventional to speak of culture being shared by groups. In this sense scholars speak of culture as a kind of normative concept. The research of anthropologists, especially in the past, was focused on identifying widely shared aspects of group cultures. Some tended to think of culture as a uniform set of rules and concepts that structured human life in an almost deterministic way. Increasingly this view was seen as unworkable.

Sharing is an important aspect of culture, one that structures cultural interactions. Think about the amount of sharing of knowledge required to perform or appreciate an activity like Chinese traditional opera or the classical Indian dance form *bharatnatyam.* There must be enough sharing of knowledge for performers and audiences to communicate. It is important to state that this emphasis on sharing, though important, also masks and de-emphasizes intracultural variation. To carry the metaphor of performance further, very few people in China or India go to the opera or dance; more important, even those who attend see it in somewhat different terms. Further, it would be interesting to know who goes and who doesn't and how meanings associated with these performances are used by participants to explain their aesthetic, social, economic, or political reasons for attending.

The idea of a cultural group can be conceptualized at many different organizational levels: nation, community, neighborhood, and even family. People routinely speak of the "organizational culture" of corporations, agencies, and schools. In recent years, social scientists have studied the culture of such organizations as nursing homes (Gubrium, 1975, 1993; Somera, 1997) and retirement communities (Keith, 1977; Thang, 2001).

Anthropologists are concerned with how cultural knowledge is distributed in specific cultural settings (Roberts, 1987). In this regard, it is important to think in terms of intracultural variation. The goal of holistic ethnographic description as produced by cultural anthropologists is impossible to achieve without identifying the differences in the cultures of men and women, rich and poor, old and young. The analysis of cultural difference among individuals of different ages has important theoretical implications. Concern for such cultural differences can be seen in various theories of social aging, including continuity (Atchley, 1999), modernization (Cowgill and Holmes, 1972), and subcultural (Rose, 1965) theories of aging.

Although people's lives are constructed culturally, it is important to recognize that people also act as agents to transform culture. People are not culturally determined automatons. They are active agents who use cultural knowledge to achieve valued ends. Through individual and group decisions, they transform the culture of which they are a part. This is the basic mechanism of social evolution.

The contexts of meaning understood by people of different ages are constructed by society as much as they are derived from their specific enculturation in the social milieus within which an individual lives. People of similar ages may have some shared experience that has resulted in a certain level of sharing of knowledge and values. One point of intracultural variation that is especially interesting for those of us who work with older adults are the differences associated with various age cohorts, what we may call "age-cohort cultures." Considering Asia, one can imagine cultural knowledge as being stratified year by year, or era by era.

For example, in his work in India, van Willigen was struck by the fact that all the older people he worked with had shared the experience of living during "British times," and many lived through the violence of the Partition of India and Pakistan. Such significant experiences led to the formation of specific attitudes. In the case of Japan, some speak in terms of which Emperor's era one was born under. In the old people's home that Thang (2001) studied, she found that, increasingly, the nursing home population is dominated by *Showa-mono* rather than the *Taisho-mono. Showa* comprises those born between 1926 and 1988 during the rule of Hirohito. *Showa-mono* are seen as being harder to please, more demanding, and less appreciative than the *Taisho-mono* born between 1912 and 1925.

CRITIQUES OF THE CULTURE CONCEPT

Although culture is an important aspect of understanding the nature of the experience of aging, there are significant problems associated with describing cultures. One of the most significant problems is that of *essentialism,* a concept associated with postcolonial studies. Essentialism involves reduction of a group of people to an "essential" idea of what it means to be a member of the group (Fuss, 1989). This essential idea is applied uniformly to all members to characterize them, and such characteristics are thought to be derived from an unchanging tradition. As Salman Rushdie (1991, p. 67) once wrote, essentialism as manifested in literary criticism "demands that sources, forms, style, language, and symbols all derive from a supposedly homogenous and unbroken tradition." Implicit within the concept of essentialism is the notion that these essential characteristics are invariable and fixed. An essentialist position implies that a person within a group has less personal agency and is more a product of cultural conditions. Labeling and characterization are important tools in colonial, class, and gender oppression. Individuals who produce behavior that deviates from the essential may be criticized as inauthentic. In talking about cultures, it is very difficult to not be an essentialist to some degree. The problem of essentialism can be addressed through methodological strategies focused on making intracultural variation more visible as well as by increasing the presence of individual voices and by using care in the characterization and labeling of sources and interpretation.

AGING AND CULTURE

Here we turn to some important aspects of aging and culture in Asia. It is not possible to comprehensively discuss cultural content. Instead, the authors will focus on a number of salient aspects of culture and aging and use materials from Asian sources to exemplify these selected aspects.

Old People Serve as an Important Source in Cultural Transmission

Because of accumulated experience, older people often have a special role to play in cultural transmission. They serve as authoritative and enculturative sources of the tradition, a role that in turn provides a foundation for prestige and power. These conditions operate widely in Asian contexts, although they are subject to rapid, pervasive change. Proponents of the modernization theory of aging argued that with the transformation of society known as *modernization,* the prestige and power of older people have declined (Cowgill and Holmes, 1972). Many scholars have become disenchanted or have rejected the idea of modernization as a progressive ideal (Kim, Liang, Rhee, and Kim, 1996; Sokolovsky, 1997); however, the knowledge environment of Asia (and the rest of the world) has been rapidly transformed in ways that resonate with the idea of modernization. These conditions are part of daily life everywhere and consist of increases in technical change, increases in the rate by which knowledge becomes obsolete, and an increase in globalization. All of these factors are causing changes in the value of local knowledge. As these transformations have occurred, the rate of the related societal change has increased and elders have become increasingly marginalized. Writing about Vietnamese elders before 1945, Truyen (1998, p. 64) asserted that older people "were the well spring of cultural experiences in a society having no science or modern techniques. They were the guardians of the moral tradition in a community where law did not prevail."

Older adults may be especially susceptible to stress caused by cultural transformations associated with structural changes in society, such as those brought on by rapid technological change. Margaret Mead's (1970) discussion of kinds of generational relationships resonate with these stresses. With rapid technological change there is a shift in generational relationships. In the first case, the young learn from the old, and culture replicates itself through the generations. In this context, older people have high prestige. She referred to this pattern as *postfigurative.* Mead argued that the technological developments associated with the industrial revolution brought about a cultural pattern in which adults and children learned mostly from their peers. She referred to this second pattern as *cofigurative.* In her conception of *prefigurative* culture, the predominant learning pattern was from young to old; Mead argued that societies affected by rapid technological change were moving toward this latter model. While it may be difficult to apply these concepts definitively in Asia, the transformations associated with these concepts have occurred.

Culture Is Subject to the Impact of Various Structural Factors

Structural changes associated with new demographic patterns affect cultural content as it relates to age and aging. The development of national and local public health infrastructures have led to increases in longevity and population aging in many Asian countries. There are suddenly many more older people. Rapid changes in the economies of many Asian nations also have had profound effects on the availability of care for elders as well as on their living arrangements. The structural changes across Asia that have had the biggest impact on elders' lives are declines in numbers of children, increased participation of women in the paid labor force, increased migration in search of employment, and the spread of Western-style attitudes of individualism through the media and education (Knodel, Saengtienchai, and Sittitrai, 1995). These changes have increased demands on the family as a support system for elders. In most Asian countries, the underlying economies have not allowed the state to easily spend on provisions for old-age security. This means that cultural solutions, as opposed to policy solutions, are important, because in the absence of sufficient state-sponsored alternatives culturally based institutions such as the family must provide for support for most old people. Cultural values may be increasingly inconsistent with the material conditions of life—a culture lag in which a dissonance in values emerges between sectors of society (Ogburn, 1950).

For example, in Japan, even though more women are employed outside the home than ever before, traditionally ascribed caregiving roles and the associated values that sustain these roles have not changed. Jenike (1997b, p. 218) wrote, "The social prescription of the daughter-in-law bearing the primary responsibility for the care of her parents-in-law persists, as does the gender-based ideological division of labor of women at home and men at work which has kept care for the elderly a woman's task." At the individual level this creates an ambivalence toward caregiving caused by the differences between cultural values and personal costs. The impact of the inconsistency between cultural values and personal goals can be mitigated by the availability of rehabilitation services for older people. In this regard, Kiefer (1987) cites as constraints to rehabilitation in Japan limited facilities, shortage of physical therapists, and the family's reluctance to subject the patient to the rigors of treatment.

Knodel and colleagues' 1995 research in Thailand showed that most of the adult caregivers the researchers interviewed recognized the effect these structural changes were having on Thai families and expected to receive less direct care from their children than they were currently providing to their parents. However, they also expected that their children would continue to recognize their familial debts. Several responded that, although children might work elsewhere, parents could expect to receive money and gifts as support. Some respondents described having more children as one way of buffering the effect of increased migration and higher female labor-force participation rates. Others stressed that the moral education of children should be sufficient to assure support as parents aged. Yet others saw smaller family sizes as beneficial so that parents could emotionally and financially invest more in each child. Within these societal changes, there is an emerging phenomenon of grandchildren living with elderly grandparents while parents migrate in search of work. Thus, even with broad changes in Thai society and shifting patterns of residence, elders are not being abandoned. In Kato's 2000 study, elders in Cambodia similarly agreed that younger family members would not be able to provide the care that was traditionally expected. On the other hand, when younger adults were asked about the care of their elders, all insisted that elders were valuable members of society. It is clear that recognition of elders' importance may not reflect actual patterns of care.

Industrialization and urbanization in South Korea have increased the spread of more individualistic attitudes toward family and society. Researchers predict that the emergence of increasingly individualistic attitudes will also lead to weakened family ties and a reduction in the care that family members provide to elders. Although elder Koreans continue to expect support from their children, elders' demands for social welfare have increased (Kim, Liang, Rhee, and Kim, 1996).

Changes in Japanese residential patterns (rural to urban), shifting alliances from intergenerational bonds to conjugal bonds between husband and wife, and changing employment opportunities result in changing values and lifestyles that directly affect the ways elders receive care. These changes have led to decreased coresidence between aging parents and adult children. Instead, families may choose to live nearby rather than together in the same household (Long and Harris, 1997). Attitudes toward the individual's relationship with his or her family have changed as a result of industrialization in Japan: Sacrificing personal interests for the interests of one's parents has shifted toward valuing individualism and nuclear families (Kamo, 1988).

Changes in gender roles are having significant impacts on the situation of older people in many Asian cultures. Migration, urbanization, and higher labor-force participation rates for women have brought about changes in the structure of families and households. One of the most salient changes has been in where and with whom older people live. Although the social support provided older people by their families is less available than in the past, care and company continue to be provided, often in new ways. Filipino elders may not be deprived of care, comfort, and support from their families, even with a shift away from coresidence with an adult child (Domingo and Asis, 1995). Indeed, Domingo and Asis document several variants of elder-care, from the traditional cultural ideal of coresidence with an adult child to the reluctant willingness of elders to continue independent living, a pattern often based on adult children's needs. Elders' resource bases are frequently spread across an array of.kin or domestic networks, even when the elders live independently.

Family structure in post-1945 Vietnam shifted as an ideology of collective agricultural production was imposed on the Vietnamese. The previous role of elders as holders of cultural and traditional knowledge was severely undermined by the emphasis Vietnamese society began to place on youth and innovation (Truyen, 1998). However, since the late 1980s, there has been a return to a productive peasant household unit and a resurgence of elders who are socially engaging with young people. Elders serve as catalysts for the revival of familial, village, and religious festivals and as pioneers in the construction of Vietnam's infrastructure (Truyen, 1998). Since the end of the Vietnam–United States War in 1975, though, the situation of Vietnamese elders has become an acute problem. The deaths of close relatives, a change from a subsistence to a market economy, longer life expectancy, and the introduction of non-Vietnamese cultural values have resulted in a rapidly growing population of homeless elders (Thang, 1998).

As these changes reverberate through Asia, governments may increase their expenditure for older people. In 1989, the Japanese government proposed a legally mandated system of family care, Gold Plan for the Welfare of the Aged, in recognition of the growing number of elders. The Gold Plan was designed to encourage family care in private homes by providing subsidies and reduced rents to encourage coresidential patterns (Long and Harris, 1997). The Gold Plan also supports homecare over institutionalization and provides practical training to teach family members how to care for elders either in multigenerational homes or small elder-friendly flats (Jenike, 1997a). Providing home-based care conforms with Buddhist conceptions of fate and the unity of life and has slowed the development of rehabilitation services in Japan. Families also were reluctant to assign biomedical diagnoses to changes in elders' daily activities and demeanors, a pattern that tended to decrease elders' participation in care services outside the home. Ideal care was envisioned as that which provided comfort to elders, not that which involved rehabilitation (Long and Harris, 1997).

Intracultural Variation Is an Important Aspect of the Relationship Between Age and Culture

Sensitivity to culture is important for understanding aging in the context of a given society; nevertheless, it is clear that one needs to go beyond a uniformist (essentialist) view of the society and consider internal diversity. One dimension of difference can be found within distinctions between ethnic groups. Also important are variations within a given ethnic group. There are relevant cultural differences between social classes, genders, and rural and urban dwellers. These distinctions can be seen in the arena of the family.

Singapore offers a unique opportunity to view the ways that membership in differing ethnic groups within a single society appears to influence elders' preferences and actual living arrangements. The population of Singapore is predominantly comprised of three ethnic groups: Chinese, Indian, and Malay. According to Metha, Osman, and Lee (1995), more than 85 percent of Singaporean elders reside with their children in patterns of coresidence closely linked to ethnocultural norms. Malay elders disproportionately prefer living with married daughters and sons-in-law, often citing better relations with their daughters than with their daughters-in-law. Yet there is flexibility in this pattern. Living with the youngest child was often considered the natural course since that child was the last one living in the house with the elder and was, therefore, the most likely to stay. Other Malay elders indicated a preference to live with the poorest child in order to assist that child by contributing to the household in whatever way possible. In circumstances of out-migration of all Malay elders' children, adoption of other children presented a viable strategy for a continuation of reciprocal care. Conversely, elders may be adopted by an unrelated family and incorporated into the family household or live in close proximity where the elder can participate in the care network. It was unlikely that Malay elders would live in an institution; all preferred to remain in their own homes or to live in the home of a married child.

Similarly, Indian Singaporean elders coreside with their children but prefer to live with a married son. This preference is based on the understanding that, after marriage, a daughter belongs to her husband's family. Circumstances such as affection and the location and availability of children strongly determined the elders' actual living arrangements. Further differences were noted between North Indian and South Indian communities. For example, the North Indian community held a strong sanction against living with a daughter. Many North Indian elders indicated that they would prefer to live alone than live with a daughter. In comparison, South Indian elders indicated that they would live with a daughter if they could not live with a son due to his out-migration or his preference for independent living. Even though there is a strong normative expectation that Indian elders will live with a married son and daughter-in-law, changing social circumstances influence their ultimate living arrangements (Metha et al., 1995).

Chinese Singaporeans overwhelmingly (88 percent) coreside with married sons. Traditionally, their preference was to live with the eldest son, but as more children choose to live independently after marriage elders are increasingly coresiding with the youngest son, presumably because he is the last to marry. Despite the high incidence of coresidence, Chinese elders indicated to the researchers that they would not rule out living alone. Their attitudes may be due to the government's policy on subsidizing the rent of families who wish to live near but not with each other. Conversely, some elders claimed that a lack of respect among younger children deterred them from coresidential living arrangements. Of all three groups interviewed, the Chinese were most receptive to the idea of living in residential institutions for elders "if the services were better and affordable" (Metha et al., 1995, p. 127).

Another dimension of intracultural variation is social rank. In Nepal, caste differences reflect how social life is organized. Nepalese Hindu families of high caste often existed as joint families—in part because of the father's control over resources. Sons who hoped to inherit from their fathers were compelled to adhere to the traditions of the joint family, such as deferring to their father's wishes, turning over all income and material wealth to the father, and providing their wives and children as laborers within the father's household. In contrast, Nepalese Hindu families of lower castes were not as likely to coreside with one another, since it was often economically advantageous to all members of the family to maintain separate households. Because low-caste families relied solely on the skills of individual members instead of on material wealth such as land, there was little incentive to remain a joint family. Although the coresident joint family was considered the norm among Nepalese Hindu families, there was much variation based on economic conditions. Interestingly, economic changes in Nepal have had a greater impact on the living patterns of high-caste elders than on low-caste elders. Within the higher-caste families, the increased availability of individual incomes (i.e., careers outside the family business) has eroded the power of fathers' monopolies over sons' productive labor. Despite these changes in living patterns, a shift toward modernization does not seem to have adverse effects on the care of elders. Indeed, increases in sons' incomes are expected to improve elders' lives (Goldstein and Beall, 1986).

Culture Constructs the Life Course

The life course is framed by what are, at the core, biological events; however, life courses are culturally constructed (Riley, Johnson, and Foner, 1972). Each culture may define a set of categories for different stages of life or age cohorts. Sometimes these categories come to be manifested in legally constituted age markers such as retirement age. The categories, in term, may influence people's cognition of the life course and proper behavior at different ages. At minimum, cultures contain conceptions of specific behaviors associated, and expected, with specific ages.

In Hindu society, for example, the cultural concepts associated with the stages of the life course are uniquely formalized and elaborated. Social involvement and disengagement are built into the four stages (*ashramas*) of life through which an individual is ideally supposed to pass: *brahmacharya* (student), *grahastha* (householder), *vanaprastha* (hermit), and *sannyasa* (renunciate). The nature and duties associated with the system of *ashrama* are described in several texts that are somewhat at variance with one another. Almost all traditional Hindus are familiar with the main themes pertaining to the four *ashramas*; these ideas are passed down through oral tradition or the literature prescribed in the early years of schooling. Because the original texts were written in Sanskrit and are not easily accessible, most people use secondary sources consisting of a translation and sometimes commentary in either Hindi or English. Few directly study the Sanskrit texts that describe *ashrama,* yet people are familiar with the overall contents of the major texts. The texts refer to the *ashramas* as male activities. In fact, some argue that women only go through the first two stages. It is nevertheless clear that both men and women are involved in the later stages.

When one examines the Hindu scriptural concept of the ideal life cycle or its contemporary version as manifested in the words of religiously unsophisticated Hindu villagers, it becomes evident that these conceptions display significant parallels to ideas put forward in certain gerontological discussions of the nature of the aging process. Disengagement theory postulates, in brief, that as a person ages a mutual withdrawal occurs between the aging individual and the society of which he or she is a part (Vatuk, 1980). *Ashrama* may represent a culturally constituted model for disengagement: Knowledge of the *ashrama* concept is almost universal and therefore shared; disengagement is sanctioned and given expression in sacred texts; *ashrama* is comprised of idealized role models that manifest a phased reduction of engagement in the social and material world over the life course; and *ashrama* is manifest in actual practice.

There are reports that some Taiwanese use the metaphor of the growth cycle of rice to conceive of the life course: The new plant grows out of the earth and subsequently decays and is recycled late in life (Thompson, 1990). Such a metaphor is consistent with a cultural emphasis on ancestors and on the continual linkages between generations.

Culture may also include conceptions about the nature of old age or the nature of older people. Younger members of the community may have conceptions of aging that are different from the experience of older people. Analysis of language can reveal significant differences in the way age is dealt with across cultures by comparing terms associated with aging. For example, a comparison of Korean and (American) English revealed significant differences in the way age is treated lexically in the two cultures (Kim, 2000). Language materials were derived from dictionaries and books of proverbs. Although the sources from the two languages were somewhat different, the findings of the comparison are of interest. The Korean-language review produced more items associated with aging than did the English-language review, but interestingly, the Korean phrases and proverbs concerning age were more negative than those in American English. Kim wrote, "one cannot help but feel that somehow the darker side of aging has attracted greater attention in Korean culture" (p. 233).

Culture Provides the Concepts of Reciprocity that Structure Important Relationships

Another component of culture that is relevant to studies of aging are concepts that provide depictions of the qualities of social relationships. In Japan, for example, the concept of *on* encompasses the idea of reciprocity, that is, it refers to a gift, favor, or other benevolence given by one person to another and the resultant obligation the recipient has toward the giver. Indeed, the Japanese language includes many words that communicate the idea of reciprocal obligations.

According to Akiyama, Antonucci, and Campbell (1997, p. 164), "*On* has had its root in the Japanese culture for at least several hundred years." This concept is manifested in a wide range of social relationships. Most relevant to studies of aging is that *on* is especially important in relationships between children and parents. Everyone establishes *on* with their parents for the care they receive as children. Akiyama et al. (1997) described such *on* as "limitless" and lifelong. The obligation to repay this moral debt to one's parents may induce lifelong commitments toward filial duties in children.

The idea of reciprocity of relationships with one's parents in this way is widespread (Gouldner, 1960; Levi-Strauss, 1969). But how does it differ from setting to setting? Akiyama and colleagues (1997) found when comparing Americans and Japanese that, despite the fact that reciprocity was an important dimension of the relationship between children and parents in both settings, this reciprocity manifested itself in different ways. The dependence of older people on the support of children was much more acceptable in the Japanese setting. In the American setting, direct and equivalent reciprocity of exchange in a short time frame was more valued. The form of reciprocity also varies.

An extension of *on* is the concept of *amae*. In the Japanese setting, the aspects of the familial role enjoyed by children are also found in the familial role of grandparents (Thang, 2001). Japanese life has been described as providing the "maximum freedom and indulgence" to both old people and babies (Benedict, 1947, p. 254, quoted in Thang). Thang argues therefore that the young and the old are the "best company" for each other (p. 5). The Japanese concept of *amae* refers to the high level of mutual dependency that can exist between people and the potential for indulgent relationships that can develop in this context. The relationship between infants and their mothers is often used to illustrate *amae*; similarly, it has been used to characterize family relationships with older people. Tsuji (1997, p. 200) notes that *amae* "enables one to presume upon other's benevolence and encourages mutual dependency among people instead of independence."

Culture Provides the Values That Support the Position of Older People in Families

Three-generation families are common in many Asian settings and are important sources for the physical care and emotional support of older people. In Japan, in the past the three-generation pattern was the norm and was supported by "Confucian moral indoctrination" (Thang, 2001, p. 3). Traditional expectations throughout much of Japanese society are that the eldest son will be responsible for care but that the daughter-in-law will actually provide it. Ideal residential patterns are influenced by patrilineal patterns of three-generation coresidence. Moreover, it is expected that the eldest son will also inherit the family's business or property. The embeddedness of Confucian moral prescriptions strongly reinforces virtues of parent care within Japanese families (Jenike, 1997a). Cultural values, norms, and precedents usually are consistent with many normal social practices. Similar values have been expressed in the Indian setting. Sharma and Dak (1987, p. viii) assert, "where [a] joint family system still prevails, the aged continue to enjoy respect and power."

In many of these settings, the legal system is structured to be consistent with these practices and to support them. Such is the case in India, where the laws concerning inheritance serve to protect the property interests of the male-dominated, patrilineal joint family even though the laws manifest a superficial gender neutrality (van Willigen and Chadha, 2003). Similarly, Ikels (1997, p. 456) writes, "Living with or at least in close proximity to one's children, especially to one's son, is a cultural ideal" in China. We need to attempt to understand the relationships among cultural content, actual practices, the conditions of economic production, and the context of law. There will, it seems, always be congruence and tension between these four elements.

Deeply engrained in Thai culture is a constant sense of awareness of the debt one owes for some benefit one individual has bestowed on another, with the debt of gratitude owed to parents being especially strong (Knodel et al., 1995). There is a strong normative expectation among Thai elders that children will provide support for them as they age. On the other hand, congruence and tension can be seen in Thai elders' living arrangements; it is often difficult to discern why an elder lives with one child and not another, since unplanned events frequently influence that decision. Knodel and Saengtienchai (1999) observed that despite Thai elders' preference for living with a daughter, for example, the elders they studied were more likely to live with a separated or divorced child regardless of the child's gender. Furthermore, poverty and relationship strains may prevent the fulfillment of Thai elders' expectations of receiving assistance from their children. The researchers found discussions of living arrangements and support to be emotion-laden topics among the elders they interviewed, especially when the level of support that the elders expected was not being provided. Interviews with adult children echoed the sense of moral obligation to take care of parents. Moreover, adult children understood the care they were to give their elderly parents represented repayment for their own upbringing.

One of the most important benefits of coresidence cited by Singaporean elders and their adult children in Metha and colleagues' 1995 study was the transfer of cultural knowledge from grandparents to grandchildren. As such, elders were seen as the chief providers of religious education through exemplary behavior and storytelling. In addition, through the examples of elders and adult children, grandchildren are enculturated into Confucian ideas of filial piety. Thus through multigenerational interactions the family shares moral education, emotional support, security, and a sense of belonging. Such intangible benefits assume a higher priority than tangible benefits in the form of income. Several elders told the researchers that financial support was meaningless if love and companionship were not freely given.

Filial piety gives shape to the framework of emotions, faithfulness, and love between parents and children and creates the hierarchically organized social relations of obedience and respect characteristic of domestic relations. Vietnamese elders, for example, are responsible for family continuity and in turn are protected in their later years by their family within the framework of filial piety. Indeed, filial piety preserves the "emotional link between recollection and transgenerational inner reality" (Liem, 1998, p. 75) and provides the rules and laws governing obedience, education, and docility. Yet, filial piety also conjures images of "retrograde Confucianism" that hinders youths' freedom, causes family failures and conflicts, increases domestic violence, and causes resentment when elders' advice is disregarded (Liem, 1998).

Researchers seeking to understand familial obligations surrounding Thai elders' living arrangements have encountered several interesting difficulties. Defining residential patterns as either coresidential or living alone loses sight of the continuum of possibilities for intergenerational assistance (Knodel and Saengtienchai, 1999). One of the most significant barriers to understanding the living patterns of elders, not only in Thailand but also within settings across Asia, is researchers' primary reliance on survey data rather than qualitative data. Qualitative data allows researchers to begin understanding ways in which cultural norms and traditions are utilized and negotiated to create living arrangements that are suitable at the individual level.

The definition of household provided by the Thai government is a group of individuals who "live and eat together." This definition fails to recognize the ways many Thais have adapted their homes to provide a better fit for family members. Knodel and Saengtienchai (1999) observed that government-mandated definitions of household structure through registration with government authorities did not always reflect economic migration patterns, especially in rural areas, nor did it reflect the additions to households or divisions of households that marriages often occasioned. Categorization of living arrangements based solely on household composition obscures the complexity and extent of intertwining network systems; attention must also be paid to who lives nearby. More than half of the Thai elders interviewed maintained intricate social contact with neighboring households containing children or other kin. Rural elders with children living and working in urban areas may diversify the types and amount of care available to elders. The familiarity that migratory children may have with more sophisticated healthcare facilities in urban areas may serve as a benefit when elders become ill. In addition, Knodel and Saengtienchai demonstrated that more distant children also play important roles in the long-term care of elders through the material assistance and remittances they provide from afar. The complexity of social networks the researchers observed can be illustrated in the example of two elders who married after their previous spouses died. Following their marriage, two step-siblings also married to create a complex system of overlapping and blended family care.

Living arrangements often exist as intergenerational exchanges rather than one-way benefits to elders (Knodel and Saengtienchai, 1999). Exchanges often are temporal, whereby first the elder provides material and nonmaterial assistance to a young family in the form of land, housing, or labor. As elders become less able to provide labor, there may be a shift in the exchange, and members of the young family may begin providing nonmaterial assistance to the elder. Application of Western notions of "dependency" to the living arrangements of Asian peoples can be misleading because interdependence seems to prevail throughout these exchanges (Knodel and Saengtienchai, 1999). Directional balances may shift within a single configuration of social and family networks. The direction and balance of the flow of support—first from parent to child, then bidirectional and, as the parent nears the end of the life course, from child to parent—reflect the strong interdependence of family relationships (Knodel et al., 1995).

Singaporean elders also indicated to Metha and colleagues (1995) that coresidence significantly benefitted all parties involved. Benefit flows such as cooking, cleaning, laundry, and childcare were often in a state of flux, with reciprocal exchange between generations shifting across the life course. Several elders expressed their preference for living with the poorest child, regardless of that child's gender. They cited the desire to experience the psychological gratification and the appreciation they derived from providing material support along with love and companionship—with the expectation that they would receive love and companionship in return.

Culture Provides Structure to the Roles of the Caregiver

Japanese culture expects elder sons to provide care. When elders live separately from sons, such residential patterns often are interpreted as neglect and mean either that parents are disliked by their son or that the son has some serious flaw (Maeda and Ishikawa, 2000). Based on such expectations, living alone brings great shame to the parents.

Traditional Hindu ideology calls for patriarchal patterns of father, mother, sons, daughters-in-law, unmarried daughters, and grandchildren to form a joint family. Within this system, children owe permanent deference to both parents, but sons and their wives are responsible for the care of the elders. Because daughters-in-law are "outsiders" they are often treated harshly and are blamed for family discord when it occurs (Goldstein and Beall, 1986).

There is great variation in who becomes the primary caregiver for Thai elders. Daughters and youngest children (especially before the child marries) are preferred providers among Thai elders due to the perception that they are emotionally closer to parents and are more dependable. However, circumstances such as having only sons or having children who could more strongly benefit from their parents' help also influence the living arrangements of Thai elders. Strong cultural norms of filial piety and reciprocal affection combine with mechanisms of control such as land or home ownership and operate to maintain family-based systems of support. That both filial piety and economic incentives for elder care exist within the same normative system is less a contradiction than a reinforcement of ideas of pragmatism that are prevalent throughout Thai culture (Knodel et al., 1995). There are numerous cases of aging parents living with a son and daughter-in-law; however, most Thai elders interviewed by Knodel and colleagues (1995) agreed that there were many more opportunities for discord under this arrangement. Thai culture stresses that the primary allegiance is to one's own parents. Thus, while the son would be fulfilling his familial duties, the daughter-in-law would be torn between providing for her parents-in-law and her own parents. Given that most caregiving is done by female family members and that women control the household money, there is considerable room in such situations for both physical and financial neglect.

Often, middle-aged women are the primary caregivers for older adults; daughters-in-law or daughters are expected to fill the role of primary caregiver within a gendered "silent system" that disproportionately burdens women. Daughters-in-law and daughters may be "exploited as caregivers to the elderly" (Jenike, 1997b, pp. 332–333). Despite Japanese laws stipulating financial support and coresidence as the primary modes for providing elder care, the apparent system of exploitation of middle-aged women as caregivers was not simply the Japanese government co-opting existing ideology to shape programs. Instead, such programs were utilizing long-held cultural traditions of family practice. Within the Japanese ideology of family care, for example, childrearing was the only socially acceptable way out of parent care (Jenike, 1997a). There are few social programs that assist daughters-in-law with the increasing burden they often assume; consequently, in-law strain is one of the most serious problems many Japanese families face (Maeda and Ishikawa, 2000).

Caregiving among Singaporean elders, however, tends to follow gendered understandings of appropriate interactions. Physical care involving intimacy, if a spouse is unavailable, tends to be based on gender-specific interactions such as son to father and daughter-in-law to mother-in-law. Other activities such as help with trips to the physician or the market may be assigned to whoever is available. Despite preferences among Singaporean Malays for daughters as caregivers and among Indian and Chinese elders for daughters-in-law, the availability of a caregiver was the primary deciding factor for coresidence among most elders (Metha et al., 1995).

Patterns of care of older people in Cambodia reflect long-held beliefs of ancestor veneration and filial piety. The structural aspects contrast with these cultural values. The pervasiveness of poverty throughout Cambodia, the lack of a social security system, and consequences of the wars and civil unrest of the past three decades have created extremely difficult circumstances for elders. Although many elders continue to work, they often increasingly rely on their youngest daughter for care. Such care is generally reciprocal. For example, elders cook, clean, gather firewood, or watch over children while the mother works for wages outside the home (Kato, 2000).

Caregiving to elders in Brunei Darussalam is strongly influenced by the inseparability of the state-sanctioned Islamic religion and the political system governing the nation (Cleary and Maricar, 2000). An ideology governing care for elders flows directly from the Qur'an and an Islamic way of life that strongly emphasizes respect and care for parents in old age. This ideology also provides forceful condemnation when family members fail to provide elders with respect, housing, or care. The Brunei government clearly expects that its elder population will be fully encased in strong family relations and, therefore, occupies a distant and indirect influence in elders' lives through the provision of pensions. In this way, the government is not absent from elders' lives, but its role is less visible. Pension payments, which are provided to all citizens over the age of 55, are channeled through local village headmen and are viewed as a traditional village-centered pattern of caring for elders rather than a bureaucratic intervention. Family members and villages, through religious and social precepts, accept the obligation to provide care. Most elder citizens of Brunei live in large extended-family housing units.

Culture Includes Beliefs About What Causes Good Health and Aging Well

There are numerous cultural beliefs concerning the practices that result in good health as one ages. Because these ideas are about how a person can live a long, healthy, and satisfying life, we could call them "ethno-theories" of aging well. There is relatively little comprehensive research on this topic, but there are examples of specific studies that deal with portions of the aging process.

Anthropologist Andrea Sankar researched the medical beliefs of Buddhist nuns in Hong Kong (Sankar, 1984). Among other concerns, she examined how old age was used as a diagnosis in China (i.e., "It's just old age"). Traditional Chinese conceptions of the universe include the dual concepts of yin and yang. "Yin and yang are the basic forces governing the universe and all things within it. Yin represents the dark, wet, cold, female, the negative. Yang is its opposite, light, warm, dry, male, the positive" (Sankar, 1984, p. 263). Each person has both yin and yang within him or her. In order for society to be harmonious it is important to keep these two forces in balance. In the context of the body, the yin-yang duality is expressed in terms of "hot" and "cold." It is important for a person to balance hot and cold foods. Hot and cold here refers to a dimension different from temperature or the amount of spice. Health is a function of maintaining a balance between these elements in the face of all the things that can disrupt it: the seasons, disposition and constitution, and most important for our consideration here, age. Loss of balance can cause disease. Western medicine is seen as useful for treating symptoms alone, not for providing an adequate explanation of the cause of disease.

One aspect of aging is loss of balance in yin and yang. Both elders and children possess less yang. Yin dominates at the beginning and end of the life course. Because of this inherent lack of balance, the young and the old are especially susceptible to diseases; additionally, they are less capable of correcting the yin-yang imbalance by adjusting what they consume or making other lifestyle choices. Presumably, as one ages one should increase the amount of hot food to counterbalance the general and inexorable tendency toward coldness. Paradoxically, Buddhist ethics encourage older adults to adopt a comprehensively vegetarian diet that tends to eliminate hot foods such as meat (Sankar, 1984).

Culture Provides Conceptions About the Aging Body

An area of analysis relevant to understanding cultural differences in aging deals with the differences in the ways people of different cultures think and talk about age-related physical conditions. Research in this area is relatively new. Noteworthy examples based on Asian populations are Margaret Lock's comparative study of menopause in Japan and North America (1993) and Lawrence Cohen's examination of dementia in India (1998). The authors of these "new classics" are medical anthropologists who share a critical perspective: In order to understand the human body we need to address its social and political dimensions as well as the biological (Cohen, 1998; Lock, 1993). In other words, bodies are both naturally and culturally produced (Lock and Scheper-Hughes, 1990). Furthermore, the discussions about physical bodies carried out in biological and medical science are seen as culturally constructed. Lock's position (1993, p. 370) is "that knowledge about the body is a product of history and culture and thus changes with location and over time." This view is contrasted with the reductionism that is associated with biological science.

Within both bodies of research, which focus on specific aging-related issues in Asian cultural settings, we find through comparison with Western life a cultural critique of Western life. One can imagine that Western healthcare providers would find reading both volumes useful and challenging. The two studies force one to think about the cultural understandings surrounding menopause and dementia in the West.

Although Lock's study makes use of a wide range of data, the core of her rhetorical strategy is based on narratives that she compiled from transcriptions of interviews with more than 100 women ages 45–55 from a number of regions in Japan. The narratives are supplemented with some survey data, secondary data, observations of life in Japan and North America, and extensive review of a wide variety of Japanese and North American literature such as medical textbooks for different eras and traditions. Her survey involved administering a questionnaire to a sample of 1,738 Japanese women. She then compared their responses to those from respondents in the United States (Massachusetts) and Canada (Manitoba), to whom she administered an identical questionnaire. Lock found that North American women reported hot flashes and night sweats much more frequently than Japanese women.

Much of Lock's discussion of menopause focuses on the Japanese concept of *konenki*. The women interviewed expressed this idea in many different ways. Lock felt that "change of life" was the best English translation of *konenki*; however, it was clear that the cognitive space covered by the term was quite different than that associated with North American use of *menopause*. Cultural differences included duration, extent of variability, symptoms and their frequency, and the extent to which the condition was seen as problematic.

Cohen's work is focused on the complex process through which a body's age comes to be important as well as how systems are "constituted by which bodily decay is experienced, named, measured, treated, and drawn into law and history and science" (1998, p. xvii). The data and experiences on which Cohen bases his interpretation were diverse, including participant observation, ethnographic interviews, use of secondary data, and deconstruction of contemporary media messages. The starting point of the analysis was Cohen's ethnographic work in a Varanasi slum. From this core he gained experience doing a wide range of dementia-related activities in India and elsewhere. The rhetorical style of the book and analytical strategy of the research make it difficult to produce a bulleted list of findings. Nevertheless, the book presents a useful understanding of dementia in the Indian setting.

Both Lock's and Cohen's discussions of the conditions they studied show the problems associated with the integration of medical research into public discourse on aging. Thus, a reasonably complete understanding of aging can only be achieved through an attempt to integrate biological and cultural processes. More important, aging processes are subjective and do not yield to the reductionist research strategy of the biomedical sciences. Cultural factors mediate age-related diseases.

CODA

Like all aspects of human life, aging has an important cultural facet. In this chapter the authors have attempted to illustrate some of the important cultural dimensions of the aging process using recent research from Asia. In addition to considering such dimensions as coresidence and reciprocity of support, it is also possible to think about culture and age in terms of an encompassing process: cultural aging.

The core of cultural aging is the life course process by which a person experiences, assigns meaning to, and understands life. The life course is the route through which learning and the creative experience allow one to experience the content and regnant meanings of human life. The core of the process is enculturation. Historically, research and theorizing about enculturation have been focused primarily on the young, seen as recipients of cultural learning. Certainly, the classic conception of enculturation emphasizes the progression by which a person, usually a child, acquires the array of knowledge, motor patterns, and emotional templates that allow social participation and use of culture-specific "webs of meaning." Although the acquisition process may be weighted to early in the individual's life, it continues over the entire life course.

To cite a platitude now obvious these days, learning occurs lifelong. Our lives are marked by a series of shifts in what kind of content is being learned; we learn different things at different stages. One of the first may be expectations associated with food and feeding, family roles, and values of generosity and support. Later in life we may become more concerned about learning spiritual matters. The ways that culture is learned at various stages have an effect on these outcomes.

At any given time the content of what people know provides a ground upon which the enculturation process unfolds. The cultural context of aging consists of the beliefs concerning age and aging held both by members of the community and by those who research and serve them. This context includes but is not limited to understandings concerning the life course, relationships within the domestic group, and causes of age-related health maintenance or decline. These beliefs will vary in important ways depending on gender, ethnicity, age, age-cohort experience, and the person's position in the political economy.

We can think about a two-sided process in which we learn cultural knowledge from the sources that we have and also share (i.e., teach or model) our cultural knowledge with others. Everybody teaches, everybody learns. Because of changing environmental structures, there are age-cohort shifts in cultural understanding. People can be thought to pass through a series of culturally formulated expectations that they use, consciously deviate from, and modify through their own choices. Early in the life course people are more usually recipients of such knowledge, and later they may be more frequently sources of cultural information. However, the intergenerational exchange of cultural knowledge is complex and does not just involve the old teaching the young. Because ways of acquiring and sharing cultural knowledge are subject to the effects of experiences accumulated throughout the life course, there are very significant cohort effects. Differences in knowledge can relate to age, but may also reflect differences in history.

As individuals age, their access to new cultural information may change. As negative examples, one can cite reduction in sensory acuity. Also, members of one's social network who share age-cohort experience may die or lose mobility. They may also have fewer social assets with which to acquire new information. This constrains an individual's access to information.

Culture is very important; however, it is equally important to recognize the role of individual agency. Addressing the cultural context of the individuals we serve or for whom we formulate policy is essential. Yet we must also guard against stereotyping and figuratively disempowering people. People act not because of culture but *within* culture according to a complex mix of self-interest and cultural expectations.

REFERENCES

Akiyama, H., Antonucci, T. C., and Campbell, R. (1997). Exchange and reciprocity among two generations of Japanese and American women. In J. Sokolovsky (Ed.), *The cultural context of aging: Worldwide perspectives* (pp. 163–178). Westport, Connecticut: Bergin and Garvey.

Albert, S. M., and Cattell, M. G. (1994). *Old age in global perspective: Cross-cultural and cross-national views*. New York: G. K. Hall.

Atchley, R. C. (1999). *Continuity and adaptation in aging: Creating positive experiences*. Baltimore: Johns Hopkins University Press.

Benedict, R. (1947). *Patterns of culture*. Boston: Houghton Mifflin.

Bernard, H. R. (1994). *Research methods in anthropology: Qualitative and quantitative approaches*. Thousand Oaks, California: Sage Publications.

Cleary, M., and Maricar, H. A. (2000). Ageing, Islam, and care for older persons in Brunei Darussalam. In D. R. Phillips (Ed.), *Ageing in the Asia-Pacific region: Issues, policies, and future trends* (pp. 322–333). London and New York: Routledge.

Cowgill, D. O., and Holmes, L. (1972). *Aging and modernization*. New York: Appleton-Century-Crofts.

Domingo, L. J., and Asis, M. M. B. (1995). Living arrangements and the flow of support between generations in the Philippines. *Journal of Cross-Cultural Gerontology, 10*, 21–51.

Fuss, D. (1989). *Essentially speaking*. London: Routledge and Kegan Paul.

Geertz, C. (1973). *The interpretation of cultures*. New York: Basic Books.

Goldstein, M. C., and Beall, C. M. (1986). Family change, caste, and the elderly in a rural locale in Nepal. *Journal of Cross-Cultural Gerontology, 1*, 305–316.

Gouldner, A. W. (1960). The norm of reciprocity. *American Sociological Review, 25*(2), 161–178.

Gubrium, J. (1975). *Living and dying at Murray Manor*. New York: St. Martin's.

Gubrium, J. (1993). *Speaking of life: Horizons of meaning for nursing home residents*. New York: Aldine de Gruyter.

Ikels, C. (1983). *Aging and adaptation: The Chinese in Hong Kong and the United States*. Hamden, Connecticut: Archon Books.

Ikels, C. (1997). Long-term care and the disabled elderly in urban China. In J. Sokolovsky, (Ed.), *The cultural context of aging: Worldwide perspectives* (pp. 452–471). Westport, Connecticut: Bergin and Garvey.

Jenike, B. R. (1997a). Home-based health care for the elderly in Japan: A silent system of gender and duty. In S. Formanek and S. Linhart (Eds.), *Aging Asian concepts and experiences past and present* (pp. 329–345). Vienna: Osterreichischen Akademie der Wissenschaften.

Jenike, B. R. (1997b). Gender and duty in Japan's aged society: The experience of family caregivers. In J. Sokolovsky (Ed.), *The cultural context of aging: Worldwide perspectives* (pp. 218–238). Westport, Connecticut: Bergin and Garvey.

Kamo, Y. (1988). A note on elderly living arrangements in Japan and the United States. *Research on Aging, 10*(2), 297–305.

Kato, E. U. (2000). Ageing in Cambodia: Tradition, change, and challenges. In D. R. Phillips (Ed.), *Ageing in the Asia-Pacific region: Issues, policies, and future trends* (pp. 360–374). London and New York: Routledge.

Keith, J. (1977). *Old people, new lives: Community creation in a retirement residence.* Chicago: University of Chicago Press.

Keith, J., Fry, C., Glascock, A., Ikels, C., Dickerson-Putman, J., Harpending, H., and Draper, P. (1994). *The aging experience: Diversity and commonality across cultures.* Thousand Oaks, California: Sage Publications.

Kiefer, C. (1987). Care of the aged in Japan. In E. Norbeck and M. Lock (Eds.), *Health, illness, and medical care in Japan.* Honolulu: University of Hawaii Press.

Kim, I. K., Liang, J., Rhee, K.-O., and Kim, C.-S. (1996). Population aging in Korea: Changes since the 1960s. *Journal of Cross-Cultural Gerontology, 11,* 369–388.

Kim, K.-D. (2000). Cultural stereotypes of old age. In V. L. Bengtson, K.-D. Kim, G. C. Myers, and K. Eun (Eds.), *Aging in East and West: Families, states, and the elderly* (pp. 227–241). New York: Springer.

Knodel, J., and Saengtienchai, C. (1999). Studying living arrangements of the elderly: Lessons from a quasi-qualitative case study approach in Thailand. *Journal of Cross-Cultural Gerontology, 14,* 197–220.

Knodel, J., Saengtienchai, C., and Sittitrai, W. (1995). Living arrangements of the elderly in Thailand: Views of the populace. *Journal of Cross-Cultural Gerontology, 10,* 79–111.

Lamb, S. (2000). *White saris and sweet mangoes: Aging, gender, and body in North India.* Berkeley: University of California Press.

Levi-Strauss, C. (1969). *The elementary structures of kinship.* Boston: Beacon Press.

Liem, L. C. (1998). On the fringe of the problem of aged people. *Vietnamese Studies, 34*(128), 73–77.

Lock, M. (1993). *Encounters with aging: Mythologies of menopause in Japan and North America.* Berkeley: University of California Press.

Lock, M., and Scheper-Hughes, N. (1990). A critical-interpretive approach in medical anthropology: Rituals and routines of discipline and dissent. In T. M. Johnson and C. F. Sargent (Eds.), *Medical anthropology, contemporary theory and methods* (pp. 41–70). New York: Praeger.

Long, S. O., and Harris, P. B. (1997). Caring for bedridden elderly: Ideals, realities, and social change in Japan. In S. Formanek and S. Linhart (Eds.), *Aging Asian concepts and experiences past and present* (pp. 347–367). Vienna: Osterreichischen Akademie der Wissenschaften.

Maeda, D., and Ishikawa, H. (2000). Ageing in Japan: Retirement, daily lives, pensions, and social security. In D. R. Phillips (Ed.), *Ageing in the Asia-Pacific region: Issues, policies, and future trends* (pp. 113–132). London and New York: Routledge.

Mead, M. (1970). *Culture and commitment: The new relationships between the generations in the 1970s.* New York: Columbia University Press.

Metha, K., Osman, M. M., and Lee, E. Y. A. (1995). Living arrangements of the elderly in Singapore: Cultural norms in transition. *Journal of Cross-Cultural Gerontology, 10,* 113–145.

Ogawa, N., and Retherford, R. D. (1993). Care of the elderly in Japan: Changing norms and expectations. *Journal of Marriage and the Family, 55,* 587–597.

Ogburn, W. F. (1950). *Social change with respect to culture and original nature.* New York: Viking Press.

Riley, M. W., Johnson, M., and Foner, A. (1972). *Aging and society, vol. 3: A sociology of age stratification.* New York: Van Nostrand.

Roberts, J. (1987). Within culture variation. *American Behavioral Scientist, 31*(2), 266–279.

Rose, A. M. (1965). *Older people and their social world.* Philadelphia: F. A. Davis Company.

Rubinstein, R. L. (1992). Anthropological methods in gerontological research: Entering the realm of meaning. *Journal of Aging Studies, 6,* 57–66.

Rushdie, S. (1991). *Imaginary homelands: Essays and criticism.* New York: Penguin.

Sankar, A. (1984). "It's just old age": Old age as a diagnosis in American and Chinese medicine. In D. I. Kertzer and J. Keith (Eds.), *Age and anthropological theory* (pp. 250–280). Ithaca, NY: Cornell University Press.

Sharma, M. L., and Dak, D. M. (1987). *Aging in India: Challenge for the society.* Delhi: Ajanta Publications.

Sokolovsky, J. (1997). Aging, modernization, and societal transformation. In J. Sokolovsky (Ed.), *The cultural context of aging: Worldwide perspectives* (pp. 179–189). Westport, Connecticut: Bergin and Garvey.

Somera, R. D. (1997). *Bordered aging: Ethnography of daily life in a Filipino home for the aged.* Manila: De La Salle University Press.

Thang, B. V. (1998). The loneliness of aged people in some post-war stories. *Vietnamese Studies, 34*(128), 69–72.

Thang, L. L. (2001). *Generations in touch: Linking the old and young in a Tokyo neighborhood.* Ithaca, New York: Cornell University Press.

Thompson, S. (1990). Metaphors the Chinese age by. In P. Spencer (Ed.), *Anthropology and the riddle of the sphinx* (pp. 137–152). London: Routledge and Kegan Paul.

Truyen, N. D. (1998). Family and social position of aged people in rural areas. *Vietnamese Studies, 34*(128), 64–68.

Tsuji, Y. (1997). Continuities and changes in conceptions of old age in Japan. In S. Formanek and S. Linhart (Eds.), *Aging Asian concepts and experiences past and present* (pp. 67–83). Vienna: Osterreichischen Akademie der Wissenschaften.

Van Willigen, J., and Chadha, N. K. (1999). *Social aging in a Delhi neighborhood.* Westport, Connecticut: Bergin and Garvey.

Van Willigen, J., and Chadha, N. K. (2003). Social networks of old people in India: Research and policy. *Journal of Aging and Social Policy.*

Vatuk, S. (1980). Withdrawal and disengagement as a cultural response to aging in India. In C. Fry et al., (Eds.), *Aging in culture and society: Comparative viewpoints and strategies* (pp. 97–119). South Hadley, Massachusetts: Bergin and Garvey.

PART II

Economic Status, Work, and Retirement

CHAPTER FIVE

Economic Status, Work, and Retirement in China

Peng Du

Change in China is proceeding at breakneck speed: Technological and economic currents are creating a forward-looking situation in Asia and in the world. These tides are converging with demographic transformations to alter the China of the past. Not only is the People's Republic of China the most populous country in the world, it also has the largest older adult population. According to the latest national census, conducted on November 1, 2000, the total population of the 31 provinces, autonomous regions, and municipalities[1] on the mainland of China was 1,265.83 million persons, or 21 percent of the world's total population. Among them are 130 million adults ages 60 and older. This figure represents 10.3 percent of the total population of China—and one fifth of the world's total older adult population (Du, 1994; Population Census Office, 2002).

Census data also revealed that in 2000, 88.11 million Chinese were ages 65 and older, accounting for 6.96 percent of the total population. Their proportion of the total population was up 1.39 percentage points since the 1990 census. Such rapid growth in the elderly population of China is the outcome of the confluence of socioeconomic and healthcare developments of the past few decades. In addition to dramatic expansion in life expectancy, there have been significant improvements in individuals' standard of living. As is classically the case with demographic transformations, the same factors are responsible for a rapid decline in fertility rates. According to a September 2000 report from the State Development Planning Committee, during the past five years China has made significant improvements in its healthcare services and the effects are profound. Just to cite one of the more significant transformations, average life expectancy in China reached 71.8 years in 2000 (State Statistical Bureau [SSB], People's Republic of China, 2000, 2001).

[1] These figures exclude the Jinmen and Mazu Islands of Fujian Province.

The findings from the 2000 census are consistent with previously published projections and estimates of the absolute and relative sizes of China's older adult population. Consequently, we can expect that the rate of population aging in China will quicken in the early decades of the 21st century. It is estimated that the number of persons ages 60 and older in China will exceed 357 million in 2030 and 439 million in 2050, at that point representing a quarter of the total population (SSB, 2000). In fact, Chinese elderly will account for one quarter of the world's population over the age of 60 (Kinsella and Velkoff, 2001; Lin and Zhai, 1996). The census data collected in China reveal that although the overall proportion of older adults in the total population is not particularly high across the board compared to that in developed countries, some large cities have sizeable concentrations of elderly residents, warranting special attention.

Despite the accelerating pace of technological and economic change, China remains an agricultural society at the time of this writing: More than 75 percent of its older adult population lives in rural areas. This figure is consistent with the level of urbanization of the overall population yet is likely to undergo a dramatic shift in the next decade or two. As has been the case since time immemorial, the majority of rural elderly continue to depend on their children for economic support and daily care in late life. Yet, because of the corollary changes already referenced, this situation too is likely to be far different by 2025.

Since the late 1970s, China's family planning policies and associated declines in fertility have received considerable attention within and outside the nation. As of 2000, the total fertility rate in China reached 1.8 births per female, and the majority of urban families had only one child (SSB, 2000). At the same time, since the time of the previous census, more than 100 million young people from rural areas have poured into cities around the nation in search of jobs and better lives, leaving their aging parents behind in their home villages. More and more rural elderly are realizing they can no longer count on their children to provide for and take care of them. Therefore, population aging, especially in rural areas, is becoming a key issue in China, and hardships are growing exponentially.

SOCIAL SECURITY IN CHINA

In the years since the Cultural Revolution, there has been a major shift from a centralized to a market economy and those changes are part and parcel of the experience of aging. Now, with China's inclusion in the World Trade Organization, the pace of economic change will quicken in all likelihood and the effects on older members of the population will be painted in even bolder relief. In general, the economic status of Chinese elderly can be judged on the basis of relative income levels compared to younger segments of the population and on primary sources of income. Due to significant regional differences in fertility and mortality levels, as well as in geography, climate, and socioeconomic development, urban and rural older adults experience differing living conditions and have widely disparate welfare, healthcare, and pension systems. In a country as vast as China, such variations can be considerable, to say the least, and reform slow to take hold (Du, 1994; Lin and Zhai, 1996).

According to regulations of the Chinese national pension system, dramatically revised in 1997 and further in 2000, retired workers—almost all of whom live in urban areas—usually receive pensions equal to about 75 percent of basic preretirement income. Such retirees are still regarded as fortunate, however, because almost all their rural counterparts have not been entitled to any pension benefits, and the majority of rural elders continue to labor in agricultural pursuits to maintain their income in later life. Given that urban-dwellers only represent a quarter of the total population, the majority of Chinese elders still consider children their best investment for old-age security (Lin, 1994). Even in large cities today, many older adults believe that a son is their most reliable security for the later life, even as their offspring are beginning to alter their perception of their obligations (Du, 1998).

Income patterns among Chinese elders also show significant urban-rural differences: The greatest percentage of urban elderly belong to the middle income bracket. However, more than 80 percent of rural elders have incomes that are classified as belonging to the lowest income bracket (SSB, 2001). Furthermore, as of 2000, 50 percent of urban elderly receive pension benefits; by contrast, less than 5 percent of rural elderly were entitled to pensions.

In addition, the younger the older adult, the higher his or her income level, because the young old have better educational backgrounds and higher labor-force participation rates and are therefore more likely to be covered under the social security system. There is a direct relationship between educational achievement and income level among the elderly, and the vast majority of older adults are classified as having only minimal education as defined in Chinese terms, despite the fact that approximately 85 percent are considered literate. Finally, and not coincidently, there are significant gender disparities in income, with older women falling disproportionately into the no-income category.

China's Retirement System

Although China began providing retirement benefits to government officials before the 20th century, such provisions never became widespread. Traditionally, and in the absence of a social security system, the responsibility for supporting the elderly has customarily belonged to families. Shortly after the founding of the People's Republic of China (PRC), the new nation issued "Regulations on Labor Insurance of the People's Republic of China" in 1951 and "Temporary Regulations on Retirement of the Staff and Workers by the State Council" in 1958. These two sets of regulations instituted basic social security for income, medical care, and social welfare for the majority of government staff and workers in state-owned enterprises. Although the PRC allotted farmers plots of land, it never established social insurance in a palpable sense in rural areas. In consequence, families and collectives continue to provide more than partial support to rural elderly.

The state and the collectives have provided "Five Guarantees" to childless and infirm older adults: food, clothing, medical care, housing, and burial expenses. Some of the old people belonging to this group have been placed in nursing homes. Despite progress made in the past few decades, however, social security inclusion in China remains relatively scarce and substantial segments of the labor force are without coverage.

Considering that China's large elderly population is expanding at a rate of 3 percent annually, that social security coverage is minimal, and that the vast majority of the rural elderly are dependent on family support, reform of old-age support systems and medical provisions is emerging as a major concern nationwide. The national Ministry of Civil Affairs issued and enacted a "Basic Scheme for Rural Social Security for Old-Age Support at the County Level" in 1992. The intent of the statute implied that raising funds for support of older persons should follow the principle of relying mainly on individual payments from personal accounts, while making collective subsidiaries through state support an official policy. At present, few people in rural areas receive social insurance, so family provisions for old age are, for all intents and purposes, the only option. In fact, family support and social security for old age are integrated and protected by the Law on the Protection of the Rights and Interests of the Elderly of the People's Republic of China, which was enacted on October 1, 1996. Revisions and reformulations of that statute are ongoing in the context of a burgeoning market economy, and it is likely that the next iteration of an integrated old-age support system in China will reflect new market-based patterns.

Emerging Aging-Policy Initiatives

China is stepping up efforts to knit together an interconnected complex of pensions and unemployment insurance to cover approximately 200 million people—making it the largest such system in the world—to replace its outdated cradle-to-grave hodgepodge of welfare provisions.

In 2000, China injected RMB 87.6 billion[2] into the program, about one-third more than it had the previous year. In 2000 the average pension benefit per month for urban elderly was RMB 661 (China Research Centre on Ageing, 2003). At the fourth session of the Ninth National People's Congress, held in March 2001, Premier Zhu Rongji identified social security as a "major task" facing China in the next five years. Under the goals laid out in the 10th Five-Year Plan (2001–05), more Chinese people will be covered by the pension system, and

[2] As of September 2003, US$1 = RMB 8.25 (yuan).

the pension system for urban employees, which integrates unified financing and individual accounts, will be further enhanced.

The previous welfare system called for state-owned enterprises to be solely responsible for the welfare of their employees, ensuring lifelong employment, medical care, and pensions. The breath of coverage for those employees was superior to what employees of other non-state entities could anticipate. The current round of reforms aims to set up a multi-tier old-age security system in urban areas that includes basic governmentally sponsored old-age insurance, employer-subsidized complementary insurance, and individual savings accounts. However, the reformed system will continue to face serious challenges: a growing elderly population, increasing demand for pensions, and the inability of enterprises with poor economic performance to pay their share of basic social security premiums for their employees.

Due to the enormous differences between rural and urban areas, the government is enacting separate aging policies in cities and in the countryside. In urban areas, it is refining the social security system and extending its reach. However, in rural areas, where the family continues to take responsibility for providing for its elderly members, the government is extending the Five Guarantees system described above to provide minimal assistance for those without family support. Currently, China's social security system is limited and problematic. Despite rapid economic growth, fund-raising channels for social insurance remain limited thus far and insurance coverage needs to be expanded to rural areas. Among the many challenges facing the national government is the standardization of local management and oversight of governmental provisions in order to ensure comparability across the vast expanse of China. Establishing a social security system independent of enterprises and institutions will be an arduous task under the best of circumstances and given the mammoth geographical and cultural differences that comprise China, even more arduous.

THE ECONOMIC STATUS OF THE ELDERLY

In traditional Chinese families, the eldest members of the family generally controlled the family's economic resources, therefore playing a dominant role. However, in the last 50 years, China has experienced a dramatic shift from an agricultural society to an industrialized society that is the fastest growing in the world. More and more young people are living in cities, separated from aging parents and exposed to global economic priorities that would have been unprecedented in China in even the recent past. Not only has the older generation lost financial control over its children, they are also losing their traditional niche in the economy. Most children work outside the family now; instead of giving their salary over to their parents, younger adults usually just give their parents an allowance for food, clothes, and daily expenses.

The strength of Chinese traditions has had a paradoxical effect on those who are currently old. The importance of the family in the past has delayed the implementation of formal governmental provisions. As a consequence, only one quarter of Chinese elders currently receive a state-sponsored pension, and the majority of Chinese elders depend on their children for economic support. In light of emerging economic priorities, many older adults now perceive themselves as an economic burden on their children, one that is impeding their children's success.

Since the 1990s, China's economy has been growing exponentially—but so has its older population. Who will provide for the elderly in China is a crucial issue today. To guarantee the economic resources of Chinese elders, the national government passed the Law on the Protection of the Rights and Interests of the Elderly of the People's Republic of China in October 1996. Article 10 of the law stipulates that the elderly shall be provided for mainly by their families, and family members shall care for and look after older relatives. Article 11 further defines "care for and look after" as providing for elders financially, taking care of them and comforting them, and catering to their unique needs, including healthcare. Providing economic support to older adults is now mandated by law in order to bolster tradition, but enforcement is challenging.

Income Level of Elders

Looking at the economic status of Chinese elderly may provide insight into their standard of living. According to data from the China Research Centre on Ageing, findings from the latest national income survey of Chinese elderly, which took place in 2000, show that the average annual income for urban elders was RMB 8,496, compared to RMB 2,232 for rural elders (China Research Centre on Ageing, 2003). Interestingly, the average annual income of urban elders is also higher than that of the average urban citizen (RMB 6,280). However, the average annual income of rural elders is quite similar to that of the average rural citizen (RMB 2,253).

The 2000 survey also revealed that the older the elderly individual is, the lower his or her economic status. For example, among the 71.5 percent of urban elderly who received a pension in 2000, those in the 60–65 age group received an average benefit of RMB 648 per month, but those in the 90-plus age group only received an average of RMB 472 per month. The survey also confirmed gender disparities in the income distribution of elders: In Chinese cities, the average monthly pension was RMB 746 for older men but RMB 529 for women.

Although the 2000 survey showed that income levels were substantially lower for rural older adults than for their urban counterparts, the benefit gap between those who were better off and those who were worse off was wider among urban elderly than among their rural age peers. Nearly half the rural elderly had average incomes less than RMB 1,000, a figure that was about three times higher than for the urban elderly. This translates into monthly incomes among rural older adults that averaged RMB 186 in 2000, about one third of that reported by urban older adults (RMB 708).

The income disparity between urban and rural elders is widening, partly as a result of the growing numbers of urban elders who receive pensions. According to data from the 2000 national census, 58 percent of city-dwelling elders live off their pensions, whereas in rural areas only 4.4 percent of all elders subsist on just their pensions. The latter figure has not changed in 10 years, but the percentage of pensioners among the urban elderly has increased 20 percent in the same time period (Population Census Office, 2002).

At the same time, the 2000 national census also revealed that adult children are still playing a very important role in providing for their old parents. Among older adults ages 60 and older, 43.8 percent depended predominantly on financial support from their children and other relatives; in rural areas this proportion was slightly higher, at 48.9 percent (Wu and Du, 2003). Recent research has also revealed that older adults who depend primarily on their children for support usually coreside with them (Du, 1999; Myers and Du, 1996; Wu and Du, 2003). This finding was especially true for rural elders and older women.

Table 1 shows the striking differences in the economic resources of urban and rural elderly in China. Rural elders are significantly more likely than their urban counterparts to depend on relatives or their own labor for their economic sustenance, and urban elders are 13 times more likely to have a pension that provides for their economic needs. These figures explain why the belief in "having a son to provide for the old" is still prevalent in rural areas.

Table 1. Primary Economic Resources of Older Adults in China, 1994 and 2000

	1994				2000			
Primary economic resource	Total (%)	City dwellers (%)	Town dwellers (%)	Village dwellers (%)	Total (%)	City dwellers (%)	Town dwellers (%)	Village dwellers (%)
Work	24.97	14.30	14.01	29.18	32.99	10.10	19.72	43.15
Pension	15.65	48.54	29.81	4.39	19.61	58.05	29.08	4.76
Family members	57.13	34.94	53.10	64.23	43.83	27.88	46.10	48.92
Other	2.25	2.22	3.08	2.20	3.57	3.97	5.10	3.17
Total	100.00	100.00	100.00	100.00	100.00	100.00	100.00	100.00

Sources: Du and Wu, 1998; Wu and Du, 2003.

One clear pattern apparent in Figure 1 is that dependence on the support of one's children increases with age. Two factors may be relevant to these findings: As the elderly age, they are usually in poorer health and must quit working; in addition, the older the person, the less likely he or she has a pension or has worked in covered employment. Clearly with the changes already afoot, the composition of economic resources of the elderly will change gradually as more and more older Chinese acquire pension benefits. This will surely improve the economic status of the elderly, but given the paucity of pension benefits among rural elders, most will continue to depend on their children for the foreseeable future (Du, 1999; Myers and Du, 1996; Wu and Du, 1996).

Figure 1 shows yet another pattern worthy of note as well. As is apparent, the elderly who remain in the labor force are most commonly the young old. At the same time, the young-old population have a much higher proportion of pensioners compared to that of the old old. As of 2000, among the elderly ages 60–64, half depended mainly on wages from work, although 22 percent regarded their pension as their main economic resource. Although the proportion of this age group who depended on their children's support was as high as 26 percent compared to other age groups, it is still the lowest rate among the elderly. Although some older adults must continue to work to maintain their economic well-being, as they age the majority of elders either withdraw voluntarily from the labor force or else become unable to secure paid employment. The figure also shows that at age 60, just over half of all Chinese elders (55.5 percent) regard the income they receive

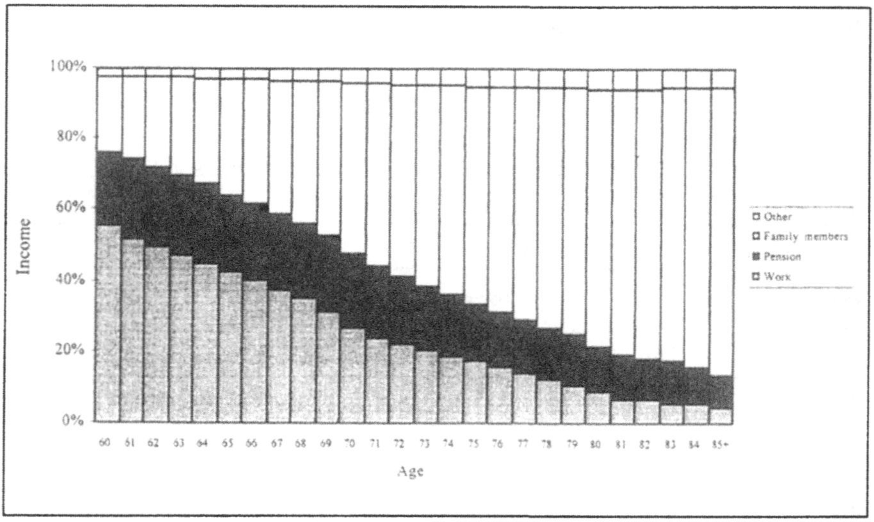

Figure 1. Economic resources of older adults in China by age, 2000. (Reprinted with permission from Wu and Du, 2003.)

from work as their principal economic resource. By age 65, this proportion has decreased to 42.5 percent, and by age 70, it has declined further, to 26.9 percent (Wu and Du, 2003).

As older people exit the labor force, they increasingly rely on the support of their children and spouses to maintain themselves. According to data from the 2000 census, the proportion of 60-year-old Chinese elderly who regarded the financial support of their family members as their main source of income was 21.4 percent. This proportion rose to 30 percent at age 64 and to 50 percent at age 71, and exceeded 80 percent at age 85. In other words, insofar as older adults must depend on the financial support of their families, it is hard to claim that they have resources to maintain their independence or even an acceptable economic status. As has been implied above, generally speaking, pensions provide an adequate economic resource for Chinese elderly who receive them. For those fortunate few, incomes are sufficient to maintain an independent quality of life, but for those without pensions, grinding dependency is the only recourse. As China improves its pension system and provides coverage to increasing numbers of people, it is reasonable to expect that the proportion of elders who can rely primarily on their pension will rise in the coming decades, strengthening the overall economic status of the elderly as a group.

Economic Status of Older Women

As is seemingly the case around the world, older women are less well off economically than older men, due to lower education levels and interrupted or lower labor-force participation rates. Although there are no significant gender differences between the salaries of male and female workers in China, there is a five-to-ten-year gender differential in mandatory retirement age. Female workers generally retire at age 50, whereas male workers continue working until age 55 or 60. Because the actual level of pension benefits is based on lifetime earnings, in China's rapidly developing economy early retirement can significantly lower pensions relative to consumer prices and purchasing power. Because older women usually have lower pensions and lower income levels than men of the same age, a higher proportion of older women are forced to depend on financial support from family. Needless to say, with the global economic currents coursing through China, their financial viability is precarious at best.

This gendered disparity in financial well-being is even more pronounced among rural elderly. In 2000, more than 64 percent of rural older women reported depending mainly on the economic support of their children or spouse. Some 32 percent were still working, regarding their income as their main economic resource, and only 1 percent of rural older women primarily lived off their pension. In contrast, among rural older men, 33 percent were still working, 55 percent saw their personal incomes as their principal financial resource, and 9 percent

Table 2. Primary Economic Resources of Older Adults in China by Gender, 2000

Primary economic resource	City dwellers (%)		Town dwellers (%)		Village dwellers (%)	
	Male	Female	Male	Female	Male	Female
Work	14.80	5.71	27.40	12.41	54.88	31.94
Pension	70.88	46.06	44.06	14.83	8.63	1.05
Family members	11.36	43.32	23.74	67.36	32.91	64.24
Other	2.96	4.91	4.80	5.40	3.58	2.77
Total	100.00	100.00	100.00	100.00	100.00	100.00

Source: Population Census Office, 2002.

lived off of their pensions (Wu and Du, 2003). Table 2 suggests that comparable gender disparities exist in both urban and rural areas across China. Overall, older urban men are the most economically independent and rural older women the least; able to provide for their own and live life on the ragged edge, depending on the kindness of their families and communities.

The findings of the National Survey on Ageing in China, conducted by the China Research Centre on Ageing in 2000, help to underscore the status of older adults within their families. In light of traditional decision making within families, the survey asked older adults who was most likely to establish the rules in the family. Drawn from the survey responses, Table 3 implies that as older adults grow older still, they lose the power to make decisions for their household—financial and otherwise. Generally speaking, the survey indicated that 53.4 percent of Chinese elderly play a leading role in family decision making; at ages 60-64, 60.3 percent retain this role, but the proportion declines to 28.2 percent by age 85. Meanwhile, the proportion of children who play the decision-maker role in family decision making increases from 15.5 percent when the eldest family member is age 60–64, to 30.0 percent at age 70–74, and further to 63.5 percent by age 80 (China Research Centre on Ageing, 2003).

Again, in regard to the older adults' role in decision making within the family, the urban-rural differences are as notable as are the financial disparities. In urban areas, 62.3 percent of the elderly play a leading role in the family, whereas in rural areas this proportion is only 45.4 percent. According to the survey, and perhaps not at all surprisingly, 20.7 percent of urban elders and 40.9 percent of rural elders felt they had financial difficulties (China Research Centre on Ageing, 2003).

Table 3. Primary Economic Decision-Makers in Households with Elderly Members, 2000

Age of elderly member	Elder (%)	Spouse (%)	Children (%)	Others (%)	No answer (%)
60-64	60.3	21.1	15.5	2.3	0.8
65-69	57.1	18.2	21.8	2.1	0.7
70-74	52.0	15.7	30.0	1.8	0.5
75-79	44.4	11.4	42.5	1.5	0.3
80-84	36.7	7.1	54.8	1.2	0.2
85+	28.2	3.3	63.5	3.9	1.1

Source: China Research Centre on Ageing, 2003.

WORK

Compared to more countries that have undergone economic development in the decades prior to China experiencing the same takeoff, China has a relatively early retirement age. As a general rule, most urban workers retire before the age of 60. However, the large numbers of elderly residing in rural areas neither face mandatory retirement nor do they have any recourse except to continue to work as long as possible. As a result, China's older adult labor-force participation rates are higher than those of other countries. According to the 2000 population census, of the total population ages 60 and older—130 million persons—43 million older adults were still working, yielding a labor-force participation rate of 33 percent (Wu and Du, 2003).

Due to the absence of available pensions in rural areas, as of 2000, 43.2 percent of rural elderly age 60 or older were still engaged with the workforce or tending their own fields. In contrast, their urban counterparts generally retire at age 50 to 60, and thus the labor-force participation rate of urban older adults is low (10.1 percent in cities and 19.7 percent in towns). As can be seen in Table 4, among the 43 million older Chinese who worked in 2000, 86.3 percent lived in rural areas (China Research Centre on Ageing, 2003; Du and Wu, 1998). While these patterns are representative of current China, in the decades ahead dramatic shifts will likely occur.

Table 4 also reveals that the 2000 labor-force participation rate for older adults living in rural areas was one to three times higher than that for elderly living in cities and towns. At the same time, tremendous gender differences can be observed across all regions: The labor-force participation rates among older men were double those among older women, and the economic consequences of

Table 4. Labor-Force Participation Rates for Older Adults in China, 2000

Residence	Total (%)	Male (%)	Female (%)
City	10.1	14.8	5.7
Town	19.7	27.4	12.4
County	43.2	54.9	31.9

Source: Population Census Office, 2002.

that pattern will pay out throughout their retirement years. Chances are that pension reforms recently enacted will alter the patterns presently in place, but until what are currently working-age cohorts cycle through to retirement, differentials will remain.

The socioeconomic development currently occurring in China will result in decreased labor-force participation rates among the elderly, especially in rural areas. The government is trying to expand the reach of its social security system to provide greater coverage for those not yet included. For example, it has established a pension system in eastern rural areas for the first time. As a consequence of such developments, the proportion of pensioners among the total older adult population in rural areas will soon start to increase. Conversely, as educational attainment, health status, and attitudes about work among elders continue to evolve, some elderly may choose to continue to remain active in the labor force.

In China, there is no significant gender disparity in labor-force participation rates among people at younger and middle age, because the state guarantees that men and women experience equal opportunity of employment and equal pay for equal work. Nevertheless, gender differences increase with age due to many practical reasons and systemic barriers of the past. For example, the retirement age for female workers continues to be 50 and that for male workers, 60. In light of legal mandates, it is not surprising that comparison of labor-force participation rates among men and women at age 60 shows a dramatic differential. However, older women most commonly take full-scale responsibility for household work and for taking care of grandchildren, making it difficult for them to work outside the home to the extent possible. As is the case worldwide, this unpaid work at home is not reflected in the above figures.

TYPES AND SECTORS OF EMPLOYMENT AMONG OLDER WORKERS

What kind of work are Chinese elderly doing? According to data from the 2000 population census, the majority of the elderly labor force is engaged in productive enterprises. Ninety percent of workers ages 60 and older are engaged in farming, animal husbandry, forestry, and fishing; 2.6 percent are engaged in commerce and other service industries, including restaurant and delivery work as well as comparable enterprises; and 2.4 percent are engaged in industry (Table 5). The industrial sector employment of the elderly population is closely associated with the general level of economic development in the country: China is a developing country, and in 2000, 64.4 percent of the total working population was engaged in farming, forestry, animal husbandry, and fishing. Between the 1990 and 2000 censuses, the proportion of the total labor force engaged in self-employed agriculture declined; however, the proportion of the elderly labor force engaged in paid agricultural work increased. As has typically been the case in countries where agriculture shifts from being a family-run enterprise where surpluses are sold in the marketplace to a market-based enterprise where agricultural workers tend the fields and crops as paid employees, self-employed agricultural pursuits are being supplanted by agribusinesses.

In 2000, 95.0 percent of older women still working were concentrated in the agricultural sector, actually a higher percentage than among their male counterparts. These figures may reflect both labor needs and more flexible policies. The second largest employment sector for older women, as it is with older men, is in commerce and retail food service (2.1 percent). Age-specific data from the 2000 census showed that at more advanced ages, larger proportions of older men were engaged in agriculture, commerce, and residential services whereas the proportions of those engaged in industry and government agencies declined, which can be attributed to the retirement policies in place for the latter sectors. Likely the same policy-based explanations help explain why as age increased among older women, the proportions of those working in industry and agriculture decreased while the proportion of those working in commerce increased.

OCCUPATIONAL PURSUITS

The majority of older workers who work are engaged in physical labor of one sort or another. According to 2000 census data, forestry, animal husbandry, and fishery workers accounted for more than 90 percent of all employed older workers (Table 6). Employment in business and service occupations accounted for 3.5 percent. Examining gender differences in occupational pursuits reveals that the proportion of older women engaged in farming, forestry, animal husbandry, and fishery (95.2 percent) was even higher than that of older men (88.7 percent). However, with advancing age, the differential between men and women declines.

It must be noted that the above figures regarding the composition of the older adult labor force are predominantly shaped by the rural elderly, because rural older people account for three quarters of the total older adult population and have higher labor-force participation rates than their urban counterparts. In another words, almost all of the rural elderly who work are engaged in agriculture, while

Table 5. Industrial Structure of the Employed Elderly Population in China, 2000

	Total population		Men ages 60+		Women ages 60+	
Industry	Number	%	Number	%	Number	%
Farming, animal husbandry, forestry, and fishery	3,842,489	91.01	2,364,083	88.67	1,478,406	95.02
Mining	7,334	0.17	6,773	0.25	561	0.04
Manufacture	99,666	2.36	79,625	2.99	20.041	1.29
Supply of power, gas, and running water	3,371	0.08	3,142	0.12	229	0.01
Construction	19,678	0.47	18,968	0.71	710	0.05
Geological prospecting	1,727	0.04	1,649	0.06	78	0.01
Transportation and telecommunication	11,881	0.28	10,953	0.41	928	0.06
Commerce, catering trade, supply and marketing of commodities and storage	108,812	2.58	76,605	2.87	32,207	2.07
Finance and insurance	2,912	0.07	2,630	0.10	282	0.02
Management of residential buildings and public facilities, residential services	2,273	0.05	1,988	0.07	285	0.02
Social services	34,057	0.81	26,427	0.99	7,630	0.49
Health, sports, and social welfare	21,273	0.50	17,209	0.65	4,064	0.26
Education, culture, and arts	26,747	0.63	22,798	0.86	3,949	0.25
Scientific research and comprehensive technical services	4,086	0.10	3,558	0.13	528	0.03
State organs, party, committees, and NGOs	32,406	0.77	26,911	1.01	5,495	0.35
Other trades	3,316	0.08	2,761	0.10	555	0.04

Note: Figures in the table are sample results from the 2000 national census. The sample ratio is 9.8465% of the total elderly population.

Source: Calculated based on data from Population Census Office, 2002.

Table 6. Occupational Structure of the Employed Elderly Population, 2000

	Total ages 60+		Men ages 60+		Women ages 60+	
Occupation	Number	%	Number	%	Number	%
Managers for state organs, party, and NGOs, enterprises and institutions	18,031	0.43	15,896	0.60	2,135	0.14
Staff for scientific and technical work	59,406	1.41	50,658	1.90	8,748	0.56
Office workers and service workers	57,353	1.36	53,258	2.00	4,095	0.26
Commercial and service workers	148,280	3.51	105,855	3.97	42,425	2.73
Workers in farming, forestry, animal husbandry, and fishery	3,847,332	91.13	2,366,146	88.75	1,481,186	95.20
Workers for production and transportation	89,550	2.12	72,614	2.72	16,936	1.09
Other nonclassified workers	2,076	0 .05	1,653	0.06	423	0.03
Total	4,222,028	100.00	2,666,080	100.00	1,555,948	100.00

Note: Figures in the table are sample results from the 2000 national census. The sample ratio is 9.8465% of the total elderly population in China.

Source: Calculated based on data from Population Census Office, 2002.

the urban elderly concentrate in productive processes, business, and social services. Among older workers, occupation is closely related to educational attainment: Among those older people with relatively little education and who remain in the labor force, 95.8 percent are engaged in farming, forestry, animal husbandry, and fishery. Among those who have graduated from universities, 60.5 percent do various kinds of scientific and technical work; 12.8 percent are managers for state organs, party, nongovernmental organizations (NGOs), and enterprises; and 11.7 percent work as office workers (Wu and Du, 2003).

RETIREMENT

In 1951, when China implemented a pension scheme in state-owned enterprises and government agencies, the dependency ratio was a scant fraction of what it is today after decades of state-mandated birth control. During the same period, China has moved from the state-run, centralized economy that characterized the People's Republic of China at the time to a rightful player on the world economic stage and a partner in the World Trade Organization. Initially, a 3 percent contribution on composite wages was sufficient to ensure adequate old-age insurance benefits. At the same time, because most workers and government servants covered under the plan were young, until 1978 only 3.14 million retirees received a pension from the scheme. By 1980 the number of pensioners had risen to 8.16 million, and then the rate of increase accelerated rapidly. By the end of 1999, there were 37.27 million pensioners throughout the nation. Add to those changes the fact that the Chinese economy suffered as the Asian bubble burst in the 1990s, and the accompanying significant hardships had a disruptive effect on existing state policies and served to set the stage for sweeping reforms in the 1990s.

According to data from the 2000 census, the total number of urban elderly in China exceeded 45.9 million. In other words, the majority of urban elders nowadays are pensioners. Early in the 1980s this pattern was becoming evident. Beginning in 1986, municipal pooling of pension obligations became a means of keeping up with migration driven by economic restructuring. Unfortunately, regional economic disparities, local pension obligations, contribution evasions, and other dilemmas soon revealed fault lines in the municipal pooling plan. Still, urban elderly have much better income security than Chinese elders of previous generations or their rural age peers, and most can live on their pensions independent of family support. Therefore, to some extent their economic status is stronger than that of past generations of elders and their contemporary rural counterparts.

Table 7 shows the growth in the number of retired workers over the past two decades. It demonstrates that the number of retired people in China has increased more than three times, from 8.16 million in 1980 to 37.3 million in 1999.

As the pension system matures and as population aging continues to occur, it is projected that the number of retirees in China will continue to increase for a long time. The total number of retired people is expected to exceed 100 million by 2012, 200 million by 2026, and 300 million by 2048 (Lin, 2001). Such demographic shifts will result in a much higher ratio of pensioners to workers. In response, China has to consider reforming the pension system as it is now structured, as well as relevant regulations on retirement.

Beginning in 1997, governmental retirement policies formally adopted a three-pillar model along lines alluded to elsewhere in this volume. The first pillar is a defined-benefit program paid for out of current wages and payrolls and paid into a municipal pool designed to provide approximately 58 percent of pre-retirement earnings; this percentage, however, is down from a previous 80 percent replacement rate. The second pillar is an individual provident-inspired savings account funded by employees at a current contribution rate of 8 percent of wages. The third pillar consists of voluntary individual contributions to personal accounts.

Table 7. Number of Retired Persons in China, 1980–1999

Year	Retired persons (1,000s)	Year	Retired persons (1,000s)
1980	8,160	1990	23,010
1981	9,500	1991	24,330
1982	11,130	1992	25,980
1983	12,920	1993	27,800
1984	14,780	1994	29,290
1985	16,370	1995	30,941
1986	18,050	1996	32,116
1987	19,680	1997	33,507
1988	21,200	1998	35,936
1989	22,010	1999	37,269

Source: State Statistical Bureau, 2000.

Not too surprisingly, numerous problems have arisen, and collections are running to about three quarters of what had been anticipated. An added complexity revolves around the problem of providing for current cohorts of retirees, the financing of their benefits, and the actual level of benefits earmarked for those who played out their work lives under the old entitlements scheme.

Various strategies are being considered for resolving the issues, which include noncompliance in more than 20 provinces. Those sorts of difficulties aside, one of the biggest headaches is to make available resources cover the number of claimants. As mentioned above, current retirement age for female workers is as low as age 50, and many workers retire before age 60, with an average of age 56. Raising the mandatory retirement age may serve to lower the numbers of pensioners and reduce expenditure on pensions. Although there has been some debate over raising the retirement age since the 1990s, in the face of an over-abundance of workers, running to about 200 million nationwide, it is virtually unfeasible to change existing regulations in the near term.

The National Social Security Fund was established at the turn of the century to manage the problem and direct pooled funds to where they are most needed. In addition, a National Council for the Social Security Fund now exists. It is charged with implementing emergency financial procedures to prop up local fiscal crises relating to pension benefits. As should be implied by just these few examples, China is facing a long, hard struggle to ensure that retirement benefits remain solvent and available to a growing older population. A number of quite far-reaching solutions are being explored, including some degree of privatization, and policymakers will not be able to escape formulating much needed solutions in the very near term.

CONCLUSION

China's existing social security system only covers residents of urban areas. The majority of the country's many rural elderly still must depend on their children for financial support and care. Older adults in rural areas are significantly poorer than their urban counterparts, and the economic status of rural older women is especially dim. Economic currents sweeping across China are only painting the problems in even bolder terms than those described here.

Despite the dark cloud looming large on China's horizon, for the first time in history, more than half of all urban Chinese elders—more than 70 percent in cities such as Shanghai and Beijing and some other municipalities—receive pension benefits and regard their pensions as their main economic resource. There can be little doubt that the social insurance provided through the pension program is playing a leading role in ensuring the quality of life of urban older adults.

Even as the number of retired workers is growing, the labor-force participation rate for older Chinese has simultaneously been increasing. The lack of a viable social security system in rural areas is principally responsible. To avoid becoming dependent on their children, rural elderly are preferring to remain involved in the workforce for as long as possible—contingent on their health and opportunities to work. Obviously, changes in China's social security system have a significant impact on the labor-force participation rate of older adults. Should the day come when adequate coverage for rural workers becomes the norm, it would be reasonable to expect labor-force participation rates to begin to approximate those observed in China's cities. With a life expectancy at birth in urban areas of China now greater than 74 years, it is becoming increasingly problematic to have mandatory retirement set as low as age 50 for female workers, an age established in the early 1950s, when retirement funding in the pay-as-you-go system was predicated on life expectancies that were no greater than 10 years following retirement. In China's rapidly aging society, there are few solutions to this quandary, other than raising mandatory retirement age for everyone to 60 or even later. Such a step will not just slow down the increase in the number of retired pensioners throughout China; it will also benefit older workers and the national economy.

With the emergence of China as a player on the global economic stage, priorities have shifted and economic development looms large. At the present time, China is the most rapidly growing economy in the world. Nonetheless, the current shortcomings in retirement benefits must be addressed, as they will only grow more intrusive as China moves forward in its quest to become a fully modernized economic power.

REFERENCES

China Research Centre on Ageing. (2003). *Data analysis of the sampling of survey of the aged population in China.* Beijing: China Standard Press.

Du, P. (1994). *The process of population ageing in China.* Beijing: People's University Press.

Du, P. (1998). Changes in living arrangements of the elderly in Beijing. *Chinese Journal of Population Science, 1*(3), 231–240.

Du, P. (1999). Survey on family structure and the elderly in China. In Economic and Social Commission for Asia and the Pacific (Ed.), *The family and older persons in China, Indonesia, and Thailand* (pp. 9–54) (ESCAP Asian Population Studies Series No. 152). New York: United Nations.

Du, P., and Wu, C. (1998). Analysis on the economic resources of Chinese elderly. *Population Research, 23*(4), 50–57.

Kinsella, K., and Velkoff, V. (2001). *An aging world* (U.S. Census Bureau Series 95/01-1). Washington, D.C.: U.S. Government Printing Office.

Lin, B. (2001). Timing and options: Adjustment of retiring ages in China. *Chinese Journal of Population Science, 4*(1), 25–31.

Lin, F., and Zhai, Z. (Eds.). (1996). *China's population, environment, and development toward the twenty-first century.* Beijing: Higher Education Press.

Lin, J. (1994). Parity and security: A simulation study of old-age support in rural China. *Population and Development Review, 20*(2), 423–448.

Myers, G. C., and Du, P. (1996, November). *Living arrangements among Chinese older persons.* Paper presented at the annual meeting of the Gerontological Society of America, Washington, D.C.

Population Census Office. (2002). *Tabulation of the 2000 population census of the People's Republic of China.* Beijing: China Statistical Publishing House.

State Statistical Bureau, People's Republic of China. (2000). *China statistical yearbook, 1999.* Beijing: China Statistical Publishing House.

State Statistical Bureau, People's Republic of China. (2001). *China statistical yearbook, 2001.* Beijing: China Statistics Press.

Wu, C., and Du, P. (1996). *Chinese elderly in the process of population ageing.* Shanghai: Press of Shanghai Normal University.

Wu, C., and Du, P. (2003). *2000 census report on Chinese elderly.* Beijing: National Census Office.

CHAPTER SIX

Economic Resources of the Elderly Within the Japanese Family

Nobuko Nagase

Many Westerners wonder at the high labor-force participation rates of older adults in Japan. In 2001, the Japanese Cabinet Office published *The Fifth International Study on the Life and Consciousness of Senior Citizens (FISLCSC)* presenting the results of its survey comparing labor-force participation rates of older adults ages 60 and older in Japan, South Korea, the United States, Germany, and Sweden. Although the sample size was 1,000 persons in each country, the findings allow for an approximate international comparison of the five countries. The labor-force participation rates for older men in Japan and South Korea were reported to be somewhat higher than the U.S. rate and much higher than those of their European counterparts (Figure 1). Labor-force participation rates for older women were also high in Japan and South Korea, though markedly lower than those of older men.

Such high labor-force participation rates have often been attributed to the size of the self-employed sector: Occupational pursuits such as farming, small retail stores, and home-based factories were once widespread in Japan. The self-employed sector, however, constitutes a much smaller share of the labor market in Japan today, while that of paid employment has increased dramatically. According to the 2000 Survey on the Employment Status of the Elderly conducted by the national Ministry of Welfare, Labor, and Health (2000), at the turn of the millennium the self-employed comprised 25.6 percent of male workers and 18.5 percent of female workers ages 60–64. In comparison, in 1983 the percentage of self-employed among the same age group was 37.7 percent for male workers and 54.7 percent for female workers.

The labor-force participation rates of older men, however, have not remained stable over time. Figure 2 shows that over the past 20 years the labor-force participation rates of men ages 60 and older have declined, whereas those of men

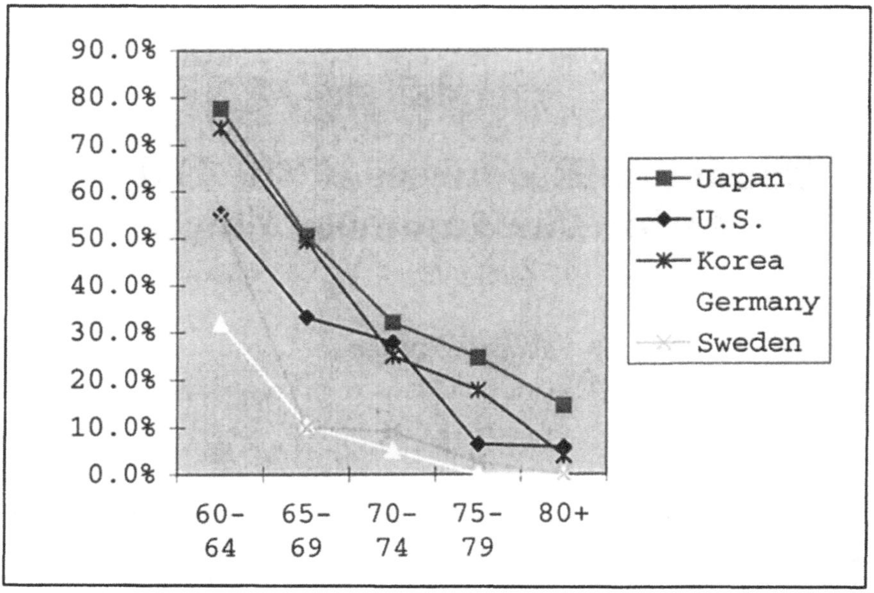

Figure 1. Labor-force participation rates of older men in the United States, Germany, Sweden, South Korea, and Japan.
Source: Cabinet Office of Japanese Government, 2001.

ages 55–59 have increased. Such changes undoubtedly reflect changes in retirement age and pension plans. During the 1980s, the national government encouraged firms to raise the mandatory retirement age and planned to raise the eligibility age for full pension benefits for all salaried workers. The public supported such changes. Firms negotiated with labor unions to keep wages stable in return for raising the retirement age so as to help accommodate the change (Ono, 1989). According to the Ministry of Labor's 1980 Survey on Employment Management, 82 percent of the firms surveyed had a "mandatory retirement system"; 60 percent of these firms set the retirement age between 55 and 59. By 1990, the proportion of firms that still retained a mandatory retirement age between 55 and 59 had declined to 36 percent, and increasing numbers of firms had raised their retirement threshold to 60. To further institutionalize the national retirement system, the government enacted the Employment Stability Law for the Aged in 1994, thus making any mandatory retirement age under 60 ineffective starting in 1998.

Such measures obviously had a significant impact on the labor-force participation rates of men ages 55–59. However, the rate for men over the age of 60 showed a declining trend: In 1970, 80 percent of Japanese men ages 60–64 were engaged in the workforce; this figure fell to a low of 71 percent by 1988. It

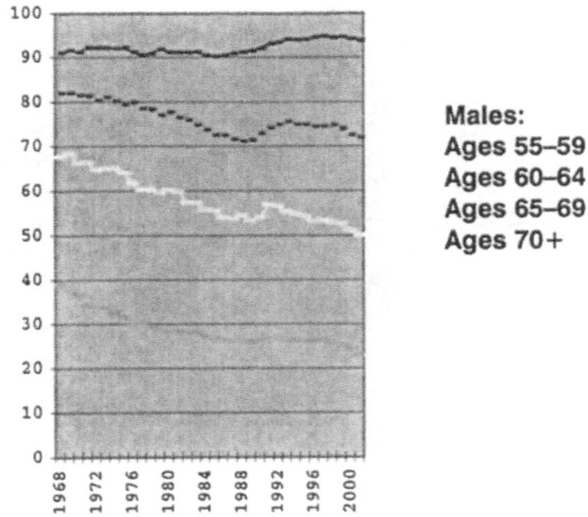

Figure 2. Labor-force participation rates of older Japanese men.
Source: Statistics Bureau, Ministry of Public Management, Home Affairs, Post and Telecommunications, Labor Party Survey (composite summary).

rebounded moderately to almost 75 percent during the economic boom of the late 1980s and early 1990s, but declined again during the deep recession, falling back to 71 percent in 2001. The labor-force participation rates of men ages 65 and older show a comparable trend. Many empirical investigations have attempted to measure the effect of Japan's public pension system on individual decisions on when to retire; these studies will be discussed later in this chapter.

The labor-force participation rates of women ages 55–59 increased even more markedly over the past two decades, and such rates for women ages 60 and older showed no decline (Figure 3). However, the labor-force participation rates of older women are much lower compared to those of older men of comparable ages.

OLDER ADULTS' ECONOMIC RESOURCES

Household Income

In modern Japan, benefits received through the public pension system constitute an important source of income for older adults. Figure 4 shows the average income structure of households consisting of adults ages 65 and older who live apart from their children. For the purposes of this chapter we will call such households an "aged household." On average, public pensions account

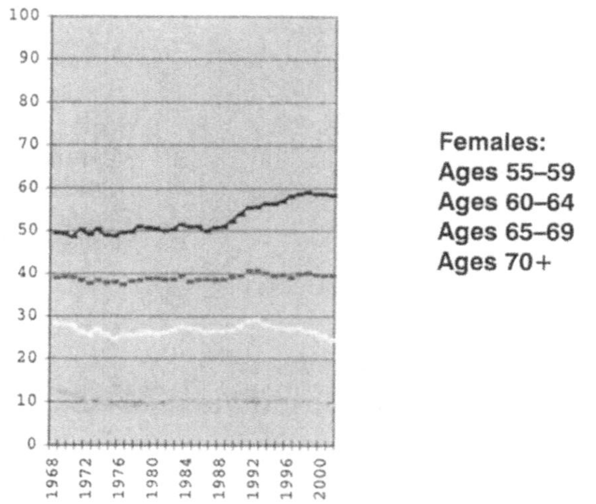

Figure 3. Labor-force participation rates of older Japanese women.
Source: Statistics Bureau, Ministry of Public Management, Home Affairs, Post and Telecommunications, Labor Party Survey (composite summary).

for 65 percent of aged households' total income; income from wages amounts to some 21 percent; and income from housing, land rent, and other assets, another 8 percent. Family transfers of wealth, private pensions, and other sources of income make up the remaining 4 percent. For 60 percent of aged households, public pensions are their only source of income.[1] As is pointed out elsewhere in this book, unlike some other countries, Japanese elders do not receive a significant portion of the income they spend on daily living from private pensions nor from income transfers from children.[2]

When average household income is compared by the age of the head of the household, the per capita income level of the aged household is lower than

[1] According to the Ministry of Welfare, Labor, and Health's *Comprehensive Survey of the Living Conditions of People on Health and Welfare,* as of 2001, 72 percent of aged households relied on their public pensions for more than 80 percent of their income.

[2] The 2001 *FISLCSC* surveyed older adults ages 60 and older, and asked respondents to list the sources of all income that the family depended on to cover daily expenses. Family transfers of wealth comprised a larger part of elders' income in South Korea than in Japan, and private pensions comprised a larger part of the income of U.S. elders. Some 39 percent of Americans, 11.1 percent of Japanese, and 1 percent of Koreans earned income from private pensions; conversely, 59 percent of Koreans, 12 percent of Japanese, and 3 percent of Americans received income from their relatives. Furthermore, 86 percent of the Americans, 85 percent of the Japanese, and 10 percent of the Koreans received income from public pensions.

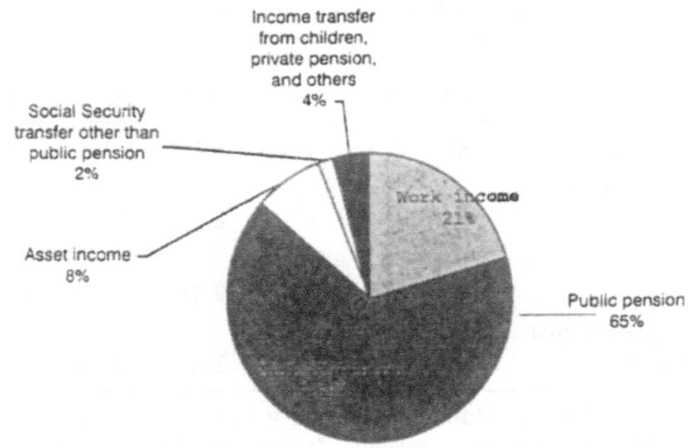

Note: Aged households are households consisting solely of individuals ages 65 and older. Aged households containing unmarried youth younger than age 19 are also included in this figure.

Figure 4. Household income construction of aged households.
Source: Ministry of Welfare, Labor, and Health, 2001.

that of households headed by people in their 50s—but higher than that of households headed by people in their 30s and 40s (Table 1). Therefore, the living condition of Japanese elders can be considered as being rather good quality. In fact, as shown in the lower part of Table 1, less than 20 percent of people living in aged households perceive daily life as "very difficult," which is lower than the same figure for members of households headed by people in the prime working ages.

Not too surprisingly, however, income distribution becomes more skewed with increasing age. This fact is evident in the increase in the Gini coefficient (measure of income inequality), which is 0.440 for household heads in the 70–79 age group as compared to 0.272 for household heads in the 30–39 age range (Quality of Life Policy Bureau, Cabinet Office, 2002).

Cross-national comparative research confirms this general pattern. Shirahase (2002) conducted a comparison of income distribution among households in the United Kingdom, United States, Sweden, Taiwan, and Japan, and pointed out that for Japanese and Taiwanese households, income distribution as evidenced by Gini coefficients become markedly unequal as the age of the head of the household increases. At the same time, such a pattern did not appear to hold for the United States, United Kingdom, and Sweden—suggesting that either financial hardships or insufficient accumulation of assets are relatively more common among the elderly in the two Asian nations than in the other three countries.

Table 1. Annual Household Income by Age of Head of Household

Age	<29	30-39	40-49	50-59	60-69	70+	65 and older
Average income (¥1,000)	3,331	5,565	7,347	8,239	5,775	4,620	4,796
Average disposable income (¥1,000)	2,818	4,703	6,111	6,691	4,791	3,942	4,120
Per capita disposable income (¥1,000)	1,726	1,734	2,008	2,615	2,172	1,894	1,935
Percentage of those who feel that daily life is "difficult"[a]	17.6%	20.0%	23.5%	22.2%	20.0%	16.5%	16.7%

[a]Survey respondents' answers to the question "Does your household consider daily life to be "very difficult," "rather difficult," "ordinary," "rather good," or "very good"?
Source: Ministry of Welfare, Labor, and Health, 2001.

Financial Assets

Table 2 shows the average financial assets and loans held by Japanese households, broken down by age of household head. As the table makes clear, financial assets increase with age. Aged households have an average of more than ¥10 million[3] in assets, and only 15 percent or so of all aged households carry outstanding loans. In comparison, half of households headed by people in their 40s and 50s have financial loans, which can be attributed to housing loans and educational costs for children. It should be mentioned, however, that although the average level of assets held by the elderly is rather high in Japan, one in three aged households has financial assets of less than ¥3 million.[4]

Severance payments, which are usually given by private firms and government agencies to employees on their retirement, have a major impact on reducing loan balances and increasing financial assets in later life. As revealed by the findings of the Central Labor Committee's Severance Pay, Pension, and Mandatory Retirement Survey of 2001, which surveyed large firms, such payments can be quite substantial.[5] The average amount of severance disbursement for employees who quit voluntarily was roughly ¥ 4.8 million for workers who had been with the company for 20 years and ¥14.7 million for employees with 30 years of service. These amounts are much lower, but still significant, at medium-size and smaller firms: ¥3.23 million for 20 years and ¥7.3 million for

[3] As of May 2004, ¥1 million = US$9,134.

[4] Comparable figures are 86 percent for household heads in the 20–29 age group, 53 percent for those ages 30–39, 46 percent for those ages 40–49, 36 percent for those ages 50–79, and 39 percent for those ages 80 and older.

[5] Firms with more than 1,000 employees or with capital larger than ¥0.5 billion were surveyed.

Table 2. Financial Assets and Loans by Age of Household Head

Age	Total	<29	30-39	40-49	50-59	60-69	70+	65 and older
Average savings per household (¥1,000)	9,265	1,370	4,090	6,604	1,075	12,547	12,257	11,951
Percentage who have no savings	8.2	15.6	8.0	6.9	7.0	8.1	8.8	8.7
Percentage who have some savings	88.1	82.1	89.7	90.0	89.8	87.7	86.2	86.5
Average loans per household (¥1,000)	4,852	1,486	6,421	8,584	5,516	3,750	2,169	2,.581
Percentage who have no loans	61.1	78.6	56.8	43.3	49.9	69.0	77.1	75.1
Percentage who have some loans	32.5	17.7	39.8	52.5	44.9	22.8	12.9	15.3

Source: Ministry of Welfare, Labor, and Health, 2001.

30 years, according to the Tokyo Metropolitan Government's 2002 Survey on Wage and Retirement of Small and Medium-Sized Firms.[6] It should also be noted that the amount of the severance payment is generally much lower for individuals retiring from firms with fewer than 30 employees or with tenures of less than a decade.

Housing Assets

The percentage of households that own their own housing also increases with age. In general, home ownership is higher in rural areas and lower in large cities, where land prices are astronomically high. Nearly 70 percent of urban households headed by people ages 70 and older—and 82 percent of all households with household heads in this age group—own their own homes (Figure 5). When the monetary value of housing is calculated according to the official price of the land, 13 percent of elderly homeowners own homes worth less than ¥5 million, about half of this cohort own housing worth ¥5 million to ¥30 million, and the rest own homes valued at more than ¥30 million (Ministry of Welfare, Labor, and Health, 2001). It is clear that many elderly, who purchased housing earlier in their lives, have benefitted from the increases in the value of their assets that high economic growth across Japan has engineered.

[6] Firms with less than 300 employees in Tokyo metropolitan area were surveyed.

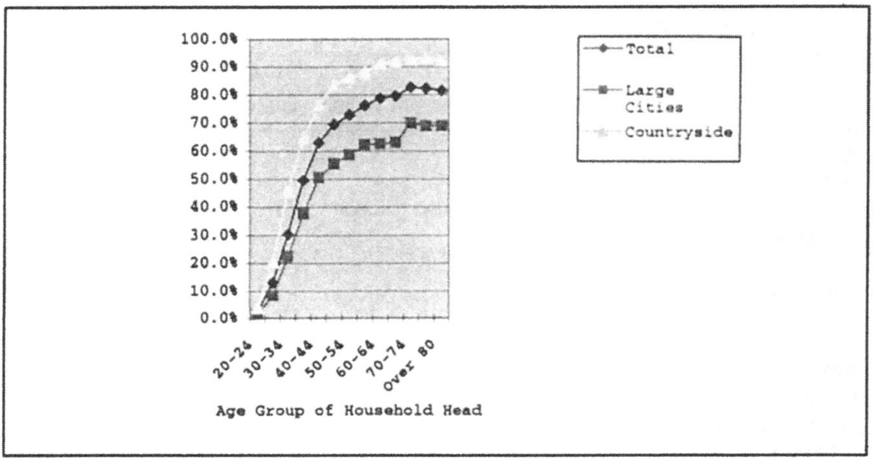

Figure 5. Percent of population who own their own homes, by age of household head.
Source: Ministry of Welfare, Labor, and Health, 2001.

The Quality of Life Policy Bureau's 2001 *White Paper on National Lifestyle* pointed out that the net financial assets of households with heads in the 60–69 age group increased during the 1990s, from an average of ¥15 million in 1989 to approximately ¥19 million in 1999. However, the net financial assets of households headed by people in their working years, especially those in their 30s and 40s, showed a decline. The author would attribute such a falling off to a combination of factors. The economic recession and the deteriorating working conditions that ensued in the late 1990s caused workers' income levels to stagnate. At exactly the same time as wages were standing still, higher premiums for social security insurance were imposed on the working-age population in order to underwrite relative increases in public pension benefits provided to the elderly. Additionally, a spike in housing prices in the late 1980s, followed by a plunge in 1990 and torpid land prices thereafter, left many young households with home loans larger than the asset value of their houses. Many of these households found themselves in a deficit situation because they purchased their homes during the boom only to see the value of their dwellings erode from under them. On the other hand, older households had accumulated more assets in the past decade, partly because of reasonably favorable public pension benefits and relatively good severance payments. Also, their assets have had sufficient time to appreciate, and any paper losses incurred during the 1990s left asset values greater than the purchase price of years previously.

Family Resources

The picture painted above, however, does not reveal the overall economic status of the aged, as it only focuses on the economic status of independent aged households and not on that of older adults living with their families. As several of the chapters in this volume point out, coresidency is still commonplace throughout Asia, even though it has been in decline for the past two decades or so.

As can be discerned in Table 3, over the past 20 years a quiet but far-reaching change has taken place in the family life of the aged. In 1985, nearly half of all households with one or more members over the age of 65 were considered "extended families," which means a complex household composed of married adults, their offspring, and their aging parents. In 2001, the proportion of extended families among all households with an older member declined to just one in four. Households consisting solely of an aged couple increased from just fewer than 20 percent to nearly 30 percent of all households with an older member, and the percentage of older adults living alone also increased.

Such a massive shift is partly a result of sociocultural changes but also is fueled by a general increase in pension benefits of retired men. Table 4 shows that in 1983, as much as 40 percent of women ages 65–69 reported being dependent on their children's income, but this figure declined to 24 percent just nine years later. Instead, in 1992, 40 percent of women in this age group replied that they depended on their husband's income (Nagase, 1999). Since the labor-force participation of older men was on the decrease, this figure means that more husbands had sufficient incomes from their pensions to support their wives. It might also be possible that children's contribution to the financial well-being of their aging parents gradually shifted during these years from direct monetary transfers within the family to national transfers through the public pension scheme.

Table 3. Households with One or More Members Age 65 or Older

Year	One-person household (%)	Married couple living alone (%)			Parents living with unmarried children (%)	Extended family of three generations (%)	Other (%)	Households consisting solely of members ages 65+
		Total	Only one age 65+	Both age 65+				
1985	12.0	19.1	8.5	10.6	10.8	45.9	12.2	23.1
1995	17.3	24.2	8.1	16.1	12.9	33.3	12.2	34.4
2000	19.7	27.1	8.0	19.1	14.5	26.5	12.3	39.9
2001	19.4	27.8	7.9	19.9	15.7	25.5	11.6	40.5

Source: Ministry of Welfare, Labor, and Health, 2001.

Table 4. Primary Income Earner and Household Size of Older Japanese Women, 1983 versus 1992

	Ages 55–59		Ages 60–64		Ages 65–69	
	1983	1992	1983	1992	1983	1992
Primarily self-sufficient	22.4	21.1	19.7	20.4	18.9	22.6
Primarily dependent on husband	58.3	65.9	44.0	58.8	31.0	42.8
Primarily dependent on children	13.0	6.3	27.8	12.9	41.5	24.2
Household size						
One	8.7	6.3	10.8	9.2	13.8	13.6
Two	31.7	32.9	33.4	38.7	25.8	34.3
Three	22.0	28.3	14.1	20.1	11.5	12.7
Four or more	37.6	32.5	41.8	32.1	48.9	39.5

Source: Nagase, 1999.

As is apparent throughout this volume, rapid social change is making itself felt across Asia. Traditionally, many older adults could be found coresiding with their adult children. However, changes in the country's industrial structure, increases in public pension benefits, and changes in family structure have interdependently affected not only the propensity to retire but also residency after retirement.

In light of these trends it is fair to ask: Is the tradition of extended families diminishing in Japan? The evidence suggests that many fewer women start their married lives amid their husband's extended family than was previously the case. *The Fourth National Survey on Household Changes,* which the National Institute of Population and Social Security Research conducted in 1999, suggests that only 16 percent of men in their late 30s who formed families live in their parental home. This figure could be interpreted to represent young couples raising their children in the traditional extended-family style.

However, when older adults become fragile, they are more likely to live with their children. Table 5 implies that we can infer from cross-sectional survey data that the number of households with four or more members increases when the age of the oldest member exceeds 80. According to the survey, the cultural preference to live with the "first boy in the family" seems to remain among this cohort: Around 60 percent of older adults who list themselves as coresidents live with their oldest son. The survey report also indicates that health issues have a great deal to do with the decision to reside with one's children. In fact, 32 percent of the elderly age 85 or older who are still residing outside of institutions express a need for supplemental assistance with the activities of daily life or even more intensive assistance, and accordingly, live with adult

Table 5. Aging-Related Changes in Coresidence with Family

	Ages 65–69 (%)		Ages 75–79 (%)		Ages 85+ (%)	
Household size	Male	Female	Male	Female	Male	Female
One	5.1	14.4	5.8	20.6	5.2	15.2
Two	47.2	44.8	43.8	29.2	24.7	14.0
Three	22.5	16.2	13.7	11.9	22.1	27.0
Four or more	25.2	24.6	36.7	38.3	48.0	43.8

Source: National Institute of Population and Social Security Research, 1999.

children. Even so, there are also signs that more and more widows are living on their own well into old age. As shown in Table 5, 20 percent of women in their late 70s currently live alone. A generation ago, this would have been an extraordinary figure.

Figure 6 depicts not only coresidence patterns amid the population ages 65 and older but also residency close by children. These data show that about 52 percent of individuals over the age of 65 live with their children and another 13 percent live near their children; only 24 percent of the aged live some distance away from their children or have no children. Though the figure for coresidence was about 10 percentage points higher a decade ago, a majority of older adults continue to live with *or near* their children. *FISLCSC* examined which child the older adult was living with, and found that 25 percent of older Japanese live with a married son, 8 percent live with a married daughter, and 20 percent live with unmarried children. Comparable figures were 28 percent, 4 percent, and 20 percent, respectively, in South Korea and 1 percent, 3 percent, and 11 percent in the United States.

Empirical studies have found that among the aged, financial need (as in low pension benefits), residency in rural areas, and engagement in certain occupations (such as running a family business) increase the probability of living in an extended family (Nagase and Takayama, 1997; Takayama and Arita, 1996). Of course the converse is true as well. One thing is certain, however; the face of the aging Japanese family is in the midst of change.

JAPAN'S PUBLIC PENSION SCHEME

As noted earlier in this chapter, public pensions constitute an important source of income for Japanese elderly. This section will describe the public pension system and its reforms as well as the distribution of actual benefits.

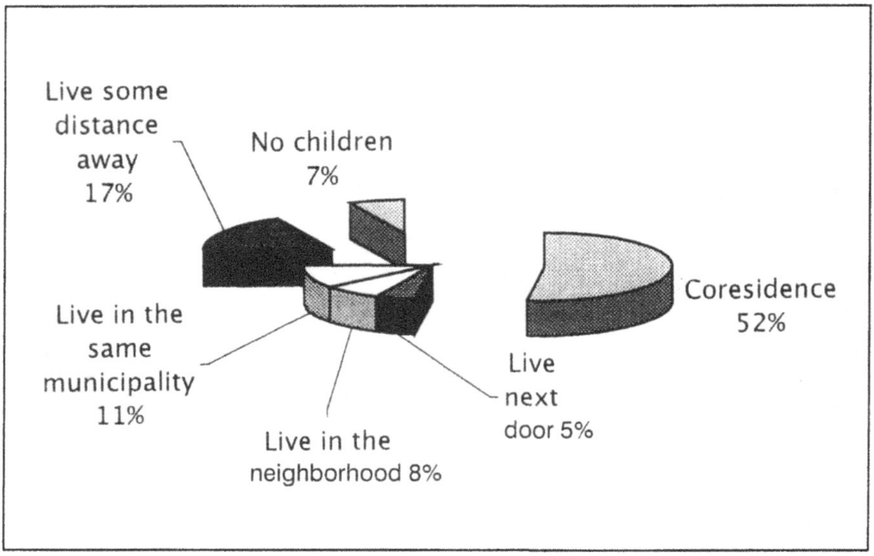

Figure 6. Distance that elderly ages 65 and older live from children.
Source: Ministry of Welfare, Labor, and Health, 2001.

At the time of this writing, sweeping reforms are being bandied about and likely as not the future may portend something different than is currently the case.

The Japanese public pension scheme for employees has an earnings-related portion based on wage or salaried work and a flat-rate portion based on years of participation in the system. Both categories of benefits are based on prorated contributions by employees and their employers, with the amount of pension benefits received by an individual reflecting his or her earnings history. Participants in the pension described (also called the Employees Pension) are called "Type Two" participants; about 50 percent of the working-age population is covered by this type of pension program (Figure 7). Another type of pension, the National Pension, is based on years of flat-rate contribution to the scheme. The National Pension covers all those ages 20–59 who are not salaried workers, such as the self-employed, part-time employees or many non-standard employees, the unemployed, and students; they are called "Type One" participants. About 30 percent of the working-age population is covered by this type of pension provision. "Type Three" participants represent a third category of pension-scheme participants: dependent spouses of Type Two participants, who are given the same flat-rate benefits as Type One participants. They consist of about 20 percent of the working-age population. The average level of retirement benefits offered by the Employees Pension is nearly twice as high as that offered by the National Pension.

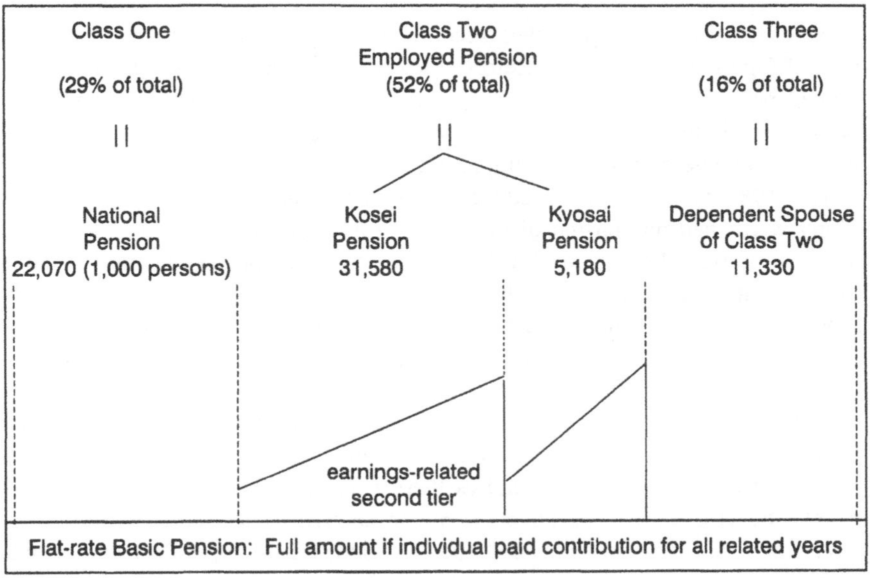

Figure 7. Public pension scheme.

Japan's public pension programs were initially operated independently by various occupational groups. For example, the Employees Pension scheme was established prior to World War II. The scheme is still divided into a "Kosei Pension" for employees from private firms and a "Kyosai (Mutual Aid) Pension" primarily for public-sector employees and schoolteachers. The National (Kokumin) Pension was first implemented in 1961 to ensure pension benefits for farmers and the self-employed, who made up nearly half the working population in those days. However, after the major pension reform of 1985, the National Pension, or so-called Basic Pension, has become the common first tier for all national pension-scheme participants.

This 1985 reform came about because of public recognition of population aging in Japan, projected budget deficits in the National Pension, the need for curtailment in future pension benefits, and the need for creating pensions for women. The reform, which was to take place over a 20-year period, consolidated isolated pension systems into one comprehensive scheme. Before 1985, the Employees Pension combined several covered-years-based benefits with an earnings-related benefit. The 1985 law ruled that the former was gradually to be reduced to the same level as the Basic Pension. Once the reform is fully implemented, all Japanese pension programs will have a common first tier, called the Basic Pension, with defined benefits yielding a flat pension annuity. If a worker were enrolled in the Employees Pension, that worker would also be eligible for the earnings-related second tier, as illustrated in the triangular area of Figure 7. The Pension Reform Law of 1985 also decreased the earnings-related pension multiplier from 10 per thousand yen of earned income to 7.5 per thousand, thus increasing the time required to qualify for a "model pension" from 30 to 40 years of covered employment.

The 1985 reform also introduced a unique pension plan for housewives. Many wives had no pension of their own or a modest one at best. The reform aimed to curtail the pension level of husbands [in employee insurance] while introducing a new pension in the name of their wives, realized by gradually reducing the yearly return of the employee's coverage-based pension benefit—therefore, explained the government, the total amount of the household's pension benefits would be unaffected.

The reform, however, had different repercussions for single-income and double-income households. In essence, it resulted in a direct reduction of benefits received relative to premiums paid as these households would not be in line to receive benefits earmarked for a dependent spouse. This aspect of the reform gave full Basic Pension rights to dependent spouses of Type Two participants without assessing the spouses nor husbands any additional premiums. The premiums for dependent spouses are now underwritten by the Type Two participants as a group.

Unfortunately, the new housewife's (Type Three) pension encourages housewives to remain reliant on their husbands. Paradoxically, if housewives earned above minimal wages, they would not have to pay the full premium but would be provided only a small-second tier pension based on their own employment history. Though the reform did increase the average pension benefit that the average woman was entitled to receive, the system produced heated discussion in later years when both the number of married women who work and the number of women who have remained single increased.[7] Type Three participants account for about one third of women in the working-age population.

The reforms have also brought the design of the Survivor's Pension scheme to national attention. Under current provisions, widows have to choose to receive either the earnings-related portion of their own pension or the Survivor's Pension for their deceased husband. Because women tend to earn less than men and thus are entitled to lower pensions, 80 percent of widows abandon their own pension to receive their spouse's Survivor's Pension. Because many working women thus end up with the same pension level as they would have received had they remained out of the labor market during their

[7] A committee was organized under the Minister of Welfare, Labor, and Health to discuss such changes, publishing a committee report, *Change in the Lifestyle of Women and the Quest for New Scheme for Women's Pensions*, in 2001. There was strong disagreement within the committee, of which the author was a member, as to what a fair pension plan for women across Japan might be.

prime working years, the Survivor's Pension scheme is often criticized for encouraging women to remain dependent on their husbands rather than seek an independent income.[8]

Recent Changes to Public Pensions

A cluster of reforms in 1989, 1994, and 1999 came on the heels of the 1985 Pension Reform Law. These latter reforms primarily raised the age of eligibility for full pensions, adjusted pension benefits, and set out to encourage late-life employment among older workers. They also increased the wage contribution rate of the working population. Prior to the reforms, the threshold for full benefits under the Basic Pension was age 65, while eligibility for Employee Pensions was set at age 60. Following the reforms, both are now set at age 65 except for "grandfathering in" those individuals born in 1941 or later. For those who turned 60 in 2001, the earnings-related portion was still available at age 60. Age of eligibility will gradually shift upward to age 65; becoming 65 for men in 2025 and in 2030 for women. The multiplier for the earnings-based pension was again slightly reduced to further diminish the earnings-related pension. Starting in 2003, the base income used for calculating contributions will include bonus payments. The multiplier was reduced to 5.481 per thousand yen earned per year of enrollment, reflecting this change.

A number of the reforms have had the effect of encouraging older adults to continue to work. If an individual below the age of 65 was entitled to a Kosei Pension but worked in the private sector full time prior to 1989, his or her pension benefit would be taxed at 20, 50, 80, or 100 percent according to income level. The 1994 reform reduced the average rate at which pension benefits were reduced but extended the wage-based stepped-in reductions on workers who remained employed all the way to age 69. Traditionally, Social Security provisions in place in the United States provide a comparable step-change policy for earned incomes between legal retirement age and age 70.

The contribution rate for the working population has risen rapidly in recent years (Table 6). The table also shows that as of 2003 the full benefit per person for the National Pension is ¥67,017 per month and the "model pension plan" for the Kosei Pension—a benchmark set by the national government—is ¥238,150 per month for a couple. The benchmark household for

[8] Upon the death of their spouses, wives of salaried workers have the right to receive the Survivor's Pension. However, if the wife had her own earnings-related pension, she would have to choose between that pension or her husband's Survivor's Pension. Critics of the Japanese pension system cite this policy as another sign that the system favors nonworking wives. The 1994 pension-law reform added a third option for widows of salaried workers: They may elect to receive half of their own earnings-related pension plus half of their spouse's Survivor's Pension. However, because many women are only entitled to a small earnings-related pension, 80 percent of widows choose the Survivor's Pension and renounce their claim to their earnings-related pension.

Table 6. Pension Contributions and Model Benefits for Selected Years

	Contribution per month		Model benefits per month	
Year	Flat rate contribution for national pension (¥)	Earnings-related contribution for employee pension (%)	National old-age pension (¥ per person)	Employees "Model Pension" (¥ per couple)[a]
1989	8,000	12.4 (11.9)[b]	55,500	197,400
1994	11,100	14.5	65,000	230,983
1998	13,300	17.35	66,625	236,758
1999	13,300	17.35	67,017	238,150
2003	13,300	13.58[c]	67,017	238,150

[a]The model pension for 2003 consists of husband's earnings-related pension of ¥104,092 and basic pension of ¥ 67,017 per person for husband and wife.

[b]Percentage in parentheses represents women.

[c]From April 2003 on, the base wage used to calculated premium payment will include bonus payment on full basis, and the decline in percentage does not mean decline in real term.

Source: Ministry of Welfare, Labor, and Health, 2002.

which the value of the model pension is calculated consists of a male worker with 40 years experience[9] who was paid at a mean wage level and lives with his dependent wife. The ¥238,150 figure is broken down into ¥104,092 from the earnings-related portion of the husband's pension, ¥67,017 from the husband's Basic Pension, and the same amount from the wife's Basic Pension (see footnote, Table 6). The replacement rate of the model pension is 59 percent of the disposable income of male workers (Ministry of Welfare, Labor, and Health, 2002). The Ministry of Welfare, Labor, and Health estimates that this model pension will cover most of the average daily expenses of a household consisting of a nonworking husband over the age of 65 and a wife over the age of 60; its figures come from the findings of the national Statistics Office's 2001 National Expenditure Survey. Using the same data, the ministry also estimates that a full Basic Pension for a couple covers basic daily expenses for food, shelter, utilities, clothing, and medicine (Ministry of Welfare, Labor, and Health, 2003).

[9]Individuals born before 1941 need less than 40 years to qualify for full pension. For example, individuals born in 1931 need to have contributed to the pension for only 30 years, since they were already 30 when the National Pension began.

Distribution of Public Pension Benefits

Do many households receive the pension level described in the "model pension"? Actual years of enrollment in the Kosei Pension vary for persons due to longer attendance in school, periods of unemployment, and changes in occupation that result in changes in the pension program in which they are enrolled.

Table 7 shows the average level of old-age pensions, granted in 2001 for those who had worked in covered occupational areas for at least 20 years. This data includes only those receiving benefits under the Kosei Pension.[10] On average, the men who are entitled to the Kosei Pension are found to receive benefits a little above the model pension. The combined benefits of the Kosei Pension and the Basic Pension total ¥196,746, which is slightly higher than the model pension as calculated by adding the husband's earnings-related plus his Basic Pension (but excluding the housewife's pension). Retired women received significantly less, an average of ¥106,000 per month.

Obviously, not all workers have the mandated 20-year work history and will therefore receive a reduced benefit. Table 8 shows the distribution of the years of coverage for Kosei Pension recipients, broken down by gender, and includes men and women who have been covered for fewer than 20 years. Table 8 clearly demonstrates that more than 40 percent of women and 22 percent of men were enrolled in the Kosei Pension scheme for fewer than 10 years. By contrast,

Table 7. Average Amount of Pension That Started Paying Benefits in 2001

	Monthly pension (¥)	
Kosei old-age pension only with second tier	Male	104,643
	Female	55,223
Kosei old-age pension with first tier	Male	196,746
	Female	106,226
National old-age pension		53,515

Source: Social Insurance Agency, 2003.

[10]The amount paid to those in the second tier in Table 7 is very close to the earnings-related portion for the model pension plan as described in the text.

Table 8. Number of Years Subscribed in Kosei Pension Scheme as of 1998

	Male (%)	Female (%)
Up to 10 years	22	43
10 to 20 years	14	32
20 to 30 years	18	20
30 to 40 years	30	5
40 years and more	16	1
Total	100	100

Source: Social Insurance Agency, 2001.

46 percent of men—but only 6 percent of women—had enrolled in the plan for more than 30 years. The number of years of coverage, combined with relative earnings history, produces a significant gender gap in pension benefits received by Japanese men and women.

Table 7 also shows that the average Basic Pension benefit is around ¥53,000 per month, lower than the full benefit of ¥67,000. This discrepancy is due to early receipt of benefits or because of a shortfall in the number of years enrolled. Some 27 percent of all new recipients of the Basic Pension in 2001 applied for an early pension; one becomes eligible for early benefits at age 60. As is apparent, average pensions received per household are reduced for claimants entitled to just the National Pension benefit and among those who live alone.

Table 9 shows total accrued public pension benefits by age and sex, and includes Kosei, Kyosai, and National pensions. The table suggests that a substantial portion of the population ages 60 to 64— more than 40 percent of men and nearly 60 percent of women—did not receive a pension at that age.[11] Most received some public pension only after turning 65.

Figure 8 shows the pension benefits received by adults ages 70–74. Some 46 percent of men in this age group receive more than ¥2 million a year, comparable to or more than the male portion of the model pension. Women received much less: Only 10 percent of women in this age group collect more than ¥2 million per year in pension benefits.

[11]The standard age for full benefits under the National Pension (primarily for the self-employed or housewives) is 65, although the standard age for the Employees Pension had been age 60. Because individuals can get a lump-sum payment reflecting foregone years during which they were entitled to coverage at the time of their retirement, Abe (1998) assumes that some of those who have enough earnings defer applying for the pension.

Table 9. Annual Total Pension Receipt by Age Group and Gender

Income (¥1000)	60 to 64		65 to 69		70 to 74		75 to 79	
	Male %	Female %	Male %	Female %	Male %	Female %	Male %	Female %
Up to 400	5	11	2	9	1	9	4	11
400 to 800	9	11	10	26	11	27	18	31
800 to 1200	5	8	11	22	14	22	10	13
1200 to 1800	8	6	13	12	14	12	10	12
1800 to 2000	4	2	5	2	4	3	5	3
2000 to 2500	9	2	14	3	10	4	9	6
2500 to 3000	10	1	14	2	12	3	11	2
More than 3000	7	0	17	1	24	3	23	2
No pension benefit	44	59	13	23	9	17	19	21
	100	100	100	100	100	100	100	100

Source: Ministry of Welfare, Labor, and Health, 2001.

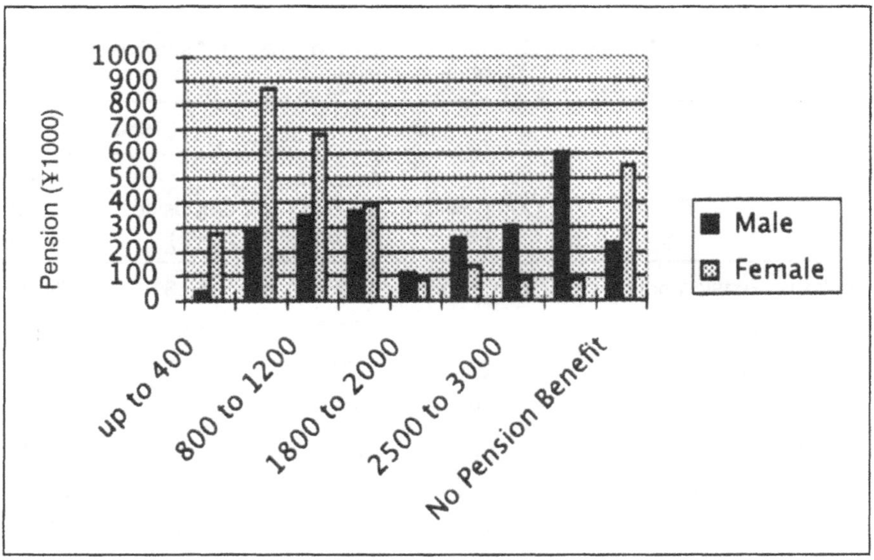

Figure 8. Total annual public pension receipt by gender, 70- to 74-year-old age group.
Source: Ministry of Welfare, Labor, and Health, 2001.

On average, women receive significantly lower annuity levels under public pensions than men. Many are eligible for no more than the first tier of benefits, about ¥400,000–¥800,000 per year.

Table 10 compares types of pensions received by women ages 65–69 in 1983 and 1992, and reveals a great deal about the work histories of Japanese women. More than 50 percent of older women in 1992 were only eligible for the National Pension, presumably because many had spent their working years as housewives or as unsalaried workers in family businesses. Reflecting the increasing numbers of women working in formal paid employment, however, the percentage of women ages 65–69 who were entitled to the Kosei Pension increased between 1983 and 1992. About 10 percent of the women surveyed in 1992 were eligible for more than two kinds of pensions, due to changes in occupation and intermittent work behavior. The respondents who were entitled to the Kyosai Pension—teachers, nurses, and those who had primarily been employees of local government agencies—collected the largest pensions. The difference in pension value may be explained by the fact that women employed in local government remain in their jobs longer than women working for private firms. In addition, the gender gap in public-sector wages is considerably smaller, so that women in the public sector accumulate greater lifetime earnings and are consequently entitled to larger pension benefits than those employed in the private sector.

Table 10. Monthly Public Pension Receipt of Women Ages 65–69, by Pension Group

	1992		1983	
	Composition (%)	Average receipt (¥1,000)	Composition (%)	Average receipt (¥1,000)
National Pension only	51.3	37.3	55.3	24.2
Kosei only	21.7	91.3	13.3	59.6
Kyosai only	3.8	171.1	3.7	107.9
National and Kosei	9	87.6	8.6	58.5
National and Kyosai	2	122.2	1.8	97.3
Kosei and Kyosai	1.6	151.7	1.2	120.6
National, Kyosai, and Kosei	0.6	135.3	0.4	133.1
Receiving no public pension	11.6	—	16.7	—

Note: The 65–69 age group was examined since 65 years of age is the standard eligibility age for the National Pension.

Source: Nagase, 1999.

When the above data were scrutinized, Nagase (1999) found that even among those who had been paid employees at age 55—roughly 30 percent of the women surveyed in 1983—approximately 40 percent were eligible for the Kosei Pension. The remaining 60 percent must have lacked Kosei coverage because they had worked part time or had been employed by small enterprises in uncovered occupations or situations.

THE RETIREMENT DECISION AND THE PUBLIC PENSION SYSTEM

The ways in which Japan's pension schemes affect worker behavior has interested many labor economists. As is apparent in Figure 2, labor-force participation rates of older men demonstrated a declining trend over time, followed by a moderate and brief increase before turning downward again. Empirical efforts have estimated the negative effect of the increase in the value of pensions on the retirement decision: as benefits increase rates of retirement also increase. However, researchers have found it difficult to ascribe the recent rise and drop in labor--force participation rates to changes in pension schemes. Similar studies have also focused on labor-supply responses to changes in the pension scheme, especially the curtailment of pensions for older adults who continue to earn work-related income. Again, however, the methodology and the findings are challenging.

Seike (1986, 1989) showed that some older salaried workers were intentionally restricting their monthly incomes so they would not reduce the amount of pension benefits they received. Seike used entitlement levels in place of actual pension receipts to measure the impact of the public pension on older workers' decision to retire. While there may be some challenges to his methodology and the parameters he established concerning elasticity in benefits claimed, his results suggest that among male claimants in the 60–64 age interval there may be a 0.20 percent–0.25 percent underreporting of wages earned in order to ensure maximum benefits received. Other empirical investigations (Shimono and Tachibanaki, 1984; Takayama and Arita, 1996) estimated elasticity approximately the same as that reported by Seike. These latter analyses also suggest that the earnings test has a greater impact on benefits received among men in the 65–69 age group.

Responding to proposals put forth by the National Social Security Council in 1989 and 1994, the National Diet passed consecutive reforms that ameliorated the discouraging effect of the earnings test on older-worker employment.[12]

[12]The earnings test and curtailment of pension were rather stringent before the 1989 reform. If an individual earned more than ¥95,000 a month between the ages of 60 and 64, his or her Kosei Pension benefit would be cut by 50 percent. As workers' earnings rise, the cut in pension increases incrementally, reaching 100 percent for individuals who earned more than ¥150,000 per month. After the 1994 reform, individuals earning less than ¥360,000 per month would only see their pension cut by about 50 percent. Those earning less than ¥95,000 on a monthly basis will now only experience a 20 percent cut.

Abe (1998) measured the effect of the 1989 reform on the labor supply of older workers in Japan to verify whether the pension reform actually caused the increase observed in their labor-force participation rates. She concluded, however, that the trend started before the reforms of 1989. Ogawa (1997, 1998a, 1998b) conducted a comparable estimation using different variables and parameters, but he, too, concluded that the reform did not have much effect. Ogawa's research found that the higher percentage of elderly living with unmarried children as well as benefit reductions per years of covered employment were supply-side reasons contributing to the rise in employment rates among older Japanese.

Other factors contributing to increases in labor-force participation rates among this cohort came from the demand side: a high demand for labor during the economic boom of the late 1980s and early 1990s and the increase in the mandatory retirement age.

Some economists cast earnings tests for the pension benefits as a penalty for working. A number of research studies, however, offer a divergent interpretation. Tachibanaki and Shimono (1994) noted that companies were able to use this earnings test to their advantage to employ older adults at such low monthly wages, less than ¥95,000. Because higher wages would result in reductions to their pension benefits, older workers were willing to work at lower wages than their younger counterparts.

Ogawa (1997, 1998a, 1998b) referred to the earnings test pension-reduction provisions for workers who remain in the labor force as an employment subsidy that directly benefitted employers and indirectly benefitted employees by creating a market for older workers' labor even if at reduced wages. Before the 1994 reform, pension annuities after the earnings test (or "subsidy" as Ogawa labeled it) were greatest when workers earned no more than ¥95,000 and dropped to zero if they earned more than ¥250,000 in monthly wages. Following the 1994 reforms, the maximum return on the subsidy remains at ¥95,000, but the upper cap has now increased to ¥360,000. In effect, the subsidy is highest for those earning reduced salaries yet receiving relatively high pension benefits. Ogawa concluded that the structure of the existing pension benefits strongly encouraged men to work at low wages.

In contrast, Ohishi (2000) examined health status as an important factor in older adults' labor-force participation decisions. She concluded that health status as well as income has a decisive impact on labor-force participation among older men. Ohishi also pointed out, however, that health conditions are a function of lifetime incomes, so the two remain connected in the retirement decision-making process much as they do in Western countries.

Significantly fewer studies have focused on pension benefits received by women or the impact of the pension program on their daily lives. Mikami (1983) and Shimono and Tachibanaki (1984) conducted some of the earliest research examining women in retirement, followed by Nagase and Takayama (1997) and Nagase (1997, 1999). Nagase and Takayama (1997) suggested that among older women, the decision to work is affected by household characteristics: A woman living alone was likely to make different decisions than one who lived in a two-person household. The same could be said of women living in households of more than three persons. Women living alone made work-related decisions that approximated those made by men. Women living in two-person households seemed to bear most of the burden of housework, and their prime activities were housework even at very old ages. Furthermore, women in larger households, who were possibly members of an extended family, were found to spend more time in leisure pursuits and other nonwork activities but less time doing housework compared to older women living in two-person households.

Using the same data as Seike (1989), Nagase (1999) found that pension benefits had a greater effect on women's decision to retire than on men's decision making about retirement, presumably because many elderly women also bear responsibilities for household maintenance. What effect would transfer of the husband's pension entitlement to the wife—as in the newly created housewife's pension—have on women's activities? Using estimated coefficients, earlier retirement was forecast for working women. However, since 74 percent of women with no salaried experience at age 55 (mostly housewives or unpaid workers in family businesses) were mainly doing housework at "retirement" age, the impact of an increase in pension level among this population was small. Yet a rise in their own pension entitlements while keeping household pension level the same was found to slightly increase leisure activities among nonworking women.

OLDER ADULTS' ATTITUDES ABOUT WORK

This chapter has not yet explained the high labor-force participation rates of Japanese men. In the author's opinion, three reasons not attributable to economic considerations account for this phenomenon: They are the attitudes of Japanese men toward work, high marriage rates among older Japanese, and the traditional division of labor between married partners.

Comparing countries using *FISLCSC* data, more Japanese elders ages 60 and older work than in four other countries examined. *FISLCSC* respondents were asked why they wanted or did not want to work. The proportion of those who reported working because they want to earn income was highest in South Korea, at 64 percent, as compared to 28 percent of U.S. elders and around 40 percent of those in other countries. For Koreans, participation in the labor force may indicate the necessity for income.

On the other hand, among elders who did not work and do not want to work, more than 50 percent of Swedish and American respondents and 35 percent of German respondents stated that they do not work "because I have other things I like to do." A significantly lower proportion of Japanese elders—16 percent of nonworking respondents—chose that option. Forty percent of nonworking

Japanese elders and 73 percent of nonworking Korean elders chose the option "because my health does not permit it."[13]

What reasons other than income necessity encouraged the elderly to work? The proportion of respondents who worked and would like to continue working "because it is good for my health or because it helps me to slow down my aging"[14] was the reason cited most frequently by the Japanese, 29 percent of whom selected this option. Comparable figures for older workers in other countries were less than 20 percent. Even among those not currently employed, a comparable attitude seems to underlie Japanese male's decision to work. In Western countries, actual labor-force participation rates among older adults were lower, and they worked only when they found work intrinsically enjoyable. Some 40 percent of these older adults chose to work "because I enjoy working or [because] it gives me vitality"; the comparable figure in Japan was 20 percent.

It seems that for Japanese males, having to work is regarded as a good routine. The belief that work is good for one's health also may have something to do with the rather clear division of labor between the sexes in Japan. To illustrate: According to the 2001 Survey on Time Use and Leisure Activities, among elders in the 65–74 age group, men did 32 minutes of housework a day, an increase of merely 13 minutes compared to full-time working men in their prime ages. Women ages 65–74, however, did 3 hours 43 minutes of housework a day (Statistics Office, Ministry of Public Management, Home Affairs, Posts and Telecommunications, 2003). This gap is outstanding compared to that observed in other countries. Because housework is not shared equitably between the sexes, paid work may give the husband some sort of daily routine and may also signify that the husband is shouldering his fair share of the couple's labor. The FISLCSC also asked who primarily did the housework in the respondents' household. Only 8 percent of male respondents in Japan claimed that they did and 8 percent claimed the tasks were shared by husband and wife. These figures were 33 percent and 15 percent, respectively, in the United States, 24 percent and 21 percent in Germany, 29 percent and 20 percent in Sweden, and 9 percent and 6 percent in South Korea. Only in South Korea were older men as unlikely as Japanese men to share housework responsibilities.

The reticence of Japanese men to share household responsibilities is captured by the derisive term "wet leaf" to refer to men who are virtually useless as far as any productive household purpose is concerned. Though clearly a bit of slang

[13]The *FISLCSC* surveyed older adults regarding the main reason they did not want to work. Participants could choose from among the following responses: "Because I have other things that I like to do"; "Because my health does not permit it"; "Because I can't find a suitable job"; and "Other."

[14]The *FISLCSC* asked survey participants who worked the main reason they wanted to continue to work. There were five possible responses: "Because I want an income"; "Because I enjoy working/because it gives me vitality"; "Because I can make friends"; "Because it is good for my health/because it helps me to slow down my aging"; and "Other."

that originated on a television show, it does resonate with the *FISLCSC* data that suggests an extended working life for Japanese men is desirable as it is one acceptable means of productivity.

This interpretation of the *FISLCSC* data also may be supported by a cross-country comparison of the respondents' marital status. Among men in the 70–74 age interval, 92 percent of Japanese respondents were married, compared to 83 percent in South Korea, 74 percent in Germany, and 65 percent in the United States and Sweden. Such a difference may be attributed to two factors: the lower mortality rate among Japanese men and the lower divorce rate among Japanese elders.[15] The fact that the marriage rates are nigh universal in Japan may contribute to creating an arena wherein strongly gendered divisions of labor predominate.

THE ECONOMIC STATUS OF THE AGED IN FUTURE YEARS

Japan's rapid economic growth and its shifting industrial structure have brought numerous changes to the lives of Japanese elders. The labor-force participation rates of older men have declined, although such rates remain high compared to their counterparts in Western countries. At the time of this writing, the ratio of self-employment to salaried employment remains moderately high in Japan—but the percentage has declined to around one in four for men in the 60–64 age group. Prior to Japan's economic takeoff, many more men over the age of 60 either had worked in the informal sector or were self-employed in small-scale operations. In fact, when comparing Japan's overall distribution of self-employed to salaried workers over the age of 60, Japan's aggregated 33 percent rate is described as medium high in comparison to other *FISLCSC* reporting countries. That figure has been more or less stable since at least 1990. Comparable figures are much lower in the United States (13 percent), Germany (12 percent), and Sweden (10 percent). However, the self-employment ratio is much higher in South Korea, at 61 percent. It is reasonable to assume these figures reflect relative levels of industrialization and modernization in the economies of these same countries.

As a consequence of budget constraints, the national government has taken steps to alter the pension system prior to Japan's postwar baby boomers reaching retirement age. Pension benefits available to those between the ages of 60 and 64 will be partly reduced for those born after 1941, and the standard employee retirement age will be raised to age 65 in the 2013–2030 window of time. Furthermore, the Pension Reform Act of 2004 will have a significant effect.

[15]For men ages 70–74, the *FISLCSC* data show that in Japan, only 7 percent lost a spouse to death, 0 percent divorced, and 0 percent never married. In the United States, the comparable figures were 15.6 percent, 11 percent, and 6.4 percent, respectively. In Germany, they were 16.7 percent, 5.1 percent, and 3.8 percent; in Sweden, 9.1 percent, 13.6 percent, and 10.2 percent; in South Korea, 17.1 percent, 0 percent, and 0 percent.

A report by the Ministry of Welfare, Labor, and Health foresees a replacement ratio provided by the Kosei "Model Pension" to drop to around 50 percent. Whether the combined effect of these changes will actually keep older workers on the job will, to a sizable extent, depend on the demand for labor and the nature of that demand.

It is still the case that a large percentage of Japanese elders—although comparatively fewer than in the past—continue to live in extended families: In the 1980s, nearly half of all households with one or more members over the age of 65 were considered extended families. In the 1990s, this proportion declined to 25 percent. More and more, older adults live just with their spouses or by themselves. Interestingly, although coresidence with adult children is declining, proximity is not; many older Japanese live either with or very near their adult children. Patterns of intergenerational transfers of wealth and familial support are changing as well, and will continue to do so as a consequence of formal policy changes and economic shifts.

The overall economic status of Japanese elders is good. Eighty percent own their own homes, and the value of those homes has appreciated due to economic growth throughout the country. Estimates are that two out of three aged households have financial assets worth more than ¥3 million. Sixty percent of elderly households receive their sole income from public pensions and can live on this income without relying on their children to provide for their fiscal well-being. The "model" or benchmark pension as determined by the Japanese government is enough to cover most daily expenses, and a recent survey shows that about 40 percent of elderly households with household heads aged 70–74 receive pension benefits equal to or higher than the model pension. Although most older Japanese are able to lead a respectable life without needing economic assistance from their children, women without husbands do represent an exception. Not unlike in the West, such women tend to fall into the lowest income stratum and are at high risk of having incomes in the lowest 10th percentile. Because of the gender gap in wages and the tendency for women to work outside the home for fewer years than men—if they did at all—the pension benefit that older women receive is often low. In addition, many older women spent their prime earning years in informal and small enterprises with no entitlement to employee pensions, thus compounding their economic need in old age. Even women who never married have a tendency to have shorter working histories due to poorer employment opportunities or caregiving responsibilities for their own parents.

As far as women and pensions are concerned, the Pension Reform Act of 2004 permits "pension splitting" for couples divorcing after 2007. Though the rewritten scheme does not provide any particular advantage to working wives, it should lessen some of the financial strain facing older divorced women.

The newest quinquennial population projections for Japan released by the Social Security Council Population Committee (2002) predicted that in 2001 marriage and childbirth rates will continue to decline and life expectancy will continue to lengthen in the early decades of the 21st century. In the future, more women may spend longer periods of time in the workforce. At the same time, however, there will be more older men and women who have never married and who subsequently cannot rely on their families for resources—resources that many older Japanese depend on today. The medium-variant projection published by the committee estimates that 30 percent of women born in 1985 may not bear children. It also projects longer life expectancy for both sexes. Attaining age 90 may not be rare, especially for women, and these women will face a number of hurdles as they age.

Given these projections, policies that encourage older adults to build community networks and engage in voluntary activities such as caregiving and community service may receive greater emphasis. Also needed are policies that support women having children without losing their jobs. Since coresidence of older adults and adult children is on the decline, so too are elders' availability for child-rearing duties, and more childcare facilities will be needed. Such policies may not only benefit the well-being of young couples and children but also may help Japan's older adults. There are many voices in Japan advocating for an increase in social security benefits for children.

Japan can be considered a unique society in which generations brought up in different stages of industrialization live together simultaneously. Japanese over the age of 80 may share family values formed before World War II—values that place strong emphasis on traditional family structures and coresidence with direct descendants. Many of the oldest old were brought up on farms. Those in the 55–65 age interval were born during or after the war, and experienced heart-rending poverty as children and young adults. However, middle-aged Japanese experienced rapid economic growth during their childhood, and many of those under 30 have spent their entire lives in an affluent society. Japan's elderly citizens today enjoy both the newly constructed public pension system and also the remaining culture of living closely with descendants. On the whole, it can be said that they have good resources. However, those ages 80 and older might be wishing for even closer, more traditional ties with their children, while those newly entering retirement may aspire to have different relations with their children.

REFERENCES

Abe, Y. (1998). 1980–1990 nendai no dansei koreisha no rodo kyokyu to zaishoku rorei nenkin seido [Worker's pension scheme and the labor supply of males, 1980–1990]. *JCER Economic Journal.*

Cabinet Office of the Government. (2001). *The fifth international survey on the life and consciousness of senior citizens, 2001.* Tokyo: Gyosei.

Central Labor Committee. (2002). *Severance pay, pension, and mandatory retirement survey of 2001.* Tokyo: Roikyokai.

Mikami, F. (1983). Joshi koreisha no rodo kyokyu pattan [Elderly women's pattern of labor supply]. *The Quarterly of Social Security Research, 19*(2).

Ministry of Welfare, Labor, and Health. (2000). *Survey on the employment status of the elderly.* Tokyo: Zaimusho Insatsukyoku.

Ministry of Welfare, Labor, and Health. (2001). *Comprehensive survey on the living conditions of people regarding health and welfare.* Tokyo: Kosei Tokei Kyokai.

Ministry of Welfare, Labor, and Health. (2002). *Report to the National Social Security Council Pension Committee on July 19, 2002* (Mimeographed Report). Tokyo: Author.

Ministry of Welfare, Labor, and Health. (2003). *Report to the National Social Security Council Pension Committee on Feb 19, 2003* (Mimeographed Report). Tokyo: Author.

Nagase, N. (1997). Koreijyosei no syugyokodo to nenkinjyukyu: Kazokukosei, syugyorireki kara mita jisshobunseki [Elderly women's labor participation and pensions]. *The Quarterly of Social Security Research, 33*(3), 272–312.

Nagase, N. (1999). The public pension and the labor supply of older women in Japan. *Review of Population and Social Policy, 8,* 27–48.

Nagase, N., and Takayama, N. (1997). Josei koreisha no kurashi to nenkin jukyu ga ataeru eikyo [Pensions and the life of elderly women: Comparison of the survey of labor participation behavior of the aged in 1983 and 1992]. *The Japan Institute of Labor Research Report,* 95–156.

The National Institute of Population and Social Security Research. (1999). *The fourth national survey on household changes.* Tokyo: Kosei Rodo Kyokai.

Ogawa, H. (1997). Nenkin to danseikoreisya no syugyokodo [Pension and elderly men's labor-force participation]. In Japan Institute of Labor (Ed.), *Nenkinseido no kaikaku ga syugyo intai kodo ni oyobosu eikyo ni kansuru kenkyu I* (pp. 17–57). Tokyo: Japan Institute of Labor.

Ogawa, H. (1998a). Nenkin ga koureisya no syugyokodo ni ataeru eikyo [The influence of pensions on the working behavior of the elderly]. *Keizai Kenkyu, 49*(3), 243–258.

Ogawa, H. (1998b). Nenkin, koyohoken kaisei to danseikoreisya no syugyo kodo no henka [The effect of pension and unemployment insurance reform on the elderly men's labor participation]. *The Monthly Journal of the Japan Institute of Labor, 40*(11), 52–64.

Ohishi, A. (2000). Koreisya no syugyo kettei ni okeru kenkoyoin no eikyo [Health and work-related decision making among the elderly]. *The Monthly Journal of the Japan Institute of Labor, 42*(8), 51–62.

Ono, A. (1989). *Nihonteki koyoukankou to rodo shijo* [Japanese employment practices and the labor market]. Tokyo: Toyokeizaishinposha.

Quality of Life Policy Bureau, Cabinet Office of the Government. (2002). *White paper on the national lifestyle, FY 2001.* Tokyo: Gyosei.

Seike, A. (1986). Koreisha shugyo no susei to koteki nenkin [in Japanese]. *The Monthly Journal of the Japan Institute of Labor, 328.*

Seike, A. (1989). Koreisya no rodo kyokyu ni ataeru kotekinenkin no koka no sokutei: Futatsu no baiasu wo nozoita odanmenbunnseki [Measurement of the effect of public pensions on the labor participation of the elderly: Cross-analysis without two biases]. *Nihon Rodo Kyokai Zasshi, 31*(8), 11–19.

Shimono, K., and Tachibanaki, T. (1984). Konenreisya no syugyokodo bunseki: Danjyo hikaku [Analysis on the labor-force participation behavior of the elderly between male and female]. *The Quarterly of Social Security Research, 19*(4), 398–413.

Shirahase, S. (2002). Nihon no shotoku kakusa to koreisha setai [Japan's income inequality and elderly households]. *Monthly Journal of the Japan Institute of Labor, 44*(500), 72–85.

Social Insurance Agency. (2001). *Annual report on social insurance.* Tokyo: Gyosei.

Social Insurance Agency. (2003). *2001 Shaki hoken jigyo and gaikyo* [General information on social insurance–2001] in http://www.sia.go.jp/inform/tokei/gaikyo2001/gaiko.pdf

Social Security Council, Population Committee. (2002). *Shorai jinko suikei no shiten* [The framework of the future population estimate]. Tokyo: Gyosei.

Statistics Office, Ministry of Public Management, Home Affairs, Posts and Telecommunications. (2003). *2001 survey on time use and leisure activities.* Tokyo: Statistics Bureau.

Statistics Office, Ministry of Public Management, Home Affairs, Posts and Telecommunications. (2003). *Labor force survey.* Tokyo: Statistics Bureau.

Tachibanaki, T., and Shimono, K. (1994). *Kojin chochiku to raifu saikuru* [Life cycle and family savings]. Tokyo: Nihon Keizai Shinbunsha.

Takayama, N., and Arita, F. (1996). *Chochiku to shisan keisei: Kakei shisan no maikuro deta bunseki* [Accumulation of savings and assets: Micro data analysis of household assets]. Tokyo: Iwanamishoten.

Tokyo Metropolitan Government. (2003). *2002 survey on wage and retirement of small and medium-sized firms.* Retrieved November 2003, from http://www.metro.tokyo.jp/INET/CHOUSA/2002/12/60CCP200.HTM

CHAPTER SEVEN

Empowering Older Adults as Key Resources in Development in Malaysia

Poo Chang Tan and Nai Peng Tey

Aging issues do not concern just the old. Yet the immediate response of most countries facing demographic transformations is to implement welfare programs for older people. Extended life expectancies can be construed as a triumph of human civilization, but sadly, the concerns of aging populations tend to concentrate on disease, disability, and morbidity. Much of the evidence indicates that in fact the majority of older people are likely to be healthy (Tan, Ng, Tey, and Halimah, 1999).

As has been made readily apparent in this handbook, the population in Asia is aging rapidly. In countries with lower levels of economic development, there is a need to initiate policies that encourage older people to remain key resources within their communities and facilitate their doing so. Few policies have been put in place to provide options for older people to continue to participate in society, have access to care, and pursue self-fulfillment in order to age with dignity and independence—goals that are congruent with the United Nations Principles for Older Persons. Such programs and policies are crucial, particularly in developing countries where social security provisions are unlikely to be adequate.

SOCIOECONOMIC CONDITIONS AND ISSUES OF POPULATION AGING IN MALAYSIA

Malaysia comprises 13 states and three federal territories. Its population is made up of Malays and other indigenous ethnic groups (66 percent), Chinese (25 percent), Indians (7 percent), and others (2 percent). The continuing challenge of political negotiations in Malaysia is customarily couched in terms of harmonizing the interests of the respective groups and lessening the strife that has characterized the country for too many years. Income inequality, poverty, and distrust among the major ethnic groups resulted in racial riots in May 1969. In the aftermath of that tumult, the government implemented the New Economy Policy aimed at eradicating poverty irrespective of race and restructuring Malay society to eliminate linkage of race with vocation and location. The main thrust of the New Economy Policy has been retained in the national government's subsequent National Development Policy (1990–2000) and National Vision Policy (2000–2010). Despite their sometimes subtle variations, each ethnic community has accorded older people a place of honor, yet each is also undergoing transformation as Malaysia assumes a role on the global economic stage. Malaysian domestic policies attempt to grapple with the impact of these changing traditions while remaining sensitive to the country's ethnic diversity (Ho, 1999). Malaysia has made tremendous economic and social advancements since the country achieved independence in 1957. Its economy grew at around 8 percent per annum throughout the 1980s and most of 1990s. Like other national economies in the region, though, Malaysia suffered a downturn during the Asian financial crisis of 1997. Having rebounded in 2000, the economy is projected to grow at about 4.5 percent in 2003 and beyond.

At the same time, the level of educational attainment has risen substantially for both men and women. According to the 2000 Population Census, by the beginning of the millennium about 53 percent of the population ages 10 and older had passed the lower secondary examination (55 percent for males and 51 percent for females), and 6.8 percent had received a tertiary education (7.6 percent for males and 6.0 percent for females) (Malaysia Department of Statistics, 2002). Educational advancement has allowed increasing numbers of women to pursue their own careers and participate in economic activities outside the home.

Simultaneously, public health has improved spectacularly, so that in 1999 the life expectancy at birth reached 70 years for men and 75 years for women. Malaysia's crude death rate, at around 4.5 per thousand population, is among the lowest in the world.

Rapid economic change and growing urbanization have dramatically affected the social fabric much as they have in other Asian nations. As a consequence of increased migration, extended families have gradually given way to nuclear families. Single-member households and female-headed households are emerging as a new norm (Tan and Ng, 1995).

The pressures of rapid socioeconomic and demographic changes have led to the breakdown of the traditional extended family system. Rising urbanization, rural-urban migration, increased education, increased labor-force participation rates among women, rising age at marriage, rising rates of nonmarriage, declines in fertility and mortality, and rising prosperity have lured many Malaysians to pursue quick gains over traditional values. In light of these changes, the family support system for the elderly is weakening and is likely to remain under siege.

The greater longevity of women raises critical welfare and economic issues for the entire society as many women remain outside the labor force and have little or no income of their own. The higher life expectancy and younger age at marriage of women as compared to men means that many older women outlive their spouses. With little or no education, little savings, little inheritance, low access to credit, and family support systems that have eroded, older women are particularly vulnerable and perhaps beyond the coverage of the Family and Child Care Service programs of the Ministry of Social Welfare.

Mandatory retirement age in Malaysia is 56.[1] With little social security available from the national government, many older adults do not have adequate financial resources for daily living once they retire, especially in light of the pressures of inflation as they affect healthcare (Tan, 1999c, 2000). This situation is made worse by rising education levels and delayed age of marriage and age of childbearing. Many adults are likely to retire with meager savings for themselves, since upon retirement they may still have school-age children or children pursuing higher education and may at the same time have to care for parents and older relatives. It is therefore clear that as a consequence of sweeping social change, the Malaysian government needs to consider new and innovative strategies for supporting older adults.

The population of Malaysia is aging gradually. More and more people will live to older ages. It is estimated that 6.2 percent of the population, or 1.45 million persons, were ages 60 and older in 2000, out of a total population of 23.3 million. By the year 2020, the proportion of those ages 60 and older is projected to rise to 12.5 percent of a projected population of 32 million, or about 4 million elders. Older women will outnumber their male counterparts due to their higher life expectancy.

Significant differentials in the aging process can be observed across the major ethnic groups in Malaysia. Malaysian Chinese have an older age structure compared to Malays and Indians, resulting from a longer life expectancy and a more rapid decline in their fertility rate. Nevertheless, in 1999, ethnic Malays ages 60 and older numbered 728,200, while the number of Indian elders in this age group was 101,400 and Chinese elders only numbered 499,300. In the decades ahead, higher fertility rates among Malays (3.8 children per woman in 1997) will cause the older Malay population to grow much faster than the older adult populations of ethnic Chinese and Indians (whose fertility rates were 2.5–2.6 children per woman in the same year).

According to the definition of demographic structures formulated by the Association of South-East Asian Nations (ASEAN), Malaysia is classified as a young country, with fewer than 6 percent of its population currently over the age of 60. As was noted in the introductory chapter of this volume, countries with comparatively young population distributions are not yet mindful of the need to develop broad-reaching ameliorative policies in support of their elderly

[1] The retirement age was increased from 55 to 56 in 2001.

citizens. That fact, combined with the relatively young retirement age of 56 plus the extension of life expectancy in Malaysia, means that more and more older Malaysians are becoming dependent.

Given the trend toward smaller family size, the current working-age population will have fewer children to help care for them in their old age. Accordingly, it is critical to consider aging-related issues for the current population of older adults from all three ethnic groups as well as for the impending spurt in the older population that will accompany the aging of Malaysia's baby boom generation. Without ameliorative intervention and more appropriate policies, problems already apparent will only be exacerbated in the years ahead.

Table 1, which breaks down the sex ratio of the population by age, shows that in 1999 there were more males than females at every age interval younger than 60. As is apparent in Figure 1, a comparable pattern holds for all ethnic groups. After age 60, females begin to outnumber males, indicating lower age-specific mortality and longer life expectancies for females as compared to males. The current figures show that at birth, males can expect to live some 70 years compared with 75 years for females (Table 2). Variations in life expectancy exist across ethnic groups: The Chinese have a longer life expectancy than ethnic Malays or Indians. For Malays, the male-female differentials are 2 years at ages 55 and 60, compared to 3 to 4 years for Chinese and Indians in the same age groups. At age 60, a man will have about 16.5 years more to live and a woman, some 19 years more. This works out to be about a quarter of his or her lifespan, or at least a third of his or her adult life.

Table 1. Population Sex Ratio by Age Group, 1999

Age group	Sex ratio	Age group	Sex ratio
0–4	107	45–49	103
5–9	107	50–54	105
10–14	105	55–59	102
15–19	106	60–64	99
20–24	103	65–69	89
5–29	101	70–74	90
30–34	100	75–79	77
35–39	101	80+	71
40–44	102	Total	103

Source: Malaysia Department of Statistics, 1999a.

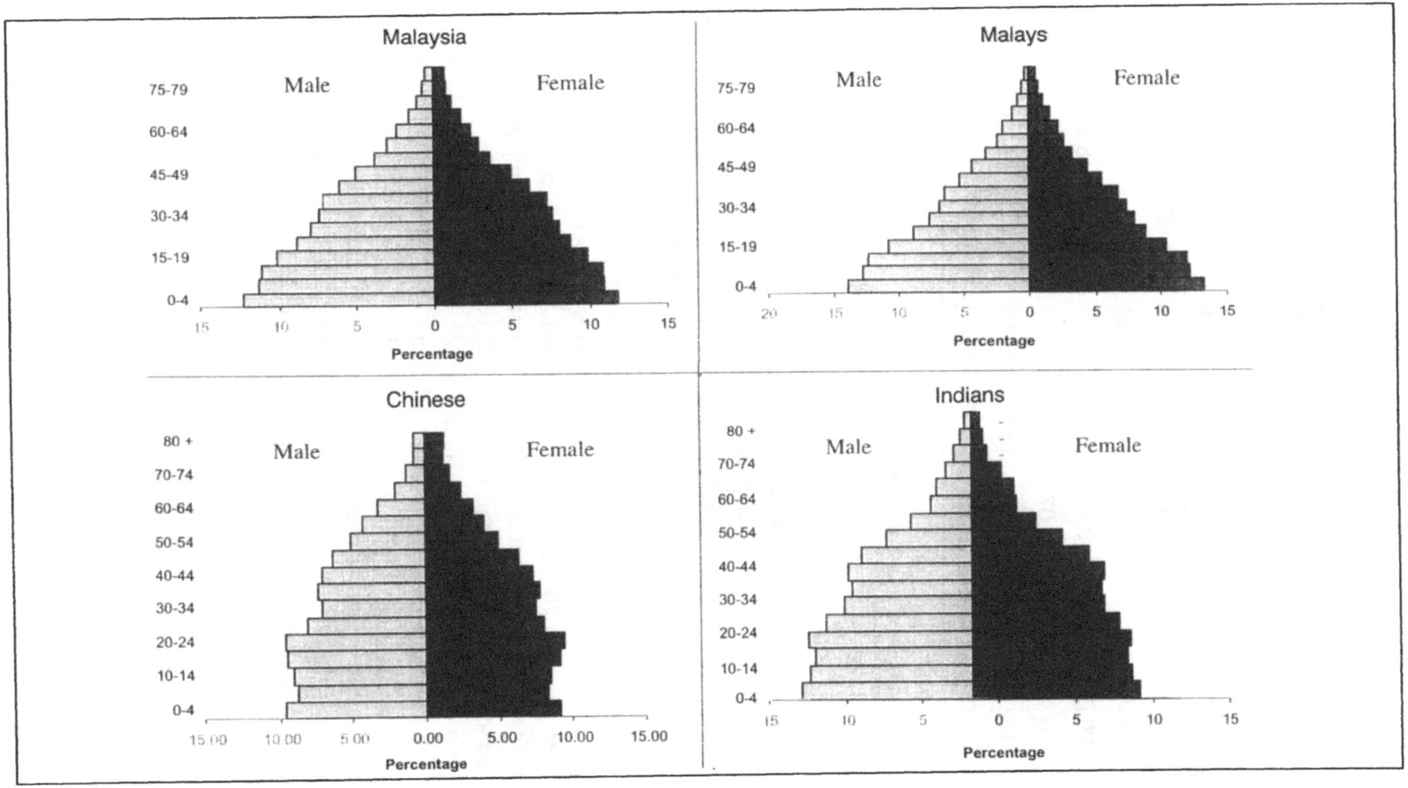

Figure 1. Population distribution in Malaysia by age group, sex, and ethnic group, 1999.
Source: Malaysia Department of Statistics, 1999a.

Table 2. Life Expectancy at Selected Ages by Sex and Ethnic Group, 1999[a]

	Total		Malays		Chinese		Indian	
Age	Male	Female	Male	Female	Male	Female	Male	Female
At birth	69.89	74.87	69.84	73.31	72.19	77.74	65.59	74.20
40	33.14	36.70	32.31	35.29	34.76	39.05	30.02	36.17
50	24.36	27.41	23.47	26.05	25.94	29.68	22.07	27.10
55	20.25	23.00	19.44	21.70	21.71	25.17	18.35	22.80
60	16.46	18.86	15.67	17.65	17.84	20.87	15.20	18.95
65	13.07	15.08	12.45	14.02	14.25	16.83	12.23	15.42
70	10.07	11.72	9.52	10.82	11.14	13.26	9.49	12.02

[a]Preliminary value
Source: Malaysia Department of Statistics, 1999b.

As is true in much of the world, age-specific death rates (ASDR) for Malaysian males were higher than for females at all ages from birth onward (Figure 2). It is interesting to note that death rates among males are higher than those among females, even during childbearing years. Male death rates outpace female death rates by a factor of two or more from age 15 to age 45. For instance, in the 30–34 age group, the ASDR for males was 2.4 per thousand compared to 0.89 per thousand for females; at ages 35–39, the rate was 3.8 per thousand for males and 1.8 per thousand for females. However, although women survive longer than men, the indication is that at various ages women tend to complain of illness more than men (Tan, Ng, Tey, and Halimah, 1999).

With improvement in education, older people in the future will be better trained (Tan and Ng, 1998). The 2000 Population Census shows that in that year about one third of the population ages 55–64 had at least a lower-secondary education. By 2020 the corresponding proportion is expected to be close to three quarters (Malaysia Department of Statistics, 2002). As has occurred in the West and elsewhere in Asia, the needs of future cohorts of older adults would be quite different from those of today. Governments and other service providers should therefore be responsive to the changes in tastes that are likely to emerge.

Generally, the labor-force participation rate declines rapidly with age. The labor-force participation rates of adults ages 55–64 are lower than those of younger adults. As is typically the case in comparable societies, labor-force participation rates in Malaysia are generally lower for females than for males at every age, despite rapidly changing labor-force participation patterns for women (Table 3).

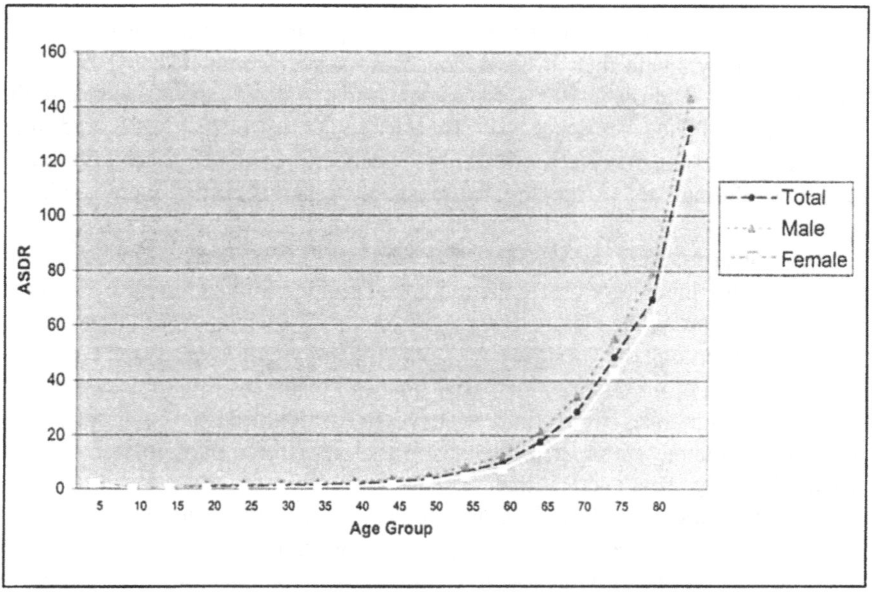

Figure 2. Age-specific death rates for males and females in Malaysia by age group, 1998.
Source: Malaysia Department of Statistics, 1998.

Table 3. Labor-Force Participation Rates by Selected Age Group, Residence, and Gender, Peninsular Malaysia, 1998

Selected	Total (%)			Urban (%)			Rural (%)		
age group	Total	Male	Female	Total	Male	Female	Total	Male	Female
40–44	74.7	98.8	50.2	75.6	98.7	52.1	73.5	99.0	47.6
45–49	72.1	97.4	45.9	72.4	97.4	46.2	71.7	97.3	45.6
50–54	65.9	93.1	37.6	64.8	91.9	35.4	67.4	94.7	40.3
55–59	49.4	72.2	26.3	44.1	65.3	21.6	55.4	80.5	31.4
60–64	38.5	61.8	16.2	30.5	50.2	12.4	47.2	73.8	20.5

Note: Malaysia comprises Peninsular Malaysia with 11 states and Sabah and Sarawak in East Malaysia.

Source: Malaysia Department of Statistics, 1999c.

Insight into the situation of many older people in Malaysia can be gleaned from how they spend their time. A household survey conducted in 1997 (Tan, Ng, Tey, and Halimah, 1999) found that most older Malaysians spend the greater part of their time at home. The large majority were healthy and able, but there were not many activities at the local level in which to involve them; and few alternatives to tending to household responsibilities were available to them.

Not too surprisingly, as Malaysia becomes more economically developed and urbanized, the labor-force participation rates of older adults are expected to fall further still. Among the factors thought to account for such an overall trend, rising literacy rates among the younger population, the introduction of a wage economy, mechanization of production, increased financial resources through savings, and increased remittances from children have been identified as being primarily responsible for the anticipated declines in the labor-force participation rates of elders (Tan, Ng, Tey, and Halimah, 1999).

Older individuals, especially older women, are painfully susceptible to poor living conditions. The rapidly rising proportion and number of older people also has serious social and economic implications for government planning in Malaysia. Women in particular need to be part of the policy agenda as they have been found to be at the lowest rung of the employment hierarchy—primarily working in informal sector jobs and earning very low income—and hence likely to live in poverty at older ages (Tan, 1999b; Tan, Tey, Kuppusamy, et al., 1995; World Bank, 1994).

As is universally the case, good health is the main contributory factor to the overall well-being of older Malaysians. Within the Ministry of Health, the Division of Health is charged with health promotion and preventive interventions. For the most part, primary healthcare is delivered through the Family Health Programme, but its principal focus is the health of children and mothers. Still, this program is also the source for healthcare for older citizens. Medical care is delivered through a series of local health facilities scattered across the country, but they are not distributed equitably. In addition to this network of outpatient facilities, there is also a network of hospitals operating under the Inpatient Programme of the Ministry of Health. The hospital system is organized into four tiers, and each provides a focused set of medical procedures, from general procedures (offered throughout the country) to narrowly focused specializations (offered in Kuala Lumpur). In addition to these public health provisions, there is a thriving private-sector medical community with physicians, nursing staff, various forms of therapy, and even private hospitals on privately held land and in major cities. These for-profit providers operate on a fee-for-service basis that is independent of governmental provisions. Unfortunately, some medical practitioners in the private sector are businesspeople first and healthcare providers second. Perhaps a community-service effort mounted by qualified medical practitioners would ensure that providers only render relevant tests, procedures, and prescriptions. Yet systemic reformulations or corrections are not currently on the horizon.

To date, social security provisions cover only a small proportion of the population and are likely to remain less than comprehensive. In any case, welfare programs may promote care and some independence but do little in terms of encouraging participation in the community, self-fulfillment, or dignity. In fact, a far more fundamental change in society needs to occur for older adults to be empowered and welcomed into a wide range of opportunities that help them enjoy a high quality of life. Unless older people are allowed to remain in mainstream society, fully integrated with younger generations, it is unlikely they will overcome their marginalized status. Older adults are seldom regarded as key resources in Malaysian community, environmental, or economic development. Older individuals who do not embody new technologies and modernized methods of production have come to be regarded as superfluous, obsolete, and a burden to society.

One of the hallmark changes associated with industrialization is the economic shift from family enterprises to wage employment (Goode, 1963). As a result, older adults no longer have control of vital productive resources, which tend to shift into the hands of younger family members with higher educational achievement and greater facility in the new economy. The movement away from family enterprises to factory and service-sector employment leaves behind those who had worked under their own aegis without formal work histories. The existing social security schemes focus disproportionately on workers in the formal sector; those with informal productive engagements are left to welfare programs—if they are considered at all. With limited welfare assistance, older adults must depend on their children's goodwill and sense of familial obligation to ensure that they are taken care of.

Countries in which development—and thus population aging—occurred earlier have a long-established pattern of providing welfare for their older citizens (Tan, 2001). In Malaysia, as in other nations just now undergoing economic and demographic transformation, such concerns have only just begun to occupy a place on the policy agenda.

The national government formulated its National Policy for the Elderly in 1995 to help create a context in which older Malaysians might find greater contentment and obtain a heightened sense of self-worth and dignity. The policy seeks to achieve its goals through optimizing elders' self-potential and ensuring that they enjoy the care and protection as members of their family, society, and nation (Prime Minister's Department, Malaysia, Economic Planning Unit, 1996). Specifically, the policy has the objectives of "improving the potential of the elderly so that they can continue to be productive in national development, and create opportunities to assist them to live independently; and encouraging the creation and availability of specific facilities to ensure the care and protection of the older person to enhance their well-being" (p. 571). Sadly, many aspects of the policy have yet to be implemented and are in fact being challenged in some quarters even before implementation.

THE COMMUNITY CENTER APPROACH: THE MALAYSIAN EXPERIENCE

The Malaysian model of engaging older people through community centers to foster productive aging can provide valuable lessons to other Asian countries. Malaysia, like many other Asian nations, does not yet have thoroughgoing aging policies, yet has been able to implement action-oriented programs such as the community centers across the nation. These programs have been rather successful in meeting their objectives, and their basic model may be adapted to other cultures and countries. These prototype programs are commonly called community centers to give them a recognizable identity, but the "centers" have no physical properties, nor do they occupy specific sites. The community center is in fact a flexible pivot point that works through smart partnership among governmental, private, and nongovernmental agencies and local communities where demonstration projects are underway. Membership in the community center is open to all, and the aim of the center is to encourage groups to cooperate in a concerted manner, tapping existing expertise and resources to meet local needs or serve local agendas.

The innovative approach of Malaysia's community centers engages older adults as central players in the family and community. The centers also recognize that the continuum of care and supportive services has to extend from the family to the community. Otherwise, many families will be hard-pressed to care for their oldest members (Tan, 1993). The experience of aging can become a triumph if the exemplary expertise and experience of older people are utilized to help design and implement innovative opportunities to meet the challenges facing them. The advantage of the community center approach is that it incorporates basic notions of life-course developmental perspectives. Younger cohorts become increasingly aware of aging issues and participate in enriching programs catering to themselves and their older parents, relatives, and friends. In turn, older adults get to turn their attention to helping their peers and those who will grow old tomorrow or the day after.

Economic Contributions

The declining trend in fertility and increasing life expectancy in Malaysia call for the productive labor force to be redefined to include more and more older workers. Rather than becoming a burden and a drain on society, older Malaysians have the potential to use their knowledge and experience to do well in many areas. Older adults should be provided with incentives and assistance to become involved in many types of business enterprises and service arenas.

An infrastructure can be provided by one or more government agency to enable older adults to venture into economic development and, in turn, provide employment opportunities to others.

Currently, many professionals retire into enforced idleness. The fundamental principle behind the concept of the community center is that older people can continue to contribute to the economy if opportunities are provided through innovative policies and programs (Tan, 1999a). The community center movement provides older adults with opportunities to serve as trainers or resource people in various fields. They need not be viewed as a threat to younger workers who aspire to take over the senior positions that the elders once held. Potentially, every company and organization could establish a relevant resource group comprising retired members to help younger workers in need of their services.

Older adults can provide education, training, and awareness programs in many areas in the community, especially those that involve the young. Older adults can become the "eyes" and "ears" of the community and assist families in such activities as overseeing young children when their parents are working, are otherwise indisposed, or during periods of sickness or emergency. Many older people can also provide support in terms of transportation, chores, and other regular or occasional forms of assistance.

Local and national governments can set up a formal infrastructure to enable older people to remain in productive employment for as long as possible. However, retaining older workers under current employment conditions may well conflict with the interests of younger workers in developing countries. It may be necessary to adopt innovative approaches in exploring new avenues to involve older adults. There are many forms of community support that older adults can provide to enhance the quality of life of the general population as well as targeted groups. There are also numerous activities that may be developed into entrepreneurship opportunities that tap the expertise of older people and provide market-based returns. Furthermore, older adults can provide support and care for family members who are busy at work. Many families, especially those in urban areas, do not have regular sources of support for their children. Consequently, many social ills have emerged, affecting the stability and well-being of families and communities. Older people can be given training and opportunities to enhance their role in caring and nurturing future generations, thereby relieving working-age women for productive employment.

Education and Training

Another fundamental notion intrinsic to the concept of community centers is that it is never too late to learn a new skill or upgrade one's foundational knowledge. Furthermore, enrichment programs, which require modest effort beyond creative thinking, are not costly to implement. Communities can begin to contribute toward the dream of continuing learning. Even older adults with little education may have substantial skills to share: For example, cooking, gardening, and even cleaning can be made enjoyable and may be turned into a bartering-based kind of sharing. With relatively little effort, these tasks can become an area of economic activity for elders that helps them maintain their dignity and provides income for them.

Still another principle inherent in the idea of community centers is that every community should provide education and training outside mere formal schooling. Older adults can and should be a primary resource for leading continuing and informal education programs. Local and national governments should encourage older people to take a leadership role in diverse education models and should acknowledge their contributions when they do so. Older people can become teachers in their community and, in turn, can themselves benefit from learning to communicate what they know and from socializing with others.

A MODEL COMMUNITY CENTER

The Petaling Jaya Community Centre (PJCC) was started in 1997 to foster partnerships among government, private, and nongovernmental agencies and the local community to benefit older adults. Starting out with the objective of providing older adults and young people with employment opportunities that contribute to the community, the PJCC is now providing a wide range of opportunities, including a number of innovative activities and self-sustaining programs. It has been widely acknowledged because of its simplicity in structure and because its model can easily be modified to meet the varied needs of the many diverse groups in the community. There are already 11 such centers to date, with the furthest being in Kuching and Sibu, Sarawak, and in Greenlane, Penang.

Environmental Services

The center's wide-ranging services now include environmental intercession in the form of a recycling operation at an environmental activity center. The environmental activity center is aimed at waste reduction; it collects all discarded items and then repairs and resells them, only recycling items that cannot be fixed. People in financial need, especially older adults, perform these recycling activities for wages. In addition, the PJCC runs two retail outlets that double as community centers, providing opportunities for young people to socialize and for older people to use the Internet. The PJCC generates additional revenue via a monthly auction as well as through an online auction (*http://pjcc.lelong.com.my*). The recycling operation has improved the surrounding environment and encouraged the local community to assume responsibility for caring for their neighborhood. Where possible, the PJCC also operates awareness and training programs to encourage others to set up similar mutual-care cooperatives.

Not only has the PJCC been able to sustain itself and provide employment to older adults through these activities, it has also been able to regularly contribute to other charities and community activities. In addition, the PJCC has a long-term objective of providing help during emergencies. When crises arise, the PJCC can send out its trained cadre of older people, who are ready to lend a helping hand and alleviate as many concerns as possible so that emergency personnel can be directed where demand is most urgent.

Another PJCC program, Environment Initiatives, has carried out a number of cooperative activities with local agencies to raise awareness about how the agencies can work together to conserve resources and reduce duplication. The PJCC also puts on an annual awareness exhibition and has embarked on programs to tackle problems related to environmental degradation and pollution. For example, in 2003, the PJCC, working with Forest Research Institute Malaysia (FRIM) and a few local councils, undertook a special program to reduce wood wastes, food wastes, and hazardous wastes such as batteries and expired medicines.

Health Programs

The PJCC also sponsors a number of initiatives, such as regular exercise programs, to improve the health of older adults. Monthly health awareness days bring volunteer health personnel together to provide screening and primary health education. Once a year, the center holds an interagency health screening and exhibition focusing on older adults and disadvantaged groups within the community. Health services, including counseling and subsidized or free tests, are provided for the needy. Both the monthly and the annual health events emphasize preventive health measures focusing on eyesight, hearing, dental health, and basic blood tests. It is believed that by having access to basic health tests, everyone will be able to live to a ripe old age, exhibiting the five U.N. principles of independence, participation, care, self-fulfillment, and dignity. In addition to these events, the PJCC partners with the University of Malaya Medical Center to coordinate health-related talks and forums throughout the year.

Another program initiated by the PJCC, the Robin Food Program, provides food at affordable prices to all adults ages 60 and older at selected hotels and food outlets. The mission of the program, which is promoted in partnership with various agencies, is to encourage older adults to visit places that they can afford and that bring them in contact with others. Another PJCC-sponsored program has arranged for the very poor to receive once a week free food that they can consume at home, but local political disagreements caused the program to be suspended in mid-2003.

Caregiving Programs

PJCC sponsors an annual Caregivers Training Program to train local service providers in the particular needs of older adults. The program, taught by clients themselves, is aimed at raising the quality of care. So far, the groups that have been trained are largely from the national Ministry of Health and private nongovernmental organizations (NGOs). Another innovative effort, the Information, Communication, and Technology (ICT) Program for Community, is attempting to bridge the age gap in knowledge and access to information technology. ICT trains youths to become key technical assistants in local schools and community organizations and works to ensure that the rapid development of information technology does not create increasing disparities for older adults. To this end, ICT has conducted a number of courses to bring technology to the most likely users. Older adults are especially encouraged to register for these courses and access the Internet at facilities in Pusat Komuniti Links.

CONCLUSION

The number and proportion of older people in Malaysia are increasing rapidly. Moreover, with general improvements in education and health, retirees at age 56 are capable of continuing to contribute many more years to national development and family welfare. Consequent upon the changing social structure, the erosion of family support for older people, the escalating cost of living, and the changing expectation and needs of older people, appropriate strategies will have to be undertaken to allow them to continue to work and be independent. Ideally, such strategies do not only benefit individuals but also their communities.

The community center movement in Malaysia, which started out with the establishment of the PJCC in 1997, has been rather successful in mobilizing human resources, particularly those of older adults, and in carrying out recycling activities for economic gain and environmental protection. These centers provide gainful employment to people who are in need, allow older people to continue to be actively involved in society, and contribute to the welfare of the needy through donations and free or subsidized services. Since 1997, community centers have expanded to provide social activities, exercise, health awareness campaigns and screening, caregiver training, and initiatives for environment conservation. More importantly, the community center movement has been instrumental in fostering smart partnerships among government agencies, NGOs, and the private sector. Such partnerships help build a caring society, encourage volunteerism, and bridge intergenerational and social gaps through the participation of young and old from differing social groups. The community centers also provide an avenue for older people to transfer their knowledge, expertise, and values to younger generations, and for younger Malaysians to communicate with their elders.

The community center movement has made a fine start in Malaysia. In the coming years, many more community centers will be set up throughout the country. These centers will be run by the people, for the people, and will return manifold dividends on their costs. Many international visitors have already come to Malaysia's community centers to learn and share their experience. Such international exchanges of ideas will help improve the effectiveness of the community centers in Malaysia and in other parts of the world.

REFERENCES

Goode, W. J. (1963). *World revolution and family patterns.* New York: Free Press.

Ho, K. L. (1999). Politics and institutions in economic policy implementation in Malaysia. In F. A. Lazen (Ed.), *Policies studies and developing nations* (pp. 57–73). Stamford, Connecticut: JAI Press.

Malaysia Department of Statistics. (1998). *Vital statistics Malaysia: 1998.* Kuala Lumpur: Author.

Malaysia Department of Statistics. (1999a). *Vital statistics Malaysia: 1999.* Kuala Lumpur: Author.

Malaysia Department of Statistics. (1999b). *Abridged life tables, 1997–1999.* Kuala Lumpur: Author.

Malaysia Department of Statistics. (1999c). *Labour force survey 1998.* Kuala Lumpur: Author.

Malaysia Department of Statistics. (2002). *Population and housing census of Malaysia, 2000— Education and social characteristics of the population.* Kuala Lumpur: Author.

Prime Minister's Department, Malaysia, Economic Planning Unit. (1996). *Seventh Malaysia plan.* Kuala Lumpur: Author.

Tan, P. C. (1993). Implications of changing family structures on old-age support in Asia. In United Nations Economic and Social Commission for Asia and the Pacific (Ed.), *Report of the Fourth Asian and Pacific Population Conference* (APSS No. 124, pp. 160–165). New York: United Nations.

Tan, P. C. (1999a, June). *Implications of policy alternatives for the wellbeing of older persons.* Paper presented at the Sixth Asia/Oceania Regional Congress of Gerontology, Seoul, South Korea.

Tan, P. C. (1999b, July). *Capacity building of older persons in community support.* Paper presented at the Regional Conference on Aging of the Japanese Organization for International Cooperation in Family Planning, Tokyo, Japan.

Tan, P. C. (1999c, September). *Social security in the context of social development in East and South-East Asia.* Paper presented at the Social Policy Research Centre Workshop on Academy of the Social Sciences in Australia, Sydney, Australia.

Tan, P. C. (2000). Implications of population ageing in Malaysia: The need to consider poverty issues. In O. Roziah (Ed.), *Poverty and ageing* (pp. 24–30). Petaling Jaya, Malaysia: National Council of Senior Citizens Organizations of Malaysia and University of Malaya, Faculty of Arts and Social Sciences.

Tan, P. C. (2001). Situation of older persons in the newly industrialized countries of East Asia. In the United Nations (Ed.), *The world ageing situation: Exploring a society for all ages* (pp. 55–69). New York: Author.

Tan, P. C., and Ng, S. T. (1995, August). *Current and emerging family patterns in Malaysia.* Paper presented at "Towards Effective Development Planning," Population Information Workshop, National Population and Family Development Board, Malaysia.

Tan, P. C., and Ng, S. T. (1998, February). *Situation of older persons in Malaysia.* Paper presented at Assisted Living Vision 2020—Aging with Dignity, Kuala Lumpur, Malaysia.

Tan, P. C., Ng, S. T., Tey, N. P., and Halimah, A. (1999). *Evaluating programme needs of older persons in Malaysia* (Monograph Series No. 1). Kuala Lumpur: University of Malaya, Faculty of Economics and Administration.

Tan, P. C., Tey, N. P., Kuppusamy, S., Lee, H. K., Ng, S. T., Noor Azina, I., Wan Sabri, W. H., and Janakky, R. (1995). *Women in the informal sector in Malaysia: Household survey.* Kuala Lumpur: University of Malaya, Faculty of Economics and Administration.

World Bank. (1994). *Averting the old age crisis.* New York: Oxford University Press.

CHAPTER EIGHT

Economic Status, Work, and Retirement Among Korean Elders

Sung-Jae Choi

Retirement is both a phenomenon and a product of modern industrial society (Donahue, Orbach, and Pollak, 1960). Industrialization is one of the most salient aspects of modernization and is a defining characteristic in all societies undergoing transformation. Previously a stable agricultural society, South Korea began to modernize with the influx of Western thought and the institutionalization of modern mass education immediately after the end of World War II. Over the past 40 years, the modernization of South Korea has been accelerated by rapid industrialization and a diffusion of basic notions of a market economy. In terms of Korea's industrial structure, products from secondary (mining and manufacturing) and tertiary (social overhead and services) industries accounted for 35 percent and 60 percent, respectively, of the gross national product (GNP) in 2000, compared to 16 percent and 47 percent in 1960. At the same time, employment in the secondary and tertiary sectors accounted for 20 percent and 69 percent, respectively, of total employment in 2000, compared to 9 percent and 28 percent in 1963. Accordingly, the GNP/GDP (gross domestic product) per capita increased from US$87 in 1960 to US$9,770 in 2000. Along with industrialization, Korea has experienced a synchronous and rapid urbanization: The proportion of the population living in urban areas has increased from 28 percent in 1960 to 88 percent in 2000.

Since the early 1960s, when the first national plan for economic development through industrialization was launched, the prolongation of life expectancy and the rise in employment in secondary and tertiary industries has been remarkable. However, while the life expectancy of the average Korean has greatly extended, the mandatory retirement age, set at 55, has for the most part remained constant. Due to the fact that the retirement age has not risen to reflect increased life expectancy and that a public old-age pension system was instituted relatively late, the majority of Korean retirees have insufficient income to maintain a minimum standard of living. Hence, the maintenance of financial wherewithal during the retirement years is an important social issue in contemporary Korean society.

POPULATION AGING IN SOUTH KOREA

Changes in the fertility and mortality rates of a specific society are associated with the process of transition from an agrarian state to an industrialized and urbanized state (Kim, 1996). Modernization tends to be associated with a demographic transition that is facilitated by the reduction in both fertility and mortality rates. Along with the decline of fertility and mortality rates associated with industrialization since the early 1960s, average life expectancy at birth has substantially increased. As shown in Table 1, life expectancy at birth for men and women increased from 51.1 years and 53.3 years, respectively, in 1960 to 72.1 years and 79.5 years in 2000. These figures are expected to reach 78.4 years and 84.8 years by 2030 as South Korea continues along its path of becoming a world economic partner.

Consequently, the sheer number of South Koreans age 65 or older has greatly increased over the past 40 years. Their proportion of the total population has grown from 2.9 percent in 1960 to 7.3 percent in 2000 (Table 2). It is estimated that older adults will make up 9.9 percent of the total population in South Korea by 2010 and 13.2 percent by 2020. Such a rate of population aging is unprecedented: It is estimated that it will take only 22 years for the proportion of older adults in the population of South Korea to double, a process that took 85 years in Sweden and 24 years in Japan (United Nations, 1996).

Table 1. Factual and Estimated Life Expectancy at Birth for South Koreans, by Selected Years

Year	Mean	Male	Female
1960	52.4	51.1	53.3
1970	63.2	59.8	66.7
1980	65.8	62.7	69.9
1990	71.7	67.7	75.9
2000	75.9	72.1	79.5
2010	78.8	75.5	82.2
2020	80.7	77.5	84.1
2030	81.5	77.5	84.8

Source: South Korea National Statistical Office, 2001.

Table 2. Factual and Estimated Size of the Older Adult Population in South Korea

Year	Total population (A) (1,000s)	Older adult population (B) (1,000s)			Percentage of older adults in total population (B/A)		
		65+	70+	80+	65+	70+	80+
1960	25,012	726	381	59	2.9	1.5	0.2
1970	32,241	991	563	101	3.1	1.7	0.3
1980	38,124	1,456	832	176	3.8	2.2	0.5
1990	42,869	2,195	1,294	302	5.1	3.0	0.7
2000	47,008	3,395	2,014	483	7.2	4.3	1.0
2010	49,594	5,302	3,514	957	10.7	7.1	1.9
2020	50,650	7,667	5,100	1,804	15.1	10.1	3.6
2030	50,296	11,604	7,892	2,571	23.1	15.7	5.1

Source: South Korea National Statistical Office, 2001.

THE INCOME STATUS OF KOREAN ELDERS

Due to such factors as the past trend toward the establishment of earlier mandatory retirement ages, underdevelopment of income maintenance policies, unstable employment throughout life, the pressing need to support the family during working years, and the burdens of supporting one's children's educations and marriages, the income status of the current generation of elderly Koreans is generally low (Choi and Chang, 2002).

The results of a national survey that Sunwoo, Chung, Oh, Cho, and Suk (2001) conducted among Koreans ages 65 and older revealed that the monthly average income of the majority of households comprised solely of older adults is below the poverty line (Table 3).[1] More than 70 percent of older adults living alone have incomes below the poverty line, and the same is true of 50 percent of older couples who live by themselves. Elder-only households comprised 45 percent of all households with elderly members as of 2000; multigenerational households with elderly members comprised the remaining 55 percent (South Korea National Statistical Office, 2002).

Furthermore, about a quarter of all South Koreans on public assistance are older adults, and some 40 percent of the households headed by an individual receiving

[1] In 2001, the poverty line set by the South Korean government was 334,000 won (US$278) per month for a single-person household and 553,000 won per month for a two-person household.

Table 3. Income Distribution of Households with Elderly Members

Household income (won)	Total (%)	Elder living alone (%)	Elder living with spouse (%)	Elder living with adult children (%)	Elder living with others (%)
Less than 300,000	27.7	72.1	25.1	7.7	32.9
300,000-500,000	14.8	18.3	27.2	6.2	19.7
300,000-700,000	10.1	5.2	16.9	8.2	15.7
700,000-1.1 million	17.2	3.2	16.4	24.6	13.1
1.1 million-2.1 million	21.8	1.1	10.4	38.3	14.6
More than 2.1 million	8.4	0.1	4.0	15.0	4.0
Total	100.0	100.0	100.0	100.0	100.0

Note: Sample size = 3,877 households.
Source: Sunwoo et al., 2001.

public assistance are headed by older adults (South Korea Ministry of Health and Welfare, 2001). As that statistic implies, older individuals have scant discretionary income and barely enough income to meet basic needs.

Elderly South Koreans living separately from their adult children draw their incomes primarily from those same adult children and from work (Table 4). Elders in single-person households mainly draw their income from a combination of sources—their adult children, work, and public assistance—and households made up of elderly couples living alone receive income from a combination of work, adult children, assets, and retirement benefits or pensions. On the whole, elderly South Koreans still rely heavily on their families for financial assistance. As the statistics shown in Table 4 do not distinguish between retirement benefits (part of a semipublic program) and pensions (part of a public program), the proportion of older Koreans who receive public pensions cannot be calculated with exact certainty. In any case, the proportion of elders who receive either kind of income is very small. Such figures attest to a number of concerns, first and foremost the underdevelopment of income maintenance policies in Korea.

THE RETIREMENT SYSTEM IN KOREA

The South Korean retirement system is directly connected to the economic status of elderly Koreans. As mentioned above, Korean society was primarily agricultural until the early 1960s. But by 2000 only 12 percent of the population

Table 4. Main Sources of Income for Households with Elderly Members

Main sources of income	Total (%)	Elder living alone (%)	Elder living with spouse (%)	Elder living with adult children (%)	Elder living with others (%)
Older person's work	51.0	21.8	36.4	72.8	30.1
Work of other family members	8.2	—	8.3	11.6	9.1
Property	6.4	6.9	11.1	3.9	7.2
Retirement benefit or pension	5.6	3.2	10.8	3.8	9.1
Non-coresident adult children	20.1	45.8	27.0	4.1	33.5
Government	7.2	20.8	5.0	2.2	9.6
Other	1.5	1.5	1.4	1.6	1.4
Total	100.0	100.0	100.0	100.0	100.0

Note: Sample size = 4,043 households.
Source: Sunwoo et al., 2001.

still lived in rural areas. During the process of industrialization, the South Korean economy has become export oriented, and salary systems for workers in most Korean industries have been based more on seniority than on individual capability. Therefore, given an option most industries preferred to retain younger workers, who tend to be lower paid than older workers, particularly in manufacturing industries (Tahk, 1984).

A retirement system has been in place across the country in both the public and private sectors since the early 1960s. However, South Korean law legislates no mandatory retirement age. In consequence, South Korean companies have instituted an almost universal practice of retiring their workers at the age of 55; this retirement age is "mandatory" only insofar as it exists in company and industry bylaws. The sole existing law covering mandatory retirement age, the Older Workers Employment Promotion Act, only recommends that companies increase the mandatory retirement age from 55 to 60 and provides some financial incentives to companies that comply. However, this recommendation has not been entirely accepted by private companies. As a result, the average age of retirement in South Korea is 56.7 (Table 5), in sharp contrast to the average retirement age of 65 or older that prevails in other developed countries. The statistical data used to calculate this figure were gathered from medium and large

Table 5. Mandatory Retirement Age of Corporations with More than 300 Workers

Retirement age	Percentage of total
Younger than 55	0.9
55	46.5
56	5.6
57	11.4
58	21.2
59	1.1
60	10.1
61 and older	3.2

Source: South Korea Ministry of Labor, 2001.

companies with more than 300 workers. If smaller-size companies were included in these data, the average retirement age of companies could have been lower than 56.7 years. Of particular note is that during the economic crisis that began in late 1997 and is continuing at the time of this writing, many workers are not even guaranteed a retirement age of 55, despite the fact that most companies' bylaws set the retirement threshold at 55.

Not only is the prevailing compulsory retirement age of 55 contrary to the trend of increasing life expectancy, so is eligibility for the National Pension: The National Pension Act sets the age at which people are eligible for full pension benefits at 60. Such a gap between retirement age and pensionable age obviously poses a number of serious problems for older South Koreans. First, family expenditure tends to peak dramatically, often outstripping income, when the primary breadwinner reaches age 55 (Choi, 1996; Min, Ryu, Choi, and Kim, 1993). Educational expenses and financial assistance given to children upon their marriage also peak at this time. Parents usually assume full economic responsibility for their children throughout university and even graduate school, and customarily pay for weddings and down payments on first homes for newly-wed couples. Second, many retired workers experience economic hardship until they become eligible to draw on their public pensions at age 60. Third, recent retirees, comparatively young at age 55, usually do not have many opportunities to be reemployed or to participate in social, recreational, voluntary, and other meaningful activities. This attenuation from employment and social activities may lead to premature aging in social and psychological terms for many of the newly retired. Without meaningful roles and opportunities, it becomes increasingly difficult to maintain a sense of satisfaction and well-being.

EMPLOYMENT STATUS OF KOREAN ELDERS

In a national survey that Chung, Cho, Oh, Byun, Byun, and Moon (1998) conducted among older adults ages 65 and older, about two-thirds of the respondents who were working said that the main reason that they continued to work was to earn income. The younger the retired elder, the stronger his or her intention to work.

In general, the elderly are characterized as those ages 65 and older. However, this age-based definition can vary according to the sociocultural and sociolegal systems of each country. In South Korea, in reality, taking into consideration the fact that the compulsory retirement age is between 55 and 60 and the age at which elders are eligible for pensions is 60, it would be more appropriate to separate the elderly into three age categories: those ages 55 and older, those ages 60 and older, and those ages 65 and older. These classifications are useful when discussing the employment status of older South Koreans.

Tables 6, 7, and 8 display data on the employment status of older South Koreans. These statistics were compiled from the *Annual Report on Economically Active Population Survey* in 2000 (South Korea National Statistical Office, 2001b). The data show that 50 percent of adults ages 55 and older are working. Of those working, almost 40 percent are engaged in paid jobs (formal employment), while the rest are in "unpaid jobs," a category that includes the self-employed and workers in casual employment. Looking at employed older Koreans ages 55 and older by occupation in the order of frequency, they are engaged

Table 6. Economically Active and Employed Population Ages 15 and Older, 2000

	Ages 15+	Ages 55–59	Ages 60–64	Ages 55+	Ages 60+	Ages 65+
Population (in thousands)	37,139	2,006	1,817	7,218	5,212	3,395
Percentage who are economically active	59.1	68.7	59.7	48.9	41.2	31.3
Percentage who are employed	56.7	66.6	58.4	47.9	40.7	31.2

Source: South Korea National Statistical Office, 2001.

Table 7. Employment Status of the Elderly, 2001

Employment status	All ages (15+)	Ages 55–59	Ages 60–64	Ages 55+	Ages 60+	Ages 65+
Paid workers						
Regular	30.4	18.7	9.2	10.9	6.3	3.5
Temporary	21.5	16.2	16.0	14.1	12.8	9.7
Daily	10.5	13.1	13.2	12.3	11.9	10.7
Subtotal	62.4	48.0	38.4	37.3	31.0	23.9
Unpaid workers						
Employer	7.4	7.4	5.5	4.9	4.1	2.8
Self-employed	21.5	32.3	41.2	43.3	49.1	56.7
Unpaid family worker	8.7	12.3	14.9	14.5	15.8	16.6
Subtotal	37.6	52.0	61.6	62.7	69.0	76.1
Total	100.0	100.0	100.0	100.0	100.0	100.0

Source: South Korea National Statistical Office, 2001.

Table 8. Distribution of Employed Older Koreans by Occupation, 2001

Occupation	All ages (15+)	Ages 55–59	Ages 60–64	Ages 55+	Ages 60+	Ages 65+
Legislator/senior official/manager	2.3	3.8	3.2	3.1	2.6	2.0
Professional	6.5	3.4	2.2	2.6	1.9	1.7
Technician/paraprofessional	9.6	3.2	2.6	2.7	2.3	2.0
Clerical worker	11.4	2.9	1.9	2.1	1.5	1.1
Service worker	12.7	12.0	8.4	9.1	7.1	5.8
Sales worker	13.4	12.4	10.7	11.3	10.3	9.8
Skilled agricultural/fishery worker	10.2	23.7	38.5	38.5	46.9	55.3
Craft and related trade worker	12.7	9.5	6.2	6.8	4.9	3.6
Plant and machine operator/assembler	10.8	9.1	5.0	4.1	3.2	1.3
Unskilled labor	10.4	20.0	21.3	19.7	19.3	17.4
Total	100.0	100.0	100.0	100.0	100.0	100.0

Source: South Korea National Statistical Office, 2001.

in skilled agricultural and fishery jobs (39 percent), unskilled labor (20 percent), sales jobs (11 percent), and other jobs in a variety of fields.

Slightly more than 40 percent of older adults ages 60 and older are working. Some 30 percent of those working are engaged in paid jobs while the rest are in unpaid work. Elders in this cohort are most frequently engaged in skilled agricultural and fishery jobs (47 percent), unskilled labor (19 percent), sales jobs (10 percent), and service jobs (7 percent).

Slightly more than 30 percent of adults ages 65 and older are working. Of those working, about a quarter are doing paid work and the rest are doing unpaid work. Fifty-five percent of workers over the age of 65 are engaged in agricultural and fishery work, 17 percent in daily labor, 10 percent in service jobs, and the rest in other fields.

Thus we can see that as their age advances, elderly South Koreans represent a smaller and smaller proportion of the economically active population, their employment rates decrease considerably, and their work status becomes increasingly irregular. South Korean elders also tend to be more engaged in primary industries (agriculture and fishery), industries with no set compulsory retirement age but also with no guaranteed incomes.

The majority of South Koreans ages 65 and older who work report that they do so for economic reasons, and the rest report that they work because they enjoy working, because they want to stay healthy, or because they want to work to pass the time (Chung et al., 1998). This means that a majority of elderly South Koreans work—and want to work—to compensate for insufficient incomes. Whether out of necessity or desire, work remains very much a part of the lifestyle of the majority of South Koreans passing into old age.

HISTORY OF INCOME MAINTENANCE POLICIES FOR KOREAN ELDERS

The history of income maintenance policies for elderly South Koreans from the years before 1960 to the present can be divided into five stages.

Before 1960

The Korean Peninsula only began to have international relationships with Western countries and to interact with Western ideas in the 1880s. However, no modern type of welfare program for older adults existed until Japanese colonialism abolished the last Korean dynasty in 1910. The Japanese colonial government ruled Korea for 36 years, from 1910 to 1945. It began to provide Japanese Royal Relief Funds on an ad hoc basis to poverty-stricken Koreans; but no systematic statutory welfare program for the elderly existed. The first old-age home was opened in 1918. Eight more opened between 1918 and 1945 (Park, 1999). However, most of these institutions were run by voluntary organizations with little assistance from the national government or the occupying forces. A modern system of public assistance was created by the Korean Relief Order, which the colonial government proclaimed in 1944. With this program, the national government began to provide some assistance to poor older adults living in institutions and in the community. During the colonial period, the most serious social problem that plagued Korea was poverty. This problem could not be solved systematically, due to budget constraints and to the colonial government's harsh treatment of Koreans. Therefore, the welfare system for the general public was mostly provisional, and accordingly, programs for the elderly were also provisional, primarily institutional care provided by voluntary organizations. During this colonial period, the problem of aging could not be recognized socially. If anything, aging-related problems may have been acknowledged only as a part of the larger problem of poverty.

Immediately after Korea was liberated from Japanese rule in August 1945, an American military government oversaw the country until 1948, when Korea reestablished its own government. However, the newly formed government did not have the financial ability to assist those in poverty because the devastation caused by the Korean War from 1950 to 1953 stripped Korea of its wealth and resources. After the war, South Korea relied heavily on foreign assistance. Throughout the 1950s, poverty continued to be the most serious and pressing social problem facing the country—more than one third of all South Koreans still lived in poverty in 1959—eclipsing any attention that might have been given to aging-related issues. During this time, the only welfare program for the elderly was institutional and some in-home relief services for the elderly. As of 1959, 37 elderly institutions around the country accommodated only 2,226 poor older adults.

The Korean Relief Order proclaimed by the Japanese colonial government was still the reference program for public assistance in Korea until 1961, when the Livelihood Protection Law, the first public assistance law, was passed. As important as that event was, it was slow to establish any kind of precedent.

The 1960s

Though the per capita GNP of South Koreans continuously rose from 1962 on due to the implementation of economic development plans, poverty continued to be one of the most haunting social problems that the country faced in the 1960s. Aging-related issues continued to be identified as part of the problem associated with poverty. Thus institutional and in-home relief under the public assistance law were the only programs available to older adults during this time and they provided little more than minimal assistance.

During the 1960s, two social insurance schemes for retirement income in old age were instituted: the Government Employees Pension, which began in 1960, and the Military Service Pension, which started in 1963. However, as these plans only covered a tiny proportion of the total number of Korean employees, the existence of these two programs did not raise awareness among the general public of the issue of retirement income security. As of 1969, about 10 percent of Koreans still lived in poverty, and 40 percent of those poor were elderly who received in-home assistance of one or another type for those suffering from disability. As of 1969 there were 43 elderly institutions spread across South Korea accommodating only 2,360 poor elderly persons (0.3 percent of the population ages 65 and older).

The 1970s

The successful implementation of a series of five-year economic development plans continued to boost the income levels of South Koreans during the 1970s. The GNP per capita rose from US$70 in 1960 to US$1,644 in 1979, representing an annual economic growth rate of 8 to 9 percent. However, poverty still remained the most serious social problem facing the country, affecting 5.3 percent of the total population in 1979.

At the end of the 1960s and the beginning of the 1970s a set of predicaments associated with aging began to be recognized as social problems (Hyun, 1992). Throughout the 1970s the following patterns of problems related to aging had been identified: economic problems, healthcare problems, alienation from the family and society, loss of societal roles and feelings of productivity, and the problems caused by the mandatory retirement age of 55. Despite the progress made in the identification of pressing social issues, not all the dilemmas faced by aging South Koreans were so recognized or accorded serious consideration.

In 1973 the National Welfare Pension Law was enacted, in response to the general public's concern for their uncertain economic security in old age. However, the law was not implemented until 1988, when it was recodified into the National Pension Law and enforced. In 1975 the Private School Teachers Pension program was initiated to secure retirement benefits for private school teachers, but its inception did not have any noticeable impact on enforcement of the National Welfare Pension Law for the general public.

The 1980s

Modernization triggered by the successful implementation of successive economic development plans resulted in a rupture of traditional family structures, the increasing participation of women in the labor force, waning of traditional family values, and the emergence of conflicts for individuals regarding care provisions for their elderly parents. Societal recognition of the problems associated with aging began to spread, and consideration of their complexity and scope became more serious. With the efforts of many leaders from voluntary aging-services organizations and from the South Korean congress itself, the Elderly Welfare Law was enacted in 1981.

The Elderly Welfare Law stipulated only modest forms of institutional care, health examinations, discounts for older adults on certain public programs, and creation of jobs suitable to the elderly. For the first time, it also classified institutions for elders into two categories: "homes for the aged" for relatively well elders and "nursing homes" for frail and ill elders. In order to implement this law, an Elderly Welfare Section was created within the Division of Family Welfare, part of the Ministry of Health and Welfare.

As awareness of aging-related problems grew, the public became much more concerned with issues surrounding retirement income and economic security in old age. The implementation of the old-age pension program created by the enactment of the National Welfare Pension Law in 1973 could no longer be postponed. Thus the law was recodified into the National Pension Law in 1986 and came into force in 1988. Under the new law, pensions are to be provided to those who have contributed to the national pension scheme for 20 years or more and who have reached the age of 60. Measures to promote the employment of older adults included the Elderly Job Bank (renamed the Elderly Employment Center in 1997) and Elderly Workshop programs created by the Ministry of Health and Welfare.

1990 to the Present

Since the 1990s, the average life expectancy of South Koreans has continued to rise, and with it has risen the percentage of older adults in the general population. The lengthening of life expectancy meant that chronic, degenerative diseases became more prevalent among older adults. The proportion of elders who do not live with their adult children also has greatly increased. Due to these developments, the problems and needs of older adults have become both more varied and more pressing. Care provisions in the home for older adults who require long-term assistance has emerged as a serious social concern.

Responding to these problems and the needs of elderly South Koreans, the government created the Elderly Persons' Welfare Division, independent from the Family Welfare Division, under the Bureau of the Family Welfare, Ministry of Health and Welfare, in 1990. The Family Welfare Division was dissolved in 1999, and the Elderly Persons' Health Division was established, again under the Bureau of Family Welfare, in 1999. Even without detailed knowledge of the situation of the elderly in South Korea, both of these moves can be seen to be portentous in their own right.

The National Pension, the national old-age pension system, was introduced in 1988. As population aging advanced in South Korea, the public began to voice worries about the depletion of National Pension funds. In response to these concerns, the National Pension Law was amended so that in the case of claimants with 40 years' contributions, the pension benefit was reduced to 60 percent of the earnings replacement rate instead of 70 percent. The new law also reduced the minimum contribution period to be eligible for any kind of old-age pension (but not the full pension) from 20 to 10 years. As a supplemental measure to find employment for older adults, thus improving their income status, the Older People Employment Promotion Law was enacted in 1992.

In order to guarantee a minimum standard of living to all South Koreans, including Korean elders, the Livelihood Protection Law, the existing public assistance law, was recodified as the National Basic Livelihood Security Law in 1999. This new law, which came into effect in October 2000, purports to recognize every citizen's right to a minimum standard of living and to provide public assistance to guarantee at least a minimal standard of living.

When the National Pension was instituted in 1988, it was designed to mature in 2008 for those who are eligible for it by virtue of contributing to the system for 20 years. However, immediately after the inception of the National Pension Law, it was recognized that citizens who have already reached pensionable age could not benefit from the system. In order to compensate for this inequitable treatment, the Old Age Allowance (OAA) was instituted in 1991. Due to budget limitations, the OAA was to be provided to low-income elderly (those who are under and slightly above the poverty line). In this sense, the OAA was a kind of public assistance, not a universal provision. In 1997, the OAA was changed to the "Elder-Respect Pension" to fully address the iniquities introduced by the National Pension system. Its coverage expanded to include not only older adults below the poverty line but also those whose incomes are above the poverty line but less than 65 percent of the average monthly income of individuals in urban workers' households.

Because of the societal norm of mandatory retirement at the relatively early age of 55, the majority of retired South Korean workers face daunting economic deprivation. A majority of those who are retired also express a strong desire to continue to work (Chung et al., 1998). In order to promote employment for older workers, in 1992 the Older Workers Employment Promotion Law was enacted. The law recommends that 3 percent or more of the workforce of each organization with more than 300 workers should be ages 55 and older. The law also established Older Worker's Banks and Older Worker's Priority Employment Job Selection programs around the nation to help older South Koreans find employment. However, because it does not mandate employment of older workers, the Older Workers Employment Promotion Law does little but suggest that companies should employ the elderly.

INCOME MAINTENANCE PROGRAMS AMONG KOREAN ELDERS

The economic problems associated with aging should be dealt with through a nation's social welfare programs and not left to individual resolutions. Currently, South Korea has six categories of income maintenance programs for older adults: public pensions, public assistance to the poor, the Elder-Respect Pension, the Senior Discount Program, employment promotion programs, and retirement benefit programs.

Public pensions and public assistance to the poor (National Basic Livelihood Security) and the Elder-Respect Pension are cash-payment programs; the senior discount program is simply a mechanism to allow the elderly to receive concessions on specified fees in the public arena and for transportation; and the employment promotion programs is a vehicle to help older adults earn income through remunerative work. The retirement benefit program is a cash-payment program but is a semipublic program that is managed by the workplace according to the Labor Standard Law. An overview of the coverage amounts and beneficiaries of the cash-payment programs is presented in Table 9.

As Table 9 summarizes, as of 2002, cash-payment income maintenance programs cover about 19.6 million South Koreans—41 percent of the total population. Public pension programs cover around 17.8 million workers. Together they account for approximately 81 percent of all employed workers. Public assistance programs cover about 1.8 million persons, or 3.7 percent of the total population. Roughly 27 percent of all Koreans ages 60 and older benefit from these income maintenance programs. Public pensions provide benefits to about 17 percent of those ages 60 and older and about 10 percent of those ages 65 and older. Public assistance programs provide benefits to about 10 percent of Koreans ages 60 and older and to 16 percent of those ages 65 and older.

Public Pensions

There are four public pension programs in South Korea, all designed to operate as contributory social insurance schemes. Occupation-specific pensions such as the Government Employees Pension, the Military Service Pension, and the Private School Teachers Pension cover only 5.9 percent of all employed workers and currently provide pensions to only 2.5 percent of elders ages 65 and older. The National Pension, the country's primary old-age pension program, is designed to cover the majority of all workers and the self-employed.

Whereas the three pension schemes for particular occupations were instituted in the early 1960s and in the middle of 1970s, the National Pension was only instituted in 1988. Furthermore, it covered only employees of companies with five or more full-time workers and those employed in agriculture and fisheries until June 2003. As of July 2003, however, the National Pension covers all those who are not insured under the three occupation-specific pension schemes.

The National Pension provides disability and survivor benefits, but its main function is that of an old-age pension. To receive benefits, individuals must have accrued 20 years or more of contributions and be 60 years old. The system has a few special categories for people who do not qualify for the full pension: A "reduced old age pension" is given to those who have contributed to the system

Table 9. Beneficiaries of Cash Payments Under Income Maintenance Programs, 2002

Program	Covered persons (A) (in thousands)[a]	Recipients ages 60+ (B) (in thousands)[a]	Recipients Ages 65+ (C) (in thousands)[a]	A/Total employed workers (%)[b]	B/Total ages 60+ (%)	C/Total ages 65+ (%)
Public pension	17,801	944	368	80.7	16.6	9.8
Government Employees Pension	931	115	63	4.2	2.0	1.7
Military Service Pension	150	38	22	0.7	0.7	0.6
Private School Teachers Pension	221	8	4	1.0	0.1	0.1
National Pension	16,499					
		783	279	74.8	13.8	7.4
Public assistance	1,785	585	585	—	10.3	15.5
National Basic Livelihood Security	1,539	441	339	—	7.8	9.0
Elder-Respect Pension	585	585	585	—	10.3	15.5
Total	19,586	1,529	953	80.7	26.9	25.3

[a]Since 339,000 out of 585,000 recipients of the Elder-Respect Pension also receive National Basic Livelihood Security (NBLS), 339,000 was subtracted from the column enumerating covered persons, the total number of recipients ages 60 and older, and the total number of recipients ages 65 and older.

[b]In calculation of the column "A/total employed workers," the number of public assistance recipients was not included in "A" because most of the recipients of public assistance are those who are not working.

for 10–19 years and have reached age 60. An "incumbent old-age pension" is provided to those who have contributed for more than 10 years, who are between 60 and 64 years of age, and who are still engaged in gainful employment. An "advanced old age pension" is provided to those who have contributed to the program for more than 10 years and whose age is between 55 and 59.

The National Pension program is financed in three ways, depending on the employment sector: For the general workforce, contributions come equally from both employees and employers; for the self-employed, contributions come solely from individuals, who pay double what employees in the general workforce contribute from their wages; and for the agricultural and fishery industries, contributions come from the worker's income and a flat per-person rate of government assistance. As of 2002, nearly 16.5 million Korean workers, or about 75 percent of the total workforce, are compulsorily covered by the National Pension (Table 9). The National Pension currently provides benefits to 783,000 Koreans ages 60 and older, or about 14 percent of this cohort, and to 298,000 Koreans ages 65 and older (7.4 percent).

As of 2002, approximately 1.3 million Korean workers, or about 6 percent of the total workforce, were covered under the three occupation-specific pension programs, and 161,000 Koreans ages 60 and older (2.8 percent of their cohort) received benefits from the three schemes.

Instituted in 1960 and amended several times since, the Government Employees Pension is the oldest public pension program in South Korea. It is financed by equal contributions from the central or local government and individual employees, and is managed by the Government Employees Pension Management Corporation. This program provides a much broader range of benefits to people who have reached the age of 60 than those offered by the National Pension. Prior to 1996, all enrolled individuals who had contributed to the pension program for more than 20 years—regardless of their age at retirement—were eligible for the full old-age pension. Currently, the program pays a reduced pension to those who retire at ages 55–59 with more than 20 years' contributions. Under the Government Employees Pension, as with the two other occupation-specific pensions, retirees eligible for benefits can choose one of three methods of payment: monthly payments, lump-sum benefits (offered at retirement), or partial retirement benefits (partial lump-sum and partial monthly payments).

The Military Service Pension program, begun in 1963, also provides much broader benefits than the National Pension. The pension is also financed by the shared contributions of the government and military professionals, and its benefits are available to individuals who have contributed to the program for more than 20 years. The program is managed by the South Korean Ministry of National Defense.

The Private School Teachers Pension program was started in 1975 and is managed by the Private School Teachers Pension Management Corporation. It covers teachers and employees at private schools (public school teachers are covered by the Government Employees Pension system). The program provides the same kinds of benefits as those of the Government Employees Pension to those who have contributed for more than 20 years. The Private School Teachers Pension is financed by three parties (teacher, school, and government) for teachers and by two parties (employee and school) for school employees.

Several issues seem worthy of mention. The self-employed tend to underreport their incomes, thereby lowering their mandated contributions to the National Pension, and there is no mechanism to investigate actual incomes reported by the self-employed. The underpayment of contributions lowers the pensions of those who have honestly reported their incomes and contributed the correct amounts. Another issue requiring both attention and redress is that the minimal guaranteed pension, even for those with a 40-year history of contributions, does not ensure finances necessary to sustain an acceptable standard of living above the poverty level. In addition, the National Pension's financial scheme is designed to pay substantial benefits even with disproportionately suppressed contributions, and thus may lead to a premature bankruptcy of the pension system. A recent estimation of the balance in the National Pension funds revealed that the funds will begin to show a deficit in 2033 and will become completely bankrupt by 2048 (Min, 2002).

Public Assistance

The National Basic Livelihood Security (NBLS) program is a public assistance program designed to guarantee a minimum standard of living for all Koreans independent of their earnings history and contributions. This program was first established by the Livelihood Protection Act in 1961 and recodified as the National Basic Livelihood Security Law of 1999. To be eligible for the NBLS program, an older person must have an income below the poverty line and have no one legally responsible for supporting him or her. Or, if the individual has someone legally responsible, that person must be unable to work themselves.

The NBLS stipulates five categories of benefits for elders: livelihood, medical, housing, self-reliance (such as employment training, loans for small businesses, job placement services), and funeral assistance. Younger Koreans may receive two additional types of benefits: educational and childbirth assistance. In 2002, 339,000 Koreans ages 65 and older received NBLS benefits (Table 9). The central government contributes 50 to 80 percent of the program costs, with the remaining 20 to 50 percent covered by local governments.

One of the hot-button issues concerning the NBLS is the right of the government to claim compensation for the support of older adults from those who are deemed responsible for such support (mainly adult children) but who have refused to provide assistance. The exercise of this right may create conflicts among family members and relatives. Another issue is the policy guideline of the "principle of productive welfare" underlying the NBLS; it implies that public assistance benefits should be related to job seeking or job training and should be provided to those who are economically active. The emphasis on work and economic productivity may therefore discourage the government from making available assistance to the elderly, who have formally exited from the labor market and are generally regarded as unproductive due to prevailing misconceptions of ageism or negative stereotypes in regards to aging in South Korean society.

Elder-Respect Pension

To be eligible for the Elder-Respect Pension, individuals must be 65 years or older as of 1998 and must not be covered by any other public pension. They also must have a mean income of the elderly household that is less than 65 percent of the mean income of individual members of urban workers' households, and must have household assets below 140 percent of the household asset eligibility limit set for NBLS self-reliance assistance. The central government contributes 50 to 70 percent of the costs of the Elder-Respect Pension, with the remaining 30 to 50 percent coming from local governments. This noncontributory pension scheme is also administered in the same way as the NBLS. In 2002, 585,000 elderly Koreans received benefits from the Elder-Respect Pension (Table 9).

The Elder-Respect Pension is set up like a universal provision for those who could not be covered under the National Pension program. In this sense, it should be provided to all elderly South Koreans who had reached age 60 by 1988. However, due to financial limitations, this pension is provided only to individuals ages 65 and older whose incomes and assets are below certain limits, and thus the amount of the pension is nominal. The limitations in the level of benefit and the number of beneficiaries is one of the issues associated with the Elder-Respect Pension. The Elder-Respect Pension is the only program for those presently ages 65 and older to get some substantial income from the government without the negative social stigma that may be associated with public assistance; the stigmatization of poverty may be much greater in the NBLS program. Saving face is an all-important consideration throughout Asia and nowhere is it a stronger value than in South Korea.

Senior Discount Program

The Senior Discount Program provides people ages 65 and older with discounts on public transportation, which is operated by the government, and on admission to public facilities such as parks and museums. It also provides elders a certain amount of cash each month as a transportation allowance. The Senior Discount Program is the only universal provision to all older Koreans and is presented as an acknowledgment of their carrying out their citizenship responsibilities. The program costs are borne solely by local governments, and the program is administered through the local governments under the supervision of the national Ministry of Health and Welfare.

The monthly allowance is a very small amount equivalent to fares for 12 rides on city buses. One issue concerning this program is whether it is desirable to provide the allowance to all South Koreans. However small the amount may be, it may be indispensable to low-income people; this is not the case with people in higher economic strata. Some argue that the transportation allowance should be paid only to low-income elders or upon request.

Employment Promotion Programs

There are five employment promotion programs that provide elderly people with the opportunity to earn income. Two are operated under the supervision of the Ministry of Health and Welfare: the Elderly Employment Center and the Elderly Workshop program. Elderly Employment Centers link employers and older job seekers. The Elderly Workshop program sets up workshops where older people can work together—generally on unskilled jobs such as pasting, sorting, and packing for small- and medium-size companies—and receive remuneration for their work.

The other three programs are operated under the supervision of the Ministry of Labor: Older Worker's Bank, Older Worker's Priority Employment Job Selection, and Older Worker Employment Quota. All three were created by the Older Workers Employment Promotion Law of 1992. The Older Worker's Bank is very similar to the Ministry of Health and Welfare's Elderly Employment Center but is particularly focused on those in the 55–64 age interval. The costs of the Older Worker's Banks are partly underwritten by the central Ministry of Labor, and all are operated by voluntary organizations.

The Older Worker's Priority Employment Job Selection program identifies jobs most appropriate to older workers and encourages employers to hire older workers for these jobs. The quota, as mentioned earlier, recommends that companies with more than 300 full-time workers hire enough older workers so that they represent 3 percent of the total workforce. However, the noncompulsory nature of these programs makes the recommendations of the law unenforceable.

Retirement Benefit

The retirement benefit program is compulsorily applicable to all workplaces under the 1953 Labor Standard Law, even though it is not rigidly applied. In the sense that it is compulsory, the program may be regarded as a semipublic program. However, it may be regarded as a private program in the sense that the system is managed by the workplace itself. The Labor Standard Law requires employers, public or private, to pay one month's salary per year into a retirement benefit fund for each worker, provided that the individual has been employed for more than one year. Therefore, any full-time worker who has worked for more than one year is eligible for the retirement benefit. The benefit is paid as a lump sum when workers leave their jobs on reaching the mandatory retirement age, or for other reasons such as changing employers. Currently, this program is the principal income source for most retirees in South Korea because the public pension has not yet matured.

As of 2002 only 47 percent of all employees were covered by this retirement benefit program. A substantial proportion of workers (about 32 percent) draw their retirement benefits in advance before they leave the workplace. Increasing numbers of companies (about 38 percent as of 2002) institute an annual salary system based on labor contracts. Therefore, the retirement benefit program is losing its original meaning of providing income security in old age. In response to this situation, the government is planning to convert the retirement benefit program to an occupational pension in the not-too-distant future.

POLICY RECOMMENDATIONS

The current generation of elderly South Koreans has suffered great hardships during their lives: They had to survive Japanese colonialism, World War II, and the Korean War. They have suffered from hunger, they have had to work hard to maintain their livelihoods and the welfare of their families, and they have spent a large proportion of their income on the education of their children. Many of them had to accept the harsh reality of low pay during the period of export-driven economic development, particularly in the 1960s and 1970s. In more personal terms, during their work lives few could afford to save for their old age, and the government could not afford to institute an old-age pension scheme prior to actually doing so. Under the best of circumstances, entering old age under such constraints would be problematic and few aging South Koreans enjoyed the best of circumstances.

South Korea currently has numerous programs aimed at maintaining a minimum standard of living for all its citizens. This is widely understood to be the primary goal of income maintenance programs, yet such a minimum standard of living was not guaranteed by national law until October 2000. Furthermore, the new National Basic Livelihood Security Law only provides for an absolute minimum standard of living for elderly South Koreans. In addition, the National Pension Program does not always guarantee a minimum standard of living, even for those who have contributed to the program for 40 years. For a substantial period of time in the future, only a small percentage of elderly South Koreans will be able to secure the extra income they need to ensure their quality of life.

The income levels of older adults in the lower-middle class must be improved so that they may enjoy a quality of life during their retirement years that is above mere subsistence. Under the current system of income maintenance for the elderly, achieving this goal means upgrading the coverage and benefit levels of the Elder-Respect Pension.

The retirement benefit program, which has existed as a semipublic program since 1953, was the main income maintenance program for older adults until the National Pension was instituted in 1988. This will remain the case until 2008, when the pension program reaches maturity. At present, employers must concurrently accumulate retirement benefits and pay National Pension premiums for their employees, which poses a troublesome burden for them. As mentioned earlier, the retirement benefit program is losing its function as a means of income security in old age. Therefore, the retirement benefit program needs to be converted to an occupational pension that may operate more flexibly as an optional fringe benefit to employees.

One of the best alternative programs to improve income maintenance for elders during retirement is to provide opportunities for older adults and the newly retired to be reemployed. Since the current Older Workers Employment Promotion Act only recommends to private companies that 3 percent or more of their total workforce should comprise workers ages 55 and over, this recommendation has not been widely taken up. It would be more desirable to make this recommendation a compulsory regulation and to provide employers with data showing the benefits of employing older workers who have considerable work and life experience (Hwang, Choi, Kim, Rhee, Ryu, and Byun, 2001). Some of these possible benefits include higher levels of diligence, lower absenteeism levels, lower salaries, and higher skill levels in jobs requiring precision.

It is also prudent to extend the compulsory retirement age to 60 and then to 65, with the eventual goal of abolishing it completely. Premature retirement, which continues to be set out in the bylaws of companies and industries, not only makes workers age prematurely but also aggravates the economic plight of retired South Koreans. Therefore, an extended mandatory retirement age needs to be clearly stipulated in the Elderly Employment Promotion Law. Furthermore, legislation of an anti-age-discrimination act would help solve the problem of premature retirement. Such legislation needs to be contingent upon adopting a system of compensation based on capability rather than on seniority.

The development of income maintenance policies for elderly Koreans needs to be supported by the conscious practice of filial piety at an inclusive societal level. The traditional value of filial piety, which emphasizes family responsibility for the economic support of elderly people and the provision of care to them by their family members, has hampered the development of a social welfare policy for the elderly in South Korea. Filial piety has customarily been emphasized at the familial level but not at the societal level. One of the most important reasons for filial piety is to repay one's parents for their love and care (Choi, 1982). At the level of the family, the role of filial piety is to support one's aging parents to repay them for their love and care. At the societal level, filial piety is the state's welfare provision to the elderly in order to repay them for their contributions to society.

For the current generation of older citizens, who have made great sacrifices during their lives for the development of the modern South Korean society, the state needs to take action on a number of fronts: expanding coverage of current income maintenance programs, improving benefit levels, and in particular, allocating more of its budget to income maintenance programs for the elderly.

REFERENCES

Choi, S. J. (1996). The family and ageing in Korea: A new concern and challenge. *Ageing and Society, 16,* 1–25.

Choi, S. J., and Chang, I. H. (2002). *Welfare of the elderly* (Rev. ed.). Seoul: Seoul National University Press.

Chung, K. H., Cho, A. J., Oh, Y. H., Byun, J. K., Byun, Y. C., and Moon, H. S. (1998). *Current status of the life and welfare needs of the elderly.* Seoul: Korean Institute for Health and Welfare.

Donahue, W., Orbach, H. L., and Pollak, O. (1960). Retirement: The emerging social pattern. In C. Tibbits (Ed.), *Handbook of social gerontology* (pp. 330–406). Chicago: University of Chicago Press.

Hwang, J. S., Choi, S. J., Kim, T. H., Rhee, K. O., Ryu, S. H., and Byun, J. K. (2001). The ways of enhancing employment for the older population. *Journal of Korea Gerontological Society, 21*(1), 98–118.

Hyun, O. S. (1992). *A comparative study on the formulation process of social welfare policy for the aged in Korea and Japan.* Unpublished doctoral dissertation, Seoul National University, South Korea.

Kim, I. K. (1996). Demographic transition and population aging in Korea. *Korea Journal of Population and Aging, 25*(1), 27–40.

Min, J. S. (2002). Pension problem and policy tasks. *Pension Forum, 4,* 5.

Min, J. S., Ryu, I. H., Choi, S. J., and Kim, Y. H. (1993). *Aging trends of Koreans and policy measures for welfare of the elderly.* Seoul: Korea Development Institute.

Park, T. R. (1999). *The welfare of the elderly: Theories and practice.* Kyungsan, South Korea: Taegu University.

South Korea Ministry of Health and Welfare. (2001). *Statistics on recipients of benefit of national basic livelihood security program.* Mimeographed manuscript. Gwacheon, South Korea: Author.

South Korea Ministry of Labor. (2001). *Statistics on retirement age of corporations.* Gwacheon, South Korea: Author.

South Korea National Statistical Office. (2001a). *Population estimate, 1960–2030.* Daejon, South Korea: Author.

South Korea National Statistical Office. (2001b). *Annual report on the economically active population survey.* Daejon, South Korea: Author.

South Korea National Statistical Office. (2002). *2000 population and housing census report, vol. 10 (The aged).* Daejon, South Korea: Author.

Sunwoo, D., Chung, K. H., Oh, Y. H., Cho, A. J., and Suk, J. E. (2001). *A study on long-term care needs of the elderly and policy measures for long-term care.* Seoul: Korean Institute for Health and Social Affairs.

Tahk, H. J. (1984). Current status and problems of the retirement system. In Asan Foundation (Ed.), *Industrializing society and retirement* (pp. 31–41). Seoul: Asan Foundation.

United Nations. (1996). *Population ageing in Asia and the Pacific*. Bangkok: Economic and Social Commission for Asia and the Pacific.

PART III

Living Arrangements, Family Caregiving, and Social Support

CHAPTER NINE

Living Arrangements and Social Support for Older Adults in India

Phoebe Liebig and P. V. Ramamurti

Issues affecting older adults in India have generally received little attention from the gerontological community, as evidenced in the literature on aging in Asia. Other than the articles cited here and a few studies of demographics, housing, and family support (Brink, 1998; Kendig, Hashimoto, and Coppard, 1992; Martin, 1988), greater attention has been paid to aging in the more developed nations such as Japan, Hong Kong, South Korea, and more recently, China. Even within India, a focus on those ages 60 and older only became pronounced during the last 25 to 30 years of the 20th century. However, the dimensions of aging in India are becoming better understood and appreciated, through recognition that together India and China will account for nearly 40 percent of the world's elderly by 2025 (Shuman, 1995).

POPULATION AGING IN INDIA

Population aging, a global phenomenon of the 20th century, will become even more dominant in this century in both developed and developing nations. In 1996, more than 43 percent of the world population ages 75 and older lived in just four countries, three of them in Asia: China, the United States, Japan, and India (Shuman, 1995). In the early 1990s, the number of Chinese citizens ages 60 and older reached 70 million. India had more than 57 million elders, with 63 percent (or 36 million) ages 60–69 and nearly 11 percent (or 6 million) ages 80 and older (Government of India [GOI], 1999).

India's older adult population grew from 12 million in 1901 to 71 million a century later, nearly a sixfold increase. In 2001, every seventh older person in the world was Indian. According to United Nations projections, India will have

198 million persons ages 60 and older by the year 2030 and 326 million by 2050 (GOI, 1999). Sustained reductions in levels of fertility and mortality, especially since the 1980s, have brought about this accelerated aging of the population in the world's largest democracy (Alam, 2000).

Although age projections for Japan are common knowledge, it is less well known that 12.6 percent of all Indians will be age 60 or older in 2025. By 2050, the proportion will be 21.3 percent, compared to 5.6 percent a century earlier (GOI, 1999; Rajan, Mishra, and Sarma, 1999). An increase by almost a factor of four, this figure nearly equals the United Nations' old-age projections for Asia (21.9 percent) in the mid-21st century (Velkoff and Lawson, 1998).

All Indian states have shown recent growth in the numbers of older adults and a simultaneous decline in the numbers of children ages 0–14 (Tracy, 1991). However, the 25 Indian states and seven Union Territories are in different stages of this demographic transition. In each of the 15 major states—whose combined populations account for more than 97 percent of the nation's total population—the elderly population exceeds the national average of 7 percent (Alam, 2000).[1] The state of Kerala has the highest proportion of older adults: 8.8 percent of Keralans are ages 60 and older. Punjab, Haryana, and Uttar Pradesh in the north; Maharashtra in the west; and Orissa in the east also have proportions of elders that are above the national average (Alam, 2000). Of these, Orissa has the highest rate of rural poverty (47 percent), followed by Maharashtra (34 percent) and Uttar Pradesh (32 percent). By contrast, Haryana and Kerala have low rates of rural poverty (12 and 10 percent respectively); Punjab has the lowest, at 4 percent (Alam, 2000). In a federal nation where 80 percent of elders live in rural areas (Kapoor, 2001; Rajan et al., 1999), these figures have important implications for national and state policymakers.

Life Expectancy and Aging of Indian Elders

Greater life expectancy also has been a hallmark of population aging around the world. In India, life expectancy at birth has shown huge gains: For men it rose from 42 years in the 1950s to 58 years in the late 1980s (GOI, 1999). By 1997, life expectancy for men had increased to 60 (Gist and Velkoff, 1997) and is projected to be 67 by 2015 (GOI, 1999). For women, life expectancy has been somewhat higher, from 58 years at birth in the late 1980s to 61 years in 1997; it is projected to rise to 69 years by 2015 (Gist and Velkoff, 1997; GOI, 1999).

In the early 1990s, life expectancy at age 60 for Indians also increased by 15 years for men and 16 years for women (GOI, 1999). As elsewhere, greater longevity in India, combined with a declining fertility rate, has enhanced the joint survival of different generations. This has led to increased numbers of

[1] The remaining states, with 3 percent of the population, have so few elders that it brings the total proportion of older adults in the population down to 7 percent.

generations who are alive at one time and decreased numbers of family members within each generation (Bengtson, 2001).

Aging of the aged is another 20th-century trend that will continue in this century. Both developing nations and developed nations report growth in the numbers of citizens ages 80 and older: In 1998 there were 8.7 million old old in the United States, 5.75 million in India, and 4.34 million in Japan. By 2025, these figures will increase to 14.4 million in the United States, 17.98 million in India (nearly triple the earlier figure), and 10.67 million in Japan. In that year, older Indian women will constitute nearly 54 percent of the old old (Velkoff and Lawson, 1998).

Socioeconomic Characteristics of the Aging Population

A brief look at several socioeconomic characteristics—literacy, economic status and labor-force participation, caste, and marital status—round out the picture of population aging in India. Education levels are positively correlated with greater longevity, higher life expectancy at birth, higher economic status, better health, and a greater capacity for self-care in old age. Literacy rates in India are low: 53 percent for men and 32 percent for women. These rates are lower for older men (41 percent) and women (13 percent), and even lower for rural elders: 34 percent for men and 7.5 percent for women, an outcome of the low quantity and quality of educational facilities in rural areas in the past (Rajan et al., 1999). Future elders are expected to be more literate, due to a greater emphasis on education as part of India's economic development strategies.

Fully 65 percent of rural men and 19 percent of rural women ages 60 and older continue to work (Alam, 2000), but at reduced hours, largely due to failing health (Rajan et al., 1999). Overall labor-force participation of adults ages 60 and older, particularly for men, has declined over the past four decades; still, 43 percent of rural and 24 percent of urban elders were working in 1991 (Alam, 2000). The 1991 census revealed that almost 80 percent of older workers in India work in the agricultural sector (Rajan et al., 1999).

Due to the overall drop in labor-force participation among elders, low rates of pension coverage (only 10 percent of all workers), and high rates of poverty for Indian families, financial problems are common for the aged. Surveys conducted in rural areas generally reveal a high degree of financial insecurity among the elderly, especially among older women (Muttagi, 1997). In poor societies such as India, women and elders often suffer from unequal sharing of family resources (Alam, 2000). It is not surprising to find a higher degree of economic hardship among older women, particularly widows. Approximately 60 percent of older widows in rural areas work, as do 69 percent of their urban counterparts (Rajan et al., 1999).

Economic security also has been found to be related to caste (Rajan et al., 1999), which defined social relations and economic status in the past and still does today, although less so. Despite Mahatma Gandhi's efforts and the passage of laws guaranteeing equal access to education and jobs, caste is still part of the national mindset, as witness the explicit media attention given to the recent election of India's first Untouchable president. There are four castes: Brahmins (priests), Kshatriyas (warriors), Vaishyas (merchants), and Sudras (artisan-laborers), each with numerous subcastes, or *jatis,* that vary regionally. Each subcaste had a distinctive tradition with strong ties to the same subcaste in other villages (Hsu, 1963). "Untouchables," who historically carried out the most menial tasks, fell outside this classification, as did tribals (indigenous groups), who primarily engaged in agriculture, crafts, and trading. Tribals, landless peasants, and untouchables, known collectively as "scheduled tribes and castes and backward classes," are likely to be very poor and to experience substandard living conditions, especially those who migrate to urban areas and end up living in slums (Muttagi, 1997). The tribal way of life has disintegrated, victim to modernization, with severe impacts on the economic status of women from these groups (Rathore, 2000).

Individuals are born into their caste or subcaste, which formerly served as an occupational monopoly. In the villages, if all inhabitants were of the same caste, the village council, or *panchayat,* also operated as a caste council (caste councils, unlike *panchayats,* traditionally made many decisions affecting families, such as marriages). Caste also served as the means by which intervillage and intravillage marriage was regulated (Hsu, 1963). Today, although perusal of marriage ads in urban newspapers indicates that caste may be somewhat less important, it is still a means by which behavioral cohesion and norms are achieved. Among the elderly, especially in rural areas, adherence to caste norms is still important for marriage.

Marital status among older Indians is an important aspect of well-being. In general, married couples are better off economically, socially, and emotionally than unmarried adults (Rajan et al., 1999). In India, as elsewhere in Asia, older men are much more likely to be married than older women. According to the 1991 census, nearly 81 percent of men ages 60 and older are married, versus 44 percent of older women (Rajan et al., 1999); 15.5 percent of men are widowers who have not remarried, compared to 54 percent of women. These latter figures reflect two tendencies in Indian society: Women generally marry men older than they, and widowed men tend to remarry. In Hindu society, due to the perception that widows are still part of their husband's bodies after death, women are expected not to remarry (Lamb, 2000). Reflecting greater longevity, the proportion (but not absolute numbers) of women ages 60 and older who are widows has shown a decline over the past 40 years, from 75 percent in 1961 to 54 percent in 1991, with a similar pattern for women ages 70 and older. In 1971, 80 percent of old-old women were widowed, compared to 67 percent in 1991 (Alam, 2000).

Marital status has major implications for living arrangements and social support. However, before addressing those issues, a description of the traditional Indian family system is required. Similar to norms in other parts of Asia, expectations and roles are different for men and women in India.

THE TRADITIONAL INDIAN FAMILY

Although some matrilinearity exists in Kerala and among tribal groups, the traditional Indian family is patrilineal, as in much of Asia. Under this system, men have ownership of resources; when women marry, they take on the identification of their husband's family. Older adults live with their oldest married sons and are cared for by their daughters-in-law when the need arises (Bongaarts and Zimmer, 2002). The Indian family follows this pattern, but its membership is more extended (i.e., comprises siblings of multiple generations and their descendants) than the stem family in Japan and other Asian nations.

The Indian concept of the joint family has a long history; in Mughal times (15th through mid-19th centuries) it was the primary source of support for older people (Muttagi, 1997; Williamson and Pampel, 1993). The joint family encompasses relationships of centrality that comprise people (including ancestors, servants, and guests), animals, family deities, household material goods, and the space of the house itself (Lamb, 2000). Such an extended family system is based on long-term bonds of reciprocal interdependence and indebtedness demonstrated through food, material goods, services, and observance of special rites such as giving of the first food and administering final rites (Lamb, 2000; Kapoor, 2001).

The joint family also comprises hierarchical relations and relations of mutuality. In the former, elder-junior interactions consist of blessings, requests and commands, advice, and affection, but also curses and complaints. Junior-elder interactions consist of blessings, compliance, deference, respectful listening, and devotion, but more negatively of withholding services and blessings and of showing disrespect. Relations of mutuality center around the sharing of food and shelter; being "the same house's people"; loving, touching, and embracing; and the sharing of gossip and conversation (Lamb, 2000). All family members live, cook, and eat together and share responsibility for managing common landholdings or a family business. Overarching family concerns take precedence over those of individuals in domains such as education, marriage, choice of careers, and disposition of property.

Gender

The traditional Indian joint family ascribes distinct roles to each gender. The typical family consists of the oldest man and his wife, his male siblings and their wives, and their children and grandchildren. The oldest man brings the entire family under his umbrella, regardless of the age of individual members. His duty is to direct, advise, and guide family members until his death, and his authority is supported by his occupational role and income (Muttagi, 1997). As head of the family, the oldest male has primary responsibility for familial interactions with his own sons; his wife usually oversees relations with his daughters-in-law (Gore, 1992).

A long tradition of *ashrama,* the four stages of life defined in the ancient Vedic scriptures also has governed the behavior of men (and to a lesser degree, that of women), especially in higher castes. Each stage is allied with specific tasks and responsibilities. After the first stage (*brahmacharya*, or childhood) comes young and middle adulthood (*grasthastha*), with its duties of marriage and the rearing and educating of children. The third stage (*vanaprastha*) denotes the time when individuals or couples leave their homes, having fulfilled their household duties, to take up lives more removed from those responsibilities, similar to the concept of retirement in Western societies (Cohen, 1998). Traditionally, this occurred at age 60; the transition from *grasthastha* to *vanaprastha* was accompanied by specific rituals and celebrations, and could involve a shift to greater participation in community affairs (Muttagi, 1997). The fourth stage (*sannyasa*) is a period of renunciation from worldly engagements to pursue more spiritual concerns, similar to the concept of disengagement much discussed in the early gerontological literature (Cumming and Henry, 1961).

In general, girls and women in India have had a marginalized status within the family, and their access to opportunities for educational and occupational advancement has been limited. That situation is gradually changing; in the 1990s the declaration of the Year of the Girl Child and the offering of 500 rupees for the birth of each female child were policies designed to change traditional thinking. Male children, however, still are preferred because they bring a higher standard of living to the family unit and thus a better return on educational investments (Gore, 1992).

In contrast, a daughter imposes costs on her family in the form of a dowry to be given to her husband's family as part of the marriage contract. In addition, because daughters are not permanent members of their family of origin (Lamb, 2000), the costs of their education do not bring the same tangible economic benefits to their parents as those spent on their brothers do. Daughters are expected to cut their family ties upon their marriage and transfer allegiance to their husband's family. They often become a servant in their husband's home, where their activities are controlled by their mother-in-law (Lamb, 2000). Traditionally, a daughter cannot care for her parents in their old age, even if they have no sons.

Greater urbanization and modernization have led to better educational and employment opportunities for women—especially among middle-class families—and, in turn, have modified traditional ideas about women's roles. In recent years, middle-class elders have begun to look to their married daughters occasionally for support; instances of unmarried daughters supporting their parents are somewhat more common (Gore, 1992). But the norm of the daughter-in-law as primary caregiver of the older couple is still dominant, especially in rural areas (Jamuna, 1992).

Traditional views of women and their gender-appropriate roles guide both men's and women's behavior. Marriage and family are important for men, but even more so for women. Arranged marriages between prepubescent children are largely in the past. The average age of marriage for women is now 20; for tribal women, this average is 13 (Desouza, 2000). As noted above, the new bride continues to join her husband's family and works for her mother-in-law, who is in charge of the household's domestic activities. Indeed, the formal authority of the older woman derives from her relationships with her daughters-in-law; however, the compliance of the younger women cannot be taken for granted (Gore, 1992). The older woman retains this position of dominance, usually until her husband dies.

Widowhood is a dreaded time of life for many older Indian women, with its many restrictions on food, clothing, and behavior. Widows may lose their children to in-laws and even their rights to their deceased husband's property, despite laws to the contrary. Widowhood may also lead to domination by a daughter-in-law, if a widow's son becomes the head of the joint family. In addition to being perceived as dangerously inauspicious by others, widows face the prospect of an economically precarious life, because they must rely on the goodwill of their sons or the brothers of their deceased husbands (Lamb, 2000). The childless widow is at even greater economic risk, especially if she belongs to an upper caste or a middle-income family, in which women traditionally have not been expected to work. By contrast, poorer, lower-caste women are more likely to seek employment, but some must depend at least partly on the help of neighbors or distant relatives and some migrate to urban areas and live on handouts (Gore, 1992). Many widows end up in places of pilgrimage because they feel they have no real family ties and are generally unable to return to their parental home, even if they are widowed at a young age (Lamb, 2000). This removal from household concerns and turn toward the spiritual in later life fits well with the traditions of *vanaprastha* and *sannyasa,* and so has not been viewed as abandonment (Cohen, 1998).

Class and Geography

Two other factors affecting the status of older Indians deserve mention: class and geography. In general, elders from propertied classes are better off; older people enjoy higher economic status—not just within the family but in the larger society as well—if they are economically self-sufficient and are not an economic burden on the family. Research since the 1970s shows that the degree of authority exercised by older men is directly related to their level of economic self-sufficiency (Cohen, 1998; Muttagi, 1997; Ramamurti, 1997).

In rural areas, where the economy is primarily agrarian, there is intergenerational continuity of occupation between fathers and sons, and the life experience of parents continues to be relevant in village society (Gore, 1992). Older men in rural areas are likely to continue working until they become incapacitated, ensuring the continuation of income, autonomy, social involvement, and familial authority as the male head of the household (Gore, 1992). The traditional joint family in rural India has undergone some stresses, primarily occasioned by younger family members migrating to other parts of India or the world in search of better-paying jobs. However, more than two thirds of rural families retain the joint family tradition (Jamuna, 1992).

The joint family in urban areas, however, has been subject to more severe pressures. The significance of elders' parental roles tends to be reduced. Pensioned retirement at age 60, or somewhat earlier in some occupations, is well defined for middle- and upper-class men, although not for women (Gore, 1992; van Willigen and Chadha, 1999). The urban environment also is more supportive of the young and of innovation; intrafamilial occupational discontinuity is more prevalent (Gore, 1992). In addition, acute housing shortages, especially in very big cities such as Mumbai (Bombay) and Chennai (Madras), undermine the tradition of the coresident joint family (although the opposite effect has been found elsewhere in Asia due to specific policies [Liebig, 2001]). Under those circumstances, older people often prefer to remain in their villages in familiar settings rather than migrate with their sons to cities in India or elsewhere.

Significantly, most research on aging and the joint family in India focuses on the problems of the aged in cities and towns (Gore, 1992). Contrasted with the ideal of the traditional joint family, the picture that this research presents of India's urban middle class is often one of estranged older parents, nuclear households, and unwanted elders (Cohen, 1998). However, as is the case with rural elders, the status of urban elders is often less dependent on their age and more dependent on their economic status and level of education (Gore, 1992). This emphasis on the urban aged, rather than looking at rural elders, has led to discussions about the decline and possible disappearance of the joint family tradition.

The Decline of the Joint Family

The breakdown of the traditional joint family and the rise of the nuclear family have received attention in Asia and elsewhere (Hareven, 2001; Kendig et al., 1992). Indian researchers (Bose, 1988; Dandekar, 1996; Gokhale, 1992; Jamuna, 1998; Kapoor, 2001) and the popular press have decried the decline of the joint family tradition. Some suggest the decline is so precipitous that the death of the joint family is nearly a *fait accompli*.

Bengtson (2001) has identified a similar perception in Western studies of family structure, starting in the 1960s, when Ernest W. Burgess identified the emergence of the modern nuclear family as an outgrowth of industrialization and modernization. Burgess hypothesized that urbanization, increased individualism, secularism, and the emancipation of women changed the family from a social institution based on law and custom to one based on companionship and love (Bengtson, 2001). The outcomes of this shift are changes in family patterns, weakening of extended kinship ties, dissolution of lineage patterns, and the development of the nuclear family as a more independent kinship unit (Bengtson, 2001; Bongaarts and Zimmer, 2002). Such changes are accompanied by a decline in family caregiving capacity and practice, a perspective shared by most Indian and Asian gerontologists.

This same view was advanced in the United States in the 1960s and 1970s, accompanied by charges that the American family was neglecting its elders and warehousing them in nursing homes (Bengtson, 2001). Yet, systematic research by Shanas (1979) and others revealed this perception to be untrue. More recently, Bengtson, Rosenthal, and Burton (1995) report that although family structure is changing, cross-generational support remains strong. The degree of sustained reciprocity and exchange is key when considering the possible decline of family solidarity (Bengtson, 2001).

Not all researchers studying aging in India consider these changes in family structure as a decline. Lamb (2000) suggests there is little or no evidence that the past was filled with harmonious joint families, submissive young women, and venerated elders. Similarly, Cohen (1998) decries the notion of the "bad family" in modern India, pointing out the lack of baseline or longitudinal data to support assertions of the widespread decline of the joint family tradition (see also Martin, 1990). Lamb indicates that the few longitudinal studies undertaken in the late 1980s revealed that, contrary to popular belief, the proportion of joint families actually increased (2000, pp. 93–94). Several researchers indicate the perceived decline of the joint family is actually an urban phenomenon rather than a rural one (Gore, 1992). Others have suggested that family structure is less important than the degree to which family members continue to operate as a caring, supportive unit (Gokhale, 2003).

Despite these varying perspectives on the robustness of the joint family, agreement exists that it is still a viable institution. As reported by Liebig and Ramamurti (2000), interviews of numerous public and private decision-makers (such as state ministers and heads of NGOs) and administrators and trustees of old-age homes yielded an overwhelming consensus that the Indian family still reveres and cares for its elders (see also Gokhale, 2003; Kapoor, 2001; Muttagi, 1997). However, there also is widespread agreement that families are changing, requiring the aged to adjust (Jamuna, 1998; Singh, 1997).

LIVING ARRANGEMENTS OF OLDER ADULTS

Across Asia, researchers have examined the living arrangements of older adults in order to define the status of the traditional family and to discern the capacity of the family to care for its elder family members. Coresidence is a central feature of housing and living arrangements for Asian—and specifically, Indian—elders (Liebig, 2001). In the developing nations of Asia (e.g., India, Pakistan, Nepal, Philippines), 66 percent of older men and 68 percent of older women reside with one or more adult children, usually with a male child. Among these elders, 80 percent of older Pakistani men and 90 percent of Bangladeshi women live in this kind of arrangement (Bongaarts and Zimmer, 2002). Some researchers posit that 90 percent of rural elders in India live in households with at least one adult child (Martin, 1988).

Researchers often determine living arrangements by examining size of household, which also serves as an indicator of coresidence (Rajan et al., 2000). Other measures of living arrangements include headship of the family and relationship to the head, the gender of the coresident child, and coresidence with kin or others. Other studies examine the proportion of elders living alone (Bongaarts and Zimmer, 2002; Rajan et al., 1995, 2000) or elders who live in housing for the aged.

Household Size

Household size can be defined in two ways: the average number of individuals per household in the population; or the number of household members in the household of the average individual, known as *average experienced household size.* In the developing nations of Asia, including India, the average household size of all adults ages 65 and older is 5.2, while the experienced household size is 5.5, compared to 6.5 for individuals of all ages. Thus, older adults live in smaller-than-average households but with several household members (Bongaarts and Zimmer, 2002).

Data for Indian elders show a similar pattern. From 1961 to 1981, average household size increased from 5.2 to 5.6 in both rural and urban areas (Rajan et al., 1999). However, if one assumes that a household of six or more members indicates the presence of older people, the proportion of that size household declined in the 1990s. Nationwide, slightly less than 40 percent of India's aged live in households with six or more members, and 14 percent live in one- or two-member households. However, fully 71 percent of India's elderly live in households with four or more members (ranging from 4.83 to 5.27), the expected minimum for a joint family. Slightly more than half of all Indian elders live with their children and grandchildren; around 4 percent live with other relatives (Rajan et al., 2000).

Head of Household

In the developing nations of Asia, 94 percent of older men are the head of their household or the parent of the head (Bongaarts and Zimmer, 2002). In India, 90 percent of men ages 60 and older hold that status (Rajan et al., 2000). Older women are far less likely to be the head of the household, but they are related to the head as spouse or parent (Bongaarts and Zimmer, 2002). More rarely, they assume headship of the household after their husband's death (Rajan et al., 2000). These data indicate that the patrilineal family is still a major social structure in developing Asian nations, including India. Indian elders still reside with their sons, which is their preference, even if the elders must make social, economic, or psychological compromises to do so (Rajan et al., 2000).

Living Alone

In the Bongaarts and Zimmer study (2002) of developing nations in Asia, slightly more than 7 percent of Asian elders (3.6 percent of older men and 10.2 of older women) lived alone. However, these figures can be somewhat misleading. Many elders living alone have kin nearby with whom they exchange support, but current data cannot capture this information.

Indian elders show different patterns of living alone than their counterparts in other Asian nations. The 1991 census indicated that slightly less than 8 percent of rural elders and 5.4 percent of urban elders live alone. Major differences occur for men and women: Nearly 12.5 percent of rural older men and 9.5 percent of urban older men live alone. By comparison, 1.43 percent of rural older women and 0.8 percent of urban older women live in single households. Older women are more likely to live in one- to two-person households than are men: 16.2 percent versus 12.5 percent (Rajan et al., 1999).

Some factors significantly affect living arrangements. Martin (1990) found that coresidence increases if elders are married and have greater numbers of children. Bongaarts and Zimmer (2002) examined the impact of several measures of economic development—higher levels of education, higher gross national product per capita, lower percentage of citizens living in rural areas, and greater life expectancy—on living arrangements. Other than education, they found little association with changing patterns of coresidence. Higher levels of education among older Asians, especially men, were associated with a downward trend in coresidence with children. Older adults with more schooling were more likely to live in smaller households with fewer children and other adults, with their spouses, or alone. Low literacy rates in India, noted earlier, may help to explain the persistence of the joint family, but the higher levels of education expected among India's future elders raise important questions about what will happen to coresidential living and whether more elders will live in old-age homes.

Old-Age Homes

Old-age homes are not new to India; they were first established in the early 18th century as free homes (Nair, 1989). They served destitute elders who had no family to care for them. Before 1900, only 29 such homes existed; that number had increased to more than 300 by 1990 (HelpAge India, 1995; Nair, 1989; Rajan et al., 2000). Other studies suggest there may now be as many as 600 or 700 old-age homes in the country (Liebig, 2003; Rajan et al., 2000).

Various directories (HelpAge India, 1995, 1998; Nair, 1989) and GOI grants lists (Ramamurti and Jamuna, 1996) reveal that homes are concentrated in the states of Kerala, Maharashtra, and Tamil Nadu; some states have none. Although old-age homes in India are located primarily in urban areas, some are found in rural areas as well (Liebig, 2003). Some homes serve other marginalized groups, such as orphans and people with mental retardation (Liebig, 2003). Nearly three fourths of these homes have been established since 1951 (Rajan et al., 1999). This rapid growth has raised concerns in the gerontological community and the media and is seen as yet another indicator of the decline of the joint family.

A 1995 survey by HelpAge India, however, indicated that fewer than 13,000 elders were living in old-age homes. Three years later, the number had increased to nearly 16,000 (HelpAge India, 1998), still less than 1 percent of the total older adult population. Despite the increased numbers of homes, the numbers of aged living in those settings remain minuscule.

The socioeconomic class of residents of old-age homes is beginning to change, as seen by the development of for-pay homes, called "pay and stay." These homes are generally smaller than free homes, are somewhat less likely to be run by Christian denominations, and cater to the more educated, emerging middle class, especially couples or childless individuals. Although some pay-and-stay homes are located in urban areas, many are found in suburban and rural areas that provide peace and quiet and beautiful surroundings (Liebig, 2003).

Nearly all residents of old-age homes, regardless of socioeconomic status, live there because their families are unable to care for them. Surveys of old-age homes, primarily free homes, indicate that resident satisfaction is often low because the aged feel abandoned, are disturbed by family conflicts, or see their lives as falling short of the expected norm of a peaceful and revered old age. The lack of emotional support from their families is keenly felt (Dandekar, 1996; Rajan et al., 1999; Ramamurti and Jamuna, 1996). However, for destitute elders, the homes provide food, shelter, and clothing that their families are unable to supply on a stable basis. Thus, economic need is a second major factor for the aged living in free homes and in homes that combine both paying and non-paying residents. In these homes, income-generating activities, such as making garlands for religious celebrations, help defray some operating costs and provide meaningful activities for residents.

A third reason given for living in old-age homes is a desire for companionship; residents of for-pay homes frequently mentioned the desire to live with their peers. In most homes, residents are expected to help provide care and caring, as they would in their own villages or neighborhoods. The for-pay homes are less likely to stress common welfare among residents and are often more focused on helping out the local community. Residents in religion-based homes, especially men, are often expected to participate in community-based programs run by the organization (Liebig, 2003).

Quality of care in old-age homes is a societal concern, especially in government-run facilities (Rajan et al., 1999). Gaining access to publicly run homes—even for short visits—is often difficult, giving rise to the perception of something to hide. Few systematic evaluations of old-age homes, however, have been conducted (Ramamurti and Jamuna, 1996). Similar to U.S. media accounts about nursing homes, anecdotal information published in *The Hindu* and other major newspapers reveals the "uncaring care" provided in government-run homes. These stories invariably mention the decline of the joint family and raise questions about support for elders if families move away from that tradition.

However, while there is no question that coresidence is a central feature of family support in the developing world (Bongaarts and Zimmer, 2002), and one that makes it easier to provide social support to elders (Hareven, 2001), the family is a process, not merely a structure (Bengtson, 2001; Gokhale, 2003). What appears to be the ascendance of the nuclear family does not mean that the aged are cut off from assistance from children and kin (Hareven, 2001).

SOCIAL SUPPORT FOR THE AGED

Krause (2001) defines social support in terms of social "embeddedness," tangible help actually provided, and membership in a network of communication and mutual obligation. These factors are measured by frequency of contact, types of support received, and feelings of self-esteem, regardless of age or role (e.g. caregiver). However, support that the elders *provide* is also important, as is family support redistributed over the life course: Embeddedness is not just support received but also what is provided within families, and this reciprocal relationship occurs over the lifespan. Elders give and receive support to society and families, and families support their members over the life course, not just at one point in time (Bengtson, 2001; Hareven, 2001; Hashimoto and Kendig, 1992).

Family support takes three forms: financial, instrumental, and emotional (Hashimoto and Kendig, 1992). In the Indian context, meaningful familial roles consist of expressive support—loving, respectful, caring relationships and performance of tasks—and material support such as food, shelter, and clothing (Gore, 1992; Muttagi, 1997). Care and welfare of the aged is closely tied to the economic capacity of their families (Sarvekshana, 1991), absent major public programs or widespread programs sustained by nongovernmental organizations (NGOs).

In tracking the extent of social support for India's aged in their families and communities, data are lacking. The 1991 census showed that two thirds of elders are cared for by their children (Rajan et al., 2000), presumably within the coresidential family, but the dimensions of the care the family provides are not spelled out. In addition, there are no data about nonresident children and their proximity to their older parents, the type of support these children may provide, and how their support may differ from support provided in coresident families.

In one study examining frequency of contact between aging parents and their adult children, 15 percent of older men and 16 percent of older women reported that their children do not visit them. Similarly, only about 20 percent of both genders reported no letter communication from their children, with the same proportion of elders reporting they never visit their children (Rajan et al., 1995). Anecdotes about the "money-order economy" indicate that younger family members living at some distance provide economic support to their older parents and relatives (Kapoor, 2001), but again almost nothing is known about the amount and sufficiency of this support. We also know little about the extent and types of support provided by extended kinship networks.

Furthermore, few studies have focused on the emotional and instrumental support that elders may receive from outside the family. One intriguing study suggests that grandfathers—but not grandmothers—in joint families have broader social networks and that interactions with friends and neighbors, rather than adult children, may result in higher morale among elders (Chadha, 2001). Another study indicates that neighborhood relations and assistance among urban elders are an important aspect of well-being (van Willigen and Chadha, 1999).

Much of what is known about social support for elders comes from surveys of destitute older residents of old-age homes, whose self-esteem is likely to be low (Dandekar, 1996; Rajan et al., 1999, 2000; Ramamurti and Jamuna, 1996); from focus groups (Rajan et al., 1999); or from anthropological studies based in particular cities, regions, or neighborhoods in north India (Cohen, 1998; Lamb, 2000; van Willigen and Chadha, 1999). The lack of multigenerational and longitudinal studies that involve younger family members and that examine the nature of support provided over time make it difficult to determine the extent to which the joint family is meeting the needs and expectations of all generations as circumstances change over the life course of the family.

Similarly, the support that NGOs provide elders in India is not well documented in many instances. Surveys of old-age homes are uneven in quality and provide information on about half of all known facilities. Daycare centers, which provide respite care for families and provide meals and health promotion, socialization, and income-generating activities for elders, have received almost no attention (Ramamurti and Jamuna, 1996). Also, little is known about the support functions provided by village *panchayats* and a variety of socioreligious organizations, despite a tradition of this community support (Williamson and Pampel, 1993). Most studies have centered on intergenerational relations in the realm of emotional support and, to a lesser degree, on elder abuse.

Intergenerational Relations

In Asia, intergenerational relations are guided by the norms of respect for older people, which require the young to care for their elders when the need arises (Martin, 1990). Filial piety in Confucian-based societies comprises respect for the parent, filial responsibility, harmonization of the family, repayment of debts to one's parents, and affection and sacrifice for parents (Sung, 1998). This practice extends to elders in the neighborhood and in the larger society.

Hindus and Moslems in India also stress the duty of children to respect, support, and love their parents. There is a strong Hindu tradition of filial piety and kinship bonds (Shuman, 1995). The value placed on reciprocity among generations—for both material assistance and psychosocial support—is high. In Hindu society, deference to old age is based on the moral instruction embedded in the Indian epics, the Ramayana and the Mahabharata, and on the Vedas, which instruct believers to treat their father and mother as God (Gore, 1992). *Seva,* or service to and respect for aged parents, is a domestic duty (Cohen, 1998). It is seen as the basis for social order, extending beyond one's parents to other family elders and all older people in the community (Muttagi, 1997). Elders in the family and in the community are the custodians of culture and the transmitters of traditions, customs, and values. They care for, rear, and train their children to become independent, active, and useful citizens (Ramamurti, 1986), and also contribute to the welfare of the joint family via grandparenting, providing advice, and representing the family at familial and community events (van Willigen and Chadha, 1999).

Several factors affect this ideal pattern of intergenerational relations: changing cultural norms and socialization patterns; differences in generational interests, concerns, and expectations; and the health and economic status of the aged (Nayar, 2001). For example, during her formative years the mother-in-law in a family may have been conditioned to assume a submissive housewife role and to wear the traditional sari. However, her daughter-in-law, like many of today's young Indian women, may have received more education, been encouraged to be assertive, and even allowed to wear Western clothes such as blue jeans (Ramamurti, 2001). These cohort differences can lead to conflicts and mutual stereotypes, hindering smooth interactions (Reddy, 1992).

Intergenerational tensions also arise from disparate educational levels, different stages in the life course, and differing expectations about appropriate roles. Younger generations are becoming more educated, creating knowledge gaps and differing lifestyles within even the poorest families (Nayar, 2001). Narasimha Reddy (1985) found that generational disconnects are mostly due to differences in family members' interests. Expectations as to what constitutes appropriate behavior and respect for elders' wishes can lead to disharmony (Reddy, 1992). This is a major problem, primarily for older women (Cohen, 1998; Dandekar, 1996; Lamb, 2000; Rajan et al., 1999; van Willigen and Chadha, 1999). Most complaints about neglect in old age are directed by mothers-in-law toward their daughters-in-law; such conflicts also occur between mothers and sons and, less often, between mothers and their married daughters (Lamb, 2000).

By contrast, few men complain about inadequate treatment from their children, although father-son conflicts do arise (Lamb, 2000). Most older men retain nominal control over household property and money until death, and are likely to be treated better by doing so (Cohen, 1998; Gore, 1992; Ramamurti, 2001). However, if sons have moved out of the family home and the father or the older couple subsequently joins a son's household, feelings of dependency can arise. This may lead to greater problems of adjustment and may generate conflicts and complaints (Gore, 1992; Muttagi, 1997). Such conflicts can be alleviated through mutual understanding, adjustment, and cooperation among the generations and through the application of good interpersonal skills (Nayar, 2001; Ramamurti and Jamuna, 2000).

Finally, the health and economic status of elders can affect intergenerational interactions (Nayar, 2001). Poor health can lead to a lack of appropriate self-care by the aged, to ageist stereotypes about elders being unhygienic and bumbling (Ramamurti, 2001), and to greater reliance on younger family members for assistance. The maintenance of good health and functional capacity can reduce dependency and improve the quality of intergenerational relationships (Ramamurti, 1997; Ramamurti and Jamuna, 2000).

Economic dependence also can lead to intergenerational tensions. Fully 51 percent of rural and 58 percent of urban elders, particularly older women, are totally dependent on their families for economic support (Rajan et al., 2000). These economic pressures have generated feelings of burden among younger family members (Rajan et al., 1999), while the elderly in such straits find the attitudes and behaviors of family members unsatisfactory (Rajan et al., 2000). Although laws require individuals to maintain their parents, subject to their economic ability, this traditional family support is weakening (Gokhale, 1992), especially in poverty-stricken families (Rajan et al., 2000). For many Indian families who live at or below the poverty level, stretching meager resources to provide for aging parents and grandparents may lead to less support for young children (Cohen, 1998).

Positive intergenerational interactions in the Indian family can lead to a better quality of life for the elderly and to a more peaceful social and familial life (Ramamurti, 2001). However, family dissonance is not absent in the joint family (Ramamurti, Jamuna, and Reddy, 1992). The joint family is a healthy institution if it generates emotional links among members of different generations, but it can also be a source of social and emotional problems for elders (Achamamba, 1987), and even elder abuse.

Elder Abuse

Decalmer and Glendenning (1997) define *elder abuse* as willful treatment (acts of commission) and neglect (acts of omission). Abuse can be physical, social, or psychological and can include exploitation and deprivation of normal privileges. Gore (1992) has laid out a characteristic path of how elder abuse in India may arise out of declining familial support. As elders are less able to contribute to household well-being, spontaneous affection may give way to formal deference. In the next stage, physical needs are taken care of, but the elder experiences psychological and social isolation, accompanied by the failure to provide nonessential but emotionally satisfying needs. The final stage is a failure to provide the basic necessities of life. Some observers (Shah, Veedon, and Vasi, 1995) view the act of moving elders to old-age homes as abuse.

A study by Padmasree (1991) revealed that elder abuse may be patent (blatant forms of mistreatment) or latent, as evidenced by veiled threats toward the elder, exploitation of the elder's weaknesses, and reduced status of the aged regarding family matters. Other studies have shown that abuse is more common when the elder is economically and physically dependent (Jamuna and Padmasree, 2000; Kapoor, 1997). In general, these and other studies of abuse or neglect in India consist of case studies based on interviews of elders (Lamb, 2000; Rajan et al., 1999); rarely are interviews conducted with the adult children, the alleged abusers. Padmasree (1991) conducted one such series of interviews and found that many adult children reported that their aged family members were authoritarian, rigid, inflexible in their ways, argumentative, and highly demanding of attention. Some indicated they were unable to keep their aging parents at home due to lack of resources or time to care for the elders.

While it may appear from these few studies and newspaper accounts that the incidence of cases of elder abuse is on the increase, most of what we know is anecdotal. Even in the United States, where this issue received widespread media attention in the 1980s and early 1990s, subsequent research showed only about 3 percent of elders are abused—most often by spouses, followed by adult children (Bengtson et al., 1995). At the present, we do not know the extent to which elder abuse occurs in India and what types are dominant. In-depth research is required on the antecedent and contextual factors influencing various forms of elder abuse.

THE FUTURE OF FAMILY SUPPORT FOR ELDERS IN INDIA

The structure of the Indian family *is* changing, raising concerns about whether the family will continue to support its elder members. This is a major concern for policymakers who value and prefer to maintain family systems of care rather than introduce potentially expensive programs of social services and healthcare (Bongaarts and Zimmer, 2002; Shuman, 1995). In India and other developing countries, the common assumption is that families will provide care, requiring strategies to strengthen the resources of these traditional caregivers (Shuman, 1995). The economic capacity of India's national and state governments is inadequate to mount massive social welfare programs; other solutions are paramount.

Several approaches have been suggested, some of which are more direct and immediate; others are less direct and more long-term in their impact. Most can help ease intergenerational tensions and promote aging with dignity, one of the goals of India's National Policy on Older Persons (NPOP), which was created in 1999. The goal of the NPOP, which took more than 15 years to develop, is to strengthen the legitimate place of elders in society and help them live their last years with purpose, dignity, and peace, similar to the goals of the Older Americans Act. Two guiding principles of the policy are to empower and involve older adults to ensure their continued contribution to their family, community, and society, and to promote an age-integrated society in which the family capacity for caregiving is strengthened. Suggested approaches include the following:

- Providing direct economic support and incentives to poverty-level families supporting aged family members
- Providing health promotion programs for elders and their families
- Initiating, expanding, and evaluating community programs designed specifically to sustain families, especially in rural areas
- Conducting research on the extent of family support in the changing family system, especially in rural areas
- Developing and strengthening local programs focused on productive aging as part of economic development and social justice
- Developing programs to raise consciousness about India's aging society and the value of older people to society
- Expanding the number of NGOs and strengthening existing organizations to develop more widespread programs for the aged

Many of these goals are mentioned in the NPOP. However, it is long on goals and overall strategies and short on the specifics of implementation, especially in the most troubling area of economic support (Gokhale, 2003).

Economic Support for Families

In 1995, the Indian government created a national old-age pension and a food-ration program to supplement similar state programs for destitute elders; many of these state-level programs had existed for 40 years. While this effort is an index of collective ability and willingness to take care of the aged, only elders *without* family support are eligible for very minimal amounts (approximately $3 per month). In poor countries such as India, where 30 percent of the population lives below the official poverty level, old-age pensions help only if they are supplements to total family income, not alternatives to family support (Gore, 1992).

In developed countries with social security plans that cover most if not all elders, helping families provide economic support is less crucial. When families are the major source of economic support, however, they may require help. Some Indian NGOs have created programs to provide food rations, clothing, and basic medical care for elders living with family members. These programs reduce the economic burden the aged may pose for their families and help elders contribute to family well-being, thereby strengthening family bonds. Such programs, however, are limited in number and geographic scope; they are no substitute for public support. Public programs—such as housing preferences and tax relief for coresident families (Liebig, 2001), medical expense rebates, and demogrants for elder care, similar to demogrants for childcare in several European nations—can be tried on a demonstration basis.

Health Promotion

The NPOP mentions health promotion as important for families. Because elders' poor health and disability can negatively affect family dynamics and economics, basic health promotion can help older adults avoid accidents and enhance self-care. Some of the estimated 400–500 daycare centers in India provide some kind of health promotion information and wholesome meals (Gokhale, 2003). In addition, some NGOs provide cataract operations as well as eye and diabetes care through mobile medical units and in a handful of geriatric hospitals or clinics. Incentives and support for more health promotion programs need to be created.

Community-Based Programs for Families of Elders

To dispel stereotypes, family members need educational programs that help them understand normal aging and learn to be better caregivers. Family counseling programs can help ameliorate intergenerational tensions and improve the acceptance of daughters as appropriate caregivers. Daycare centers can provide respite for families, enabling them to work and attend school knowing their elders are safe and occupied during the day. With help from international NGOs such as HelpAge International and from GOI grants, a few homecare programs have been developed in large cities. They train disadvantaged young adults to provide this care. However, similar programs need to be developed in rural areas and should provide technical assistance provided to *panchayats,* an area of community programming not fully addressed in the NPOP. Training of program personnel, supported by NGO-government partnerships, is needed for both entry-level or basic-care workers and professionals such as counselors.

Research on Family Support

The NPOP calls for further research, but does not specify studies that focus on enhancing family support. The GOI sponsors a few training grants to develop a cadre of researchers to fill the gaps in knowledge about aging. This support, however, needs to be expanded and targeted to studies of the following: the types of *actual* support that resident and nonresident family members provide, the roles of extended kin and neighbors in supporting elders, and differences between rural and urban communities and between regions. The results should be used as the basis for future interventions to assist families in caring for their elders. In particular, longitudinal studies of multigenerational family exchange and solidarity need to be conducted to track changes over time.

Promotion of Productive Aging

The NPOP names productive aging as one of its goals; the concept of productive aging envisions elders not just as society's beneficiaries but as contributors to the well-being of their communities. Again, though, the NPOP is short on specifics. Enhancing the productivity of older women through their inclusion in local economic development schemes does not receive the attention it should. HelpAge India has created a handful of programs that involve older women, but the type of support that Grameen Bank provides[2] should be offered to women's cooperatives that include elders. Income-generating activities, such as those developed by HelpAge India and other NGOs, need to be expanded so elders can help support themselves and their families.

Also, the NPOP pays little attention to the resources of the expanding middle class, through mechanisms such as Japan's Senior Corps, which mobilizes elder volunteers to help communities solve their problems and gives them technical assistance to achieve their goals. Federations of existing senior clubs, such as those in Kerala and Maharashtra, can be funded to develop these programs, especially in rural areas. Peer programs specifically targeted to addressing other elders' problems, such as isolation and feelings of loneliness, also need to be created.

Valuing Older People

As suggested in the NPOP, educational campaigns need to be mounted in the media and in the schools. Aging advocacy organizations, located primarily in urban centers, can play important roles in developing media campaigns about normal aging, working in connection with other NGOs and the national and state governments. Some schools have already initiated "Adopt a Granny" programs linking students with residents of old-age homes, and some homes have already developed youth-oriented programs for their residents (e.g., providing childcare to members of the community and teaching in schools). Elementary-school curricula also can be created to increase understanding about aging and to instill greater appreciation of elders and their contributions to the community.

Strengthening NGOs

The NPOP relies heavily on NGOs to help meet the challenges of India's aging society, a time-honored tradition in Asia (Riker, 1995). However, the capacity of

[2] The Grameen Bank provides small, very low-interest loans to women in developing countries to promote local economic development and individual self-sufficiency.

these organizations to do so is limited. Elder-focused NGOs are heavily concentrated in some states and lacking in others, especially in rural areas. Some are indigenous, while others (e.g., HelpAge India, Indian Federation on Ageing, Rotary) are affiliated with international organizations. All need additional funding to carry out current programs and develop new ones, especially those centered on strengthening the family.

Several strategies might be employed to strengthen NGOs' capacity to serve the aged in India. The national and state governments, working with major corporations, need to engage NGOs more fully and help them actively seek support from international NGOs and foundations. Future media campaigns should include appeals for greater financial support for NGOs so that they can expand their elder-oriented efforts. Promoting capacity-building among NGOs, particularly new ones, is vital to ensure their stability and accountability. Public and private sources can fund a training and technical-assistance program, to be administered by NGOs, that is similar to existing programs aimed at improving public administration in India.

The NPOP has provided an overall framework for several areas that need to be addressed to improve the well-being of India's aging population. The next step is to develop a strategic plan that will place specific emphasis on strengthening family support for elders and on developing mechanisms for enabling elders to contribute to their families and communities. In particular, this plan must articulate and strengthen the roles and capacities of NGOs to bring about the goals of India's ambitious policy statement.

REFERENCES

Achamamba, B. (1987). Social and emotional problems of men and women in joint and nuclear families. In K. S. Rao and V. Prabhaker (Eds.), *Ageing—A multifactorial discussion* (pp. 97–102). New Delhi: Association of Gerontology (India).

Alam, M. (2000). Ageing in India: A country profile. *Bold, 10*(3), 5–22.

Bengtson, V. L. (2001). Beyond the nuclear family: The increasing importance of multigenerational bonds. *Journal of Marriage and Family, 63,* 1–16.

Bengtson, V. L., Rosenthal, C., and Burton, L. (1995). Paradoxes of families and aging. In R. H. Binstock and L. K. George (Eds.), *Handbook of aging and social sciences* (4th ed., pp. 253–282). San Diego, California: Academic Press.

Bongaarts, J., and Zimmer, Z. (2002). Living arrangements of older adults in the developing world: An analysis of demographic and health survey household surveys. *Journal of Gerontology: Social Sciences, 57B*(3), S145–S157.

Brink, S. (1998). *Housing older people: An international perspective.* New Brunswick, New Jersey: Transaction Publishers.

Bose, A. B. (1988). Policies and programmes for the aging in India. In A. B. Bose and K. D. Gangrade (Eds.), *Aging in India: Problems and potentialities* (pp. 58–63). New Delhi: Abhinav Publications.

Chadha, N. K. (2001). Intergenerational issues and social support networks. In A. Chaudhary (Ed.), *Active ageing in the new millennium* (pp. 40–46). New Delhi: Anugraha.

Cohen, L. (1998). *No aging in India: Alzheimer's, the bad family, and other modern things.* Berkeley: University of California Press.

Cumming, E., and Henry, W. E. (1961). *Growing old: The process of disengagement.* New York: Basic Books.

Dandekar, K. (1996). *The elderly in India.* New Delhi: Sage.

Decalmer, P., and Glendenning, F. (1997). *The mistreatment of elderly people.* New Delhi: Sage.

Desouza, S. (2000, May). *Women's identity: Tradition and modernity in maternal health.* Paper presented at the Third International South Asian Women's Conference, Los Angeles.

Gist, Y. J., and Velkoff, V. A. (1997). *Gender and aging: Demographic dimensions.* Washington, DC: U.S. Bureau of the Census.

Gokhale, S. D. (1992). Toward productive and participatory aging in India. *Caring,* 86–89.

Gokhale, S. D. (2003). Towards a policy for aging in India [Special issue on aging in India]. *Journal of Aging & Social Policy, 15*(3/4), 213–234.

Gore, M. S. (1992). Family support to elderly people: The Indian situation. In H. L. Kendig, A. Hashimoto, and L. C. Coppard (Eds.), *Family support for the elderly: The international experience* (pp. 260–270). New York: Oxford University Press.

Government of India. (1999). *National policy on older persons.* New Delhi: Ministry of Social Justice and Empowerment.

Hareven, T. K. (2001). Historical perspective on aging and family relations. In R. H. Binstock and L. K. George (Eds.), *Handbook of aging and the social sciences* (5th ed., pp. 141–159). San Diego, California: Academic Press.

Hashimoto, A., and Kendig, H. L. (1992). Aging in international perspective. In H. L. Kendig, A. Hashimoto, and L. C. Coppard (Eds.), *Family support for the elderly: The international experience* (pp. 3–14). New York: Oxford University Press.

HelpAge India. (1995). *Directory of old-age homes in India.* New Delhi: Author.

HelpAge India. (1998). *Directory of old-age homes in India.* New Delhi: Author.

Hsu, F. L. K. (1963). *Clan, caste, and club.* Princeton, New Jersey: D. Van Nostrand.

Jamuna, D. (1992). Caring for the disabled elderly. In S. K. Chowadary (Ed.), *Problems of the aged and old-age homes.* Bombay: Akshan Pratiroop Pvt. Ltd.

Jamuna, D. (1998). Challenges of changing socio-economic and psychological status of the aged. *Research & Development Journal, 5*(1), 5–13.

Jamuna, D., and Padmasree, V. (2000). Psychosocial profiles of abused elderly. *Indian Journal of Gerontology, 10*(3), 11–19.

Kapoor, P. (1997). Elderly abuse: Some counseling tips. *Research & Development Journal, 3*(3), 13–23.

Kapoor, R. N. (2001). Multigenerational relationships—Indian context. In A. Chaudhary (Ed.), *Active ageing in the new millennium* (pp. 22–31). New Delhi: Anugraha.

Kendig, H. L., Hashimoto, A., and Coppard, L. C. (Eds.). (1992). *Family support for the elderly: The international experience.* New York: Oxford University Press.

Krause, N. (2001). Social support. In R. H. Binstock and L. K. George (Eds.), *Handbook of aging and the social sciences* (5th ed., pp. 272–294). San Diego, California: Academic Press.

Lamb, S. (2000). *White saris and sweet mangoes: Aging, gender, and body in North India.* Berkeley: University of California Press.

Liebig, P. S. (2001). International perspectives on housing frail elders. *Journal of Architectural and Planning Research, 18*(3), 208–222.

Liebig, P. S. (2003). Old-age homes and services: Old and new approaches to aged care [Special issue on aging in India]. *Journal of Aging & Social Policy, 15*(2–3), 159–178.

Liebig, P. S., and Ramamurti, P. V. (2000, November). *Social and cultural perspectives on aging in India.* Paper presented at the annual meeting of the Gerontological Society of America, Washington, DC.

Martin, L. G. (1988). The aging of Asia. *Journal of Gerontology: Social Sciences, 43,* S93–S113.

Martin, L. G. (1990). The status of south Asia's growing elderly population. *Journal of Cross-Cultural Gerontology, 5,* 93–117.

Muttagi, P. K. (1997). *Aging issues and old age care.* New Delhi: Classical Publishing Company.

Nair, T. K. (Ed.). (1989). *Care of the elderly: Organisations caring for the elderly in India.* Madras: Madras Institute on Ageing.

Narasimha Reddy, K. L. (1985). *Intergenerational preferences as a function of value and interests.* Unpublished master's thesis, S. V. University, Tirupati, India.

National Sample Survey Organization. (1991). Socioeconomic profile of the aged persons: NSSO 42nd round (July 1965–June 1987). *Sarueh Shana, 15*(2). New Delhi: Author.

Nayar, P. K. B. (2001). Active ageing, intergenerational integration, and related issues: Theoretical and empirical considerations. In A. Chaudhary (Ed.), *Active ageing in the new millennium* (pp. 3–14). New Delhi: Anugraha.

Padmasree, V. (1991). *A study of incidence of elder abuse and some factors related to abuse.* Unpublished master's thesis, S. V. University, Tirupati, India.

Rajan, S. I., Mishra, U. S., and Sarma, P. S. (1995). Living arrangements among the Indian elderly. *Hong Kong Journal of Gerontology, 9*(2), 20–28.

Rajan, S. I., Mishra, U. S., and Sarma, P. S. (1999). *India's elderly: Burden or challenge?* New Delhi: Sage.

Rajan, S. I., Mishra, U. S., and Sarma, P. S. (2000). Ageing in India: Retrospect and prospect. *Indian Social Science Review, 2*(1), 1–47.

Ramamurti, P. V. (1986). *Human resources for a happy aging.* Proceedings of the 74th Indian Science Congress, Bangalore, India.

Ramamurti, P. V. (1997). Coping with aging. *Indian Journal of Medical Research, 106,* 376–380.

Ramamurti, P. V. (2001). Intergenerational relationships and active ageing. In A. Chaudhary (Ed.), *Active ageing in the new millennium* (pp. 15–21). New Delhi: Anugraha.

Ramamurti, P. V., and Jamuna, D. (1996). *Evaluation of old-age homes, day care centers, and mobile medical units in Andrha Pradesh* [Report to the Government of India]. Tirupati, India: Centre for Research on Ageing.

Ramamurti, P. V., and Jamuna, D. (2000). New perspectives of ageing. In P. D. Kulkarni (Ed.), *Pilgrimage of light—A versatile life* (pp. 277–288). Pune, India: Ameya Prakashan.

Ramamurti, P. V., Jamuna, D., and Reddy, L. K. (1992). Psychological aspects of caregiving and disability among the elderly in India. In D. Krishan and K. Mahadevan

(Eds.), *The elderly population in the developed and developing world: Problems and perspectives.* New Delhi: D. K. Publications.

Rathore, S. D. (2000, May). *The status of tribal women in India: Problems of integration and the prospect for change.* Paper presented at the Third International South Asian Women's Conference, Los Angeles.

Reddy, L. K. (1992). Does attitude towards ageing per se determine our preference for the elderly? *Personality Study and Group Behaviour, 11,* 7–10.

Riker, J. V. (1995). From cooptation to cooperation and collaboration in government-NGO relations. In N. Heyzer, J. V. Riker, and A. B. Quizon (Eds.), *Government-NGO relations in Asia* (pp. 91–130). New York: St. Martin's Press.

Shah, G., Veedon, R., and Vasi, S. (1995). Elder abuse in India. *Journal of Elder Abuse & Neglect, 6*(3/4), 101–118.

Shanas, E. (1979). The family as a social support system. *The Gerontologist, 19,* 169–174.

Shuman, T. (1995). Third world aging. In G. Maddox (Ed.), *The encyclopedia of aging* (2nd ed., pp. 934–937). New York: Springer.

Singh, Y. (1997). Changing trends in Indian families and adjustment of the aged. *Research and Development Journal, 3*(2), 31–42.

Sung, K. (1998). Filial piety: The traditional ideal of parent care in east Asia. *Aging & Spirituality.* Retrieved March 2002 from http://www.asaging.org/networks/forsa/a&s-101.htm

Tracy, M. B. (1991). *Social policies for the elderly in the third world.* New York: Greenwood Press.

Van Willigen, J., and Chadha, N. K. (1999). *Social aging in a Delhi neighborhood.* Westport, Connecticut: Bergin and Garvey.

Velkoff, V. A., and Lawson, V. A. (1998). *Gender and aging: Caregiving.* Washington, DC: U.S. Bureau of the Census.

Williamson, J. B., and Pampel, F. C. (1993). *Old-age security in comparative perspective.* New York: Oxford University Press.

CHAPTER TEN

Living Arrangements and Social Interaction of the Elderly in Taiwan

Te-hsiung Sun and Ming-cheng Chang

With the progressive modernization and effective promotion of family-planning programs in East Asia, the total fertility rate in the region has finally dipped below replacement levels. Simultaneously, the proportion of the population ages 65 and older has reached 8 percent, exceeding the level (7 percent) set by the United Nations above which a population is regarded as aged. It is expected that the economic and social modernization occurring across East Asia will continue to bring about an aging of the population. As was noted in the chapter on demography, this shift in the age structure of the population arouses great concern and political deliberation over how to take care of the growing older adult population. Taiwan provides a good case in point of the nature of the dilemma.

Situated in the middle of East Asia, Taiwan started its demographic transition during the 1920s, when the birthrate was about 45 per thousand and the death rate was greater than 20 per thousand. By 1990, these two rates were brought down, in respective order, to 16.6 per thousand and 5.2 per thousand. As a result of this shift, the proportion of the population ages 65 and older has increased from 2.8 percent in 1920 to 6.2 percent in 1990, further rising to 8.5 percent by 2000. It is expected that this proportion will grow to 9.9 percent in 2010, 13.8 percent in 2020, 19.6 percent in 2030, and 21.6 percent in 2036. The absolute number of older adults in Taiwan is expected to triple, climbing from 1.9 million to 5.6 million, in the same 36-year time span. Furthermore, the old-age dependency ratio, which measures the size of the working population (ages 15–64) against that of the older population (ages 65 and older), will shift from 8:1 in 2000 to 3:1 in 2036. This means that each elder will be supported by far fewer people of working age.

Dealing with the rapidly increasing elderly population in Taiwan will become a serious social issue, encompassing many aspects of society, including healthcare, welfare, living arrangements, leisure activities, psychological support, and manpower utilization. The adjustments include far more than demographic change. They entail political, economic, and social ramifications as well. This chapter will focus primarily on living arrangements and social interactions of the elderly in the face of the transformations Taiwan is undergoing.

CULTURAL BACKGROUND

In Taiwanese society, which is strongly rooted in Chinese culture, adaptations to population aging depend largely on elders' families. Therefore, it is also important to understand changing familial values and family structure in Taiwan.

The Influence of Confucianism

Confucianism underpins many aspects of Chinese culture. This philosophical belief system emphasizes the importance of family and relationships among family members. As a patriarchal society, Chinese culture places great importance on having a male heir. Children, especially sons, should express filial piety toward their parents by demonstrating respect and taking good care of them. Most elderly people in societies influenced by Confucianism are part of a stem family or an extended family, and very few live alone. Thus, they are taken care by their children or younger relatives. So the care of older adults has not been as much of a social problem in Confucian societies as it is in Western societies. However, modern currents are beginning to challenge long-established traditions.

During the 17th century, when ethnic Chinese from the mainland started to migrate to Taiwan in large numbers, they brought with them the traditional Confucian family system and values. In the early stages of the Chinese settlement, people in Taiwan tried to form extended families based on long-cherished principles. However, many obstacles prevented Chinese migrants from achieving this ideal family structure: Forming and maintaining a large family was expensive, thus beyond the reach of most migrants, who were poor tenants. It also required strong leadership to maintain peace in the extended family. The high mortality rate in early Taiwan also was unfavorable to the formation of extended families. Therefore, extended families were maintained mainly among the upper class, made up primarily of landlords and government officials. Families in the lower and middle classes commonly formed stem families that included three to four generations instead.

Judging from the fact that average family size only increased from 5.2 persons in 1905 to 5.8 persons in 1930, it could be said that the family structure in Taiwan did not change appreciably in the first part of the 20th century, a period in which agricultural expansion prevailed.

Changes in Family Structure

Many sociological and anthropological studies of the family have pointed out that regardless of where the family is situated, as societies modernize, the formation, structure, and function of the family as well as the relationships among its members change dramatically (Freedman, Chang, and Sun, 1982; Goode, 1963; Greenfield, 1961; Levy, 1949, 1965; Wei and Reischl, 1981). Some investigators maintain that modernization erodes traditional family functions, increasing the proportion of nuclear families, changing relationships among family members, and eventually leading to the dissolution of the family as an institution. Others, however, think that modernization may actually expedite formation of extended families (Gallin, 1966; Lavely, 1982).

After World War II, Taiwan's economy underwent significant changes and at unprecedented speed, resulting in rapid industrialization and urbanization as well as a rise in standards of living, educational levels, and life expectancy. The effects of this rapid development on family structure are quite significant (Table 1).

Many studies have asserted that modernization has some effect in reducing the proportion of extended families and increasing the proportion of nuclear families. Freedman, Chang, and Sun (1982) pointed out that such is true in Taiwan. This shift is actually more significant than it initially appears. Due to the declining mortality rate, more parents and brothers have survived to form extended families. In theory, this should increase the proportion of extended families. To the contrary, however, there has been a slight increase in the proportion of nuclear families, because the proportion of parents and married brothers who have chosen not to live with their married sons or brothers has increased substantially.

Another factor that obscures what may be happening in Taiwan is the criteria used for classification of family structure (Table 2). It is possible for family members to live together but not share a common economy. There is a large difference in the distribution of specific family types among the population, depending on whether classification was based on family economy or on association per se. For example, if the families included in the Taiwan KAP (Knowledge, Attitude, and Practice of Family Planning) surveys[1] were classified on economic bases (i.e., those who lived and ate together), the proportion of families classified as nuclear increased from 50 percent in 1965 to 59 percent in 1998. However, if families are classified on the basis of association, for example those who lived together but might not necessarily eat together, then the proportion of nuclear families increased from 41 percent in 1965 to 59 percent in 1998. In the latter instance, even though some family members live under one roof,

[1] The KAP was a series of sample surveys carried out by the Taiwan Provincial Institute of Family Planning for the evaluation of family-planning programs. The survey was administered from 1965 to 1998 to a representative island-wide sample of about 4,000 married women in the reproductive ages at three- to six-year intervals.

Table 1. Indicators of Social and Economic Development in Taiwan, 1952–1998

	1952	1965	1975	1985	1998
Economic indicators(%):					
Per capita GNP	100	186	366	716	1,689
Agricultural production index	100	190	245	306	323
Total industrial production index	100	465	2,010	5,220	11,535
Percent of labor force in primary industry	56	47	30	17	8
Percent of labor force in secondary industry	17	22	35	42	37
Percent of labor force in tertiary industry	27	21	35	41	5
Education indicators (%):					
Illiteracy rate (age 6 and above)	15	14	12.9	8.4	4.7
Percent with junior high education or better	10.2	23	35.5	50.8	64.9
Communication and transportation indicators (per 1,000 population):					
Daily newspaper circulation	28[a]	60	89	195	209[b]
Automobile ownership (sedan, truck, and wagon)	1	3	17	70	240
Motorcycle ownership	0	5	105	342	497
Telephone ownership	3	8	51	219	547
Household amenities (%):					
Household with piped water	29	38	50	78	90
Power consumption per person year (kwh)	32	88	317	674	1,488
Health indicators:					
Life expectancy at birth:					
Male	57.4	65.1	68.3	71	72.3
Female	60.3	69.7	73.4	75.9	78.1
Calories per person per day	2,078	2,410	2,722	2,614	2,891
Persons served by each physician	1,584	1,901	1,492	1,130	703
Total fertility	6,615	4,825	2,832	1,885	1,555
Percent of population in urbanized areas	30	50	63	73	80

[a]1955. [b]1977.

Source: Council for Economic Planning and Development, 2000.

they are economically independent, not pooling their resources to any significant extent. Even in the latter arrangement, though, it is still accepted practice to help care for elderly relatives living nearby.

Modernization has exerted both compositional and substantive alterations on family structure. It has also brought a kind of relativity whereby families of different circumstances evolve divergent family structures. So, for example, there is a tendency for families of different economic and social strata to develop

Table 2. Household Types in Taiwan, 1965–1998 (Selected Years)

Household type	1965	1973	1980	1985	1998
On associative basis:					
Nuclear	41	49	53	58	59
Stem	31	35	34	34	27
Extended	28	16	13	8	14
On economic basis:					
Nuclear	50	60	61	62	59
Stem	35	33	33	32	28
Extended	15	7	6	6	13

Source: Taiwan Provincial Institute of Family Planning, 1989.

particular types of families due to their particular status and the characteristics of that stratum. Interestingly, even in the face of these disparities, the family structure specific to that stratum can be quite stable provided social change is moderate. That is, the distribution of family types within that stratum does not change much provided social conditions are unwavering. But when social change is rapid, not only will the social-strata compositions change and affect family structure (a compositional effect), the family structure within a stratum will also change (a substantive effect).

These two effects can be seen in Tables 3 and 4, tabulated from Taiwan KAP survey data of 1965, 1973, and 1980. Table 3 uses an economic basis and Table 4 uses an associative basis to classify family type. The husband's educational level, the level of urbanization of a respondent's living place, and the husband's occupation were used as indicators of socioeconomic stratum.

From Table 3, in which family type is classified on an economic basis, we can see that, from 1965 to 1973, in terms of education, the proportion of husbands who completed junior high or higher levels of education increased significantly (from 25 percent to 37 percent). This change, combined with the fact that those with higher education are more likely to live in nuclear families, pushed up the proportion of nuclear families in the whole society, from 50 percent to 60 percent. At the same time, the proportion of nuclear families in each educational stratum also increased, especially among Taiwanese with primary school or lower educational attainment (from 48 percent to 58 percent).

The effect of urbanization has been comparable to that of education. As the proportion of Taiwanese living in urban areas has increased, so too has the proportion of nuclear families, especially in cities.

Although educational achievement and urbanization continued to rise from 1973 to 1980 and the proportion of Taiwanese engaged in industry and commerce

Table 3. Family Type Composition in Taiwan (Classification on Economic Bases), 1965, 1973, 1980

Indicators of social strata	1965					1973					1980				
	Family type (%)			Sample		Family type (%)			Sample		Family type (%)			Sample	
	Nuclear	Stem	Extended	Number	% of total	Nuclear	Stem	Extended	Number	% of total	Nuclear	Stem	Extended	Number	% of total
Husband's education:															
College or university	73	20	7	165	3	68	29	3	458	8	66	29	5	541	14
Sr. high	54	33	13	490	11	67	26	7	851	15	54	37	9	793	21
Jr. high	52	38	10	525	11	59	32	9	745	14	64	29	7	541	14
Primary	46	36	18	2,620	58	56	36	8	2,886	52	59	23	8	1,736	46
Literate	46	41	13	46	1	72	24	4	168	3	77	21	2	90	2
Illiterate	55	32	13	758	16	62	35	3	417	8	66	30	4	119	3
Level of urbanization:															
National and prov. city	58	33	9	892	19	67	29	4	1,571	28	67	27	6	1,078	28
County-level city	58	30	12	387	8	70	26	4	723	13	71	25	4	657	17
Urban township	48	34	18	1,404	30	55	35	10	1,289	23	54	36	10	842	22
Rural township	45	37	18	1,930	42	54	38	8	1,953	36	54	39	7	1,244	33
Household head's occupation:															
Technological	67	30	3	43	1	64	32	5	149	3	68	•27	5	113	3
Managerial	53	31	16	374	8	63	29	8	1,151	21	63	30	7	963	25
Clerical	62	28	10	893	19	66	30	4	516	9	63	31	6	419	11
Sales	55	30	15	336	7	58	35	7	291	5	59	35	6	167	5
Personal services	66	29	5	70	2	76	20	4	205	4	75	23	2	146	4
Skilled	47	43	10	306	7	66	28	6	1,502	27	61	32	7	1,224	32
Manual labor	51	35	14	1,079	23	62	35	3	435	8	63	34	3	272	7
Agricultural, fishery	37	39	24	1,450	32	45	44	11	1,271	35	47	44	9	509	13
Unemployed	66	21	13	62	1	44	56	—	16	0	25	63	12	8	0
Total	50	35	15	4,613	100	60	33	7	5,536	100	61	33	6	3,821	100

Source: Taiwan Provincial Institute of Family Planning, 1989.

Table 4. Family Type Composition in Taiwan (Classification on Associative Bases), 1965, 1973, 1980

Indicators of social strata	1965 Family type (%)			1965 Sample		1973 Family type (%)			1973 Sample		1980 Family type (%)			1980 Sample	
	Nuclear	Stem	Extended	Number	% of total	Nuclear	Stem	Extended	Number	% of total	Nuclear	Stem	Extended	Number	% of total
Husband's education:															
College or university	68	23	9	165	3	65	32	3	458	8	63	31	6	541	14
Sr. high	50	31	19	490	11	61	28	11	851	15	50	28	12	793	21
Jr. high	47	38	15	525	11	52	34	14	745	14	56	32	12	541	14
Primary	35	34	31	2,620	58	42	38	20	2,886	52	49	33	19	1,736	46
Literate	28	28	44	46	1	65	26	9	168	3	66	24	10	90	2
Illiterate	44	28	28	758	16	45	38	17	417	8	55	35	10	119	3
Level of urbanization:															
National and prov. city	52	33	15	892	19	60	29	11	1,571	28	63	28	9	1,078	28
County-level city	53	32	15	387	8	62	30	8	723	13	66	25	9	657	17
Urban township	41	32	27	1,404	30	45	34	21	1,289	23	48	38	14	842	22
Rural township	33	33	34	1,930	42	39	41	20	1,953	36	40	40	20	1,244	33
Household head's occupation:															
Technological	67	30	3	43	1	61	31	8	149	3	60	33	7	113	3
Managerial	48	30	22	374	8	56	31	13	1,151	21	59	30	11	963	25
Clerical	58	28	14	893	19	59	31	10	516	9	58	33	9	419	11
Sales	46	30	24	336	7	50	37	13	291	5	51	37	12	167	5
Personal services	60	26	14	70	2	73	20	7	205	4	73	23	4	146	4
Skilled	42	40	18	306	7	56	31	13	1,502	27	52	33	15	1,224	32
Manual labor	38	34	28	1,079	23	48	37	15	435	8	51	36	13	272	7
Agricultural, fishery	26	35	39	1,450	32	27	45	28	1,271	23	32	43	25	509	13
Unemployed	63	16	21	62	1	31	63	6	16	0	25	63	12	8	0
Total	41	31	28	4,613	100	49	35	16	5,536	100	53	34	13	3,821	100

Source: Taiwan Provincial Institute of Family Planning, 1989.

continued to increase, family type seems to have stopped changing. Little substantive change occurred during this period.

However, when families were classified on associative bases rather than on economic bases, we see somewhat different results, mainly in the period between 1973 and 1980. The primacy of nuclear families in the majority of educational, occupational, and geographic strata continued to increase slightly, suggesting that the traditional extended family of Chinese custom is beginning to wane. Across the period shown (1965–80), the proportion of nuclear families in Taiwan as a whole rose from 41 percent to 53 percent, and the proportion of extended families declined from 28 percent to 13 percent. However, the shift was less significant in the second period (1973–80) than in the first period (1965–73).

To assess the impact on families of factors associated with economic and social modernization, a multivariate technique known as Multiple-Classification Analysis (MCA is a subroutine available with SPSS) was utilized by Sun and Liu (1991) to examine changes in family structure. MCA permits examination of the relationship between one or a set of predictor variables and a dependent variable while controlling for the effects of other predictor variables. The results suggest that modernization factors such as urbanization and higher educational achievement each have an effect in fostering nuclear family structures, and the impact of these factors is greater among workers employed in occupations associated with the export economy or in other white-collar or service-sector jobs associated with "modern" markets (as opposed to traditional agricultural and fishing pursuits). Another factor having an effect on family structure has to do with higher employment rates for women; when women are involved in the paid labor force, family structures move away from the extended type. It appears that the shift may have passed its peak impact around 1973; the effect of the same factors, especially higher educational achievement, on family structure has been on the decline since that time. However, urbanization and occupation have continued to have some effect (Sun and Liu, 1991).

Other researchers have also pointed out that the representation of nuclear families in the total population of Taiwan was positively correlated with education, level of urbanization, and nonagricultural activities (Freedman, Chang, and Sun, 1982). Although nuclear families have continued to increase, most older Taiwanese still lived with married sons: In 1980, 72 percent of older adults in the best-educated stratum, 68 to 71 percent of elders in large cities, and 87 to 89 percent of elders in rural areas lived with their married sons.

Changes in Parent-Child Relations

Three of the five value principles emphasized in Chinese tradition are directly related to family relationships: parent-child, husband-wife, and brother-sister. The parent-child relationship emphasizes *filial piety,* which entails supporting, serving, respecting, and obeying one's parents, as well as continuing the family line by bearing children. The husband-wife relationship emphasizes *the obedience of the wife to her husband*; in this principle, men are responsible for external affairs and women for internal matters. The division of labor is quite pronounced and well established. The brother-sister relationship stresses that the elder siblings should *love and care for* the younger ones, while the younger siblings should *obey and respect* the elder ones. As is noted in a number of the chapters, modernization has significantly affected parent-child relationships and thus the care of elders across Asia, and the situation in Taiwan is not different.

The Taiwan KAP surveys show that 74 percent of married women ages 20–39 in 1973, and 81 percent of this same cohort in 1980, had parents-in-law (the subject's husband's parents) living in Taiwan. The percentage of these parents-in-law who were not living with a married son increased from 19 percent in 1973 to 24 percent in 1980. The proportion of parents-in-law not eating with their married sons increased from 29 percent to 32 percent. These findings show that more of the older adults lived apart from their married sons in 1980 than did so in 1973, and that by 1980, 8 percent to 10 percent of older adults were living with married sons but were not eating with them.

Separate living, however, does not indicate severed family ties. Most married children maintain ties with their parents through mutual visits and the exchange of money. According to the 1973 and 1980 KAP surveys, of those couples who did not live with the husband's parents, 41 percent in 1973 and 35 percent in 1980 visited their parents at least weekly; only 2 percent (in both years) reported never visiting their parents. Even though transportation in Taiwan is now quite convenient, the number of visits tended to decrease as the amount of available free time among the working-age population decreased. But even then, families were not out of touch with their older members; they would compensate for reduced visitations by telephoning each other more often.

Another characteristic of Taiwanese family relations is the reciprocal flow of money. According to tradition, children have worked the family holdings in order to contribute to the family economy. In fact, in agricultural societies there may be a net flow of wealth from children to parents as the children are serving as family laborers. In contemporary Taiwan, however, it is quite expensive to rear children, and very few children can contribute to the family's fiscal well-being prior to adulthood. Thus resources flow primarily from parents to children in a unidirectional fashion.

According to KAP surveys, 10 percent of the 1973 respondents expected that unmarried sons who had completed their education would work in the family business or on the family farm until they married; 73 percent expected their sons to work outside the family and contribute to the family economy; and only 16 percent of respondents reported that they would leave decisions about contributions to their sons themselves. The corresponding proportions for unmarried daughters were 9 percent, 76 percent, and 15 percent, respectively. Nine percent of respondents expected that their *married* sons would work in the family business or family farm; 67 percent expected these sons to work outside the family but contribute to the family economy; and 24 percent would leave the decision to their married sons. Higher proportions of survey respondents who had more modern residential, educational, and occupational characteristics were willing to leave family-economy decisions to their sons, especially in the 1980 survey. These findings suggest among other things that parents' expectations about the filial responsibilities of their sons are decreasing.

KAP survey data also show that the proportion of respondents who regularly sent money to their parents increased from 32 percent in 1973 to 42 percent in 1980. Furthermore, the proportion of couples who occasionally sent money also increased from 32 percent to 43 percent in the same time period, and the proportion of couples who never sent money decreased from 35 percent to 16 percent. The willingness to share financially with aged parents might reflect the fact that the relative affluence of most Taiwanese increased during this period.

Conversely, while the same low proportion (3 percent) of couples in the 1973 and 1980 samples accepted money regularly from their parents and the proportion of couples who never received money from parents remained relatively constant (86 percent in 1973 and 85 percent in 1970), the proportion of couples who received money from their parents once in a while rose from 9 percent in 1973 to 12 percent in 1980. When asked whether the money respondents sent to their parents was of any help to the parents, the 1980 survey results show that 19 percent of the respondents who sent money thought it was quite helpful, 43 percent thought that it was of some help, and 38 percent thought it was only modestly helpful. By contrast, 77 percent of those who received money from their parents reported that they only received small sums; only 3 percent received substantial amounts from their parents. Therefore, it can be concluded that before children graduate from school, money mainly flows one way from parents to children. After the children graduate, the direction of money flow reverses, though in a smaller stream.

The 1980 KAP survey findings also showed that 43 percent of the married female respondents ages 22–39 expected to have to depend on their own savings for their financial needs in old age (Table 5). Only 27 percent expected that they will depend on their children, 16 percent thought they would depend on income from their business or property, and 12 percent planned to rely on their pensions.

The difficulty in living with or being supported by children in old age is also reflected in the expectations of the respondents. The proportion of married women ages 22–39 who expected to live with their married children in old age decreased sharply from 94 percent in 1965 to 47 percent in 1985. Similarly, the proportion of this cohort who expected their children to support them financially in their old age also decreased from 81 percent in 1973 to 61 percent in 1985. These proportions were even lower for women with higher educational levels and for those women who lived in cities. Among respondents who might be described as

Table 5. Expectations of Support in Old Age Among Married Women Ages 22–39

	Expectations in old age							
	Live with children (%)					Be supported by children (%)[a]		
	1965	1967	1973	1980	1985	1973	1980	1985
All respondents	94	87	56	41	47	81	65	61
Education								
None	99	94	71	56	75	93	84	83
Primary	93	89	57	44	56	84	72	76
Jr. high	82	63	37	37	43	58	59	58
Sr. high and above	66	45	21	22	28	38	36	37
Level of urbanization								
Rural township	99	93	64	50	53	90	73	70
Urban township	93	85	60	47	53	83	77	73
Small city	96	85	43	37	44	67	58	58
Large city	87	80	51	28	37	74	54	48

[a]No figures available for 1965 or 1967.
Source: Taiwan Provincial Institute of Family Planning, 1989.

participants in the global or market economies of Taiwan, even fewer respondents expected family support in old age to be forthcoming. Among the better-educated and more affluent respondents, the decline in those anticipating financial support from children were even more marked.

Survey respondents' opinions regarding the willingness of Taiwanese youth to observe traditional customs about children being obligated to shoulder filial responsibilities to their parents also changed over time. Increasing numbers of married women ages 22–39 felt modern young people were less willing to fulfill filial duties, live with parents after marriage, support parents in their old age, give part of their salary to their parents before marriage, or adhere to their parents' opinion. The proportion of women with lowered expectations of Taiwanese youth was considerably higher among those with more education and among those who lived in cities, and rose between 1970 and 1980 (Table 6). However, the degree to which expectations were lowered and the pace of change varied according to the nature of the expectations. More respondents reported that they expected Taiwanese youth to fulfill such basic duties as filial piety and supporting their parents in old age, and indeed these opinions were slower to change. But higher proportions of respondents felt that Taiwanese youth were unwilling to

Table 6. Proportion of Married Women (Ages 22–39) Who Think That Modern Youth Are Less Willing to Fulfill Traditional Obligations

Traditional obligation of children	Year	Total (%)	Education (%)				Urbanization (%)			
			None	Primary	Jr. high	Sr. high	Rural	Town	Small city	Large city
Filial piety	1970	22	17	25	30	28	17	20	25	33
	1973	39	35	41	43	43	37	37	43	43
	1980	n/a	—	—	—	—	—	—	—	—
Live with parents after marriage	1970	47	34	49	72	82	35	48	57	66
	1973	70	62	70	82	87	65	65	84	74
	1980	71	66	69	74	79	70	59	79	76
Support parents in old age	1970	11	9	12	18	14	10	11	11	17
	1973	28	25	28	29	29	26	24	33	29
	1980	25	28	24	26	26	29	16	33	23
Give part of salary to parents before marriage	1970	29	23	32	41	33	27	24	31	39
	1973	45	39	46	48	44	43	41	46	46
	1980	44	44	43	44	46	47	28	50	47
Listen to parents' opinions	1970	35	28	37	41	55	26	35	42	51
	1973	49	41	50	54	64	41	45	55	59
	1980	58	54	56	59	64	58	41	70	63

Source: Taiwan Provincial Institute of Family Planning, 1989.

fulfill other traditional obligations, such as living with parents after marriage or listening to parents' opinions, and these proportions increased more rapidly over the years. Despite the variations, the KAP survey findings also suggest that in Taiwan some traditional values continue to exist and that modernization is changing primarily peripheral behaviors and attitudes.

LIVING ARRANGEMENTS OF THE ELDERLY AND FAMILY SUPPORT

The rapid demographic, social, and economic changes that have occurred in Taiwan in the past 50 years or so have manifold implications for current and future patterns of support for Taiwanese elderly. For example, the increases in income that most Taiwanese have seen allow parents and children to achieve greater privacy via separate households if they so choose. At the same time, the increasing industrialization of the country and the migration of children from rural to urban employment make coresidence more difficult. Increases in the average age at marriage mean that unmarried children are likely to live in the parental home for longer periods. In addition, the rising labor-force participation of married women may limit the amount of support daughters-in-law can provide for their in-laws even when they share a residence. On top of familial changes affecting the relationship between adult children and their parents, there is another set of factors having to do with the rapidly evolving social welfare provisions available in Taiwan. As is the case in many modern economies, the availability of publicly sponsored options is offsetting the need to depend on traditional forms of care-giving within families.

Living Arrangements

There is little evidence that the economic and social changes described above have dramatically affected the living arrangements of Taiwan's older adults to date, although changes are clearly underway. Sufficient data to discern long-term trends regarding household composition are not available, but Table 7 presents an overview of the pattern that change in household composition has taken since 1976, based on two sources: the household data collected as part of the Survey of Income and Expenditures (Lo, 1987) and the 1989 Survey of Health and Living Status of the Elderly and follow-up interviews in 1996 and 1999 (Taiwan Provincial Institute of Family Planning, Population Studies Center, and Institute of Gerontology, 1989). Despite the limited scope of the surveys and lack of complete comparability between the two sources, these surveys offer clear evidence that greater numbers of Taiwanese elders are living independently, either alone or with a spouse. Concomitantly, the proportion of older adults who reside with one or more married children has declined from about two thirds of the total older adult population to a little less than one half. However, it is difficult

Table 7. Living Arrangements of the Elderly, 1976–1999 (Select Years) (%)

Living arrangements	1976	1978	1980	1982	1984	1985	1989	1996	1999
Alone or with spouse only	8.8	8.9	12.8	12.8	15.4	17.3	22.8	27.7	30.1
With married children	66.9	64.5	60.6	59.6	56.8	55.3	56.6	50.5	48.9
With unmarried children	16.8	20.6	21.0	22.3	22.4	23.0	14.1	17.0	13.8
Other arrangements	7.5	6.0	5.6	5.3	5.4	4.4	6.6	4.8	7.3
Total	100.0	100.0	100.0	100.0	100.0	100.0	100.1	100.0	100.1

Note: Sources may not be totally comparable. May total slightly more than 100%.
Sources: Data for 1976–1985 from Lo, 1987. Data for 1989–1999 from special tabulations of Taiwan Provincial Institute of Family Planning, 1989.

to determine whether the elderly are opting to live with an unmarried child. The 1985 Survey of Income and Expenditure data suggest an upward trend in the latter, but the results of the 1989–99 Survey of Health and Living Status show a substantial decrease in the numbers of elders living with an unmarried child. Explaining the differences is problematic but likely have something to do with how the questions were posed.

Though not shown on Table 7, further analysis of the 1989–1999 data demonstrates that older adults who are male, younger, Mainlander Chinese, never married, divorced, or childless are more likely to live alone or only with a spouse. On the contrary, those who are female, older, widowed, or have two or more children are more likely to live with their children. Older adults with more economic independence are more likely to live alone or with just their spouse. However, several groups of elderly—those with higher educational achievement, those who live in urban areas or rural townships, and those who are engaged in farming—tend to live independently only if they are living with a spouse. In addition, older adults in better health (measured in terms of subjective self-rating of their physical health) and those who have fewer limitations in activities of daily living (ADLs) or instrumental activities of daily living (IADLs), as well as fewer functional limitations, tend to undertake independent living only if they live with their spouse.

It should be mentioned that these increases in independent living patterns apply mostly to elders who coreside with a spouse, not to elders who live alone. The proportion of elders who live alone remained approximately the same between 1989 and 1999 (from 9.9 percent in 1989 to 11.0 percent in 1999), while the proportion of older adults who lived independently with their spouse increased from 12.5 percent of the overall elder Taiwanese population in 1989 to 19.1 percent in 1999.

Research by Chang (2001) indicated that declining rates of widowhood have a salutatory effect insofar as they enable more of the elderly to live independently with their spouse, but have a negative effect on the proportion of the elderly who live alone without a spouse. At the same time, increases in educational level and economic independence also foster more independent living among the elderly who have living spouses, while these factors are unfavorable for the elderly who live alone without a spouse. These patterns are consistent with those of Chen (1994), whose findings indicated, ". . . a substantial proportion of the elderly are satisfied with living alone, or with their spouse. They are characterized as being younger, better educated, male, in good health, and economically independent" (p. 47). The findings are also consistent with qualitative data generated through 21 focus-group discussions conducted in Taiwan in the early 1990s, in which many participants expressed interest in the freedom and privacy that independent living confers (Lee, Lin, and Chang, 1995). It should be mentioned that the elderly who lived in rural townships are more likely than elderly in other geographic areas to transition from coresidence with children to independent living with a spouse (Chang, 2001). This finding suggests that increasing industrialization and the migration of children from rural to urban jobs make coresidence problematic.

Living Arrangements and Types of Support

Ideally, an investigation of support arrangements for elderly Taiwanese would include the following elements:

- Assessment of needs across several dimensions
- Inventory of potential providers (ranging from elders themselves and their families to community resources and governmental programs)
- Inventory of characteristics of potential providers (e.g., for individual care providers, such characteristics as location, family status, education, and income)
- Assessments of the nature and magnitude of the specific kinds of support provided by each provider

Few studies attempt to obtain this full array of data, and there is little agreement at present on the requisite procedures for data collection.

Although the questionnaire employed in the 1989 Taiwan Survey of Health and Living Status of the Elderly collected considerable data on each of the major elements described above, it was far from exhaustive. The information the survey collected is based on a national probability sample of more than 4,000 men and women ages 60 and older who were residing in the nonaboriginal areas of Taiwan; the sample included elderly in institutions as well as those living in households in the community. The survey collected detailed information on characteristics of all individuals residing in the same household as the elderly respondent; the characteristics and location of close relatives not in the household, as well as the frequency of contact between the respondent and those relatives; and the exchanges that took place between respondents and others.

More specifically, each respondent was asked whether he or she received any of the following assistance: (a) help with activities of daily living (bathing, dressing, using the toilet); (b) help with certain instrumental activities of daily living (household chores, shopping, meal preparation, transportation, and managing finances); (c) money; and (d) food, clothing, or other goods. In each case, the respondent was asked to identify all the people who provide such support as well as the most important provider. Those receiving support of any kind were asked to characterize the adequacy of that support, and those not receiving any support were asked if they needed this type of assistance.

Analyzing these data, Hermalin, Ofstedal, and Chang (1996) indicated that the elders' living arrangements highly influenced the type of support they received as well as the providers of such support. Unfortunately, the set of questions regarding ADLs, IADLs, and financial support in the 1989 questionnaire were not repeated in the 1999 survey. Instead, in 1999 respondents were asked whether they had trouble with ADL tasks (bathing, dressing, eating, and using the toilet) and IADL tasks (household chores, shopping, meal preparation, transportation, and managing finances). If respondents answered in the affirmative, they were asked whether they received assistance with ADLs or IADLs. In each case, the respondent was asked to identify the most important provider of support and to characterize the sufficiency of the support they received.

Table 8 presents a broad overview of elders' self-perceived needs and the sufficiency of the support they received for ADLs and IADLs, distinguished by living arrangement and ethnicity. A very high proportion of the respondents in both 1989 and 1999 claimed that they needed no support for ADLs. Respondents who had come from the mainland after World War II (Mainlanders) were slightly less likely to need or receive this type of support than were those who had been born on the island of Taiwan. Similarly, those who lived in nuclear family situations were less likely to require support than elders in other living arrangements. Due to the increase in the older adult population, especially those ages 75 and older, prevalence rates for ADL limitations were higher in 1999 than they were in 1989, regardless of living arrangement or place of birth.

Although caution is in order when looking at results from investigations with relatively small sample sizes from which results are generalized, there do appear to be variations based on living situation and place of birth. In general, native Taiwanese were more likely than Mainlanders to report that they received a sufficient support. In addition, among the native Taiwanese, respondents living with a spouse, an unmarried child, or a married child were more likely to receive sufficient support with ADLs than were those living alone or with other relatives or friends.

Table 8. Support and Sufficiency of Support for ADLs[a] and IADLs[b] Among Older Adults in Taiwan, 1989–1999

Type and sufficiency of support	Living arrangement															
	Native Taiwanese (%)								Mainlander (%)							
	Alone		R/U/S[c]		R/M[d]		Other		Alone		R/U/S[c]		R/M[d]		Other	
	1989	1999	1989	1999	1989	1999	1989	1999	1989	1999	1989	1999	1989	1999	1989	1999
ADL:																
Does not need nor receive support	92.9	91.4	95.1	94.7	91.8	89.4	89.2	72.9	97.3	91.2	96.6	94.2	96.2	90.2	95.6	73.7
Receives sufficient amount of support	25.4	11.2	65.3	43.6	70.7	39.7	40.7	8.2	18.5	22.5	52.9	30.1	42.1	24.3	65.9	33.3
IADL:																
Does not need nor receive support	91.4	75.1	87.3	85.7	72.0	71.3	75.6	63.8	98.0	84.7	92.5	90.6	87.2	78.5	94.1	62.0
Receives sufficient amount of support	90.1	33.1	93.4	59.4	94.6	66.8	92.6	34.4	40.0	21.3	94.7	50.0	94.2	57.4	85.5	53.9
Total *N*	152	193	963	978	1,752	1,372	164	576	153	102	441	260	179	140	118	22

[a]ADL = Activities of daily living: bathing, dressing, eating, or using the toilet.
[b]IADL = Instrumental activities of daily living: household chores, shopping, meal preparation, transportation, or managing finances.
[c]R/U/S = Respondent lives with unmarried child and/or only with spouse.
[d]R/M = Respondent lives with married child (spouse may or may not be present).

As with ADLs, the proportion of elderly survey respondents who reported needing assistance with IADLs increased between 1989 and 1999. The proportion of elders who required IADL assistance was much higher than that of elders who needed assistance just with ADLs. Again, there is considerable variation in how likely respondents were to be receiving assistance with IADLs but less variation in terms of their perceptions about the sufficiency of the support they received (except for those living alone). Respondents from both island-born and Mainlander groups were most likely to receive IADL support when living with a married child and least likely when living alone. However, those born on the mainland were less likely than native Taiwanese to receive support when living with others. Additionally, the sufficiency of IADL support declined slightly between 1989 and 1999 for elderly in all living arrangements, regardless of nativity.

In 1989, spouses and daughters-in-law were the most common providers of assistance with ADLs (Table 9). Daughters-in-law were reported to be the most prominent individual provider of support when they lived with the older person; the spouse assumed this role when the daughter-in-law is not in the household. Children (sons and daughters) played less prominent but nonetheless important roles as providers of ADL support. By 1999, however, children emerged as more important providers of support with ADLs. A similar pattern exists for IADL support. In 1989, daughters-in-law and spouses were respectively the first and second most common providers. Children were significantly less likely

Table 9. Elderly Whose Major Income Sources Are from Children and the Sufficiency of Financial Support

	1989		1999	
	Major source of income from child support (%)	Sufficiency (%)	Major source of income from child support (%)	Sufficiency (%)
Living arrangements				
Alone	28.0	67.0	25.0	61.8
With spouse only	34.5	68.3	30.0	69.1
With married children	69.9	77.3	43.1	65.9
With married and unmarried children	58.2	80.3	40.5	62.5
With unmarried children	40.4	67.3	30.6	63.8
Other	22.4	60.6	37.5	54.4
Total *N*	4,048	2,054	3,186	1,149

to provide assistance with IADLs than they were for ADLs; mostly, responsibility seemed to fall to daughters-in-law. However, in 1999 adult children were playing a more active role in taking care of their parents.

With respect to financial support, a large proportion of elderly couples living with their married or unmarried children received financial support from them. Coresidence allows children to provide economic benefits to their elderly parents in a number of ways beyond the mere transfer of funds. Parents may live rent free in their children's homes and may have food provided at no cost. Even elderly who live alone may have their housing or other costs paid for by their children, greatly reducing the demands on their own meager incomes. Nevertheless, sufficiency of financial support varied along the lines of respondents' living arrangements; the elderly who lived alone were least likely to receive sufficient financial support, and those living with married children were most likely to receive sufficient amounts. However, between 1989 and 1999 the amount of financial support provided to the elderly, as well as its sufficiency, significantly declined. In addition, the authors' panel data, tabulated from the 1989 and 1999 Surveys of Health and Living Status of the Elderly, indicate that reliance on children decreased during this time period, suggesting that complex shifts in sources of support across the life course are occurring, meriting further study.

In summary, living arrangements are closely correlated with the expressed level of support needed and received. Furthermore, as might be expected, the need for support is highly correlated with living arrangement. The elderly are most likely to receive (or need) each type of support when living with a married child, and least likely when living alone. Overall, changes in family structure in Taiwan appear to have reduced the willingness of offspring to be the sole source of support for their older family members, a trend which will continue, in light of competing demands faced by the working age population, which is both occupationally and geographically mobile.

SOCIAL INTERACTION

Given the cultural traditions of the Chinese in Taiwan, it is not surprising that even with the conflicting pressures that are rife on the island, and despite declines over the past half century, older adults continue to interact with their family members quite intensively. But of course family contact is not the elders' only form of interaction. Another question that might be asked: How do older people interact with society outside the family context?

To examine this issue, the authors analyzed data from the 1996 Survey of Health and Living Status of the Middle Aged and Elderly in Taiwan, which was conducted by the National Institute of Family Planning, part of the National Department of Health, in the Executive Yuan (Cabinet). The survey was conducted with a representative sample of Taiwanese adults ages 50 and older, but only the data for those ages 60 and older will be discussed below.

In the early stages of industrial development in Taiwan, when most people worked on farms, very few activities were organized outside the family circle, and older adults traveled very little. In these pretelevision days, most of the older people were illiterate; only a few could even read newspapers. At that time, elderly people, mostly men, were commonly found after a day's work congregating with other elderly at the temple or perhaps a grocery store to share information, gossip, or exchange points of view. Many elderly participated in Taoist and Buddhist religious activities and presumably derived satisfaction from the social opportunities provided in that environment. However, as Taiwanese society has modernized, the social activities of older adults have changed.

Today, Taiwanese elders usually interact with society through their work, leisure activities, travel and sightseeing activities, volunteer activities, social groups, or the social assistance they receive from others. The popularity and intensity of these activities change with time, and also vary according to the older person's cultural background and age.

Working Situation

Many of today's elderly in Taiwan once made their living as farmers. About 26 percent of men in the 65–74 age group and 40 percent of men ages 75 and older formerly made their livelihood from agriculture. The corresponding proportions for older women are 28 percent and 36 percent, respectively. Other common occupations held by older men during their working years were managerial (about 19 percent for both the younger and the older age groups), semiskilled (18 percent and 10 percent, respectively), and clerical (11 percent for both groups). Women engaged in a diverse array of occupations, none of which involved more than 10 percent of the female population. However, about 36 percent of the elderly women in both age groups never worked for pay outside of the home. Relatively larger proportions of women in the 65–74 age group held more modern occupations such as skilled, semiskilled, or service work, which provided them with greater opportunity to interact with people other than their families (Table 10).

As for the current working situation of older adults in Taiwan, in 1996 only about 25 percent of men ages 65 and older and 6 percent of women in the same cohort were still employed on a full-time basis. Of those who worked, around 30 percent were engaged in agriculture, 23 percent were in the service sector, and 15 percent in managerial work. In addition, 25 percent of adults ages 65 and older (13.7 percent of older men and 37.7 percent of older women) held part-time jobs in 1996. The main reasons that survey respondents gave for continuing to work were to contribute to the family economy (67 percent of workers ages 65–74 and 55 percent of those 75 and older) and to pursue their own interests or enterprises (41 percent of younger workers and 64 percent of older workers).

Table 10. Past and Current Occupational Categories of Taiwanese Elderly, 1996

	Major occupation in past				Current occupation	
	Male		Female		Male	Female
Occupation	Ages 65–74	Ages 75+	Ages 65–74	Ages 75+	Ages 65+	Ages 65+
Agricultural	25.5	39.8	28.2	35.6	35.5	31.5
Managerial	19.4	18.8	4.9	6.1	15.4	12.2
Professional	5.9	3.9	2.3	1.7	7.2	3.6
Clerical	11.5	11	3	0.9	3	1.2
Skilled	6.8	6.2	5.5	4.3	4.3	6.5
Semiskilled	18.9	10.5	3.1	1.5	2.6	8.6
Sales	3	3.4	3	2.6	2.3	3.6
Services	3.9	1.4	7.3	3.9	22.2	23.9
Laborer	3.8	4.3	5.8	7.2	7.5	8.9
Unemployed	1.5	0.7	36.9	36.2	n/a	n/a
Sample (N)	762	280	570	295	256	53
% currently working	n/a/	n/a	n/a	n/a	24.6	6.1

Source: National Institute of Family Planning and Population Studies Center, 1996.

Among survey respondents ages 60–64, 37 percent (54 percent of men and 21 percent of women) were currently employed on a full-time basis and 34 percent (11 percent for men, but 57 percent for women) on a part-time basis. Interestingly, some 37 percent of elderly in this age group who still worked maintained that they experienced no particular stress or pressure from doing so. In fact, 79 percent received some satisfaction from work, and 74 percent would not stop working even if their incomes were sufficient to allow them to stop. Some 67 percent felt that they could still improve at their jobs by learning new knowledge or gaining additional skills.

Three quarters (76 percent) of all respondents ages 60 and older who were still working indicated that they would continue to work as long as their health permitted; 8 percent planned to retire at retirement age and 15 percent remained uncertain about when to retire. Only 13 percent of the respondents expressed certainty that there would be a pension waiting for them when they did decide to retire. About one third of the older respondents who were no longer working had retired before the age of 60, and most of the early retirees were female.

Leisure Activities

As the Taiwan economy modernizes, leisure activities become increasingly significant, much as they have in other industrial and postindustrial economies. Today, almost all families have at least one television set, and there are close to 100 cable channels available to the average viewer. In a culture that pays rapt attention to electronic forms of entertainment, it is not too surprising that the vast majority of older adults (94 percent) spend the bulk of their discretionary time watching television or videotapes. Despite its important place in their earlier lives, only 34 percent of older adults listen to the radio regularly; this proportion is even lower among women, those with lower education, and rural elderly (less than 29 percent for all three groups).

A smaller group of elderly spends time reading newspapers and magazines: 55 percent of men and 14 percent of women. Married older persons are nearly twice as likely (42 percent) as their single counterparts (24 percent) to read for enjoyment. Obviously educational level makes a difference; about 80 percent of elders with junior high or better education, as opposed to 20 percent of those less educated, read for leisure. Both place of residence and nativity also make a difference: 42 percent of urban dwellers as opposed to 23 percent of those in rural areas, and 71 percent of Mainlanders versus 29 percent of native Taiwanese, read for pleasure. Those who read newspapers have a higher level of awareness of political and social issues, which comes from these leisure pursuits.

As is the case in the West, religious activities are still important among older Taiwanese. Approximately 70 percent of older women participate in religious activities, compared to 48 percent of men. The proportion of elders who participate in religious activities is inversely related to educational achievement, degree of urbanization, and age. Part of the Chinese tradition is that on the 1st and 15th of each lunar-calendar month or on the birthdays of particular gods, people (mostly women) bring token gifts (formerly sacrifices) to the temple as acts of veneration. These occasions are also social opportunities for people to interact and socialize. In addition to attendance at religious observations, both Taoism and Buddhism place emphasis on adherents helping to build and maintain places of worship. Even though less than 5 percent of the population in Taiwan consider themselves to be Christians, there are more than 4,700 churches across Taiwan and these institutions, too, provide opportunities for voluntary association. In both Eastern and Western religions, relatively larger numbers of church members are older adults. Estimates are that little more than half of all church members regularly attend and participate in church-related activities.

Another important leisure activity for Taiwanese elderly is visiting friends or getting together with neighbors to drink tea and talk. Tea drinking is quite popular among older men in Taiwan. Those who engage in "elder's tea," as it is popularly called, use a special tea set consisting of a teapot and small cups. The process to make good tea requires quite an elaborate procedure, and only elderly people with sufficient leisure time can afford to participate. More than 60 percent of elderly men who participated in the 1996 survey said that they enjoy drinking tea and gossiping with friends. Almost the same proportion of older female respondents (58 percent) said they also enjoy visiting friends and gossiping.

About 30 percent of older survey participants enjoy gardening or flower arrangement. This proportion is especially high among those with higher levels of education (46 percent of those who completed senior high school or better). Elderly women often attend flower arrangement classes and take pleasure from their interaction there with other classmates. In fact, 66 percent of women ages 65–74 who completed junior high or higher levels of education reported taking such courses as a form of leisure education. Elderly men enjoy mostly gardening or horticulture.

Among forms of outdoor activities that older adults in Taiwan participate in, the most popular is walking. About 60 percent of survey respondents reported they regularly walk for pleasure, a rate that is even higher (74 percent) among those with at least a high-school education, with a comparable percentage of the Mainlanders reporting that walking is a source of pleasure. Aside from walking, about 17 percent of the elderly reported engaging in individual athletic activities including jogging, mountain climbing, and playing tennis or golf. The proportion was higher among men (22 percent), elders ages 60–64 (22 percent), those with higher levels of education (32 percent of those who completed junior high or better education), and Mainlanders (26 percent). One in 12 elderly also participates in such group activities or exercises as dancing, singing, shadow-boxing, or Chinese kung fu. These activities usually take place in small groups in a park or a playground early in the morning, with participants remaining on site afterward to socialize with others.

Only about 5 percent of older adults in Taiwan attend concerts or the theater. The attendance rate might have been influenced by the popularity of television. Comparable to patterns found throughout the world, the proportion of elders who engage in these types of cultural activities is slightly higher in urban areas and among elders with higher levels of education. In earlier times, puppet troupes used to tour around rural villages in Taiwan, especially at temples during special occasions. There were usually many older adults in the audience at these free outdoor shows. Nowadays, puppet shows are available only on television, but they are no less popular.

Sightseeing and Traveling

Resorts and other tourist destinations are rapidly becoming more fashionable around the country, and sightseeing and traveling are popular pastimes among the elderly in Taiwan. The 1996 survey showed that one third of the respondents ages 60 and older made one or more one-day trips to a Taiwanese resort during the previous year. The proportion was slightly higher among those who were younger (38 percent of those ages 60–64), those who traveled with their spouse (35 percent), those with better education (43 percent of those with at least a high-school education), or members of the Hakka[2] ethnic group (43 percent).

A little more than 30 percent of the respondents reported that they had made at least one sightseeing trip that lasted two or more days during the previous year. Similarly, the proportion was somewhat higher among those who were ages 60–64 (36 percent), men (33 percent), those who had a spouse with whom they could travel (33 percent), the better educated (38 percent among those with a junior high education or better), or Hakka (36 percent).

International traveling is more convenient than it was in the period shortly after World War II and far more feasible than it had been prior to that time. Travel agencies regularly organize tour groups to other countries. Group tours are relatively inexpensive these days, and contribute greatly toward increasing elders' knowledge about the world. Some 29 percent of respondents had traveled to China or other countries in the previous year, a slightly lower proportion than that of elderly who had made sightseeing trips within Taiwan. The proportion is especially high among men (33 percent versus 24 percent of women), those with a spouse with whom they might travel (33 percent versus 22 percent of those without a spouse), elderly living in urban areas (32 percent versus 23 percent of rural elders), and among Mainlanders (43 percent). Many Mainlanders visit their birthplace in China to see relatives and sightsee.

Volunteer Activities

Very few elderly in Taiwan—just 4.4 percent of survey respondents ages 60 and older—reported to be participating in volunteer work. The participation rate was somewhat higher for younger elderly (5.6 percent of those ages 60–64, compared to 2.7 percent of elders ages 70 and older), those with higher education (7 percent of adults with a junior high education or better), and those in the Hakka ethnic group (6.1 percent). Several charity organizations in Taiwan, especially a Buddhist organization called Chhu-chi ("Merciful" in Chinese), regularly recruit volunteers to work in hospitals, for welfare programs, in times of disaster, and for traffic control. However, this is one area of activity that lags behind rates of participation found in Western countries.

About 40 percent of those who reported volunteering worked in the area of religion, 15 percent in community activities, 12 percent in charity, 10 percent in healthcare programs, 9 percent in safety-maintenance activities, and 7 percent in environmental programs. As for the frequency of participation, about 40 percent

[2] The Hakka people originally came from Guangdong (Canton) Province in mainland China. They speak a different dialect than those from the Fukien Province and have different customs and a stronger sense of ethnic solidarity. The Hakka compose about 13 percent of Taiwan's total population.

of the volunteers participated in such activities every week, 36 percent every month, and 26 percent on an annual basis. The average time spent in voluntary activities was approximately 17 hours per month. Men and elders in the 65–74 age group reported spending relatively more time volunteering than the average older person who volunteered.

For those who did not participate in volunteer work, only 10 percent expressed an interest in doing so in the future. This proportion decreases with age: 18 percent of respondents ages 60–64, 9 percent of those ages 65–74, and 2 percent of those ages 75 and older felt they might volunteer for something in the future. Greater numbers of men (13 percent), elderly who were currently married (12 percent), those with a junior high education or better (24 percent), and Mainlanders (16 percent) reported a likelihood of joining some kind of volunteer effort in the future. The possibility is greatest among those elderly ages 60–64 with a junior high education or better (48 percent).

Participation in Social Groups

The most common type of social association that Taiwanese elders join is known as an "older people's group," often called the Evergreen Club or Pine-Age Fellowship. Twenty-one percent of survey respondents ages 60 and older reported being members of this type of organization. The proportion of those ages 65 and older rose to 24 percent, and that of men ages 75 and older reached 28.5 percent. Participation rates are also higher among rural elderly (25 percent), Hakka elders (25 percent), elderly from the Fukien ethnic group (24 percent), and men ages 75 and older who did not complete a junior high education (31 percent). In addition to the older people's groups, almost all Taiwanese Christian churches have fellowship groups for older members that meet regularly. The Presbyterian churches in Taiwan also organize a Pine-Age University program that offers courses of interest to elderly church members and elderly people in the community. There are about 50 such "universities" in Taiwan, attracting about 5,000 elderly students. Each county in Taiwan also has an Elderly People's Activity Center that provides many opportunities for older adults to meet and many activities in which they may participate.

Other popular organizations are the Farmers' Association, the Fishermen's Association, and Lions Clubs. About 12 percent of the survey respondents reported participating in one or more of these three associations. The participation rate was relatively higher among older men (18 percent), elderly with a primary school education or better (16 percent), Hakka elders (25 percent), and rural elderly in the 60–64 (30 percent) and 75-and-older (34 percent) age groups. The Farmers' Association has been quite active in Taiwan, contributing greatly to the development of the country's agriculture. Most farmers are members of this association. The same is true for the Fishermen's Association, with most of those who have plied the trade belonging. Both groups also have specialized programming for their older members.

According to the survey, religious organizations such as temples and churches involve about 10 percent of the elderly in Taiwan. The biggest such organization is the above-mentioned Chhu-chi, which has more than a million members in Taiwan and overseas. The participation rate for religious organizations is higher among young widows (18 percent), women ages 65–74 with a junior high education or better (23 percent), and native Taiwanese (17 percent).

Older adults reported equal rates of participation—8 percent—in political parties and clan associations whose members have the same family name. Participation in political parties was higher among men (15 percent, compared to 1 percent for women), adults ages 65–74 (11 percent), those with a junior high education or better (22 percent), and Mainlanders (30 percent). These rates were as high as 34 percent for older men with a senior high education or better and 35 percent for male Mainlanders. Participation in clan associations is higher among Mainlanders (18 percent), men (13 percent), and those with a junior high education or better (17 percent), especially men with a senior high education or better (23 percent).

Some respondents (3.3 percent) reported being members of their community's "friendly group," which gathers together often for a variety of activities, such as singing karaoke, dancing, playing games, and arranging flowers. Women were more likely to participate in the friendly groups (5.6 percent, compared to 1.3 percent of men), especially women ages 60–74 living in rural areas (9.6 percent), female Mainlanders (9.9 percent), and better-educated women ages 60–64 (12 percent for those with a junior high education or better).

AWARENESS AND DEMAND FOR WELFARE SERVICES

Welfare services for the elderly in Taiwan, although still in the early stage, do exist to a certain extent. However, not all older adults are aware of them. In the June 18, 1997, revisions to the Taiwanese National Welfare Law of the Elderly, the age at which a person is defined as "elderly" has been reduced from 70 to 65. The revised law demands that the government at all levels should provide services and welfare programs to older adults, including housing, pensions or subsidies, homecare services, healthcare services, transportation services, employment services, opportunities for social activities, and protection of frail elderly. The implementation of the law, of course, depends largely on the availability of funds, but many forms of welfare service have been carried out in small scale if not in a fully developed fashion. In the 1996 Survey of Health and Living Status of the Middle Aged and Elderly in Taiwan mentioned above, the respondents were asked whether they were aware of the availability of certain services and what types of welfare services they thought the government should provide older adults (Table 11).

Table 11. Awareness Among Taiwanese Elderly of Welfare Services Provided by the Government, 1996

Respondent characteristics	Economic assistance	Discount on transp. and entrance fees	Leisure-activity services	Homes for poor and sick elders	Opportunity for continued learning	Special medical care services	Support for daily living	Encourage volunteer services	Job-finding services
Sex									
Male	95.0	93.1	70.8	59.0	53.4	53.4	46.2	37.4	28.9
Female	92.3	90.9	53.8	45.5	37.6	37.6	29.5	24.2	12.6
Age									
60–64	91.8	90.6	62.4	53.0	45.0	45.0	40.0	33.4	18.7
65–74	95.2	92.4	64.9	55.4	48.9	48.9	40.8	33.5	24.6
75+	92.4	93.7	57.4	45.6	40.9	40.9	30.5	22.3	17.6
Education									
Illiterate	91.5	89.6	47.0	35.6	33.5	33.5	24.7	16.7	9.5
Literate, primary	93.7	93.1	64.9	52.4	47.1	47.1	39.6	31.5	20.6
Jr. high	96.5	94.0	78.9	74.7	62.8	62.8	54.4	48.2	36.5
Sr. high	96.7	93.6	85.9	86.3	64.9	64.9	61.8	59.8	47.4
Residency									
Urban	93.5	91.2	65.9	58.4	46.3	46.3	39.7	34.6	24.9
Rural	94.0	94.2	55.2	39.7	46.0	46.0	36.1	23.7	13.3
Ethnicity									
Fukien	92.5	90.9	57.4	47.1	41.1	41.1	33.5	26.7	16.2
Hakka	96.1	95.3	63.6	64.1	47.7	47.7	37.2	30.8	15.9
Mainlander	95.5	93.2	81.3	74.1	63.5	63.5	58.1	49.7	45.3
Aborigines	91.6	91.6	47.4	6.4	29.7	29.7	29.3	4.0	6.4
All respondents	93.6	92.1	62.8	52.8	46.2	46.2	38.6	31.4	21.5

Source: National Institute of Family Planning and Population Studies Center, 1996.

Virtually every respondent from every geographic, educational, and occupational category knew that the government provides economic assistance to the elderly as well as a 50 percent discount on public transportation and entrance fees to public exhibitions. Not only did the older respondents know of these forms of assistance, they utilized them as well.

However, only slightly more than 60 percent knew that the government provided leisure activities for older adults and homes for poor or ill elders in need of long-term care. The proportion of respondents who knew of these services varied by sex and ethnicity and was also positively correlated with educational achievement.

About half the respondents knew that the government provides older adults with opportunities for lifelong learning (53 percent) and long-term healthcare services at medical institutions (46 percent). The proportion of respondents who were aware of these services also varied by sex and ethnicity and was once again positively associated with educational achievement.

About one third of the respondents know that the government provides services to help older people who live alone to meet their needs for daily living (38.6 percent) and that it encourages older adults to participate in volunteer activities (31.4 percent). The proportion of elderly aware of these issues varied greatly by sex and ethnicity and was strongly correlated with educational levels.

Very few (21.5 percent) of the respondents knew that the government also provides services to older adults seeking employment. The proportion of elderly aware of such services was relatively high among elderly men, respondents ages 65–74, those with a junior high education or better, and Mainlanders.

As for the welfare services that respondents thought the government should provide older adults, it is interesting to see that a comparison of Tables 11 and 12 shows that the demand and supply of welfare service seems to match quite well. The most needed service, according to the respondents, was economic assistance; 88.9 percent mentioned the need for it. The demand was especially high among elderly women (92 percent), illiterate elders (94 percent), rural elders (94 percent), and native Taiwanese (96 percent).

Economic assistance was followed by "half price for public transportation and entrance fees to public exhibitions," the need for which was mentioned by 85.9 percent of respondents. There was not much variance across social strata, except for native Taiwanese, 94 percent of whom cited the need for such services.

The proportion of elderly who mentioned that they needed leisure activities and long-term medical care services was much lower, at 66.8 percent and 66.1 percent, respectively. This lower demand for the latter might be related to the fact that all older adults are already covered by national health insurance.

About half the respondents (55.5 percent) cited the need for "provision of services to meet the needs of daily living" and homes for indigent elderly (54.7 percent). The proportion of elderly who reported a demand for these services

Table 12. Taiwanese Elders' Demand for Welfare Services, 1996

Respondent characteristics	Economic assistance	Discount on transp. and entrance fees	Leisure-activity services	Special medical care services	Support for daily living	Homes for poor and sick elders	Opportunity for continued learning	Encourage volunteer services	Job-finding services
Sex									
Male	86.5	86.7	70.2	66.9	56.6	56.1	40.5	35.4	32.1
Female	91.8	84.5	62.7	65.2	54.4	53.0	36.7	29.2	22.5
Age									
60–64	88.4	85.0	69.0	69.8	60.6	60.7	42.4	37.4	31.9
65–74	88.4	85.8	66.7	65.2	53.7	53.1	39.1	32.4	28.2
75+	91.0	86.4	63.2	62.3	51.9	48.6	31.5	24.9	19.1
Education									
Illiterate	94.4	84.0	58.7	63.2	51.2	48.9	26.5	21.0	19.4
Literate, primary	90.5	87.4	70.8	66.9	56.4	55.1	39.9	34.2	29.7
Jr. high	79.1	85.8	72.5	71.6	59.7	64.0	53.4	45.6	35.1
Sr. high	74.6	83.1	69.1	60.7	61.4	62.3	57.4	48.6	37.5
Residency									
Urban	86.7	85.0	66.5	66.3	56.5	56.0	43.0	36.5	32.0
Rural	94.0	87.3	67.4	65.7	53.3	51.6	28.6	23.2	17.5
Ethnicity									
Fukien	91.6	85.8	67.0	67.4	58.2	56.6	36.9	32.2	27.1
Hakka	92.5	86.5	70.6	61.1	46.6	45.4	42.3	29.4	22.9
Mainlander	76.0	84.3	63.2	61.1	54.4	56.8	43.9	38.0	35.7
Aborigines	76.0	94.0	62.6	67.0	64.7	58.2	10.4	10.4	4.4
All respondents	88.9	85.9	66.8	66.1	55.5	54.7	38.8	32.6	27.2

Source: National Institute of Family Planning and Population Studies Center, 1996.

was somewhat higher among those ages 60–64 and those with better educations, but was significantly lower among the Hakka (46 percent).

About one third of the respondents expressed a desire for opportunities for continued learning (38.8 percent) and for encouragement to participate in volunteer activities (32.6 percent). The proportion was somewhat higher among elders ages 60–64, those with higher educational achievement, those living in urban areas, and Mainlanders, but was particularly low among native Taiwanese.

The least desired services, according to the respondents, were job-finding services, mentioned only by 27.2 percent of the respondents. The proportion was a bit higher for men than for women, as well as among elderly in the 60–64 age group, those with better educations, urban dwellers, and Mainlanders, reflecting the increased need of these groups to find jobs. Conversely, the demand for job-finding services was very low among native Taiwanese.

CONCLUSION

Older people in Taiwan today, and for several decades to come, face a complex situation. First, their numbers will triple in the next four decades and their proportion of the total population will increase from 9 percent to more than 20 percent. In other words, there will be a relatively large number of elderly people needing support who will rely on relatively fewer working-age Taiwanese to provide it. Whether the responsibility for furnishing adequate care to the growing older adult population rests with the family or with society as a whole is a topic sure to generate spirited debate.

Second, today's older adults are encountering rapid changes in Taiwanese society, including rapid economic development, modernization, urbanization, and lifestyle changes. The interactions of these factors affect their financial, social, and physical well-being. The rapid economic developments of the past half century have brought more affluence to the elderly, but other changes have eroded the customary function of the family and traditional cultural values, both of which have long played important roles in ensuring adequate support for older people in Taiwan. It is encouraging to see that per capita income has increased from only about US$200 in 1965 to US$14,000 in 2001, which has generally raised the standard of living for all Taiwanese, including the elderly. However, increasing numbers of older adults are living alone, and the willingness of younger people to support their aging relatives is flagging. Crowded living environments and the rising cost of accommodations in the nation's expanding urban areas has made it more difficult for older adults to live with their married children.

Third, developments in medicine are extending the life expectancy of older people so that greater numbers require chronic or long-term care. Such care in turn demands more trained staff and greater numbers of institutional structures to assist those elderly facing physical problems or mental declines. These increased demands will cause medical expenditures to skyrocket, becoming a heavy burden to families and society at large.

Societies in the process of modernization—Taiwan is one such society, but other nations in Asia are soon to follow—are encountering comparable hurdles. However, these scenarios might not be as pessimistic as they seem. As a nation, Taiwan may refer to the experiences of more developed countries in the West or in Asia for examples of how to cope with the aging of its population. As long as the Taiwanese have the will to solve the country's problems, solutions are always available. For example, the elderly may find it increasingly difficult to live with their married children in the same house, but they can still live as neighbors in the same community. Sometimes this situation is even better for both parties because it provides more privacy and prevents conflict between the generations. With well-developed transportation and electronic communication systems, even distance need not pose an insurmountable obstacle to familial interaction. Finally, in the face of chronic conditions that befall long-living populations, the government—and, in fact, society as a whole—should develop adequate facilities to accommodate elders who need intensive care and should provide economic assistance to poor older adults.

However, as the Taiwanese economy continues to improve, people also should prepare to live to old age by setting aside assets of their own and paying more attention to their health before it begins to decline. Because people are living longer, it is increasingly important for them to maintain healthy lifestyles by participating in such activities as outdoor exercises, group activities, leisure activities, sightseeing trips, and volunteer activities. By maintaining healthier and happier lives as they age, the elderly can lessen the social and economic burdens their aging places upon their families and upon society as a whole.

REFERENCES

Chang, M.-c. (2001, March). *Living arrangements of the elderly and types of support in Taiwan: Cross-sectional and time-serial analysis.* [In Chinese.] Paper presented at the "Symposium on Population Aging and Its Strategy in China and Taiwan," sponsored by the Population Association of Taiwan, Taipei, Taiwan.

Chen, C. (1994). The determinants of satisfaction with living arrangements for the elderly in Taiwan. *Journal of Population Studies, 16,* 29–52.

Council for Economic Planning and Development. (2000). *Taiwan statistical data book.* Taipei: Manpower Department, Council for Economic Planning and Development.

Freedman, R., Chang, M.-C., and Sun, T.-H. (1982). Household composition, extended kinship, and reproduction in Taiwan. *Population Studies, 36,* 395–411.

Gallin, B. (1966). *Hsin Hsing, Taiwan—A Chinese village in change.* Berkeley: University of California Press.

Goode, W. K. (1963). *World revolution and family patterns.* New York: The Free Press.

Greenfield, S. M. (1961). Industrialization and the family in sociological theory. *American Journal of Sociology, 67,* 312–322.

Hermalin, A. I., Ofstedal, M. B., and Chang, M. C. (1996). Types of supports for the aged and their providers in Taiwan. In T. K. Harven (Ed.), *Aging and generational relations: Life-course and cross-cultural perspectives* (pp. 179–215). New York: Walter de Gruyter.

Lavely, W. R. (1982). *Industrialization and household structure in rural Taiwan.* Unpublished doctoral dissertation. Ann Arbor: University of Michigan.

Lee, M.-l., Lin, H.-s., and Chang, M.-c. (1995). Living arrangements of the elderly in Taiwan: Qualitative evidence. *Journal of Cross-Cultural Gerontology, 10,* 53–78.

Levy, M. J. Jr. (1949). *The family revolution in modern China.* Cambridge, Massachusetts: Harvard University Press.

Levy, Marion J. Jr. (1965). Aspects of the analysis of family structure. In A. Coale, L. Fallers, M. Levy Jr., D. Schneider, and S. Silvan (Eds.), *Aspects of the analysis of family structure* (pp. 1–63). Princeton, New Jersey: Princeton University Press.

Lo, J. C. C. (1987). *The changing patterns of household structure and economic status of the elderly: 1976 to 1985.* In the Institute of Economics, Academia Sinica, Conference on Economic Development and Social Welfare in Taiwan (I) (pp. 375–401). Taipei: Academia Sinica.

National Institute of Family Planning. (1999). *1996 survey of health and living status of the middle aged and elderly in Taiwan.* Taiwan aging studies series, no. 8. Ann Arbor: National Institute of Family Planning, University of Michigan.

Sun, T.-H., and Liu, Y. H. (1991). Changes in intergenerational relations in the Chinese family: Taiwan's experience. In L. J. Cho and M. Yada (Eds.), *Tradition and change in the Asian family* (pp. 320–361). Honolulu, Hawaii, and Tokyo: East-West Center and University Research Center, Nihon University.

Taiwan Provincial Institute of Family Planning, Population Studies Center, and Institute of Gerontology, University of Michigan. (1989). *1989 survey of health and living status of the elderly in Taiwan: Questionnaire and survey design* (Comparative Study of the Elderly in Four Asian Countries: Research Report No. 1). Ann Arbor, Michigan: Author.

Wei, H. C., and Reischl, U. (1981). The impact of industrialization on family structure in Taiwan. *Industry of Free China, 56*(3), 11–26.

CHAPTER ELEVEN

Intergenerational Support Mechanisms for Filipino Elderly

Mercedes B. Concepcion and Aurora E. Perez

The gradual process whereby a society moves from a period of high fertility and mortality rates to one of low rates is customarily termed *demographic transition.* As was noted in the chapter on demography, this transition is distinguished by reductions in infant and child mortality as infectious and parasitic diseases are brought under control. When fertility rates fall and mortality rates in all age groups improve, the population begins to age.

Swiftly mounting numbers of older adults in the global population represent a social phenomenon without historical precedent. The world's elderly population, defined here as people ages 60 and older, was estimated to have reached 606 million at the end of the 20th century and is expected to approach 1.2 billion by 2025. As a result of declining fertility and lengthening life expectancy, the number of older adults in the majority of countries is expanding faster than the population as a whole, thereby causing a shift in the age structure of the country. For the first time in human history, the population of older adults is projected to outnumber the population ages 0–14 by the year 2050.

As was noted earlier in this volume, to date, population aging has been foremost an issue in the industrialized nations of Europe, Asia, and North America. In at least 44 such countries, 15 percent or more of the total population is age 60 or older. These nations have keenly debated such issues as social security costs, provision of healthcare, and educational investment, which are directly associated with the changing age structure of the population. What is not broadly realized is the fact that population aging is also taking place in developing countries and that the older cohorts in most of these countries are growing much more quickly than their counterparts in developed nations.

Demographic transformation in the Philippines has been relatively slower than that observed among its neighbors. Nonetheless, the Philippines has experienced significant increases in life expectancy at birth, from 55.5 years among males and 59.1 years among females in 1970 to an estimated 67.2 years for males and 71.4 years for females at the turn of the 21st century (United Nations [U.N.], 2001). Furthermore, there have been indications of improved infant and child survival, with infant mortality rates declining to 35.3 deaths per 1,000 live births around 1995, down from 45.3 deaths per 1,000 live births a decade earlier (Philippine National Statistics Office and Macro International, 1998). This has translated to a modest change in reproductive behavior among Filipinos: The total fertility rate has declined from 6.0 children per woman around 1970 to 3.7 in 1996. A continuation of such trends into the future means a growing proportion of older adults. In 1970, the proportion of the Philippine population ages 60 and older was 4.6 percent; it had increased to an estimated 6.0 percent by 2000. In absolute numbers, this represents an increase from 1.7 million elders in 1970 to 4.6 million at the century's end. By the year 2030, Filipino elders are projected to number 14.3 million, and their numbers will almost double to 26 million by the middle of the 21st century (Philippine National Statistics Office, 1999).

GLOBALIZATION AND URBANIZATION

Citizens of both developed and developing countries, rich and poor, young and old, worker and retiree, feel the impact of globalization. As resources are redistributed across and within nations, traditional class divisions are shifting. An avenue to participation in the new global economy is through access to information and technology. In the era of digital transfers, capital is increasingly detached from visible investments in people, places, and things, becoming a free-floating element that flows across national borders with the stroke of a computer key in quantities difficult to fathom. Concurrently, as localized costs mount and public resources diminish, governments strain to sustain at least minimum expenditures for maintaining the welfare of the population in general, for the elderly, and in the area of universal targeted healthcare provisions (Dixon-Mueller, 2001).

For many nations, but especially the Philippines, the global economic crisis that occurred during the 1990s, in combination with the stringent conditions of structural adjustment policies and the escalating numbers of the poor, presents an insuperable obstacle between the countries' aspirations and their probable achievements. As the demand for services swells, resources tail off and economic inequalities multiply. Analysis of the situation of the elderly must be placed in this context.

In accord with the worldwide trend toward increased urbanization, the older populations of both developed and developing regions have become more concentrated in cities over the past two decades. At the same time, however, many rural areas have become disproportionately "old" as young adults move from rural areas to urban centers. Such rural-to-urban population shifts can have unforeseen effects for elders in rural areas, who may find themselves without direct familial support, and in some cases, with the added responsibility of raising grandchildren whose parents have migrated to urban areas in search of work (Gist and Velkoff, 1997).

In many countries, older women are more likely to reside in towns and cities than are older men. In part, this gender difference in residential concentration appears to be related to life-cycle stages. Older women are more likely to be disabled and to be widowed than are older men. Among older Filipino women, the 1980 Philippine census revealed that 43 percent were widowed urban dwellers. In contrast, only 15 percent of older men were widowers living in urban areas (U.N., 1993). It may be that residing in cities provides older women, especially widows, the benefits of being close to their children and in close proximity to specialized health and social services (Kinsella and Taeuber, 1993).

This chapter provides an overview of the demographic and socioeconomic profile of the elderly in the Philippines with the goal of generating relevant polices and programs for older Filipinos. The authors depend heavily on census reports, census data, and analyses generated from the 1996 Philippine Elderly Survey (PES), the first national representative sample of the elderly (ages 60 and older) and near elderly (ages 50–59). The study formed part of a larger project, Comparative Study of the Elderly in Four Asian Countries (Singapore, Taiwan, Thailand, and the Philippines), sponsored by the U.S. National Institute on Aging (Hermalin, 2002). Population projections discussed in this chapter are based on the medium variant of official national projections and those prepared by the United Nations for the Philippines.

DEMOGRAPHIC PROFILE OF FILIPINO OLDER ADULTS

Although the growth rate for the elderly population in the Philippines surpassed that of the entire population, the aging of the population does not seem to be an immediate problem for government agencies. People ages 60 and older comprised 5.5 percent of the country's population in 1995. While the present level has not reached crisis proportions, this should change dramatically in the year 2030 when the elderly are expected to reach 14.2 percent of the total population, at which time the median age will be 33.3 years (Philippine National Statistics Office, 1999).

While these figures indicate moderate levels in absolute terms, they assume quantitative significance. Some 3.7 million persons were identified as being 60 or older during the 1995 Census of Population. This number is expected to triple to 10.8 million by the year 2020. This is suggested by the fast rate of growth exhibited by the incoming cohorts of older people, particularly among those ages 40–49, whose rate of growth between 1990 and 1995 exceeded not only that of the older cohorts but also that of the total population.

Due to their growing magnitude, older adults pose a burden on the productive age group, those ages 15–59, a burden that is expected to be more cumbersome in the future. Available population data indicate an increasing old-age dependency ratio accompanied by a falling dependency ratio of young people. In 1970, 11 economically active persons supported each older adult; that number decreased to 10 economically active persons by 1995. In the year 2030, there will only be six economically active persons per older person. This increasing old-age dependency pattern has significant implications, considering the low social security coverage for the elderly in the Philippines. The task of providing revenues for elder care then is left primarily to the younger segments of society.

Several additional demographic characteristics of elderly in the Philippines must be considered when discussing their needs and the development of national policy for older adults: sex ratio, life expectancy, marital status, and residence patterns.

Sex Ratios

As pointed out earlier in this volume, one notable characteristic of the worldwide elderly population is the numeric dominance of women over their male counterparts. This is particularly true in developed regions, where, in 1990, there were three female elders to two male elders. The low proportion of older men observed in Western countries presumably reflects a history of extensive war losses in Europe, Japan, and the former Soviet Union (Concepcion, 1988). The predominance of older women in the population is less marked in developing regions, where there are five female elders to every four male elders. In the Philippines, the sex ratio for the elderly (represented as the number of men per 100 women) stood at 87 in 1995.

One important aspect of aging common to both developed and developing regions has been the increasing feminization of the older population. This global pattern, however, is expected to change in the 21st century as indicated by projections that manifest an evening out of sex ratios. While a general rise in the sex ratios of Asian populations as well as in other parts of the world will prevail, the sex ratio will continue to fall in the Philippines. This means that the population of older women will continue to increase faster than that of their male counterparts. Middle-level projections indicate that the sex ratio will decline from the 1995 level of 88 to 85 by the year 2020.

Another interesting pattern is that with advancing age women make up progressively greater proportions of the older population. On the global level, in 1997 women made up just over half of the 60–69 age interval but accounted for 65 percent of the oldest old (those ages 80 and older). The gender imbalance was more pronounced in developed countries, where the 1997 sex ratio of the population ages 60–69 was 85, as compared to 96 in developing countries (Gist and Velkoff, 1997). If the mortality trend in the developing countries approximates that observed in the West, the gap between male and female life expectancy would be expected to widen in the future. One likely consequence would be an increasing proportion of women among the oldest cohorts of the elderly population. However, should the life expectancy of men in developed countries rise somewhat faster than that of women, there will be resulting reductions in the female proportion of the population at older ages.

The age-specific feminization pattern is likewise true in the Philippines, although the differentials are not as marked as those observed in the developed world. As of 1995, the sex ratio recorded for 60-to-69-year-olds was measured at 92, compared to 77 among those ages 80 and older.

Life Expectancy

Due to improved healthcare over time, a greater proportion of the population now reaches what is nominally defined as old age. This pattern is clearly indicated by the increasing life expectancy of the population, with women enjoying a universal margin of advantage over men. In 2000, the average woman in the developing world could expect to reach at least age 65, some three years beyond that of her male counterparts (U.N., 2001). The feminine advantage stems from the fact that women currently have lower mortality rates than men in every age group and for most causes of death (Kinsella and Gist, 1995).

Not only do more people stay alive to reach their later years, those who do can expect to live longer. That the elderly themselves are aging is clearly illustrated by the increasing remaining years a person can expect to live after reaching age 60. In 1995, a Filipino woman who reached age 60 could expect to live another 19 years on the average, as compared to 17 years for her male counterpart; in fact, this gender gap had widened between 1970 and 1990 (Cabigon and Flieger, 1999). This discrepancy suggests that health improvements may have benefitted women more than men.

Marital Status

The marital status of older individuals is an aspect of family structure that deeply affects their living arrangements, support systems, and well-being. Marital status is also likely to have a profound impact on retirement from the labor market, on pensions provided by the government, and on general social support (Kinsella and Gist, 1995).

Distinct gender differences can be seen in terms of Philippine marriage patterns. Although being married is the predominant marital status among Filipino elders—almost two thirds of whom are married—older men are more likely to be married than women. As can be seen in Table 1, at least four out of five older men reported being currently married, compared to approximately one in two women. The proportion of older women who were widowed came close to that of women who were married. This statistic may be due to a

Table 1. Distribution of Male and Female Elderly by Selected Characteristics, 1996

Characteristics	Male (%)	Female (%)
Marital status		
Never married	2.9	8.1
Married	81.5	49.2
Widowed	14.7	41.5
Divorced/separated	0.9	1.2
Educational attainment		
Elderly (ages 60+)		
None	19.1	19.3
Elementary	58.2	60.7
Secondary/vocational	15.7	13.6
Postsecondary/tertiary	7.0	6.4
Near-elderly (ages 50–59)		
None	12.5	6.7
Elementary	52.1	63.7
Secondary/vocational	24.7	19.4
Postsecondary/tertiary	10.8	10.2
Labor-force participation		
Currently working	52.3	28.1
Not currently working	46.0	50.2
Never worked	1.7	21.7
Occupation		
Professional	2.2	2.0
Administrative/clerical	1.7	1.0
Sales, commerce, trade	5.9	20.6
Agriculture	57.2	18.7
Production, crafts	7.5	9.3
Service	1.7	2.2
Never worked	2.5	36.7
Retired	16.5	7.1
Out of work/other	4.8	2.4
Self-assessed health status		
Excellent/very good	17.6	12.7
Good/fair	68.2	71.4
Poor	14.2	15.9

Table 1. (Cont'd.)

Characteristics	Male (%)	Female (%)
Leisure activities		
Daily		
Listen to radio	51.5	43.4
Read newspapers, books, etc.	13.6	7.9
Meditate, pray	75.2	90.1
Watch TV	30.2	36.3
Weekly		
Exercise	34.3	26.7
Gamble	13.5	8.0
Attend religious services	48.3	64.4
Attend socials	15.7	11.6
Important income source		
Work earnings	30.5	22.8
Pension	10.3	5.5
Annuity/severance pay	0.4	0.3
Rental, savings, real estate	1.6	2.3
Family business	5.2	4.8
Farm	26.7	17.7
Children/relatives in-country	20.0	36.9
Children/relatives abroad	4.4	7.9
No information	1.0	1.8
Support from coresident children		
Percent receiving money	83.9	88.1
Percent receiving food, clothing, other gifts	84.2	92.1
Support from non-coresident children		
Percent receiving money	78.6	82.0
Percent receiving food, clothing, other gifts	77.2	86.3

Source: Hermalin, 2002.

combination of factors: women marrying men older than themselves, the longer life expectancy of women, and the greater tendency of widowed men to remarry (Domingo, 1995).

Worth noting is the substantial fraction of older adults who have remained unmarried; as reported in the 1996 PES, women who have not married outnumbered their male counterparts (8.1 percent as against 2.9 percent). However, this pattern may become less prominent in the near future, since there are now fewer unattached individuals among those ages 50–59 than among people ages 60 and older (4.8 percent versus 5.6 percent).

Migration

The geographic mobility of Filipino older adults, especially elderly widows, is worth examining given their wish to coreside with their children or seek their support. The PES data revealed that nine out of ten Filipino older persons had moved at least once in their lifetime. Two thirds of those who had moved were lifetime migrants, that is, they had left their birthplace and later settled in another village/town/city at the time of the interview; one third had lived in the same village after moving. Most of the elderly lifetime migrants transferred from their birthplace to their last address between the ages of 20 and 49. Evidently, few of the older study participants had made residential changes in recent years.

A study by Ogena and Williams (1999) revealed that when those who moved after age 50 were asked why they had moved, the most commonly cited reasons given were: (a) to settle in their own home; (b) to be reunited with their children or other relatives; and (c) to take advantage of better living arrangements. In general, men tended to move closer to their place of work or to a new house or lot they owned, whereas women often moved to join children or other relatives. The latter move is probably due to family life-cycle changes such as the death of a spouse and the expectation that children would take care of the respondents during their widowhood.

The data also disclosed that recent migrants—those who moved to their present address within the past two to five years preceding the interview—were likely to be women, single, and far from close relatives. Such migrants have not received from, or given financial and material support to, their relatives prior to their move. That is, those who made recent moves were actually seeking support, with coresidence with children appearing to be the most desirable form of support.

When asked of any plans to change homes in the next two years, less than one in 20 reported any intention of moving in the near future. Those likely to move in the next two years were respondents with at least a high school diploma; those living with their spouses and children; the unemployed; and the retired.

SOCIOECONOMIC PROFILE OF FILIPINO ELDERLY

As agents and beneficiaries of progress, today's Filipino elderly require opportunities and support systems including those for income generation, social security, and healthcare. This section describes selected socioeconomic characteristics of older women and men—their educational attainment and occupation, living arrangements, health and leisure, social security, and pension schemes—in order to generate relevant policies and programs.

Educational Attainment and Occupation

Participation in the labor force among the elderly reflects changes in the educational system and shrinking job opportunities due to reduced productivity with advancing age or to the shifting of the labor force away from agriculture. An assessment of the educational status of the elderly and near elderly (those ages 50–59) indicates that their modal (most common) educational attainment is sixth grade (Table 1). Attesting to significant improvements in educational attainment over time, the 50–59 cohort, when compared against the 60-plus cohort, showed lower proportions of those who were unschooled and higher proportions of those who completed high school. About one fifth of the older adults claimed to be illiterate; there were no gender differentials for this statistic. Interestingly, the fraction of those who lacked any formal education was highest among near-elderly men (13 percent), nearly double that of their female counterparts (7 percent). This pattern supports the apparent headway that Filipino women in their 50s have made insofar as education is concerned, an indicator of the initial success of basic education in reducing illiteracy among women. Nevertheless, men in their 50s continue to demonstrate a slight advantage when it comes to secondary vocational and postsecondary (tertiary) educational achievement. This picture is likely to change in the future. In 1990, women ages 20–24 exhibited an edge over their male counterparts (3.2 versus 2.2 percent) in terms of tertiary-level enrollment (Xenos and Raymundo, 1999).

As far as employment of Filipinos ages 60 and older is concerned, substantial age- and sex-related patterns are common. For both sexes, work participation declines with advancing age. Men have a clear advantage over women. Starting at age 50, the proportion of men employed exceeded that of women, ranging from 50 percent more to greater than 200 percent more depending on the work sector (Table 1). Farming remained the primary occupation of older adults, particularly men. Older women were predominantly engaged in sales and commerce. Worth highlighting is the fact that one in three older women reported never having worked outside the home for pay or profit. However, this figure masks the real situation. It is likely that women consider their unpaid activities on family farms or in other household enterprises to be part of their domestic responsibilities. Hence, their participation in economic activity as well as their contribution to economic production continues to be underreported or inadequately acknowledged in official statistics.

Living Arrangements

Another important indicator of the well-being of Filipino elderly in terms of economic support, emotional support, and healthcare is their living arrangements. Undoubtedly, living with family members is the best arrangement for older people, given the support and care supplied by coresident children and the help given by non-coresident children. While Filipino elderly predominantly live in extended family households, it cannot be denied that the proportion of older adults living in one-person households is growing. United Nations reports indicate that local variations notwithstanding, almost one third of all one-person households in the world are composed of older individuals. Casterline et al. (1991) analyzed results of a 1984 Association of South-East Asian Nations (ASEAN) survey that showed that the percentage of Filipino elderly living alone rose with age, from 15 percent among those ages 60–64 to 23 percent among those ages 75 and older. A greater number of older women than older men lived alone—19 percent versus 14 percent among the 60–69 cohort and 23 percent versus 19 percent among the 70-plus cohort, respectively.

Despite the fast pace of urbanization and the growing number of young Filipinos joining the ranks of the international workforce, it is comforting to note that most Filipino elderly do not live in isolation. The PES results showed that more women (6 percent) than men (4 percent) reported living alone. Seven out of ten (69 percent) older respondents lived with their children and another one in thirteen (8 percent) resided next door. Moreover, 96 percent of the children of the elderly respondents were adults capable of providing support to the respondents (Perez, 1999a). The phenomenon of the "empty nest," which describes couples whose children have moved away from the family home to establish their residence elsewhere, was apparent only among a few older respondents. However, older women were less likely to be living with a spouse (7 percent as against 9 percent among men), again underscoring the fact that many women outlive their spouses.

Nevertheless, more than two fifths (43 percent) of older survey respondents expressed the opinion that living alone would be ideal. That proportion declined with age and increased with degree of dependence. Although three quarters of the elders considered homes for the aged to be a good idea, less than one third told researchers they would actually stay in one (de Guzman, 1999).

The considerable proportion of older adults who coreside with their children can be traced to cultural norms that view children as primary caregivers for their elderly parents. In the Philippines, the strongly instilled sense of reciprocity that children feel toward their parents is clearly illustrated in the value of *utang na loob* (debt of gratitude or shared humanity), a potent cultural mechanism (Asis, Domingo, Knodel, and Mehta, 1995).

Non-coresidence with children does not necessarily imply total loss of support and contact. A fair amount of contact exists between older adults and non-coresident children. More than a quarter of older individuals (27 percent of older men and 31 percent of older women) acknowledged that they either visit or are visited by a non-coresident child daily (Perez, 1999b). Although the other three fourths may not receive frequent visits from their children, family reunions usually take place at Christmas and during Holy Week.

Health and Leisure

The increasing numbers of older adults who are expected to live longer lives will naturally result in more health-related problems, which will further burden the country's already limited healthcare services. Although lengthening life expectancy can be viewed as good news, recent studies indicate that longer lives do not necessarily translate into healthier lives (Crimmins, Hayward, and Saito, 1996). Moreover, the aggregated medical costs of the aged exceed those of the young. One common finding emerging from various studies of changes in health status and health inequalities within and among the elderly of various nations is that women who reach older age can expect live more disability-free years than their male counterparts. Despite women having longer life expectancy at any given older age than men, the disability-free portion of life expectancy at age 65 tends to be somewhat greater for men (Kinsella and Gist, 1998).

To ascertain how older adults view their physical health, respondents in the 1996 PES were asked to self-assess current health status (Table 1). The method may be somewhat biased considering that no effort was made to substantiate the respondents' reports with supportive medical records. Quite expectedly, respondents ages 60 and older were more likely to evaluate their health more negatively than those ages 50–59. Most of the older respondents rated their health as "good" or "fair." Interestingly, women assessed their health in more negative terms than did men: One out of six older men considered his health to be "excellent" or "very good," as compared to only one out of eight older women.

How older adults spend their leisure time is one important dimension in discussing their health and sense of well-being, as retired individuals are free from the demands of routine work or many prescribed duties. The results of the PES revealed that after retirement many older adults turn to religious activities such as praying and meditating daily; women are once again more likely to do so than men. To a lesser degree, older adults also listen to the radio, watch television and read. Some older adults, especially men, exercise regularly to prevent or slow deteriorations in their health.

Social Security and Pensions

The Philippine social security system dates back to 1936, when the Government Service Insurance System (GSIS) was established for all government employees. Later, workers in the private sector were covered under the Social Security System (SSS), implemented in 1954. Both systems provide mandatory basic coverage of the defined-benefit type. The benefits under GSIS cover retirement, separation, unemployment, disability, and death. Employees who are at least 60 years old and who have rendered 15 years of service are eligible for retirement benefits. Compulsory retirement is at age 65. Those who elect to retire at age 65 with 35 years of service can receive a pension of close to four fifths of their final salary up to a specified wage ceiling. Retirees can claim benefits under two basic options, each of which combines a lump-sum payment plus a lifetime annuity. The SSS provides benefits for death, disability, sickness, and childbirth. Unfortunately, both national social security programs are beset with financial and administrative problems that must be addressed to assure compliance among recipients and solvency of the program.

Many Asian countries have barely begun to develop programs to address the social security of their older citizens. Unhappily, many of these nations lack the legal framework, financing, and administrative ability required to institute broad and efficacious programs (Mason, Lee, and Russo, 2000). The family support system, particularly in the Philippines, has attended to the needs of the elderly with ample success. However, this traditional approach will become an increasingly unappealing option in postindustrial societies where both occupational and geographic mobility are the norm. Given the pace of the aging of the Philippine population, only a relatively short period remains for the nation to develop and implement requisite policies and programs to protect the economic security of its older citizens.

INTERGENERATIONAL SUPPORT WITHIN FAMILIES

The Filipino home remains central in the exchange network of support and care between young and old. When families include young children, working adults, and older adults living under one roof, the reciprocal flow of support is assured. The assumption is that they are bonded by relationships of mutual economic, social, and emotional interaction with an expectation that those who have will help provide for those in need.

The flow of support varies across time and stages of the life course and with competing demands, of course. A traditional notion in Filipino culture is that when the elderly parent cannot contribute to household expenditures, ownership of the dwelling itself may be viewed as tantamount to his or her share.

Flow of Support from Children to Parents

One of the facilitating factors for the continued reciprocal flow of support between Filipino elders and their adult children is the physical proximity between the two and the amount of contact they have. The data in Table 2, based on findings from the PES, focus on material and financial support that older Filipinos receive from their children. Of those older people who received support from their children, the proportion receiving money was relatively high (67 percent).

Older adults who lived with their spouse only or with their children received more monetary support than those who lived alone or with other kin. The percentage of elderly who received financial assistance increased with age and number of children. However, age differentials were minimal and gender differentials nonexistent. Unexpectedly, older people with just a primary education were more likely to receive monetary support than those who were unschooled or those who had obtained at least a high school diploma. Rural elders were more likely to receive money from their children than urban elders. Not surprisingly, older parents who worked or who rated their health as excellent or very good were less likely to receive support in the form of money than those who were not working or who rated their health as poor. In general, the fraction of older people who received material support—food, clothing, and the like—surpassed that of elders who received money. Women, married and widowed elderly, rural residents, and those not working were more likely to receive such support. Self-rated health status and living arrangements were shown to have minimal effect on receipt of material support.

As Table 2 illustrates, the high proportion of elderly living apart from children who received support from non-coresident children suggests that the intergenerational bond is not delineated by the boundaries of "home." In fact, the magnitude of such support is indicative of the degree to which children who have left home fulfill obligations to provide for elderly parents. An analysis of support exchanges between elderly parents and non-coresident children by Natividad and Cruz (1997) showed that a high proportion of elderly parents received monetary support from at least one non-coresident child in the year prior to the PES survey. Similarly, the proportion of older adults who received material support was higher (64 percent) among those ages 60 and older than among those in their 50s (59 percent).

In a more recent multivariate analysis of the probability of whether Filipino elders will receive monetary support from non-coresident adult children, using predictor variables combining parents' and children's characteristics, the findings revealed that only three of the older adults' characteristics were statistically significant: work status, educational attainment, and self-assessed health status (Perez, Arguillas, and Williams, 1999). As expected, children were more likely to support parents who were not working (65 percent) compared to 53 percent among children whose parents were working. Moreover, working children (63 percent)

Table 2. Respondents Ages 60 and Older Receiving Money and Material Goods, 1996

Characteristics	Receiving money (%)	Receiving material goods (%)
Age		
60–69	87.3	89.7
70 and older	89.3	91.8
Sex		
Male	88.0	87.0
Female	88.3	93.2
Living arrangements		
Alone	84.2	90.7
Spouse only	87.8	87.0
With children	89.0	91.7
Other	84.8	87.8
Marital status		
Married	87.5	89.3
Widowed	90.7	93.4
Other	74.9	82.3
Number of adult children		
None	58.7	68.3
1	80.0	83.6
2–4	88.8	92.7
5 or more	90.7	92.4
Education		
No formal education	86.0	89.9
Any primary	90.5	91.7
Secondary and above	81.3	87.3
Urban/rural		
Rural	90.4	91.2
Urban	85.3	89.8
Self-rated health		
High	88.4	92.3
Moderate	87.5	89.7
Low	91.1	93.0
Work status		
Working	86.0	85.9
Not working	89.6	93.8

Source: Hermalin, 2002.

were more disposed to assist their elderly parents than those children who were not working (56 percent). Interestingly, the lower the educational achievement of the parents, the less likely they were to receive monetary support. A plausible explanation may be that parents with little education probably have less-educated children who may not be in a position to provide monetary support. In addition, children tended to support healthier parents. It may be that children are more likely to support healthier elderly who can engage in entrepreneurial activities that yield earnings or who can otherwise reciprocate. Another explanation is that monetary support is motivated by the anticipation of a future inheritance.

With regard to children's characteristics, Perez et al. (1999) demonstrated that daughters were more inclined to provide monetary support to their elderly parents than were sons. The higher the level of the children's education, the greater was their ability to provide financial support. Working children, those staying in the same village as their parents, and those with more frequent face-to-face contact with their parents demonstrated greater likelihood of providing monetary support to parents.

The other continuous variables assessed in the study, such as the children's age, the number of adult children's offspring, and the number of the adult children's siblings, manifested statistically significant effects on the probability of monetary assistance. As age increases, the probability of children providing monetary support increases slightly. As expected, the larger the family size of the adult children, the less they are able to provide financial assistance to their elderly parents; "sandwich couples" often find themselves caught in a situation where they have to provide for both children's and parents' needs. Adult children with many siblings were shown to provide less support to their aging parents, suggesting that in families with a large number of siblings, each child waits for the others to pitch in, resulting in substantially diminished levels of support.

Clearly, Filipino adults remain constant caregivers for their aging parents. The 1996 PES data indicated that 44 percent of elderly survey participants received care of one kind or another from their children. In 1984, this proportion was 35.1 percent. The constancy of intergenerational support is deeply entrenched in Filipino family values and is not expected to fade easily. This situation will only change if the elderly begin to view themselves as a burden to others and prefer to live alone in old-age institutions or if children increasingly detach themselves from their parents.

As evident in Table 1, Filipino elderly derive their income from multiple sources. Among such sources, children and relatives residing in the Philippines (30 percent), earnings from work (27 percent), and farm income (22 percent) were considered most important. A greater fraction of older men considered their earnings from work, farm income, and income from children and other relatives as their most important sources of income. More women depended primarily on monetary transfers from children and other relatives. A relatively low proportion of the elderly relied on pensions, reflecting the limited impact of the country's pension and retirement benefits.

The PES demonstrated that 64 percent of elders with at least one living child derived income from their children and 37 percent claimed their children to be their main source of income. Children were also primary sources of nonmonetary support (Table 3). There appeared to be a positive (though not monotonic) relationship between the number of living children and the elderly parents' likelihood of deriving income from children. However, the proportion of elderly with more than two living children who cited their children as their most important source of income (37 percent) did not vary significantly as the number of children increased.

Generally, the PES projects a very active exchange of support between older parents and their children in both monetary and nonmonetary terms. Intra-household rather than inter-household exchanges seemed most pronounced, as evidenced by the findings that showed that older adults, regardless of sex, were more likely to receive support from their coresident children than from their non-coresident children (Table 1). Moreover, a higher proportion of children, whether coresident or not, were more inclined to provide food, clothing, and other forms of material support than they were money.

Table 3. Elders Receiving Money and Material Support from Children, 1996

Number of living children	Percent considering their children as most important income source	Percent receiving material support from children
1	27.5	71.2
2	36.9	87.1
3	32.2	93.4
4	29.9	88.3
5	39.2	79.5
6	35.5	91.0
7	39.0	90.1
8	40.0	86.1
9+	37.1	89.1
Total	36.6	87.3

Source: Hermalin, 2002.

Flow of Support from Parents to Children

What is clearly borne out by these data is that the flow of support between younger and older generations is not unidirectional. The prominence of the children-to-parent flow is supported by PES data showing that 44 percent of both monetary and material support constitute this type of exchange and a mere 7 percent of support flows from parents to children. It is remarkable that 44 percent of the elderly reported both receiving and providing support. Almost one third (29 percent) of Filipino elders gave money to one or more non-coresident children and nearly two fifths (39 percent) provided material support. Among older providers of support, men, those who were currently married, and urban-dwellers were most likely to give monetary support. The same was true for material support, except that rural elders were in a better position than their urban counterparts to provide food, clothing, and other personal gifts to their children.

Although the more predominant flow of support is from children to elderly parents, the reciprocal flow of support continues to this day. Two fifths of Filipinos ages 50–59 provided food, clothing, and other personal gifts to their children as compared to one fourth of those ages 60 and older. This difference suggests that older adults' ability to provide material support varies inversely with age. Such a pattern is further reinforced by the commonly held expectation in Filipino society that children should, in appreciation and gratitude, provide more support to parents as the elderly age, particularly in their retirement years.

One popular form of support that elderly parents provide to their children is the care of grandchildren. PES data disclosed that three tenths of Filipino elders took care of three or more grandchildren. On average, they spent 44 hours weekly providing such care. The traditional grandparenting role of Filipino elderly has become a support mechanism in modern times, when mothers are often compelled to work in both domestic and international labor markets. Thus the unpaid care of grandchildren that grandparents provide indirectly augments family income and may contribute to family solidarity in the face of many social changes that can weaken family ties.

The amount of financial contributions that Filipino elderly make to their household expenditures is associated with age and income source. Couples ages 60 and older contributed significantly less than couples in their 50s. Older adults with very stable incomes, such as from annuities and family businesses, reported the highest levels of financial contribution (median contributions of PHP 3,817 and PHP 3,000, respectively),[1] whereas elderly who were financially dependent on their children reported the lowest levels of contribution (median contribution of PHP 378). The ability of this financially vulnerable group to contribute despite their apparently low incomes suggests that for older Filipinos, the notion of well-being is not limited to their own individual welfare but encompasses that of

[1] The peso-dollar exchange rate in 1996 was PHP 26.22 per US$.

the entire family or household. This concept seems to explain the active intergenerational flow of resources observed in households with older members. Such a network of support likewise reflects the older person's role as a conduit for the redistribution of family income in order to maximize overall family welfare. In a sense, the older adult serves as an economic buffer for the entire family (Cruz, 1998).

Whereas the majority of older Filipinos contributed financially to their household on a monthly basis, a significant proportion (23 percent) did not contribute any amount to household funds. This group includes those who did not respond or whose reply was "don't know." Although older adults' contribution to household expenditures in absolute terms may be considered low, it is rather substantial in relative terms. On the average, adults over the age of 60 covered more than half (54 percent) of the monthly operating expenses of their households while those in their 50s covered three quarters, as reported by Cruz (1998). Even with low incomes, the elderly are still helping to sustain their household.

COMMUNITY SUPPORT PROGRAMS FOR OLDER ADULTS

One of the positive developments promoting community support provisions for the elderly is the emergence of a "gray lobby" and the organization of the elderly into vocal proponents of supportive services. The Department of Social Welfare and Development (DSWD) has developed the Federation of Senior Citizens Association of the Philippines, a community-based organization composed of older adults. This organization has been set up not only at the *barangay* (village) level but is also found all the way up to the national level. It has been mobilized to participate in the delivery of community-based services for older people through voluntary service providers.

One of the more commendable efforts of another group, the Coalition of Services for the Elderly, a nongovernmental organization (NGO), is the establishment of group homes for older adults. The group homes were established with financial assistance from HelpAge International, under the auspices of the Medical Mission Sisters together with the DSWD. Although each home only serves 10 or fewer older women, the homes are a wonderful demonstration of an integrated approach to meeting the needs of disenfranchised and abandoned older women. The residents are actively engaged in generating revenue to maintain their new home through whatever enterprise is appropriate for their skills and level of functioning. A parallel group home has recently been created to shelter older men and street children together in an interdependent community. These latter are involved in vegetable farming as a way to help underwrite expenses and for personal income of the residents.

The *Bahay Pag-Ibig* (House of Love) is another community of caregivers, older adults, and street children established by the Roman Catholic Archdiocese of San Fernando, Province of Pampanga. The staff, volunteers, and the priest-director work together to restore and protect the dignity of the 59 older adults (mostly women) and street children under their care. Since 1988 the community has been housed in six buildings, two of which have been recently renovated with the help of the Rotary Club organization and private benefactors. Another home in a nearby village has been constructed to house the street children, some of whom are autistic or disabled, under the care of the religious sisters.

PHILIPPINE PUBLIC POLICY REGARDING OLDER ADULTS

Article 15, Section 4, of the 1986 Philippine Constitution states, "It is the duty of the family to take care of its elderly members while the State may design programs of social security for them." Furthermore, Article 8, Section 11, states, "The State shall adopt an integrated and comprehensive approach to health development which shall endeavor to make essential goods, health, and other social services available to all people at affordable cost. There shall be priority for the needs of the underprivileged, sick, older persons, disabled, women, and children." To that end, several national laws and initiatives have been passed or are underway.

Laws Supporting the Welfare of Older Adults

To date, several landmark bills have passed in the Philippine Congress and signed into law.

Republic Act no. 7432 was enacted in 1992 "to maximize contributions of senior citizens to nation building," "to grant benefits and special privileges [to senior citizens]," and to "mobilize their families and the community to care for the senior citizens." Under this act, older adults receive a 20 percent discount in the use of transportation services; in hotels, lodging establishments, restaurants, and recreation centers; and in the purchase of medicines. Elderly Filipinos are also exempt from payment of individual income tax if their income does not exceed the poverty threshold. They are also exempt from paying training fees for socioeconomic programs. The elderly may gain access to medical and dental services at no cost as well as other benefits, including housing assistance, provided by either of the two national social security programs.

Republic Act no. 7876 was passed in 1995 to establish a "senior citizens center" in all cities and municipalities in the country. These centers will be used as venues for the delivery of integrated and comprehensive social services to all older adults.

Signed into law July 1997, Republic Act no. 8425 "institutionaliz[es] the social Reform and Poverty Alleviation Program, creating for the purpose the National Anti-Poverty Commission."

Republic Act no. 344, known as the "Accessibility Law," was approved in December 1982. This act provides the minimum requirements and standards to render buildings, facilities, and utilities for public use accessible and safe to people with disabilities, including older adults who are confined to wheelchairs and those who have difficulty in walking or climbing stairs.

The National Health Insurance Act was passed in 1995 to provide health insurance coverage to the entire Philippine population through the turnover of the Medicare Program to the Philippine Health Insurance Corporation. The National Health Insurance Program seeks to provide people with a viable means of helping them pay for adequate healthcare through a Health Insurance Fund that covers a certain proportion of the costs of a member's hospital care. Careful scrutiny of the exclusions in the benefit package indicates a bias against the elderly in regard to access to homecare, rehabilitation services, and optometry services, for which this population has the greatest need.

Current Initiatives

In time for the celebration of the United Nations' International Year for Older Persons in 1999, the DSWD collaborated with other government agencies, NGOs, grassroots organizations serving the elderly, businesses, and older individuals to draft the Philippine Plan of Action for Older Persons. The plan addresses the need to institute appropriate policies, strategies, mechanisms, and programs to ensure that the rights of older adults are upheld, their needs and concerns addressed, and their roles as active participants in nation building fully recognized.

The plan addresses the areas of concern specified in the Macau Plan of Action on Aging, adopted in October 1998 by delegates and observers representing government agencies, NGOs, and other organizations. The seven major areas of concern are the following: the social position of older adults; older adults and the family; health and nutrition; housing, transportation, and the built environment; income security, income maintenance, and employment; consumer concerns; and social services and the community.

In addition, the national government has created a number of programs to improve the living conditions of older Filipinos. These include substitute family care; assistance for the physical restoration of older adults; self-enhancement; livelihood development services; integrated daycare for older persons and children; volunteer services among elders; income security, income maintenance, and employment initiatives; healthcare; and nutrition programs.

CURRENT POLICY AND POLICY RECOMMENDATIONS FOR THE FUTURE

Past mortality and fertility patterns have fashioned an unalterable future marked by the increasing population of older people in the Philippines. Apart from the numeric change, the future generation of Filipino elders will represent a different qualitative profile from previous generations. The 1996 PES discredits the stereotypic notion that the majority of the older adults are idle, weak, and unproductive. As a result of past policies geared toward expanding educational opportunities for all Filipinos, the next cohort of elders will be better educated and thus expected to be more active in the labor force. Improvements in economic conditions and lengthening longevity ensure that future elderly will be healthier and are expected to outlive their predecessors.

The preponderance of women in the older adult population, together with the apparent disadvantage of females in the education and employment arenas, will place many older women in an onerous position. As many older women are widowed and are not in the productive labor force, they lack financial resources to maintain their independence. Service providers and policymakers in the Philippines would do well to keep older women's particular concerns in mind when developing care for the aged else they do more harm than good.

The good news is that Filipino elderly are closely connected to their families, either living with them or receiving monetary and nonmonetary support from them. The data underscoring the absence of marked differentials in support observed among the elderly with varying family sizes indicate that such familial support is expected to continue in the near term even as fertility levels decline.

Filipino culture has a convention of strong family bonds that anchor the custom of caring for elderly parents when need arises. Interestingly, mothers are more likely than fathers to receive support from adult children, however. In a society in which filial piety is an unwritten family principle, reciprocity of intergenerational obligations and support find firm grounding nonetheless.

In fact, as has been seen throughout this volume, in most Asian societies, the family bears primary or exclusive responsibility for providing old-age security. The majority of older adults live in extended, multigenerational families and until recently preferred it that way. They have been comfortable relying on their adult children, the children's spouses, and other family members for both material needs and personal care, and the call for assistance has seldom been challenged in any systematic way. Even when adult children live independently of their parents, contact is more frequent and resource flows more substantial than in developed countries of the West. These characteristics are certainly spot on for Filipino society. All things considered, the family-based approach continues to be remarkably successful in providing for Filipino elders' needs. Despite its success, however, the long-established family support system is under extreme pressure from demographic, social, and economic changes. These pressures are likely to intensify in the coming years. As life expectancy continues to lengthen, most adults will have surviving elderly parents. Declines in fertility signify that sons and daughters will have fewer siblings with whom to share the responsibilities of parental care.

Furthermore, economic forces are intensifying the impact of these socio-demographic shifts. The young are relocating in search of jobs, leading to greater physical distance from their parents. Women are joining the labor force, diminishing the time they are able to spend on family care. Exposure to the West is likely introducing groundbreaking ideas about marriage, family, and individualism. The salience of these issues cannot be overestimated, nor can the need for a coordinated and centralized governmental response. One of the more pressing questions insofar as elder care in the Philippines is concerned is whether in the face of increasing and permanent urbanization, will norms of family care for elders remain intact? Should Filipino society begin making alternative arrangements for elder care? Can the government provide sufficient resources for non-family-based elder care options? Will competing demands eclipse the needs of the elderly?

A review of the basic socioeconomic characteristics of older adults and intergenerational support in the Philippines suggests several directions for future policy regarding elders.

Older Women

Women make up a disproportionately large segment of the older adult population in the Philippines. Women tend to outlive men, but their advantage in life expectancy is often offset by the prospect of potential age-related disability. Hence, older women are vulnerable to situations that require greater assistance from the government and from community organizations. Older women's health demands attention, especially in a society where the primary caregiver within the family is the wife, mother, or daughter.

Eye and Ear Care

A common physical impairment among older adults in the Philippines is the weakening of eyesight and hearing. These sensory deficits can prevent older adults from participating in activities that demand interaction with other people as well as from engaging in activities that promote active aging. Community-based eye and ear care that does not require older individuals to go to health centers or clinics can help them maintain levels of eyesight and hearing necessary for daily interaction with other people.

Isolation Among the Elderly

Care of the elderly should integrate training for them on how to deal with feelings of isolation and loneliness. Perhaps these feelings can be partially assuaged by social activities such as bingo socials after Sunday religious services and weekly gatherings for ballroom dancing.

Images of Aging

Popular images of old age and of the roles and capabilities of older adults require reshaping. The mass media have an important role to play in conveying the concerns of elders and not merely focusing on the crimes and illegal acts committed by older adults. Newspapers, magazines, and radio and television programs can interview active older adults to highlight their contributions to their families, their community, and to society at large.

Retirement Housing

Given the propensity of Filipino elders for returning to their birthplaces following retirement, it might be a good idea to have retirement villages in such areas with housing structures that are carefully designed to meet the needs of the elderly, for example, one-floor structures with a thoughtfully laid-out plan ensuring easy entry and exit into rooms, manageable floor areas, nonslippery flooring, and specially designed bathroom fixtures.

Tax Burden

For older adults who rejoin their children, tax exemption claims for children supporting aging parents appear reasonable, particularly to cushion the financial impact of elder care among "sandwich couples." Such tax incentives could be used for renovating sections of the children's homes to ensure they are elder-friendly or simply to encourage retention of family bonds.

As mentioned throughout this volume, the forces of social change associated with modernization and urbanization may erode the traditional family support system, which is based on values of altruism and intergenerational exchange. Advocacy efforts by the media may come in the form of two-minute television spots promoting such Filipino family values as filial piety. Moreover, separate modules on Filipino family values may be integrated into courses on social history or Philippine society at the primary, secondary, and tertiary educational levels.

Likewise, it is recommended that the Philippine government develop sustainable social protection programs for elders. Such programs can be seen as a safety valve in the event that intergenerational relations become substantially weakened. A review of present pension schemes is needed immediately.

The Philippine government and Filipino society together must enable older adults to maintain their economic independence as much as possible. The government may need to proscribe employment policies that prompt early retirement from the labor force, reduce employment opportunities for the elderly, and lower job mobility for older workers. The government can also establish a regulatory base to stimulate the development of financial instruments that will allow workers to save for their own retirement. Discriminatory practices that undermine independence of older women can be eliminated, including those governing education, employment, property ownership, and inheritance. Finally, the government must design programs that rely on public-private partnerships, ensuring an efficient and equitable support system for Filipino elderly.

REFERENCES

Asis, M. M., Domingo, L. J., Knodel, J., and Mehta, K. (1995). Living arrangements in four Asian countries: A comparative perspective. *Journal of Cross-Cultural Gerontology, 10,* 145–162.

Cabigon, J. V., and Flieger, W. (1999). *1995 gender-specific life tables for the Philippines, its regions, and provinces.* Manila: National Statistics Office.

Casterline, J. B., Hermalin, A. I., Cheung, P., Domingo, L. J., Knodel, J., and Ofstedal, M. B. (1991). *Differences in the living arrangements of the elderly in four Asian countries: The interplay of constraints and preferences* (Comparative Study of the Elderly in Asia Research Report No. 91-10). Ann Arbor: University of Michigan, Population Studies Center.

Concepcion, M. B. (1988). Emerging issues of aging in the Asian region. In *Economic and social implications of population ageing* (United Nations Publication ST/ESA/Ser.R/85, pp. 399–417). New York: United Nations.

Crimmins, E. M., Hayward, M. D., and Saito, Y. (1996). Differentials in active life expectancy in the older population of the United States. *Journal of Gerontology: Social Sciences, 51B*(3), S111–S120.

Cruz, G. T. (1998, April). *Economic well-being of the Filipino elderly.* Poster presentation at the Population Association of America Annual Meeting, Chicago.

De Guzman, E. A. (1999). *Living arrangements of the Filipino elderly.* Quezon City, Philippines: University of the Philippines Population Institute/Demographic Research and Development Foundation.

Dixon-Mueller, R. (2001). Gender inequalities and reproductive health: Changing priorities in an era of transformation and globalisation (Policy and Research Paper No. 16). In *International Union for the Scientific Study of Population (IUSSP) Contributions to Gender Research.* Liège, Belgium: IUSSP.

Domingo, L. J. (1995, July). *The family and welfare of the Filipino elderly* (Professorial Chair Paper Series No. 95-10). Unpublished paper presented for the Metro Manila Commission Professorial Chair, Manila, Philippines.

Gist, Y. J., and Velkoff, V. A. (1997). *Gender and aging: Demographic dimensions* (International Brief No. 1B/97-3). Washington, DC: U.S. Bureau of the Census.

Hermalin, A. I. (Ed.). (2002). *The well-being of the elderly in Asia: A four-country comparative study.* Ann Arbor: University of Michigan Press. (See chap. 1, p. 20, for a description of the comparative project and the specific surveys, including PES.)

Kinsella, K., and Gist, Y. J. (1995). *Older workers, retirement, and pensions: A comparative chartbook* (Census Publication No. IPC 95-2). Washington, DC: U.S. Bureau of the Census.

Kinsella, K., and Gist, Y. J. (1998). *Gender and aging: Mortality and health* (International Brief No. IB/98-2). Washington, DC: U.S. Bureau of the Census.

Kinsella, K., and Taeuber, C. M. (1993). *An aging world II* (International Population Report No. P/95/92-3). Washington, DC: U.S. Bureau of the Census.

Mason, A., Lee, S.-H., and Russo, G. (2000). *Population momentum and population aging in Asia and Near-East countries.* Unpublished report submitted to the U.S. Agency for International Development (USAID).

Natividad, J. N., and Cruz, G. T. (1997). Patterns in living arrangements and familial support for the elderly in the Philippines. *Asia-Pacific Population Journal, 12*(4), 17–34.

Ogena, N. B., and Williams, L. (1999). *Migration of the elderly in the Philippines.* Unpublished manuscript, University of the Philippines Population Institute, Quezon City.

Perez, A. E. (1999a). *Intergenerational support for the elderly.* Quezon City, Philippines: University of the Philippines Population Institute/Demographic Research and Development Foundation.

Perez, A. E. (1999b, July). *Who are the Filipino elderly: A socio-economic and demographic profile of the elderly and their successors.* Paper presented at the National Academy of Science and Technology Forum, Bicutan, Taguig, Metro Manila, Philippines.

Perez, A. E., Arguillas, F. O., and Williams, L. (1999, April). *An analysis of monetary transfers between the elderly and non-coresident children in the Philippines.* Poster presentation at the Population Association of America Annual Meeting, New York City.

Philippine National Statistics Office. (1999). *1995 census-based national, regional, and provincial population projections.* Manila: National Statistics Office.

Philippine National Statistics Office and Macro International. (1998). *National demographic and health survey 1998 preliminary report.* Manila: National Statistics Office.

United Nations [U.N.]. (1993). *Demographic yearbook 1993. Special issue on population ageing and the situation of elderly persons, table 4* (United Nations Publication Sales No. E/F/92.XIII.9). New York: Author.

U.N. (2001). *World population prospects: The 2000 revision, vol. 1, comparative tables* (United Nations Publication Sales No. E.01.XIII.8). New York: Author.

Xenos, P., and Raymundo, C. M. (Eds.). (1999). *Adolescent sexuality in the Philippines.* Quezon City, Philippines: University of the Philippines Office of the Vice-Chancellor for Research and Development.

CHAPTER TWELVE

Welfare Policy for Older Adults and Caregiving Burden in South Korea

Ka-Oak Rhee

South Korea is far from exempt from the worldwide phenomenon of population aging. The country has experienced rapid aging in a short time: It is expected to take 22 years for the proportion of South Koreans ages 65 and older in the total population to double, from 7 percent to 14 percent. In addition, because the health of older adults deteriorates with aging, dramatic increases in life expectancy have led to an increase in the number of older Koreans needing long-term care. As the earlier chapters on South Korea make clear, as one of Asia's *so called* economic tigers, South Korea is faced with a number of conflicting priorities.

In South Korea, family members, especially adult children who reside with aged parents, have traditionally cared for elderly relatives. However, economic and social changes mean that recent years have seen a dramatic increase in the number of elders living apart from their adult children. Subsequently, growing numbers of elders do not have family caregivers and therefore have relatively few options for support.

Although most elderly Koreans have family caregivers, a large proportion of family caregivers report that they feel deleterious emotional consequences of caregiving, such as burnout. In particular, when caregivers feel that their caregiving tasks are stressful, the quality of the care they provide deteriorates, and as a result, the health of the impaired elderly in their care declines. In the worst cases, caregivers may neglect or abuse their elderly care recipients (Rhee, Cha, Choi, Yoon, Suh, and Park, 1999).

Despite the increase in the number of elders who do not have a caregiver and the large number of family caregivers who experience a severe emotional burden, long-term care services are not readily available for most impaired elderly and their families due to the underdevelopment of welfare policy for older adults in South Korea. There is an urgent need to develop social policy for long-term care, as a family-based approach is no longer viable in either practical or affective terms.

DEMOGRAPHIC CHARACTERISTICS OF ELDERLY KOREANS

It is clear that the number of South Koreans ages 65 and older has grown rapidly (Table 1), from 991,000 in 1970 to 3.37 million in 2000. By 2020, it is expected that this population will grow to 6.9 million, nearly doubling. Decreased birthrates and death rates have resulted in a spike in the proportion of elderly Koreans in the total population. In 1970, Koreans ages 65 and older represented 3.1 percent of the total population. This figure rose to 7.1 percent in 30 years and is expected to reach 13.2 percent in 2020 (Table 1).

This aging phenomenon has caused the old-age dependency ratio to skyrocket. Approximately 5.7 persons ages 65 and older were dependent on 100 persons ages 15–64 in 1970, but by 2000, 10.0 older adults relied on the same number of young persons. Moreover, every 100 young persons will be supporting nearly 20 older adults in 2020.

Table 1. Older Adults in the General Population, South Korea

	1970	1980	1990	2000	2010	2020
Total population (in thousands)	32,241	38,124	42,869	47,275	50,618	52,358
Adults ages 65+ (in thousands)	991	1,456	2,195	3,371	5,032	6,899
The proportion of those ages 65+	3.1	3.8	5.1	7.1	9.9	13.2
The proportion of those ages 75+	0.9	1.1	1.5	2.3	3.5	5.0
Aged dependency ratio	5.7	6.1	7.4	10.0	14.2	18.9
Aging index	7.2	11.2	20.0	32.9	49.9	76.5

Sources: South Korea National Statistical Office, 1997; South Korea National Statistical Office, 1999.

The average age of the population and life expectancy at birth have lengthened as well (Table 2). In 2000, the average age in South Korea was 32.9 and the average life expectancy was 74.9; these figures represent increases of 10 or more years since 1970 and can be attributed to improvements in health and economic conditions. Life expectancy in Korea will be close to 80 in 2020, certainly comparable to industrialized countries around the world.

As is true elsewhere, female elders also outnumber male elders (Table 3). In 2000, the ratio of male to female elderly was nearly 6:10, and will continue to be unbalanced, considering that women live an average of seven years longer than men. There is also a remarkable difference in martial status between male and female elders. In 1990, just 26.0 percent of female elders were currently married, but more than 80 percent of male elders were married. This difference results

Table 2. Average Age and Life Expectancy at Birth (in Years)

	1970	1980	1990	2000	2010	2020
Average age	23.6	26.0	29.5	32.9	36.3	39.5
Male	22.9	25.1	28.5	31.7	35.1	38.5
Female	24.3	26.9	30.6	34.1	37.4	40.6
Life expectancy at birth	63.2	65.8	71.6	74.9	77.0	78.1
Male	59.8	62.7	67.7	71.0	73.3	74.5
Female	66.7	69.1	75.7	78.6	80.7	81.7

Sources: South Korea National Statistical Office, 1997.

Table 3. Sex and Marriage Status of Elderly Koreans

	1970	1980	1990	2000	2010	2020
Sex ratio	102.4	101.8	101.3	101.7	101.8	101.6
Koreans ages 65+	62.1	59.5	60.0	62.4	72.3	78.5
Koreans ages 75+	55.8	51.0	52.6	53.9	63.9	71.2
Percentage of elderly (ages 65+) who are	41.6	45.0	47.2	—	—	—
Male	73.5	79.9	82.6	—	—	—
Female	21.7	24.3	26.0	—	—	—

Note: Sex ratio = (the number of men/the number of women) × 100.
Sources: South Korea National Statistical Office, 1990, 1997, 1999.

from several factors, such as the gap between the life expectancy of men and women, the comparatively low remarriage rate of female elders, and a gap between the age of first marriage for older men and women (women's spouses are usually older than they are).

SOCIAL CHANGES

As noted above, the family has traditionally supported the elderly in economic, physical, and emotional respects, and has long played the most important role in satisfying elders' caregiving needs. However, changes in family structure resulting from industrialization and urbanization have altered these roles (Table 4).[1] Of those households that include an elderly member, the proportion of elderly living alone has increased dramatically (from 16.2 percent in 1994 to 20.1 percent in 1998), whereas the proportion of elders who live with their children has decreased slightly (from 55.9 percent in 1994 to 53.2 percent in 1998). Such a slight reduction of the proportion of elders who live with their children may contribute to an increase in the number of older adults who want to be—but are not—cared for by their children.

The increase in the proportion of women in the labor force also deserves attention (Table 5). In 1960, 28 percent of females participated in the labor force, but nearly 50 percent did in 1998. Since women have had the traditional role of caring for the elderly, this phenomenon may result in a reduction of the pool

Table 4. Living Arrangements of Adults Ages 65 and Older

	1994 (%)	1998 (%)
Living alone	16.2	20.1
Living with spouse	22.8	21.6
Living with children	55.9	53.2
Other	5.1	5.1
Total (number of households)	100.0 (1.12 million)	100.0 (1.96 million)

Source: Rhee, Suh, Ko, and Park, 1994; Chung, Cho, Oh, Byun, Byun, and Moon, 1998.

[1] These changes in family structure can be summarized as an increase in the proportion of nuclear-family households and single-person households, a decrease in the proportion of patrilineal family households and three-generation family households, and a reduction in the number of family members (Rhee, Kwon, Kwon, and Lee, 1990.

Table 5. Labor-Force Participation Rates in South Korea[a]

	1960	1970	1980[b]	1990	1998
Adults ages 15 and older	50.1	56.1	56.5	60.0	60.7
Male	72.9	73.0	71.3	74.0	75.2
Female	28.0	39.7	42.8	47.0	47.0

[a]Labor-force participation rate: (adults ages 15 and older participating in the labor force) / (adults ages 15 and older in total population) × 100.

[b]The 1980 labor-force participation rate was computed on the basis of adults ages 14 and older.

Sources: Economic Planning Bureau, 1960; Ministry of Finance and Economy, 1970, 1980, 1990, 1998.

of female family members available to take care of the elderly. In combination, these trends suggest that more older women will become dependent on formalized caregiving services and fewer will be able to shoulder responsibilities for providing care.

WELFARE BUDGETS FOR THE ELDERLY

Needless to say, it requires substantial financial support from the government to carry out formalized welfare policies. However, in 1999 South Korea's social security budget represented just over 1 percent of its gross domestic product (GDP) and only 7.3 percent of the national budget, even though those proportions have increased slightly since the mid-1990s (Table 6). The 1990s saw a slight increase in the proportion of the national budget allocated to support for the elderly (Table 6).[2] Although the amount spent on welfare for the elderly increased from 6.9 billion won in 1989 to 191.7 billion won in 1999, such expenditures still represented less than 1 percent of the national budget in 1999. Despite pressing needs and growing demand, competitive priorities for centralized revenue support imply that the difficulties will be exacerbated in the years immediately ahead. Although the composition of welfare budgets for the elderly has changed (Table 7), the portion of this budget allocated for community-care services, including home help services, daycare services, and respite care services, remained at about 1–2 percent in the late 1990s. The restricted budget available

[2]Many factors prohibited the proportion of welfare budgets from increasing. One main factor was the national defense budget. Since the Korean War (1950–53), the South Korean government has allocated a large portion of its budget to national defense, for example, 17.1 percent in 1999 (Ministry of Health and Welfare, 2000c).

Table 6. Welfare Budgets for the Elderly

	1989	1991	1993	1995	1997	1999	2000[a]
National budget / GDP (%)	13.8	15.4	14.1	14.2	16.1	18.0	—
Social security / GDP (%)	0.5	0.8	0.9	0.9	1.0	1.3	—
Social security / national budget (%)	5.2	7.0	6.4	5.9	6.2	7.3	9.1
Welfare budget for the elderly / national budget (%)	0.03	0.13	0.22	0.12	0.19	0.24	0.31
Welfare budget for the elderly / social welfare services budget (%)	10.5	28.2	37.7	22.9	26.7	35.9	37.7
Welfare budget for the elderly (hundred million won)	69	827	827	612	1,300	1,917	2,771

[a]The 2000 South Korean GDP was not calculated at the time of publication.

Sources: Ministry of Health and Welfare, 1989a, 1991a, 1993a, 1995a, 1997a, 1999a, 2000a; Ministry of Finance and Economy, 1989, 1991, 1993, 1995, 1997, 1999, 2000.

for community-care services prevented them from expanding in any appreciable manner despite what appears to be a pressing need.

When the Old Age Allowance, which provided cash benefits for the elderly in the low-income group, was introduced in 1991, it represented 10.9 percent of the welfare budget for the elderly. By 1997, it had increased to 62.1 percent. The next year, the Old Age Allowance was abolished, replaced by non-contribution pensions termed the Elder-Respect Pension. Elder-Respect Pension benefits represented 72.1 percent of the welfare budget for the elderly in 2000.

An interesting form of governmental assistance in South Korea was inaugurated in 1990 in the form of support for traffic expenses, which was justified as a means of elevating honor and respect for older adults. The idea was to ensure a kind of independence by enabling older Koreans to commute on their own. The program provides all community-dwelling elders with a monthly sum equal to 12 bus trips. Interestingly, this program represented more than 50 percent of the national welfare budget for the elderly in the early 1990s, but responsibility for funding the program was transferred from the central government to the local governments in 1994.

Table 7. Composition of National Welfare Budgets for the Elderly

	1988	1989	1990	1991	1992	1993	1994
Total budget (in million won)	4,544	6,955	37,861	39,272	57,715	82,654	46,203
Allocation (%)							
Support for traffic expenses[a]	—	—	75.9	63.6	50.9	52.7	—
Old Age Allowance[b]	—	—	—	10.9	27.8	27.6	49.4
Elder-Respect Pension	—	—	—	—	—	—	—
Community-care services	0.2	0.5	0.1	0.2	—	—	0.1
Residential care facilities	73.8	60.1	13.2	13.5	10.7	11.8	36.1
Other	26.0	39.4	10.8	11.8	10.6	7.9	14.4
	1995	**1996**	**1997**	**1998**	**1999**	**2000**	
Total budget (in million won)	61,223	84,665	129,972	169,081	191,714	277,050	
Allocation (%)							
Support for traffic expenses[a]	—	—	—	—	—	—	
Old Age Allowance[b]	55.5	55.5	62.1	22.3	—	—	
Elder-Respect Pension	—	—	—	43.9	78.3	72.1	
Community-care services	0.2	2.2	2.4	2.2	1.7	1.4	
Residential care facilities	32.3	31.3	25.2	21.8	13.0	18.9	
Other	12.0	11.0	10.3	9.8	7.0	7.6	

[a]Support for Traffic Expenses has been provided by the local governments since 1994.
[b]The Old Age Allowance was abolished in July 1998 when the Elder-Respect Pension was introduced.

Sources: Ministry of Health and Welfare, 1988, 1989b, 1990, 1991b, 1992b, 1993b, 1994, 1995b, 1996, 1997b, 1998, 1999b, 2000b.

WELFARE PROGRAMS FOR THE ELDERLY

Welfare programs for the elderly in South Korea include income security programs, healthcare programs, residential care services, and community-care services.[3] In light of the economic turmoil in the South Korean economy, it is unlikely that dramatic revisions to existing programs will be implemented in the next few years. In all likelihood, only as the economy rebounds will further relief be provided.

Income Security Programs

Income security programs for older Koreans are comprised of social security programs and the Aged Honor Program (Table 8). Social security programs

[3] There are also leisure programs for the elderly, but this chapter will not discuss them.

Table 8. Income Security Programs for Older Koreans, 2000

Social Security Programs	Public assistance	Proportion of elderly who receive public assistance: 7.8% (1999) Maximum amount of cash benefits: 261,000 won per person per month
	Public pensions	Proportion of Korean elders who receive benefits from the Government Employees Pension, Military Service Pension, and Private School Teachers Pension: 4.3% The National Pension was introduced in 1988, and will start distributing old-age pensions to Koreans in 2008. Only 5.2% of the elderly currently receive National Pension benefits (including disability pensions).
	Elderly Pensions	Proportion of elderly who receive Elder-Respect Pensions: 20.6% Amount of cash benefits: 30,000–50,000 won
Aged Honor Program		Support for Traffic Expenses: Every Korean ages 65+ receives cash benefits adequate to 12 bus rides Subways, palaces, national museums, and national parks are free to the elderly Railways give discounts to the elderly

Sources: Ministry of Health and Welfare, 2000b.

include public assistance, public pensions, and the Elder-Respect Pension. Approximately 7.8 percent of Koreans ages 65 and older received public assistance in 1999.[4] Public assistance programs are means-tested, and the amount of cash benefits each elder received was determined by the individual's income. Public assistance programs for elders have been criticized for their strict eligibility criteria and the low level of benefits they provide.

The national public pension system consists of four distinct pension schemes: Government Employees Pension, Military Service Pension, Private School Teachers Pension, and the National Pension (Table 8). The first three pensions are for those who have been employed in specific job sectors such as government agencies and public schools, the military, and private schools. Just 4.3 percent of all older Koreans receive one or another of these pensions. The National Pension, a national contribution pension program, was introduced in 1988 and has expanded incrementally. By April 1999 it enrolled all South Koreans ages 15–59 who were participating in the labor force. Nevertheless, many elderly do not receive any pension benefit now, as they were not eligible for the National Pension when it was first implemented based on their age at the time.[5]

To solve this problem, the Elder-Respect Pension program was introduced in July 1998. Its main goal is to provide noncontribution pensions for the elderly who are otherwise ineligible to receive public pensions but who are nonetheless categorized in the low-income group of South Koreans as defined by a specified formula. The criteria for Elder-Respect Pension recipients are as follows: Total monthly household income, divided by the number of household members, should be less than 60 percent of the average monthly per-person income of workers in urban areas in the previous year. In addition, the assets of all family members living with the elder should be less than 140 percent of the asset criterion for public-assistance recipients. All elders receiving public assistance are eligible for Elder-Respect Pension benefits as well.

The amount of cash benefits that the Elder-Respect Pension provides differs between public-assistance recipients and the low-income group. Public-assistance recipients ages 65–69 receive 40,000 won[6] per month, and those ages 80 and older receive 50,000 won per month. By comparison, elders from the low-income group receive 30,000 won per month, and if both members of a married couple receive the Elder-Respect Pension, one spouse receives 100 percent of the total amount and the other receives 75 percent. Only 20.6 percent of Koreans over the age of 65 received the Elder-Respect Pension in 2000. Moreover, the amount

[4] The proportion of elders receiving public assistance demonstrates that the economic situation of Korean elderly is usually worse than that of the general population. About 8 percent of Korean elders are receiving public assistance, whereas public-assistance recipients represent 2.6 percent of the general population.

[5] Workers ages 45 and older were excluded from National Pension when it was initiated in 1988.

[6] As of May 2004, 1,000 won = US$0.84.

of the cash benefit is extremely low compared to the minimum National Pension benefit, which is 64,500 won per month.

The Aged Honor Program includes Support for Traffic Expenses benefits and some free or discounted programs. Other programs targeting adult children supporting elderly parents include tax exemptions, a "Parent Allowance" for government employees, and tax credits for purchasing houses.

Healthcare Programs

South Korea has two national healthcare programs: Medical Assistance and Medical Insurance. Medical Assistance was created in 1979 to provide healthcare benefits to individuals receiving public assistance, and Medical Insurance was implemented in 1977. In the beginning, Medical Insurance covered individuals who were working at large private companies. It was extended to all except public-assistance recipients in 1989. Today, all South Koreans can receive medical benefits through one of the two programs and they function in a manner akin to Medicare and Medicaid in the United States. The programs have helped older Koreans gain access to medical services (Table 9).

However, as is often the case elsewhere, some medical treatments are not covered by Medical Insurance. In addition, some Medical Assistance recipients must pay 20 percent of the total fees for inpatient medical treatment. These subsidies and payments may prevent some elders from going to the hospital. More critically, the current medical system is designed to serve those suffering from

Table 9. Healthcare Programs for the Elderly, 2000

Program	Benefits
Medical assistance	Public assistance recipients: All services free of charge
	Elders in the low-income group: – Inpatient services: Patients pay 20% of charge for medical treatment – Outpatient services: Patients pay 1,500 won per visit to primary-care hospitals
Medical insurance	Inpatient services: Patients pay 20% of charge for medical treatment
	Outpatient services: If medical expense is less than 12,000 won, patients pay 2,200–4,800 won per visit (older adults pay 1,200–2,100 won for primary hospitals); if medical expense is more than 12,000 won, patients pay 30–55% of charge.

Source: Ministry of Health and Welfare, 2000b.

acute illness. Therefore, it has difficulty in satisfying the medical needs of elders with chronic illness. Furthermore, Medical Insurance does not cover the costs of long-term care. In addition to Medical Insurance and Medical Assistance, there are health examination programs for older adults, and a 10-year national plan to develop services for elders with dementia is underway.

Residential Care Services

As of 1999, 0.3 percent of older Koreans (12,751 persons) were living in 229 residential care facilities (Table 10). Residential care facilities are for elders who have no limitations in activities of daily living (ADL) but do not have families with whom they can live. Residential care facilities are not for older adults who need long-term care but who nonetheless may benefit from a sheltered living environment.

Nursing homes are divided into intermediate-care facilities and skilled-nursing facilities. Intermediate-care facilities are designed for frail and impaired elders who require nursing services. Skilled-nursing facilities are designed for elders with dementia or paralysis who need nursing services.

Elders are eligible for free-of-charge, low-cost, or full-fee residential care facilities according to their economic status. Free-of-charge facilities are for those ages 65 and older who are receiving public assistance and do not have any caregivers. A budget for free-of-charge facilities was created by the central

Table 10. Residential Care Facilities for the Elderly, 1999

		Free of charge[a]	Low-cost[a]	Full fee[a]
Residential care homes	Facility for elders who have no limitations in ADL and do not have any family members to live with.	92 (4,779)	4 (98)	22 (836)
Nursing homes	Intermediate-care facility: Nursing and personal services are provided for frail and impaired elderly.	73 (4,413)	13 (688)	4 (144)
	Skilled-nursing facility: Nursing and personal services are provided for elders with dementia and paralysis.	21 (1,793)	—	—
	Total		221 (12,751)	

[a]Unit: Number of institutions (number of residents)
Source: Ministry of Health and Welfare, 2000b.

government under the Welfare Act for the Elderly, but in reality, this budget is not enough for the facility to provide even basic services (such as heating and meals) for residents. Low-cost facilities are for elders in the low-income group. The charge for these facilities is relatively low, and each facility receives 24 million won from the government every year. Full-fee facilities are for elders ages 60 and older. These facilities receive no financial support from the government.

Most nursing homes serve either elders receiving public assistance or elders in the low-income group. As of 1999, there were 73 free-of-charge and 13 low-cost intermediate-care facilities in the country, compared to just 4 full-fee ones. As pointed out by Byun, Chung, Cho, Oh, Lee, and Lee (1999), intermediate-care facilities and skilled-nursing facilities tend to provide only personal services for residents, although many residents are in need of nursing and rehabilitation services as well.

Community-Care Services

Community-care services available in South Korea include home help services, daycare services, and respite care services. Like residential care facilities, community-care services are free of charge, low cost, or full fee based on economic status. Home help services, which started in 1987, include personal, homemaking, and befriending services. They serve older adults who receive public assistance or who belong to the low-income group and whose physical or mental problems cause limitations in their activities of daily living. Like residential care services, home help services primarily target elders receiving public assistance: 93 percent of those who use home help services are public-assistance recipients (Chung, Cho, Oh, Byun, Byun, and Moon, 1998).

People who deliver home help services are classified into two groups: paid and unpaid (voluntary).[7] Unpaid home helpers have played an important role in delivering home help services because of a nationwide shortage of paid home helpers.[8] Because delivery of these services usually depends on unpaid home helpers who are less trained than paid home helpers, home help services are generally regarded as a kind of friendly visiting. Elders accessing home help services received an average of 2.8 hours of befriending visits, 2.1 hours of homemaking services, and 1.0 hour of health-related services per month. Helpers

[7] In order to become a paid home helper, it is necessary to attend a 40-hour training course for certification; unpaid home helpers must attend a 20-hour training course. In 2000, there were about 600 paid home helpers and 34,500 unpaid home helpers in South Korea.

[8] Home help services were started in 1987 by a privacy agency, the Korea Senior Citizens' Association, which received assistance from HelpAge International in Britain to set up and oversee such services. In those days, the government provided no financial support, and thus home help services were delivered by unpaid volunteers. The government now regards it as natural that home help services are delivered by unpaid home helpers, and therefore does not give home help service centers sufficient support to hire paid home helpers.

also provide an average of only 0.1 hours of bathing services and 0.1 hours of hygienic services per person per month (Chung, Cho, Oh, Byun, Byun, and Moon, 1998).

Daycare services are for frail or disabled elders who cannot be cared for by their family during the day. When introducing daycare services, the government believed many Koreans would utilize daycare services because these services were free for public-assistance recipients and the fee was extremely low (about 50,000 won per month) for elders not receiving public assistance. Contrary to expectations, utilization rates for daycare services turned out to be amazingly low. A majority of elderly living alone or with just a spouse were so poor that they were thought to be unable to afford daycare services. As for older adults living with children and relatives, family caregivers might be unlikely to spend money on such services for the elderly, perhaps out of a perception that family members should shoulder the burden of caring for the older person. Without continuing financial support from the government to cover service fees, it would be unreasonable to expect future increases in the utilization rates of daycare services.

Respite care services are for frail or disabled elders whose families cannot care for them for short periods (up to 45 days). Respite care services became popular mainly because there is less stigma surrounding respite care services, and family and relatives may feel less guilty using them than they do about institutional care. However, the act does not allow elderly to stay at a respite care facility more than 45 days. Many elderly move into one respite care facility to another to avoid the prohibition article of the act. It implies institutional care facilities should be developed to meet needs of elderly and their families.

FACTORS ASSOCIATED WITH EMOTIONAL CAREGIVING BURDEN

Using a subsample of the caregivers identified in their earlier study of family caregivers of impaired elderly South Koreans (Rhee, Cha, Choi, Yoon, Suh, and Park, 1999), Rhee and Lee (2000) examined emotional caregiving burden among 404 family caregivers of impaired elderly. Guided by Lazarus and Folkman's Transactional Model of Stress and Coping (1984), the authors hypothesized that emotional caregiving burden is affected by three factors: stressors, resources, and other background variables. Their analysis showed that respondents' sense of emotional caregiving burden increased as the number of stressors increased. Stressors included the impaired elder's limitations in ADLs, his or her mental problems, and the presence of other household members in need of care, such as children (Kramer, 1995, 1997; Miller, McFall, and Montgomery, 1991; Thompson, Futterman, Gallagher-Thompson, Rose, and Lovett, 1993). By contrast, frequency and duration of caregiving did not have a statistically significant relation to perceived caregiving burden. Caregivers who reported such resources as good health and social support from other family members or relatives were found to have less perceived caregiving burden, presumably because they could deal with the situation better than their counterparts deprived of some social-familial resources (Kramer, 1997; Montgomery, Gonyea, and Hooyman, 1985; Thomson, Futterman, Gallagher-Thompson, Rose, and Lovett, 1993; Vaux, 1988).

Other background variables identified as associated with caregiving burden were the gender of the caregiver and the combination of family ties (between the caregivers and the impaired elderly) and coresidence (with children of the elderly). Female caregivers tend to express a greater caregiving burden than male caregivers (Miller, McFall, and Montgomery, 1991; Thompson, Futterman, Gallagher-Thompson, Rose, and Lovett, 1993). According to Rose-Rego, Strauss, and Smyth (1998), caregiving tasks have traditionally been regarded as a woman's job, so female caregivers are inclined to feel greater responsibility for them. Male caregivers are likely to provide impaired elderly family members with delimited help such as transportation assistance, while women tend to perform personal services that are repetitious, time-consuming, and do not have sharply defined parameters. The result, it seems, is that women tend to feel more caregiving burden than do men.

Studies on Western societies (Ingersoll-Dayton, Starrels, and Dowler, 1996; Miller, McFall, and Montgomery, 1991; Seltzer and Li, 1996; Thompson, Futterman, Gallagher-Thompson, Rose, and Lovett, 1993) are divided over whether child or spouse caregivers experience greater caregiving burden. Rhee and Lee (2000) hypothesized that in South Korea, spousal caregivers have the greater caregiving burden. If children are the primary caregivers of impaired elderly, they are likely to feel emotional rewards derived from their filial responsibility as defined by their Confucian belief system. Spousal caregivers would not necessarily have a comparable traditional system of beliefs. Multiple-regression analysis of the data suggested that adult children caring for impaired elderly parents who coreside with them have the least caregiving burden; these caregivers may have access to additional family members, such as their children, to help with caregiving tasks. The analysis suggested that spouse caregivers of impaired elderly who live separately from their children experience the greatest caregiving burden.

CONCLUSION

The number of South Korean elders who require long-term care is rapidly increasing. Although family caregivers still assume responsibility for caring for their aging family members, a significant proportion of them are experiencing severe caregiving burden as traditions and customs are assailed by competing demands.

Currently, the South Korean government only targets long-term care services to low-income elders who do not have family caregivers available. However, in order to reduce caregiving burden of family members of impaired elders and help them carry out their caregiving tasks, the government should set up long-term care policy for elders in the upper-middle income group and elders who have a family caregiver as well.

Along with expansion of the target group for long-term care services, both residential care facilities and community-care services should be expanded. What is more, consideration should be given to the introduction of transitional-care facilities for impaired elderly who are unable to return to their community because they still need rehabilitation services after their release from a hospital or a residential care facility. Under current arrangements, they fall into the cracks and depend on unenviable options not suited to their condition.

The government also should provide financial support to reduce the financial burden of impaired elderly who want to use long-term care services. At present the government only provides financial support to elders receiving public assistance in order for them to use residential care services or community-care services. However, as the vast majority of the elderly do not receive any pension benefits, they do not have sufficient economic resources to pay long-term care services. Currently, Medical Insurance does not cover the expenses associated with long-term care. In order to solve these problems, the Korean government should expand Medical Insurance to cover the cost of long-term care services; eventually, it should implement long-term care insurance as the German and Japanese governments have.

REFERENCES

Byun, J. K., Chung, H. E., Cho, A. J., Oh, Y. H., Lee, Y. K., and Lee, Y. H. (1999). *The current status of residential care services in Korea.* Seoul: Korea Institute for Health and Social Affairs.

Chung, K. H., Cho, A. J., Oh, Y. H., Byun, J. K., Byun, Y. C., and Moon, H. S. (1998). *A research study on the status of the elderly people's life and their welfare needs.* Seoul: Korea Institute for Health and Social Affairs.

Economic Planning Bureau. (1960). *Population and housing census report.* Seoul: Author.

Economic Planning Bureau. (1970). *Population and housing census report.* Seoul: Author.

Economic Planning Bureau. (1980). *Population and housing census report.* Seoul: Author.

Ingersoll-Dayton, B., Starrels, M. E., and Dowler, D. (1996). Caregiving for parents and parents-in-law: Is gender important? *The Gerontologist, 36*(4), 483–491.

Kramer, B. J. (1995). Eldercare and work-role conflict: Toward an understanding of gender differences in caregiver burden. *The Gerontologist, 35*(3), 340–348.

Kramer, B. J. (1997). Differential predictors of strain and gain among husbands caring for wives with dementia. *The Gerontologist, 37*(2), 239–249.

Lazarus, R. S., and Folkman, S. (1984). *Stress, appraisal, and coping.* New York: Springer.

Miller, B., McFall, S., and Montgomery, A. (1991). The impact of elder health, caregiver involvement, and global stress on two dimensions of caregiver burden. *Journal of Gerontology, 46*(1), 9–19.

Ministry of Finance and Economy. (1970). *Annual report of participation in the labor force: 1970.* Seoul: Author.
Ministry of Finance and Economy. (1980). *Annual report of participation in the labor force: 1980.* Seoul: Author.
Ministry of Finance and Economy. (1989). *Annual budget summary: 1989.* Seoul: Author.
Ministry of Finance and Economy. (1990). *Annual report of participation in the labor force: 1990.* Seoul: Author.
Ministry of Finance and Economy. (1991). *Annual budget summary: 1991.* Seoul: Author.
Ministry of Finance and Economy. (1993). *Annual budget summary: 1993.* Seoul: Author.
Ministry of Finance and Economy. (1995). *Annual budget summary: 1995.* Seoul: Author.
Ministry of Finance and Economy. (1997). *Annual budget summary:1997.* Seoul: Author.
Ministry of Finance and Economy. (1998). *Annual report of participation in the labor force: 1998.* Seoul: Author.
Ministry of Finance and Economy. (1999). *Annual budget summary: 1999.* Seoul: Author.
Ministry of Finance and Economy. (2000). *Annual budget summary: 2000.* Seoul: Author.
Ministry of Health and Welfare. (1988). *Annual guidelines of the welfare policy for the elderly: 1988.* Seoul: Author.
Ministry of Health and Welfare. (1989a). *Annual business report summary: 1989.* Seoul: Author.
Ministry of Health and Welfare. (1989b). *Annual guidelines of the welfare policy for the elderly: 1989.* Seoul: Author.
Ministry of Health and Welfare. (1990). *Annual guidelines of the welfare policy for the elderly: 1990.* Seoul: Author.
Ministry of Health and Welfare. (1991a). *Annual business report summary: 1991.* Seoul: Author.
Ministry of Health and Welfare. (1991b). *Annual guidelines of the welfare policy for the elderly: 1991.* Seoul: Author.
Ministry of Health and Welfare. (1992). *Annual guidelines of the welfare policy for the elderly: 1992.* Seoul: Author.
Ministry of Health and Welfare. (1993a). *Annual business report summary: 1993.* Seoul: Author.
Ministry of Health and Welfare. (1993b). *Annual guidelines of the welfare policy for the elderly: 1993.* Seoul: Author.
Ministry of Health and Welfare. (1994). *Annual guidelines of the welfare policy for the elderly: 1994.* Seoul: Author.
Ministry of Health and Welfare. (1995a). *Annual business report summary: 1995.* Seoul: Author.
Ministry of Health and Welfare. (1995b). *Annual guidelines of the welfare policy for the elderly: 1995.* Seoul: Author.
Ministry of Health and Welfare. (1996). *Annual guidelines of the welfare policy for the elderly: 1996.* Seoul: Author.
Ministry of Health and Welfare. (1997a). *Annual business report summary: 1997.* Seoul: Author.
Ministry of Health and Welfare. (1997b). *Annual guidelines of the welfare policy for the elderly: 1997.* Seoul: Author.
Ministry of Health and Welfare. (1998). *Annual guidelines of the welfare policy for the elderly: 1998.* Seoul: Author.

Ministry of Health and Welfare. (1999a). *Annual business report summary: 1999.* Seoul: Author.

Ministry of Health and Welfare. (1999b). *Annual guidelines of the welfare policy for the elderly: 1999.* Seoul: Author.

Ministry of Health and Welfare. (2000a). *Annual business report summary: 2000.* Seoul: Author.

Ministry of Health and Welfare. (2000b). *Annual guidelines of the welfare policy for the elderly.* Seoul: Author.

Ministry of Health and Welfare. (2000c). *Reference for annual business report summary.* Seoul: Author.

Montgomery, R. J. V., Gonyea, J. G., and Hooyman, N. R. (1985). Caregiving and the experience of subjective and objective burden. *Family Relations, 34,* 19–26.

Rhee, K. O., Kwon, J. D., Kwon, S. J., and Lee, W. S. (1990). *Study on the support for the elderly..* Seoul: Korea Institute for Health and Social Affairs.

Rhee, K. O., Suh, M. K., Ko, K. H., and Park, J. D. (1994). *Analysis of living status of the Korean elderly and policy implications.* Seoul: Korea Institute for Health and Social Affairs (in Korean).

Rhee, K. O., Cha, H. B., Choi, S. J., Yoon, H. S., Suh, H. K., and Park, K. S. (1999). *Long-term care needs of the elderly and emotional caregiving burden of family caregivers.* Seoul: Sungkonghoe University.

Rhee, K. O., and Lee, M. J. (2000). A study on caregiving burden among family caregivers of impaired elderly. *Journal of Korea Gerontological Society, 20*(2), 215–228.

Rose-Rego, S. K., Strauss, M., and Smyth, K. (1988). Differences in the perceived well-being of wives and husbands caring for persons with Alzheimer's disease. *The Gerontologist, 38*(2), 224–230.

Seltzer, M. M., and Li, L. W. (1996). The transitions of caregiving: Subjective and objective definitions. *The Gerontologist, 36*(5), 614–626.

South Korea National Statistical Office. (1990). *Population and housing census report.* Seoul: Author.

South Korea National Statistical Office. (1997). *Statistics of population dynamics, Jan. 1997.* Seoul: Author.

South Korea National Statistical Office. (1999). *Korea statistical monthly book, June 1999.* Seoul: Author.

Thompson, E. H. Jr., Futterman, A., Gallagher-Thompson, D., Rose, J., and Lovett, S. (1993). Social support and caregiving burden in family caregivers of frail elders. *Journal of Gerontology, 48*(5), 245–254.

Vaux, A. (1988). *Social support: Theory, research, and intervention.* New York: Praeger Publishers.

PART IV

Health and Long-Term Care

CHAPTER THIRTEEN

Health Insurance in South Korea

Sang-soo Bae and Tae-jin Lee

Located on the eastern edge of the Asian continent, South Korea lies in the southern end of the Korean Peninsula and includes more than 3,400 surrounding islands. As of 2000, the population was estimated to be 47 million. Left devastated after the Korean War, the country has experienced rapid economic development and industrialization since the 1960s. In fact, South Korea has been labeled one of the "economic tigers" in Asia. By 2000, the country's gross domestic product (GDP) had reached US$461.6 billion with a per capita GDP calculated as US$9,764 (Organization for Economic Cooperation and Development [OECD], 2001).

South Korea's economic growth is complemented by striking improvements in the overall health status of the population. Life expectancy has been increasing steadily, from 53.7 years in 1960 to 79.2 years in 1999 for females and from 51.1 years to 71.7 years for males. Concurrently, infant mortality rates have dramatically decreased: In 1999, the infant mortality rate was 7.7 deaths per 1,000 live births, compared to 89.2 per 1,000 live births in 1962. The four main causes of death in South Korea in 2001 were (in descending order) cancer, cerebrovascular diseases, cardiovascular diseases, and diabetes, which accounted for 50.4 percent of all deaths in 2001 (South Korea National Statistical Office, 2002).

The South Korean healthcare system is market oriented and dominated by the private sector. The government plays a limited role in providing public health services or in developing health promotion campaigns. In 2000, there were 72,503 doctors and 218,676 hospital beds in the country. About 90 percent of physicians work in the private sector, and the vast majority of hospital beds are privately administered.

The proliferation of private-sector healthcare services is mainly attributed to the government's laissez-faire policy toward healthcare and to the establishment of the National Health Insurance (NHI) system in South Korea. By improving access to healthcare for the entire population, the NHI is thought to have contributed to the global improvements in the health status of the population. However, with the South Korea economy experiencing difficult times, the NHI is currently suffering from a financial crisis. Even so, it is faced with escalating needs for healthcare and long-term care. Whether the NHI can and should meet the needs of older Koreans for long-term care is emerging as a significant societal issue.

OVERVIEW OF THE NATIONAL HEALTH INSURANCE PROGRAM

Although the national Health Insurance Act was first implemented in South Korea in 1963, access to healthcare was slow to expand. Until the compulsory provision of health insurance in all companies with 500 or more employees became the law of the land in 1977, there were only a few voluntary health insurance societies (Table 1).

In 1979, a separate health insurance fund was created for government employees and teachers at private schools (public-school teachers were regarded as government employees). Meanwhile, health insurance for private-sector workers continued to be extended to increasingly smaller companies: first to companies with more than 300 employees in 1979; next to companies with 100 employees in

Table 1. Evolution of National Health Insurance in Korea

Year	Event
1977	Introduction of health insurance for employees of private companies
1979	Introduction of health insurance for government employees and school teachers (GE&T)
1988	Introduction of regional health, health insurance for rural residents
1989	Extension of regional health insurance to self-employed urban residents, effectively creating National Health Insurance
October 1998	Integration of GE&T insurance with insurance for the self-employed, creating the National Medical Insurance Corporation (NMIC)
July 2000	Integration of NMIC with insurance for corporate employees, creating the National Health Insurance Corporation (NHIC)

1981; then to companies with 16 employees in 1983; and finally to companies with as few as 5 employees in 1988.

In order to ensure equal access to healthcare, regional health insurance societies were organized to cover residents of rural areas in 1988 and subsequently expanded to the urban self-employed in 1989, when the South Korean government launched a compulsory national health insurance program for the entire population.

A national health insurance system was thus implemented in only 12 years after the first introduction of compulsory insurance but was not being operated efficiently, as it was fractured and administered by many small funds. After years of fierce political debate, the government followed the recommendation of the Committee on Health Reform and decided to integrate all funds into a single unit, thereby improving efficiency and creating a socially cohesive policy. As a first step, regional health insurance plans for the self-employed and the health insurance program for government employees and school teachers were integrated in October 1, 1998, to create the National Medical Insurance Corporation (NMIC). All private-sector workers' health insurance societies combined with the NMIC in July 1, 2000, creating the National Health Insurance Corporation (NHIC), which is a special public organization.

The insurance provided by the NHIC has the following characteristics.

Mandatory and Universal Enrollment

Enrollment in NHI is compulsory. The NHI covers employees in all kinds of enterprises and government divisions, the self-employed, and their dependents. As of 2001, the NHI covered 46.3 million persons, or 96.9 percent of the entire population of South Korea. The Medical Aid Program, funded by taxes, covers the remaining 3.1 percent, or 1.5 million persons. Between the two, the entire population of South Korea is guaranteed at least a modicum of access for their health needs.

Limited Benefits Coverage

In response to increased demand for healthcare, the coverage of benefits in the NHI has been expanded. Benefits currently covered by the NHI include inpatient and outpatient care, dental services, traditional Asian forms of healthcare, prescription drugs, laboratory tests, and some essential preventive services such as health screening.

However, the benefits coverage provided by the NHI has significant limitations. Taking into account the availability of insurance funds, the government generally determines the range of services covered under the NHI each year. Uninsured services are mostly new or expensive high-technology medical interventions such as magnetic resonance imaging and ultrasonograph. Patient meals, hotel fees, and specialist services are not covered by the NHI, so patients still face considerable out-of-pocket expenses. In addition, treatment days[1] covered by the NHI are limited to 365 days a year. Due to this limitation, patients with chronic diseases, primarily older adults, face substantial out-of-pocket payments to cover needed healthcare.

High Copayment Rates

Even covered conditions under the NHI are far from being cost free. Partly because of insufficient insurance reserves and partly to reduce unnecessary service utilization, a cost-sharing scheme exists whereby all patients are required to pay for part of the costs of the health services they receive. As is the case in many national health insurance programs around the world, there are two types of cost sharing: deductibles and coinsurance.

As of 2001, the coinsurance rate is 20 percent of total inpatient costs, regardless of healthcare provider (Table 2). Patients must pay from 30 percent to 65 percent of total healthcare costs for outpatient care, depending upon the type of provider. In the case of prescription medicine dispensed at pharmacies, coinsurance is also 30 percent of medicine-related costs[2] exceeding 10,000 won[3]; below that amount there is a deductible of 1,500 won. Therefore, despite the existence of the NHI, patients still pay a high proportion of the healthcare costs at the time of service utilization.

Fee-for-Service Payment

The predominant way of paying providers through the NHI is fee-for-service reimbursement. It is generally recognized that physicians paid according to a fee-for-service model have an incentive to induce demand for services to maintain or increase their income. Since the beginning of the NHI, the government has regulated the level of fees for insured services in order to make it possible to implement the health insurance scheme with rather limited funding. Before 2001, a schedule regulating fees for all medical services and materials was set unilaterally by the national Ministry of Health and Welfare (MOHW). After 2001, a resource-based relative-value scale has been set for all insured services, and the level of fees is negotiated annually between the NHIC and representatives of healthcare professional associations.

The NHIC pays providers on the basis of the fee schedule. In order to ensure the quality of care, the insurer has recently introduced decreasing reimbursement

[1] Treatment days include the number of visits for outpatient care or days of stay for inpatient care and medication days without medical treatment. Conceptually, it is possible that, without restrictions, treatment days of patients—especially those with chronic diseases—may exceed 365 days a year.

[2] Medicine-related costs include the cost of the pharmaceuticals dispensed and several types of dispensing fees for compensating pharmacists for their services.

[3] In 2002, the average exchange rate for US$1 was 1,251 Korean won.

Table 2. Copayments Under National Health Insurance

	Copayment
Inpatient	20% of total treatment cost
Outpatient	
General hospital[a]	- Per-visit consultation fee + 45% of treatment cost if total cost is more than 25,000 won - 60% (or 65% for university hospitals) of total cost if total cost is 25,000 won or less
Hospital	40% of total treatment cost
Clinic	30% of total treatment cost (3,000 won if total cost is less than 15,000 won)
Pharmacy	30% of total pharmacy cost (1,500 won if total cost is less than 10,000 won)

[a]A hospital with 100 or more beds is called a *general hospital* in South Korea.
Source: Ministry of Health and Welfare, 2001.

rates for doctors at clinics depending on the number of patients they see per day. For example, when doctors treat 75 or fewer patients a day, 100 percent of claimed amounts are paid. However, the reimbursement rate reduces to 90 percent, 75 percent, and 50 percent respectively when doctors treat 76 to 100, 101 to 150, and more than 150 patients daily.

Single-Payer Insurance

At about the time the NHI was instituted, there were more than 400 independent insurance societies in South Korea. There was no competition among them for beneficiaries, but there was considerable variation in their financial status. Some well-capitalized societies could accumulate surplus revenue while some poor societies suffered deficits. In addition, small insurance societies incurred high managerial costs. In order to reduce financial inequality and administrative inefficiencies, an integration policy was implemented. The first stage of integration in 1998 reduced the number of societies to 143, and the second integration stage of 2000 created a single insurer. As of 2002, however, total financial integration was tentatively deferred, mainly because of differences in ways of calculating contribution rates for employees versus the self-employed. Given the current economic turmoil and the political wrangling that has accompanied it, financial integration is unlikely to take place in a few years.

Finance

The NHI is financed through three sources: the insured, employers, and the government. For employees of governmental agencies, schools, and corporations, contributions are shared equally by employees and employers. As of 2001, the contribution rate was 3.4 percent of the individual's wages. In comparison, the contributions of the self-employed are calculated on the basis of household income, property value, and car ownership. The government is obligated to subsidize 50 percent of the insurance contribution for the self-employed.

Although the NHI has operated under a single-payer corporation since July 2000, the methods of calculating contributions differ for self-employed individuals and employees, and the management of reserve funds remains separate among these two categories of the insured.

THE CURRENT STATUS OF THE NHI

Healthcare utilization rates have continued to increase over the past decade due to a combination of factors, including increases in per capita income, aging of the population, and the enhanced access to healthcare that compulsory national health insurance brought about. As shown in Table 3, the number of medical claims per person per year more than doubled, from 3.23 in 1990 to 7.10 in 2001, representing average annual increases of 7.4 percent. Increases in health utilization rates caused NHI expenditures to rise 16.9 percent annually on average during the period between 1990 and 2000.

Because of certain coverage exclusions and copayment schedules, the proportion of healthcare expenses that patients pay for out-of-pocket is very high. In 2001, patients had to shoulder more than half of their healthcare costs at the time services were rendered (Choi and Shin, 2002). Because of this, some hold a negative view of the merits of the NHI, saying that the way the current NHI system operates is not a proper form of insurance but merely a discount for treatment. This is the inevitable result of the "low contribution, low benefit" policy that has been maintained since the inception of the compulsory insurance. Such a policy has implications for the redistribution of wealth: Whereas insurance

Table 3. Annual Utilization of Medical Services, 1990–2001

	Annual utilization							
Variable	1990	1995	1996	1997	1998	1999	2000	2001
Medical claims per person	3.23	4.46	4.88	5.19	5.31	5.98	6.32	7.10
Medical visit days per person	7.91	9.50	9.94	10.35	10.51	11.56	11.59	13.16

Source: NHIC, 2002.

contributions are income proportional, out-of-pocket payments are not. Expanding benefit coverage and reducing out-of-pocket expenses are urgent challenges that the South Korean NHI faces.

Paradoxically, out-of-pocket expenditures provided the largest source of funding for healthcare in South Korea; they represented 44 percent of national healthcare expenditures in 1999 (Figure 1). Social security, including the NHI, paid about a third of total health expenditures, while the government's share was about 11 percent. Private insurance has played a limited role in funding healthcare to date. Supplementary health insurance plans offered by private insurance companies have been marketed for several years but have had limited appeal.

The public sector's share of healthcare funding, which includes both government and social security expenditures, has increased continuously but is still less than half of total outlay (Table 4), which is relatively low in comparison to international patterns.

Healthcare financing through health insurance has been a major factor in the rapid increase in healthcare expenditures in South Korea. As shown in Figure 2, the proportion of resources spent on healthcare in relation to the national GDP was 4.26 percent in 1985 and increased to 5.40 percent in 1999 (Jung, Lee, and Kang, 2000). Although the 1999 figure is still relatively low compared to that of OECD countries, it is expected to reach the average expenditure rate of OECD countries within a few years due to the effects of recent healthcare reforms.

Looking into health insurance expenditures by service type, outpatient care consumed almost half of health insurance expenditures in 2001, and inpatient care and pharmaceuticals each consumed about a quarter.

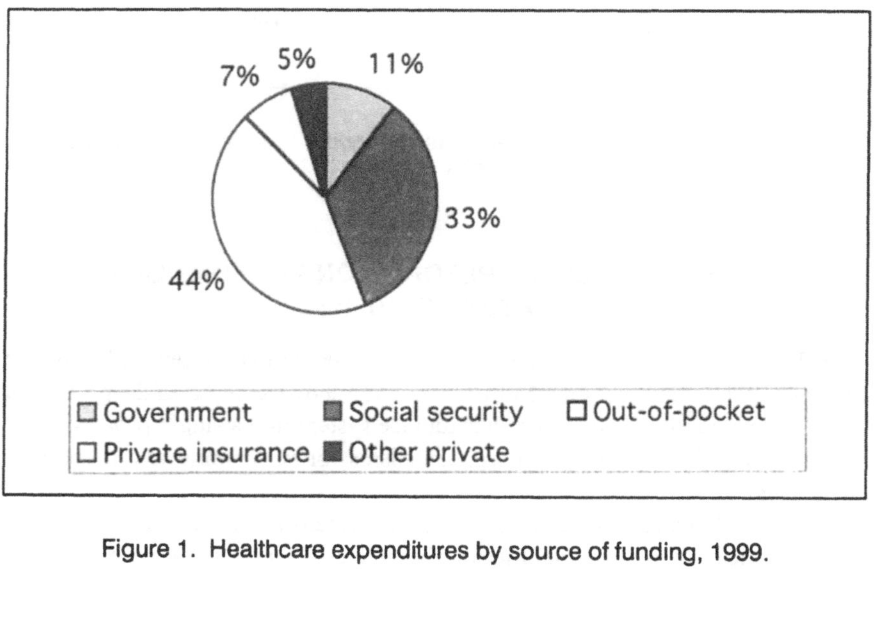

Figure 1. Healthcare expenditures by source of funding, 1999.

Table 4. Trends in Healthcare Expenditures by Source of Funding, 1985–1999

	Percentage of total expenditures							
Source of funding	1985	1987	1989	1991	1993	1995	1997	1999
Public (total)	26.6	25.6	32.0	33.3	33.4	36.5	41.0	43.9
Government	5.8	6.1	8.7	8.3	9.9	11.1	11.5	10.6
Social security	20.9	19.5	23.3	25.1	23.5	25.4	29.5	33.3
Private (total)	73.4	74.4	68.0	66.7	66.6	63.5	59.0	56.1
Out-of-pocket	59.9 5.0	61.3	57.3	56.4	54.9	51.1	46.1	43.8
Private insurance	8.5	5.2	5.4	5.3	5.9	5.8	6.7	7.4
Others		7.9	5.3	5.0	5.9	6.6	6.2	5.0

Source: OECD, 2001.

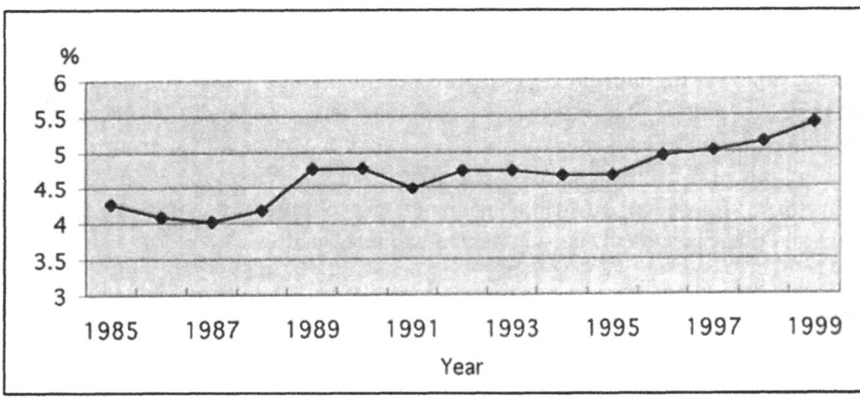

Figure 2. Trends in total healthcare expenditures as percent of GDP, 1985–1999.

IMPACT OF RECENT REFORMS ON THE FINANCIAL STATUS OF THE NHI

In July 2000, the Korean government implemented two sweeping healthcare reform policies. "Integration reform," mentioned above, completed the process of reorganizing a multiple-fund health insurance system into a single-payer system. "Separation reform" separated the mechanisms for prescribing and dispensing medicines.

Before the latter reform, the prescribing and dispensing of medicines took place simultaneously in medical facilities or pharmacies. From a consumer viewpoint, direct purchase of medicine at pharmacies represented a low-cost way to access healthcare, replacing comparatively expensive medical services. Absent prescriptions written by physicians, however, it was easy for people to misuse or overuse medicines. This practice in medical facilities also caused higher prescription rates, especially for antibiotics, than were regarded as appropriate.

Separation of prescribing and dispensing mechanisms was conceived as a remedy for this situation. The government was determined to put the separation into effect by July 2000, though many stakeholders were worried about its tremendous impact on the entire healthcare system. After medical professionals engaged in several strikes protesting the separation policy and then conducted a four-month-long campaign to impede implementation, the separation system was finally put into operation in 2000 with some details deviating from what was originally planned. It is too early to assess the long-term consequences of these reforms. However, a glance at the short-term effects reveals that, after the reforms, NHI expenditures skyrocketed by about 40 percent, from 10 trillion won in 2000 to 14 trillion won in 2001, when the NHI recorded a deficit of 2.4 trillion won (Table 5).

FUNDING LONG-TERM CARE FOR THE ELDERLY

As has been noted earlier in this volume, the South Korean population is aging rapidly due to decreases in fertility rates and in mortality rates at older ages. The average number of children a woman has during her childbearing years has decreased over the last decade, notably dropping from 1.47 in 2000 to 1.30 in 2001 (South Korea National Statistical Office, 2002). Such a decline in the fertility rate implies an acceleration of the population aging process

Table 5. Financial Status of the Health Insurance Fund

	Amount (billion won)							
	1993	1995	1996	1997	1998	1999	2000	2001
Revenue (A)	4,116	5,435	6,326	7,297	7,849	8,692	9,529	11,642
Expenditure (B)	3,364	5,054	6,413	7,679	8,709	9,561	10,538	14,051
Balance (A–B)	752	381	−88	−382	−860	−869	−1,009	−2,409
Ratio of expenditure to revenue	81.7	93.0	**101.4**	**105.2**	**110.9**	**110.0**	**110.6**	**120.7**

Source: NHIC, 2002.

and a reduction in the ability of the society to support its elderly members in the future. Concurrently, life expectancy continues to lengthen for both males and females: As of 1999, life expectancy was 79.2 years for females and 71.7 years for males (South Korea National Statistical Office, 2001a). The proportion of the population ages 65 and older was 7.2 percent in 2000, and is projected to reach 14 percent in 2019 and 20 percent in 2026 (South Korea National Statistical Office, 2001b). Thus it will take less than two decades for the 2000 figure to double.

The rapid aging of the population alluded to here and discussed earlier has many implications for the Korean healthcare system. Above all, the increase in the elderly population puts significant pressure on the healthcare system. A nationwide survey showed that 86.7 percent of Korean elders were suffering from one or more chronic diseases in 1998 (Jung, Cho, and Oh, 1998). Healthcare service utilization of older adults has increased over the last decade. In the early 1990s, the number of medical claims per person showed little difference between older adults and younger cohorts. However, the medical utilization rate of South Koreans ages 65 and older has increased more rapidly than that of younger South Koreans ages 0–64. In 2000, the average annual number of per-person medical claims for older adults was almost two times that for younger Koreans, and there is every reason to believe no significant reversal in that trend will occur (Table 6).

In addition, healthcare expenditures per NHI claim for patients ages 65 and older were 1.54 times greater than those ages 64 and younger in 2001, and tended to increase with successive age intervals (Table 7). Moreover, the per capita health expenditures of the elderly were 2.9 times those of younger groups. Consequently, the elderly, who represented about 7 percent of the population, accounted for 17.7 percent of total NHI expenditures in 2001. It is estimated that when elders ages 65 and older reach about 10 percent of the population in 2010, they will consume approximately 30 percent of annual NHI expenditures (Ministry of Health and Welfare, 2001).

Table 6. Medical Claims per Person by Age Group

Age group	Medical claims per person										Rate of annual increase (%)
	1991	1992	1993	1994	1995	1996	1997	1998	1999	2000	
0–64	3.17	3.38	3.64	3.72	4.20	4.61	4.94	5.01	5.67	5.92	7.17
65+	3.52	3.96	4.48	4.92	5.88	6.83	7.64	8.45	11.30	11.81	14.39

Source: NHIC, 2001.

Table 7. Older Adult Population and Healthcare Expenditures, 2001

Age	Percentage of population	Percentage of utilization	Percentage of healthcare expenditure	Treatment cost per episode of illness (won)	Treatment cost per person (won)
0–64	93.07	87.7	82.3	29,121	340,120
65+	6.93	12.3	17.7	44,906	983,368
65–69	2.87	5.3	7.3	43,053	983,149
70–74	1.83	3.6	5.2	45,147	1,091,697
75+	2.23	3.4	5.2	47,539	894,934

Source: NHIC, 2002.

PROPOSALS FOR FUNDING LONG-TERM CARE OF THE ELDERLY

Although both the healthcare utilization rates for older adults and the insurance expenditures for healthcare services for this population continue to increase, benefits coverage for the elderly is hardly comprehensive under current NHI guidelines. The elderly are entitled to the same types of benefits as younger cohorts, including medical care, dental care, traditional Asian healthcare services, and pharmaceutical services. The benefits coverage for the two groups differs little, apart from a small discount for out-of-pocket payments made by older adults. Despite the increased demand for long-term care of the elderly resulting from rapid population aging, however, such services as homecare, home help services, daycare services, and short-stay services are not provided under the current NHI scheme.

Currently, the primary providers of long-term care for older South Koreans are their families. According to Rhee (1999), the average primary caregiver for an impaired older adult is 57.8 years old, and nearly half of such caregivers are spouses of the care recipient. Some 70 percent of family caregivers for impaired elders have provided informal care for three years or longer. This responsibility must place huge emotional and economic burdens on informal caregivers. Although there are some social services available to older adults, only a few caregivers recognize and use them (Chapter 12).

Such low rates of social service utilization are, on the one hand, a result of strong family ties. On the other hand, they reflect the absence of a formal caregiving system. However, the perception that the family is responsible for supporting the elderly is weakening among younger generations of South Koreans much as it is throughout Asia. Family size continues to decline, and the participation of women in the labor force continues to increase. South Korea can no longer depend heavily on family support for long-term care of the elderly without developing its formal caregiving system. Formal strategies for relieving the caregiving burden of families are desperately needed but will not be implemented without lengthy political deliberation.

Strategies for Funding Long-Term Care

Unfortunately, South Korea does not have unlimited resources available to provide long-term care to its older citizens. In developing a formal long-term care strategy with such limited resources, two considerations must be kept in mind: the availability of informal care and the urgency of individual need for long-term care. Although it is true that the support function of families is declining, the importance and availability of family provisions for older adults should not be overlooked. It is important to maintain an optimal balance between informal and formal long-term care. Even if it is desirable to make formal long-term care available to every older person in need, it is more realistic to provide such care on the basis of urgency of need. That is, the more severely limited an elder's daily life, the higher priority it should be to provide him or her with access to formal long-term care.

Table 8 shows a hypothetical model for providing stepwise long-term care based on urgency of need and availability of informal care. According to the model, bed-bound elderly who have no informal caregivers or whose main caregiver is their spouse, and chair-bound elderly who have no caregivers or whose main caregiver is a spouse age 70 or older, should benefit first from formal

Table 8. A Proposal for Gradual Provision of Long-Term Care

	Caregiver characteristics				
		Informal caregiver present			
		Spouse		Children	
Severity of impairment	No informal caregiver	Ages 70+	Ages <70	Employed	Unemployed
Moderate[a]	A1	A2	A3	A4	A5
Severe (chair-bound)[b]	B1	B2	B3	B4	B5
Severe (bed-bound)[c]	C1	C2	C3	C4	C5

Source: Byun and Sunwoo, 2000.
[a]Older person with limitations in instrumental activities of daily living (IADLs) only.
[b]Older person with limitations in one to five activities of daily living (ADLs).
[c]Older person with limitations in all ADLs.

long-term care services. Depending upon the availability of resources, long-term care coverage could then be expanded to older adults with less severe conditions and to those whose caregivers are unemployed adult children.

Options for Funding Long-Term Care

Few mechanisms for funding long-term care are well developed in South Korea. A small number of wealthy elderly use expensive private long-term care facilities or services. In addition, a small number of impoverished elderly benefit from tax-funded public long-term care facilities or services. However, the supply of long-term care facilities and services, private or public, does not come close to meeting the demand. The vast majority of older adults in need of long-term care rely heavily upon the informal care of their families. In order to extend the provision of long-term care facilities and services, more resources must be made available.

There are several options for funding long-term care.

Extension of NHI Coverage

Because of the current financial crisis of the NHI, further extension of coverage to include long-term care is unlikely for the time being. The government anticipated that it would take five years to overcome the crisis, but their forecast is generally seen as optimistic. Moreover, even if the crisis is resolved, priority should be given to meeting the increasing demand for other health services. In order for long-term care to be included in the NHI benefit package, substantial increases in both individual and employer contributions are inevitable. Taking into account the public's unfavorable opinion of contribution increases, however, the NHI is not likely to be capable of providing comprehensive long-term care for the elderly in the immediate future.

Taxes

Another option is to create a tax-based long-term care system. However, it is expected to be very difficult to establish a system completely funded by taxes, since additional tax-based funding for long-term care places a huge burden on the government. Some European countries, including the United Kingdom, have already withdrawn from a tax-based long-term care system, and are searching for an optimal public-private mix to cover long-term care. In addition, the progressiveness of the South Korean tax system may be questioned because the portion of indirect tax is as high as 50 percent of total tax revenues. Therefore, it is reasonable that tax revenues should play a limited role in building long-term care facilities or providing long-term care services for low-income older South Koreans.

Private Long-Term Care Insurance

Although private long-term care insurance has the potential to provide an alternative to a tax-based long-term care system, its prospects are not rosy. Despite the immense probable market for private health insurance created by the low coverage offered by the NHI, private insurance has only played a limited role in financing healthcare in South Korea, and this pattern is expected to extend to long-term care insurance. If the government were to offer tax subsidies to encourage purchase of private long-term care insurance, the financial implications would in fact be fairly regressive, placing an inordinate burden on those who could least afford but might most need private coverage. It is unlikely that private long-term care insurance will be a popular option for funding long-term care in South Korea in the near future.

Medical Savings Accounts (MSAs)

Medical savings accounts (MSAs), developed in Singapore to fund healthcare, may be appropriate for funding long-term care in South Korea. MSAs permit individuals to shelter income set aside to meet their long-term care needs or those of their family, thus relieving future generations of undue burden. Emphasizing individual and family responsibility for long-term care of the elderly, MSAs do not promote so-called moral hazard[4] but encourage economical utilization of resources. MSAs would also correspond well with South Koreans' high regard for personal savings (OECD, 2002). However, since MSAs rely on individuals' ability to set aside current resources, low-income individuals may be unable to accumulate adequate savings. Without governmental subsidies, low-income elderly could be left as vulnerable as they are now.

Public Long-Term Care Insurance

Another option for funding long-term care is to develop public long-term care insurance to supplement the NHI. The principle of public long-term care insurance goes hand in hand with that of the current NHI, since it emphasizes collective responsibility for long-term care of the elderly. Income-proportional contributions for public long-term care insurance would contribute to social solidarity by subsidizing high-risk individuals to increase their access to long-term care. However, public insurance is susceptible to moral hazard representing excessive use of services. More importantly, the willingness of South Koreans and their ability to pay for additional contributions need to be considered.

[4] Moral hazard is a kind of consumer response to the reduced price of healthcare services. For example, health insurance reduces the price of healthcare services, leading consumers to increase the use of those services. In the case of MSAs, this kind of consumer incentive hardly exists.

CONCLUSION

The Korean National Health Insurance system is facing several challenges. Above all, finding effective solutions to the current financial crisis is essential. The functions of insurance such as risk pooling and income protection also need to be strengthened through expanding the terms of insurance coverage. These efforts will help restore the public's trust in the NHI. Nevertheless, it is difficult to expect the NHI will meet the increasing need for long-term care of the elderly, which is the result of population aging and other social changes. A separate funding mechanism for long-term care needs to be developed in order to relieve the NHI of the cost of social hospitalization wherein there is no immediate medical intervention required and to improve older adults' access to homecare, nursing homes, and the like. Whether South Koreans would be willing or able to pay for additional contributions to long-term care is a vital question. The greatest challenge for South Korea is to have sustainable health and long-term care systems in place. The challenges are both knowledge-based, requiring additional information and planning, and political.

REFERENCES

Byun, J. K., and Sunwoo, D. (2000). *A study on policy development of long term care services for older persons.* Seoul: Korea Institute for Health and Social Affairs.

Choi, B. H., and Shin, H. W. (2002). *Health insurance crisis: An evaluation and measures for financial stabilization.* Seoul: Korea Institute for Health and Social Affairs.

Jung, K. H., Cho, A. J., and Oh, Y. H. (1998). *The 1998 national survey on the living standard and need for social care of the elderly.* Seoul: Korea Institute for Health and Social Affairs.

Jung, Y. H., Lee, K. J., and Kang, S. W. (2000). *Korea's national health expenditure account.* Seoul: Korea Institute for Health and Social Affairs.

Ministry of Health and Welfare. (2001). *Measures for stabilizing the financial crisis of the National Health Insurance.* Seoul: Author.

National Health Insurance Corporation. (2001). *Statistical yearbook 2000.* Seoul: Author.

National Health Insurance Corporation. (2002). *The 2001 major statistics of the National Health Insurance.* Seoul: Author.

Organization for Economic Cooperation and Development [OECD]. (2001). *OECD health data 2001* [CD-ROM]. Paris: Author.

OECD. (2002). *Review of the Korean health care system.* Paris: Author.

Rhee, K. O. (1999). *Long-term care needs of the elderly and emotional care-giving burden of family caregivers.* Seoul: Sungkonghoe University Institute of Elderly Welfare.

South Korea National Statistical Office. (2001a). *Life tables for Korea.* Seoul: Author.

South Korea National Statistical Office. (2001b). *The future estimated population in Korea.* Seoul: Author.

South Korea National Statistical Office. (2002). *Annual report on the vital statistics.* Seoul: Author.

CHAPTER FOURTEEN

Long-Term Care Insurance in Japan

Koichi Hiraoka

The Long-Term Care Insurance Act was passed in Japan in December 1997 and took effect in April 2000. Under terms of the act, all Japanese adults ages 40 and older are now enrolled in a new compulsory social insurance scheme, and all frail elders ages 65 and older and some disabled people aged 40–64 are entitled to receive community-care or institutional care services. With the enactment of this long-term care legislation, Japan became the first country in Asia whose government bears essential responsibility for the social care of its elderly citizens.

Until the 1970s and 1980s, Japanese citizens held the firm belief that families should bear the full responsibility for the care of their elderly members, yet only 20 years later the central government introduced its new system of long-term care services. This chapter will describe Japan's innovative Long-Term Care Insurance (LTCI) scheme, will examine the extent to which its goals have been attained, and will describe the problems that have arisen through its implementation.

HISTORICAL BACKGROUND

The Japanese welfare state witnessed the establishment of its institutional framework in the 1960s, in the midst of a period of rapid economic growth lasting from the mid-1950s to the early 1970s. The government's Nationwide Universal Health and Pension Insurance Plan, designed to cover the entire nation under one or another public health insurance and pension scheme, was realized in 1961 when the 1959 National Pension Act came into effect.

A series of amendments to social security legislation in the 1960s and the 1970s improved pension and health insurance benefits. For example, a 1973 alteration introduced a mechanism of automatic price adjustment into the pension schemes. The Free Medical Care Scheme for the Elderly (ages 70 and older) was also introduced the same year.

The 1960s saw the passage of three major pieces of social welfare legislation: the Law for the Welfare of People with Mental Retardation (1960), the Law for the Welfare of the Aged (1963), and the Law for the Welfare for Fatherless Families (1964). The rapid expansion of child daycare services was realized in the 1960s and the 1970s.

However, during this period long-term care services for the elderly remained in the early stages of development. In 1963, the Special Care Home for the Aged program was initiated to respond to the need for long-term care services. By 1975 the number of places in special care homes for the aged (nursing homes) had reached 41,606, but this figure only amounted to 0.47 percent of the population ages 65 and older. At the beginning, although eligibility for the program was not determined by income level, admission to homes was restricted to frail older individuals who had no family members able to provide appropriate care in their own homes. In addition, a national program for home help service was started prior to the enactment of Law for the Welfare of the Aged. However, it was intended to accommodate elders' housekeeping needs, and access to the program was restricted to low-income households until 1982.

The main reason for the delay in the development of long-term care services in Japan was the assumption underlying government policymaking that the family should bear full responsibility for the care of its aged members and that long-term care services should be predicated on exceptional cases where family care was not possible through any means. This assumption was based on traditional family norms in Japan, according to which a married son (normally the eldest son) and his wife and children were obliged to live with his aging parents, and it was the daughter-in-law's duty to care for them when they became frail.

The validity of this assumption, however, gradually eroded as Japan's rapid economic growth brought about corresponding changes in its social structure. As a result of the increasing mobility of the population, growing housing shortages in urban areas, and changes in family values, the number of three-generation households began to decline, and the number of older adults living alone increased. In addition, as greater numbers of married women entered the labor force, the capacity of the family to care for its aged members tended to diminish.

Furthermore, advances in medicine and improved access to medical services, coupled with the enhancement of living standards and environmental hygiene, lengthened life expectancy—but also resulted in the rise in the number of older adults who required intensive personal care or who developed dementia. Together these factors combined to increase the call for long-term care services. The noticeable aging of population accelerated the growth of these demands: During the period from 1960 to 1980, the population ages 65 and older in Japan almost doubled from 5.4 million to 10.6 million, and as a proportion of the total population it rose from 5.7 percent to 9.1 percent.

The central government's response to the growing need for long-term care services was far from swift, however. At the end of the 1970s, less than 1 percent of the older adult population resided in special care homes for the aged or used home help services. The government began subsidizing short-stay (respite care) services in 1978 and daycare programs for the aged in 1979, but it was not until the 1990s that these programs became accessible nationwide.

Social Hospitalization and the Upsurge in Healthcare Expenditure

One of the serious consequences of the delay in developing long-term care services was the growth in the number of elderly patients who were hospitalized for long periods. Between 1970 and 1980, the number of elderly hospital inpatients rose from 158,800 to 432,200, an increase of 272 percent (Takagi, 1993). This sharp rise in hospitalization rates among the elderly was partly attributable to the improved access to hospital treatment that the Free Medical Care Scheme for the Elderly inaugurated in 1973.

This scheme ended in 1982. The subsequent Health and Medical Service Law for the Aged, enacted in 1982, introduced a small copayment system for both outpatient and inpatient treatment. But even after the start of this system, the number of elderly hospital inpatients continued to increase (Steslicke, 1984). In 1990, the Ministry of Health and Welfare (MHW) conducted a nationwide patient survey of hospitals. The findings revealed that 4.7 percent of elders ages 65 and older were hospitalized for some time and that 43 percent of elderly inpatients remained in hospital for more than six months (Takagi, 1993).

The greater portion of these long-term patients did not require intensive medical treatment, but stayed in the hospital because adequate family care was not available. As has been the case in the West, strong stigma attached to the social welfare institutions induced frail elders and their relatives to choose hospitals rather than special care homes for the aged. In addition, there was a shortage of special care home beds, particularly in metropolitan areas. A considerable proportion of older adults on the waiting lists for these beds were hospitalized until they could secure admission. The term *social hospitalization* was coined to describe the situation whereby hospital stays were the preferable option (Shimizu and Wake, 1994).

Increasing reliance on social hospitalization gave rise to a couple of problems that resisted easy solution. The first dilemma was the low quality of care provided in the hospital for patients in need of personal care. Most of the hospitals that accommodated elderly long-term inpatients lacked appropriate facilities for social care such as dining halls, lounges, and rehabilitation facilities. Another issue revolved around the fact that hospitals tended, on the one hand, to over-medicate patients and, on the other hand, to not provide adequate personal care since the cost of drugs was covered by health insurance but the cost of employing additional care workers was not. Also, hospitals often assessed elderly inpatients additional charges for personal care, which was in violation of rules regulating hospital care under the health insurance system but was tacitly recognized by the government (Campbell, 1984; Takagi, 1994).

The increase in social hospitalization also caused an upsurge in medical care expenditures. Total expenditures for medical care for those ages 70 and older in Japan increased by 5.7 times from 1973 to 1981, and by 79 percent from 1983 to 1990 (Kosei Tokei Kyokai, 1999). Per-person medical care expenditure for this cohort increased by 3.9 times from 1973 to 1981, and by 37 percent from 1983 to 1990.[1]

The central government has implemented various changes since the 1980s to cope with the rising costs of medical care for the elderly. A new system of "geriatric hospitals" with lower staffing requirements and lower medical fee structures was introduced in 1983. Under the Health and Medical Service Law for the Aged enacted in 1983, community health services were gradually expanded. In addition, 1988 saw the introduction of Geriatric Healthcare Facilities, which cater to older inpatients' need for rehabilitation and recuperation after discharge from acute-care hospitals and facilitate their return to homecare settings (Shimizu and Wake, 1994).

The Gold Plan

All in all, these measures were not effective in curtailing social hospitalization. More effective measures were required to promote community care. However, it was getting more and more difficult to shift the burden of caregiving from social and medical services to the family. That the burden of care for frail older adults predominantly fell on female relatives was increasingly perceived as a symbol of an inequitable division of labor between men and women in Japan. There was increasing awareness among policymakers, professionals, and researchers in the field of long-term care that a shift in policy was desirable to cope with the growing problems surrounding long-term care. Be that as it may, in the political climate of the 1980s, when a reorganization of the Japanese welfare state was undertaken, and a reconstruction of state financing was given the highest priority in government policymaking, significant expansion of long-term care services seemed unrealizable.

Yet, paradoxically, an important policy shift occurred at the end of 1989. The government and the ruling Liberal Democratic Party, deeply concerned with the unpopularity of a Consumption Tax introduced in April 1989, decided to draw up a plan for the expansion of long-term care services, an aspect of policy generally seen as lagging behind other areas of social security, to show the public that the new tax would mainly be used to fund government programs addressing the needs of the rapidly growing elderly population. On December 21, 1989, the

[1] In comparison, the consumer price index rose by 99 percent from 1973 to 1981 and by 12 percent from 1983 to 1990 (Kosei Tokei Kyokai, 2001).

Ten-Year Plan for the Promotion of Health and Welfare Services for the Elderly, later called the "Gold Plan," was circulated, reflecting a negotiated agreement among the Minister of Health and Welfare, the Minister of Finance, and the Minister of Home Affairs.

The Gold Plan was an ambitious proposal to significantly expand community-care and institutional care services for the elderly between 1990 and 1999 (Table 1). It is important to note that the government's intention to promote community care was reflected in the service targets laid out in the plan. The plan called for home help services, short-term stay services, and adult daycare centers

Table 1. Main Service Targets of the Ten-Year Plan for the Promotion of Health and Welfare Services for the Elderly

		Service target (in 1999)	
	1989	Gold Plan (1989)	New Gold Plan (1994 revision)
Home helpers (persons)[a]	31,405	100,000	170,000
(per 1,000 elderly population)	(2.2)	(4.7)	(8.0)
Short-term stay services (beds)	4,247	50,000	60,000
(beds per 1,000 elderly population)	(0.3)	(2.4)	(2.8)
Daycare services	1,080	10,000	17,000
(per 1,000 elderly population)	(0.1)	(0.5)	(0.8)
Homecare support centers	—	10,000	10,000
(per 1,000 elderly population)		(0.5)	(0.5)
Visiting nurse stations	—	—	5,000
(per 1,000 elderly population)			(0.2)
Special care homes for the aged (beds)	162,019	240,000	290,000
(per 1,000 elderly population)	(11.3)	(11.3)	(13.7)
Geriatric healthcare facilities (beds)	27,811	280,000	280,000
(per 1,000 elderly population)	(1.9)	(13.2)	(13.2)
Care houses[b] (persons)	200	100,000	100,000
(per 1,000 elderly population)	(0.0)	(4.7)	(4.7)
Elderly population, ages 65 and older (1,000)	14,309[c]	21,156[d]	21,156

[a]Includes part-time home helpers.
[b]Sheltered accommodation for the elderly.
[c]**Source:** Statistical Bureau, Management and Coordination Agency, *Population Estimates of Japan.*
[d]**Source:** National Institute of Population and Social Security Research, 1998.

to grow at a higher rate than the growth of the elderly population. Among institutional care services, geriatric healthcare facilities, designed to facilitate transitions from hospital care to homecare, and "care houses," offering assisted living options, were given priority over special care homes for the aged. Beds in the latter type of institution were supposed to increase in equal proportion to the elderly population.

THE LEGISLATIVE PROCESS LEADING TO THE LONG-TERM CARE INSURANCE ACT

Long-term care policy in the early 1990s was structured to facilitate goals of the Gold Plan and to extend long-term care services to all older adults in need of care, regardless of caring capacity of their families. The idea was to provide blanket coverage without attempting to embed fine gradations of need into national policy.

In order to accomplish the goals of the Gold Plan, the Law for the Welfare of the Aged and the Health and Medical Service Law for the Aged were both revised in 1990, and both stipulated that each prefecture and municipality publish a "Health and Welfare Plan for the Elderly" and include in it services goals for the provision of major health and welfare services for older persons.

The national Ministry of Health and Welfare (MHW) issued its *Revised Guidance on Management of Home Help Services* in 1990 and the *Handbook on the Management of Home Help Services* in 1992, both of which made it clear that the ministry intended to extend the prospect of long-term care services to all those in need of care and that the municipalities should not restrict the provision of home help services to those whose family members were not able to care for them.

Envisioning a Long-Term Care Insurance Scheme

Early in the 1990s, the MHW started to examine the possibility of creating a new system of service delivery that would be more congruent with this shift in policy. The outline of the new system was described in a report titled *A Welfare Vision for the 21st Century: Toward a Low-Fertility and Aged Society,* issued in March 1994 by a private advisory body set up by the MHW (Korei Shakai Fukushi Vijon Kondan-kai, 1994). This report proposed revisions of the Gold Plan to upgrade its service targets, and to create a new system of long-term care services within which "easy access in the local settings to whatever care services [are] needed is guaranteed to all those who need it." The announcement of this new principle was taken to mean that the MHW intended to pursue the realization of the goal of socialization of care, which academics, professionals, and activists working in long-term care had long advocated.

However, given the projected rapid aging of population, the prospects for securing enough resources for the accelerated expansion of long-term care services seemed bleak to MHW staff unless a new source of funding could be created. For comparative purposes, academics and welfare bureaucrats within the government had long alluded to the long-term care insurance scheme in (then West) Germany. In 1992, the MHW set up an informal working group to draft a comparable initiative in Japan (Eto, 2000).

At this stage, the introduction of a long-term care insurance scheme was not regarded as the exclusive option for securing funds for the expansion of long-term care services. Another viable option was to increase the consumer tax. However, as discussions of funding new services progressed within the MHW, the arguments being advanced in favor of the former option gradually emerged as the favored option.

What were the arguments that shifted opinion about appropriate recourse? First, considering the Japanese political culture and the attitude of the Japanese public toward taxes, it was natural to think that imposing new insurance contributions would be more acceptable to the public than the raising of the tax rate. Second, management of long-term care insurance funds would be within the purview of the MHW. Thus the establishment of a new social insurance scheme meant the creation of "a rich and controllable source of revenue" for the ministry (Yoshihara, 1997, p. 81). Third, the establishment of a long-term care insurance program was considered to be an effective means for expanding the supply of long-term care services as well as for making the existing service delivery system more flexible and user directed.

Under the previous patchwork program of long-term care, older adults were not automatically granted access to long-term care services. Municipalities were given much discretionary power to set eligibility standards and to prioritize need (Eto, 2000). This system was sometimes seen as a barrier for the expansion of long-term care services, and hence, for the achievement of the service goals of the Gold Plan. By introducing an insurance scheme within which access to long-term care benefits was universally contracted, it was hoped that barriers to access would be removed. In addition, since service users would be given a right to choose service providers under the insurance scheme, a market for long-term care would be created, and competition would function to improve the quality and efficiency of services. Moreover, it was also hoped that transferring the costs of social hospitalization from the health insurance system to a newly created LTCI system might permit the design of more appropriate services and ease the financial difficulties faced by the heath insurance system (Eto, 2000; Yoshihara, 2000).

In April 1994, the MHW set up the Office for Eldercare Measures to assume supervisory responsibilities for the revision of the Gold Plan and the creation of a new arrangement of long-term care. At that time, the ministry had not yet ruled out the option of a tax hike to fund the expansion of long-term care services.

However, when the Murayama cabinet decided to raise the consumer tax rate from 3 percent to 5 percent in July 1994, not to 7 percent as Prime Minister Hosokawa had proposed five months earlier,[2] the prospects for securing sufficient funds by means of taxation became bleak. The establishment of the LTCI scheme turned out to be the only option left (Masuda, 2001).

Henceforth, MHW staff took the lead in the government's process of establishing a LTCI system.[3] They undertook various measures to pave the way for the introduction of the new scheme: They published leaflets and organized lectures to share information intended to convince the public of the necessity of long-term care insurance. They also consulted closely with ruling coalition political parties as well as with major organizations in the fields of health, welfare, local administration, business, and labor to obtain widespread support for the issue (Masuda, 2001).

In February 1995, the MHW presented a draft bill to the Council on Health and Welfare for the Elderly to review. Members of the council represented universities, major professional organizations in health and welfare, local government bodies, business organizations, and labor unions. The council agreed on the establishment of an LTCI arrangement, but opinion was divided as to the concrete institutional design of the new scheme, particularly on the following issues (Eto, 2001; Kyogoku, 1997):

1. *Who will take on the role of insurer?* The MHW wanted the municipalities to assume fiduciary responsibility for being the insurer underwriting the provision of prescribed services. As might be expected, mayors were reluctant to take on such an accountability as it implied further dilution of available resources. They were not confident about the financial viability of the new plan and were concerned about the projected gap between the demand and supply of long-term care.
2. *What ages will be covered?* According to the MHW proposal, everyone ages 20 and older would contribute to the plan, but only individuals age 65 and older would be entitled to receive benefits. Some members of the council regarded this as discriminatory and unfair.
3. *Should employers pay their employees' contributions?* The MHW proposed that employers pay half of each employee's insurance contribution. Council members representing the interests of employers were naturally opposed to this plan.

[2] At a midnight press conference in February 1994, Prime Minister Hosokawa announced his plan to raise the consumer tax from 3 percent to around 7 percent (and to rename it the "national welfare tax"). Soon after, faced with strong opposition from the parties within the ruling coalition parties as well as from opposition parties, he was forced to withdraw his plan.

[3] Several other political actors played important roles in the decision-making process. See Eto (2001) for an analysis of the roles played by two citizen action groups and a group of reform-oriented mayors.

4. *Should family caregivers be given the right to claim cash benefits as a substitute for formal care services?* The ministry, as well as female members of the council, spoke out against the introduction of cash benefits. Other members of the council argued that it would be inequitable not to provide cash benefits to family caregivers who do not rely on formal long-term care services.

After much wrangling, the final report of the Council on Health and Welfare for the Elderly was submitted to the MHW in April 1996. After 30 meetings, the council was unable to reach consensus regarding appropriate resolution of the controversial issues and elected instead to pass the task of finding acceptable compromises back to MHW. The council's final report recorded the divergence of opinions on these issues, which resulted in a rather inconclusive tone.

Enactment of the Long-Term Care Insurance Act

The lack of consensus within the council did not discourage the ministry from struggling on to give life to the LTCI scheme. They decided to make substantial revisions to the original plan to address the contentious points, and presented the revised plan to the interested parties to garner their support. Although the MHW was forced to give up the idea of presenting the bill to the National Diet during the session that ended in June 1996, it revised the plan a second time and finally achieved consensus among all interested parties. The Long-Term Care Insurance Bill was introduced in the Diet in November 1996, and the Diet approved it on December 17, 1997.

The Long-Term Care Insurance Act was to come into effect on April 1, 2000. The period between December 1997 and March 2000 was to be devoted to indispensable preparatory work needed for the implementation of the LTCI scheme. However, in the fall of 1999, certain quarters of the ruling Liberal Democratic Party expressed the opinion that the implementation of the LTCI scheme be postponed or revised. These judgments were apparently based on concerns over the reaction of the electorate against new levies or the negative impact of socialized care on traditional family values.

For good or for ill, the government refused to postpone the implementation of the new insurance scheme, but added "Special Measures for the Smooth Implementation of the LTCI," which included reducing home help charges for certain low-income users and adding a nominal cash benefit for those who do not use long-term care services but deliver comparable services themselves. In addition, the government postponed the collection of LTCI contributions from those ages 65 and older until October 2000, and halved the amount that this cohort would contribute toward the scheme during the period from October 2000 to September 2001. In lieu of user contributions, costs were to be covered from general revenues collected by the national government, but that strategy would also have resulted in an increase in deficit spending.

OUTLINE OF THE LONG-TERM CARE INSURANCE SCHEME

Japan's Long-Term Care Insurance program was thus implemented in April 2000. The outline of the scheme below is based on the laws and regulations effective as of March 31, 2003, and may not necessarily reflect revisions made since.

Insurer and Insured

The insurer that manages the LTCI system is the municipality (cities, towns, villages, or special wards in Tokyo). The municipality is allowed to execute part or almost all of its duty as insurer in collaboration with other governmental administrative units. All residents of the municipality ages 40 and older are enrolled in this plan on a compulsory basis. Those ages 40–64 who receive medical assistance benefit as part of public assistance are excluded from health insurance and hence from LTCI as well. Insured individuals are divided into type I (those ages 65 and older) and type II (those ages 40–64). Benefits for type II insured individuals are provided only in cases where dependency arises from age-related diseases and several other conditions and diseases specified by the Ministry of Health, Labor and Welfare (MHLW).[4] Examples of covered conditions include early-stage dementia, cerebrovascular disorder, amyotrophic lateral sclerosis, and Parkinson's disease.

Financing LTCI

The LTCI scheme is financed by both individual contributions and general revenue from central and local governments. In principle, 17 percent of the total expenses (excluding user charges) are borne by type I insured and 33 percent by type II insured. The central government pays 25 percent of total expenses, one fifth of which is distributed to municipalities according to a certain formula in order to make necessary adjustment for differences in the municipalities' financial capabilities. In addition, the prefecture pays 12.5 percent and the municipality pays 12.5 percent of total expenses. However, it should be noted that, because of the differences in the older adult population among municipalities, actual proportions of the expenses borne by the central government, prefecture, municipality, type I insured, and type II insured differ from one municipality to another.

Municipalities determine the amount of insurance contributions imposed on type I insured in accordance with government guidelines. These amounts are normally calculated according to the individual's income bracket with five

[4] As part of the reorganization of the central government, the former Ministry of Health and Welfare (MHW) and the former Ministry of Labor were integrated into the Ministry of Health, Labor, and Welfare (MHLW) in January 2001.

stipulated income brackets. The national average of the monthly standard contribution amount of type I insured (i.e., the contribution amount imposed upon those belonging to income bracket 3) in April 2000 was estimated to be around ¥2,900. Individuals from income brackets 1, 2, 4, and 5 contribute 50 percent, 75 percent, 125 percent, and 150 percent, respectively, of the standard contribution amount. In principle, the municipalities are responsible for the collection of contributions from type I insured, but the contributions of type I insured whose yearly old-age pension exceeds ¥180,000 (about 85 percent of all type I insured) are automatically deducted from their pensions.

The insurance contributions imposed on type II insured are collected by the individual's healthcare insurance scheme. In accordance with rules stipulated in the formal plan, these insurers determine copayment amounts. Half of the contributions of individuals who are employed are normally borne by their employers.

Procedures for Service Utilization

In order to receive LTCI benefits, insured individuals must apply to the municipality for a formal assessment of their degree of dependence. The municipality then makes a determination of the applicant's physical and mental status by means of home visitations conducted by assessment officers. In addition, the applicant's family doctor is required to submit a diagnostic appraisal and rate the applicant's need for supportive services.

The initial assessment consists of two stages. In the first stage, the data derived from the investigation (an 85-item questionnaire) is analyzed according to MHLW procedures and guidelines. The applicants are automatically classified into seven categories: "nonapplicable" (independent), "in need of support," or "in need of care" (grades 1 through 5). In the second stage, an assessment panel consisting of five experts or so in health, medicine, and welfare reviews the results of the first-stage assessment using the information derived from the family doctor's statement and additional comments by the assessment officer. The panel is free to change the result of the first-stage assessment, but only in accordance with government guidelines.

Those judged by the panel to be "nonapplicable" are not entitled to receive LTCI benefits. Those judged to be "in need of support" are allowed to use only community-care services. Those judged to be "in need of care," grades 1 through 5, can use both community-care and institutional care services. Once judged to be in need of support or care, the applicants are automatically eligible to use community-care or institutional care services to which they are now entitled. They can get in touch directly with service providers and enter into contract with them. Service users accessing community-care services are strongly encouraged to use care management, which is provided free of charge. Individuals who do not use the care management service may make their own care plan, or they may use long-term care services without making a care plan. In the latter case, service users have to pay all expenses at the point of service use and seek reimbursement from the municipality afterward.

Services Covered and the Upper Limits of Benefits

The long-term care services covered by Japan's LTCI scheme are shown in Table 2. They are comprehensive, covering both community-care and institutional care services, some types of healthcare services, and social-care services. Except in special cases, benefits are paid directly from the municipality to service providers.

Individuals judged to be "in need of care" can use any of the three types of institutional care services without undergoing any further needs assessment by the municipality.

Those judged to be "in need of support" or "in need of care" (all grades) can utilize community-care services within limits set by the government. The upper limits of services for 9 out of 14 types of community-care services (nos. 1–5, 7–9, and 12 on Table 2) have been set in monetary terms, or more accurately, in terms of service "units" (Table 3). Elders can choose freely among these services

Table 2. Long-Term Care Services Covered by the LTCI Scheme

Community-Care Services
1. Homecare
2. Visiting bathing service
3. Visiting nurse services
4. Visiting rehabilitation services
5. Day rehabilitation services
6. Visiting medical management and guidance
7. Daycare services
8. Short-term stay services (at nursing homes)
9. Short-term stay services (at healthcare facilities)
10. Group homes for people with dementia
11. Care services at fee-charging homes for the aged or care houses
12. Rental of technical aids
13. Purchase of technical aids
14. Housing improvement
Institutional Care Services
1. Special care homes for the aged
2. Geriatric healthcare facilities
3. Long-term care geriatric hospitals

Table 3. Upper Limits of Monthly Long-Term Care Insurance Benefits for Community-Care Services

Category	Benefits cap[a]
In need of support	6,150 units (¥61,500–¥65,930)
In need of care	
Grade 1	16,580 units (¥165,800–¥177,440)
Grade 2	19,480 units (¥194,800–¥208,830)
Grade 3	26,750 units (¥267,500–¥286,760)
Grade 4	30,600 units (¥306,000–¥328,030)
Grade 5	35,830 units (¥358,300–¥384,100)

[a]1 unit = ¥10.00 to ¥10.72, depending on the area where the service provider is located and on the type of service provided.

until they reach the monthly limits shown in Table 3.[5] The maximum number of uses of visiting medical management and guidance services has been set separately from the other nine types. As to the purchase of technical assistance, the yearly limit of benefit (excluding user charges) is ¥90,000. The annual benefits cap for housing improvement (excluding user charges) is ¥180,000.

Care services provided at "fee-charging homes for the aged," unauthorized old-age homes set up by for-profit or private nonprofit agencies or care houses, which offer assisted living options, are regarded as community-care services covered by LTCI if they meet the governmental criteria. Elders who reside in group homes for elders with dementia are provided benefits within the limits set according to the degree of dependence of the individual.

User Charges

Individuals who use long-term care services (excluding care management) are normally obliged to copay 10 percent of the cost of the services they use. The maximum amount of monthly user charges for non-low-income households is ¥37,200. For low-income households (mainly those households belonging to income brackets 1 and 2 as discussed before), the upper limit is either ¥24,600 or ¥15,000, depending on family income level. Those who cannot afford to pay any user charges can apply for public assistance, subject to a rather strict means test.

As mentioned above, the government has taken additional measures to lessen the fiscal burden of low-income service users. There are temporary transitional

[5] When the LTCI scheme started in April 2000, the benefits cap for short-term stay services was set separately from those of the other eight types of community-care services. Starting in January 2002, however, these benefits limits were consolidated.

measures for those who have been residing in special care homes for the aged or using homecare services since before the start of the LTCI scheme. In addition, certain nonprofit organizations that assess low-income service needs provide public or private subsidies to offset copayments faced by those individuals below certain income minimums.

Regulation of Service Providers

In order to receive remuneration for community-care services from LTCI, service providers have to apply to the prefectural governor to receive "designated care agency" status (akin to preferred provider status within U.S. regulations). In order to obtain this status, service providers must be incorporated (apart from exceptional cases specified by rules and regulations) and must meet certain criteria as to their staffing, facilities, and management. Designated care agencies may be for-profit or private nonprofit organizations. Prefectures are primarily in charge of inspecting and auditing designated care agencies.

Institutional care services are among the most strictly regulated. For-profit enterprises are not allowed to manage any of the three types of long-term care institutions: special care homes for the aged, geriatric healthcare facilities, or long-term care geriatric hospitals. Only governmentally approved and legally recognized organizations may be authorized to manage special care homes for the aged. Social welfare corporations having such authorization are under strict regulation of the central and local governments as to their activities, management, accounting, and personnel policies.

Remuneration paid to the service providers is, from the providers' viewpoint, remunerations for services provided. Remuneration amounts are set by the central government according to a schedule of the type or content of the service provided and the conditions (e.g., hours of service or staff-to-client ratio) under which the services are rendered. Regional variations in price levels and labor costs are taken into account to reflect the relative cost of services in urban and nonurban locales.

Complaints Procedure

The LTCI system includes a complaints or ombudsman procedure to deal with injustices. Service providers are obliged to take necessary measures for resolving complaints, including setting up contacts within their agencies for handling complaints. The municipality assumes the primary responsibility for handling complaints that cannot be resolved between providers and users. If the municipality cannot resolve the complaint, the appropriate prefectural federation of the National Health Insurance (one of the quasi-governmental organizations that take charge of the inspection of claims and the payment of benefits) assumes final responsibility for resolution.

LTCI Implementation Plan

The LTCI Act stipulates that each municipality draw up and publish successive five-year plans for implementation of the LTCI scheme. These plans should include the projected number of insured in the area and projected benefit levels and amounts, as well as measures to ensure availability of adequate services and to ensure that service delivery functions effectively. Revisions of five-year plans are to occur on a rolling three-year schedule so that adjustments are continually under review.

THE ACHIEVEMENTS AND PROBLEMS OF THE LTCI SCHEME

The MHW (and later, the MHLW) expected that the LTCI system would be an effective means for expanding long-term care provisions throughout Japan. To what extent has this goal been achieved?

During the first year of the implementation of the LTCI scheme, major community-care services expanded substantially. The total amount of home help services used in May 2001 was 6.45 million hours, which represented an 84 percent increase over the yearly average amount of hours per month used in fiscal year 1999. In the same manner, the total amount of daycare services increased by 54 percent from an average of 2.5 million attendances per month in fiscal year 1999 to 3.8 million attendances in May 2001. The number of group homes for people with dementia increased from 266 at the end of fiscal year 1999 to 1,312 in September 2001.[6]

Expansion of long-term care services continued during the second and third years of implementation. Table 4 shows changes in the expenses (the sum of benefits provided by the insurers and user charges paid by service users under the LTCI scheme) for long-term care services. Between the first half of fiscal year 2000 and the first half of fiscal year 2002, the average monthly expenses of community-care services increased by 74 percent, from ¥99.7 billion to ¥173.8 billion. The largest increase was realized in the case of group homes for people with dementia. As compared to homecare and daycare services, the rate of increase for visiting nurse services was small. Average monthly expenses for institutional care services increased by 17 percent in the same period, from ¥215.5 billion to ¥251.3 billion.

Changes in the Balance of Care

As is shown in Table 4, the growth of institutional care services has been slow compared to growth of community-care services. Does this mean that governmental efforts to shift resources from institutional care to community care has achieved a fair measure of success? Not necessarily, and the answer to that

[6] The MHLW statistics presented to the Long-Term Care Benefit Subcommittee of the Social Security Advisory Council on October 22, 2001, retrieved September 23, 2003, from http://www.mhlw.go.jp/topics/kaigo/shingi/syakai/1022-1.html

Table 4. Changes in the Expenses of Long-Term Care Services

	Average expenses per month (¥100 million)					Average expenses per month (index)				
	4/2000–9/2000	10/2000–3/2001	4/2001–9/2001	10/2001–3/2002	4/2002–9/2002	4/2000–9/2000	10/2000–3/2001	4/2001–9/2001	10/2001–3/2002	4/2002–9/2002
Community-Care Services: Total	997.1	1,159.8	1,361.3	1,490.0	1,737.9	100	116	137	149	174
Homecare	209.5	274.0	333.2	372.8	433.5	100	131	159	178	207
Visiting bathing service	32.9	34.9	39.1	39.0	43.4	100	106	119	119	132
Visiting nurse services	81.7	87.1	92.4	92.7	99.2	100	107	113	113	121
Visiting rehabilitation services	2.7	3.3	3.7	3.8	4.2	100	122	134	140	155
Daycare	247.5	270.9	319.0	338.9	394.9	100	109	129	137	160
Day rehabilitation services	203.3	212.3	231.2	234.2	256.0	100	104	114	115	126
Rental of technical aids	19.5	36.4	53.0	67.4	84.2	100	187	273	346	433
Short-term stay services	73.9	91.9	114.2	141.4	188.5	100	124	155	191	255
Visiting medical management and guidance	12.7	14.7	15.5	16.3	17.4	100	115	121	128	137
Group homes for people with dementia	10.2	16.2	27.1	37.5	53.4	100	159	266	368	525
Care services at fee-charging homes for the aged or care houses	14.7	18.2	22.4	26.3	31.6	100	123	152	179	215
Care management	88.5	99.9	110.5	119.6	131.5	100	113	125	135	149
Institutional Care Services: Total	2,154.6	2,277.7	2,360.7	2,396.6	2,512.6	100	106	110	111	117
Special care homes for the aged	953.5	991.8	1,035.8	1,050.5	1,088.5	100	104	109	110	114
Geriatric healthcare facilities	748.3	799.7	827.2	841.5	863.5	100	107	111	112	115
Long-term care geriatric hospital	452.8	486.2	497.7	504.7	560.6	100	107	110	111	124
Total	3,151.6	3,437.5	3,722.0	3886.6	4,250.5	100	109	118	123	135

Note: Calculated from *Kaigo kyufu to no jokyo* [Statistics on long-term care benefits], by Kokumin Kenko-hoken Chuo-kai [All Japan Federation of National Health Insurance], 2001–2003.

question is more complex that it might appear. The main reason for the slow growth of institutional care is that the establishment of care facilities is regulated through mechanisms of authorization and planning as well as through a system of government subsidy for construction costs of care facilities.

The number of applications for admission to care facilities, particularly to special care homes for the aged, has been increasing sharply since the implementation of LTCI. One of the main reasons for this increase is that the criteria for admission to special care homes for the aged were loosened at the inception of the LTCI program. Older adults classified as "in need of care," grades 1 through 5, can now move into these homes regardless of their family circumstances or economic conditions. The waiting lists for special care homes for the aged have been getting longer and longer all over the country. The government has not published numbers of people on the waiting lists, so firm conclusions are difficulty to draw. However, according to the result of a survey conducted by the newspaper *Asahi Shinbun*, at least 230,000 elderly persons, roughly equivalent to 69.8 percent of the 329,664 persons (Kosei-rodosho, 2003) actually residing in homes nationwide, were on waiting lists at the end of 2002. The shortage of beds in the special care homes is particularly serious in metropolitan areas. For example, in one special ward in Tokyo, the net number of older persons on the waiting lists for admission to special care homes was 1,013 as of August 1, 2002, which far exceeded the number of elders actually staying in local homes at the time—621.

The only steps the MHLW has taken so far to cope with this problem is to change its regulations on admission to care facilities and to instruct local governments and care facilities to jointly set criteria for determining admissions priorities. These criteria take into account not only an individual's degree of dependence but also his or her family circumstances and the amount of community services he or she currently utilizes.

It is critical to assess the last criterion because the greater part of those entitled to use community-care services do not use them fully. According to a survey of LTCI benefits usage conducted nationwide by the MHLW in May 2002 (Kosei-rodosho, 2002), the average ratio of actual benefits used to the upper limit for such benefits set by the government was 42 percent. In a survey in Sumida Ward in Tokyo, only 45 percent of those on the waiting lists for special care homes for the aged were actually using the maximum amount of community-care services for which they were eligible (Hiraoka et al., 2002).[7]

[7] The survey that I conducted with my colleagues (Hiraoka, Takagawa, Takechi, Fukimura, Shizume, and Tsukahara, 2002; Hiraoka, Takegawa, Nakatani, Fujimura, Shizume, and Tsukahara, 2003) consisted of a questionnaire mailed to the LTCI division of 444 municipalities in urban areas (conducted from December 2000 to January 2001, with an effective response rate of 64 percent), case studies of 5 municipalities (conducted from June 2000 to March 2003), and interviews with 877 frail elderly persons in Sumida Ward in Tokyo (conducted from January to February 2002). Our research was supported by the national Ministry of Health, Labor, and Welfare through its Health Sciences Research Grants (Research on Policy Planning and Evaluation, H12-011).

There are several likely reasons for such underutilization of community-care services. User charges are one obvious reason, but not the primary one. Another, more relevant issue is that relatives of older adults are generally reluctant to have outsiders such as home helpers come into their home, even to assist them with eldercare tasks. This may be the principal reason why utilization ratios for homecare services for elders living with their children are considerably lower than those for daycare services. Furthermore, analysis of the survey data showed that utilization ratios for homecare services among elders with severe dementia are not necessarily higher than the ratios among those with no symptoms of dementia (Hiraoka, Takegawa, Nakatani, Fujimura, Shizume, and Tsukahara, 2003). This result seems to indicate that family caregivers think that homecare services are not effective for elders with severe dementia.

Changes in the Compilation of Welfare Options

In introducing the LTCI scheme, the central government took various deregulatory measures as to the entry into the market of long-term care services in order to expand and diversify private-sector services (Hiraoka, 2001). To what extent has deregulation achieved its aim?

Table 5 shows the distribution of welfare services for the elderly provided by various types of service agencies as of September 2000. The greater part of long-term care services are provided by the nonprofit and voluntary sector. However, in view of the fact that for-profit agencies played an insignificant role in providing homecare services before the initiation of the LTCI scheme,[8] it is notable that private enterprises account for 25.7 percent of homecare services. Within the nonprofit sector, social welfare corporations (governmentally approved and legally recognized organizations that had virtually monopolized the nonprofit sector provision of social welfare services until the 1980s) and medical corporations (governmentally approved and legally recognized organizations that run private hospitals) are the dominant service providers, but it seems that new types of service agencies—such as NPO corporations (small-scale nonprofit organizations incorporated under the 1998 Law to Promote Specified Nonprofit Activities) and cooperatives—are gradually expanding their share of service provision.[9] From these results it can be concluded that the government's aim to expand and diversify the private sector has been achieved to a certain degree.

[8] The *Survey of Demands for Health and Welfare-Related Services* conducted by the MHW in 1994 showed that only 6.6 percent of those using homecare or home help services were using services provided by for-profit agencies.

[9] See Hiraoka (2001) for the historical development of these agencies and more recent changes in the welfare mix in Japan.

Functioning of the Market Mechanism

It has often been pointed out that the LTCI scheme introduced a free-market mechanism into Japan's long-term care system. However, in view of the following factors, *quasi-market* (as defined by Le Grand and Bartlett, 1993) might be a more appropriate term to describe the mechanism through which long-term care services are provided under LTCI. First, some 90 percent of the expenses of long-term care services are borne by insurance and taxes, not by point-of-service user fees. Second, service providers include private nonprofit and public agencies as well as for-profit agencies. Third, the extent of government intervention in the market is considerable and includes price regulation. Agencies are allowed to provide long-term care services at discount prices in accordance with government regulations only if they comply with certain procedures. They are not allowed to collect extra payment or extra user charges for higher-quality services.

Extensive research on how this long-term care quasi-market is actually functioning under the LTCI scheme has not yet been conducted, but the results of our survey of the LTCI division of municipalities and our case studies of municipalities revealed a few insights (Hiraoka, Takegawa, Takechi, Fujimura, Shizume, Tsukahara, 2002; Hiraoka, Takegawa, Nakatani, Fujimura, Shizume, and Tsukahara, 2003).

First, on the whole, users now have a wider choice of service providers. But there are considerable variations in the number of agencies operating in each local area. Certain metropolitan areas have more than 40 homecare agencies. By contrast, many rural communities often have only one comparable homecare agency. Second, price competition has rarely occurred. The obvious question is the degree to which the absence of a competitive market has resulted in overall improvement in the quality of services. The answer depends in part on the type of services or local circumstances. Third, a number of new agencies, especially for-profit agencies and NPO corporations, entered the market with the start of the LTCI scheme. However, this did not result in the rapid decline in the market share among existing care agencies. Service users proved to be cautious about switching to new agencies. But those who start using long-term care services may not hesitate to choose new agencies. There are indications that, as time passes, competition is gradually starting to occur. Fourth, there is little scope for competition among service providers in the institutional care sector, because demand for institutional care far exceeds supply almost everywhere in the country.

The Role of Municipalities

Municipalities have a triple role to play within the long-term care system. First, as insurers of the LTCI scheme, municipalities bear responsibility for its administration. Their performance as far as administrative duties are concerned—such as collection of contributions, assessment of individuals' degree of

Table 5. Proportion of Services Provided by Different Types of Care Agencies, September 2000

	Public sector (%)	Nonprofit and cooperative sector (%)					Commercial sector (%)	Others (%)	Total (%)
	Prefecture and municipality	Quasi-governmental body and social insurance organization	Social Welfare Corporation	Medical Corporation	NPO Corporation	Cooperative	Private enterprise		
Number of agencies and institutions									
Homecare service agencies	6.6	0.0	43.2	10.4	2.1	4.6	30.3	2.7	100.0
Visiting nurse stations	5.1	3.3	10.4	53.3	0.3	4.3	6.0	17.3	100.0
Daycare centers	22.2	0.0	66.0	4.2	1.3	1.1	4.5	0.7	100.0
Group homes for people with dementia	3.6	—	37.5	31.1	5.5	0.3	21.2	0.9	100.0
Care management agencies	11.9	0.3	35.0	25.1	0.9	3.3	18.1	5.5	100.0
Special care homes for the aged	12.7	0.1	87.2	—	—	—	—	—	100.0
Geriatric healthcare facilities	5.5	2.1	15.8	73.0	—	—	—	3.6	100.0
Long-term care geriatric hospitals	4.2	1.2	—	70.7	—	—	—	24.0	100.0

Amount of services									
Homecare services[a]	7.7	0.0	50.1	6.3	1.6	3.4	25.7	5.2	100.0
Visiting nurse services[a]	4.6	3.8	9.9	49.1	0.2	5.1	3.2	24.2	100.0
Daycare services[a]	21.0	0.0	71.0	3.6	0.4	0.8	2.7	0.4	100.0
Group homes for people with dementia[a]	3.0	—	41.2	33.1	4.1	—	18.2	0.5	100.0
Special care homes for the	13.7	0.2	86.2	—	—	—	—	—	100.0
Geriatric healthcare facilities[b]	4.5	2.0	16.3	73.4	—	—	—	3.7	100.0
Long-term care geriatric hospitals[b]	2.3	1.1	—	80.5	—	—	—	16.0	100.0

[a]Service users (total number of visits or attendances), [b]Number of places. Calculated from tables in *Heisei 12nen kaigo saabisu shisetsu jigyoshos chosa* [2000 Survey of long-term care institutions and agencies by Kosei-rodosho Tokeijohobu [Ministry of Health, Labor, and Welfare, Division of Statistics and Information], 2002.

dependence, and payment of benefits—is generally highly regarded, although, in the first few months there was some confusion as to handling of the claims and payments.

Municipalities have little discretion as to the scope of these administrative duties. However, they are allowed to introduce "special benefits" such as the provision of diapers, meal services, or transportation services in addition to standard types of services (as shown in Table 2). Municipalities also are allowed to raise the benefits cap beyond the standard amounts (as shown in Table 3) as they deem appropriate. All additional costs incurred by these changes must be born by type I insured. Because of this arrangement, only a few municipalities have introduced special benefits or raised the upper limit of benefits. According to Hiraoka and colleagues' (2002) survey of municipalities in urban areas, only 2.3 percent have introduced special benefits, and 0.6 percent have raised the upper limit of benefits.

Second, municipalities also assume the role of provider of long-term care services. This role had already diminished substantially before the inception of the LTCI scheme. As of October 1, 1999, 92.7 percent of special care homes for the aged were run by nonprofit agencies (Koseisho, 2000a). As of March 31, 1999, less than 10 percent of home helpers were employed by municipalities (Koseisho, 2000b). The introduction of LTCI accelerated the shrinkage of this role.

Third, municipalities have been entrusted with a range of new duties as "enablers" of long-term care services. Given the basic principle of the LTCI scheme that service utilization is based on the contract between users and service providers, the most important of these new duties may be those concerned with protection of users' rights and in providing quality assurance.

Our survey of municipalities in urban areas showed that most had provided information on local service providers to those insured by distributing leaflets or through other means. In addition, most had introduced a system for accepting and resolving complaints and had organized care agencies or care management agencies. About three fourths had already conducted a survey of users to ascertain their level of satisfaction with the quality of services. However, only 5.1 percent of the municipalities had introduced a system of service evaluation (Hiraoka, Takegawa, Takechi, Fujimura, Shizume, and Tsukahara, 2002).

Assessment of the Degree of Dependence

In October 1999, when the LTCI scheme began assessing insured elders for their degree of dependence in order to determine benefits, the media criticized the effort for alleged deficiencies of the first-stage assessment procedures, which involved computer-aided assessment. This procedure was developed by a group of researchers in collaboration with the MHW in the mid-1990s using data from a large-scale study of caregiving in care facilities. The computer-assisted assessment procedure classifies applicants into seven grades based on the estimated time needed for providing care to them in long-term care facilities.

In the author's view, the validity, fairness, and transparency of the assessment process was considerably improved as compared with the system that had existed before the start of LTCI, which depended heavily on discretionary judgments of municipality officers. However, it is certainly true that this procedure needs further refinement. In particular, the time that family caregivers spend looking after older adults with dementia—which does not include time spent on physical care—was appreciably undervalued. In response to such criticism, the MHLW made minor revisions to the procedure, with revised procedures implemented in April 2003.

Care Management

The introduction of care management for all service users signified a major advance in the long-term care system in Japan. Judging from the results of user satisfaction surveys, the majority of users of long-term care services are satisfied with their quality (Hiraoka, Takegawa, Nakatani, Fujimura, Shizume, and Tsukahara, 2003). However, from the viewpoint of professionals and researchers, the present system of care management needs further improvement. The amount of remuneration for care management was established on the assumption that each care manager has a caseload of approximately 50 individuals. In fact, many care managers consider their caseloads too heavy and complain that they are forced to spend too much time on benefits management and other administrative tasks.[10] In addition, many critics have pointed out that the knowledge and skills of care managers are sometimes inadequate.

A third criticism has been that care managers are not guaranteed to be neutral in their choice of service agencies. A considerable proportion of them are employed by organizations that also provide community-care or institutional care services.

Cooperation and Coordination Between the Health and Welfare Sectors

As a result of the establishment of LTCI, substantial improvements have been made in the levels of cooperation and coordination between the health and welfare sectors. The LTCI scheme has unified admission criteria for the three types of care facilities (special care homes for the aged, geriatric healthcare facilities, and long-term care geriatric hospitals). Additionally, care management agencies now function as a single point of entry to various types of long-term care services,

[10] Starting in April 2003, the amount of remuneration for care management was considerably upgraded, which may result in a decrease in the number of caseloads that each care manager has.

and every service user now receives an integrated care plan that covers both health and welfare services.

However, several problems remain unresolved. First, proper division of functions among the three types of care facilities mentioned above is not easy to achieve because the geographic distribution of these three types is often uneven. Second, significant numbers of care managers are unable to coordinate services properly among different care agencies due to excessive caseloads or a lack of appropriate knowledge and skills. The increase in the number of care agencies and the diversification of the independent sector have made the care manager's task of coordination more complex and time consuming. Third, because of the inadequate level of community-care services and the shortage of beds in special care homes for the aged, the problem of social hospitalization remains unsolved.

Measures for Low-Income Households

As is apparent, the government has taken several measures to ease the burden that contributions and user charges place on low-income households. Whether these measures are enough is currently in dispute. The results of our survey in the Sumida Ward of Tokyo suggest that the proportion of respondents who stated that they did not use their full allocation of community-care services due to difficulties in paying for user charges was considerably higher among low-income households (Hiraoka, Takegawa, Nakatani, Fujimura, Shizume, and Tsukahara, 2003).

In addition to measures taken by the central government, as of April 2002, 13 percent of all municipalities had instituted additional efforts for reducing insurance contributions or exempting certain individuals from them. Similarly, 26 percent of the municipalities have instituted steps to reduce user charges or provide exemptions.

Financing the LTCI Scheme

Fundamental to the future of the LTCI program is the question of whether the present system of financing will be sustainable in the long run. Increasing utilization of community-care services presents one noticeable threat. In 1996, the Council on Health and Welfare for the Elderly estimated that the average ratio of benefits used to the upper limit of benefits allocated to each individual would rise from 40 percent in 2000 to 80 percent in 2010, and that, with such increases in service utilization, the total amount of service expenses (the sum of benefits and user charges) would increase from ¥4.8 trillion to ¥10.0 trillion.

In April 2003, municipalities all over Japan revised the copayment schedule for individual insurance contributions. It is estimated that the national average of monthly insurance contributions for type I insured (those ages 65 and older) increased from ¥2,911 to ¥3,241 (an increase of 11.3 percent), and those for type II insured rose from ¥2,918 to ¥3,043 (an increase of 4.3 percent).

It is generally believed that, given the financial capacity of elderly households, the amount of insurance contributions for type I insured will reach its practical limit in the near future. Under such circumstances, if neither an increase in user charges nor a reduction in the benefits cap is undesirable or politically risky, one possible solution to the financing crisis is to lower the age limit of type II insured from 40 to 30 or even 20.

CONCLUSIONS

As of April 2003, three years have already passed since the introduction of the LTCI scheme. It is safe to say that this new initiative has been firmly established in Japan as an integral part of its system of social security, even if financing is not entirely secure.

More and more Japanese have come to think that long-term care services will be an essential element in their lives in their later years. Such an attitude was inconceivable to most Japanese before the start of the Gold Plan in 1989. As far as the administrative aspects of its system are concerned, the performance of LTCI seems satisfactory. In addition, there has been a substantial increase in the amount of community-care services available to elders. The expansion and diversification of the private sector has been realized as was intended by the government.

However, it is becoming clearer with the passage of time that a national long-term care insurance scheme cannot be the final solution to vicissitudes of long-term care, as some of its enthusiastic supporters claimed in the policy debates of the 1990s. Demand for institutional care services seems to have increased at a higher rate than the demand for community-care services. Convincing evidence exists that the use of community-care services has not relieved families' care-giving burden as markedly as was expected (Hiraoka, Takegawa, Nakatani, Fujimura, Shizume, and Tsukahara, 2003; Kondo, 2002). On the one hand, the LTCI scheme has enabled frail older individuals in the upper- and middle-income strata to use long-term care services at lower rates. On the other hand, the new scheme has raised the financial burden imposed upon some lower-income elders. Moreover, the long-term financial sustainability of LTCI is in question.

However, it should be recognized that, even within the present framework of the LTCI scheme, there is still ample opportunity for additional initiatives to improve the quality of care management and care services and to improve cooperation and coordination among caregiving agencies. The government, having recognized the need to improve the capacity of care managers, has implemented national programs to train and support them. In addition, the quality of services can be improved if the government takes additional measures to improve the system of training care workers and if it requires service providers to employ sufficiently trained workers. Furthermore, by establishing a system of quality assurance for the services that each agency provides, and by offering the findings of quality-assurance reviews to service users, the government will ensure that each service user can choose among service providers based on more adequate and objective information.

It seems that, under these circumstances, policymakers in Japan are faced with the dual task: to improve the present LTCI initiative while exploring the possibility of introducing a new system of financing and service provision that will not only be sustainable in the long run, but also will foster development of community care comparable to that identified with Scandinavian countries.

REFERENCES

Campbell, R. (1984). Nursing homes and long-term care in Japan. *Pacific Affairs, 57,* 78–89.

Eto, M. (2000). The establishment of the Long-Term Care Insurance. In H. Otake (Ed.), *Power shuffles and policy process: Coalition government in Japan in the 1990s* (pp. 21–50). Tokyo: Japan Center for International Exchange.

Eto, M. (2001). Public involvement in social policy reform: Seen from the perspectives of Japan's elderly-care insurance scheme. *Journal of Social Policy, 30*(1), 17–36.

Hiraoka, K. (2001). Long-term care insurance and the welfare mix in Japan. *Ochanomizu University Studies in Arts and Culture, 54,* 133–147.

Hiraoka, K., Takegawa, S., Takechi, H., Fujimura, M., Shizume, M., and Tsukahara, Y. (2002). *Kaigo saabisu kyokyu sisutemu saihensei no seika ni lansuru hyoka kenkyu: Heisei13-nendo sokatsu-buntan hokokusho* [A study on the effects of the reorganization of the system of long-term care services: 2001 report]. Tokyo: Ochanomizu University, Department of Sociology.

Hiraoka, K., Takegawa, S., Nakatani, H., Fujimura, M., Shizume, M., and Tsukahara, Y. (2003). *Kaigo saabisu kyokyu sisutemu saihensei no seika ni kansuru hyoka kenkyu: Heisei14-nendo sokatsu-buntan hokokusho* [A study on the effects of the reorganization of the system of long-term care services: 2002 report]. Tokyo: Ochanomizu University, Department of Sociology.

Kondo, K. (2002). Kaigo hoken seisaku donyu no inpakuto 2: kaigosha eno shukanteki shakudo eno inpakuto [Impact of the establishment of the Long-Term Care Insurance scheme 2: Impact on the subjective scales]. In Nihon Fukushi Daigaku CCP Kenkyukai [CCP Research Group of Nihon Fukushi University] (Ed.), *Kiso jichitai ni okeru kaigo hoken seido no koritsuteki unyo to seisaku sentaku no hyoka kijun ni kansuru kenkyu heise 11-13 nendo hokokusho* (pp. 83–90). Mihama, Aichi, Japan: Nihon Fukushi University, CCP Research Group.

Korei Shakai Fukushi Vijon Kondan-kai [Welfare Vision Discussion Group]. (1994). *21-seiki fukushi vijon: Shoshi korei shakai ni mukete* [A welfare vision for the 21st century: Toward a low-fertility and aged society]. Tokyo: Koseisho [Ministry of Health and Welfare].

Koseisho [Ministry of Health and Welfare]. (2000a). *Shakai fukushi shisetsu-to chosa hokoku 1999* [Report of national survey of social welfare institutions, 1999]. Tokyo: Kosei Tokei Kyokai [Health and Welfare Statistical Association].

Koseisho [Ministry of Health and Welfare]. (2000b). *Shakai fukushi gyosei gyomu hokoku 1998* [Report of social welfare administration, 1998]. Tokyo: Kosei Tokei Kyokai [Health and Welfare Statistical Association].

Kosei-rodosho [Ministry of Health, Labor, and Welfare]. (2002). *Kaigo kyufu-hi jittai chosa geppo heisei 14 nen 5 gatsu-sinsa-bun* [Provisional report of the LTCI benefit expenditure, May 2002]. Tokyo: Author.

Kosei-rodosho [Ministry of Health, Labor, and Welfare]. (2003). *Kaigo hoken jigyo jokyo hokoku (zantei) heisei 15 nen 2 gatsu-bun* [Provisional report of the LTCI implementation, February 2003]. Tokyo: Author.

Kosei Tokei Kyokai [Health and Welfare Statistical Association]. (1999). *Kokumin eisei no doko* [Trends of national health]. Tokyo: Author.

Kosei Tokei Kyokai [Health and Welfare Statistical Association]. (2001). *Kokumin no fukushi no doko* [Trends of national welfare]. Tokyo: Author.

Kyogoku, T. (1997). *Kaigo hoken no senryaku.* [Strategies of the Long-Term Care Insurance scheme]. Tokyo: Chuo Hoki Shuppan.

Le Grand, J., and Bartlett, W. I. (1993). *Quasi-markets and social policy.* London: Macmillan Press.

Masuda, M. (2001). Kaigo hoken no seisaku keisei katei no tokucho to kadai [Characteristics and issues of the policymaking process for the Long-Term Care Insurance system]. *Kikan Shaki Hosho Kenkyu* [The Quarterly of Social Security Research], *37*(1), 44–58.

Shimizu, Y., and Wake, J. (1994). Japan. In J. I. Kosberg (Ed.), *International handbook on services for the elderly* (pp. 227–243). Westport, Connecticut: Greenwood Press.

Steslicke, W. F. (1984). Medical care for Japan's aging population: An introduction. *Pacific Affairs, 57,* 45–52.

Takagi, Y. (1993). Reinforced care capacity in geriatric hospitals and changes in costs and manpower. *Review of Social Policy, 3,* 1–17.

Yoshihara, M. (1997). Kouteki kaigo hoken kosou o meguru seiji katei to non ajenda [Political process and non-agenda in the process of planning the public Long-Term Care Insurance program]. *Shakai Mondai Kenkyu* [Studies on the Social Problems], *46*(2), 71–95.

CHAPTER FIFTEEN

Healthcare and Long-Term Care Financing in Singapore

Kai Hong Phua

Financing care for older adults has surfaced as a critical issue in many Asian countries experiencing rapid population aging. Rapid demographic and epidemiological transitions across the continent have tremendous implications for the future employment, financial security, and care of the aged. Such population aging is expected to result in increased need for long-term care services and in intensifying demand and expenditure for healthcare. Therefore, many countries are finding it necessary to develop appropriate, cost-effective services for their growing older adult populations. The need for bold and innovative approaches to the organization and financing of healthcare and long-term care is urgent.

Two decades ago, Singapore began to recognize the impact an aging population would have on its society. Following its philosophy of visionary planning, the government responded by setting up an Inter-Ministerial Population Committee in 1984 and, four years later, forming a National Advisory Council on the Aged to undertake a comprehensive review of the status of older adults in Singapore. One of the key recommendations proposed by the advisory council was that a National Council on Ageing, with the character and authority of a statutory board, should be established to effectively plan and coordinate policies and programs for older adults. Other proposals included raising the retirement age from 55 to 60 to help preserve older adults' sense of worth, dignity, and financial independence; adjusting the seniority-based wage system to a performance-based model so that more older people would be employed; strengthening public education programs on aging to inculcate the right attitudes toward older people; making land available for voluntary organizations to set up homes for elders; lengthening term leases for homes; studying the feasibility of providing health and medical services for frail older adults living in their own homes; and increasing the dependency tax rebate for families who look after older people. In terms of the way Singapore had structured aged services in the past, these initiatives were indeed innovative.

The 1990s saw the development of two milestone policies implemented to deal with problems related to the social welfare and health of older people. The first, a significant piece of legislation called the Maintenance of Parents Act, was introduced in 1994 after much deliberation by various constituencies leading up to its consideration by a Parliamentary Select Committee. The policy imposed a legal obligation on children to support their parents. Such social policy, unique to Asia, is intended to preclude neglect of elderly parents. In 1996, amendments to the Women's Charter (the 1967 parliamentary act that established women's rights) provided channels for elderly parents to exercise legal action if they found themselves victims of physical, mental, or psychological abuse from their children.

The second policy, which covered medical care for the terminally ill, was implemented in 1996. Under the Advanced Medical Directive Act, individuals who have been medically certified to be brain-dead can now be relieved of life support if they had signed an advance directive beforehand. Such a progressive policy reduces unnecessary suffering for both terminally ill older adults and their families. As importantly, however, is the fact that it signals a new mindset in Singapore.

Singapore's national aging policy has taken shape through several successive rounds of policy review. The policy formation process as it plays out in Singapore has revealed two distinct characteristics. First, the various committees involved in policy development and review have had the benefit of representation from various constituencies, allowing the committees to receive diverse inputs and formulate implementable decisions. Historically, cross-sector representation has worked well in local contexts and is a standard attribute of the national government's problem-solving approach. Second, the committees were given much publicity and visibility. Public awareness of the issues was thereby heightened, especially when the committees offered controversial recommendations. The public's enhanced discussion of aging-policy changes has resulted in an increasing emphasis on the social care of older adults in Singapore. Public input thus has become an important consideration in the committees' deliberations. The most recent Inter-Ministerial Committee on the Ageing Population, formed in 1998, has revisited many of the earlier recommendations of various committees on aging matters and proposed a more coordinated, comprehensive plan to deal with challenges presented by Singapore's aging population.

FUNDING SERVICES FOR OLDER ADULTS

In terms of funding services for older adults, as well as services for the general population, the state applies Western-style copayment principles wherever possible. Individual consumers or their families are expected to pay a portion of the charges for services; the government subsidizes the rest. This principle applies to Medisave, a compulsory medical savings scheme administered under the rubric of the Central Provident Fund (CPF), the Singaporean social security system. As the fund is tantamount to a flexible spending plan, individuals may use their Medisave funds to pay for their own or their parents' hospitalization expenses, including expenses incurred at hospices.

A sliding-fee scale based on household income is imposed for such community-based services as home nursing, daycare, and rehabilitation services. Recipients of Public Assistance (PA), a financial scheme targeted at destitute, frail, and disabled elderly and disbursed by the Ministry of Community Development, are entitled to free medical service at government polyclinics, one-stop medical centers providing a wide range of medical, dental, and mental health care. All Singaporeans ages 60 and older are entitled to a subsidy of 50 percent off polyclinic fees.

The Medisave scheme for basic healthcare coverage is augmented by a voluntary backup MediShield insurance scheme to cover catastrophic conditions. For the needy and indigent without adequate Medisave or MediShield funds, public subsidies are complemented from a medical endowment fund known as Medifund. Together, these three programs are labeled as the 3-M healthcare financing system (Phua, 1997).

FINANCIAL SECURITY AND CARE OF THE ELDERLY

Many surveys of older adults have implied that most are in favor of raising the retirement age (Ministry of Social Affairs, 1983). The principal reasons that older survey respondents gave for withdrawing from the labor force were adequacy of financial support or ill health. The 1995 National Survey of Senior Citizens in Singapore found that financial problems and boredom were cited as major concerns during retirement. According to survey results, 2.1 percent of the older respondents found their incomes inadequate for their expenses either due to the high cost of living (57.7 percent of this cohort) or to high medical costs (16.5 percent) (Ministry of Health, 1996). Some 9.4 percent of respondents also cited high medical costs as contributing to their feelings of financial insecurity. Prolonging work life by postponing retirement should not only alleviate some of these problems but also should maximize elders' productive capacity while taking advantage of the experience of older workers. It also would increase older adults' financial and social independence and provide them with the economic means to lead an active, healthy life in the community. As improvements in life expectancy continue, there will be a greater need to raise the retirement age and to extend the working life of older adults. Various forms of inducement need to be developed to encourage employers to retain older workers as active employees for as long as possible.

In Asia, only the more economically developed countries have public programs set up for the expressed objective of providing financial security in old age or in the face of permanent disability. However, several sectors of the workforce still are not covered by these formal systems: the self-employed, workers in family businesses, casual laborers, and others who do not have permanent employment. With only rare exceptions, depending on how much these types of workers save or whether they have private health insurance, they often lack financial security, which potentially could pose problems for the government in the future (Advisory Council on the Aged, 1989).

The lack of financial security among the present generation of older adults has certain implications concerning healthcare. The degree of this cohort's dependency on families and government services will continue to be high in the foreseeable future. In addition, until personal savings for old age become the norm, the present cohorts of the employed will have to shoulder the increasing costs for the support of older adults who do not have personal savings.

As is the case in many countries of the world, the healthcare needs of older adults, both those that are treated through formal health services and those that are unmet, are much greater than is typically the case for the rest of the population. Singapore expects to see a rise in the demand for healthcare, intensified by both the increasing proportion of older adults in the total population and by the aging of the older adult population itself, that is, the growing number of older adults who live long enough to be classified as old old. The elderly are particularly vulnerable to chronic debilitating diseases and severe disability and are more likely than their younger counterparts to need long-term care (World Health Organization [WHO], 1982, 1999). It thus becomes necessary to plan for appropriate levels and types of healthcare services required by older adults. Innovative approaches to the organization and financing of healthcare are urgently needed as the demand side of the equation is only going to escalate.

Even though the evidence indicates that the overall health of older people in the rapidly developing countries of Asia is generally improving, that scenario could well take a dramatic turn for the worse, even become critical, given demographic trends. However, the prevalence and severity of the reported conditions, as inventoried by WHO (1999) and other Asian governmental bodies, are uncertain for the future, since the actual epidemiology depends on lifestyle, social acceptance of disease and disability in old age, cultural adjustments to related problems revolving around such factors as nutrition, and other ancillary influences as well as medical advances (Siegel and Hoover, 1982).

In the 1995 National Survey of Senior Citizens in Singapore, approximately 7 percent of respondents ages 55 and older reported that they had been hospitalized in the preceding year. This proportion increased with age, from 5.5 percent among those ages 55–64 to 8.2 percent among those ages 65–74, and to 9.2 percent among those ages 75 and older. Nearly 30 percent of the respondents also indicated that they had been receiving regular treatment from doctors for a long-standing illness. The medical problems reported by this cohort were, in descending order, high blood pressure (52.2 percent), diabetes (31.7 percent), heart conditions (16.7 percent), rheumatism and arthritic conditions (10.9 percent), and stroke (3.0 percent) (Ministry of Health, 1996).

Several things influence elders' utilization of healthcare services and subsequent healthcare expenditures. Foremost among them, one must consider the extent of medical benefits provided by employers and whether the benefits cover retirees, pensioners, or elderly dependents of employees. The bottom line is that if older adults and their families do not have sufficient income or savings to pay for their increased medical needs—especially chronic long-term care and catastrophic illnesses—a larger public safety net will have to be laid. Rising healthcare costs will thus result in increased demand for private health insurance or increased public pressure for government subsidies and social insurance.

Meeting the costs of healthcare and hospitalization for Singapore's rising older adult population promises to be a major hurdle. Individuals ages 65 and older comprised 7 percent of the population of Singapore in 1995 but accounted for 17 percent of all hospital admissions and 19 percent of outpatient polyclinic visits. The average length of hospitalization for older adults was 11.3 days, which was substantially higher than the overall average of about 5.0 days. In addition, older adults consume a disproportionate share of healthcare services due to an increased prevalence of diseases that are chronic and more severe. As Singapore's older adult population grows, such demand-side demographic and epidemiological factors will exert economic pressures that are also likely to be aggravated by supply-side factors such as the introduction of life-sustaining but costly medical technologies. This situation calls for innovative strategies for providing older adults with cost-effective healthcare and for more sustainable methods of financing care through the old-age security system.

Singapore has responded to these impediments by enlarging the scope of mandatory individual savings to cover the social objectives of providing old-age security. One of these objectives is coverage of healthcare costs, especially the high costs of hospitalization. Policymakers have determined that traditional healthcare financing through taxation or personal payments is not going to be adequate to pay for high-quality healthcare. Individual savings plans and responsibilities have had to be enforced to meet the rising costs of medical care. These considerations form the underlying basis for the National Health Plan of Singapore, formulated in 1983. Its key element, the Medisave scheme, imposed compulsory savings and restructured existing arrangements for financing medical care. The main objectives of the National Health Plan are to secure a healthy, fit, and productive population through disease prevention and health promotion activities, and to improve the cost efficiency of healthcare services. In addition to promoting individual responsibility for maintaining good health, the plan aims to build individuals' financial resources so that they have the means to pay for medical care during periods of illness, especially in old age.

Medisave funds also can be used to pay for the hospital expenses of immediate family members. This dovetails in with two Singaporean cultural norms: The family is seen as the basic social and economic unit of society, and care for the welfare of ill and aged members continues to be seen as first and foremost a family responsibility. The aim of the National Health Plan is to preserve certain desirable cultural values, such as filial piety, that enhance the stability of an essential societal structure amid rapid economic, social, and demographic changes. However, in cases where the entire family is unable to cover the medical expenses of its sick and elderly members, the state steps in to subsidize costs using funds from public taxes (Phua, 1986).

The findings from the 1995 National Survey of Senior Citizens in Singapore showed that Medisave has become the most important provision that older Singaporeans rely on to finance their healthcare. According to reliable estimates, Medisave funds accounted for 74.9 percent of respondents' healthcare financing provisions. More than half (55 percent) of the respondents ages 55 and older depended on their children's Medisave accounts to cover their medical expenses; 17.9 percent depended on their own and 2 percent on their spouse's Medisave. Overall, older claimants tended to rely more on their children's Medisave than on their own. Proportionately more women (65 percent) depended on their children's Medisave than did men (43.8 percent). Since men were likely to have accumulated more money in their Medisave account during their working years, the proportion of men (30.1 percent) depending on their own Medisave for financing their healthcare was higher than that of women (6.9 percent). However, a small group (7.9 percent) of older respondents reported that they had not made any financial provisions for healthcare. Nearly 42 percent of this group indicated that they were not able to do so because of unemployment or low income, and another 42 percent had not done so because they felt that they could rely on their children to pay their medical bills (Ministry of Health, 1996).

Singapore has sought to meet rising demand for healthcare services and expenditures through implementation of social policies that balance supply and demand factors in the health sector. On the supply side, by engaging in manpower and facilities planning, and on the demand side, by mobilizing individual savings, steps are being taken to ramp up the ability of healthcare providers to meet the escalating demand for healthcare. Demand also has been rationed implicitly by augmenting consumer purchasing power. The need to balance supply and demand is felt acutely in Singapore, where rising expectations for higher quality healthcare have surfaced with growing affluence (Phua, 1987a, 1987b).

In anticipation of future demands presented by population aging, a Committee on the Problems of the Aged, chaired by the Minister of Health, was convened in 1983 "to recommend measures to prevent, ameliorate, or deal with such problems." Among the recommendations made in its 1984 report, the committee called for development of a national policy for the elderly to address employment, financial security, health and recreational needs, social services, institutional care, and family relations (Ministry of Health, 1984). The Advisory Council on the Aged (1989) subsequently released a report recommending development of community-based programs for health promotion, disease prevention, and rehabilitative and social support for the elderly. Concomitant with the release of the council's recommendations were other related developments such as the implementation of the National Health Plan and the 3-M financing system. These national programs reflected an integrated, consistent policy of ensuring that savings through the CPF would form the backbone for viable long-term financing of healthcare for older Singaporeans.

The 1999 *Inter-Ministerial Committee Report on Health Care for the Elderly* concluded that the most viable option for future of long-term care financing should be along the lines of the MediShield scheme. Like MediShield, the prospective Long-Term Care Insurance Scheme, also known as "ElderShield," was slated to be voluntary, with automatic enrollment for all Singaporeans but ensuring optional withdrawal. In addition, deductibles and coinsurance were to be built into the scheme to discourage overuse of services and unnecessary procedures. The latest Inter-Ministerial Committee on the Ageing Population has also supported the establishment of additional financing for long-term care, which the committee calls "step-down care." Step-down care refers to healthcare provided to elders who have been discharged from the hospital but require continuing intermediate care to successfully return to the community (Appendixes A and B). Proposed financing strategies included the introduction of an insurance scheme to help individuals and families defray the high costs of step-down care required by those few elderly who were stricken by severe functional disabilities. In many parts of the world, step-down services are known as palliative or rehabilitative care, but in all instances the goal is to facilitate return to the best possible level of functioning. The same report called for consideration of capital funding for voluntary welfare organizations (VWOs) to build step-down care facilities, a means test to channel government subsidies for step-down care to those patients in greatest need, and government subvention to cover home medical care and home nursing services. The details of the financing proposals are being evaluated by governmental representatives at the time of this writing, especially insofar as they entail significant financial obligations for the government.

CURRENT HEALTHCARE FINANCING ARRANGEMENTS

The healthcare financing system in Singapore emphasizes personal responsibility and family support; as was intimated above, yet the community and the national government help the indigent and poor who cannot afford to pay for their basic healthcare needs. Current schemes for financing elder care adopt very much the same principle (Table 1).

Table 1. Sources of Funding for Elder Care

Individuals and families	Direct payment
	Medisave (medical savings scheme linked to CPF accounts)
	MediShield (catastrophic illness coverage, whose premiums are payable from Medisave)
	Private supplemental insurance
Community	Financial assistance provided by VWOs and community development councils
Government	Subsidies and subventions for public-sector health services
	Medifund (endowment fund for the poor and indigent who have no family support)

The current system of subsidies serves to ensure that lower-income and middle-income elders have access to affordable healthcare. In the public hospitals, the subsidies range from 20 percent to 80 percent of fees charged, depending on the class of ward providing the care. In government polyclinics, older patients pay only nominal fees; on average, the government provides a 75 percent subsidy. It is expected that with Medisave funds and Medisave coverage, which the majority of adults now have, future generations of older adults will have sufficient financial resources to meet their expenses for acute care. For those who do not have sufficient Medisave funds, MediShield coverage, or family support, public welfare in the form of the Medifund and other alternative forms of financial assistance or charity must suffice.

At the time of this writing, there is presently no comprehensive system for financing long-term care in Singapore. In recent years Medisave has been revised and extended to provide fairly limited coverage for selected forms of long-term care, such as nonacute inpatient care in community hospitals, hospices, and rehabilitative services provided by the Home Nursing Foundation, but an inclusive program has yet to be implemented. Currently, therefore, financing and subsidies for long-term care derives from the following patchwork of sources:

- Direct payment from individuals and families
- Community assistance from VWOs, accumulated through fund-raising activities available to cover up to 50 percent or more of recurring expenditures)
- Government funding through subventions and grants to VWOs: capital funding (up to 90 percent of capital costs) and recurrent funding (up to 50 percent of government cost norms and 75 percent for Public Assistance cases)

Current Methods of Financing Acute Care

The 3-M financing system provides coverage for costly hospitalization and restricted coverage for outpatient procedures, including select forms of nonacute care in community hospitals and hospices as well as some rehabilitative care. Most types of long-term care, other than some forms of rehabilitation and post-hospitalization follow-up services, are excluded. Medisave withdrawals are limited to a maximum of SN$300 per day of hospital stay and up to the capitation level of approved costs as set by the government for the type of procedure performed. These ceilings have not been adjusted despite several revisions in hospital fees. Due to the fixed limits, increasingly larger amounts of medical expenses will have to be paid out-of-pocket.

Individuals are allowed to voluntarily opt out of MediShield. This option allows an element of choice for those who may have alternative coverage or those who may not be able to afford the MediShield premiums, which are risk adjusted according to age. No doubt this may place older cohorts at a disadvantage, but poor older adults who are uninsured for catastrophic illnesses can still rely on Medifund as a last resort. In 1996, the Ministry of Trade and Industry's Cost Review Committee became concerned that one in four older Singaporeans over the age of 60 had opted out of MediShield. Since this group is more likely than younger cohorts to require healthcare, the committee noted that such high opt-out rates were undesirable.

Certain segments of the population are currently excluded from the Medisave and MediShield schemes, such as retired older adults and especially housewives or those who work outside of the sphere of formal wage employment. Due to stringent requirements, these indigent groups may not qualify for Medifund coverage and must therefore depend on other forms of financial assistance to receive health services.

Financing Long-Term Care

There is a dearth of statistics providing insight into the types and quality of informal care provided to older Singaporeans in their own homes. It is not inconceivable that most of the care is performed by untrained relatives and domestic help. Lower-income families who cannot afford household help may be hard-pressed to provide even reasonable care for their elderly. Since the current 3-M financing system only covers hospitalization, there can be a perverse incentive to hospitalize elders. The present hospital subsidy system may also explain the longer average lengths of stay observed in groups unable to cover the costs of alternative provisions that remain in palliative wards in lieu of going without medical attention.

If a voluntary long-term care insurance scheme is instituted, there is a modicum of concern that the number and proportion of those who opt out could mirror what is seen with MediShield. Of greater concern is the large number of young people who have opted out of MediShield despite their relatively less costly age-adjusted premiums. Differential premiums are justified as it would be unfair for those remaining in the lower risk pool to bear the burden of carrying the risks of the elderly, especially if those who have opted out and have not contributed earlier are allowed to claim benefits later without penalty.

The introduction of more inclusive insurance and third-party coverage of various sorts could potentially pose moral hazards involving excessive consumption and abuse on both the demand and supply sides of services. Because long-term care is not well defined and can involve multiple providers and settings, there is greater room for overlap of services and disputes among consumers, healthcare providers, and insurance administrators. Preventing fraud would involve more auditing and more administrative oversight, resulting in higher transaction costs. In addition, the availability of new financing for long-term care could have an inflationary effect on the costs of covered services, resulting in differential price increases. Similarly, equity issues concerning access to more costly care could surface, as was the case when higher fee schedules were implemented in restructured hospitals following the introduction of Medisave. As governmental subsidies became available, fees increased, as frequently appears to happen whenever publicly funded payments are implemented.

Report of the Inter-Ministerial Committee on Healthcare for the Elderly

As reprinted in Appendix A, the Inter-Ministerial Committee (IMC) on Health Care for the Elderly has recommended that VWOs expand the scope of individuals served beyond their traditional clientele of low-income elderly to include middle-income elderly, whom they could charge for services. However, to do so the VWOs would also have to raise substantially more funds to cover the increased volume of patients and to improve the quality of care provided if they are to attract higher-income individuals and families. Currently, most VWOs are able to solicit between 20 percent and 50 percent of their operating expenditures through voluntary contributions from the private sector. It is problematic whether they would be able to maintain higher-level fund-raising into the future.

At present, the Singapore government may provide funding for up to 90 percent of the capital costs, but does not differentiate between the types of institutional residential care, such as quality of amenities or level of comfort in the actual facilities. The IMC's recommendation to fund such services on a "cost per bed" basis also does not take into consideration special requirements and needs of different service levels to be provided. Government funding for recurring costs also neglects to specifically differentiate the case mix of patients or such factors as age, gender, severity of disease, and compounding conditions. One recommendation is that it may be desirable to target limited government subsidies to those with greatest need and to have a more refined subvention formula that could balance affordability figures for patients and families. Clearly, there are demonstrable difficulties in administering a means test to differentiate who should receive subsidized services. An obvious question is whether the test should be based on personal or household income. Should other financial assets and sources of support be taken into account? Since subventions for home medical care and home nursing care are not yet available, there still exist mixed incentives to institutionalize patients who otherwise could be served more cost effectively in their own homes. Private contractors able to provide residential healthcare are not yet widespread due to a lack of financial incentives and problems in obtaining suitable premises and in recruiting staff. Land and rental costs are also quite prohibitive, and labor costs for specialized and trained personnel are high compared to any possible fee structure that might be put in place.

Resource Allocation

Singapore has enjoyed a lower rate of growth in healthcare spending relative to gross national product than in other countries in Asia and throughout much of the world. There appears to be reasonable consensus among relevant decision-makers that the country's 3-M healthcare financing system has contributed to more effective healthcare spending by reducing unnecessary consumption of services and by streamlining the process. In essence, Medisave provides an additional source of personal financing for medical expenditures. Since the public thus assumes a greater share of healthcare costs, tax revenues can be redirected to meet other priorities and to contribute to a better targeting of subsidized health services.

Not surprisingly, such a cost-sharing plan may also help control demand for healthcare services. Under the Medisave scheme, payment for healthcare is made at the point of consumption. This tangible nexus between payment and utilization is intended to reflect real costs of healthcare, thereby preventing overutilization. Medisave also helps accommodate consumer preferences regarding the level of care provided at public and private hospitals. The scheme can therefore be used to provide complete coverage for lower-cost wards and facilities providing only the basic essential services or to subsidize more expensive wards within certain limits reimbursed from selected nongovernmental resources.

Through Medisave, reimbursement for private hospitalization is pegged to rates set by the more pervasive public hospital sector, which is itself subject to strong budgetary controls through governmental oversight. With the imposition of limits on daily charges and on the types of procedures performed at private hospitals, abuses can be prevented, avoiding excessive Medisave claims. However, with such price caps in place, might there also be added incentive on the part of providers to increase the volume or lower the quality of the services provided? Medisave withdrawal limits also may need to be adjusted periodically to reflect rising costs; otherwise, the balance will have to come increasingly from out-of-pocket payments, which will primarily burden lower-income individuals. Similarly, withdrawal limits may be adjusted to take into consideration the higher differential costs of medical care for the elderly. Further fine-tuning and revisions could also be affected in order to improve reimbursement procedures as they evolve out of individual facilities. In particular, attention might profitably be directed to the introduction of case-mix funding or diagnosis-related-group-type payments and fee schedules based on relative-value scales for healthcare providers. Such reformulations in the way payment is made will help offset the problem of "balance-billing" (i.e., charges assessed in addition to the set rates), and preclude such a procedure from becoming serious.

Financial Burden

Additional recommendations for healthcare reform must also take financial onus into consideration. Although it may not be particularly innovative, there is a straightforward resolution available that would help place the obligation on those who are utilizing healthcare services. Unlike social insurance and tax-based financing, a savings approach to cover long-term care for the elderly would not place an unduly heavy burden on the disproportionately decreasing number of younger, productive members of society, and would free public expenditure for such care from the vagaries of economic cycles. Under this prospective system, the present generation of wage earners is obliged to save for the future, instead of relying on the uncertain taxes of the next generation to help provide support to them in later life. This paradigm is in line with the Singapore government's policy of promoting financial independence among the aged even as their medical needs are expected to increase in the years ahead. However, the introduction of a long-term care savings scheme in addition to the existing Medisave and MediShield programs would also mean that both employees and employers would have to be squeezed hard to make contributions to this new plan on top of rising wage costs, subtracting from private incomes and profits. In addition, the present cohort of wage earners could be doubly affected by such a scheme, since they not only have to save for their own old age but also have to provide for their elderly dependents, who do not have substantial savings (Phua, 1987a).

FUTURE FINANCING OPTIONS

Given the still-popular and traditionalist assumption in Singapore that the family is the primary source of care for older adults and that the state provides a safety net only as a last resort, even if a long-term care savings plan were introduced many people would refuse to recognize the need to personally save for their old age. Besides, when faced with unpleasant possibilities such as catastrophic illness and long-term debilitating conditions, denial is a common response in almost all cultures. Unless steps are taken to increase public awareness of the costs of elder care, the probability of people opting out of any new long-term care insurance scheme remains fairly high. Perhaps the government should also mandate that participants could begin contributing the moment they start working so that they only need to pay low monthly premiums.

Since most caregivers are female, women tend to sacrifice their financial independence, losing out in terms of paid employment, in order to fulfill their unpaid familial obligations as housewives or caregivers. Therefore, those who do not work for pay outside the home and certain others, such as women who stay at home, should be encouraged to join a medical savings plan through being allowed to pay lower premiums or use their spouses' incomes to contribute. As these women will form a large proportion of the future older adult population, it makes sense for them to start saving long before they reach old age or before their spouses die.

In view of projected demographic, epidemiological, social, and economic trends facing Singapore, existing tax-based healthcare financing would have to support the growing needs implied by these trends. The Singapore model attempts to avoid the problems of increasing the tax burden on the productive—both employers and employees—while not subjecting social expenditure to the vagaries of economic cycles. Present generations of younger wage earners are mandated to save for their own inevitable healthcare needs in old age, instead of relying on the uncertain taxes of future generations. By implementing such a multilayered healthcare and long-term care financing system, together with varying levels of cost sharing and subsidies in a public-private mix of health services, it is hoped that the economy of Singapore will be able to withstand the increasing burden of healthcare costs even as the country provides a sustainable degree of social security for its aging population (Phua, Seow, and Lee, 1996).

Much like MediShield, which provides for optional coverage of high-cost benefits, the proposed ElderShield scheme would be integrated with Medisave and Medifund to offer more protection for care provided outside hospitals. ElderShield would be limited to provide insurance coverage only for severe disabilities, defined on the Katz index score of three or more. Thus, individuals and families would continue to share a substantial amount of the costs through Medisave for long-term care for people with mild disabilities, and MediShield insurance would continue to be specifically targeted at treating catastrophic diseases and severe disabilities.

THE WAY AHEAD

The World Bank policy research report *Averting the Old Age Crisis: Policies to Protect the Old and Promote Growth* has sounded the alarm about the potential crisis facing old-age security systems in many countries in the region. The study recommends a mix of three systems or "pillars" to support the basic functions of old-age security systems: redistribution, savings, and insurance. The first pillar is a mandatory, publicly managed, and tax-financed system; the second pillar is a mandatory, privately managed, and fully funded individual savings system; and the third pillar is a voluntary system of occupational or personal savings plans. Together, these three pillars coinsure individuals against the risks of old age without impeding economic growth in aging societies (World Bank, 1994).

Considering that individuals' healthcare needs are expected to be greater in future generations of old people, might not the same recommendations apply to the next steps in healthcare financing? The three basic functions of redistribution, savings, and insurance are just as applicable for financing healthcare as for old-age security. Even though the relative risks and uncertainties may be distinct for healthcare systems, an analogous mix of financing methods can still be recommended to offer more protection while simultaneously promoting growth. These considerations have formed the basis for the existing integrated systems of old-age security and healthcare financing in Singapore and they represent the future as well.

Commensurate innovative strategies for financing need to be explored to guarantee cost effectiveness of providing supplementary essential services for the aged, straddling the full range of diverse types and levels of long-term care in various settings (e.g., acute versus chronic care; nursing home, residential, or home-based care; and preventive, curative, and rehabilitative care). In developing multifaceted forms of care for the elderly, more economic checks and balances would inevitably be introduced in response to increasing expenditure because of the insatiable competition for scarce resources. Fiscal responsibility will need to be an integral ingredient in any proposed alternative. A related and particularly relevant component will be the introduction of acceptable methods of cost sharing or cost containment aimed at balancing supply and demand. As is the case in economically advanced portions of the world, the rapid aging of Singapore's population poses a global challenge as the 21st century unfolds. As the editors pointed out in their introduction, the same pattern holds throughout Asia. This will require bold and innovative policies, financing, and programs on healthcare, especially long-term care for the elderly.

CONCLUSION

The rapid aging of Singapore's population poses a challenge for not only Singapore, but the rest of Asia in the next millennium. The demographic transitions require policies and programs on healthcare for the elderly that are able to respond not only to their needs, but also to the higher expectations that seemingly accompany economic development. Singapore is in many respects a role model for other Asian governments in that it has undertaken advance planning on a number of fronts prior to the emergence of crisis situations brought on by desperate straits among various segments of its population. Singapore is fortunate in that its economic fortunes parallel those of its most affluent counterparts in Asia, but it has also experienced the depths of the economic downturn with the Asian bubble burst. Not to be discouraged, governmental agencies continued apace with their planning efforts so as to be ready to implement optimal changes with the economic rebound.

APPENDIX A. INTER-MINISTERIAL COMMITTEE ON AGEING POPULATION

Excerpted from Ministry of Community Development, 1999

The Inter-Ministerial Committee (IMC) on Ageing Population was formed in October 1998 to identify the challenges posed by Singapore's rapidly aging population, develop policy directions, and lead a coordinated national response to address these challenges.

The IMC on Ageing Population is chaired by the minister for national development, Mah Bow Tan, with the minister for health, Lim Hng Kiang, and the minister for community development, Abdullah Tarmugi, as deputy chairs. The IMC members comprise representatives from ministries, statutory boards, and nongovernmental agencies.

From November 1998 to February 1999, the IMC carried out a broad audit of present policies and programs concerning aging matters and older people. Various ministries, statutory boards, and service-sector organizations—elder care voluntary welfare organizations, Singapore National Employers Federation, and National Trades Union Congress—have briefed the IMC on issues such as employment, financial security, housing, transportation, social services, healthcare, and the integration of older people into society.

Minister Mah announced the formation of six IMC workgroups in March 1999 to conduct in-depth policy reviews and develop recommendations on key issues.

APPENDIX B. REPORT OF THE IMC WORKGROUP ON HEALTH CARE

Excerpted from Ministry of Health, 1999

The number of elderly Singaporeans aged 65 years and above is projected to increase from the current 7 percent to 8 percent in 2010 and 19 percent in 2030. Apart from primary care and hospital care, the needs of many elderly people would be more appropriately met by health care services delivered in "step-down" settings, such as community hospitals, nursing homes, day care and day rehabilitation centres, and home medical and nursing care. More than 90 percent of the elderly in Singapore are found to be independent and able to perform basic activities of daily living. However, it is estimated that 8 percent of the elderly will require step-down care of differing levels of intensity, of which 2.7 percent will require institutional step-down care and 5.3 percent will require community-based step-down care.

The rapid aging of the population will pose a challenge to health care planners to provide adequate health care facilities, services, and support systems. The National Health Expenditure is also expected to increase from the current level of 3 percent to 7 percent of GDP in 2030.

Needs of the Elderly

The future elderly are better educated, enjoy better health, and are financially independent. Viewed as assets, many elderly can continue to contribute to society and benefit the wider community. The National University of Singapore's Gerontology Research Programme can undertake research on future trends and needs of the elderly.

Care for the elderly should emphasize health promotion and disease prevention to enable the elderly to remain healthy and active in the community. There should be greater use of information technology to disseminate information on health promotion, disease prevention, and services.

Service Delivery

Whilst the needs of the elderly will center mainly on health and social services, policies of various ministries and organizations in areas like housing, transportation, land use, town planning, employment, and financing will have significant impact on the elderly in the community.

There is adequate networking amongst ministries and agencies. Therefore, no extra barriers or bureaucratic layers should be created between the service providers and the administering ministry as these lead to delays and inefficiencies.

Nevertheless, coordination and integration of the multiple organizations and agencies involved in elderly care are important for a seamless continuum of planning, service provision, and care to meet the needs of the elderly. The Inter-Ministerial Committee on Ageing Population is recommended to take on the role as the Central Coordinating Committee with the Elderly Development Division of the Ministry of Community Development as its operational arm to coordinate policy planning, implementation, and monitoring of programmes for the aging population.

The workgroup (WG) endorses the recommendation of the IMC on Health Care for the Elderly (IMCHE) to set up multi-service centres, integrating appropriate health, social, and other services under one roof.

It is proposed that care management services be developed further as a placement and monitoring service to assist the elderly with multiple needs.

Publicity on elderly issues should also be coordinated to reduce information overload and confusion.

The roles of voluntary welfare organizations (VWOs) and the private sector in the provision of health care services for the elderly should be defined such that the VWOs provide services for the poor and lower income groups and private operators provide services for the middle and high income groups.

The WG recommends that ministries, as regulatory authorities, set minimum output or outcome-based targets as measures of standards of care rather than stipulate fixed measures for inputs, processes, or methods to deliver the services or programmes. Service providers should also be allowed some flexibility in service delivery to achieve higher efficiency.

Service Providers

Currently, health care services for the elderly are provided by the government, VWOs, and the private sector.

The government, while continuing to be the main provider of health care services for the elderly, will also ensure that various policies, measures, and provisions to meet the varied needs of our elderly are well coordinated and effectively implemented.

The WG recommends that VWOs be encouraged to strengthen their capacities in providing services for the elderly through pooling of resources for common needs, better costing, accounting and management information systems, and colocation of common services.

Besides VWOs, the WG also recommends greater involvement of private-sector operators. The WG recommends that land should be zoned for health care purposes and commercial operators allowed to tender and develop nursing homes and other facilities. In order to remove the uncertainties inhibiting such investments and the upgrading of facilities, extended tenancy and lease terms should be given. Also, the WG recommends that Government develop nursing homes and lease them out to private operators. Similar incentives could also be given to cooperatives to enter this sector.

Manpower

The provision of health care is labour intensive and to provide better health care services, manpower is an important consideration.

The WG recommends that multi-task staff be trained in multiple areas such as nursing, rehabilitation, and care management to meet the different needs of the elderly. Since time and commitment are often problems for such staff, part-time courses could be developed to encourage staff to upgrade. Training programmes and resources of VWOs could be pooled to better optimize expertise. Training of health personnel in VWOs and commercial homes should be under the Skills Development Fund and Skills Redevelopment Programme. The WG also recommends that VWOs be networked in clusters so that experienced personnel could be tapped in the appropriate areas. General practitioners should also be encouraged to pursue geriatric training and hospital geriatricians to supervise community geriatricians to ensure continual training and skill development.

For informal carers, support services should be made more easily available. Besides enhancing the range of services, training and equipping the informal caregivers through Web pages, training courses, and seminars should be made available to them.

Financing Health Care for the Elderly

The philosophy of financing health care for the elderly in Singapore emphasizes personal responsibility and family support, with the community and the government helping the indigent and the poor who cannot afford to pay for their basic health care needs. The existing financing framework is adequate in ensuring affordable acute health care for the elderly as well as the young.

With an aging population, it is important to ensure that an equally effective financing framework for step-down care is put in place. The IMCHE has made a number of recommendations on the financing of step-down care. These include an insurance scheme to help individuals and their families defray the high costs of step-down care required by those few elderly who acquire very severe functional disabilities. Other recommendations include a review of capital funding for VWOs to build step-down care facilities, a means test to channel government subsidy for step-down care to those patients who need financial help the most, and government subvention to cover home medical care and home nursing services.

The WG on Health Care endorses the general approach as recommended by the IMCHE, and as currently being implemented by the Ministry of Health. To enhance the effectiveness of what has already been recommended, the WG recommends the following measures: (a) to accompany the launch of the insurance scheme against severe functional disabilities with a comprehensive public communications strategy; and (b) to conduct ongoing research on the aged population.

Conclusion

The rapid ageing of Singapore's population poses a challenge for our society in the next millennium. This will require policies and programmes on health care for the elderly to be able to meet their needs and higher expectations.

REFERENCES

Advisory Council on the Aged. (1989). *Report on the Advisory Council on the Aged.* Singapore: Author.

Ministry of Community Development. (1999). *Report of the Inter-Ministerial Committee on the Ageing Population, November 1999.* Singapore: Author.

Ministry of Health. (1984). *Report of the Committee on the Problems of the Aged.* Singapore: Author.

Ministry of Health. (1996). *The national survey of senior citizens in Singapore: 1995.* Singapore: Author.

Ministry of Health. (1999). *Report of the Inter-Ministerial Committee on Health Care for the Elderly.* Singapore: Author.

Ministry of Social Affairs. (1983). *Report on the national survey of senior citizens.* Singapore: Author.

Phua, K. H. (1986, May). Singapore's family savings scheme. *World Health.*

Phua, K. H. (1987a). Saving for health. *World Health Forum, 8,* 38–41.

Phua, K. H. (1987b). Ageing: Socio-economic implications for health care in Singapore. *Annals of the Academy of Medicine, 16*(1), 15–23.

Phua, K. H. (1997). Medical savings accounts and health care financing in Singapore. In G. Schieber (Ed.), *Innovations in health care financing* (World Bank Discussion Paper No. 365, pp. 247–255). Washington, DC: World Bank.

Phua, K. H., Seow, A., and Lee, H. P. (1996). Issues and challenges of public health in the 21st century in Singapore. In Y. Khairuddin, Y. L. Low, and S. N. Zulkifli (Eds.), *Issues and challenges of public health in the 21st century.* Kuala Lumpur: University of Malaya Press.

Siegel, J. S., and Hoover, S. L. (1982). Demographic aspects of health of the elderly to the year 2000 and beyond. *World Health Statistics Quarterly, 35*(3/4), 140–141.

World Bank. (1994). *Averting the old age crisis: Policies to protect the old and promote growth.* New York: Oxford University Press.

World Health Organization [WHO]. (1982). [Special issue on Public Health Implications of Ageing]. *World Health Statistics Quarterly, 35*(3/4).

WHO. (1999). *Ageing and health: A global challenge for the 21st century.* Kobe, Japan: WHO Centre for Health Development.

PART V

Community Social Services

CHAPTER SIXTEEN

Family Support and Community Services for Older Adults in China: Integration and Partnership

Joe C. B. Leung

For centuries, it has been a cherished and deep-rooted Chinese practice for the elderly to be supported by their offspring. Accordingly, formal social services for older adults were regarded as unnecessary and therefore slow to develop (Chen, 1996; Chow, 1991). Following the formation of the People's Republic of China in 1949, a comprehensive employment-based social security system covering retirement and medical care was introduced. However, the market-oriented economic reforms that began in the 1980s have rendered the traditional social welfare system, based on the work unit, increasingly inadequate and inefficient.[1] With the turn of the 21st century, China has experienced a dramatic influx of manufacturing and assembly work, and the organization of such enterprises represents a dramatic break with traditional forms of labor. In the context of a globalized economy, China is now actively in search of a pluralistic, effective, and affordable social welfare system that will be compatible with both a thriving market economy and a resilient political structure. Meanwhile, China's aging population poses formidable challenges to the government, which must find ways to meet the present and impending financial and long-term care needs of the elderly. A national network of community-based social welfare services is emerging to meet those needs, and will soon become the dominant source of social welfare for the care of older people in China.

[1] Under China's centrally planned economy which was modeled on the Soviet Union, "work units" were workplaces such as government offices and state economic enterprises. Urban residents would be assigned jobs in these units, which guaranteed lifelong employment and generous welfare benefits and services.

THE SOCIOECONOMIC TRANSFORMATION OF CHINA

Over the past two decades, China's economy has become one of the fastest growing in the world. Between 1978 and 1999, China's gross domestic product (GDP) grew at an average rate of almost 10 percent a year. Unlike many of its neighbors, China has enjoyed almost uninterrupted economic growth since the initiation of market reform in the 1980s.[2] Currently, China is the seventh largest economy in the world and ranks ninth in terms of volume of trade. While the world economy has undergone a widespread slowdown, China is still expected to benefit from an average annual growth rate of 6 to 8 percent in the coming decade. More significantly, according to a 1998 report of the World Bank, as reported in the *China Daily* (August 13, 2001), the per capita GDP of China has reached US$860. As the World Bank sets an upper threshold for low-income countries at US$785 per capita, China now ranks for the first time as a middle-income country.[3] Most notably, China has led the developing world in the use of direct foreign investment in the last decade, and the foreign exchange reserve of China has been rated second in the world after that of Japan (*People's Daily,* September 4, 2001).

In terms of the Human Development Index produced by the United Nations Development Program, in 2001 China was ranked 87th out of 162 countries—in contrast to its 1995 rank of 111th among 174 countries—despite having a per capita GDP that ranked only 94th (*The Economist,* July 14, 2001, p. 98).[4] The wages and income of peasants and urban residents have soared appreciably in the last decade.[5] Impressively, China has reduced its rural poverty-stricken population from 250 million in 1978 to only 30 million in 2000 (the poverty line is defined as an annual per capita income of RMB 625[6]) (China Internet Information Center, 2002). According to figures compiled by the State Statistical Bureau, in 2000, 14.8 million urban residents, representing 3.8 percent of the urban population, lived below the poverty line, with an average per capita annual

[2] In the 1980s and early 1990s, the average annual rate of growth for the GDP was greater than 10 percent, while the average annual population growth rate during this period was only about 1.4 percent. Thus, the per capita GDP almost quadrupled over this period (Khan and Riskin, 2001). The average annual GDP growth rate in the period between 1995 and 2000 slowed to 8.3 percent (*China Daily,* March 6, 2001).

[3] The Chinese government expects that the per capita GDP will reach US$1,140 by the year 2005 (*People's Daily,* October 19, 2001). Shanghai is performing even better than the rest of the country: In 2000, the city's per capita GDP was US$4,180, and its annual growth rate in the 1990s reached 12 percent (*People's Daily,* February 7, 2001).

[4] The Human Development Index combines three indicators of welfare: life expectancy, GDP per capita, and educational attainment.

[5] Between 1990 and 2000, average wages increased 4.4 times, net incomes of peasants 3.3 times, and disposable incomes of urban residents 4.2 times (Ministry of Civil Affairs, 2001a, p. 81).

[6] In September 2003, US$1 = RMB 8.3 (yuan).

income of RMB 2,310 (*China Civil Affairs,* 2001, vol. 8). In its 10th Five-Year Plan (2001–2005), China proclaimed that poverty alleviation is now a high priority for the national government.

Beginning in the 1980s, market-oriented economic reform focused on the deliberate liberalization of the economic structure and the enlargement of the production and management autonomy of state-owned enterprises.[7] With the introduction of a more pluralistic economy, the state sector has ceased to be the major economic force. In 1999, the state sector only contributed about 26.1 percent of China's gross industrial output value, down from 76 percent in 1980. In terms of employment, only 40.8 percent of urban employees worked in the state sector in 1999, compared to 76.2 percent in 1980 (State Statistical Bureau, 2000). Now, collectively owned enterprises (mainly owned by township governments) and privately owned enterprises (owned by individuals and foreign corporations) have become the engines of economic growth. In fact, the Chinese Communist Party announced at the 15th Party Congress in 1997 that non-state-owned enterprises are an integral part of the socialist market economy. The Chinese Constitution was amended in 1999 to recognize that privately owned enterprises can have status and treatment equal to that of state-owned enterprises.[8] The Law on Enterprises Funded Exclusively by Individuals, which came into effect in 2000, gives further incentives to private businesses. Meanwhile, the performance of state-owned enterprises has been disappointing, with mounting losses brought on first by the Asian economic crisis at the end of the 1990s and then by the increasing globalization of the economy at the start of the 21st century. Many of these state ventures are currently ridden with debt. From 1998 to 2000, state-owned business enterprises laid off a total of 23 million employees (*People's Daily,* September 24, 2001). Looking into the future, the Chinese economy will become increasingly privatized, with collectives and the private sector constituting the largest share of the economy.

Market reform has also transformed the structure of the Chinese economy. In terms of production value, the primary industries (farming and agriculture) have continued to decline in importance. In 1999, they only constituted 17.7 percent of the total output value, down from 28.4 percent in 1978 (State Statistical Bureau, 2000). Although tertiary industries (largely the service sector) have already made significant advances, their contribution to the total output value was only 33 percent in 1999, compared to 23 percent in 1978. It is envisaged that the output value of the tertiary sector will increase to 36 percent by 2005, while the primary industry will continue to decline to 13 percent (*People's Daily,* October 19, 2001).

[7] "State-owned enterprises" refers to enterprises whose entire assets, or a majority share, are completely owned by the state.

[8] The Chinese Communist Party is actively considering admitting capitalists of private enterprises as party members (*The Economist,* August 11, 2001, p. 23).

The 10th Five-Year Plan on Economic and Social Development declares that a viable social security system is the foundation for development of a socialist market economy. The government has repeatedly pledged to improve living standards and establish a sound social security system. Specifically, the state should ensure that basic living allowances for laid-off workers from state-owned enterprises and basic pensions for retirees are paid in full and on time (*China Daily,* March 6, 2001; *People's Daily,* September 25, 2000). The Chinese government is showing increasing concern for the widening income imbalances accompanying the market-oriented economic reforms (Khan and Riskin, 2001; Riskin, Zhao, and Li, 2001). In 2000, the Gini coefficient, a measure of income disparities, reached 0.397, indicating a notable gap in income levels among paid workers (*China Civil Affairs,* 2001, vol. 8). The presence of inequalities of this magnitude are widely thought to threaten social stability (*People's Daily,* March 12, 2001, and October 18, 2001; Perry and Sheldon, 2000).

One consequence of China's active population-control policy is the rapid increase in the proportion of the population classified as elderly. The low birthrates and natural growth rates that have continued for more than two decades have caused the proportion of children ages 0–14 in the national population to decline from 33.6 percent in 1982 to only 22.9 percent in 2000.[9] According to the 2000 census, the population of mainland China was 1.266 billion people at the beginning of the millennium. The average annual population increase since the 1990 census was 1.07 percent, representing approximately 12.79 million people (*People's Daily,* March 29, 2001). However, natural growth rates vary from −1.1 per 1,000 population in Shanghai, 0.9 per 1,000 population in Beijing, and 3.6 per 1,000 population in Jiangsu to 15.8 per 1,000 population in Tibet, 14.2 per 1,000 population in Guizhou, and 13.9 per 1,000 population in Qinghai (State Statistical Bureau, 2000) (Table 1). According to the 10th Five-Year Plan on Economic and Social Development, the government pledged to maintain the size of the national population within 1.33 billion people, the net increase of the population within 56 million, and the natural growth rate under 9 per 1,000 population over the coming five years (*People's Daily,* August 10, 2001).

The low death rate, meanwhile, has increased the proportion of people ages 65 and older in the national population from 4.9 percent in 1982 to 5.6 percent in 1990, and further to 6.96 percent in 2000, representing 88.11 million people. In Shanghai alone, the older adult population of the city reached 11.5 percent in 1999, representing 1.8 million people (State Council, 2001).

In a country the size of China, regional variations in population aging are substantial. In general, coastal provinces and cities have a much higher proportion of people ages 65 and older (Shanghai, 11.5 percent; Jiangsu, 8.8 percent;

[9] In 2000, the birthrate was 15.2 per 1,000 population, the death rate 6.5 per 1,000 population, and the natural growth rate 8.8 per 1,000 population. The birthrate and the natural growth rate were 33.4 per 1,000 population and 25.8 per 1,000 population respectively in 1970.

Table 1. Natural Growth Rates and Proportion of the Population Ages 65 and Older by Province, 1999

Province	Natural growth rates (per 10,000 persons)	Proportion of the elderly population (%)
Anhui	8.60	7.45
Beijing	90.00	8.36
Chongqing	4.96	7.90
Fujian	5.21	6.54
Gansu	9.17	5.00
Guangdong	9.92	6.05
Guangxi	8.03	7.12
Guizhou	14.24	5.79
Hainan	12.03	6.58
Heibi	6.73	6.86
Heilongjiang	5.06	5.42
Henan	7.72	6.96
Hubei	5.20	6.31
Hunan	4.60	7.29
Inner Mongolia	7.24	5.35
Jiangsu	3.56	8.76
Jiangxi	9.49	6.11
Jilin	5.23	5.85
Liaoning	3.33	7.83
Ningxia	12.32	4.47
Qinghai	13.90	4.33
Shaanxi	6.13	5.93
Shandong	4.81	8.03
Shanhai	–1.10	11.53
Shanxi	9.86	6.20
Sichuan	6.78	7.45
Tianjin	2.95	8.33
Tibet	15.80	4.50
Xinjiang	11.80	4.53
Yunnan	11.66	6.00
Zhejing	4.29	8.84

Source: State Statistical Bureau, 2000.

Zhejiang, 8.8 percent) than do the western provinces (Tibet, 4.5 percent; Ningxia, 4.5 percent; Xinjiang, 4.5 percent) (State Statistical Bureau, 2000). Regarding the old-age dependency ratio—the ratio of the number of people ages 65 and older to the number of people ages 15–64—the national average in 1999 was 11.15 percent, a significant increase from 9.3 percent just five years earlier (State Statistical Bureau, 2000).

Life expectancy across China currently stands at an average of 71 years: 69 years for men and 73 years for women (*China Daily,* April 1, 2001). The average annual rate of increase for the population ages 60 and older is 3 percent, which is more than three times the average rate of natural increase in the national population. For those ages 80 and older—who numbered 11 million in 2000—the average rate of increase is 5.4 percent (*China Daily,* March 1, 2001; *People's Daily,* December 14, 2000). Adults ages 65 and older will make up 9 percent of the total population by 2010 and 22.4 percent by 2050 (Zhang, 2000) (Table 2). The number of urban retirees has soared from 3 million in 1978 to 37.3 million in 1999. Likewise, expenditure on pensions jumped from RMB 5 billion in 1980 to RMB 242 billion in 1999 (State Statistical Bureau, 2000).

Being one of the most rapidly aging societies in the world, China has to face all the social and economic issues of elder care found in developed countries but must deal with numbers that are far greater. Yet its economy is still that of a developing nation. Faced with an emerging market economy, both the pension system and formal social services for older people are woefully inadequate. Some 71.4 percent of older people have to rely on their children as their principal source of financial support. The reliance on children for financial support is particularly prominent for women and older people in rural areas. Not surprisingly, the old old are more likely than the young old to rely solely on their families for economic support. Only 16.9 percent of older people receive pensions and only 6.2 percent can count on public relief (Zhang, 2000). In rural areas, peasants have no actual retirement age and remain engaged as long as they are able.

Table 2. Changing Population Structure of China

	Year							
Age	1953 (%)	1964 (%)	1982 (%)	1990 (%)	2000 (%)	2010 (%)	2020 (%)	2030 (%)
0–14	36.3	40.7	33.6	27.6	22.9	20.0	20.3	17.7
15–64	59.3	55.7	61.5	66.8	70.1	71.1	67.5	66.2
65+	4.4	3.6	4.9	5.6	7.0	8.9	12.2	16.1
Median age	21.7	20.2	22.9	25.3	—	—	—	—

Sources: State Council, Information Office, 2001; Yu, 1995.

Over the last decade, the government has attempted to transform the existing work unit–based social security system implemented by the Maoist government into an independently funded national program in which both employers and employees make contributions into individual accounts. Retired workers can now obtain their pension annuities from local banks or post offices and need not depend on centralized agencies. The amount received is largely determined by savings and contributions accumulated in personal accounts. Despite reform initiatives, the present program is still marked by problems of narrow coverage, undue reliance on employers, uneven participation by employers, poor management and investment of funds, low transferability of funds, and inability to collect contributions on time (Chow and Xu, 2001; Yin, Lin, and Gates, 2000).

A nationwide survey in 1994 showed that some 8 percent of people ages 60 and older—9 million people altogether—still depended on others to take care of them, and 25 percent of this population reported being in poor health (China Research Center on Aging, 1994). As expected, only 3.16 percent of people ages 60–69 were bedridden, while the percentage rose to 4.3 percent for those ages 80 and older. Some 78.4 percent of older adults ages 60 and older reported that they depended on their children to take care of them during periods of illness.

A 1994 study of family caregivers revealed several characteristics of family care. In terms of daily activities, women tended to be more capable of self-care than men in both cities and villages, and spouses were most likely to be the caregiver within the family. Urban older men were more dependent than urban older women on their spouses as caregivers; wives often had to take care of their own needs. Further, older people in villages tended to rely more on their children than those in cities did. Urban-dwelling daughters were more likely to provide care to older relatives than their rural counterparts, though daughters-in-law were more often the caregivers in villages, perhaps due to the way land is passed between fathers and sons. In either case, however, women were shown to be primary caregivers (China Research Center on Aging, 1994). On the whole, the majority of older people, influenced by traditional beliefs, still prefer to live with their married sons and receive financial assistance from them. At the same time, many older people expect female members of the family to take care of their day-to-day needs.

Overall, older people in China still largely rely on their families for support and care, as is typically the case across Asia. Insofar as the family is able to assume these responsibilities, the problem of elder care has not surfaced as a major issue compared to such pressing social issues as unemployment, income disparities, drug abuse, poverty, and housing shortages (Chow and Leung, 2000). Yet, with the rapid pace of economic reform, the willingness and the ability of the family to shoulder filial responsibilities are invariably being put under considerable pressure.

CHANGING PATTERNS OF FAMILY SUPPORT

Traditional Chinese society comprised a multitude of family groups that formed the basic unit of the country's social, economic, and political structure. Few secondary organizations existed outside the family to serve an individual's social needs. The Chinese family, and its extended network of blood-related kin, has operated as a self-sufficient, self-regulating, and self-governing "little society" upon which one had to depend for work, education, support, and assistance in times of difficulty (King and Bond, 1985). The dominant principle of filial piety placed a moral obligation upon junior members of the family to respect and take care of elderly parents, as expressed by a cherished saying, "The elderly are cared for." The Chinese saying "Raise children to protect old age" also characterized how heavily older people customarily have relied on families as their leading source of financial support.

The time-honored Chinese concept of filial piety prescribed that children had the responsibility to take care of their older parents during their lives as well as after their deaths. Accordingly, filial piety consisted primarily of economic support, respect and obedience, and care during periods of illness (Zhang, 2000). For their part, family elders were obligated to look after the welfare of other members of the family by settling domestic disputes, disciplining nonconformists, arranging marriages and careers, assigning social and economic responsibilities, distributing income to family members, allocating relief to those in need, and so on. Elderly family members held a place of honor in the family of almost omnipotent authority. In return, junior members enjoyed complete protection and security. The continuation of this family tradition required parents to take care of their children, and then the children, when they were grown up, would take care of their aging parents. The reciprocal sense of responsibility was tantamount to a "feedback model" of family care, in contrast to the "relay model" of the West. This social contact between generations has been carried on for thousands of years (Fei, 1988).[10]

When the People's Republic of China was established in 1949, one of the government's most pressing tasks was to redirect the primacy of the individual's loyalty from family and kinship groups to the state. In addition to the nationalization of family businesses in cities and the collectivization of family farming in villages, the government introduced employer-based comprehensive social welfare coverage to urban workers. The Marriage Law of 1950 provided the freedoms of marriage and divorce, and further undermined the conventional influence of elders over family members' choices of employment and spouses. In

[10] Fei identified two models of the parent-child relationship. In the Western relay model, generation A takes care of generation B, which in turn takes care of generation C, and so forth. In the feedback model of China, generation B must care not just for generation C, but also for generation A when the latter gets old. Formal support for older adults in China is based on this model of care.

successive political movements and during the Cultural Revolution (1966–76), young people were encouraged to denounce their own parents as a way of demonstrating their fresh loyalty to the regime (Whyte, 1997).

Yet, despite the overwhelming effort of the Maoist government and the political machinery to enforce virtually any mandate, the family continued to be the primary social unit, often interacting in subtle and wily ways. The fact that lifelong employment impeded geographic mobility and that the government required localized household registration abetted the survival of family linkages. The absence of social services such as nurseries and housing meant that families were still the prime source of care for children and elders despite collectivist guidelines. A severe housing shortage in the cities, coupled with a widespread policy of allocating housing to workers with the most seniority, meant that adult children had little choice but to live with their parents, even after marriage. In rural areas, despite collectivization in the form of communes, families were often allowed to cultivate private plots and engage in sideline production. In addition, organized cadres of community members, most commonly party members as well, would use administrative measures to mediate marital disputes and enforce family obligations to provide care to children and elderly parents. With little need to consider economic efficiency, work units could, and would, support employees in their caregiving duties, for example, by providing family leave for employees to take care of their sick parents (Leung, 1997; Leung and Lam, 2000).

Even in the most dire of times, many people saw their parents as a resource rather than a burden. In living together, aging parents helped their children with finances, domestic chores, and childcare. All along, the intergenerational relationship can be best described as one of mutual interdependence (Whyte, 1997). One recent survey carried out in a Chinese city showed that some 41 percent of older people were financially independent from their children, 10 percent adopted mutual financial support, 41 percent received financial support from their children, and 8 percent provided financial support to their children (Zhang, 2000). In reality, contemporary intergenerational relationships involving financial support are more complicated, and support is not always one-sided.

Recent demographic and social changes are doing what the previous regime was unable to accomplish, affecting the capacity and willingness of the family to provide care to the elderly. In 2000, the majority of individuals lived in small families, that is, households made up of one to four persons; the average household size was 3.44 persons (2.88 persons in Shanghai), down from 4.4 persons in 1982 (*People's Daily,* March 27, 2001). A smaller family size means fewer potential caregivers. Furthermore, the number of divorces granted in 2000 reached 1.2 million, three times that number in 1981 (Ministry of Civil Affairs, 2002). In addition, women, who are usually the primary caregivers in the family, have been encouraged to participate actively in the workforce. By 1999, 46.7 percent of the workforce was female and 90 percent of women ages 20–44 participated in the labor force, a rate similar to that of their male counterparts (*People's Daily,* October 8, 2000).

Under the household registration system in place between 1958 and 1978, it was difficult for people to move from place to place to seek work. With the relaxation of restrictions on peasants' moving into cities and towns and on urban workers in the western and central provinces seeking jobs in coastal provinces, rural-to-urban and city-to-city migration has become increasingly common. In fact, the government now intends to grant permanent urban residential status to migrant workers who currently have a stable job and source of income as well as a permanent address (*People's Daily,* August 28, 2001). As more rural young people, particularly men, migrate to the cities in search of work, their aged parents risk being left behind and, in effect, abandoned. Some migrants maintain responsibility for the care of their aging relatives by sending home remittances; others just disappear and contact is attenuated at best (Leung, 1997).

Paradoxically, economic reform has also carried with it the reemergence of poverty and unemployment in China. In cities, conservative estimates put the number of people living in poverty at 12 million. While many of them became poverty stricken due to unemployment, others, despite being employed or retired, have fallen into poverty as a result of low wages and low pensions (Leung and Wong, 1999). The official unemployment rate in 1999 was reported as 3.1 percent, representing 5.75 million people, yet unofficial estimates put the figure at greater than 10 percent (State Statistical Bureau, 2000). To enhance the efficiency of state-owned enterprises, more workers are being laid off, and some 60 percent of those laid off are women (Leung, 1996). With the deepening of economic reform and the shift to more cost-effective forms of production dictated by the influx of foreign interests, the number of workers in state-owned enterprises has decreased from 70 million in the early 1990s to less than 50 million in 2000 (*Beijing Review,* 2001, vol. 7). In addition, the State Council allows—and even encourages—workers within five years of their retirement age to retire early. From January 1998 to August 1998, some 35 percent of the 2 million newly retired workers were classified as having taken early retirement (Song and Liu, 1999).

These economic trends impose a double bind on the Chinese family. Unemployment rates among women imply that a greater number are available to serve as caregivers, yet the same trends are imposing real economic and employment insecurities that tend to counter willingness to assume the caregiver role with all the responsibilities it entails. Today's older people were born no later than the 1930s, generally married by the 1950s, and had a sizable number of children as part of China's own baby boom. Therefore, they have three to four children on average (3.5 in cities and 3.7 in villages) who in theory can share caregiving responsibilities for them (China Research Center on Aging, 1994). In contrast, their children, who themselves married and had children in the mid-1970s and the early 1980s, will probably reach old age a few decades hence with only one child to look after them. This is one of the inevitable and daunting consequences of the one-child policy implemented in 1980, and it is the harbinger of an even larger social issue in the future. The Chinese media and demographers alike characterize the phenomenon as "four-two-one": The responsibility of caring for the four grandparents and two parents will rest on a single grown-up child.

Despite the trends outlined above, the preponderance of older people in China do still live with adult children. According to the 1987 national survey, 82.2 percent of adults ages 60 and older lived with their children. In 1997, a similar survey showed that the percentage had dropped to a still substantial 76.7 percent. Another 11.7 percent of elderly lived with their spouses, 1.2 percent with relatives, and 0.3 percent with other people. More importantly, 11 percent of Chinese elders lived alone (State Statistical Bureau, 1998) and in the cities some 25 percent of urban elderly do not live with their children (*China Daily,* March 1, 2001; *People's Daily,* December 14, 2000).

Clearly the causes of this phenomenon come from both directions. More young people, whether single or married, are choosing to live away from their parents and likely some parents prefer to live independently, especially those who have been exposed to Western views. They make up a significant proportion of Chinese families in some large cities: 34 percent in Beijing and 33.6 percent in Shanghai (*People's Daily,* December 4, 2000). It is estimated that by 2020, when those parents with only one child enter old age, almost half of the elderly will live apart from their children. Indeed, in the West, a growing number of older people who are economically and physically independent prefer to live separately from their children (Hareven, 1987; Sher, 1984; Unger, 1993). Perhaps the same pattern will follow in China where joint residency does not automatically mean responsible care, just as it does in the West. Likewise, even though more older people in East and West prefer to live separately from their adult children, it does not mean ties are severed or that their relationships are deteriorating. Many elderly prefer intimacy at a distance, content to live relatively near their children. When their spouse passes away or their health deteriorates, proximity helps. Some elderly Chinese choose to live in homes for the aged where their family members can visit them on weekends (*China Daily,* February 22, 2000).

WELFARE SERVICES FOR THE ELDERLY

Under the centrally planned economy largely modeled after that of the Soviet Union, the system of public ownership, full and lifelong employment, job creation and assignment, and restricted labor mobility that Mao Zedong established was regarded as one of the better features of socialism. Since social welfare was employment centered, each work unit functioned as a self-sufficient welfare agency within which individuals received employment and income protection, and enjoyed heavily subsidized benefits and services including housing, food, and education.[11] They could also obtain social security benefits in the event of sickness, maternity, work injuries, invalidism, death, or old age. Based on distribution decisions made by the local administration, a basic, egalitarian security network—the aptly named "iron rice bowl"—with high employment, high welfare, and low wages was established (Leung and Nann, 1995; Lu and Perry, 1997; Walder, 1986). As such, the function of the government in regard to older adults was remedial; it was only responsible for taking care of older people who had no work-unit or family support (Ikels, 1992). In fact, the domination of work unit–centered welfare rendered centralized governmental social services for the elderly minimal and those provided by nongovernmental organizations unnecessary.

From the beginning of the 1980s, the iron rice bowl, which involved "everyone eating from the same big pot," came to be viewed as impeding economic efficiency and productivity, acting virtually as a disincentive. Today, greater numbers of urban residents are living and working outside the protection of the state sector. In 1999, only 12 percent of the national workforce—41 percent of the urban workforce—were employed in the state sector (State Statistical Bureau, 2000). For all the good they may have done, work-unit welfare excludes rural migrants, employees in private and foreign-owned enterprises, and self-employed laborers. More importantly, as the government reforms state-owned enterprises, layoffs and early retirement have become widespread at a time when it is getting harder to claim benefits from work units. The necessity to develop other forms of welfare services is urgent and growing (Croll, 1999; Guan, 2000; Lei, 2001; Philion, 1998).

Currently, centrally administered social welfare services consist principally of welfare institutions for the destitute and welfare factories for people with physical disabilities. By tradition, welfare institutions provided free residential care for those classified as "three no's"—those with no working ability, no source of income, and no family support. They included people with mental illness, those with mental disabilities, orphans, and childless older people. In that sense, residential care was not based on physical or healthcare needs. Since 1983, these institutions also have been open to people who can afford to pay out of pocket with their own resources.

In 2000, approximately 40,000 residential homes across China provided a total of 1.13 million residential places, 90 percent of which were designated for older people. Neighborhood governments were responsible for the oversight and financing of 77.7 percent of these facilities. (In China, township governments in rural areas and "street offices"—an extension of the district people's government—in urban areas are both regarded as semigovernmental organizations.)

[11] Currently, one third of schools and two fifths of hospitals in China are operated by work units, including 18,000 primary and secondary schools (enrolling a total of 6.1 million students) and 3,700 medical institutions (containing one third of the nation's hospital beds) (Chi, 2000).

Private organizations funded and managed another 2.7 percent of the places for older adults; Local Civil Affairs departments maintained the remaining 19.6 percent. Although the growth rates of all the residential care homes for elders have been moderate in recent years (Table 3), the number of places available in privately operated residential care homes soared from 16,626 in 1999 to 30,940 in 2000, representing a growth rate of 86.1 percent (Ministry of Civil Affairs, 2002).

In 2000, the average residential care home operated by a neighborhood had 17.4 residents; government-operated homes were much larger, housing an average of 66.5 residents. With an occupancy rate of only 75.6 percent, all these old-age homes were largely underutilized. Privately operated homes had even lower occupancy rates, averaging only 63 percent. This phenomenon reflects in part the traditional reluctance of older people in China to live in institutions. According to a study, the low quality of care provided in these homes and the high fees charged were other factors leading to their underutilization (*China Civil Affairs,* 2000, vol. 3). Given the fact that the population of adults ages 60 and older in China was 126 million in 2000, the institutionalization rate of older people was extremely low, representing about 0.6 percent of the total older adult population. The government pledged in 2000 to increase capacity within residential care homes for older persons to a rate of 10 beds per 1,000 urban elderly, representing an institutionalization rate of 1 percent (*China Civil Affairs,* 2000, vol. 4). Furthermore, recognizing the remaining unmet need, the government recently committed itself to increasing the number of places to 1.8 million by the end of the 10th Five-Year Plan, which concludes in 2005 (*People's Daily,* August 10, 2001).

Table 3. Development of Social Welfare Institutions Over the Last Two Decades

	1983	1998	1999	2000
Number of institutions	22,117	40,741	38,367	39,154
Government	—	1,364	1,677	1,958
Neighborhoods	—	39,377	36,690	37,196
Capacity (beds)	335,056	993,695	996,401	1,040,064
Government	—	145,421	154,049	170,669
Neighborhoods	—	848,274	842,352	869,395
Actual residents	312,226	654,669	750,343	777,525
Government	—	115,571	119,450	130,244
Neighborhoods	—	639,098	630,893	647,281

Source: Ministry of Civil Affairs, 2002.

According to estimates provided by the Ministry of Civil Affairs, the proportion of older people who perceived that they required residential care reached 11 percent, or 14 million elders, in 2000 (*China Civil Affairs,* 2000, vol. 3). In a survey of residential care needs in Guangzhou, 90 percent of the elderly respondents stated that there was no need for them to live in a home for the aged. Sixty percent of this group reported that they did not need residential care because they were satisfied with the care their children provided. Ten percent of the respondents showed a desire to live in a home for the aged, justifying their preference on the basis of partiality for collective living and the better living environment of residential homes. The same survey revealed that those who lived in homes tended to be older than the general elderly population and had more difficulty with self-care. Ironically, the survey also found that 70 percent of older people did not have sufficient income to pay the fees charged by the homes. The average monthly fees for these homes are close to the average monthly wage in Guangzhou city. Therefore, high fees are a major deterrent to older adults gaining the benefits of institutional care (Guangzhou Sociology Society and Guangzhou Civil Affairs Bureau, 1999). Other potential forms of formal care services designed specifically for frail older people, such as nursing homes, home help, and daycare centers, are largely underdeveloped in China.

To promote higher standards of institutional care, in 2001 the Ministry of Civil Affairs published its *Standards of Social Welfare Institutions,* prescribing basic quality standards for residential homes for the aged. The standards set up formal classifications for different types of homes—social welfare institutions for the aged, homes for the aged, hostels for the elderly, homes for the device-aided elderly, nursing homes, and homes for the elderly in rural areas. They also established quality guidelines for food, personal care, rehabilitation, social life, management structure, staffing, facilities, and space. All these services for the aged require administrative supervision from social workers, rehabilitation personnel, and medical personnel (Ministry of Civil Affairs, 2001b).

In the 1990s, welfare reform was carried out under a policy called "socialization." Loosely speaking, socialization refers to a shift from a work unit–centered welfare system to a more open, pluralistic social welfare system with more diversified responsibilities. To be more specific, socialization refers to the diversification of working targets (traditionally, the ministry was only responsible for taking care of those without families and sources of income), funding sources, modes of management, and service personnel. The role of the government becomes that of enabler and coordinator. This policy shift is marked by a shift in how Chinese people identify themselves, from being members of work units to being members of society or, even better, members of their local community. In 2001, the Ministry of Civil Affairs issued a statement that summarizes the direction that aging services must take under the policy of socialization:

> In extending the new frontiers of social welfare services for the older persons, the core service framework operated by the government and the collectives has been gradually established, with the new social sector acting as the growing points. The social welfare system for the older person with Chinese characteristics is based on home care, supplemented by community-based services (Ministry of Civil Affairs, 2001c).

Under this directive, the Chinese government acknowledged the importance of homecare and community-based services. Even though the government and the collectives (semigovernmental organizations) will remain the core providers of services for the elderly, emerging nongovernmental organizations and the private sector are expected to play a more active part. As such, partnerships between different sectors and the integration of services become paramount considerations for future policymakers.

THE EMERGENCE OF COMMUNITY SERVICES

In pre-socialist China, successive regimes relied on a decentralized system of local organizations to help govern and control the citizenry. The neighborhood system was responsible for tax collection, military conscription, and moral education, as well as regular reports to government officials on births, deaths, marriages, movements of people, and unlawful activities. After establishment of the People's Republic of China in 1949, street offices and residents' committees were set up in urban neighborhoods. Their primary function was political: identifying and locating counterrevolutionaries, runaway criminals, and landlords, as well as mobilizing residents in political movements and campaigns. In addition, they were responsible for overseeing the neighborhood environment and providing care to residents who had no work units, such as the unemployed, housewives, and the childless elderly. The government believed that work units would eventually replace this neighborhood system and that the neighborhoods' limited role in providing welfare would become unnecessary in the future (Lei, 2001; Leung, 2000; Leung and Nann, 1995; Whyte and Parish, 1983).

Yet the neighborhood system has persisted. Currently, each urban neighborhood of about 50,000 residents is administered by a street office. As an extension of the district people's government, the street office is staffed by government cadres. In addition to the street offices, there are independent residents' committees covering an average of 500–700 households; their members are elected by local residents (Leung, 2000).[12] The street office, supported by the residents' committees within its purview, is responsible for the provision of a variety of public, commercial, and social services. Public services for general residents

[12] In China's 668 cities in 2000, there were 5,902 street offices, 108,000 residents' committees, and 484,000 committee members.

include fire and policing patrols, environmental management, sanitation improvement, marriage registration, household registration, family planning, family and neighborhood mediation, bicycle parking, and recreational and cultural activities. Fee-based commercial services include the delivery of milk and fuel; household cleaning; employment referrals for domestic helpers; the running of restaurants, shops, laundries, and guest houses; and home and electrical-appliance repair work. Welfare services administered by the street office are targeted for older people, people with disabilities, the young, military veterans, poverty-stricken families, and the unemployed. Since the 1980s, the Ministry of Civil Affairs has encouraged street offices and residents' committees to develop welfare services specifically for such vulnerable populations as poverty-stricken families, people with disabilities, and frail older people. The street offices often establish community-service centers providing welfare, educational, and health services as well. Similarly, residents' committees also provide community-service stations offering convenient and easily accessible welfare services for vulnerable populations.

The major strengths of these localized community services are their ability to identify all vulnerable people living in the community and need of assistance and then employing local residents as caring staff to deliver aid. Each street office, through household registration procedures, keeps detailed records of the members of each household in the neighborhood. As such, they typically have dependable information on older adults and people with disabilities who live in the area. Because most of the caring staff are permanent residents in the neighborhood, they, too, have good knowledge of the needs of the vulnerable populations in their midst. More importantly, the neighborhood can, in theory, provide an integrated and coordinated package of community-based and user-centered services, including healthcare, housing, social welfare, cultural and educational services, and cover remedial, supportive, preventive, and developmental functions. Often, the street offices can establish community-service working groups that bring together representatives from different community sectors such as government departments, the Women's Federation, the Communist Youth League, work units, and the unions to share insights.

By 2000, the number of community-service facilities in China had increased to 181,000, which included 12,674 community-service centers—up from 148,042 community-service facilities and 6,154 community-service centers in 1998. Some 750,000 employees and 3.8 million volunteers were involved in the operation of community-service programs (Ministry of Civil Affairs, 2002). However, community-service facilities are located mainly in coastal cities and are not evenly distributed across China. As of 2000 there were only 3 community-service facilities in Tibet, 170 in Yunnan province, and 267 in Qinghai province, compared against 13,572 in Jiangsu province, 13,094 in Zhejiang, 10,006 in Shanghai, and 11,602 in Jilin province (State Statistical Bureau, 2000).

With limited financial support from city governments, each neighborhood is dependent on its own efforts to develop public and social welfare services. In general, city government allocations for community services only account for 30 percent of their total operating cost. Profits derived from commercially based services and fee-based public and welfare services managed by the street offices are used to underwrite overall operations. The principle is well described by the Chinese saying "Use profit-making services to support services that are free of charge." In fact, in the 1990s many street offices expanded the fee-based community services they offered while significantly reducing free services. In 1993, 14 government ministries and commissions jointly issued a report titled *Views Concerning the Speeding up of the Development of Community Service,* and in 2000 the State Council issued *Memorandum Concerning the Views of Promoting Community Building.* Both policy papers envisioned community services as a form of tertiary industry that offered both commercial and welfare functions.

Another major source of financing for community services is the city welfare lottery fund. Since the introduction in 1987 of welfare lotteries where net revenues are directed to service provision, the government has raised a total of RMB 9.5 billion for welfare spending (*Beijing Review,* 2000, vol. 3). In 2000, sales of lottery tickets amounted to RMB 11.3 billion, of which RMB 4.2 billion were allocated for welfare (Ministry of Civil Affairs, 2002). Lottery revenues are usually used to finance capital costs of welfare projects, such as homes for the aged and community-service centers in the neighborhoods. In Shanghai, about two fifths of the lottery allocations go toward supporting community services, and throughout China lotteries have become a major source of revenue for community services (Xu, 2001).

Under the Star Light Project introduced by the Ministry of Civil Affairs in 2001, local governments, often funded through the lotteries, provide financial support to community initiatives for developing service facilities for the elderly, such as building homes for the aged and establishing activity centers and rehabilitation stations. The projects, which specifically target older people, are usually small, local, and flexible enough to respond to urgent social needs. Initially started in larger cities, these services and facilities are expected to provide a unified service design, appearance, and structure so as to facilitate monitoring, accessibility, and publicity (*Beijing Review,* 2001, vol. 7; *China Civil Affairs,* 2001, vols. 7, 8, and 9). The government has pledged to invest a total of RMB 10 billion in the Star Light Project, with the funds coming mainly from local governments (Ministry of Civil Affairs, 2002).

Furthermore, community services can receive preferential treatment from city governments in terms of taxation and credits. As such, it is exceedingly difficult to separate the welfare and profit-making commercial functions of community services. Because the provision of welfare services is largely dependent on the ability of the street offices to develop a profitable local revenue base, the quality and quantity of welfare services provided can vary substantially from neighborhood to neighborhood. Generally, street offices in commercial districts and city centers generate much higher proceeds. Some street offices have even established charity funds for welfare functions, with revenue coming from public donations, profits from welfare enterprises, and street office allocations. In general, community services are both informal and loosely structured, and the quality of services is not standardized.

Because of fluctuating financial situations, community services not only vary significantly from city to city, from district to district, and from street office to street office, they are also difficult to maintain continuously. Some community services are forced to close down periodically because of a lack of financial support or a lack of users (Lei, 2001).

The quality of community services is also plagued by the limited skills of the neighborhood cadres who staff them. The majority of the cadres are retirees and redundant workers laid off from ailing state enterprises. This is particularly true of residents' committees (Leung, 2000). More than one third of the employees in street offices are workers laid off from underperforming state enterprises. Social work educators in China have long advocated the need to professionalize community cadres in order to overcome the shortcomings of a well intentioned but ill trained volunteer base (Leung, 2001; Xu, 2001).

The following are a few of the typical services that street offices provide to older people.

Homes for the Aged

Homes for the aged can provide care to older people in need. These homes are usually small in size, many having only a few residents. Many homes are informally organized and may simply employ a domestic helper to render care to the residents. Only individuals who are defined as "three no's" are admitted to these homes free of charge. According to the government's plan, street offices with a population of less than 60,000 residents should have one home for the aged with the capacity of 30 beds (*China Civil Affairs,* 2000, vol. 4).

Social Assistance

To establish a last-resort welfare safety-net in cities, the government restructured the conventional social assistance program in 1993 to extend its coverage, raise the level of benefits provided, and secure financial commitment from local governments. The new Minimum Living Standard Guarantee System provides assistance to those with urban household registration status. Under the system, work units are responsible for providing assistance to individuals who still have connections to them. The level of assistance the program provides is calculated according to the local minimum standard of living, often based on expenditure surveys of low-income households and on financial capacity of the local government. At subsistence levels, this assistance merely covers the basic costs of food and clothing, and may take into account fuel, rent, medical care, and tuition expenses. In reality, the level of assistance can hardly cover these expenses. In 2001, the highest standards of living were found in coastal cities and the lowest were in cities in the western provinces.[13] In some neighborhoods, social assistance recipients are given food stamps that they can use to purchase food and fuel at reduced prices from designated local vendor shops.

The city and district governments finance the program, but its administration is community based. Cadres from the street offices are responsible for evaluating eligibility, delivering benefits, and periodically reviewing the recipients' situations. Based on a principle of deterrence involving a certain amount of humiliation, the provision of such services is unpleasant and harsh so that it discourages all but the most desperate. To facilitate public monitoring of recipients' situations, their names and amount of benefits received are also posted on neighborhood bulletin boards (*China Civil Affairs,* 2001, vol. 6; Leung and Wong, 1999). A breakdown of the background of public-assistance recipients in Wuhan city in 1998 showed that only 0.15 percent of the city's population received assistance from the program, of which 71 percent were unemployed; the rest were primarily childless elders and people with disabilities (Yang and Zhang, 1999).

By 1999, all the 688 cities in China had implemented the Minimum Living Standard Guarantee System. In 2001, some 4.16 million urban residents received assistance from the program, compared to only 2 million people in 1997. The average monthly allowance per person they received rose from RMB 48 to RMB 60 in the same period (Ministry of Civil Affairs, 2002).

Care Groups

For individuals classified as "three no's"—often older people living alone and not institutionalized—the street office can make arrangements to establish a care group. Care groups comprising cadres and volunteers circulate through the area providing basic services such as home help, meal delivery, escorts to the doctor's office, haircuts, electrical-appliance repair, laundry, and housecleaning.

Family Mediation

The Chinese government is convinced that the family should shoulder primary responsibility for the care of older adults. Article 183 of the Criminal Law (1979) makes it an offense, punishable by a sentence of not more than five years' criminal detention, for adult children to refuse to carry out their obligation to support an aged family member. The role of adult children, including adopted children, to support their parents was reiterated in the revised Marriage Law (1980). In 1996, the government passed the Law on the Protection of the Rights

[13] The highest standard of living is found in Shenzhen (RMB 319 per person per month), and the lowest in Qianxi county in Guizhou (RMB 78 per person per month). The average assistance line is between RMB 130 and RMB 150 per person per month (Ministry of Civil Affairs, 2002).

and Interests of the Elderly. Chapter 2 of the law, "Maintenance and Support by Families," reiterated the responsibility of adult children to support their parents as well as their parents-in-law. Children are expected to take care of the financial, medical, housing, and social needs of older relatives (Leung and Lam, 2000). The enforcement of these family obligations rests on the mechanism of the mediation service operated at the neighborhood level in cities and villages and in work units. Whenever there is a dispute involving the care of an older person, the neighborhood cadre brings all family members together for a family meeting to work out arrangements for support and care. Family members have to sign a "caring agreement" that is monitored by the neighborhood cadres.[14]

In principle, the mediation service has to be accepted by both parties. Education and persuasion is the basic approach, and no coercive sanction should be employed. The neighborhood mediator should be impartial and neutral. The outcome of mediation carries no authority in regard to acceptance. Any person who does not accept the agreement can take his or her case to court (Leung and Lam, 2000).

In 1999 there were almost 974,000 people's mediation committees in China. Some 8.8 million mediators handled a total of 5.2 million cases, down from 7.3 million cases in 1989. These committees function informally, and most of the mediators work on a part-time basis. About 37 percent of the cases in 1999 involved family issues. Some 7.2 percent (372,193 cases) involved the care of the elderly, compared to 5.6 percent (409,235 cases) in 1989 (State Statistical Bureau, 2000). On the whole, there is an increasing tendency for people to resolve their social conflicts through legal means rather than through informal mediation.

Other Community Services

Other rapidly developed community services for the elderly in recent years include the neighborhood clinics, daycare centers, recreational and educational activity centers, canteens, legal advice services, marriage referral services, hotline

[14] Chapter 2, Article 17, of the Law on the Protection of the Rights and Interests of the Elderly states the following:

> Supporters may conclude an agreement between themselves on their duty to provide for the elderly, subject to approval by the latter. Neighborhood committees, villagers' committees, or the organizations of the supporters may supervise the fulfillment of the agreement.

In addition, Chapter 5 ("Legal Responsibility"), Article 45, states:

> When the elderly have disputes with their family members over their support, or over housing or property, they may ask the organizations where their family members are employed, the neighborhood committees, or the villagers' committee to mediate. They may also bring a lawsuit directly to the People's Court. . . . If the family members are found to be in the wrong through mediation of the disputes mentioned in the preceding paragraph, they shall be educated through criticism and ordered to correct their mistakes (China National Committee on Aging, 1996).

services, and help bells for older people living alone. To use the development in Shanghai as an illustration, the community services in Shanghai in 1999 included the following:

- A community-service hotline network
- 115 community-service centers and 2,441 activity subunits
- 162 daycare centers providing care for 1,334 older persons
- 2,230 medical consultation stations serving 570,000 older persons
- 315 community clinics serving 120,000 older persons
- 21,000 family beds serving 21,000 older persons
- 107 elderly rehabilitation centers serving an average of 954 older persons each day
- 6,600 volunteers serving 426,000 older persons
- 8,500 caring groups serving 35,000 older adults
- 5,000 elderly mutual-help groups serving 21,000 older adults
- 69 canteens for the elderly serving 2,000 meals each day
- 368 bathrooms serving 2,200 older persons each day
- 2,400 legal advice stations for the elderly serving 146,000 persons
- 366 homes for the aged with a total of 11,500 residents
- 35 nursing homes serving 2,200 older people (Shanghai Committee on Aging, 1999)

A study of community-service needs of older people in Tianjin city showed that 94 percent of the respondents claimed to depend on their family members for care in the event of sickness and poor health. Some 2 percent reported domestic helpers were their caregivers. About 10 percent preferred that the street office take care of them (the respondents were allowed to indicate two choices). Some 42 percent of the respondents had received care from community services and neighbors. The assistance they received included social conversation, visits during festivals, medical consultation and advice, help with laundry, assistance in contacting relatives, care during periods of illness, meal preparation, and escorts to the doctor (Tianjin Elderly Livelihood Survey Group, 1998). A study carried out by this author in Guangzhou found that most older people had used some form of community services. Forty-two percent of the respondents perceived that community services for older people were essential (Chow and Leung, 2000). Because of escalating needs and the underdevelopment of social services operated by the government, nongovernmental organizations, and for-profit businesses, community services are becoming a vital source of social support for older people.

CONCLUSION

Because China is experiencing a conflict between traditional values and modern worldwide economic ideologies, social welfare services for the aged in China have been slow to develop. As a consequence, the Chinese government has had to resort to legislative mandates to enforce family support for elders. To be sure, family obligations do not need to be—and cannot be—enforced solely through rule of law. Filial obligation values are still intact, and there is no evidence that children are becoming less willing to provide care to their older parents. Yet, with smaller families, more working women, growing divorce rates, and a restructured economy, the pool of potential caregivers is shrinking, affecting the capacity of families to provide care and support to dependent elderly family members. In fact, family care has been taken for granted by Chinese policymakers, who assume it is natural, and relatively few studies have been conducted in China on the changing nature of family care.

The most crucial issue insofar as elderly welfare is concerned is how best to sustain or even maximize informal family care. Although most of the existing welfare services are targeted at those classified as "three no's," there is an urgent need to develop formal social services that support the family, rather than simply relying on coercive legal action and appeals to morality to enforce the responsibility of family care. With the escalating long-term care needs of older people, a staggering number of elders, even those still living with their families, face certain risks.

In particular, Chinese elders express a resounding reluctance to enter into institutional care. They have a strong desire to live with their children and in the community. That is why homes for the aged in China are largely underutilized. Still, policymakers in China are preoccupied with the paradigmatic notion that building more homes for the aged is the solution to the problem of elder care. Only recently have policy documents such as *Concerning the Views on the Speeding up of the Socialization of Social Welfare,* issued by the State Council in February 2000, recommended that the basis of care should be in-home services (*China Civil Affairs,* 2000, vol. 4).

Therefore, community-based and in-home services directed at frail older people should enable them to continue living with their family and in the community. To be specific, more community-based services should be developed to support family caregivers and address their needs. The roles, functions, contributions, and needs of family caregivers have to be acknowledged by policymakers. Family caregivers even play a significant role in enhancing the quality of life of older people living in residential settings.

Many family caregivers are in fact elders themselves. They include the relatively healthier spouses of frail elders, as well as elderly children who take care of their old-old parents. In such situations, both the caregiver and the care recipient are simultaneously becoming increasingly frail. As is the case elsewhere in the world, family caregivers require not only tangible material aid, informational advice, and emotional support, but also training to handle the complications involved in providing care, such as coping with bedridden, frail, or demented older people.

Currently, in-home services for older people, such as home help, community nursing, meal delivery, and daycare centers, are still not fully developed. There is an urgent need to institutionalize these informally organized and loosely structured community-based services. In short, community services and family support should be complementary rather than mutually exclusive. Faced with the heterogeneous and complex needs of older people, there is a paramount need for the development of a coherent and integrative policy on family care and community-based services in order to maintain older people in their own homes and neighborhoods for as long as possible. The primary goal of social care is to maintain the greatest degree of personal independence and self-sufficiency, rather than fostering dependency.

As in many other countries, older adults represent a large potential market for private business in China. Older adults' annual incomes from pensions, reemployment, and endowments from relatives and friends are estimated to amount to RMB 300–400 billion (*Beijing Review,* 2001, vol. 7). Local governments can employ preferential policies and support to facilitate the development of private-sector social-care services for older people.

Both the quality and the quantity of community services have been rapidly improving, particularly in coastal cities where the economy is booming. But services are still largely underdeveloped in cities in the hinterland. Looking into the future, the government has to provide more active support to those poor neighborhoods where welfare needs are more urgent.

It also appears that as social welfare services become more "socialized" in accordance with national policy, the development of welfare services for older people will increasingly come from the nongovernmental sector. As mentioned before, the development of the community services and for-profit sector in elderly care has been thriving. Furthermore, it appears the government prefers to reduce its role in direct-service provision. Yet such a reduction will not mean the diminution of its responsibility to Chinese elders. There is an urgent need for the government to assume leadership in overall policy formulation and service planning, strengthening and orchestrating partnerships between different service providers, and to ensure the integration of services that respond to the changing needs of elders.

REFERENCES

Beijing Review. (2000). Issue cited: 3.

Beijing Review. (2001). Issue cited: 7.

Chen, S. Y. (1996). *Social policy of the economic state and community care in Chinese culture.* Aldershot, United Kingdom: Avebury.

Chi, A. M. (2000). An exploration into the welfare policy reform of state-owned enterprises. *Journal of the China Mining University, 1,* 25–28.

China Civil Affairs. (2000). Nos. cited: 3, 4.

China Civil Affairs. (2001). Nos. cited: 6, 7, 8, 9.

China Daily. (2000). Issue cited: February 22.

China Daily. (2001). Issues cited: March 1, March 6, April 1, August 13.

China Internet Information Center. (2002). *The development-oriented poverty reduction program for rural China*. Retrieved from http://www.china.org.cn/e-white/fp1055/index.htm

China Research Centre on Ageing. (1994). *A data compilation of the survey on China's support systems for the elderly*. Beijing: Hualing Press.

China National Committee on Aging. (1996). *Law of the People's Republic of China on protection of the rights and interests of the elderly*. Beijing: Hualing Press.

Chow, N. (1991). Does filial piety exist under Chinese communism? *Journal of Aging and Social Policy, 3*(½), 209–225.

Chow, N., and Leung, J. (2000). *Report on welfare reforms in China: The case of Guangzhou city*. Hong Kong: University of Hong Kong, Department of Social Work and Social Administration.

Chow, N., and Xu, Y. B. (2001). *Socialist welfare in a market economy: Social security reforms in Guangzhou*. Aldershot, United Kingdom: Ashgate.

Croll, W. (1999). Social welfare reform: Trends and tensions. *The China Quarterly, 159*(1), 684–699.

Fei, X. T. (1988). Patterns and issues of elderly support. In Policy Research Department, Chinese National Committee on Aging (Eds.), *Caring for the elderly, developing the undertaking* (pp. 112–116). Beijing: Beijing Science Press.

Guan, X. P. (2000). China's social policy: Reform and development in the context of marketization and globalization. *Social Policy and Administration, 34*(1), 115–130.

Guangzhou Sociology Society and Guangzhou Civil Affairs Bureau. (1999). *The study on the elderly care in Guangzhou city*. Unpublished monograph.

Hareven, T. (1987). Reflections on family research in the PRC. *Social Research, 54*, 663–689.

Ikels, C. (1992). Family caregiving and the elderly in China. In D. Biegel and A. Blum (Eds.), *Aging and caregiving: Theory and practice* (pp. 270–284). Newbury Park, California: Sage Publications.

Khan, A. R., and Riskin, C. (2001). *Inequality and poverty in China in the age of globalization*. New York: Oxford University Press.

King, A., and Bond, K. (1985). The Confucian paradigm of man: A sociological view. In W. S. Tseng and D. Wu (Eds.), *Chinese culture and mental health* (pp. 29–45). London: Academic Press.

Lei, J. Q. (2001). *The transition of the grassroots community organizations in cities: A study of the grassroots community organization and community development in Beijing City*. Beijing: Peking University Press.

Leung, J. (1996). The emergence of unemployment insurance in China: Problems and issues. *Canadian Review of Social Policy, 38*, 5–17.

Leung, J. (1997). Family support for the elderly in China: Issues and challenges. *Journal of Aging and Social Policy, 9*(3), 7–101.

Leung, J. (2000). Community building in China: From welfare to politics. *Community Development Journal, 45*(4), 425–427.

Leung, J. (2001). Training social development cadres in China. *Regional Development Dialogue, 22*(1), 16–26.

Leung, J., and Lam, D. (2000). Enforcing family care obligations for the elderly in China through mediation. *Asia Pacific Journal of Social Work, 10*(1), 77–89.

Leung, J., and Nann, R. (1995). *Authority and benevolence: Social welfare in China.* New York: St. Martin's Press.

Leung, J., and Wong, H. (1999). The emergence of a community-based social assistance program in urban China. *Social Policy and Administration, 33*(1), 39–54.

Lu, X. B., and Perry, E. (Eds.). (1997). *Danwei: The changing workplace in historical and comparative perspective.* Armonk, New York: M. E. Sharpe.

Ministry of Civil Affairs. (2001a). *China civil affairs statistical yearbook.* Beijing: State Statistical Press.

Ministry of Civil Affairs. (2001b). *Standards of social welfare institution.* Beijing: China Society Press.

Ministry of Civil Affairs. (2001c). The situation of social welfare services for older people in China. In *China's social welfare services.* Beijing: Author.

Ministry of Civil Affairs. (2002). No title. Retrieved from http://www.mca.gov.cn

People's Daily. (2000). Issues cited: September 25, October 8, December 4, December 14.

People's Daily. (2001). Issues cited: February 7, March 12, March 27, March 29, August 10, August 28, September 4, September 24, October 18, October 19.

Perry, E., and Sheldon, M. (Eds.). (2000). *Chinese society: Change, conflict, and resistance.* New York: Routledge.

Philion, S. (1998). Chinese welfare state regimes. *Journal of Contemporary Asia, 28*(4), 518–536.

Riskin, C., Zhao, R. W., and Li, S. (Eds.). (2001). *China's retreat from equality: Income distribution and economic transition.* Armonk, New York: M. E. Sharpe.

Shanghai Committee on Aging. (1999). *Statistical report on the basic conditions of elderly welfare services in Shanghai in 1999.* Shanghai: Author.

Sher, A. E. (1984). *Aging in post-Mao China.* Boulder, Colorado: Westview Press.

Song, Q. Z., and Liu, F. (1999). Early retirement and its impact on retirement insurance funds. *China Social Security, 6,* 18–19.

State Council, Information Office. (2001). *China's population and development in the 21st century.* Retrieved from http://peopledaily.com.cn

State Statistical Bureau. (1998). *China statistical yearbook: 1998.* Beijing: China Statistical Publishers.

State Statistical Bureau. (2000). *China statistical yearbook: 2000.* Beijing: China Statistical Publishers.

The Economist. (2001). Issues cited: July 14, August 11.

Tianjin Elderly Livelihood Survey Group. (1998). The dependency of the livelihood of urban elderly on family and community. *China Social Work, 3,* 27–29.

Unger, J. (1993). Urban families in the eighties. In D. Davis and S. Harrell (Eds.), *Chinese families in the post-Mao Era* (pp. 25–49). Berkeley, California: University of California Press.

Walder, A. (1986). *Communist neo-traditionalism: Work and authority in China's industry.* Berkeley, California: University of California Press.

Whyte, M. (1997). The fate of filial obligations in China. *The China Journal, 38*(7), 1–31.

Whyte, M., and Parish, W. (1983). *Urban life in contemporary China.* Chicago: University of Chicago Press.

Xu, R. X. (2001). *Community development in China.* Shanghai: East China Normal University Press.

Yang, Z. C., and Zhang, Q. L. (1999). The analysis of the study on the implementation of the Minimum Living Standard Guarantee System in Wuhan. *Economic Forum, 4,* 99–103.

Yin, J., Lin, S., and Gates, D. (Eds.). (2000). *Social security reform: Options for China.* Singapore: World Scientific.

Yu, X. J. (1995). *The study on the economics of the aging population in China.* Beijing: China Population Publishers.

Zhang, W. F. (Ed.). (2000). *The problems and responses of population aging in China in the first half of the 21st century.* Beijing: Hualing Press.

CHAPTER SEVENTEEN

Community Services for Older People in Australia

Hal Kendig and Susan Quine

The development of services for older people around the world is best understood in the context of each country's cultural traditions and economic development. Most of the international literature is based on European and North American countries, which have postindustrial economies and governments with long-standing involvement in healthcare and aged-care concerns. By contrast, countries in Asia have relied overwhelmingly on family-based support for older adults, but are now facing structural changes as they are experiencing an unparalleled pace of economic development and population aging. Australia provides a useful point of comparison for Asia because it has a European tradition and an Asian future. Countries in the Asian region facing the need for developing community services for older adults may find the Australian experience illuminating.

OLDER ADULTS IN AUSTRALIAN SOCIETY

Australia has a relatively small population, approaching 20 million, 90 percent of whom are concentrated in coastal urban areas, notably Sydney and Melbourne. Because most of the arid continent is unoccupied, the population density is only 2 people per square kilometer, compared to 471 per sq km in South Korea and 335 per sq km in Japan. Apart from the 2 percent of the population that is indigenous, Australia is a country populated by successive waves of immigration, beginning with the arrival of settlers and prisoners from Britain at the end of the 19th century. After the two world wars, many more immigrants arrived from Central and Southern Europe and, more recently, from Asia. These postwar immigrants and their children now represent more than 40 percent of the population.

Overall, Australians enjoy a reasonably high standard of living. In the 2001–02 Australian fiscal year,[1] real net national disposable income per capita amounted to A$29,161 (US$18,955) (Australian Bureau of Statistics, 2002a), with the gross domestic product (GDP) increasing at a steady rate of 2.4 percent per year from 1991 to 2001 (Australian Bureau of Statistics, 2002b). In 2002 the recorded unemployment rate was 6 percent. Seventy percent of women of workforce age are currently employed in the paid workforce. In addition, a high proportion of older men remain in the workforce: approximately 80 percent of those ages 55–59 and 60 percent of those ages 60–64. Approximately half of all adults have completed either vocational or higher education.

Population Aging

The Australian population has been aging at a modest rate over the past few decades, mainly because of the continuing arrival of younger immigrants and a continuing baby boom from 1946 to 1965. The population ages 60 and older increased only modestly from 9 percent in 1976 to 12 percent in 1997. Population aging has been hastened more recently with the aging of first-generation post–World War II migrants, declining fertility rates, and increasing life expectancy at older ages. Australia now has a demographically mature population comparable to that of the United States of America. It will take another two decades before the aging baby boom cohort swells the older population from 2.3 million in 1998 to a projected 4.0 million (18 percent of the total population) in 2021. As emphasized in the landmark *Intergenerational Report* recently published by the Australian treasurer (Costello, 2002), the aging of the population does not pose an economic crisis for Australia, but there is a clear need for long-term planning.

One can make inferences about the aged-care needs of the population by looking at the size of the population ages 80 and older. By this measure, Australia's old-old population grew reasonably quickly from 1985 to 1995, at 5 percent per year, although the growth of this cohort is projected to slow to 3 percent per year over the next decade (Gibson and Goss, 1999). Overall, according to a 1999 report by the Australian Institute of Health and Welfare (AIHW), only 20 percent of Australians ages 65 years and older in 1998 were found to have a substantial disability, that is, any difficulty with the core activities of self-care, mobility, or communication. Another 8 percent were reported to have mild levels of disability and generally have needs only with household and property-related responsibilities. Less than 10 percent of older people are socially isolated (Gardner, Brooke, Ozanne, and Kendig, 1998).

[1] The Australian fiscal year begins in July and ends in June.

Household Arrangements and Needs

In 1998, the national Disability, Ageing and Carers[2] survey of 30,000 people showed that 91 percent of older people lived in private households, 6 percent in healthcare establishments such as nursing homes, and 3 percent in other accommodation, such as boarding houses (Australian Bureau of Statistics, 1999). However, among the minority of older people with a substantial disability, most resided in some form of long-term care accommodation, including hospitals, nursing homes, hostels, and the care-intensive sections of retirement villages. Widows and never-married older men were more likely to be in residential care than married older people and never-married older women, thus reflecting the important influence of informal care. Overall, less than half of the people entering old age are projected to ever live in a nursing home or hostel (Liu, Braun, and Mason, 2004).

Analyses of the Disability, Ageing and Carers Survey (Australian Bureau of Statistics, 1999) found that among older people who have substantial disabilities and live in private households, more than half are married and only a third live alone, again indicating the importance of informal support. Relatively few of this cohort live with an adult child, reflecting older people's wishes to remain independent, their financial capacity to do so, and Australian cultural norms of "intimacy at a distance." They have extensive needs for assistance, however, ranging from help with property maintenance (60 percent), housework (46 percent), healthcare (44 percent), and transportation (42 percent) to assistance with self-care (29 percent) and meal preparation (18 percent). Some 54 percent of older people with a substantial disability living in the community report that all their needs are met, 30 percent that needs are partially met, and 12 percent that none of their needs are met (Bridge, Kendig, Quine, and Parsons, 2002).

Informal Support

Family members, notably spouses and adult daughters, are the primary source of assistance for older people who live with substantial disabilities in the community. Fully 77 percent of these older people have some informal support from family or friends and a third receive assistance only from these sources (Bridge et al., 2002). Just over half (53 percent) receive some formal support from community services or privately purchased assistance, and 9 percent have only formal assistance. The single most common arrangement, reported by 44 percent of this group, is the combination of both formal and informal assistance. Only 12 percent report that they do not need any assistance and 2 percent say they do not have any support (Bridge et al., 2002).

According to a report published by AIHW and the National Disability Administrators (2000), nearly 500,000 people served as the primary caregivers

[2] Caregivers are called "carers" in Australia.

of people with disabilities of all ages in 1998. Furthermore, more than a third of caregivers reported spending 40 or more hours weekly on caregiving tasks. The monetary value of this work was estimated at A$16.60 billion (US$11.07 billion) in the 1995–96 fiscal year.

There is considerable controversy about the value base and sustainability of informal support for older Australians. Yet the available research indicates that middle-aged children have strong values of family obligation for frail older parents who wish to remain independent (Kendig, 2000a). A survey of older people in Melbourne conducted by Charleton and Kendig (1995) found that 75 percent of the respondents reported that they wished to stay in their own homes should they need care; 60 percent believed that adult children should help aging parents in need; and 60 percent believed that government can replace some family care. Further, for the next few decades people in advanced old age will have relatively large numbers of adult children. However, paid employment among middle-aged women does limit their capacity to care for older people with significant needs.

Housing

Housing is particularly important for older Australians. On the one hand, fully three fourths of older Australians own their homes and 10 percent live in public housing. Owning one's home obviously keeps housing costs low, which is particularly important because only one out of five older Australians has a personal income greater than A$12,000 (US$8,000) a year. Many older homeowners are "asset rich but income poor," which means that their wealth generally is not available unless they sell their homes and move. On the other hand, because so many older people live in single-family houses with gardens in suburban areas, their needs for assistance with property maintenance, housework, and transportation are extensive (Kendig, 2000b).

Staying in their own homes can be central to older people's identity and sense of independence (Davison, Kendig, Stephens, and Merrill, 1993). Although the single-family home can be difficult to maintain, frail older people can evince remarkable inventiveness in adapting their home environments to compensate for impaired abilities. Those who choose to move to retirement villages (Gardner, 1994) or public housing (Brooke, Davison, Kendig, and Reynolds, 1998) by and large benefit significantly. However, older Australians show a marked resistance to entering nursing homes: One recent study reported that most respondents claim they would prefer to die rather than enter a nursing home (Salkeld et al., 2000). These intense views are shaped by a fear of dependency as well as of nursing home conditions.

Care Relationships

An intensive qualitative study of very frail older people receiving community care reported that their views of dependency and care depended on earlier life experiences and interpretations of caring experiences (Kendig and Brooke, 1999). Difficult interpersonal negotiations center around accepting enough support to maintain adequate care at home and, if necessary, resisting the efforts of family and service providers who may urge moves to residential care. Caregiving typically begins when a long-term relationship of mutual support between an older person and a close relative, usually a spouse or a daughter, is changed by dependency into reduced mutuality.

The demands of caregiving can generate considerable stress, particularly in situations of coresidency (Schofield et al., 1994). In many cases, entry into residential care reflects the difficult decisions made by caregivers more than by older people themselves. In a longitudinal study of older users of community services, caregiver stress was found to be a main reason for entry to residential care (Wells, Swerissen, and Kendig, 1999).

THE LEGACIES OF PUBLIC POLICY AND PROGRAM DEVELOPMENT

The community services available to older people today reflect approximately 50 years of policy developments, intertwined with political initiatives and pressures from interest groups. Central to these Australian developments are three factors: the division of responsibilities between national and state governments; long-standing focus on institutional rather than community care; and separations between health and welfare services.

In Australia's federal system of government, the Commonwealth (national) government receives the bulk of all revenue collected, mainly through income taxes. In the area of health, the Commonwealth provides block grants to the states, Medicare benefits for general-practitioner services, and pharmaceutical benefits to individuals (Kendig and Duckett, 2001). The six state governments generate fewer financial resources, but the Australian Constitution provides them with primary authority to deliver health, housing, and most other direct services. They are thus well positioned to deliver and coordinate care for older people, public-hospital care, and related services. As a result of the differing resources and responsibilities of the two levels of government, there can be considerable contention between the two in terms of policy development and payment for services.

Australia also has a legacy of substantial investment in residential care, provided by both the voluntary and private sectors and sustained by massive government funding, since the 1960s. By comparison, community-care services developed in a modest, fragmented way with little government funding until the 1980s. Over the last 25 years, aged-care policy has aimed to rein in residential care costs and build up community-care services. Increasing government policy interest in community care and more funding for it has been accompanied by increasing central direction, which has been resisted by some care providers.

As outlined in Kendig and Duckett (2001), community-care services and other aged-care services have developed in Australia along the following long-term trends:

- Increasing involvement by government in health and welfare services.
- A shift in the leadership of the aged-care industry, first from voluntary providers to more private for-profit providers, and then to government funders.
- The rising expectations and financial resources of increasingly significant proportions of older people anticipating and requiring care.
- Recognition of caregivers as central to the provision of aged care, and to social equity between men and women.
- The rising expectations of older cohorts for their quality of life and their rising personal capacities and economic resources for achieving their expectations.

Voluntary Traditions

The immediate postwar period was an era of family responsibility for aged care and there was optimism for making a better world, particularly for returned servicemen and their families. Old people during this time, who had begun their lives in the 19th century, had low expectations for standards of living and government services. Early prototypes of the aged-care services that were to emerge were found in homes for independent older couples, which some churches provided to their members. It was virtually unquestioned that single people would live with their families, and "sick" older people would go to the hospital. As compared to benevolence homes for the sick, poor, and neglected, these church homes were convincing models for supporting well older people in the community. The church homes demonstrated to the public and the government the potential value of aged-welfare accommodation and services.

Government involvement in aged care began under the conservative Menzies government. The Aged Persons Homes Act (1954) provided grants to the politically popular and vocal voluntary sector, most visibly in the lead-up to difficult elections. These small beginnings set into motion rising public expenditure on aged care. However, with the act also began persistent problems: the domination of the institutional sector in aged care; inequities caused by older people having to match public subsidies with their own money; and provider dominance in aged-care services. Aged-care services were not integrated with mainstream state services, and there was a divide between health services and welfare services.

During the 1950s and early 1960s, the Menzies era of political conservatism was not conducive to the development of health or welfare policy. Some legislation for home nursing was introduced in 1956, but it was not followed up on until a politically harried government passed legislation much later for homecare (1969), paramedical services (1969), and meals services (1970) (Healy, 1990). The modest, supplementary grants that the Commonwealth provided directly to service providers largely perpetuated the fragmented development of services for older people. The modest public debate centered on whether or not government had any useful part in what was assumed to be family responsibility for care of older people.

The Nursing Home Industry

Arguably the most significant postwar development in aged care was the introduction of public funding to develop and sustain a nursing home industry comprised largely of private providers. In the early 1960s, national subsidies for nursing homes proved to be a politically palatable response to rising pressure on private health insurers and hospitals to provide aged-care services. The consequent laissez-faire period of nursing home policy, such as it was, inevitably led to rapid cost increases as a result of the burgeoning nursing home industry (Howe, 1990). There was virtually no policy coordination between Commonwealth and state governments in the regulation of nursing homes, nor in the provision of community services and acute healthcare.

Throughout the 1970s, relatively few developments in community services were introduced by either the Labor government of Gough Whitlam or by the Conservative Fraser government that followed it.

The 1980s Reforms

On the return of Labor in 1983, the Australian national government began to take aged-care reform seriously. At that time the concept of integrated aged care was developing among professionals frustrated by service fragmentation. Aged care took on wider political significance in the developing women's movement and new caregiver-advocacy and dementia-advocacy organizations. The Combined Pensioners and Superannuants Association and the Australian Council on the Ageing (COTA) argued strongly for universal aged-care provision. Academic research supported the case. At the same time, the government was increasingly concerned about the cost escalation of residential care services, scandals regarding patient mistreatment, and inappropriate placement of older people in nursing homes. Community care for older people thus emerged along with income maintenance and health support for older people on the political agenda.

In the Labor government's 10-year reform of aged care, a major platform was the 1985 Home and Community Care (HACC) program, which incorporated existing funding for community services into a joint Commonwealth-state effort (Healy, 1990). HACC established the objective of preventing inappropriate and premature entry into residential care, which was seen to enhance individuals' independence and limit costs to the government. The target groups included frail older people, younger people with disabilities, and their caregivers. The range of services was widened to provide more comprehensive services, funding for services was increased substantially, and program management was strengthened.

Other major initiatives were the consolidation of hostels and nursing homes into one residential care program, and the expansion of Geriatric Assessment Teams that restricted inappropriate admission to institutions and enhanced referrals to community services.

In 1992, the Commonwealth government initiated the Community Options Program, which aimed to provide community alternatives for older people at high risk for entry into residential care. This program, which provides high levels of services, has been funded entirely by the Commonwealth government out of its residential care program.

From 1985 to 1994, aged-care funding increased by more than 50 percent after adjusting for inflation. In her review of the 10-year Aged Care Reform Strategy, Howe (1997) concluded that the reforms had succeeded in shifting the balance of aged care toward community care. Her review also voiced continuing concern for the poor interface between the aged-care and acute-care sectors, shortfalls of community services, reform fatigue, and the slow pace of ongoing reform.

Recent Directions

On the return of a Conservative government in 1996, population aging was initially portrayed as a national crisis that required constraints on future government expenditure. Consideration also was given to devolving aged-care service delivery from the Commonwealth to the state governments. However, neither of these bold proposals went very far. Devolution to state governments was undermined by opposition from both provider and consumer groups, who were concerned about a possible lessening of their influence on service delivery. There were also deep suspicions between the Commonwealth and the states as to which government would ultimately bear the financial and political costs.

The new Howard government's "Recognizing Older Australians" budget statement featured a theme of "aging in place" that focused heavily on residential care. The government's Aged Care Act 1997, as the centerpiece for its Aged Care Structural Reform Strategy, again focused mainly on reforming residential care. In 1998, amid continuing controversy over these residential care reforms, the government launched a popular "Staying at Home" package that provided for additional community care including dementia and caregiver support. Provision of these new services directly by the national government avoided the need to coordinate (and share political credit) with state governments.

These reform initiatives increased expenditure on community care, but the balance of total aged-care expenditures continued to tip toward residential care (Howe, 2000). A two-year review of the reforms, which Gray conducted in 2001, concluded that they had ". . . delivered substantial improvements to the aged-care system" (p. xxxi). The review specifically noted that access to community services had improved for people who wished to stay in their own homes, and access to residential care improved for those having high levels of need.

In 1998 the national government launched the National Strategy for an Ageing Australia and produced discussion papers on the topic, including *World Class Care* (Bishop, 2000). The most recent stage of the strategy plan, released by the new minister for aging (Andrews, 2002), again listed "world-class care" as one of four goal areas. The minister's plan noted chronic diseases as the underlying cause of disability, the impacts of changing technology on illness and service delivery, and a likely increase in the expectations and resources of the next cohort of older Australians. The plan projected a doubling of real expenditure on community-care services for older people over the next 40 years.

In the campaign for the 2001 national election, the Coalition government—which was reelected—made commitments as part of its "Better Care for Older Australians" program. The commitments included 6,000 more Community Aged Care Packages (CACPs), which provided high levels of community services worth A$68 million over the next four years, and A$80 million for caregivers and dementia care.

NATIONAL COMMUNITY-CARE AND AGED-CARE SERVICES

For some years, Australia has been making a substantial investment in health and welfare for older people. In 1995–96 government expenditure for such services represented 5.1 percent of Australia's GDP and 13.4 percent of total government outlays (Choi, 1998), rising only modestly from the 1975–76 figure of 4.8 percent.

While levels of government pensions have risen in real terms, costs to government were limited by more stringent means tests (Kalish, 2000). Similarly, use of residential care has been increasingly restricted to older people having high levels of need (Gibson, Liu, and Choi, 1993).

Aged care is a relatively small part of Commonwealth and state government expenditure on older people (Kendig and Duckett, 2001). In 1995–96, income support accounted for nearly two thirds of the government expenditure on older people. Health-related areas of expenditure included hospitals (15 percent of total aging-related expenditure), medical services (6 percent), and pharmaceuticals (3 percent). By comparison, a modest 10 percent of aging-related expenditure was spent on residential care and only 3 percent on community care. Overall, aged care in 1996 amounted to A$3.85 billion, or around 0.7 percent of the GDP, with residential care comprising 76 percent of these costs (Commonwealth Department of Health and Aged Care, 1998).

In its 2002–03 budget, the Commonwealth government announced that funding for aged care and community care had grown by 83 percent from 1996–97 to 2002–03; expenditure on the nonresidential sector (HACC and CACPs) had grown relatively faster, at 106 percent. Over this period, Commonwealth expenditure increased from A$423 million to A$674 million for the HACC program, from A$33 million to A$265 million for the CACPs, and from A$140 million to A$321 million for other purposes, including respite funding, dementia support, and support for caregivers. Total aged-care expenditure in 2002–03 was projected to be A$5.5 billion (Australian Department of Health and Ageing, 2002).

Expenditure on Community Care

Community care for the aged and disabled is funded primarily through the HACC program. In 1997–98, a total of A$786 million was spent on HACC, approximately 60 percent of which was paid by the Commonwealth government. Howe (2000) has stated that 20 percent of the program is funded by user charges. She also estimated that that HACC-funded services are used by approximately one third of the frail older people in the community who might benefit from them and by a smaller proportion of younger people with disabilities. Bridge et al. (2002) reported similar findings, and added that older people had higher levels of service use than did younger adults.

In 1997–98, HACC was responsible for the vast majority of government expenditure on community services, which included community nursing (23 percent); home help (20 percent); respite care (13 percent); program support (12 percent) including education, training, information, and coordination; and a range of other services (25 percent) including meal delivery, home maintenance, transportation, and paramedical services (Duckett, 2000). The Community Options Program, while not part of HACC, amounted to 7 percent of total government expenditure on community services.

Community-Care Provision

Community-care services are delivered by a large number of organizations in the voluntary and public sectors. Almost 60 percent of the HACC-funded organizations employ fewer than three persons (Duckett, 2000). This fragmentation reflects the legacy of the voluntary era and suggests the difficulties in ensuring consistency and economies of scale in service delivery of community care.

The most widely used type of service is home help: About 10 percent of Australians ages 70 and older receive an average of four hours a month of home help. This contrasts with day-center care services, which are provided to 4 percent of older people at an average usage rate of 18 hours per month per person. Six percent of older people receive meal services, an average of 15 meals per person per month. Overall, 64 percent of HACC clients receive assistance from only one organization, while almost one sixth are seen by three or more separate organizations. Concerns for service coordination apply primarily to the minority of users who have relatively extensive needs. According to some reports, wide variation exists among the states in the rates of provision for HACC services. These disparities reflect the varied traditions of community services and the joint Commonwealth and state management of the HACC program (Duckett, 2000).

Community-Care Clients

Agency records show that nearly 70 percent of HACC clients are women, and their average age is 74 (median age: 78) (Bridge, Kendig, Quine, and Parsons, 2002). The average age of older men served was slightly younger, at 69.9 (median age: 75). Although younger people with disabilities also are eligible for the program, the average age for the total population of HACC users was 72.4 (median age: 77). More than half (58 percent) of those receiving HACC assistance reside with a caregiver, and many caregivers are older adults themselves. In 1998 it was estimated that 133,330 Australians ages 75 and older cared for people with disabilities (Bishop, 2000).

It is difficult to predict individuals' service use or the costs they pay out-of-pocket for community care. A Sydney study conducted by Broe, Grayson, Waite, Creasey, Edelbrock, Bennett, and Brooks (2002) found that the most significant predictor of community-service use among older people was the individual's disability level, with modest additional use predicted by marital status and veteran status—older unmarried women and veterans make higher claims. Older migrants from non-English-speaking countries are relatively less likely to use community-care services (Kendig and Russell, 1998). In a Melbourne study of Community Options Program clients, per-person service-delivery costs were directly related to dependency levels (including incontinence), whether the primary caregiver was a male, and the duration of the period in which services had continued (Kendig, Wells, Swerissen, and Reynolds, 1999).

The appropriate "targeting" of the HACC program has increasingly come under question. On the one hand, no formal assessment is required to restrict use to people with high levels of need. On the other hand, there has been increasing demand to provide high levels of support for small numbers of very frail people. The Community Options Program model has demonstrated the considerable capacity of case management and individually targeted service packages in maintaining people with intense needs in the community with acceptable quality of life. Howe (2000) reported that one half to two thirds of HACC clients receive only 20 to 30 percent of the total resources available, whereas 5 to 10 percent absorb up to half of the resources.

Community Aged Care Packages

The Commonwealth CACP program parallels the HACC program. It provides "packages" of case management and flexible services tailored for individuals who are assessed as needing low-level residential care, but who strongly prefer to remain at home (AIHW, 2002). The care packages are viewed by the Commonwealth as an alternative to placement in residential facilities and count toward planning and funding residential care, at a rate of 10 CACP places for every 1,000 persons ages 70 and older. Gibson and Mathur (1999) concluded that the CACPs serve a less dependent clientele than either hostels in the residential care program or Community Options Program clients in the HACC program.

The number of care packages increased rapidly from a few hundred in 1992 to 10,000 in 1998 and 27,000 in 2002 (AIHW, 2002; Australian Department of Health and Ageing, 2002). The 2002–03 Commonwealth Budget funded the 2001 election commitment to provide an additional 6,000 places by 2005–06. The Community Options Program and the CACP program are popular among older people who prefer to remain in their own homes. The programs offer cost advantages to the government because, relative to residential care, no capital investment is required. Provision varies considerably across states, and places are more common in remote areas, where their flexibility assists in dealing with shortages of institutional care and other infrastructure. Some CACP places are provided specifically for older Aboriginal and Torres Strait Island people, and the recent budget approved additional places as a pilot program in retirement villages.

Caregiver Support and Benefits

In Australia, the Commonwealth and state governments support frail older people in the community primarily through services rather than through direct payments. However, there has been increasing recognition of the value of cash payments that enable caregivers to continue providing support. The means-tested Carer Payment provides the equivalent to the Age Pension for those who provide full-time care to an adult who has a long-term, severe disability and who otherwise would need full-time professional care (Australian Department of Family and Community Services, 2002). In 2002, 65,000 persons received the Carer Payment; a third of them were caring for a frail older person. The 2002–03 budget for Carer Payment was A$730 million.

A Carer Allowance is provided to help parents and guardians care for a disabled child or adult at home. This allowance is not asset- or income-tested, and payments are set at a relatively low rate of A$80 per fortnight, indexed annually. A quarter of a million persons received this allowance in 2002, of whom two thirds were caring for one or more children. The 2002–03 budget for the Carer Allowance was A$737 million.

The 2002–03 aged-care allocation fulfilled the government's 2001 election commitment to provide an additional A$80 million of funding over four years in support of its National Respite for Carers Program. Thirty million dollars were committed to respite centers for caregiver support, covering specialized equipment, transportation, and counseling services. An additional A$20 million was allocated to support caregivers of people with dementia, subsidizing access to aged-care homes for respite and increased coverage of psychogeriatric units. An additional A$30 million was committed to the support of aging caregivers of people with disabilities, pilot education and training programs for volunteer caregivers, purchase of care packages through CACP, and help with the costs of respite, transportation, and equipment. These funds supplemented those that HACC already directed to support caregivers.

A State Perspective: New South Wales

States have primary responsibility for the management of the national HACC program. Every year, each of the six Australian states prepares an annual plan that provides accountability and sets priorities. In New South Wales (NSW)—the largest Australian state, which includes Sydney—the annual HACC State Plan is the responsibility of the NSW Department of Ageing, Disability, and Home Care.

As shown in the 2001–02 New South Wales HACC State Plan, the states "purchase" services from nonprofit service providers in each of their state regions, which are broadly equivalent to American counties (NSW Department of Ageing, Disability, and Home Care, 2002). The 2001–02 plan paid particular attention to intersections and gaps between aging and disability programs. This is understandable, given potential cost shifting between levels of government. Two additional priorities were the development of a Minimum Data Set to monitor client profiles and shifts from input to output funding. Other areas for detailed work concerned pooling of funds and cooperation between services, assessment and coordination of existing services, development of a quality manual, targeting strategies especially for high-need clients, and attention to special-needs groups. Plans were underway for service type reviews, analyses of client data, and a capital development review.

The NSW HACC program was allocated a substantial A$318 million for 2000–01, an increase of A$26 million over the previous year. Funds are allocated to 16 regions as well as to statewide developments that support service provision in all regions. Major service categories eligible for expenditures included domestic assistance (A$72 million), personal care (A$51 million), respite care (A$50 million), home nursing (A$42 million), food services (A$16 million), and home maintenance (A$14 million). In addition, A$14 million was allocated for "other" support services and A$10 million for administration and other program underwriting. The HACC program also has supported Community Care Demonstration Projects that explore innovative ways to better integrate services and address fragmentation problems (Fine, 1999).

In New South Wales, community-care services also are provided by the state health department, which is responsible for public hospitals, mental health services, and various community health services. The NSW Department of Health (2001) has identified several problems with the existing structure of services, including insufficient coordination between hospital and community care, incentives for cost shifting between levels of government, some duplication of services for individual patients, and the lack of incentives for Area Health Services to engage in long-term, comprehensive planning. The department proposed an integrated health service model that would ". . . determine and deliver the most appropriate mix of services to meet the health needs of people in a particular geographic region, regardless of who provides or funds the service" (p. 3). Community health services are included in this service model.

CURRENT POLICY ISSUES IN COMMUNITY CARE

A number of proposals have been advanced for fundamental reform to deal with intergovernmental problems and to address difficulties of accountability, integration, and continuity of aged-care services (Kendig and Duckett, 2001). Some policymakers propose that one level of government should take full responsibility for aged care, but such radical proposals are unlikely to gain political acceptance. Discussion presently focuses on more intermediate approaches such as the pooling of regional funds for community-care, residential care, and related services. More incremental approaches, as described by Fine (1999), include general-practice referral systems, assessment and referral systems, information strategies, community networking and interagency meetings, case management and service brokerage, and larger-scale reforms such as Coordinated Care Trials (a form of funds pooling) for specified kinds of healthcare needs.

The interface between aged care and the health sector is important because older people are major users of public hospitals. For example, large amounts of care are provided for short-term needs after a person is discharged from an acute-care hospital. This post-acute care was once termed a "no growth" area for the HACC, leaving a legacy that such community care was to be restricted to ensure that HACC resources were not used to minimize hospital costs. Similar issues arise concerning rehabilitation care and residential care. In addition to a variety of state pilot efforts, the Commonwealth has an Innovative Pool Initiative that funds new approaches to these friction points in aged care. The Commonwealth is also testing the pilot Extended Aged Care at Home program for older people requiring nursing home–level care.

There are ongoing pressures to expand the HACC program to satisfy more of the unmet demand. Increases in Commonwealth and state expenditure and the introduction of new programs, such as the Veterans Home Care Program, have helped considerably. Ongoing requests include one by the Council on the Ageing (Australia) (2002) to increase HACC funds by 20 percent in the 2002–03 budget. The actual increase of 8 percent for 2002–03 was enough for modest expansion. Together with the rapid growth of the CACP program, provision of care in the community has increased.

Consideration has also been given to tighter rationing of HACC resources. In her report on HACC targeting, Howe (1999) recommended that funds be specified for "Basic" HACC users (the 80 percent of clients who use present HACC services); HACC "Plus" clients (the 15 percent or so who are referred to more resources after assessment), and a category of "Exceptional Clients" who would receive 2 percent with funds pooling on case-by-case bases. This approach has been supported by the Council on the Ageing (Australia) (2002), and the NSW government is exploring its application. However, it has not been adopted by the Commonwealth government.

User charges have long been a controversial aspect of the HACC program. The National Fee Principles introduced program guidelines following the 1996–97 Commonwealth Budget aimed at securing user contributions with means tests that ensured access and affordability. From 2000 on, all clients were required to contribute to the cost of HACC services unless their incomes and assets met stringent means tests. While the Commonwealth requires that states set fee targets, it is not clear how the user charges are being implemented, nor is there much information on how they may or may not have generated resources or discouraged service use. The NSW State Department of Ageing, Disability, and Home Care (2002) conservatively estimated its 2001–02 fee income at A$31 million, or 10 percent of program expenditure.

Outcome standards have long been an aim for HACC services, and instruments and procedures are slowly being implemented to determine outcomes (Jenkins, Butkus, and Gibson, 1998). Quality control also is becoming increasingly important given the rising numbers of vulnerable older people in the community and the difficulty of monitoring workers in clients' homes. In the 2002–03 budget, the Commonwealth set plans to enhance quality assurance for CACPs and to strengthen national monitoring of service standards.

For many years the HACC program has been challenged regarding its efficiency and professionalism and the lack of integration of its services. If the program was administered by fewer, larger agencies, improvements might be seen in these areas. Such a structure also might address fragmentation and discontinuities of services. Some state governments have followed recent HACC funding agreements between Commonwealth and state governments by implementing more contestable tendering arrangements, including performance requirements. Meetings of service providers frequently discuss possible consolidation of the industry. Aged and Community Services Australia, or ACSA (2002), notes the need for administrative streamlining of community-care programs.

The Myer Foundation (2002) reported on the views of aged-care experts in a report titled *2020: A Vision for Aged Care in Australia.* With regard to community care, which was the first of the priority areas in the five-point plan the foundation laid out, it recommended increasing funding, establishing an integrated national program, ensuring equity across services and regions, improving efficiency through comprehensive care providers, recognizing the key role of hospitals, and supporting the central role of caregivers. It also emphasized the importance of improving housing arrangements including separating housing and care components; ensuring consistency and streamlining of administration; and implementing a funding model that would increase and broaden the resource base by drawing on consumer as well as public resources. An industry plan for aged-care providers proposed an expanded role for community care and improved integration across the community-care, residential care, and hospital sectors.

A major gap in the integration of aged care concerns the crucial nexus between housing and care: A home is required as a base for community care (Bridge et al., 2002). Both consumer and provider organizations have argued strongly for increased public housing and other housing assistance for non-homeowners. However, the availability of public housing has been falling, and successful pilot programs linking housing and care have not expanded. Very little has been done to advance barrier-free design of housing and neighborhoods (Kendig, 2000b). To address some of these issues, Kendig and Duckett (2001) proposed the "unbundling" of care and accommodation services so that appropriate policy treatment and funding could be provided to both areas.

In addition, many aged-care providers in both the community-care and residential care sectors are concerned that available funds do not enable them to pay sufficient salaries to attract and retain good staff (Aged and Community Services Association of New South Wales and Australian Capital Territory, 2001). High-quality care depends on a skilled and dedicated workforce. In its 2002–03 budget the Commonwealth began small initiatives to fund education and training for aged-care workers and nurses, particularly in rural areas.

VISIONS FOR THE FUTURE

The *National Strategy for an Ageing Australia* (Andrews, 2002, pp. 57–59) has raised issues likely to have a significant bearing on directions for community care:

- The importance of instituting system wide changes to improve coordination and integration among the health and care systems, community care, hospital-based geriatric and rehabilitation services, and general-practitioner services.
- A focus on disease prevention, restoration of function, and maintenance of quality of life and independence for older Australians.
- Trends toward increasingly high levels of care being provided in the community.
- Responsiveness to the diversity of older Australians, including people in rural and remote areas, indigenous Australians, those from culturally and linguistically diverse backgrounds, and people aging with lifelong disabilities.
- Informal caregivers continuing as a foundation of Australia's system of care.
- Government funding as the primary source of funding for aged care, with access to services provided on the basis of need regardless of income. In the future more older people might choose to purchase care that is different from, or additional to, publicly funded care.

The Australian Department of Health and Ageing (2003) subsequently released for consultation a document titled *A New Strategy for Community Care* after conducting an internal review of its community-care programs. The department's aim was to establish a national framework for bringing together all current programs into ". . . an easily accessible, streamlined, and cost-effective system" (p. 3). The framework proposes to reorganize Commonwealth-funded services into three tiers to meet three distinct levels of need: access, information, and support; basic community care; and packaged community care. Additional elements of the strategy are the development of a Regional Access Center network and standardization of administrative requirements such as standards, fees, and accountability processes. The review did not address issues concerning the interface between general practitioners, hospitals, residential aged care, housing, and disability support programs.

In its 2002 discussion paper *A Vision for Community Care,* ACSA suggests desirable directions for community-service development from the viewpoint of service providers in the voluntary sector. The paper emphasized that debate on community-care reform is being driven by a coalition that includes professional organizations, consumer groups, and industry groups. ACSA states, "Community care of the future will support lifestyle choices to enable people who need support and their caregivers to live in their own community" (p. 2). Older people and caregivers need to be at the center of decision making, with their capacities acknowledged and strengthened and with flexible services tailored to each individual. Community-care services need to relate closely to primary and hospital-based healthcare, high-quality housing, and community planning. In June 2003 ACSA and The Myer Foundation convened a National Community Care Summit to make recommendations in response to the growing call for community care reform. (That report is expected to be placed on the ACSA website at *www.agedcare.org.au.*)

These visions for the future of aged-care services in Australia emphasize the value of research in guiding policy development. Earlier Australian research has done a good deal to guide and improve policy and program development in community care and has identified and promulgated best practices (Kendig, 2001). Research funding has been scarce over recent years, but there is some commitment to conduct additional strategic research in the near future. The ACSA paper (2002) states,

> There needs to be greater support for Australian research that will provide the evidence for the effectiveness of alternative models in supporting people to live in their own homes. Good research is also the most reliable way of making sure the voices of those most affected by community-care provision are heard, regardless of how faint those voices may be (p. 2).

CONCLUSION

Australia has made great advances in its provision of community-care services since Home and Community Care was introduced in 1985. Few commentators at that time would have anticipated the far-reaching successes of the program and the growing recognition of the importance of community care, dementia care, and support for caregivers. While HACC was once seen as subsidiary to residential care, it has deeply demonstrated the capacity of community services to meet frail older people's preferences to remain in their own homes and receive high-quality care. Community services now are the mainstay of aged care for older Australians, and only a minority of older Australians ever enter residential care.

Notwithstanding these important achievements, community care and aged care in Australia appear to be at a crossroads. Major improvement is difficult because of the fundamental division of responsibilities between the Commonwealth and the states under the Australian federal system of government. However, the practical success of community care is generating its own momentum for further improvements. Governments are encouraging innovations to deal with problems of coordination and interface between community services, hospitals, and residential care. However, as the ACSA (2002) report stated, community care now works *despite* the existing system. New directions for community care include the design of supportive built environments and health promotion activities that enhance older people's capacity for independence.

Countries in the Asia region will need to make their own judgments on the relevance of Australian community care to their cultural traditions and forms of government. While the experience of every country is distinctive, other countries may be able to avoid the imbalances and fragmentation of care in Australia caused by the early predominance of residential over community care and the separate development of health and welfare services. More positively, there is strong evidence in Australia that the provision of community services has strengthened rather than undermined family relationships. Furthermore, consumer advocacy and applied research have been invaluable in establishing the need for community care and for finding ways to improve services in Australia (Quine and Kendig, 1999). The development of a strong Asian literature on care in the community can facilitate comparisons that inform policy development for all countries in the region (World Health Organization Kobe Centre for Health Development, 2001).

REFERENCES

Aged and Community Services Australia [ACSA]. (2002). *A vision for community care: Discussion paper.* Canberra, Australia: Author.

Aged and Community Services Association of New South Wales and Australian Capital Territory. (2001). *Staffing and quality in aged care services, seminar report.* Sydney: Author.

Andrews, K. (2002). *National strategy for an ageing Australia.* Canberra, Australia: Commonwealth of Australia.

Australian Bureau of Statistics. (1999). *Survey of disability, ageing, and carers.* Canberra, Australia: Author.

Australian Bureau of Statistics. (2002a). *Australian systems of national accounts* (Catalogue No. 5204.0). Canberra, Australia: Author.

Australian Bureau of Statistics. (2002b). *Labour force Australia* (Publication No. 6203.0). Canberra, Australia: Author.

Australian Department of Family and Community Services. (2002). *Portfolio budget papers.* Retrieved April 20, 2002, from http://www.facs.gov.au/budget2002

Australian Department of Health and Ageing. (2002). *Portfolio budget papers.* Retrieved April 22, 2002, from http://www.health.gov.au/budget2002

Australian Department of Health and Ageing. (2003, March). *A new strategy for community care: Consultation paper.* Retrieved August 3, 2003, from http://www.health.gov.auacc/research/commcare.htm

Australian Institute of Health and Welfare [AIHW]. (1999). *Australia's welfare 1999: Services and assistance.* Canberra, Australia: Author.

AIHW. (2002). *Community aged care packages 2000–01: A statistical overview.* Canberra, Australia: Author.

AIHW and National Disability Administrators. (2000). *Disability and ageing: Australian population patterns and implications.* Canberra, Australia: AIHW.

Bishop, B. (2000). *The national strategy for an ageing Australia: World Class Care discussion paper.* Canberra, Australia: Commonwealth of Australia.

Bridge, C., Kendig, H., Quine, S., and Parsons, A. (2002). *Housing and care for younger and older adults with disabilities: Final report.* Melbourne: Australian Housing and Urban Research Institute.

Broe, G. A., Grayson, D. A., Waite, L. M., Creasey, H., Edelbrock, D., Bennett, H. P., and Brooks, W. S. (2002). Determinants of service use among the elderly in the Sydney Older Persons study. *Australasian Journal on Ageing, 21*(2), 61–66.

Brooke, L., Davison, S., Kendig, H., and Reynolds, A. (1998). *The support needs of older people in high rise public housing.* Victoria, Australia: Aged, Community, and Mental Health Division, Human Services Victoria.

Charleton, F., and Kendig, H. (1995). *Older people's use of community services.* Paper presented to the Aged Care Conference, Victoria, Australia.

Choi, C. (1998). *Government health and welfare expenditure on older Australians* (Welfare Division Working Paper No. 20). Canberra, Australia: Australian Institute of Health and Welfare.

Costello, P. (2002). *Intergenerational Report 2002–03* (Budget Paper no. 5). Canberra, Australia: Australian Department of Treasury.

Commonwealth Department of Health and Aged Care. (1998). *Budget paper no. 1.* Canberra, Australia: Commonwealth of Australia.

Council on the Ageing (Australia). (2002). *Health and ageing budget submission 2002–03.* Victoria, Australia: Author.

Davison, B., Kendig, H., Stephens, F., and Merrill, V. (1993). *It's our place: Older people talk about their homes.* Canberra, Australia: Australian Government Publishing Service.

Duckett, S. J. (2000). *The Australian health care system.* Melbourne: Oxford University Press.

Fine, M. D. (1999). Coordinating health, extended care, and community support services: Reforming aged care in Australia. *Journal of Aging and Social Policy, 11,* 67–90.

Gardner, I., Brooke, E., Ozanne, E., and Kendig, H. (1998). *Improving health and social isolation in the veteran Australian community.* Canberra, Australia: Department of Veteran's Affairs.

Gibson, D., and Goss, J. (1999). The coming crisis of Australian aged care: Fact or fiction? *Australasian Journal on Ageing, 18*(3), 19–25.

Gibson, D., Liu, Z., and Choi, C. (1993). *Changing patterns of residential care, 1985–1992: Supply and utilisation.* Canberra, Australia: Australian Institute of Health and Welfare.

Gibson, D., and Mathur, S. (1999). Australian innovations in home-based care: A comparison of Community Aged Care Packages, Community Options Projects, and hostel care. *Australasian Journal on Ageing, 18*(2), 72–78.

Healy, J. (1990). Community services: Long-term care at home? In H. L. Kendig and J. McCallum (Eds.), *Grey policy: Australian policies for an ageing society* (pp. 127–149). Sydney: Allen and Unwin.

Howe, A. L. (1997). The aged care reform strategy: A decade of changing momentum and margins for reform. In A. Borowski, S. Encel, and E. Ozanne (Eds.), *Ageing and social policy in Australia* (pp. 301–326). Cambridge, United Kingdom: Cambridge University Press.

Howe, A. L. (1999). *Targeting in the home and community care program* (Aged and Community Services Development and Evaluation Reports No. 37). Canberra, Australia: Commonwealth Department of Health and Aged Care.

Howe, A. L. (2000). Rearranging the compartments: The financing and delivery of care for Australia's elderly. *Health Affairs, 19,* 57–71.

Jenkins, A., Butkus, E., and Gibson, D. (1998). *Developing quality measures for home and community care.* Canberra, Australia: Australian Institute of Health and Welfare.

Kalish, D. W. (2000). *Social policy directions across the OECD region: Reflections on a decade of change* (Policy Research Paper No. 4). Canberra, Australia: Department of Family and Community Services.

Kendig, H. (2000a). Family change and family bonding in Australia. In W. Liu and H. Kendig (Eds.), *Elderly care, the family, and human values: East meets West* (pp. 107–125). Singapore: Singapore University Press.

Kendig, H. (2000b). Ageing and the built environment. In P. Troy (Ed.), *Equity, environment, efficiency: Ethics and economics in urban Australia* (pp. 97–109). Melbourne: Melbourne University Press.

Kendig, H. (2001). Policy and service-oriented research for community health care in an ageing society. In World Health Organization Kobe Centre for Health Development (Ed.), *Community health care in an ageing society* (pp. 180–191). Kobe, Japan: World Health Organization Kobe Centre for Health Development.

Kendig, H., and Brooke, L. (1999). Social perspectives on community nursing practice. In R. Nay and S. Garratt (Eds.), *Nursing older people: Issues and innovations* (pp. 133–150). Sydney: Maclennan and Petty.

Kendig, H., and Duckett, S. (2001). *Australian directions in aged care: The generation of policies for generations of older people* (Australian Health Policy Institute Commissioned Paper Series, No. 5). Sydney: University of Sydney.

Kendig, H., and Russell, H. (1998). Aging, ethnicity, and health policy in Australia. In A. Wister and G. Guttman (Eds.), *Health systems and aging in selected Pacific Rim countries: Diversity and change* (pp. 19–42). Vancouver, Canada: Simon Fraser University Press.

Kendig, H., Wells, Y., Swerissen, H., and Reynolds, A. (1999). Costs of community care services for individuals with complex needs. *Australasian Journal on Ageing, 18,* 86–92.

Liu, Z., Braun, P., and Mason, F. (2001). *The probability of using residential aged care services over a long time* (Australian Institute of Health and Welfare Publication No. 36). Canberra, Australia: AIHW.

The Myer Foundation. (2002). *2020: A vision for aged care in Australia.* Melbourne: The Myer Foundation.

New South Wales Department of Health. (2001). *Healthshare: A discussion paper for New South Wales.* Sydney: Author.

New South Wales Department of Ageing, Disability, and Home Care. (2002). *New South Wales Health and Community Care program, 2001–02 state plan.* Sydney: Author.

Quine, S., and Kendig, H. (1999). Stakeholders in policy research for older Australians. *Hallym International Journal of Aging, 1*(2), 16–25.

Salkeld, G., Cameron, I., Cumming, R., Seymour, J., Kurrle, S., and Quine, S. (2000). Quality of life related to fear of falling and hip fracture in older women: A time trade-off study. *British Medical Journal, 320,* 341–345.

Schofield, H., Bloch, S., Herrman, H., Murphy, B., Nankervis, J., and Singh, B. (Eds.). (1994). *Family caregivers: Disability, illness and ageing.* Sydney: Allen and Unwin.

Wells, Y., Swerissen, H., and Kendig, H. (1999). Client outcomes in case managed care: Who benefits most? *Australasian Journal on Ageing, 18*(2), 79–85.

World Health Organization Kobe Centre for Health Development. (2001). *Community health care in an ageing society.* Kobe, Japan: Author.

CHAPTER EIGHTEEN

Community-Care Services in Japan

Daisaku Maeda and Hisanori Ishikawa

Japan has undergone rapid economic development and urbanization since the mid-1950s. According to the Japanese National Census of 1950, 48 percent of the population was engaged in primary industries. Thirty-five years later, the 1985 National Census showed that the proportion of the population working in primary industrial areas had declined to just 10 percent. The impact of this change on Japanese society was so profound that it is occasionally referred to as the "second industrial revolution" (Oouchi, Arisawa, Wakimura, Minobe, and Naito, 1971). Naturally, the economic transformation of the country and the rapid urbanization that accompanied it greatly affected the lives of Japanese older people, and eventually the country's social security, healthcare, and welfare systems. This chapter will discuss a number of the important changes that occurred in Japan over the past half century, as well as the development of community-care services for the elderly. Like all Asian societies, Japan is a country undergoing even further change as political and global economic transitions occur.

DEMOGRAPHIC CHANGES IN JAPAN

As a consequence of improvements in the overall standard of living as well as advances in medical science, since the early 1950s the number of Japanese ages 80 and older has increased significantly. Such an increase in the numbers of the old old has brought about a proliferation in the demand for various forms of care services for the elderly. Increased demand for services was accelerated by the decreased capability of family caretakers; as Japanese elders reached advanced ages, so too did their caregiving children. In many cases, the children themselves had become old enough that their own health was no longer adequate enough for them to provide needed care for their parents. Of course, traditional value orientations have also undergone changes, though not so conspicuous as the structural changes that have occurred in Japan.

The reduction in the portion of the population engaged in agricultural occupations during the decades following World War II brought about a number of socioeconomic shifts, including the migration of younger people from rural to urban, industrialized areas. As a result, the fraction of older people living alone or only with a spouse increased significantly. Paradoxically, however, it is unique to Japan that the proportion of older people living alone or with a spouse in rural areas is still much lower than in urban areas, a pattern not replicated in other industrialized countries in East Asia such as Taiwan and South Korea (Aoi, 1976). In addition to the migration of the younger generation from rural to urban areas, the development of manufacturing and shifting labor markets led to a dispersion of industrial sites across the country in the years following the early 1960s. A large number of younger people were forced to move to other locales where industrial production was situated to find jobs. Thus, even people who were born and raised in urban locations often found it difficult to obtain employment in the same urban vicinity where their parents lived.

Industrialization has fostered geographical mobility for working people in Japan; traditionally, Japanese people tended to stay in one place throughout their lives. In industrialized societies, people change jobs more frequently than members of agricultural societies and must move to where employment opportunities are greatest. Even when employees remain in the same firm, they are often obliged to move to other locations in order to remain employed. In such cases, often their aging parents prefer to remain at their original residence rather than move to an unfamiliar place with a child's family in order to continue to live together. Moreover, in Japan's industrialized areas, houses for workers are generally not spacious enough to accommodate three generations.

Another noticeable change in Japanese society has been the growing number of women in the paid workforce. Because of the shortage of male workers, many married, middle-aged women who had been the most faithful caretakers of dependent older parents gradually began to work outside the home. In addition, the number of married women who were engaged in full-time professional jobs increased significantly. Women in full-time positions seldom quit their jobs to take care of their aging parents, as is sometimes the case with women working in part-time or unskilled jobs.

Improvements in education, higher living standards, and the cultural influence of Western industrialized countries have awakened a sense of selfhood in the general public, which has played an important role in the changing living arrangements of Japanese elders. For example, in the past several decades, increasing numbers of both older and younger generations have come to prefer to live separately from each other, primarily for the sake of independence and personal freedom (Takahashi, 2002).

The number of children in Japan has been decreasing rapidly since 1950. As a result, people with fewer children are now gradually acceding to the ranks of the older adult population. Obviously, when older people have fewer children, their probability of depending on their descendants in their old age is reduced. This factor has made the need for elder-care services, both community-based and institutional, more and more pressing.

DEVELOPMENT OF COMMUNITY-CARE SERVICES FOR THE ELDERLY, 1950–1980

The rapid and profound social changes that began in the early 1950s drew attention to the need for a universal public retirement pension system and a universal public health insurance arrangement. After long and strenuous efforts by scholars, unions, and self-help organizations, the national media began to publicize and eventually to endorse the movement for universal public pensions and health insurance provisions. In response to this growing social movement, the national Ministry of Welfare and Health initiated efforts to realize these two fundamental systems in the late 1950s, and succeeded in the early 1960s.

Thus, by the early 1960s, Japan managed to succeed in meeting the basic health and economic needs of its citizens. At the same time, the national government put into place the fundamental legislative and administrative framework needed for protecting basic human rights: the Livelihood Protection Law, a national public assistance law (1950); the Child Welfare Law (1947); the Law for the Welfare of Handicapped People (1949); universal health insurance coverage (1961); and universal coverage of public retirement pension insurance (1961). Subsequently, both the national government and local governments began to pay more attention to the social and humanistic aspects of people's lives. Various public services were developed to improve quality of life for the citizenry of Japan, which included meeting older adults' needs for social, cultural, and recreational services.

However, until the 1980s government efforts to develop public services for the elderly were designed to catch Japan up with the industrialized countries of Western Europe and North America. With the exception of a few unique actions, Japan essentially followed the trails that these countries had blazed in promoting the well-being of the elderly. Among the key legislative changes that occurred, certain developments stand out as being particularly important.

Law for the Welfare of the Aged

In 1963, the national government enacted the Law for the Welfare of the Aged (*Rohjin Fukushi Hoh*). This law effectively separated all services designed to meet the needs of the elderly from the public assistance provisions, except for public assistance in the form of cash payments to elders living in the community. Accordingly, the assets test for aging-related services was abolished, the procedure for income testing was greatly simplified, and a fee scale based on personal income was introduced so as to enable all older Japanese to receive needed services regardless of income. These measures allowed older adults who needed public services to apply for them free of the shame that almost always accompanies receiving public assistance.

However, the coverage of the Law for the Welfare of the Aged at the time of enactment was very limited compared to the scope of services that became available to Japanese elders in subsequent years. The statutory services established under the law were health checkup services, institutional care services, and community centers for the elderly. Although old people's clubs and home help services for destitute older adults had already been included under national subsidies before the Law for the Welfare of the Aged was passed, they were not designated statutory services under the law.

The Birth of Community-Care Services for the Elderly

The first community-care service for the elderly in Japan was a home help service for destitute older adults. It was started in a small city in central Japan in 1955, and soon was replicated by two large city governments, Osaka (1958) and Tokyo (1961) (Fukushi Bunka Gakkai, 1995). In 1962, the national government initiated national financial backing for the home help program. However, home help services spread slowly, because at that time most destitute older adults needing them were institutionalized. By 1980, there were still only 9,700 home helpers employed by local governments across Japan (Maeda, 2001). This means that the average local government employed only three home helpers to provide services within its catchment area.

Daycare and short-term stay services for the elderly were introduced significantly later. The first pioneering program in daycare and short-term stay services was started in 1975 by a nursing home run by a voluntary organization in a suburb of Tokyo (Fukushi Bunka Gakkai, 1995). Shortly after its inception, however, the national government acknowledged the importance of these services, and established a national subsidy for short-term stay services in 1978 and one for daycare services a year later. Again, the pace of development for the two types of services was slow, mainly due to scarcity of financial resources, until the implementation of the national Long-Term Care Insurance scheme in 2000.

DEVELOPMENT OF COMMUNITY-CARE SERVICES FOR THE ELDERLY, 1980–PRESENT

By 1980, older adults made up more than 9 percent of the total population of Japan. Although the proportion of older adults in the general population was still low compared with that of other industrialized countries, the impact of population aging became increasingly clear. It was soon recognized not just by those working directly with the elderly, but also by leaders in various sectors of Japanese society.

Around that time, projections that Japan would become one of the most aged countries in the world within 40 years began to be published. In view of the rapid progress of population aging in Japan and its anticipated economic and social impact on society, in 1986 the national government adopted a Policy Statement on the National Long-Term Program to Cope with the "Society of Longevity" (*chohju shakai taisaku taikoh*). Though the content of the program was not new for social gerontologists, who were already well informed about aging policy in Western Europe and North America, this policy statement exerted a significant impact on several bodies within the Japanese national government. The statement significantly accelerated the development of social policy for the elderly, including various types of community-care services, and served to raise the visibility of the issues already on the horizon.

Ten-Year Plan for the Promotion of Health and Welfare Services for the Elderly

In 1990, another significant development in aging services in Japan occurred: the promulgation of the Ten-Year Plan for the Promotion of Health and Welfare Services for the Elderly, commonly called the "Gold Plan." Under the Gold Plan, the development of community-care services for older adults was given priority status, as these services were significantly less developed than institutional care, educational, or recreational services.

The reason the national government promulgated the Gold Plan was that it recognized the existence of a gap between the pace of population aging in Japan and that of the development of social policies for the elderly. In order to close the anticipated gap between supply and demand of services, the government planned to introduce a "Consumption Tax." To persuade the public of the necessity for the new tax, the government proposed the Gold Plan as a long-term strategy to cope with the coming aging of Japanese society, presenting it to the public with considerable media support and outlining costs entailed in the Gold Plan. The latter, in itself, mandated a new tax policy, one capable of generating revenues necessary to underwrite corresponding outlays of the Gold Plan.

The Gold Plan was extensively revised only five years later, in 1995, as the previous plan proved to be markedly inadequate in light of the predicted expansion of the need for public care services for the elderly in the 21st century. The revised New Gold Plan was made public in December 1994. Its goals, like the goals of the original Gold Plan, were to be reached before the end of fiscal year 1999 and were to provide inclusive coverage to older Japanese citizens (Table 1).

Between 1989 and 1999, the government intended to increase the number of home helpers across Japan from 31,400 to 170,000 to achieve a 1:128 ratio of the number of home helpers to the number of Japanese ages 65 and older. For comparative purposes it is helpful to know that in Sweden this ratio was roughly

Table 1. The Gold Plan of 1990 and New Gold Plan of 1994:
Goals for 1999

Service	Gold Plan	New Gold Plan
Community-care services		
Home helpers (persons)	100,000	170,000
Short-term stay services (beds)	50,000	60,000
Daycare centers	10,000	17,000
Homecare support centers	10,000	10,000
Visiting nurse stations	—	5,000
Institutional care services		
Special care homes for the aged (beds)	240,000	290,000
Geriatric healthcare facilities (beds)	280,000	280,000
Care houses (beds)	100,000	100,000
Multipurpose senior centers in depopulated areas	400	400

Source: Maeda, 2003.

1:50 (Tanaka, 1993), and Japan's goal included part-time workers.[1] Despite the revisions, the ratio still meant that Japan's level of home help would be far below the levels found in other advanced countries in Western Europe.

The revised New Gold Plan also called for the number of daycare centers for older adults to increase from 1,080 in 1989 to 17,000 in 1999. When the goal was reached, Japan would have one such center for every 1,300 older persons; in other words, a typical medium-size city of 100,000 would have approximately 13 daycare centers. In addition, the number of beds for short-term stay (respite care) services was to increase from 4,274 in 1989 to 60,000 a decade later. The New Gold Plan also called for the establishment of 10,000 homecare support centers that would provide guidance, counseling, and care management for community-dwelling older adults and family caregivers.

Growing Concern Over Care Security

The most conspicuous trend after 1990 with regard to social security, healthcare, and social services was the public's growing concern regarding the need for *kaigo hosho* ("care security") as Japan's population aged. The concept of care security refers to a multitiered public social service system that meets all older adults' care needs, including both institutional care and homecare, regardless of income. With its Gold Plan of 1990 and New Gold Plan of 1994, the

[1] The ratio between home helpers and the number of old people ages 65-plus in Sweden was calculated by the author using the data included in Tanaka's paper.

national government attempted to respond to these concerns for a sense of security that provisions are adequate.

Only two out of the nine goals set by the New Gold Plan of 1994 were attained in the target year of 1999 (Table 2). In order to catch up with the continuing rapid increase in the aging population, the national Ministry of Welfare, Labor, and Health promulgated a new long-term plan—called the "Gold Plan 21"—in 1999; it will be discussed in detail later in this chapter.

Public Long-Term Care Insurance

The national government established in 1994 a special task force for the development of a comprehensive elder-care service delivery system within the Ministry of Welfare, Labor, and Health.

In June 1996, the ministry released the first draft of its plan to create a national long-term care insurance (LTCI) scheme. After protracted negotiations with a number of government advisory councils, political parties, and representatives of local governments, the Ministry of Welfare, Labor, and Health finalized its

Table 2. The Status Quo of Community-Care Services in 1999 and the 2004 Goals of Gold Plan 21

Services	1999 goals of 1994 plan	Status quo in 1999	2004 goals of Gold Plan 21
Community-care services			
Home helpers (persons)	170,000	176,450	350,000
Short-term stay services (beds)	60,000	57,085	96,000
Daycare centers	17,000	13,350	26,000
Homecare support centers	10,000	6,648	10,000
Visiting nurse stations	5,000	4,470	9,900
Institutional care services			
Special care homes for the aged (beds)	290,000	296,937	360,000
Geriatric healthcare facilities (beds)	280,000	230,092	297,000
Care houses (beds)	—	—	3,200
Group homes for people with dementia (beds)	100,000	44,176	105,000
Multipurpose senior centers in depopulated areas	400	266	1,800

Note: The figures for status quo are the actual number at the end of the fiscal year 1999 (March 31, 2000).

Source: Maeda, 2003.

draft in November 1996 and presented it to the National Diet. The Diet finally passed the Long-Term Care Insurance Act in December 1997.

The Long-Term Care Insurance Act came into effect April 1, 2000. The LTCI scheme covers both community-care and institutional care services for adults ages 40 and older. Without LTCI, the core of the Japanese community-care system—that is to say, the services that provide care for elders living in the community—would never even exist, because LTCI is virtually the single source of funding for these services. (For additional information on the development and specifics of the LTCI scheme, see the chapter by Hiraoka dealing with recent developments in Japanese healthcare.)

Gold Plan 21

As the target year of the New Gold Plan arrived, the national government released the Gold Plan 21 in 1999. It was promulgated for almost the same reasons as the plans of 1990 and 1994. However, this time the need for a new plan was more acute. The creation of the LTCI scheme meant that the demand for elder-care services would increase at an even faster rate. Table 2 outlines the goals of the Gold Plan 21 in comparison with the goals of the New Gold Plan of 1994. The numerical goals of the new plan were slated to be reached by the end of fiscal year 2004.

Under the Gold Plan 21, the number of home helpers will increase from 176,450 in 1999 to 350,000 in 2004. Once this goal is attained, the ratio between home helpers and the older adult population (ages 65 and older) will be 1:69.7, far lower than the 1:128 ratio targeted in the previous plans. Such coverage means that Japan will attain a level of homecare services much more comparable to that of Sweden than before. However, the figures for Japan include a large number of part-time home helpers. Therefore, the actual gap between Japan and Sweden is, to a large extent, wider than it appears at first glance. The government also plans to increase the number of daycare centers from 13,350 in 1999 to 26,000 five years later. Once this goal is reached, Japan will have one such center for every 938 older adults; in other words, a typical medium-size city of 100,000 will have 20 daycare centers.

The number of beds allocated for short-term stay services will be increased from 57,085 in 1999 to 96,000 in 2004 under the Goal Plan 21. It is believed that when this goal is reached, the most pressing shortfall for these services will be met. At present, short-term stay beds are insufficient to meet such an acute need as a sudden illness of a family caregiver.

The new plan also aims to double the number of visiting nurse stations, an increase from 4,470 in 1999 to 9,900 five years later. Japan will thus have one visiting nurse station for every 2,460 older persons, or approximately eight stations within a typical medium-size city of 100,000.

Under the Gold Plan 21, the number of beds allocated for long-term institutional care, including beds in group homes for people with dementia, will also be increased significantly as shown in Table 2. Due to the rapid increase in the older adult population, however, the proportion of Japanese ages 65 and older who are institutionalized—2.7 percent of the older adult population—will remain at almost the same level as in 1999. These projections mean that the serious shortage of long-term care beds, especially in such large metropolitan areas as Tokyo, Yokohama, and Osaka, will not be eased at the time of this writing. Without recourse, the plight of older adults living in metropolitan areas will be exacerbated even more.

PRESENT-DAY COMMUNITY-CARE SERVICES FOR THE ELDERLY

The LTCI scheme covers five types of community-care services for the elderly: in-home services, daycare services, short-term stay (respite care) services; provision of technical aids to impaired older adults living in the community, and housing improvement for impaired older adults. In addition to these five types of services, the LTCI also covers the care provided in group homes for people with dementia and in *yuhryo rohjin* homes (comparable to retirement facilities in the United States). Insured elders whose level of impairment is assessed as being above a certain level are entitled to use these services, paying only a 10 percent copayment. In addition, a national network of homecare support centers plays an important role in providing information and counseling for older adults and their families.

If we apply a broader definition to community-care services for the elderly, educational services, recreational services, meal delivery services, and services that provide opportunities for elders to be engaged in gainful occupations should also be added to the list. Each service is described in brief below.

In-Home Services

In-home services in Japan consist of four services: home help services, visiting bathing services, visiting nurse services, and visiting rehabilitation services.

Home help services, along with short-term stay services and daycare, are considered to be the core community-care services for Japanese elders. They are sometimes referred to as the "three pillars" of community care for the elderly.

A national subsidy to help local governments provide home help services to destitute older adults was initiated in 1963, and in 1982 the government abolished service utilization limits and instituted a sliding-scale fee system (Fukushi Bunka Gakkai, 1995). However, the growth of home help services continued to be sluggish before LTCI started in April 2000.

Currently, round-the-clock home help services are available in many communities, especially in large metropolitan areas. They consist of two types of support: domiciliary services (such as cleaning, washing, cooking, and housekeeping) and physical care (such as bathing, cleaning of the body or hair, and changing diapers). The latter has now become the main component of home help services. Supporting clients emotionally through informal conversation is also regarded as an important part of all home help services, though the sliding scale laid down by the national government is so rigid that it is hard for home helpers to exchange informal conversation with the users.

Visiting bathing services are very popular in Japan because many seriously impaired older persons are cared for by their families in their homes. These services can be conducted in the home or at a nursing home. In the first instance, a team of two or three persons visits the home of the client in a special automobile equipped with a bathtub and water heater. Seriously impaired older adults who need a specially designed bathtub are transported from their homes to a nursing home where such bathtubs are installed and available to those elderly not residing within the facility.

Visiting nurse services are now developing rapidly in Japan. As of October 1, 2000, there were 4,730 visiting nurse stations around the country, and this number is anticipated to double before the end of fiscal year 2004. Visiting nurse services are covered by LTCI.

Though visiting rehabilitation services are covered by LTCI, they have yet to develop in Japan due to a serious shortage of qualified professional workers.

Daycare

Daycare is regarded as one of the most important components of the Japanese social welfare system for frail and impaired elderly living in the community. The national government started a national subsidy program for daycare services in 1979, and daycare is now covered by LTCI. When the Gold Plan was promulgated in 1990, there were only 1,080 daycare centers in Japan; their number increased to 13,350 by 1999. Under the Gold Plan 21, the latter figure will be doubled by the end of fiscal year 2004.

The purpose of daycare is to promote independent living, eliminate loneliness, maintain elders' physical and mental functioning, and reduce caregiver burden. Daycare centers also offer transportation services, bathing services, meal services, training in activities of daily living, and training in care skills for family caregivers. Some centers provide evening care services for older adults with dementia in order to alleviate the caregiving burden of families. In addition to daycare services, day rehabilitation services are also available in Japan, though they are not as popular as daycare services because of the shortage of qualified professionals.

Short-Term Stay Services

Short-term stay services are also quite popular in Japan, and are covered by LTCI. They are mainly provided at nursing homes. The number of beds for short-term stay services has increased more than twelvefold since 1989, and the goal of the Gold Plan 21 is to increase the number of beds to 96,000 by the end of fiscal year 2004. However, the introduction of LTCI expanded the need for this service exponentially, and there is currently a serious shortage of short-term stay beds across the country. The need in large metropolitan areas is especially acute, because urban families have relatively weak mutual-help networks.

Assistive Devices for Impaired Older Adults Living in the Community

A national subsidy program for the provision of technical aids (assistive devices) to impaired older adults living in the community was started by the national government in 1969 (Fukushi Bunka Gakkai, 1995). In 1989, it was extended to cover healthy older adults living alone or only with an older spouse. Before the start of LTCI, local governments provided such aids to elders without charge or with only a slight charge according to a sliding scale. At present, 15

Table 3. Technical Aids Covered by Long-Term Care Insurance

Type of support covered	Technical aids
Rental	Wheelchairs
	Specially designed bed for seriously impaired older adults
	Air pads and other items for the prevention and cure of bedsores
	Tools for changing a lying posture (for the prevention of bedsores)
	Handrails for toilets, corridors, bathrooms, etc.
	Ramps
	Walkers
	Canes
	Lifts to move seriously impaired elders
	Electronic wireless sensors for wandering people with dementia
Reimbursement of purchase	Toilet chairs
	Specially designed electronic urinals
	Tools to assist bathing
	Specially designed bathtubs
	Parts for lifts to move seriously impaired older adults

types of technical aids are covered by LTCI and available on the basis of documented need (Table 3).

In addition to these 15 aids, local governments provide four technical aids not covered by LTCI: fire alarms, automatic fire extinguishers, electromagnetic cookers, and specially designed telephones for hearing-impaired older adults. These four aids continue to be provided to healthy older individuals living alone or only with an older spouse, and their distribution continues to be subsidized by the national government.

Housing Improvement for Impaired Older Adults

Housing improvement services, which are covered by LTCI, assist impaired elders with minor improvements to their dwellings. These improvements include installing handrails to staircases, bathrooms, and toilet rooms; removing steps in the house; resurfacing floors to prevent slipping; remodeling swing doors into sliding ones; and replacing Japanese-style toilets with Western-style ones.

Group Homes for People with Dementia

The Japanese LTCI scheme covers the care services provided at group homes for people with dementia, but service users are obliged to bear the charges for their rooms.

The public support for group homes for people with dementia started very recently in 1997. Until then, the only public institutions that accepted older adults with dementia were nursing homes, where elders with dementia were cared for alongside cognitively unimpaired older adults. It is difficult for older adults with dementia to enjoy a high quality of life in such an environment. Moreover, in Japan it is believed that living in group homes can contribute toward curbing the progress of senile dementia because such homes offer an environment similar to a normal private home, as well as skilled care provided by trained care workers.

The target users of group homes are elders with no more than moderate impairment due to dementia or other cognitive declines who are capable of being independent in their activities of daily living but find it difficult to live independently in the community, or those whose families have difficulty providing care in their own homes. Care staff supply necessary assistance in activities of daily living so that residents can maintain their quality of life in a peaceful, homelike environment.

The capacity of a group home ranges from five to nine residents, as stipulated by the national government. Every group home has a dining room, kitchen, and bath, and all bedrooms should be single occupancy.

Homecare Support Centers

The national government started the national subsidy program for homecare support centers in 1988 (Fukushi Bunka Gakkai, 1995). Their purpose is to support family caregivers by offering counseling or advice, providing information on homecare, and referring cases to the appropriate social services agencies when necessary. Each center is required to have an exhibition space for technical aids for impaired older adults and to have at least two workers: for example, a public health nurse and a social worker, or a trained nurse and a trained care worker.

Education and Recreation

Educational opportunities for the elderly are very popular in Japan. The national Ministry of Education, Culture, Sports, Science, and Technology provides underwriting for local governments so that they can offer a variety of educational options to the older adults in the community. Most educational activities are provided as a part of the local adult education program. In addition, some prefectural governments have special programs or facilities for older adult education. For example, Inamino Gakuen (the Inamino School for Older Adults) of Hyogo Prefecture in western Japan is famous for its excellent programs and facilities.

Two additional resources for the elderly in Japan are community welfare centers and neighborhood centers for the elderly. The main function of community welfare centers for the elderly is to provide recreational and educational services. Most of them have some sort of facility for rehabilitation therapy mainly for stroke patients living in the community. Most also have a free public bath. In addition, many centers provide counseling and advice services to the elders with financial difficulties or such psychosocial needs as trouble with a daughter-in-law, neighbors, or friends. As of October 2000, there were 2,271 such centers around the country. Their construction is subsidized by the national government.

There also are quite a number of small-scale neighborhood welfare centers for the elderly (*rojin ikoino ie,* literally translated as "rest and relaxation house for the elderly"). These small centers are places where older adults can visit one another and enjoy various recreational activities. As of October 2000, there were 4,619 such centers throughout Japan. Local governments may obtain low-interest loans from the national government to construct these relaxation houses.

In the 1950s and 1960s, there were only a few community welfare centers or neighborhood centers for the elderly in Japan. In order to help older adults become engaged in self-help activities for mutual assistance, education, and recreation, the national government inaugurated a subsidy to cover the establishment and operational expenses of old people's clubs in 1963. As of March 2001, there were 133,138 such clubs around the nation, with a total of 8.7 million members—approximately 29 percent of the population ages 60 and older. In addition to its national subsidy, the national government provides financial support to the Prefectural and National Federations of Old People's Clubs. They provide guidance to local clubs through providing consultation; organizing conferences; dispatching leaders for various activities; and publishing periodicals, bulletins, or pamphlets for the purpose of public relations.

Other Community-Care Services

A number of additional services are available to Japanese elders, including meal services, occupational assistance, and emergency alarms.

Meal services are not as well developed in Japan as similar services available in industrialized Western countries, primarily because of the limited number of frail and impaired older Japanese who live alone or only with an older spouse. Most frail and impaired elders move in with their adult children. Meal services are not covered by LTCI, nor are they supported by national government subsidies. Therefore, in most cases, existing meal delivery programs are supported by grants from local governments.

Generally speaking, Japanese elders, especially older men, want to continue to work as long as possible in order to live a meaningful life as well as to earn extra income. To meet these needs, a number of employment-oriented services for older adults are provided by the Ministry of Welfare, Labor, and Health. Among them, the Silver Human Resources Center (*Shirubah Jinzai Sentah*) is worthy of special mention. Silver Human Resources Centers, which can now be found in most cities with populations of 100,000 or more, provide opportunities for elders to be engaged in light, part-time gainful work. According to the regulation of the national government on the requirements to be qualified for this subsidy, each center is to be run by a nonprofit organization established by retired older adults themselves.

The technology employed for Japanese emergency-alarm systems, which are the same as those used in the United States, consist of an electronic device attached to a telephone and a small pendant with a button that electronically transmits a signal to the device when the button is pressed. The signal transmitted by the pendant is automatically retransmitted to an emergency alarm center that is open 24 hours a day, seven days a week.

There are four emergency-alarm agencies in Japan. One is the public Fire Defense Agency located in each prefecture. The other three agencies are for-profit companies. By purchasing the services of these four agencies, most local governments, especially those located in urban areas, provide emergency-alarm services to impaired or frail elderly or people with disabilities who live alone or with an older spouse, relatives, or friends. Often there is a modest fee, but when an individual's income level is below a specified level, the service is provided free of charge. The fee scale is, generally speaking, very lenient.

No statistical data are available as to how many people receive the alarm service from local governments, nor as to how many purchase the service directly from private agencies. It is generally believed that the number of the latter is very small, as the fees for direct purchase are high.

CONCLUSION

Public community-care services for the elderly in Japan have been developing over the past 60 years. During this period Japan has experienced profound ideological, demographic, economic, and social changes. Sixty years ago, when World War II ended, Japan was only one of the underdeveloped countries of East Asia. Since then, Japan has transformed from a poor, ultranationalistic, totalitarian country into one of the wealthiest, most democratic, and most pacifistic countries in the world.

When Japan started rebuilding itself after the war, it was determined to become a pacifistic welfare state that was exactly the opposite of its prewar national identity. Therefore, Japan immediately began to invest in the development of public health, social security, and social welfare services. However, the direction of Japan's development, especially in the area of care for the elderly, could not help but differ from that of the advanced countries of Western Europe and North America. This is because Japanese culture, deeply rooted in traditional stem-family customs as well as in Confucianism, was not as easily changed as the formal structure of Japanese society. Many Japanese still believe that families should take care of their aged parents when they become frail or impaired and can no longer continue to live independently (Takahashi, 2002).

Because of such cultural beliefs, the need for welfare assistance and supportive services has only gradually come to light or according to priority status in national policy. Even in this enlightened era of Japanese society, many of these needs remain latent, as family members, especially coresiding daughters-in-law, meet most of elders' care needs. However, the significant caregiving duties that women are expected to assume have helped retard the progress of women's rights in Japan as compared to other industrialized countries.

These days, the explicit need for public care services for elders is emerging in the form of long waiting lists for admission into nursing homes and short-term stay services, especially in large metropolitan areas. However, traditional Japanese customs of family care for impaired older adults have been declining slowly but steadily over the past several decades. This decline is expected to continue, due to social changes brought about by the further industrialization and urbanization of Japanese society.

In addition to these sociological changes, the Japanese population continues to age rapidly. Not only does Japan now have to fill the existing gap between supply and demand for community-care services, it also must expand the total volume of services to catch up with the rapidly increasing numbers of older Japanese, especially the old old. Such expansion of services will place a tremendous economic burden on younger generations. Japanese society is on the forefront of nations facing this challenge, and it is one that we can only hope future generations will be able to successfully meet.

REFERENCES

Aoi, K. (1976). *Nihonno kazokuno tokuchoh* [Characteristics of the Japanese family]: Vol. 46. *Komyunitii* [The community]. Tokyo: Chiiki Shakai Kenkyusho.

Fukushi Bunka Gakkai. (1995). *Koureisha seikatsu nenpyou, 1925–1993* [Chronological Table of the Life of the Elderly, 1925–1993]. Tokyo: Nihon Editah Sukuhru Shuppanbu.

Maeda, D. (2001). Koureisha fukushi sahbisno hatten [Development of welfare services for the elderly]. In Japan Aging Research Center (Ed.), *Study on the development of population aging and the social policies for the elderly: History of the development of care service systems in Japan and Sweden.* Tokyo: Japan Aging Research Center.

Maeda, D. (2003). Social security, health care, and social services for the elderly in Japan. In Japan Aging Research Center (Ed.), *Aging in Japan: 2003.* Tokyo: Japan Aging Research Center.

Oouchi, H., Arisawa, H., Wakimura, G., Minobe, R., and Naito, M. (1971). *Nihon keizai zusetsu* [Japanese economy illustrated] (5th ed.). Tokyo: Iwanami Publishing Co.

Takahashi, S. (2002). Kazoku [Family]. In F. Miura (Ed.), *Zusetsu koureisha hakusho, 2002.* Tokyo: Zenkoku Shakaifukushi Kyougikai [National Council of Social Welfare].

Tanaka, S. (1993). Zaitaku fukushi [Home care]. In F. Miura (Ed.), *Zusetsu koureisha hakusho, 1993.* Tokyo: Zenkoku Shakaifukushi Kyougikai [National Council of Social Welfare].

Contributors

ABOUT THE EDITORS

Jon (Joe) Hendricks is an academic dean and professor of sociology at Oregon State University. Previously he taught at Kentucky, with appointments in Arts and Sciences and the Medical School. He has held elected positions as chair of the Gerontological Society of America's Behavioral and Social Sciences section, the American Sociological Association's Section on Aging and the Life Course, and as President of the Association for Gerontology in Higher Education.

Dr. Hendricks has published extensively in the field, currently edits the *Society and Aging* series for Baywood Publishing, and is on the editorial boards of a number of journals in gerontology. Dr. Hendricks is a fellow in the Gerontological Society of America and in the Association for Gerontology in Higher Education, which presented him with its 2004 Clark Tibbitts Award for distinguished contributions to the field. His email address is *hendricj@onid.orst.edu.*

Hyunsook Yoon received a graduate degree from the School of Social Work, University of Washington, and a doctoral degree in the field of gerontology at Ewha Women's University in Seoul, South Korea. Dr. Yoon started her professional career as a social worker for hospitalized elderly and troubled families, Dr. Yoon now teaches graduate social work and gerontology at Hallym University and directs the gerontology and geriatrics program there.

Dr. Yoon is the founding editor-in-chief of the *Hallym International Journal of Aging*. She has published widely in the United States and in Asia on aging families, social support, caregiving burden, and depression. Her email address is *hyyoon@sun.hallym.ac.kr.*

ABOUT THE AUTHORS

Sang-soo Bae received his Ph.D. in public health from Seoul National University. Currently he is professor in the Department of Preventive and Social Medicine and dean of the School of Public Health at Hallym University in South Korea. Dr. Bae has published many articles and monographs in the area of health-services research, including long-term care of the elderly.

Ming-cheng (Jack) Chang currently serves as chair and professor of the Taichung Health Care and Management University in Taiwan, as well as the deputy director general of the country's Bureau of Health Promotion, Department of Health. He holds a doctorate in demography from the University of Pennsylvania, and has been the recipient of many research awards from the Taiwanese National Science Council. Dr. Chang has published more than 100 papers in numerous journals in Taiwan and abroad.

Yung-Ping (Bing) Chen has held the Frank J. Manning Eminent Scholar's Chair in Gerontology at the University of Massachusetts, Boston, since 1988. He was the recipient of a Warren C. Scoville Distinguished Teaching Award (Economics) at the University of California, Los Angeles. Dr. Chen participated as a delegate, consultant, or both in the 1971, 1981, and 1995 White House Conferences on Aging and the 1998 White House Conference on Social Security. Dr. Chen also served on the panel of actuaries and economists for the 1979 Advisory Council on Social Security. An economist with training in law and in mental health sciences, he is a fellow in the Gerontological Society of America (chair, Economics of Aging Interest Group, 1992–93; editor of its newsletter, 1988–93) and a founding member of the National Academy of Social Insurance (and its visiting scholar in 1989). His research covers Social Security financing, private pension coverage, funding of long-term care, home equity conversion, and phased retirement. He is currently a member of the board of directors of the National Council on the Aging.

Sung-Jae Choi is professor of social welfare at Seoul National University in South Korea. He earned his doctorate from Case Western Reserve University. Currently Dr. Choi serves as chair of the Asia/Oceania Region, International Association of Gerontology, and as president of the Korean Academy of Social Welfare. In addition, he is currently cochair of the Social Welfare Advisory Committee, Seoul Metropolitan Government, and has served as an advisor to the Minister of Health and Social Welfare in the South Korean government. His major research areas range from social policy and services for the elderly and social welfare research methods to program evaluation research and social welfare administration. Publications include "The Family and Ageing in Korea: A New Concern and Challenge," in *Ageing and Society* (1996); "The Role of Gerontological Associations in Korea," in *Australasian Journal on Ageing* (1998); and "Aging in Korea: Issues and Policies" in *Aging in the Asia-Pacific Region: Issues, Policies, and Future Trends,* edited by David R. Phillips (2000).

Mercedes B. Concepcion, Professor Emerita, College of Social Sciences and Philosophy, University of the Philippines, is currently a Commissioner of the Philippine Commission on Population (POPCOM). Dr. Concepcion was the first director of the University of the Philippines Population Institute, established in 1994 with a grant from the Ford Foundation to engage in research on critical population issues. POPCOM offers an master's degree program in demography, and serves as the focal point for all information concerning population in the

Philippines. Dr. Concepcion obtained her Ph.D. in sociology from the University of Chicago in 1963 and has been active in teaching, research, and extension activities since 1955. She was elected president of the International Union for the Scientific Study of Population, 1981–1985, and was deeply involved in the World Fertility Survey as a member of its Technical Steering Committee. Although retired from the University of the Philippines, Professor Concepcion remains active in the realm of population policy and advocacy. Her e-mail address is *concepcionmb@edsamail.com.ph.*

Koichi Hiraoka is professor in the Department of Sociology at Ochanomizu University in Tokyo, where he teaches social policy and social welfare. He earned a master's degree in sociology in 1980 from the University of Tokyo. Professor Hiraoka has been in his current position since 1999. He has recently been involved in evaluative studies examining the Long-Term Care Insurance scheme in Japan. His publications include *Igirisu no shakai fukushi to seisaku kenkyu* (British Social Welfare and Policy Studies, 2003) and numerous articles on the planning and evaluation of social services.

Hisanori Ishikawa is professor in the Department of Social Work at Japan Lutheran College in Tokyo. His major fields of study are social work administration, statistical analysis, and social gerontology, most notably community-care issues for the elderly. Dr. Ishikawa received his Ph.D. from the Japan College of Social Work in 1997.

Hal Kendig serves as dean of the Faculty of Health Sciences at the University of Sydney. He is a fellow of the Academy of Social Sciences in Australia; Honorary Life Fellow of the Australian Council on the Ageing; and cochair of the International Association of Gerontology's Social Research and Planning Section, Asia-Oceania. His collaborative research includes the Melbourne Longitudinal Surveys of Healthy Ageing (with Colette Browning and others) and studies of caregivers, falls prevention, housing, and aged-care policies.

Sang-Hyop Lee received his Ph.D. from Michigan State University and is currently assistant professor of economics at the University of Hawaii at Manoa, and adjunct fellow at the East-West Center. He has studied several aspects of the consequences of government influence on labor markets, population, child health, and education. Dr. Lee's current research is examining the impact of change in population structure on income inequality and economic growth. His most recent articles have appeared in leading labor economics journals such as *Labor Economics* and *Industrial Relations*.

Tae-jin Lee received his doctorate in health services management from the University of Manchester in the United Kingdom. He is currently assistant professor in the Department of Preventive and Social Medicine at Hallym University in South Korea. Dr. Lee's research interests include health insurance, healthcare financing and payment, and long-term care.

Joe C. B. Leung received his Ph.D. from the University of Hong Kong and is currently head of the Department of Social Work and Social Administration of the

University of Hong Kong as well as senior faculty associate of the university's Centre on Aging. His publications focus on social security, social work training, family support for the elderly, social development, community services, and the work of nongovernmental organizations in China. He is coauthor (with R. Nann) of the book *Authority and Benevolence: Social Welfare in China* (1995) and has published a number of other books and articles.

Denise C. Lewis is a doctoral candidate in the gerontology program at the University of Kentucky. Lewis' research interests include family relations, social networks, informal care of elders, immigrant health, and rural elders' health beliefs and behaviors. She is coordinator for the Kentucky Aging Research and Information Service (KARIS) and is currently writing her dissertation using field research data she collected in a community of Khmer elders on the American Gulf Coast.

Phoebe Liebig is associate professor of gerontology and public administration at the University of Southern California in Los Angeles. Her research interests include housing and long-term care for older adults and people with disabilities; income, tax policy, and the elderly; intergovernmental relations in aging and disability services; and aging in India, the latter as a result of her Fulbright Senior Scholar award in 1997–98. She is coeditor, with S. I. Rajan, of *An Aging India: Perspective, Prospects, and Policies* (2003); with Jon Pynoos, of *Housing Frail Elders: International Policies, Perspectives, and Prospects* (1995); and with William Lammers, of *California Policy Choice for Long-Term Care* (1990). She has published articles in numerous scholarly journals, encyclopedias on aging, and books. She is the recipient of the 2003 Clark Tibbitts Award for excellence in the field of aging and is a fellow of both the Gerontological Society of America and the Association for Gerontology in Higher Education. Her e-mail address is *liebig@usc.edu*.

Daisaku Maeda is professor emeritus at Japan Lutheran College and the Japan College of Social Work. He has also served as director of the Social Welfare Research Institute at Rissho University and of the Department of Sociology at the Tokyo Metropolitan Institute of Gerontology. Dr. Maeda is currently a member of the leadership councils for a number of national and international gerontological associations, and has served on several advisory councils for the Japanese national government. He has also been a member of the editorial boards for *Ageing and Society, Gerontology and Geriatrics Education*, and the *Journal of Cross-Cultural Gerontology*.

Andrew Mason is professor and former chair of economics at the University of Hawaii at Manoa, as well as senior fellow and former director of the Program on Population at the East-West Center. His most recent books are *Sharing the Wealth: Demographic Change and Economic Transfers Between Generations*, coedited with Georges Tapinos (Oxford University Press), and *Population Growth and Economic Development in East Asia: Challenges Met, Opportunities Seized* (Stanford University Press). Dr. Mason's research has focused on the interrelationships between long-term demographic, social, and economic trends. Much of his research has concentrated on the countries of East and Southeast Asia, especially Japan, South Korea, Thailand, Indonesia, and the Philippines. In addition, Dr. Mason has served on advisory committees and as a consultant to the World Bank, the Asian Development Bank, the U.S. National Academy of Sciences, the U.S. Agency for International Development, and the United Nations. He was a visiting professor at the Institut d'Etudes de Politique de Paris in 1998 and a visiting scholar at the Massachusetts Institute of Technology in 1983–84. He received his Ph.D. from the University of Michigan in 1975.

Nobuko Nagase received her Ph. D in economics from Tokyo University and is currently associate professor at the Graduate School of Humanities and Sciences, Ochanomizu University, Tokyo. Her primary research interest is family labor supply and social policy. She teaches and researches in the areas of labor and social policy. Much of her work focuses on the analysis of patterns of labor-supply behavior of Japanese women, childcare support programs, and social policy. Dr. Nagase's recent and forthcoming publications include papers on women and the pension system, analysis of supply of childcare facilities, and the estimation of child cost. She is a member on the Specialist Sub-Committee under the Council for Gender Equality in the Cabinet Office in Japan.

Laura Katz Olson has been professor of political science at Lehigh University since 1974. She has published five books: *The Political Economy of Aging: The State, Private Power and Social Welfare*; *Aging and Public Policy: The Politics of Growing Old in America*; *The Graying of the World: Who Will Take Care of the Frail Elderly*; *Age Through Ethnic Lenses: Caring for the Elderly in a Multicultural Society*; and *The Not So Golden Year: Caregiving, the Frail Elderly, and the Long-Term Care Establishment*. She has published widely in the field of aging and women's studies on such topics as pensions, Social Security, the problems of older women, and long-term care. Olson has been a scholar at the U.S. Social Security Administration, a gerontological fellow, and a Fulbright scholar. She also has lectured throughout Pennsylvania on Social Security, Medicare, and long-term care policy, funded by the Pennsylvania Humanities Council.

Peng Du is professor and deputy director at the Population and Development Studies Center at Renmin University of China, as well as deputy director of the university's Gerontology Institute. Previously, he served for two years as visiting scholar at the Center for Ageing Studies, Flinders University, Australia. Dr. Du is the author of *Ageing Issues and Policies in the European Union* (2000), *Who Will Provide for the Chinese Elderly?* (2000), *Chinese Elderly in the Ageing Process* (1996), and *The Process of Population Ageing in China* (1994). He also coauthored *Social Gerontology* (1999) and *The Ageing of the Population in China* (1991).

Aurora E. Perez is a social demographer by training. After completing her doctoral degree from Brown University in Providence, Rhode Island, she put into practice the principles of social demography while serving as director of the University of the Philippines Population Institute and ex-officio board member of the Philippine Commission on Population (POPCOM) from 1996 to 1999. While in the academy she helped promote research on the elderly and wrote on the policy aspects of the well-being of Filipino elderly as part of the four-Asian country study coordinated by Albert I. Hermalin of the University of Michigan. Currently on leave from the University of the Philippines, Dr. Perez is the long-term advisor and country director of a U.S. Agency for International Development–funded project on population and family planning policy advocacy. Dr. Perez is based in the Philippines and can be reached through her e-mail address: *aeptfg@compass.com.ph*.

Kai Hong Phua is associate professor of health policy and management at the Department of Community, Occupational, and Family Medicine, and the Lee Kuan Yew School of Public Policy at the National University of Singapore. He was also appointed as an adjunct fellow/senior fellow at the Institute of Policy Studies from 1988 to 2000. He received his master's degree from the Harvard University School of Public Health and his doctorate from the London School of Economics and Political Science (social administration, specializing in health economics). Dr. Phua's area of specialization include the economics of healthcare, and he has written more than 100 publications and papers in the field of health policy and management and related areas, including the history of health services, health and population aging, health economics, and financing. He has been appointed to many national advisory committees, including the Medical Hub Committee of the Economic Development Board and National Science and Technology Board (2001), Workgroup on Resource Funding in the Inter-Ministerial Committee on the Ageing Population (1999), Government Parliamentary Committee Resource Panel on Health (1988–96), National Advisory Council on the Family and Aged (1989–94), Review Committee on National Health Policies (1991–92), Health Advisory Council (1989–92), and the Health Financing Subcommittee of the Economic Policy Review Committee (1989). Internationally, he is serving as chairman of the Technical Advisory Group on Health Sector Development of the World Health Organization Western Pacific Regional Office, and moderated the Ministerial Roundtable at the 2000 WHO Regional Meeting. He is active as chair of the executive board of the Asia-Pacific Health Economics Network (APHEN), Asian Health Systems Reform Network (DRAGONET).

Susan Quine is associate professor, sub-dean, and postgraduate coordinator of research in the School of Public Health, Faculty of Medicine, at the University of Sydney, Australia. Professor Quine has a background in sociology, social psychology, and social anthropology, as well as extensive experience in survey and questionnaire design and attitude measurement. She has published widely in specialist and multidisciplinary journals, using qualitative and/or quantitative methods on a variety of health-related topics. Professor Quine has a strong interest in investigating the health of disadvantaged groups, particularly the aged and disabled, and in translating research into practice. She is currently a chief investigator on two major projects on healthy aging being funded by the Australian National Health and Medical Research Council.

P. V. Ramamurti is professor emeritus in the Department of Psychology and honorary director of the Center for Research on Ageing at S. V. University in Tirupati, India. As a pioneer in aging research in India, he was responsible for initiating the inclusion of gerontology as a master's and doctoral-level specialization at his university. He has to his credit a score of research projects and more than 100 publications in the field of aging. Dr. Ramamurti was involved as an expert consultant for the formulation of India's National Policy on Older Persons (NPOP), enacted in 1999, and is a member of the National Council for Older Persons, which oversees the further development and implementation of the NPOP. He also is a member of the Expert Consultant Group, which has been preparing a research agenda on aging for the United Nations and has been a key faculty member in the U.N.–Malta training program in aging. Dr. Ramamurti is the recipient of several national and international awards for his contribution to aging, including a Sandoz project award in 1989.

Ka-Oak Rhee serves on the faculty of the Graduate School of Civil Society and Welfare and the Department of Social Welfare of Sungkonghoe University in Seoul, South Korea. Dr. Rhee's Ph. D. is from Johann Wolfgang von Goethe-Universitaet, Frankfurt, Germany. He has been active as an organizer in the Asia-Oceania Regional Committee of the International Association of Gerontology and has published and presented research on older families and caregiving.

Gerard Russo is an adjunct fellow at the East-West Center and associate professor of economics at the University of Hawaii at Manoa. He received his Ph.D. in economics from Northwestern University. Dr. Russo has conducted research and published widely on household healthcare spending and health-service utilization in the Southeast Asian countries of Indonesia, the Philippines, and Thailand.

Te-hsiung (Tom) Sun currently serves as a professor at both National Taiwan University and National Chung-Cheng University, as well as president and chair of numerous associations in Taiwan. Previously, he held positions as chair of the Research, Development, and Evaluation Commission in the Taiwanese Executive Yuan (Cabinet), as well as directorship of the Taiwan Provincial Institute of Family Planning. Over the course of his career he has published close to 100 scholarly articles and books in the fields of demography, sociology, family planning, social welfare, human geography, and public administration.

Poo Chang Tan was a professor at the Department of Applied Statistics, Faculty of Economics and Administration, University of Malaya, Malaysia. Dr. Tan, whose doctorate was in demography, was well known internationally for her research on aging issues. Her research studies were published by such international agencies as the United Nations, ESCAP, and the AARP. Dr. Tan helped found the Petaling Jaya Community Centre in Malaysia. She also sat on the advisory board of the National Council of Senior Citizens Organisation Malaysia, and was one of the pioneering members of the Malaysian Gerontological Society and the Community Support Network. Dr. Tan passed away in May 2003.

Nai Peng Tey is associate professor in the Department of Applied Statistics at the University of Malaya, Malaysia. Prior to joining the faculty at the university, he was director of the National Population and Family Development Board's Population Studies Centre, and has consulted with numerous corporations and NGOs. Mr. Tey's research foci include demography and socioeconomic and survey research; he is currently engaged in a number of research projects on population aging.

John Turner is a senior policy advisor in the Public Policy Institute at AARP. Previously, he worked at the International Labor Office in Geneva, Switzerland, where he coedited the book *Social Security Pensions: Development and Reform*. He has also worked in research offices at the U.S. Social Security Administration and the U.S. Labor Department, where he served as deputy director of the pension research office for eight years. Turner holds a doctorate in economics from the University of Chicago, and has taught as an adjunct lecturer at George Washington University. He has published more than 100 articles on pension and social security policy, and his articles have been translated into seven languages. One of his articles received an award for the best article of the year in the *Journal of Risk and Insurance*. He has authored or edited ten books, one of which is now required reading for an examination given by the Society of Actuaries.

John van Willigen received his Ph.D. from the University of Arizona and is professor of anthropology at the University of Kentucky at Lexington, where he is also appointed to the Department of Behavioral Science, College of Medicine and the Gerontology Center, and the Health Ph.D. Program. Dr. van Willigen has conducted field research with older people in rural Kentucky and India. One of his recent publications is *Social Aging in a Delhi Neighborhood* (1999), written with psychologist N. K. Chadha of the University of Delhi. Dr. van Willigen received the 2003 Sol Tax Distinguished Service Award from the Society for Applied Anthropology.

Index

For Product Safety Concerns and Information please contact our EU representative GPSR@taylorandfrancis.com Taylor & Francis Verlag GmbH, Kaufingerstraße 24, 80331 München, Germany